BY
THE HOUSE OF COLLECTIBLES, INC.

We have compiled the information contained herein through a *patented computerized process* which relies primarily on a nationwide sampling of information provided by noteworthy collectible experts, auction houses and specialized dealers. This unique retrieval system enables us to provide the reader with the most current and accurate information available.

EDITOR
THOMAS E. HUDGEONS III

FIFTH EDITION
THE HOUSE OF COLLECTIBLES, INC., ORLANDO, FLORIDA 32809

IMPORTANT NOTICE. The format of **THE OFFICIAL PRICE GUIDE SERIES,** published by **THE HOUSE OF COLLECTIBLES, INC.,** is based on the following proprietary features: **ALL FACTS AND PRICES ARE COMPILED THRU A COMPUTERIZED PROCESS** which relies on a nationwide sampling of information obtained from noteworthy experts, auction houses, and specialized dealers. **DETAILED "INDEXED" FORMAT** enables quick retrieval of information for positive identification. **ENCAPSULATED HISTORIES** precede each category to acquaint the collector with the specific traits that are peculiar to that area of collecting. **VALUABLE COLLECTING INFORMATION** is provided for both the novice as well as the seasoned collector: How to begin a collection; How to buy, sell, and trade; Care and storage techniques; Tips on restoration; Grading guidelines; Lists of periodicals, clubs, museums, auction houses, dealers, etc. **AN AVERAGE PRICE RANGE** takes geographic location and condition into consideration when reporting collector value. **A SPECIAL THIRD PRICE COLUMN** enables the collector to compare the current market values with last year's average selling price indicating which items have increased in value. **INVENTORY CHECKLIST SYSTEM** is provided for cataloging a collection. **EACH TITLE IS ANNUALLY UPDATED** to provide the most accurate information available in the rapidly changing collector's marketplace.

All of the information, including valuations, in this book has been compiled from the most reliable sources, and every effort has been made to eliminate errors and questionable data. Nevertheless the possibility of error, in a work of such immense scope, always exists. The publisher will not be held responsible for losses which may occur in the purchase, sale, or other transaction of items because of information contained herein. Readers who feel they have discovered errors are invited to **WRITE** and inform us, so they may be corrected in subsequent editions. Those seeking further information on the topics covered in this book are advised to refer to the complete line of Official Price Guides published by The House of Collectibles.

Published by: The House of Collectibles, Inc.
Orlando Central Park
1904 Premier Row
Orlando, FL 32809
Phone: (305) 857-9095

Printed in the United States of America

Library of Congress Catalog Card Number: 83-82799

ISBN: 0-87637-268-X / Paperback

TABLE OF CONTENTS

ACKNOWLEDGEMENTS

The House of Collectibles would like to thank the following persons and establishments for contributing to the compilation of this title: The Musical Museum, Deansboro, New York, composed of the Saunders family's collection; Bellm's Cars and Music of Yesterday, Sarasota, FL; Don Mudd and Manor House of Galleries, Houston, TX; Thomas Edison Winter Home, Fort Myers, FL; Leah S. Burt at the Edison Historic Site, West Orange, NJ; Paul Spigel and Peter Press.

PHOTOGRAPHIC RECOGNITION

Ainslee's Advertiser, 1907; Alan C. Lungstrum, West Covina, CA; Bellm Cars and Music of Yesterday, Sarasota, FL; *Circle Magazine,* 1907; *Delineator,* 1907; Kalman Detrich; Edison Laboratories, East Orange, NJ; Edison Winter Home, Ft. Myers, FL; Gould and Hundermark; *Harper's Weekly,* 1905; Manor House Galleries; Metropolitan Museum of Art; *Munsey's Magazine,* 1905; Musical Museum, Deansboro, NY; Paul Spigel Collection; Price Collection; Smithsonian Institution; Steve Freeman Collection; Vestal Press.

Cover Photograph: Photographer — Bernie Markell, Orlando, FL 32809;
Courtesy of: Bellm Cars & Music of Yesterday, Sarasota, FL;
Lancaster-Miller, Inc., Berkeley, CA 94703.

MARKET REVIEW

Music collectors are fortunate. The music market is strong for the upcoming year especially in the areas of 18th century musical instruments and early 1900s music machines. Memorabilia of famous singers from opera to rock and roll comprises another section of highly valuable music collectibles.

Music is an interesting collectible field because of the vast array of items offered to collectors. From instruments to jukeboxes, sheet music to records, this collectible area offers any hobbyist the satisfaction of purchasing items that will usually increase in value. For example, an Edison Model A Home Phonograph made in 1901, is bringing $100 to $150 more over last year's prices. Its current selling price is between $500 and $700. An unusual musical vanity set that plays three different tunes when its lid is lifted brings about $640 to $750 on the current market.

Jukeboxes are an especially prized collector's item. Rarely found in restaurants or other public establishments, these colorful machines brighten any collection of music collectibles. Currently, jukeboxes in good condition are selling higher than last year. For example, a Wurlitzer Model 1015 jukebox made in 1947 is selling for $6,000 to $7,500, a jump of $1,000 to $1,500 over last year. This same machine owned by ex-Beatle member John Lennon can bring as much as $9,000 at auction.

Musical instruments will usually bring a premium at auctions. Although many 1800s instruments are museum pieces or for buyers with exquisite tastes, these beautiful instruments are worth mentioning. Violins are especially noteworthy. A handsome model made by Italian Francesco Ruggieri in the early 1700s usually brings between $40,000 and $45,000 at auction.

For the less extravagant collector, banjos, one of the most familiar instruments of folk music, is a good item to collect. Not only affordable, these instruments can be found crudely crafted or rather extensively decorated. Most American banjos from the late 1800s and early 1900s run from $150 to $300 depending on the wood, decoration and condition.

Other items more affordable to the average collector are memorabilia of music stars. In the rock and roll genre, The Beatles followed by Elvis Presley are the most collectible stars. Rolls of Beatles wallpaper, now hard to find, sell for $100 to $125 at auction, Four tickets to an August 23, 1966 Beatles concert at Shea Stadium sells for $200, while the Beatles gold album commemorating the sale of more than 500,000 copies of "Hey Jude", is selling for $8,000 to $10,000.

An Elvis Presley autographed photograph taken in the early 1970s currently sells for $250 on the music market, while a gray coat and velour hat owned by "the King" sells for $4,000.

Not only are Beatles and Elvis collectors growing immensely, but opera collectors are buying extensively. Although there are many big names in the opera area that are collectible, the biggest name is Enrico Caruso. Caruso autographs are one of the highest price items in this market bringing as much as $2,000 at auction.

Other opera items that beginning collectors can usually find and afford are signed paper programs, unreleased records and authorized limited edition statues or busts. Of course, the value of these items which can range from a few dollars to thousands of dollars depends on the artist.

Records, especially 78's are fetching higher prices over last year. Although still affordable, these thick black records are becoming quite collectible. For example, Gene Autry recordings take $100 to $150 at auctions while Duke Ellington 78's go for $50 to $75.

Old records is a new hobby still in its infancy. Most people bought them to add an authentic touch to their phonographs, which they did collect. This has changed. Records are becoming a viable market on its own.

Although the music collectible market is immense, areas collectors should watch include memorabilia of country and western singers, opera recordings of stars like Caruso, John McCormack and Geraldine Farrar and most Beatles memorabilia including 1960s manufactured items like dolls and lunch boxes.

STANDARDS USED IN THIS BOOK

All collectors' items are not created equal, and even those which may have started out equal in life are not always found in that condition today. It is impossible in a book of this nature to give valuations on every class of item in a wide range of conditions. Therefore, we have tried to arrive at certain standards and the user of this guide can, by applying our standards and prices to any items he may encounter, form a fairly accurate idea of the value.

MUSICAL INSTRUMENTS. It is not expected that antique instruments, especially those dating before about 1890, be in the same condition as when they left the factory. The use to which instruments — especially hand-held instruments — were placed resulted in some surface wear, which is inevitable on nearly every specimen, and is not considered to detract from the desirability. Instruments should, however, be **complete,** and in good operating condition.

RECORDINGS. Usually, the older a record, the less that can be expected of it condition-wise. "Very fine" for a recording of 1905 would mean still listenable but with surface noise, scratches, etc. Early wax records can be found in mint condition but this is rare. On the other hand, condition standards are pretty tight on rock records of the 1950's; these should be in virtually new condition.

BOOKS AND OTHER PAPER ITEMS. Depends upon the nature of the item and its age. More information will be found in the appropriate sections.

The values given for 8 x 10 signed photographs are for specimens with signature only, or signature plus a very brief message, such as "best wishes." Photographs carrying lengthy inscriptions are worth higher prices than those stated, sometimes double the amount or even more. This varies with the celebrity, so it is impossible to give overall guidelines.

THE PHONOGRAPH RECORD: ITS DEVELOPMENT

The phonograph, one of mankind's most historic inventions, has been with us for slightly more than 100 years. Disc records, however, are just approaching their 100th birthday, which will occur in 1987. But phonographs and records as we know them now — with stereo, vinyl, 45's and LP's — are of much more recent origin. None of these concepts existed as recently as 40 years ago. The many changes undergone by phono records add, of course, to their collecting appeal. And the fact that their beginnings are not TOO ancient is a plus for the hobbyist; the very oldest discs turn up in the marketplace and are available for collecting. One can zero in on any phase of recorded music that appeals to him, from Edison's scratchy cylinders to vinyl rock, and find it on the market. There's another plus, too: nearly every modern phonograph will play the old 78's. If you collect cylinder records, you'll need to buy a cylinder player if you want to listen to them. This, though, is no real problem. The auction sales and antiques shops frequently offer cylinder players in operating condition. If you can do your own restoration work, or know someone who can, you could save hundreds of dollars by buying a non-operating cylinder player and fixing it up.

Even today, heading towards the close of the 20th century, the phonograph is too recent an invention to be properly appraised. Centuries from now it will probably be considered just as monumental an invention as the printing press, which has been around since the 1400's. There are even some who believe that recorded words will eventually take the place of the printed word! Almost right up until the phonograph's invention, the world at large considered such a machine an impossibility. It was just as much a dream as going to the moon. Writing in the late 1700's, biographer James Boswell lamented that there was no way to preserve the voice of his idol, Samuel Johnson, for posterity. He put forward the suggestion that some method of special notations should be developed, which would indicate tones of voice and characteristics of speaking. Never did he envision a *machine* to capture the human voice — it was too improbable! Yet in less than 100 years thereafter, just such a machine was in existence, and was capturing the human voice.

During the 19th century — the "Age of Invention" as historians call it — developments occurred which led gradually up to the phonograph. Mankind acquired more knowledge of science and machinery, and each new invention pointed the way toward fresh worlds to conquer. Again and again, clever inventors accomplished the seemingly impossible — with the steam engine, the photo-camera, and so many other things. Stampedes were made upon the U.S. Patent Office, and many a patent holder went literally from rags to riches. This encouraged some people to set themselves as fulltime inventors, and secure as many patents as possible on a wide range of products. By far the most successful was Thomas A. Edison of Orange, New Jersey, to whom credit belongs for bringing the phonograph into being. While the idea for such a device may not originally have been his; while he was not, probably, the first to tinker and experiment in that direction; nevertheless he was first in building a workable model, and the first to take out a patent on a phonograph. This was U.S. Patent #200,251, issued on February 10, 1878. Actually, Edison's machine had been perfected the previous year. Thanks to the voluminous, careful accounts kept by the Edison staff, we even know the exact date upon which his phonograph played for the first time: December 7, 1877.

Recorded sound would, of course, have presented untold possibilities in any age. Ancient Greeks could have recorded the speeches of Demostheses. Elizabethan Britons could have made records of Shakespeare's plays with the REAL original casts. Napoleon's stirring addresses would have been a natural for preservation. But the age in which the phonograph *was* invented offered even greater potential for its use. The entertainment industry was growing as never before. Theatres were opening all over the country, even in very remote areas and "one horse towns." America was discovering classical music; promoters were luring Europe's top opera talent to the U.S. with contracts that look attractive even by today's standards (tickets for Jenny Lind's concerts were sold for as much as $100 each, in an era when a suit of clothes cost $5 or $6). Minstrel shows and other live acts were touring the nation. Barnum was going strong with his circus, and competitors were putting on circuses of their own. Publishers were bringing out sheet music in wholesale quantity, and sales of musical instruments were at unprecedented levels. The American people of the 1870's were very much in to entertainment — and it was no accident. The rise of the Middle Classes, due to our industrial revolution, had made for more leisure time and more spending money for millions. Much of this extra cash was channeled into entertainment. The phonograph, which could bring entertainment into the home and do it fairly inexpensively, seemed too good to be true.

Of course, the early phonographs had plenty wrong with them, compared with their descendants. You couldn't get much volume; tone was non-existent; music warbled; and the surface noise sounded like the Wabash Cannonball coming through your living room. But, looking at things in perspective, you have to realize that our ancestors were amazed simply by the fact that the phonograph *worked.* It was very remarkable indeed to have a wooden box which talked or played music. What we see as serious defects in antique phonographs and records were largely overlooked by listeners of that time. Edison himself (and other phonograph makers) did not overlook them; he kept on improving his product until the day of his death, many years later. Each improvement brought a new flurry of sales. The phonograph industry quickly established itself as one of America's biggest money-makers, simply because (as with autos, which came a little later) everybody wanted the latest and the best. People were willing — even anxious — to discard a phonograph they had bought just two or three years earlier, to get the latest model. This brought multi millions of dollars annually into the industry, and touched off many battles for supremacy in the phono-world.

Cylinder phonographs were compact and handsome to look at. But cylinder recordings presented a storage problem. If you owned more than a few, they started taking up a great deal of space. They were also easily damaged, as it was difficult to handle them without touching the grooves. The obvious solution was a flat record disc, which could be easily stacked. A prototype already existed in the metal discs used in coin-operated "music machines" or jukeboxes of that time. In 1887, a patent was taken out for a phonograph using zinc discs — but not by Edison. Developer of the disc record was Emile Berliner. However, the Edison Company very soon was producing disc phonographs and records, and garnered the lion's share of sales for them throughout the 1890's and early 1900's. Thereafter, one development followed hot on the heels of another. In 1894 Columbia Records was established and became one of Edison's main competitors. About that same time, Berliner was bringing out 7-inch records and selling them for half a dollar each. His records were blank on the reverse side and played at 70 revolutions per minute, to conform with the turntable speed of his phonographs. This is an interesting little sidelight about the pioneer phonograph trade, and about the competitiveness of Big Business even in the 19th century. Each record manufacturer cut his records at a different speed than the competition, so they could be played to their fullest advantage only on HIS phonographs. There was a possible drawback to this: if you already owned an Edison phonograph, you might not want to buy Berliner records and hear them slightly cockeyed. But the philosophy of manufacturers was: sell the phonograph FIRST, then sell the records. Companies which made only records (not phonographs to go with them) were very few at first. They tried to take a neutral position and cut their discs at middle-of-the-road speeds, so they wouldn't sound TOO bad no matter whose machine you played them on. Luckily the listeners did not have overly critical ears. In this kind of situation the music fan of today would be banging his head against the wall.

As expected, the novelty of the phonograph wore off quickly. Those who bought phonographs in the 1880's were fascinated by whatever issued forth from them — even if they had to strain to catch the words or guess about what the melody was supposed to be. As the public became more discriminating — edged on by press critics, who habitually poked fun at the phonograph — it was obvious that better records had to be put out, not only better-sounding but records of a more diverse, interesting character. Many early records were recitations or readings, such as someone reciting The Gettysburg Address. When music was used, it was often played by rank amateurs and wouldn't have sounded too good even on the best equipment. There were singers who couldn't sing, too, and all sorts of theatrical sins committed on early records. So another battle started up, to produce good records that would have wide-ranging popular appeal. And in time the sale of records far overshadowed the sale of phonographs. Professional talent was hired and, before too long, the BEST professional talent, recruited from the opera and music-hall stages. By 1905, nearly every major theatrical celebrity was making phonograph records.

The biggest step in this direction was taken by a man named Eldridge Johnson — not very well known compared to Edison, but whose legacy in the industry was awesome. Johnson had worked for Emile Berliner, then went off to found his own company. In 1901 he started up the Victor Record Company, the ancestor of RCA-Victor. In the 1920's he was bought out by Radio Corporation of America and retired with a huge fortune, to pursue his hobby of collecting rare books and prints. Johnson's Victor company made phonographs as well as records, but its records made its reputation. Johnson used different color labels on his records to indicate the type of record, and introduced "Red Seal" records for celebrity recordings. The Victor Red Seal records were the most prestigious of their time. In sound quality they were really no better than anyone else's, but the stable of artists that Johnson succeeded in signing up read like a show business Who's Who. His top selling (and by far most glamorous) artist was Enrico Caruso. In 1903, Caruso's Red Seal recording of "Vesti la giubba" became the first million-selling record in history. This was no small feat. It is very doubtful that, in 1903, as many as a million households had phonographs. Literally everybody who owned a phonograph bought "Vesti la giubba," and some must have bought more than one copy. This is the equivalent of a modern-day record selling 40 or 50 million copies, which no record has come near selling in a single run on the charts (Bing Crosby's "White Christmas" is over 100 million in sales, but this represents numerous repressings over a nearly 40-year span). Caruso cut many dozens of records for Victor, and their sales alone would have made the company very, very successful. But Johnson had many other top artists in his camp, from opera, vaudeville, the minstrel halls, and you-name-it. In less than five years he built a recording empire that even Edison must have envied.

In 1906 Eldridge Johnson added another feather to his cap. Victor brought out the first phonograph (a console model) with an enclosed horn.

Of course there were still advances left to be made, even though the industry had, in three and a half decades, come a remarkably long way. Two years later (1908) another giant stride was taken by Columbia Records with introduction of the double-sided disc. This type of record — made of pressed wax, and double-sided — remained standard until after World War II. It played at approximately 78 r.p.m. and differed not too much from — say — a 78 by Frank Sinatra or Perry Como. It was somewhat thicker and heavier, and of course the sound quality was not quite equal to that of later records. But in physical appearance it was much closer to modern records than it was to its ancestors, the cylinder and zinc disc.

Victor and Columbia were again at the forefront of progress, when the slower-playing vinyl record came along. In 1948 Columbia introduced the 33⅓ "long play" record. It had an option on the 45 r.p.m. disc but did not follow through, believing that the 45 had limited sales potential. So in 1949 Victor picked up the 45 and began experimenting with it. Very few 45 singles were released until the early fifties, when a number of companies were putting them out. The usual practice was to issue records in both 78 and 45. Companies wanted to phase out 78's as quickly as possible but could not rush things, since many record buyers had phonographs which played only 78's.

Thus the way was clear for the record boom of the sixties, seventies and eighties, which now accounts for billions upon billions of dollars in annual sales.

AUCTION SALES

Almost all varieties of musical collectibles can be purchased through auction sales. Sales devoted entirely to recordings are held by specialist auctioneers in various parts of the country and, in addition, there are opportunities to buy musical instruments, recordings, and memorabilia at many estate sales that are not billed as music sales. Any serious musicana enthusiast must follow the estate sales in his area closely and attend as many as possible to avoid missing good opportunities. Remember that the items you fail to purchase will be bought by dealers and you will pay them a 50 percent or higher profit. Don't be afraid of auctions. On the other hand, don't go blindly into an auction sale. Attend the presale exhibition, carefully examine any items on which you intend to bid, then decide on the top price you care to pay. At the sale, stay within these limits. Be especially thorough in inspecting mixed or bulk lots of records, music sheets, etc. It is quite likely that a batch of 100 music sheets will contain just one rarity that makes the whole lot worthwhile, and which other bidders have not noticed. A collection of old 78 recordings may appear at the surface very uninteresting but could contain a few first-rate gems. Once the sale is over, it's too late.

PITFALLS

The chief dangers are buying mechanical instruments that fail to operate, and personality autographs or other memorabilia that are not authentic.

The buyer of mechanical instruments should always insist on a demonstration before making a purchase, or putting down a deposit. When purchasing by mail, have some arrangement with the seller whereby a refund will be made if the item does not prove to be operable. A reputable dealer in mechanical instruments will provide a written guarantee, but this is seldom obtainable from a general antiques dealer who sells instruments only occasionally.

Personality autographs are, unfortunately, often faked. This is something of which the public is not fully aware, believing that a forger would not bother with items that retail for small amounts of money. True enough, a counterfeit Washington or Lincoln letter could be sold for thousands of dollars, while a faked Fabian autograph is worth perhaps a dollar or two, but the latter is much simpler to sell. It is almost impossible to successfully pass off Washington or Lincoln material, but a faker can, very easily, take an 8 x 10 publicity shot of any pop singer, which he purchases for $1, add a signature, and sell it for a profit. There is no defense against this sort of thing except to gain a good knowledge of celebrity autographs, study out genuine specimens, and acquire, when possible, either from respected dealers or from collectors who have obtained the autographs directly from the stars. There are many collectors who have duplicate autographs that they are willing and anxious to trade.

"Why buy?" is the motto of some hobbyists, who prefer to get their star signatures from the source — the stars themselves. This insures authenticity and provides a spark of excitement, too. Sometimes you can have the item personally autographed to you, which is a thrill that a purchased autograph will never have. There are various ways to go about this. The best, of course, is to approach the celebrity in person. When that cannot be done, a good alternative is to send a personal letter requesting his or her autograph, along with a stamped return envelope. Stars can be addressed in care of the recording studio for which they work, a TV network, motion picture studio, or even sometimes through a magazine. The best way to get a letter to a star is to find out the name of his agent and send it in care of the agent.

SOME TIPS ON USING THIS BOOK

There's an almost encyclopedic amount of information in *The Official Price Guide To Music Collectibles.* It's been arranged for maximum convenience, and especially convenience-under-fire (when you're at a flea market, for example, and need to find a listing FAST). All items are grouped into categories and the categories are alphabetized throughout the book. Within each section, the items are listed by artist or manufacturer or by "type," whichever is applicable. As there are numerous different types of collectibles listed, no single system could be workable for every category. Flip through the book and in a couple of minutes you'll get the hang of it!

A few general comments:

With all of the items listed, condition counts. The prices shown are (in cases where no reference is made to contrary) for specimens in well-preserved condition. Any object which is broken, has parts missing, is badly stained, etc., can normally be expected to sell for less than the price range indicated — usually much less. On the other hand, a perfect mint specimen with no signs of use will often sell for a higher price than shown in our ranges.

In the case of the 45 r.p.m. records, when reference is made to PICTURE SLEEVE, the price indicated is for the record PLUS THE SLEEVE. In most instances we also give the value for the record alone. You can easily compute the value of the sleeve alone (with no record), by deducting the price of the record from the price of the record-with-sleeve. The sleeves themselves are definitely collectors' items.

Values for LP albums are for specimens WITH THE JACKETS OR SLEEVES. The records by themselves are worth considerably less, in most cases only about ½ as much.

ABOUT THE PRICES

Who agrees about the values of collectors' items? Nobody — and that's the reason for the OFFICIAL GUIDE series of collectors' handbooks, to serve as an independent monitor of the market. Thousands upon thousands of actual sales and dealers' offerings were reviewed, to arrive at fair market values for the listings in this book. Each price is a RETAIL value — the sum charged by dealers when selling to the public. When selling TO a dealer, you would naturally receive less than these amounts, owing to the dealer's operating costs and profit margin. Instead of a single or "flat" price, a range is shown for every item in this book. This approach is (we feel) fairer to both buyer and seller, since the prices of collectors' items DO vary from sale to sale. It is entirely possible that some, or many, of these items can be found selling for higher or lower than the indicated range. If you're lucky enough to find a $30-45 record at a garage sale, it might be going for $1 or $2. Sales of this type are not considered when computing market values, since they occur outside the normal collector market. By the same token, in an auction sale, a $30-45 item could reach $50, $75 or even more, if bidding is intense. Nothing is certain in the world of collecting. That's why this book is presently only a guide — a map to a road which YOU will need to travel yourself, to see what the terrain is really like.

*

SID GLICKMAN
1-914-591-5371
42 BUTTERWOOD
IRVINGTON, N.Y.
10533

DEALER IN ANT.
MCL. INS'S

IMPORTANT MESSAGE

TO ______________________________

DATE ____________ TIME ________ A.M. / P.M.

WHILE YOU WERE OUT

M ______________________________

OF ______________________________

Area Code
& Exchange ______________________

TELEPHONED		PLEASE CALL	
CALLED TO SEE YOU		WILL CALL AGAIN	
WANTS TO SEE YOU		URGENT	
	RETURNED YOUR CALL		

Message ______________________________

____

____

____

____

Operator ______________________________

MECHANICAL MUSIC MACHINES

Music has always been very important to mankind. Not until the many and varied inventions of modern mad in the last hundred or so years was one able to enjoy "live" music without the aid, studied knowledge or musical expertise of those present at the "performance". This is then what is meant by "Mechanical" Music. The player piano, Encore banjo, even orchestrions are basically actual musical instruments with the addition of self-playing mechanisms.

Other machines were invented specifically to make music mechanically, for example: music boxes and roller organs.

The phonograph, though it does not actually fall into either of these categories, was a singularly monumental breakthrough in bringing a wide range of entertainment into the homes of a large segment of the population. This is the primary reason for its survival even today.

The common element in all these machines is that they produce musical entertainment without the live presence of a human musician.

DETERMINING VALUE

The most important factors in determining the value of a machine are: rarity, popularity and condition. Condition is a crucial determining factor in the mechanical musical field. "Fine original working condition" (as it left the maker's hands) is the most desirable state for a machine. It is quite rare that a machine has survived many decades without some needed repair or restoration, as in the case of most pneumatically operated machines. A player piano in original unrestored condition is not worth as much as expertly restored examples.

Unless otherwise described, the value range given in each entry is for a machine in "fine working condition" as close to the original as possible.

Our prices come from many sources such as auctions, dealer catalogues, publications in the field, and our own experience. There can be great differences between the auction and dealer price for a specific machine. Many rare items just don't seem to come up for sale anywhere else than these sources. One can reasonably allow a 10 percent leeway either way on the prices given to account for geography, inflation and other variables.

It is difficult to determine the value of a machine that is not in working condition. If the "problem" is just a minor adjustment or missing winding tool (eg. crank, key, etc.), a fair value should be considerably higher than a machine that needs total restoration. It is up to the buyer and seller to educate themselves so they can exercise discretion as well as recognizing a bargain when they see it. (See "Repair and Restoration Guidelines" and "Future Trends"). One noteworthy exception where we have included both "Unrestored" and "Restored" prices is the section on "Pianos-Self Playing". The reason for this is that so many examples are found in unrestored condition and the difference in the value in a player piano between unrestored and restored condition is considerable.

A willing buyer and seller can set their own values. In the case of rare desirable items of "Museum Quality", it is a seller's market and very difficult to evaluate. We have given it our best shot. A landmark auction tomorrow could change everything.

One must not let greed or the imagined prospect of a windfall profit cloud his reason. The reality of the market place is that it is rare that one can actually get the listed value of an item. Why? In any particular instance so many variables come into account, not the least being the personality of the parties involved.

The antique field has always been a place where "haggling" over the price is part of the pleasure in making the "deal". A guide is useful as a point of reference and in determining relative values of machines within a specific area.

DATING

As this book is meant only as a guide to the field of mechanical musical machines, very brief historical information is given. When dates are given at the beginning of each section and in some of the entries, they are meant as a point of reference. The "Further Reading" section contains some excellent reference tools for in-depth historical information.

BUYING AND SELLING GUIDELINES

Both the buyer and seller of mechanical musical machines use the same outlets to further their interests.

The private buyer has the same opportunity to purchase machines at an auction as a dealer and at the same price. Sometimes one can come away with a real bargain and other times the excitement of the moment can cause the bidders to bring the price higher than "up-to-date" retail values. It can depend on the basic character of the bidding audience and the over-all quality of the merchandise being auctioned off. An audience of mostly dealers can be good for a private buyer as you are not concerned with profit margins and may be prepared to bid higher. For the seller, consigning machines to an auction house, an audience of private buyers and collectors can bring higher prices. You should attend specialized auctions before you decide to consigne your machines to them. (See "Auctions").

The best way to gauge your chances for success at an auction is to keep the following points in mind:

Where and how much advertising you saw for the auction.
Is the audience enthusiastic about the merchandise.
Is the buying lively or is the auctioneer working hard to seel the items.
What is the percentage the auctioneer receives in commission.
Is there a buyers commission on the winning bid.

Buying and selling through special interest publications, society bulletins, collector's newsletters, and similar classified advertising is an excellent way to reach an interested readership and a receptive market. Through correspondence and business dealings one gets to meet and know fellow enthusiasts. One does not have to join the various mechanical musical societies to advertise in their publications. One does have to join the society to receive the publication on a regular basis. (See "Mechanical Musical Societies and Their Publications" and "Publications and Sources for Facsimile Reprints").

Specialized antique shows are a good way to meet some of the people one has corresponded with through the special interest publications. They are also an excellent place to see a wide variety of mechanical musical items from all over. (See "Antique Shows")

Dealers and restorers are fo course an excellent source for buying and selling machines and parts. For some very specialized and rare items, dealers are the primary and maybe the only way to locate them. They have cultivated sources and contacts the ordinary buyer doesn't know about. Dealers can help you locate restorers with the special expertise you may require. Restorers are also a good source for contacts with other interested buyers and sellers. (See "Dealers and Restorers")

DEALERS AND RESTORERS

Most of the machines in this book require and deserve expert repair and restoration, when needed, to insure and enhance their value. The following are guidelines for finding and choosing a restorer:

1. Mechanical Musical Societies can direct you to fellow members and restorers whom members have used and are satisfied with.
2. Local museums or state museums may be familiar with restorers who have done work for them.
3. Yellow pages and other directories may provide you with a starting point; for example, a local dealer who sells the type of thing you need restored.
4. Dealers and restorers listed in the accompanying section (though this is a very incomplete listing).

A word of caution: *When you have made a selection of a restorer, ask to hear and see work in progress and completed work to be sure you have chosen wisely. The list of dealers and restorers was compiled from many sources. The inclusion or exclusion from this listing of any particular company or person does not constitute a judgement about them.*

ARIZONA

WENDELL MOORE, 3085 W. Highway 89A, Sedona, Arizona 86336. Phonographs for sale.

ARKANSAS

K. R. Powers, 28 Alton Circle, Rogers, Arkansas, 72756. Disc and cylinder music box restoration sales and supplies.

CALIFORNIA

ANTIQUE JUKEBOX CO., 2363 East Olympic Boulevard, Los Angeles, California.

ANTIQUE MUSIC BOX RESTORATION, 1825 Placentia Avenue, Costa Mesa, California 92627. Varied mechanical musical machines.

BROADMOORE AUTOMATIC INSTRUMENT RESTORATIONS, 1709C 1st Street, San Francisco, California 91340. Orchestrions and reproducing pianos.

CARL FRICK, 940 Canon Road, Santa Barbara, California 93110. Catalog of parts and literature.

MUSIC BOX DOCTOR: ANTHONY J. CIUFFINI, 28810 Crestridge Road, Rancho Palos Verdes, California 90274. Musical box repairs.

MUSICAL AMERICANA TALKING MACHINE CO., 354 East Campbell Avenue, Campbell, California 95008. Large list of phonograph parts and repair services.

STEPHEN OLIPHANT, 5255 Allott Avenue, Van Nuys, California 91401. Phonographs for sale.

URBAN ANTIQUES, 1861 Union Street, San Francisco, California 94123. Variety of mechanical musical machines for sale.

VINTAGE TALKING MACHINES (STEVE AND JUDY FARMER), P.O. Box 558, San Luis Rey, California 92068. Phonographs for sale, complete restoration including coin-ops.

COLORADO

ART REBLITZ PIANOS, 3916 N. Azalea, Colorado Springs, Colorado 80907. Restoration services for automatic pianos and organs.

FRERES D'METATRON, 610 Downing Street, Denver, Colorado 80218. Music Box restoration.

CONNECTICUT

MECHANICAL MUSIC CENTER, INC., 25 King Highway North, Box 88, Darien, Connecticut 06820. One of the largest dealers in mechanical musical machines. Showroom and periodic illustrated catalogs.

MECHANTIQUES, 26 Barton Hill, East Hampton, Connecticut 06424. Buy, sell, trade mechanical musical machines.

YANKEE PHONOGRAPH CO. (SCOTT ZAHNER), 39 Florence Street, Rockville, Connecticut 06066. Phonographs for sale, restoration service.

FLORIDA

RINKY-TINK AMUSEMENTS, 14086 S.W. 142 Avenue, Miami, Florida 33186. Player piano and jukebox repair and sales.

GEORGIA

D. B. MUSICAL RESTORATIONS, 230 Lakeview Avenue N.E., Atlanta, Georgia 30305. Music boxes (restoration services).

ILLINOIS

JUKEBOX SATURDAY NIGHT, 1552 N. Wells, Chicago, Illinois 60610. Jukebox sales and restoration.

PHOENIX OLDE TIME MUSIC-SALES AND SERVICE, 60 Martin Lane, Elk Grove Village, Illinois 60007. Specializes in organettes and barrel organs.

REGINA MUSIC BOX CO., INC. (J. HARRY AND NANCY CARMEL), 7013 W. Crandall Avenue, Worth, Illinois 60482. Disc music boxes, parts, new discs.

INDIANA

CLARENCE W. FABEL, Box 202, Route 3, Morgantown, Indiana 46160. Cylinder music box restoration.

IOWA

TOM FRETTY, Highway 9 and 65, Manly, Iowa 50456. Musical antiques.

JUKEBOX JUNCTION, Box 1081, Des Moines, Iowa 50311. Parts, Reprints, etc.

STEVE LOOTS, P. O. Box 119, Des Moines, Iowa 50301. Jukebox sales, parts, reprints.

KANSAS

HILL'S PLAYER AND GRAMOPHONE SERVICE, 1535 Campus Road, Manhattan, Kansas 66502. Restoration of player and reproducing pianos, also phonograph repairs.

PLAYER PIANO COMPANY, INC., 620 East Douglas, Wichita, Kansas 67202. Large illusstrated catalog of piano and player piano parts.

FLOYD'S BAND ORGAN REPAIR AND COMPANY, 2736 N. 66 Terrace, Kansas City, Kansas 66104. Band organ rebuilder.

KENTUCKY

AUTOMATED MUSIC SPECIALISTS, 204 N. Madison, Middletown, Kentucky 40243. Repair and restoration of automatic pianos and organs.

LOUISIANA

SHREVEPORT MUSIC CO., 109 Kings Highway, Shreveport, Louisiana 71104. Piano repair.

MARYLAND

DAHLBERG'S KEYBOARD SPECIALISTS AND SERVICE, 12613 Chanler Lane, Bowie, Maryland 20715. Restoration of organs and player pianos.

ART AND HELEN MUELLER, P.O. Box 9450, Cantonville, Maryland 21228. Sales of Music Boxes and related items.

THE NOOK FOR MUSIC BOXES (CAROLE W. FETTIG), 4849 Cordell Avenue, Bethesda, Maryland 20814. Music boxes, buy, sell, repair.

MASSACHUSETTS

ALAN PIER PLAYER PIANO SERVICE, 8 Skyline Drive, Billerica, Massachusetts 01821. Restoration service, specializing in pneumatic instruments.

OLD SOUND, Route 134 near 6A, East Dennis, Massachusetts 02641. Phonograph display, sales and service.

THE PIANO SHOP (JOHN SPRINGER), P.O. Box 411, 438 Spring Street, Athol, Massachusetts 01331. Pianos and players: restoration, buy and sell.

ROLAND A. TRIFF, 11 Warwick Road, W. Newton, Massachusetts 02165. Music box sales and restoration service.

MICHIGAN

PIANO PLUS (RICHARD F. LUTIN), 916 North Third, Miles, Michigan 49120. Player piano, reed organ and music box sales and service.

MINNESOTA

JERRY MADSEN, 4624 West Woodland Road, Edina, Minnesota 55424. Phonographs and related items for sale.

MECHANICAL MAESTRO (ANGELO P. RULLI), 1300 East Third Street, St. Paul, Minnesota 55106. Music Box repair.

MISSOURI

CRAIG BROUGHER, 3500 Claremont, Independence, Missouri 60532. Complete piano and player restoration.

WILLIAM T. SINGLETON, PIANOS, 1101 South Kingshighway, St. Louis, Missouri 63110. Pianos, nickelodeons, music boxes: restoration.

NEW JERSEY

AUTA MUSIQUE LTD. (JERE AND STEVE RYDER), P.O. Box 65, Cranford, New Jersey 07016. Music box sales and restoration.

GOULD PIANO CRAFTSMEN, 391 Tremont Place, Orange, New Jersey 07050. Complete piano service and sales. Specializing in player and reproducing pianos as well as other pneumatic instruments. Pianocorders Installations, sales and service.

CHARLEY HUMMEL, 61 Laurel Drive, Wayne, New Jersey 07470. Buy, Sell, Trade, Repair Phonographs and related items.

MEEKINS MUSIC BOX COMPANY, *P.O. Box 161, Collingswood, New Jersey 08108. Music boxes, especially "Regina", restoration services.*

OLDE TYME MUSIC SCENE, 915 Main Street, Boonton, New Jersey 07005. Variety of phonographs and records for sale.

FLOYD SILVER, P.O. Box 274, Vincentown, New Jersey 08088. Buy, Sell, Trade, Repair Phonographs and related items. Also mail order auction sales with emphasis on cylinder and disc records.

NEW MEXICO

ELEMENTS OF TIME (A. PARK SHAW III), 109 Romero N.W., Albuquerque, New Mexico 87104. Music box sales and repair (also clocks and watches).

NEW YORK

ANTIQUES MECHANICAL (RESURRECTED) LTD., "Mainspring House" on the corner of Spring and Main Streets, South Salem, New York 10590. Music boxes bought, sold and repaired.

ANTIQUE PHONOGRAPH SHOP, 320 Jericho Turnpike, Floral Park, New York 11001. Buy, sell, repair spring operated phonographs.

BORNAND MUSIC BOX CO., 139 Fourth Avenue, Pelham, New York 10803. Swiss and disc music boxes for sale (restoration services).

F. & L. ANTIQUES (FRANK AND LORE METZGER), Box 47, Harrison, New York 10528. Music boxes and automata. Buy, sell and restoration services.

RITA FORD, 19 East 65 Street, New York, New York 10021. Music box sales.

LEONARD ANTIQUES, Box 127, Albertson, Long Island, New York 11507. Variety of mechanical music items.

MUSICAL MUSEUM, (THE SANDERS FAMILY), State Route 12B, Deansboro, New York 13328. Museum Shop Repair Service for mechanical musical machines. Sale of Music Rolls for grind organs.

PANCHRONIA ANTIQUES, P.O. Box 73, Warners, New York, 13164. Music boxes and parts, restoration services, discs.

PLAYER PIANO REPAIR, 12 East 12th Street, New York, New York 10003. (12th Floor), also pipe organs.

TREASURE ISLAND ANTIQUES (LEOPOLD AND VALERIE LYSLOFF), 378 South Country Road, Brookhaven Hamlet, New York 11719. Antique music boxes, also clocks, watches, dolls.

VICKI GLASGOW, 135 Plymouth Drive, Scarsdale, New York 10583. Mechanical Musical items for sale.

WAVES, 32 East 13 Street, New York, New York 10003. Early radios and phonographs.

NORTH CAROLINA

ANTIQUE PHONOGRAPH CO., 612 South Mulberry Street, Statesville, North Carolina 28677. Dealer of mechanical musical items.

OHIO

MUSIQUE MECHANIQUE, 2960 North High Street, Columbus, Ohio 43202. Music box sales.

PIANO WORKSHOP, 3166 West 33 Street, Cleveland, Ohio 44109. Piano and player piano restoration.

PLAYER PIANO SHOP (JAMES R. HOCKENBERGER), 776 Carlton, Toledo, Ohio 43609. Rebuild and sell player pianos, nickelodeons.

PENNSYLVANIA

MUSIC CURIO REPAIR SHOP, 23 N. Sycamore Street, Box 488, Macungie, Pennsylvania 10862. Music boxes, small organs.

SOUTH CAROLINA

M. LYNN REID PIANOS, 110 Highway Drive, Union, South Carolina 29379. Automatic instrument restoration.

SOUTH DAKOTA

MICHAEL V. EDWARDS, THE PIANO MAN, 2019 1st Avenue, Rapid City, South Dakota 57701. Player piano rebuilding.

TENNESSEE

GEORGE E. KURZ, 4703-A, Sabrina Lane, Chattanooga, Tennessee 37343. Pump organs, organettes, singing birds: repair and restoration.

TEXAS

AUTOMATIC MUSIC CO. (ED GAIDA), 600 Fredericksburg Road, San Antonio, Texas 78201. Buy, sell, repair player pianos.

BEAU-DAN IMPORTS, 2040 The Promenade, Richardson, Texas 75240. Music Boxes.

VERMONT

PORTER MUSIC BOX CO., 5 Mound Street, Randolph, Vermont 05060. Make and restore music boxes, also discs for Polyphone, Regina and Porter Music Boxes.

REED ORGAN SERVICE, Box 3, Back Street, Jamaica, Vermont 05343. Reed organ parts and repair.

WASHINGTON

MUSICAL AUTOMATA OF YESTERYEAR, 1901 S.E. Sedgwick Road, Port Orchard, Washington 98366. Repair and sales of mechanical musical machines.

WISCONSIN

JOHN HOVANCAK, JR., 705 N. Union, Dodgeville, Wisconsin 53533. Mechanical music repair and restoration.

AUSTRALIA

ANTIQUE CLOCK REPAIR AND ANTIQUES. 22 Ascot Blvd., Bowral, N.S.W. 2576 Australia. Music Box restoration (also watches, clocks, automata).

BELGIUM

ARTHUR PRINSEN, 15 Oostjacktpack, St. Niklass, 2700 Belgium. Music Boxes and organs.

CANADA

FRANKLIN H. FOLEY, Box 1476, Belleville, Ontario K8N5J2, Canada. Buy, sell and trade mechanical musical instruments.

THE GREAT CANADIAN NICKELODEON CO. LTD., Highway 135, Industrial Park #90, Box 33, London, Ontario N6A4B8, Canada. Repair, restoration and sales of coin pianos.

PLAYER PIANO CENTRE AND MUSEUM, 3399 Dunbar Street, Vancouver, British Columbia, Canada V6S2B9. Restoration services. Specialty: Wurlitzer.

DENMARK

MEKANISKMUSIC MUSEUM (CLAES O. FRIBERG), Box 14, Rungsted Kyst DK 2960, Denmark. Automatic musical instruments, buy, sell, repair.

ENGLAND

JOHN COWDEROY ANTIQUES, 42 South Street, Eastbourne, East Sussex, England BN214X. Music boxes (restoration services).

JACK DONOVAN, 93 Portobello Road, London W11 England. Mechanical music antiques buy and sell.

KEITH HARDING, 93 Hornsey Road, London, England N76DJ. Music boxes, parts and publications (restoration services).

NORFOLK POLYPHONE CENTRE, Wood Farm, Baudeswell, East Dereham, Norfolk, England. Mechanical musical items buy and sell.

THE TALKING MACHINE, 30 Watford Way, Hendon, Central London, NW4 England. Buy, sell early phonographs and music boxes.

JAPAN

NOF ANTIQUES SHELLMAN, INC., (NORIO ISOGAI), 14-16 Ginza 3-chome, Chuo-Ku Tokyo 104 Japan. Mechanical Musical Instruments.

NETHERLANDS

W. J. VAN OS AND H. M. G. YU, Nieuwe Spiegelstraat 68, Amsterdam, Netherlands. Antique music box sales.

SCOTLAND

MONKTON HOUSE ANTIQUES, Monkton House, Old Craig Hall, Musselburgh, Midlothian, Scotland. Buy and sell variety of mechanical antiques and curios (by appointment only).

SWITZERLAND

RETONIO'S INTERNATIONAL GALLERY, Zielstrasse 38, CH-9050 Appensell, Switzerland. Mechanical Musical items for sale.

This list of Dealers and Restorers has been compiled from many sources. The inclusion or exclusion from this listing of any particular company or person does not constitute a judgement about them. ***EACH READER MUST MAKE THEIR OWN CHOICES BASES ON THE GUIDELINES PREVIOUSLY ENUMERATED.*** *We know this list will be expanded in time. (Your recommendations are welcome.)*

ANTIQUE RECORD DEALERS

For those with specific types of interest in the record field, there are classified sections in many of the phonograph publications listed in "Publications and Reprints" where dealers and collectors advertise their records for sale.

Listed below are just a few dealers who issue price and/or auction lists:

PAUL C. BURGESS (disc and cylinder records)
Box 12-A, Friendship, ME 04547

DENNIS DEVINE (cylinder records)
722 Pierce Street, Council Bluffs, IA 51501

ELECTROPHONE CYLINDER RECORD COMPANY
320 Jericho Turnipike, Floral Park, NY 11001.
Newly made, pre-recorded cylinder records, modern artists

MUSIQUE
1177 Bay Street, Rochester, NY 14609
Cylinder and disc record mail auctions

JOHN A. PETTY (RECORD AUCTION BY MAIL)
Route 1, Box 54-A, Catawba, NC 28609

ARTHUR SANDERS, MUSICAL MUSEUM
Deansboro, NY 13328

THE 78 SHOP: DENNIS TICHY
Box 242, Murrysville, PA 15668
Sells records by artists or type by the "case".

RICHARD SIMONTON (diamond discs)
4209 Burbank Boulevard, Burbank, CA 91602

CARL A. TESSEN (all types)
1620 Columbia Avenue, Oshkosh, WI 54901

VERTIGO HILL RECORDS
Vertigo Manor, 581 Arch Street, New Britain, CT 06051
Pre-1935 records, mail auctions

YANKEE RECORD CO.
39 Florence Street, Rockville, CT 06066
Mail auctions of cylinder and disc records and related items (1900-1935).

PIANO ROLL DEALERS

Player Piano rolls can still be found at flea markets, auctions and in antique shops and there are dealers who specialize in rolls. (Dealers are especially useful if one has specific artists, roll labels or types of music in mind.) There are excellent recuts being made today especially of hard to find popular artists and music styles; e.g.: Ragtime, Gershwin, etc.

Average 88 note roll $1.00 and up; average reproducing roll $3.00 and up.

AMICA FOUNDING CHAPTER ROLL AUCTION
4271 N. First St., Space #1, San Jose, CA 95134. Periodic mail order piano roll auctions, extensive selection with emphasis on reproducing and expression rolls.

AUTOMATIC MUSIC ROLL CO.
P. O. Box 3194, Seattle, WA 98114. Old and new Reproducing Rolls and related literature.

L. CORDELL (PIANO ROLL AUCTIONS BY MAIL)
2240 Lorain Road, San Marino, CA 91108

JOHN T. DONOHUE (PIANO ROLL AUCTIONS BY MAIL)
Box 168, Southampton, NY 11968. Also has reproducing pianos for sale on consignment.

ELECTRIC PIANO ROLL CO.
Harold E. Davis, Box 1, Leslie, MI 49251

KLAVIER MUSIC ROLL (THE POWELLS)
9700 Glenoaks Boulevard, Sun Valley, CA 91352. Recuts of reproducing rolls and regular 88 note rolls..

PLAY-RITE MUSIC ROLLS, INC.
2121 S. El Camino Real, San Mateo, CA 99403. Make and sell player piano rolls.

QRS MUSIC ROLLS
1026 Niagara Street, Buffalo, NY 14213. They are the only one of the old companies still in business. Write to them for name of local dealer.

DON RAND AND ED OPENSHAW
Old Piano Roll Auction and Collector's Classics (Limited edition recuts — beautiful). By mail 3222 Larga Avenue, Los Angeles, CA 90039.

MIKE AND FRED SCHWIMMER AUCTIONS BY MAIL
241A Harbor, Glencoe, IL 60022. Monthly roll auctions.

VI & SI ANTIQUES
8970 Main Street, Clarence, NY 14031. Rolls and records (all types), auction lists (by mail).

MISCELLANEOUS ROLLS DEALERS

EDWARD FREYER
Box 373 (Route 31), Flemington, NJ 08822. Recut rolls for nickelodeons (Type A, G, 4x rolls).

MUSICAL MUSEUM (ART SANDERS)
State Route 12B, Deansboro, NY 13328. Music rolls for grind organs.

SCHMIDT'S MUSIC ROLLS
Edward M. Schmidt, 5010 Elsmere Place, Bethesda, MD 20814. Manufacturer of Music for organettes, paper roll and strip instruments.

AUCTIONS

DON P. BRITT, Auctioneer,
3125 S. Virginia, Suite #1, Reno, Nevada 89504. Auctioneer for the three Bellm Museum Auctions, among others.

CHRISTIE'S EAST
219 East 67 Street, New York, NY 10021. Periodic actions containing fine quality mechanical musical machines.

CHRISTIE'S SOUTH KENSINGTON, LTD.
85 Old Brompton Road, London SW73JS England. Regular auction sales of mechanical musical items. Catalogues available, bidding by mail accepted.

MANOR HOUSE GALLERIES
West Memorial Park Plaza, 8570 Katy Freeway, Suite 119, Houston, Texas 77079. Don Mudd, Auctioneer. Occasional large auction sales of mechanical musical instruments, very entertaining.

RETONIO INTERNATIONAL GALLERY
Zielstrasse 38, CH 9050 Appenzell, Switzerland. Periodic auctions of mechanical musical machines. Illustrated catalogue issued.

SOTHEBY PARKE BERNET
1334 York Ave., New York, NY 10021. "Collector's Carrousel" Auctions usually contain mechanical musical items.

SOTHEBY'S BELGRAVIA
19 Motcomb Street, London SW1S8LB, England. Auction sales of mechanical musical items. Catalogues available, bidding by mail accepted.

SOTHEBY'S LOS ANGELES
7660 Beverly Boulevard, Los Angeles, CA 90036. "Fine collectibles 'Auctions' ".

Special auctions of mechanical musical machines are widely advertised in antique publications, e.g.:

Antique and Auction News
Antique Trader
Collectors News

ANTIQUE SHOWS

SEVEN ACRES ANTIQUE VILLAGE AND MUSEUM
Route 20 and S. Union Road, Union, IL 60180. Annual antique phonograph and music box show.

TRI STATE MUSIC COLLECTIBLES SHOW
put on by TRI STATE EXHIBITIONS, INC.
P. O. Box 76, Livingston, NJ 07039. Periodic shows held in metropolitan New York area.

REPAIR AND RESTORATION GUIDELINES

In the field of mechanical musical machines, restoration is a key element. For the enterprising collector (especially one with limited financial resources) the satisfaction of restoring a potential "silk purse" is very satisfying. The prices for complete but unrestored machines are much more accessible and have not increased at a significant pace in the last few years. In fact in some cases their value has actually gone down. Though there is the additional investment in time, expertise, and supplies required in restoring a machine expertly it is really one of the best parts (and rewards) of collecting.

It is impossible to comprehensively describe here how to evaluate the condition one might find a particular type of machine (especially in a field as broad as mechanical musical machines) and what would be the best way to restore it. A machine that does not play may require only a minor adjustment, or more importantly, a major repair.

There are some fundamental guidelines to keep in mind. First and by far the best way to evaluate the condition of a machine is to play it. One may think appearance is a more important factor but in general it is easier to correct cosmetic problems than mechanical ones. To return to playing condition, DO NOT TRY TO PLAY THE MACHINE YOURSELF. Have the owner (dealer) play it for you. The old saying "you break it, you buy it", can be a costly way to satisfy your curiosity. BE CAREFUL of situations where the "owner" doesn't have the appropriate thing to play on the machine (piano roll, disc or cylinder record, music box disc, wooden cob, etc.) but is sure it "just needs a little adjustment to work fine". It is in your best interest to have educated yourself. There really aren't any easy instant alternatives to preparation unless you just bring an expert with you.

Preparation can consist of visiting mechanical musical machine collections that feature demonstrations of various types of machines, learning from fellow collectors about their machines and experiences in fixing them up, attending specialized antique shows and auctions and most important of all reading about your area of interest (both historical treatments as well as "how to fix" it guides). With this experience you will be able to evaluate how well a machine plays, how extensive the needed repairs are going to be and most important whether you feel able to meet the challenge of doing the restoration yourself.

Directly related to evaluating the restorable condition of a machine is the quality of previous repairs made to it (are they obvious?, sloppy?, consistent with the age, design, and type of machine, etc.). Did someone, for example install an electric motor in an early model phonograph that was only made crank wound? You should be aware of the differences between original condition and alterations made to accomodate someone's personal needs. This is not to say that you shouldn't buy such machines but their worth is dramatically affected by such alterations. Besides you must know what the original condition of a machine is to know what has been done (or undone) to it and what it will take to restore it to its former glory. Some bad repairs can be undone; others may be irreversible.

THE VALUE OF A MECHANICAL MUSICAL MACHINE IS DIRECTLY RELATED TO THE AUTHENTIC QUALITY OF THE OVERALL MACHINE, ITS COMPONENT PARTS AND PLAYING PERFORMANCE.

To further your experience and knowledge refer to the following sections: "Auctions, Antique Shows, Publications and Reprints, Buying & Selling Musical Societies, Further Reading and Dealers & Restorers".)

FUTURE TRENDS

While the values of mechanical musical machines enjoyed a rather rapid growth in the last few decades, the recent economic conditions have checked this trend.There are many factors involved not the least of which is a sluggish demand because of the discouragingly high prices in some circles. There is a point at which the price for a formerly popular item just reaches its peak and in some instances bottoms out. Buyers want fine quality machines for the high prices they are paying.

There has been a very definite leveling off of prices especially in the more common models of particular machines, eg. Edison Homes and Standards Model B and C, Victor inside horn table and floor models of the simple mahogany case variety, simple tune cylinder music boxes, unrestored player pianos, etc.

Barring the improbable miracle of someone finding a warehouse full of as yet unknown mechanical musical items, the future trends seems to be for collectors to branch out into related areas of collecting. For example: a music box collector may become interested in phonographs or roller organs. A phonograph collector may become more deeply interested in records and related items.

As far as new areas to conquer, the phonographs of the 1920's and '30's are still quite reasonable, and many, especially the floor model styles, were quite elaborate in case decoration, gold plating, etc. Columbia, Brunswick,

Edison, Sonora and Victor to name a few, manufactured lovely floor and console model disc phonographs with elaborate period decorations. There are also early electrically operated disc phonographs, notably the Victor Orthophonic table and floor models, starting to appear on the market.

Jukeboxes of the post classic or 1950's period are physically and financially accessible as are the pre-classic examples of the early 1930's.

MECHANICAL MUSICAL MUSEUMS AND COLLECTIONS OPEN TO THE PUBLIC

UNITED STATES

ARIZONA
ARIZONA HERITAGE CENTER: 949 East 2nd Street, Tuscon, AR. Varied collection of mechanical musical instruments.

ARKANSAS
MILES MUSICAL MUSEUM: U.S. Highway 62 West, Eureka Springs, AK. Varied collection of 250 musical items.

CALIFORNIA
ANGELUS CLOCKWORK MUSIC: 420 Second Street, Old Town, Eureka, CA. Varied collection of musical items.

THE DIALS: 190 West J Street, Benicia, CA. Small collection of mechanical musical machines.

KNOTT'S BERRY FARM AND GHOST TOWN: Two miles south of Santa Ana Freeway on California Route #39. Thirty-five various items.

MUSEE MECHANIQUE: 1090 Point Lobos Avenue, San Francisco, CA ("Historic Cliff House"). Collection of music machines including nickelodeons, orchestrions, and music boxes.

TOWER OF BEAUTY AT SAN SYLMAR: 15180 Bledsoe Street, San Sylmar, CA. Small collection of nickelodeons.

WELCH'S MOUNTAIN FANTASY: 23551 Highway #243, Alandale, CA.

COLORADO
PIKES PEAK GHOST TOWN: 1803 N. Cascade Avenue, Ghost Town C Highway 24 West at S. 21 Street exit, Colorado Springs, CO. Small varied collection.

CONNECTICUT
THE AMERICAN MUSEUM OF MECHANICAL MUSIC: 26 Barton Hill, East Hampton, CT. Collection of music boxes, some coin operated music machines.

MUSEUM OF THE MUSICAL BOX SOCIETY INTERNATIONAL: 295 West Avenue at the Lockwood Mathews Mansion, Norwalk, CT. Varied collection with emphasis on music boxes. Also a reference library of mechanical musical literature.

DELAWARE
DELAWARE STATE MUSEUM: Bank Lane and New Street, Dover, DE. Eldridge Johnson phonograph collection.

FLORIDA

BELLM'S CARS AND MUSIC OF YESTERDAY: 5500 North Tamiami Trail, Sarasota, FL. Very extensive collection of 1300 mechanical musical machines with demonstrations and coin operated automatic instruments.

EDISON WINTER HOME AND MUSEUM: 2350 McGregor Boulevard, Fort Myers, FL. Large phonograph collection. Also tours of the home, garden and laboratories.

ELLIOTT MUSEUM: 825 N.E. Ocean Boulevard, Stuart, FL. Small collection of music machines.

LIGHTNER MUSEUM: City Hall Complex 25 Granada, St. Augustine, FL. Varied collection of musical items.

ST. PETERSBURG HISTORICAL MUSEUM: 335 Second Avenue, N.E., St. Petersburg, FL. Small varied collection.

YESTERDAY IN REVIEW: Box 505, 8 miles S.W. of Kissimmee on Highway 17 and 92, Intercession City, FL. 200 mechanical musical instruments, varied collection.

GEORGIA

ANTIQUE AUTO AND MUSIC MUSEUM: Stone Mountain, GA. 35 mechanical musical instruments.

IDAHO

MANGUM'S MUSICAL ARCADE: Two miles north on Highway 91, Blackfoot, ID. Varied collection of musical items.

ILLINOIS

PEDALS, PUMPERS AND ROLLS: 675 W. Street, Elmhurst, IL. Varied collection of music machines.

RINGER AND SON MUSEUM: Broadway and Melody Lane, New Berlin, IL. Large varied mechanical musical collection.

SEVEN ACRES ANTIQUE VILLAGE AND MUSEUM: 8512 S. Union Road, Union, IL. Large collection of phonographs.

SVOBODA'S NICKELODEON TAVERN: ½ mile west of Dyer, IN on Route 30, Chicago Heights, IL. 150 various machines.

THE TIME MACHINE: Clock Tower Inn, 7801 East State Street, Rockford, IL. Small varied collection.

INDIANA

HISTORICAL MUSEUM OF THE WABASH VALLEY: 1411 S. 6 Street, Terre Haute, IN. Small varied collection.

JULIA MEEKGAAR WAYNE COUNTY INDIANA HISTORICAL MUSEUM: 1150 North A Street, Richmond, IN. Small varied collection.

MIDWEST PHONOGRAPH MUSEUM: 2245 State Road 252, Martinsville, IN. Large phonograph collection.

IOWA

PLYMOUTH COUNTY HISTORICAL MUSEUM: U.S. Route 75 South, Le Mars, IA. 500 instruments some mechanical.

TOM'S MECHANICAL MUSIC WONDERLAND: Highway 9 and 65, Monly, IA. 50456. Varied collection.

KANSAS

BOOT HILL MUSEUM, INC.: Front Street, Dodge City, KA. Small varied collection of machines.

KANSAS MUSEUM OF HISTORY: 6425 SW Sixth, Topeka, KA. Small collection.

MAINE

MUSICAL WONDER HOUSE: 18 High Street, Wiscasset, ME. large collection of 200 mechanical musical machines.

WELLS AUTO MUSEUM: Route 1, (Box 496), Wells, ME. Small collection mainly nickelodeons.

MARYLAND

MARYLAND HISTORICAL SOCIETY: 201 W. Monument Street, Baltimore, MD. Small collection of music boxes.

MASSACHUSETTS

YESTERYEARS MUSEUM ASSOCIATION, INC.: Main and River Streets, Sandwich, MA. 40-50 mechanical dolls and toys, some musical.

MICHIGAN

BILL'S MAGICAL MUSICAL ANTIQUES MUSEUM: 3209 Lowden, Kalamazoo, MI. Varied collection.

HENRY FORD MUSEUM: 20900 Oakwood Boulevard, Dearborn, MI. 25 musical machines.

THE MUSIC HOUSE: 7377 U.S. Route 31 North (6 miles north of Traverse City), Acme, MI. Varied collection in historic setting.

MINNESOTA

STAGE COACH MUSEUM: Route #1, Shakopee, MN. Small varied collection.

MONTANA

WORLD MUSEUM OF MINING: Box 3333, Butte, MT. Two player pianos.

NEVADA

HAROLD'S CLUB GUN COLLECTION AND MUSICAL MUSEUM: 250 North Virginia, Reno, NV. Small varied collection, mainly nickelodeons and orchestrions.

HARRAH'S AUTOMOBILE COLLECTION: Glendale Road, Reno, NV. Varied collection of coin operated machines.

VIRGINIA CITY MUSEUM: Virginia City, NV. Small collection of pianos and nickelodeons.

NEW HAMPSHIRE

CLARK'S TRADING POST: One mile north on Route 3, North Woodstock, NH. Small varied collection, mainly nickelodeons and orchestrions.

NEW JERSEY

ANTIQUE AUTO MUSEUM: State Highway 34 and Ridgewood Road, Wall Township, NJ. Small varied collection of mechanical musical machines.

EDISON NATIONAL HISTORIC SITE-EDISON LABORATORIES: Main Street and Lakeside Avenue, West Orange, NJ. Small phonograph collection. Walking tour of the machine shops, laboratories, library, museum exhibits, etc.

NEW YORK

MAHOPAC COUNTRY STORE, FARM AND MUSEUM: Route 6 and Baldwin Place Road, Baldwin Place, NY. Small collection of mechanical musical instruments.

MARGARET WOODBURY STRONG MUSEUM: 700 Allen Creek Road, Rochester, NY. Large varied collection mainly music boxes and automata.

METROPOLITAN MUSEUM OF ART-ANDRE MERTENS GALLERY: Fifth Avenue at 82 Street, New York, NY. Varied collection with emphasis on musical instruments.

THE MUSICAL MUSEUM (The Sanders Family): State Route 12-B, Deansboro, NY. Large collection of mechanical musical machines, demonstrations, very pleasant atmosphere.

Q.R.S. MUSIC ROLLS, INC.: 1026 Niagara Street, Buffalo, NY. Player and reproducing pianos on display, also perforating roll equipment.

NORTH CAROLINA

ANTIQUE MUSIC AND WHEELS MUSEUM: Route I-85 Exit 164, 12 miles west of Durham, NC, Daniel Boone Antique Village, Hillsborough, NC. Large variety of mechanical musical machines.

NORTH DAKOTA

STATE HISTORICAL SOCIETY OF NORTH BISMARK: North Dakota Heritage Center, Bismark, ND. Music Boxes (small collection).

OHIO

MUSIQUE MECHANIQUE: 2960 North High, Columbus, OH. Large variety of mechanical musical machines.

SNYDER'S ANTIQUE AUTO PARTS: 12925 Woodworth Road, New Spring, OH. Small collection of coin operated machines.

OKLAHOMA

CHUCKWAGON MUSEUM: 201 S. Miss. Highway, Atoka, OK. Varied collection mainly orchestrions.

NATIONAL COWBOY HALL OF FAME AND WESTERN HERITAGE CENTER: 1700 Northeast 63 Street, Oklahoma City, OK. Small collection, mainly nickelodeons.

PENNSYLVANIA

CAROUSEL MECHANICAL MUSIC MUSEUM: Village Mall Route 420, Morton, PA. Small varied collection.

HERSHEY MUSEUM OF AMERICAN LIFE: 300 Park Boulevard, Hershey, PA. Small collection.

INTERCOURSE MUSIC WONDER WORLD: 3457 Old Philadelphia Pike, Route 340, P.O. Box 417, Intercourse, PA 17534. Large collection of mechanical musical machines especially phonographs.

MILL BRIDGE VILLAGE: Ronk Road at Soundersburg Road, Strasburg, PA. Varied collection, Ragtime Festival July 4th.

PERELMAN ANTIQUE TOY MUSEUM: 770 S. 2nd Street, Philadelphia, PA. 50 automated toy music boxes.

SOUTH DAKOTA

OLD WEST MUSEUM: Box 275, Chamberlain, SD. Small varied collection.

PIONEER AUTO MUSEUM AND ANTIQUE TOWN: Junction of Interstate 90, U.S. 16 and 83, Murdo, SD. 50 piece collection.

TENNESSEE

HOUSTON ANTIQUE MUSEUM: 201 High Street, Chattanooga, TN. Small varied collection.

TEXAS

OLDEN YEAR MUSICAL MUSEUM: 131 Fair Meadows, Duncanville, TX. Varied collection.

VERMONT

SHELBURNE MUSEUM: ½ mile south on Route 7, Shelburne, VT. Small varied collection.

VIRGINIA

THE MARINERS MUSEUM: One mile south of Route 64 and Route 17, Newport News, VA. Very small display.

WASHINGTON STATE

BARTLESS MUSEUM: Second and Morris, La Conner, WA. Small varied collection.

MUSEUM OF HISTORY AND INDUSTRY: 2161 East Hamplin, Seattle, WA. Small collection of music boxes and phonographs.

WASHINGTON, D.C.

SMITHSONIAN INSTITUTION-NATIONAL MUSEUM OF HISTORY AND TECHNOLOGY: Varied collection.

WISCONSIN

HISTORIC CHANDLER HOUSE: 151 W. College Avenue, Waukesha, WI. Varied collection.

HOUSE ON THE ROCK: Three miles east on U.S. 14, six miles south on U.S. 23, Spring Green, WI. Small varied collection.

KALVELAGE SCHLOSS: 2432 W. Kilburn, Milwaukee, WI. Small varied collection.

FOREIGN

AUSTRIA

TECHNICAL MUSEUM FOR INDUSTRY AND COMMERCE: Mariahilferstrasse 212, Vienna, Austria. Varied collection.

THE VIENNA CLOCK MUSEUM: Schulhof 2, 1010 Vienna, Austria. Small varied collection with emphasis on music.

BELGIUM

THE INSTRUMENTAL MUSEUM OF BELGIUM: 17 Place du Petit-Sablon, Brussels. Very large collection of musical instruments.

INSTRUMENTAL MUSEUM OF THE ROYAL CONSERVATORY OF MUSIC OF BRUSSELS: Av. Broustin 19, Brussels, Belgium. Large collection of mechanical musical machines with emphasis on music boxes.

NATIONAL MUSEUM FOR MECHANICAL ORGANS: Robert Vaudemmestrate 45, Koksijde, West Vlaanderen. Large varied collection.

ORGAN MUSEUM ST. NIKLASS: Oostjacht Park 15, St. Niklass, Belgium. Mechanical Organ collection, various types.

BRITISH ISLES

BIRMINGHAM MUSEUM OF SCIENCE AND INDUSTRY: Newhall Street, Birmingham, West Midlands, England. Small varied collection.

THE BOWES MUSEUM: Barnard Castle, County Durham, England. Small varied collection.

BRITISH MUSEUM: Great Russel Street, London, England. Small varied collection.

THE DEVON MUSEUM OF MECHANICAL MUSIC: Mill Leat, Thornbury, Nr. Holsworthy, Devonshire, England. Varied collection.

MUSEUM OF MECHANICAL MUSIC: Church Road, Portfield, Chichester, England. Varied collection.

THE NATIONAL MUSICAL MUSEUM (THE PIANO MUSEUM): Charitable Trust, 368 High Street near Kew Bridge, Brentford, Middlesex, England. Large collections mainly keyboard mechanical instruments.

PAUL CORIN MUSIC MUSEUM: St. Keyne, Liskeard, Cornwall, England. Collection of mechanical musical items.

ST. ALBANS ORGAN MUSEUM: 326 Camp Road, St. Albans, England. Small varied collection.

SCIENCE MUSEUM: Exhibition Road, London, England. Large collection with emphasis on phonographs.

TOY MUSEUM: 18A North Parade, Matlock Bath, Derbyshire, England. Collection includes phonographs and music boxes.

VICTORIA AND ALBERT MUSEUM: South Kensington, London, England. Small collection mainly music boxes.

WELSH FOLK MUSEUM OF MECHANICAL MUSIC: Gears Lane off North Road, Goldsithney, Penzance, Cornwall. Varied collection.

CANADA

EBERDT MUSEUM OF COMMUNICATIONS HISTORY: 30A Rue Principale S., Sutton, Quebec, Canada. Varied collection.

PLAYER PIANO CENTER AND MUSEUM: 3399 Dunbar Street, Vancouver, British Columbia. Large varied collection.

FRANCE

GRANDE EXPOSITION MUSEE D'INSTRUMENTS DE MUSIQUE MECHANIQUES: 13 Rue Bramtone, Paris, France. Varied collection.

MUSEE DE PHONOGRAPHE ET DE LA MUSIQUE MECHANIQUES: Parc St. Donat, Rt du Muy, Sainte-Maxime Var, Cote d'azur. Large collection with emphasis on phonographs.

MUSEE NATIONAL DES TECHNIQUES: 292 Rue Saint Martens. Large varied collection.

ITALY

MUSEO DI INSTRUMENTI MUSICALLI MECCANICI: S.S. Adriatica N. 16 KM 163, Savio, Italy. Varied collection.

MONACO

NATIONAL MUSEUM: Avenue Princess Grace. Collection of Automatons and dolls.

NETHERLANDS

KIJK EN LUISTER MUSEUM: Verenigingsgebouw, Bennekom, Netherlands. Large music box collection.

NATIONAL MUSEUM-FROM MUSIC BOXES TO STREET ORGANS: Achter den Dom 12, Utrecht, Netherlands. Large collection of mechanical musical machines.

NORWAY

RINGVE MUSEUM: Lade alle 60, Trondheim, Norway. Varied collection with emphasis on music boxes.

SWITZERLAND

FREDY'S MECHANISCHER MUSIK SALON: Hauszur Frohburg, Lichtensteig (St. Gallen), Switzerland. Varied collection.

MUSEE D'ART ET D'HISTOIRE: Quai Leopold Robert, Neuchatel, Switzerland. Jacquet -Droz automata.

MUSEE BAUD S. A.: L'Auberson, Vaud, Switzerland. Varied collection.

RETONIO'S MECHANISCHES MUSIK UND ZAUBERMUSEUM (Retonio Breitenmoser): Gerbestrasse 4, Appenzell, Switzerland. Varied collection of mechanical musical machines.

WEST GERMANY

DAS MUSEUM DER MECHANSICHEN MUSIK BRAUNSCHWEIG: Ziegenmarkt 2, Braumschweig. Large varied collection.

DEUTSCHES MUSEUM: Museumsinsel 1, Munchen 26 West Germany. Varied collection.

DEUTSCHES UHRENMUSEUM FURTWAGEN: Gerwigstrassell, Furtwangen, Baden Wurttemberg. Small mechanical music collection.

MECHANISCHES MUSIK MUSEUM: Kasseler Strasse 76A Fuldatal Simmershausen, Hessen, West Germany. Orchestrion collection (ten pieces).

MUSEUM FUR MECHANISCHE MUSIKINSTRUMENTE: Sofienstrasse 40, Baden-Baden. Large varied collection.

MUSIKWISSENSCHAFFLICHES MUSEUM: Fur Selbstspielende Instrumente, Bronsart Str. 32, Hannover, West Germany. Large varied collection by appointment.

SIEGFRIEDS MECHANISCHES MUSIKKABINETT: Ober Str 29, Rudeshiem am Rhein, Hessen, West Germany. Large varied collection.

MECHANICAL MUSICAL SOCIETIES AND THEIR PUBLICATIONS

AUTOMATIC MUSICAL INSTRUMENT COLLECTORS' ASSOCIATION
International and 10 Regional (State) Chapters
Write: Bobby Clark, Jr., Membership Secretary, P. O. Box 172, Columbia, SC 29202

AMICA NEWS BULLETIN
Published by Dorothy Bromage, P.O. Box 387, La Habra, CA 90631

CITY OF LONDON PHONOGRAPH AND GRAMOPHONE SOCIETY
Hillandale News: Official Journal
Write: Treasurer-B. A. Williamson, 157 Childwall Valley Road, Liverpool, L161LA, England.

MUSICAL BOX SOCIETY INTERNATIONAL
Bulletin published three times a year, also MBS News Bulletin six times a year. Write: Mrs. C. W. Fabel, Route 3, Box 202, Morgantown, IN 46160 (also local chapters).

MUSICAL BOX SOCIETY OF GREAT BRITIAN
Journal, The Music Box published four times a year. 40 Station Approach, Hayes Bromley, Kent BR27EF, England.

PHONOGRAPH SOCIETY OF SOUTH AUSTRALIA
P. O. Box 253, Prospect 5082 Australia. The Phonographic News published six times a year.

VINTAGE PHONOGRAPHIC SOCIETY OF NEW ZEALAND
Journal, The Phonographic Record
Write: Mrs. L. Drummond, P. O. Box 5175, Papanui, Christ Church, New Zealand.

VINTAGE RADIO AND PHONOGRAPH SOCIETY
Write: Secretary VRPS, P.O. Box 5345, Irving, TX 75062. Monthly Journal "The Reproducer"

PUBLICATIONS AND SOURCES FOR FACSIMILE REPRINTS

TO RETAIN THE VALUE OF YOUR MACHINE WE SUGGEST THAT YOU ACQUIRE AS MUCH INFORMATION AS POSSIBLE ABOUT YOUR INSTRUMENT BEFORE YOU ATTEMPT A DO-IT-YOURSELF REPAIR. THE FOLLOWING ARE SOURCES OF PRINTED MATERIAL AVAILABLE TO ASSIST YOU.

Mechanical Musical Societies all issue their own regular bulletins and journals with historical and technical information articles. Many also issue reprinted catalogues, etc. See section on Mechanical Musical Societies for further information.

ANTIQUE PHONOGRAPH MONTHLY (APM)
Allen Koenigsberg, 502 East 17 Street, Brooklyn, NY 11226. Informative articles and classified ads relating mainly to phonographs and records. Facsimile reprints and original books on the subject also available.

AUTOMATIC MUSIC ROLL CO. (Frank Adams)
P. O. Box 3194, Seattle, WA 98114. AMR Catalog of Publications: Reprinted catalogs, manuals and other items related to pianos.

EDISON PHONOGRAPH MONTHLY
Wendell Moore, RR #, Box 4744, Sedona, AZ 86336. Reprinted bound volumes of the original monthly publication. Also phonograph related prints.

JEAN'S MUSICAL NEWS
Box 366, Mason, MI, 48854. Mainly classified advertising relating to phonographs. Some information articles.

JUKEBOX TRADER *(monthly)*
2545 J M S.E. 60 Court, Des Moines, IA 50317. Monthly, for collectors.

"LOOSE CHANGE" MAGAZINE
Mead Co., 21176 South Alameda Street, Long Beach, CA 90810. Monthly magazine, articles on coin operated music machines, jukeboxes, etc.

CHARLES MANDRAKE
P. O. Box 955, Ashtabula, OH 44004. Facsimile catalogues, mainly phonographs.

MUSICAL MARKET PLACE
Bob Fulwider c/o MMP 561 Washington Street, Santa Clara, CA 95050. Monthly classified ads.

TALKING MACHINE REVIEW INTERNATIONAL
19 Glendale Road, Bournemouth, England BH64JA. Bi-monthly publication dealing in all areas of the antique phonograph field, issue list of Reprints and Books.

ZONOPHONE NEWSLETTER
Box 955, Ashtabula, OH 44004.

FURTHER READING: A BRIEF BIBLIOGRAPHY

BAUMBACH, ROBERT W.—*Look for the Dog; an Illustrated Guide to Victor Talking Machines,* Woodland Hills, CA; Stationery X-Press (P.O. Box 207, Woodland Hills, CA 91364), 1981. Fully illustrated informative history. 326 pp.

BAYLY, ERNIE—*The EMI Collection,* Bournemouth, England; The Talking Machine Review 1977. 282 Phonographs illustrated with photographs by Brian Willison, notes by Mr. Bayly. Many interesting European models.

BEZDECHI, ADRIAN—*Pianos and Player Pianos; an informative guide for owners and prospective buyers.* 64 pp. 58 illustrations. Order from Player Piano House, 4001 N. Interstate, Portland, OR 97227. Basic information.

BOWERS, Q. DAVID—*Encyclopedia of Automatic Musical Instruments,* Vestal, NY; The Vestal Press, 1972. The single most important guide in the field, 1008 pages profusely illustrated. (Does not cover phonographs, jukeboxes, etc.)

BOWERS, Q. DAVID—*Put Another Nickel In,* Vestal, NY; The Vestal Press, 1966. Comprehensive illustrated history of coin operated pianos and orchestrions.

CHEW, V. K.—*Talking Machines* 1877-1914; London, England. Her Majesty's Stationery Office, 1967. Some aspects of the early history of the Gramophone, Illustrated.

DETHLEFSON, RON—*Edison blue Amberol Recordings, 1912-1914,* Brooklyn, NY; APM Press, 1980. 206 pp.

DETHLEFSON, RON—*Edison Blue Amberol Recordings, 1915-1929,* Brooklyn, NY; APM Press, 500 pp.

DeWAARD. R.—*From Music Boxes to Street Organs,* translated from Dutch by Wade Jenkins, Vestal, NY; The Vestal Press, 1967. Mainly about pipe and reed organs, Carillon and Pierement street organs.

FROW, GEORGE and ALBERT F. SEFL—*The Edison Cylinder Phonograph; a detailed account of the entertainment models until 1929.* Kent; George L. Frow, 1978. 207 pp. Comprehensive illustrated history with detailed information about the models. George L. Frow, publisher, "Salterns", Seal Hollow Road, Sevenoaks, Kent TN13 3SH England.

FROW, GEORGE—*The Edison Disc Phonograph and the Diamond Disc,* George L. Frow, 1982, 286 pp.

FROW, GEORGE L.—*A Guide to the Edison Cylinder Phonograph; A Handbook For Collectors,* Cornwall; Francis Antony Ltd, 1970 (Mr. Frow: Sevenoaks, Kent, England). Invaluable guide to the various models of Edison cylinder phonographs.

GELATT, ROLAND—*The Fabulous Phonograph, From Edison to Stereo,* New York; Appleton-Century, 1954, 1965. Illustrated history.

GIVENS, LARRY—*Rebuilding the Player Piano.* New York; The Vestal Press, 1963. Basic guide.

GIVENS, LARRY—*Re-Enacting The Artist . . .* A story of the Ampico Reproducing Piano, Vestal, NY; The Vestal Press, 1970. Illustrated history of the Ampico.

HAZELCORN, HOWARD—*A Collector's Guide To The Columbia Spring-Wound Graphophone 1894-1910,* New York, APM (Monographs in the History of Recorded Sound No. 2), 1976. Illustrated comprehensive guide.

HOOVER, CYNTHIA—*Music Machines — American Style,* a catalogue of the exhibition, Washington, DC; Smithsonian Institution Press, 1971 (Stock No. 4700-0182), Supt. of Documents. Illustrated history.

KRIVINE, J.—*Jukebox Saturday Night,* Secaucas, NJ; Chartwell Books, Inc. 1977. Beautifully illustrated (in color) history of the jukebox.

LYNCH, VINCENT and BILL HENKIN—*Jukebox — The Golden Age.* Berkeley; Lancaster-Miller, 1981. 112 pp. Glorious photographs by Kazuhiro Tsuruta. Covers jukeboxes of the "classic" 1937-1948 period.

MARTY, DANIEL—*The Illustrated History of Phonographs;* New York; Vilo, Inc. 1979. (translated from the French) 102pp.

McTAMMANY, JOHN—*The Technical History of the Player,* New York; Musical Courier, 1915 (Available from the Vestal Press).

MOSORIAK, ROY—*Curious History of Music Boxes,* Chicago; Lightner Publishing Co., 1943. Interesting sections: Checklist of makers, music box related patents, etc.

MUSICAL BOX SOCIETY INTERNATIONAL—*Silver Anniversary Collection,* Summit, NJ, Musical Box Society International, 1974. Anthology of 188 articles from past issues of the Society's Bulletin, over 1,000 pp. Fully illustrated.

OBERCHAIN, ELAINE—*"The Complete Catalog of Ampico Recording Piano Rolls",* Darien, CT; William H. Edgerton (Box 88, Darien, CT 06820), 1977. 197pp. Listings of titles.

ORD-HUME, ARTHUR W. J. G.—*Collecting Musical Boxes and How to Repair Them,* NY; Crown Publishers, 1967, concise history, descriptions and practical restoration techniques.

ORD-HUME, ARTHUR W. J. G.—*The Mechanics of Mechanical Music,* London; published by the author, 1973.

ORD-HUME, ARTHUR W. J. G.—*Musical Box, A History and Collector's Guide",* published by Geo. Allen and Unwin. 200 illustrations.

ORD-HUME, ARTHUR W. J. G.—*Player Piano; The History of the Mechanical Piano and How to Repair It,* NY; A. S. Barnes, 1970, comprehensive guide with illustrations.

PEARSALL, RONALD—*Collecting Mechanical Antiques,* New York; Arco Publishing Co., 1973, 197 pp. 92 illustrations. Section on mechanical machines musical.

PETTS, LEONARD (compiled by)—*The Story of Nipper and the 'His Master's Voice' picture painted by Francis Barrard,* Bournemouth, England. 2 edition, 1982. (Published by Ernie Bayly for The Talking Machine Review International, 19 Glendale Road, Bournemouth BH64JA England). Illustrated history.

PROUDFOOT, CHRISTOPHER—*Collecting Phonographs and Gramophones,* New York, Mayflower Books, 1980. (Christie's International Collectors Series), 116 pp. Emphasis on European examples, very good color photographs.

REBLITZ, ART and Q. DAVID BOWERS—*Treasures of Mechanical Music,* New York; The Vestal Press, 1981. 630 pp., 700 illustrations, including 450 tracker scales. (Also available from the authors)

ROEHL, HARVEY—*Player Piano Treasury;* The Scrapbook history of the Mechanical Piano in America, Vestal, NY; The Vestal Press, 1973 edition. Compilation of advertising through the years, as well as a wonderful chapter called "The Melodies Linger On", a beautifully illustrated section on Musical Museums.

READ, OLIVER AND WELCH, WALTER L.—*From Tin Foil to Stereo; Evolution of the Phonograph,* Indianapolis; Howard Sams & Co. and Bobbs-Merrill Co., Inc., 1959-1976. Comprehensive illustrated history of the phonograph and recording industry.

SCHLICK, LAWRENCE A.—*A Portfolio of Early Phonographs,* Published by Mr. Schlick, 1966. Glossy large photographs with descriptions (50 pp).

SITTER, BOB—*"Dusting Off a Little History; Spring Type Phonographs",* Yorba Linda, CA. Phonograph Collectables, (18242 Timberlane, Yorba Linda, CA 92686), 1981. 65pp.

THOMSON, ALISTAIR G.—*Phonographs and Gramophones.* A commemorative catalogue of the exhibition held at the Royal Scottish Museum, Edinburgh 1977. Beautifully illustrated catalogue with descriptive notes.

WEBB, GRAHAM—*The Cylinder Musical Box Handbook;* London; Faber & Faber, 1968. Illustrated guide with detailed repair diagrams and descriptions.

MUSIC BOXES

The Cylinder Music Box originated in the 18th-century in Switzerland. The period from the mid-1800's to 1890 saw its growth and development but by the onset of World War I the cylinder music box's popularity was at an end, surpassed by the disc music box and other forms of home entertainment.

The basic mechanism is a metal cylinder with a specific arrangement of tiny metal pins protruding from it. When the cylinder revolves, these pins pluck the teeth of a tuned metal comb which causes a specific set of notes to play. The longer and larger the cylinder and comb or combs, the more elaborate the musical arrangement.

The disc music box was popularly produced from the 1880's to the 1920's. Many of the manufacturers were German based firms. There were three companies that stand out in this field. Each produced a wide variety of models. They are Symphonion, Polyphone and Regina.

The disc music box works essentially on the same principle as the cylinder box. The steel tuned comb or combs are activated by the projections in specific arrangements, on flat metal discs. As the disc turns, the projections pluck the comb creating the music.

Most models of both types of music boxes are spring wound.

Some music box terms used to describe the entries:

1. Interchangeable cylinder box has more than one cylinder, allowing for a wider variety of musical tunes. There is usually storage space for the extra cylinders.
2. Long playing musical movement is usually found on bigger boxes. The box does not have to be wound as often because it has either a heavy duty larger spring or multi springs.
3. Manivelle is a hand cranked musical movement (no springs), usually found in small simple boxes originally made as children's toys.
4. Sublime-Harmonie is the particular way in which double combs are tuned and arranged to create a louder more brilliant tone.
5. Tune cards are decorated paper cards attached to the inside of the lid of the cylinder music box, listing the tunes on the cylinder.
6. There are extra devices incorporated in some boxes to enhance and vary the musical performance, for example—pianoforte, zither, mandolin, harp, piccolo comb, bells, drum, etc.
7. Disc Shifting Music Boxes (e.g. Sirion): The disc is shifted on a central spindle after it is played thus altering its position which utilizes a different sequence of projections on the disc. In this way one disc plays twice as many tunes.

CYLINDER MUSIC BOXES

	Price Range	
☐ **A. B. H. ABRAHAMS** *6 tune 6¼" cyl, 3 bells with butterfly strikers, grained case with transfer decoration on lid, colored tune sheet*	400.00	750.00
☐ *10 tune 6½" cyl, 3 bells with butterfly strikers, walnut veneered case with marquetry and transfer decoration, tune sheet, 18" wide.*	250.00	600.00
☐ *12 tune 13" cyl, drum, 5 bells with butterfly strikers, castanets, zither attachment, walnut veneer case, transfer decoration on lid, tune sheet, coin operated*	750.00	1500.00

	Price Range	
☐ **ALEXANDRA** *4 tune 6" cyl, interchangeable cyls (6), sleeve type, rosewood inlaid case, 4 bells, insect strikers, storage inside case to left of mechanism for extra cylinders, inner glass lid.*	1350.00	1650.00
☐ *6 tune 6" cyl, interchangeable cyls (6), c. 1890, hollow cylinders that fit over brass mandrel, single comb, inner lid of glass, two compartments on either side of mechanism with pegs for extra cylinders.*	1600.00	2500.00
☐ **D. ALLARD—J. SANDOZ** *8 tune 13" cyl, interchangeable cyls (3), some case decoration, wide base moulding hides storage drawer for extra cylinders.*	2250.00	3500.00
☐ **(GEO.) BAKER & CO. (Switzerland)** *6 tune 11" cyl, sublime harmony combs, tune sheet, tune indicator and tempo control, double spring barrel, stop/start and change levers, maple case, simple case decoration, inner glass lid.*	1400.00	2000.00
☐ **BAKER-TROLL** *2 tune, crystal and gilt metal decanter, movement in base, c. 1880, 10¾" high.*	300.00	600.00
☐ *6 tune, Sublime-Harmony Piccolo, walnut case with mother-of-pearl decoration, inner glass lid.*	1250.00	1800.00
☐ *6 tune 17" cyl, interchangeable cyls, 6 bells, bee strikers, walnut case with brass inlay decoration, matching storage table, three part comb.*	2500.00	3750.00
☐ *6 tune 19½" cyl, interchangeable cyls (7), ornately inlaid case with brass, pewter and copper decorations, matching cabinet (wide, floor standing) for extra cylinders, decorative moldings, one large comb for cylinder and one for 10 bells, double spring drive, start/stop.*	4500.00	7500.00
☐ *8 tune 13", c. 1880, interchangeable cyls (3), early maple and ebony case with drawer for cyls, decorated tune sheet, inner glass lid, double spring, rachet wind movement, carrying handles.*	3400.00	4500.00
☐ *8 tune 15" cyl, sublime harmony double comb, interchangeable cyls (6), c. 1870, double spring and zither attachment, tune indicator, burl walnut on ebony and rosewood case, inlaid decoration, matching table with cabriole legs, storage drawer for cylinders*	6000.00	8000.00
☐ **BORNAND (New York)** *6 tune 10" cyl, simple case style, decorative tune card key wind.*	750.00	1400.00
☐ **BREMOND** *4 tune 7" cyl, simple case, tune card (92 teeth comb), case 15" long.*	350.00	750.00
☐ *4 tune 9" cyl, orchestral, 17 brass flute and piccolo pipes, 13 organ reeds.*	600.00	1200.00
☐ *6 tune 3½" cyl, inlaid rosewood veneer case, inner glass lid, stop/start and change levers, single comb (42 teeth).*	250.00	500.00
☐ *6 tune 8" cyl, lever wind, simple fruitwood case, tune sheet, case 15" wide.*	500.00	750.00
☐ *6 tune 10¾" cyl, hidden drum and bells, inner glass lid (½ size), simple case lines with inlaid decoration on lid and front panel, tune sheet.*	1250.00	2250.00

	Price Range	
☐ *6 tune 11″ cyl, tune sheet, lever wind, rosewood with floral decoration.*	1500.00	2000.00
☐ *6 tune 11″ cyl, 16 note organ, colored inlay, 21″ long, inner glass lid.*	1500.00	2250.00
☐ *6 tune 11″ cyl, drum with 8 beaters, 6 bells, three part comb, stop/start, rosewood case inlaid with musical motifs and other decoration.*	2250.00	3500.00
☐ *6 tune 13″ cyl, interchangeable cyls (6), serpentine case, burled veneer, inlays, matching table with storage drawer for extra cylinders, c. 1860.*	3000.00	5000.00
☐ *6 tune 14″ cyl, mandolin attachment, 7 bells, stop/start and change levers, tune card, inlaid decoration on rosewood case, late 19th century.*	3500.00	4000.00
☐ *6 tune 16⅛″ cyl, interchangeable cyls (6), 3″ diameter (fat) cylinder, tune card, drum, 6 bells with bee strikers, castanets, 18 note organ, single massive spring, rosewood case with inlaid decorations, matching tiered table with storage drawers for extra cylinders, curved legs.*	3500.00	5500.00
☐ *6 tune 17¼″ cyl, mandoline attachment, tune sheet, lever wind, rosewood with floral motif.*	2250.00	2850.00
☐ *6 tune 17½″ cyl, (fat cyl), c. 1880, burl walnut and ebony case, tune sheet, carrying handles on sides, triple comb, double spring, lever wind, tune indicator, stop/start and repeat levers.*	2250.00	2850.00
☐ *6 tune with hidden drum and bells, decorated case, floral inlay lid and on the front of case.*	1500.00	1750.00
☐ *8 tune 11″ cyl, simple case 20″ long, tune card.*	500.00	750.00
☐ *8 tune 13″ cyl, c. 1880, mahogany case with rosewood and mother-of-pearl inlay, single comb, tune card.*	1000.00	1750.00
☐ *8 tune 13″ cyl, interchangeable cyls (2), floral inlay design on lid and front, large inside glass lid, tune card, matching table with storage drawer for cylinders*	2500.00	3500.00
☐ *8 tune 14½″ cyl, c. 1870, hidden saucer bells and castanet, serpentine shaped case with inlay decoration, tune sheet inside lid, stop/start and repeat levers.*	2250.00	2750.00
☐ *8 tune 15″ cyl, "Piano-Forte", double comb, inner glass lid, some marquetry decoration.*	1500.00	2500.00
☐ *8 tune brass and pewter inlay decoration on case.*	1000.00	1250.00
☐ *10 tune 8″ cyl, interchangeable (4) cyls, rosewood and ebony with inlaid decoration, c. 1870, double barrel spring movement, tune indicator, organ movement.*	3400.00	4500.00
☐ *12 tune 13½″ cyl, c. 1875, rachet wind, rosewood and ebony case with floral marquetry on lid, tune sheet, stop/start and repeat levers.*	1200.00	1800.00
☐ *14¾″ cyl, interchangeable (4) cyls, organ attachment, walnut and ebony case with burl walnut trim, matching table (turned legs), storage drawer for extra cylinders, double spring tune indicator.*	4500.00	5500.00
☐ **CONCHON (Switzerland)** *6 tune 11″ cyl, mandoline zither attachment, operatic selections, veneered and decorated case, inlaid lid, base molding, tune sheet.*	1200.00	1600.00

	Price Range	
☐ *8 tune 13" cyl, interchangeable cyls (7), lever wind, double spring, zither attachment, six saucer bells, stop/start and repeat levers, tune indicator, burl walnut case with ebony trim on slant top (drop front) desk, four drawers on side hold cylinders, inner glass lid, tune sheet ("S" shaped supports).*	7500.00	9500.00
☐ *8 tune 17¼" cyl, c. 1880, double springs, 4 combs, tempo control, tune selector, tune card, rosewood case with simple inlay decoration, inner glass lid, zither attachment (Quatuor Expression Zither).*	2750.00	4250.00
☐ *Orchestra box, c. 1880, drum, bells, castanets, 16 note organ, inlaid decoration, ornate case.*	2250.00	2750.00
☐ **DAWKINS** *6 tune 13¼" cyl, interchangeable, burled walnut, gold painted decoration, inlay on cover, tune card, one cylinder.*	2250.00	2500.00
☐ *10 tune 8¼" cyl, with 5 bells, walnut with inlay decoration.*	1250.00	2000.00
☐ *12 tune 13" cyl, drum, bell, wood block, inlay on cover, tune card, large case.*	1750.00	2500.00
☐ **DUCOMMON GIROD** *4 tune 8" cyl, simple case, inlay on lid*	750.00	1500.00
☐ *6 tune 6" cyl, simple case, tune sheet, stop/start and change levers, c. 1880.*	500.00	1000.00
☐ *6 tune 11¼" cyl, c. 1840, walnut case, three control levers, simple case style.*	600.00	800.00
☐ *6 tune 13" cyl, 7 bells, drum with eight beaters, stop/start and change levers, 123 tooth comb, single spring barrel with crank, burl walnut veneer with some decoration.*	1500.00	2000.00
☐ *8 tune 16¼" cyl, 3 bells, castanet, inlaid case, full glass inner lid.*	1500.00	2000.00
☐ *12 tune 19" cyl, rosewood veneered case with enamel and brass inlay decoration, operatic selections, tune sheet.*	1500.00	2500.00
☐ **ECKARDT** *2 tune Musical Christmas Tree Stand, c. 1910, German, clockwork mechanism, tree holder revolves and plays.*	200.00	300.00
☐ **GLORIA** *8 tune 11" cyl, 3" diameter cyl, zither attachment, double spring, flower inlay on lid, tune card, tune indicator, selector, 27" long case.*	1000.00	1500.00
☐ **J. H. HELLER (Bern, Switzerland)** *6 tune 4½" cyl, walnut decoration, floral motifs, inner glass lid.*	450.00	650.00
☐ *6 tune 6" cyl, simple case, some decoration, inner glass lid, tune indicator.*	500.00	750.00
☐ *6 tune, 13" cyl organ box, walnut with inlay on front and lid.*	1500.00	2750.00
☐ *8 tune 10¾" cyl, rosewood case, simple design with inlay decoration on lid, single comb and spring, tune card, inner glass lid.*	650.00	1500.00
☐ *8 tune 17¼" cyl (2¼" fat cylinder), orchestral box, drum, 6 bells, castanet, 18 note reed organ, inner glass lid, burl walnut, rosewood inlay.*	3500.00	5000.00
☐ *8 tune 19½" cyl, two piece comb tune sheet, lever wind, rosewood with fruitwood decoration, piccolo-harp, c. 1880.*	1700.00	2500.00
☐ *10 tune 13" cyl, burled veneer walnut case with some inlaid decoration, zither attachment, decorated tune sheet.*	1500.00	2000.00

	Price Range	
☐ **IMHOF AND MUKLE (Trade Label)** *8½" cyl, spring driven movement, rosewood and ebony case, marquetry decoration, c. 1880.*	300.00	500.00
☐ **JUNOD** *4 tune 5⅛" cyl, inlaid rosewood case with musical motif, tune indicator, 2 bells, decorated figural tune card, inner glass lid.*	800.00	1250.00
☐ *24 tune 13¼" cyl, "fat" diameter cylinder, zither attachment, double spring, rachet wind, decorated tune card, tune indicator, start/stop and change levers, rosewood case with floral motif, inner glass lid.*	1250.00	2000.00
☐ **LANGDORFF & FILS (Switzerland)** *4 tune 13" cyl (3" diameter fat cyl), interchangeable cylinders (2), 180 note comb, brass bedplate, inlaid decoration on carved case.*	3000.00	3750.00
☐ *8 tune 17¼" cyl, three sectioned comb, zither attachment, tune card, tune indicator, double spring barrel, burled walnut case.*	2500.00	4250.00
☐ **LECOULTRE (Geneva, Switzerland)** *2 tune, SNUFF BOX, tortoise shell case, c. 1860-1880.*	1250.00	1500.00
☐ *4 tune 8¼" cyl, key wind, early plain box, instant stop and change levers.*	750.00	1000.00
☐ *4 tune 12" cyl, 3" wide diameter cyl, keywind, pianoforte, inlaid lid, tune card, 16" long.*	3250.00	3750.00
☐ *6 tune 8" cyl, keywind, simple case.*	750.00	1000.00
☐ *6 tune 11" cyl, simple case, some decoration, 18" long case, inner glass lid, lever wind.*	1000.00	1500.00
☐ *6 tune 13" cyl, two sectioned comb, tune sheet, stop/start, change and instant stop levers, rosewood case, inlaid lid and other decoration.*	1000.00	1750.00
☐ *8 tune 11" cyl, simple case 18" long.*	750.00	1000.00
☐ *8 tune 13" cyl, winding lever under inner glass lid, 20" long simple case.*	1000.00	1250.00
☐ *8 tune 13" cyl, walnut case, with inlay.*	1250.00	1750.00
☐ *8 tune 14" cyl, interchangeable cyls (6), tune card, 9 bells struck by birds, tempo control, stop/start levers, burl walnut with fruitwood marquetry case, gilt metal handles, two tiered matching table with storage drawers on curved legs.*	4000.00	6000.00
☐ *12 tune 18¼" cyl, wide diameter cylinder, 190 tooth comb, brass bedplate, Bremond winding handle, inlaid case with enamel decoration.*	1250.00	2000.00
☐ **L'EPEE (France)** *4 tune 5" cyl, simple case.*	350.00	400.00
☐ *6 tune 6" cyl, inlaid floral decoration on simple wood case, stop/start and change levers, tune indicator, 51 tooth comb.*	750.00	1000.00
☐ *8 tune 6" cyl, single comb, operatic selections, tune indicator, change/repeat and stop/start levers, inlaid wood case, ornate tune card, c. early 1900's.*	500.00	800.00
☐ *8 tune 9" cyl, 6 bells, single comb, pictorial tune card, bird and flowers inlaid motif on lid, inner glass lid.*	1000.00	1500.00
☐ *12 tune 13" cyl, zither attachment, simple wood case with some decoration.*	750.00	950.00

	Price Range	
☐ **M. M. & CIE** *10 tune 13″ cyl, double spring, some inlay decoration, tune card and indicator, 28″ long case.*	750.00	1000.00
☐ **J. MANGER & CO. (Switzerland)** *8 tune 13″ cyl, interchangeable cylinders (10), c. 1880, 6 bells with bee strikers, two piece comb, four spring barrels, crank wind outside, speed adjustment, ornate case decoration with ebony, fruitwood and mother-of-pearl decoration, inner glass lid, matching storage table, with two drawers side-by-side for cylinder storage, turned legs.*	8500.00	11000.00
☐ **MERMOD FRÉRES (St. Croix, Switzerland)** *4 tune 6″ cyl, simple rosewood case, inner glass lid, ornate tune card, stop/start and change levers, late 19th century.*	500.00	1000.00
☐ *6 tune 3½″ cyl, c. 1900, crank wind, simple wood case with decal decoration.*	200.00	400.00
☐ *6 tune 7½″ cyl, simple case, inner glass lid, some decorations on case, tune card.*	750.00	1250.00
☐ *6 tune 7½″ cyl, interchangeable cyl, inlaid rosewood, tune indicator, Peerless Forte Piccolo.*	750.00	1750.00
☐ *6 tune 7½″ cyl, interchangeable cyls, zither attachment, tune selector, Jacquot safety check, single comb, oak case with base molding and case decoration, inner glass lid, ornate tune card.*	1000.00	1875.00
☐ *6 tune 8¼″ cyl, c. 1900, tune sheet, zither attachment, lever wind, rosewood case, floral inlay, guitar zither attachment.*	600.00	800.00
☐ *6 tune 9″ cyl, interchangeable cyl, zither attachment, inlaid rosewood, tune indicator, Peerless Forte Piccolo.*	2000.00	2500.00
☐ *6 tune 10½″ cyl, interchangeable cyl, walnut with inlay, Mandolin Piccolo, inner glass lid, 32″ long.*	2250.00	2500.00
☐ *6 tune 11″ cyl, Ideal Sublime-Harmony, double comb, Mahogany inlay.*	1500.00	2000.00
☐ *6 tune 11¼″ cyl, interchangeable cyls (2), c. 1890, burled walnut case with storage drawer in wide base moulding, inner glass lid, slow/fast lever, tune indicator, zither attachment, crank wind.*	2000.00	2500.00
☐ *6 tune 11¼″ cyl, interchangeable cyls (4), Ideal Sublime Harmony combs, c. 1895, original tune sheet, zither attachment, tune indicator, crank wind, oak case.*	2000.00	3000.00
☐ *8 tune 5½″ cyl, 3 bells, simple case, tune indicator, 16″ long case, tune skipper.*	1000.00	1250.00
☐ *8 tune 6″ cyl, coin operated, 17″ long oak case.*	750.00	1250.00
☐ *8 tune 9″ cyl, inlaid rosewood, 6 bells, 19″ case, tune indicator, tune skipper.*	1250.00	1500.00
☐ *8 tune 9″ cyl, 2½″ diameter cyl, double springs, crank wind, inner glass cover, tune indicator, zither, inlaid rosewood.*	1250.00	1500.00
☐ *8 tune 11″ cyl, rosewood case with decorative moulding, 6 bells, tune skipper, drum, 27″ case.*	1200.00	2400.00
☐ *8 tune 11″ cyl, 2¼″ diameter cyl, interchangeable cylinder, 26″ long case (called "The Concerta"), simple inlay banding decoration.*	3000.00	4000.00
☐ *8 tune 11¼″ cyl, coin operated, c. 1900, tune changer, slow/fast adjustment, crank wind, oak case.*	1500.00	2500.00

	Price Range	
☐ *8 tune 13½" cyl, c. 1900, crank wind at side, tune changer, zither attachment, walnut veneer case with inlay musical motifs.*	700.00	1500.00
☐ *8 tune 14" cyl, simple rosewood case, inner glass lid, ornate tune card, stop/start and change levers, late 19th century.*	1250.00	2250.00
☐ *10 tune 5½" cyl, outside crank, tune selector, simple case, 17½" long.*	750.00	1000.00
☐ *10 tune 7½" cyl, simple case, inner glass cover, crank wind, 20" case.*	600.00	1000.00
☐ *10 tune 9" cyl, inlaid rosewood, crank wind, inner glass lid, tune indicator, zither attachment, 21" case.*	1000.00	1500.00
☐ *10 tune 11" cyl, rosewood with decorative moulding, 6 bells, coupled mainspring, large cyl, 27" case.*	1450.00	1950.00
☐ *10 tune 11" cyl, carved oak case, crank wind, inner glass cover, 2½" diameter cyl, tune indicator, skipper, moderator, zither attachment.*	1350.00	1850.00
☐ *10 tune 13" cyl, rosewood, drum and castanets, decorative moulding, tune indicator and skipper, moderator, large cylinders, Sublime-Harmony, double spring.*	2500.00	3000.00
☐ *10 tune 13" cyl, Sublime-Harmony, tune selector, double spring barrel, tune indicator, musical motif on inlay cover.*	1500.00	2000.00
☐ *10 tune 14" cyl, piccolo, zither attachment, inner glass lid, decoration on case and lid, 27" box, original tune card.*	1000.00	1250.00
☐ *10 tune 17½" cyl, 6 bells and drum, walnut case, musical instruments motif on cover (inlay).*	2500.00	4000.00
☐ *10 tune 13½" cyl, oak carved, brass handles, outside crank wind, orchestral box, bells, drums, castanets, mandolin attachment, coin op, c. 1896.*	3000.00	4000.00
☐ *10 tune 16" cyl, two sectional comb, mandoline attachments, stop/start and change levers, burled walnut case with rosewood decoration, inner glass lid.*	1500.00	2000.00
☐ *11" cyl, interchangeable cyls, zither attachment, tune selector, tempo control, rosewood case with fruitwood marquetry decoration, "ideal piccolo".*	3000.00	3500.00
☐ *11⅜" cyl, interchangeable cyls, matching table with cabriole legs, crank wind, zither attachment, slow/fast and tune indicators, carved case decoration, storage drawer in table.*	3750.00	5500.00
☐ *11¼" cyl, interchangeable cyls, crank wind, sublime harmony combs, 6 bells struck by 3 automaton mandarins, single comb, simple case with some decoration.*	1500.00	3000.00
☐ *12 tune 10" cyl, imitation rosewood, tune indicator, crank wind, simple case.*	1000.00	1500.00
☐ *12 tune 13" cyl, carved oak case, zither attachment, inner glass lid, crank wind, tune indicator, skipper moderator.*	1250.00	1750.00
☐ *12 tune 16" cyl, interchangeable cyls (4), inlay decoration, tune sheet inside lid.*	3500.00	5500.00
☐ *12 tune, coin operated, ornately carved, tune card, orchestral box, 6 butterflies, 6 drums, 6 bells, 6 castanets (and bee strikers).*	4000.00	5200.00
☐ **H. METERT (France)** *Forte-Piano cylinder box, very simple mahogany case, hinged side of case folds down for key winding, c. 1850.*	650.00	1000.00

	Price Range	
☐ **NICOLE FRERES** *2 tune SNUFF BOX, tortoise shell case, c. 1825.*	1000.00	1500.00
☐ *3 tune 9¼" cyl, ideal sublime harmony, tune sheet, tune indicator, crank wind, oak case, zither attachment, c. 1895.*	1000.00	1750.00
☐ *4 tune 6" cyl, double spring, inlaid case, tune card.*	850.00	1250.00
☐ *4 tune 8" cyl, keywind, 15" case with inlay and banding decoration, tune card.*	1250.00	1500.00
☐ *4 tune 11" cyl, simple rosewood case with some decoration, single comb, trills.*	1000.00	2000.00
☐ *4 tune 11⅞" cyl, 3¼" diameter cyl, overture box, simple case style.*	1250.00	2250.00
☐ *4 tune 12" cyl, overture box, inlaid lid, tune sheet.*	1500.00	2500.00
☐ *4 tune 16⅜" cyl, "fat" diameter cylinder, rosewood case with mother-of-pearl and brass with enamel inlay decoration, brass tune sheet, "OVERTURE" box, stop/start, change and instant stop levers.*	3000.00	5500.00
☐ *6 tune 11" cyl, 18" plain case, lever wind, some inlay decoration, tune card.*	1250.00	1500.00
☐ *6 tune 13" cyl, 3¼" diameter cyl, 24½" case, keywind, inlay, tune sheet.*	2000.00	2750.00
☐ *6 tune 13" cyl, interchangeable cyls (6), inlaid walnut case with decorative marquetry, matching table with storage drawer for extra cylinders, single comb, inner glass lid.*	4000.00	6000.00
☐ *6 tune 18" cyl, inlay brass and enamel on rosewood, mandolin attachment.*	2500.00	3000.00
☐ *8 tune 6 bells, double spring, rosewood case, tune card, inlaid front and lid.*	2000.00	2500.00
☐ *8 tune 13" cyl, inlay, lever wind, tune sheet, 20" case.*	1000.00	1400.00
☐ *8 tune 13" cyl, operatic selections, key wind, simple fruitwood case style.*	1500.00	1750.00
☐ *8 tune 17¼" cyl, interchangeable cyls (4), decorated inlaid case with matching table, drum, bells, castanet, 31 key organ, tune indicator and selector, speed control.*	5500.00	7500.00
☐ *8 tune 17½" cyl, "Forte-Piano", key wind, grained case with inlaid decoration on lid, inner glass lid, tune sheet.*	1200.00	2500.00
☐ *10 tune, wide diameter cylinder, simple case with some inlay decoration, inner glass lid.*	2000.00	2500.00
☐ *12 tune 12" cyl, 3" diameter cyl, floral inlay, tune card, 22" case, inner glass lid.*	2000.00	2500.00
☐ *12 tune 12" cyl, 3¼" ("fat") diameter cylinder, "Mozart opera selections, key wind, simple burled walnut veneer case with inlaid lid, rachet crank-winder, single comb, inner glass lid.*	1750.00	2400.00
☐ *12 tune 13" cyl, 6 bells, drum, double spring, burled walnut, 26" case.*	2500.00	3750.00
☐ *12 tune 14" cyl, multiple combs, 6 bells, 3" diameter ("fat") cylinder, inlaid case, "Piano-Forte", inner glass lid.*	2500.00	4500.00
☐ *12 tune 19½" cyl, reed organ, inlaid case, metal tune card, 34" case.*	2500.00	3000.00
☐ *12 tune, Victorian Bracket Clock, ornately carved decoration and fretwork on walnut case, piano forte movement in base.*	2500.00	3750.00

	Price Range	
☐ *18 tune 19½" cyl (3⅜" diameter fat cylinder), plays two tunes per turn, lever wind, figural inlay motif.*	2000.00	3000.00
☐ *18 tune 3" wide cyl, two part comb, inlay case.*	1800.00	2000.00
☐ *11" cyl, keywind, simple case.*	1000.00	2000.00
☐ *13" cyl, keywind, sectional comb, cob organ.*	1500.00	2500.00
☐ *16½" cyl, simple case with floral marquetry on lid, double comb, start/stop and repeat/change levers.*	1000.00	1500.00
☐ **ORPHEA (American)** *6 tune 18" cyl, c. 1875, interchangeable cyls (3), walnut and ebony case with drawer for extra cyls, crank wind, double comb, tune indicator, revolving tune sheet.*	3000.00	3750.00
☐ **PAILLARD** *2 tune 1¾" cyl, Musical Photograph Album, c. 1900. Art Nouveau case decoration, single comb, album sits on ornate corner feet.*	100.00	300.00
☐ *4 tune 19" cyl, 3" diameter cyl, glass inner lid, Sublime-Harmony, interchangeable cyls (2), 47" case.*	3500.00	5000.00
☐ *6 tune, "Amobean" interchangeable cyls (6), simple burled walnut case with some decoration, drawers open out from sides to store extra cylinders, inner glass lid, decorated tune sheet.*	2500.00	3500.00
☐ *6 tune 6" long cyl, 4 bells, inlay case, 18" long.*	1000.00	1500.00
☐ *6 tune 10½" cyl, interchangeable cyls (4), double spring, tune indicator, tune selector, zither attachment, inlaid rosewood case with matching table, storage for cylinders.*	3000.00	4000.00
☐ *6 tune 13" cyl, zither, pianoforte, glass inner lid, painted grain, 22" case.*	1500.00	2000.00
☐ *6 tune 13" cyl, interchangeable cyls (4), zither attachment, stop/start and change levers, inlaid burled walnut veneer case with matching table with storage drawer for extra cylinders, table has carved decoration on curved legs.*	2500.00	3500.00
☐ *6 tune 13" cyl, 3" wide cyl, 4 part spring, two part comb, case decoration and inlay.*	2250.00	2750.00
☐ *8 tune 5½" cyl, "Columbia", rachet wind from the right, single comb, tune indicator, decorated tune card, inner glass lid, delicate floral and musical inlay on lid and front of box, carrying handles on sides.*	400.00	800.00
☐ *8 tune 8¼" cyl, zither attachment, simple stained wood box, tune card.*	500.00	800.00
☐ *8 tune 9" cyl, inlay decoration, tune card.*	500.00	1000.00
☐ *8 tune 10¾" cyl, c. 1860, lever wind, rosewood case with floral decoration.*	600.00	1000.00
☐ *8 tune 15" cyl (3" diameter fat cylinder), serpentine case style, elaborate metal inlay decoration, tune sheet, tune indicator.*	4000.00	5000.00
☐ *10 tune 11" cyl, bird inlay on lid, tune card, 19¾" case.*	750.00	1000.00
☐ *10 tune 13" cyl, Sublime-Harmony walnut inlay, pictorial lithograph, inner glass lid.*	750.00	1250.00
☐ *10 tune 14⅛" cyl, "Piccolo-zither", mahogany case, ebony molding with inlay decoration on lid, spring barrel, inner glass lid, decorated tune card, tune indicator, side carrying handle.*	1750.00	2750.00

	Price Range	
☐ *12 tune 8" cyl, 6 bells with bee strikers, tune selector, double comb, inlaid with handles.*	1400.00	1800.00
☐ *12 tune 11" cyl, double spring, long play, tune card, walnut cabinet, inlay musical motif on lid.*	1000.00	1500.00
☐ *12 tune 13" cyl, tune card, inlay, 20" case.*	1000.00	1250.00
☐ *12 tune 13" cyl, zither, tune card, inlay and banding, 26" case.*	1000.00	1500.00
☐ *12 tune 15" cyl, "Voix Celeste," 12 key double reed organ, two combs, spring barrel, rosewood case, banded and inlay decoration of scenes of swans and figures, inner glass lid, tune indicator.*	1750.00	2500.00
☐ *12 tune 16¼" cyl, zither attachment, two sectioned comb, stop/start and change levers, rosewood marquetry case, tune card, double spring barrel, tune indicator.*	1250.00	2250.00
☐ *24 tune 13" cyl, zither, double spring, some decal and inlay decoration.*	1250.00	1750.00
☐ *9" cyl, c. 1890, interchangeable cyls (3), crank wind, zither attachment, tune indicator, oak case carved decoration, drawer holds extra cylinders.*	750.00	1500.00
☐ *11" cyl, bells, chinese drum, some case decoration.*	1000.00	1500.00
☐ *13" cyl, 6 bells, bird strikers, lever wind, inlaid box.*	1250.00	2000.00
☐ *13¼" cyl, interchangeable cyls (2), double spring, walnut, tune sheet, storage drawer under box for extra cylinders.*	2400.00	3250.00
☐ *15½" cyl, 22 note organ, multiple combs, simple case style with some decoration.*	2250.00	3200.00
☐ *20½" cyl, interchangeable cyls (6), 9 bells, 58" base matching stand with storage for extra cylinders, tune indicator, tune selector, inlaid and painted case decoration.*	5000.00	7750.00
☐ **PEERLESS** *9" cyl, interchangeable cyls (2), "Forte Piccolo", carved decoration on mahogany case, tune sheet.*	1000.00	1500.00
☐ **RIVENC** *6 tune 13" cyl, interchangeable cyls (5), tune card, zither attachment, double spring barrel, burled walnut panels on walnut case, inner glass lid, matching table with storage drawer for extra cylinders, turned legs, mother-of-pearl, ebony and brass decoration.*	4000.00	6000.00
☐ *6 tune 13" cyl, interchangeable 4" wide ("fat") cylinders, simple case style with some decoration.*	2750.00	4000.00
☐ *8 tune 6" cyl, duplex cylinder box (cylinders placed end to end), two combs, inlaid floral decorations on lid, marquetry borders on lid and sides.*	2000.00	3250.00
☐ *8 tune 11" cyl, interchangeable cyls, stop/start and change levers, mandolin attachment, tune indicator, brass figures of griffons, tune card, burled walnut case inlaid with satinwood swallows.*	1250.00	3500.00
☐ *17½" cyl, with organ, basket case.*	1000.00	1500.00
☐ **SERINETTE** *6 tune, simple walnut case on feet, 10¾" wide.*	250.00	500.00
☐ **THIBOUVILLE-LAMY** *6 tune 11" cyl, long inner glass lid, winding lever under glass lid, 19" plain case.*	750.00	1000.00

	Price Range	
☐ *8 tune 12" cyl, simple case, inner glass lid.*	750.00	1500.00
☐ *8 tune 15" cyl, 6 bells, drum with 9 beaters, three-section comb, tune card, inlaid rosewood case.*	1250.00	2000.00
☐ *10 tune 16" cyl, 25" rosewood inlaid case, tune card.*	2000.00	2500.00
☐ *12 tune 15" cyl, plain case, inlay on cover, tune card, 25" case.*	1500.00	2000.00

☐ **TROLL AND BAKER** *See Baker-Troll.*

☐ **(CHARLES) ULLMAN (Switzerland)** *8 tune 11" cyl, tune sheet, stop/start and change levers, tune indicator, rosewood case with handles, inlaid lid decoration.*	500.00	750.00
☐ **UNIVERSELLE** *1 tune 6½" cyl, interchangeable cyls (8), capstan wind, 3 bells, simple stained wood case with embossed ornament on lid, single comb, c. 1891.*	1500.00	3000.00

CYLINDER MUSIC BOXES — MAKERS UNKNOWN

☐ *3 tune 4¼" cyl, walnut, very simple, unadorned box.*	500.00	750.00
☐ *4 tune 3⅝" cyl, small box, mahogany (or walnut), decoration on lid, small inside glass lid, tune card, tune indicator.*	400.00	600.00
☐ *4 tune 5" cyl, simple case design, 11½" long.*	400.00	650.00
☐ *4 tune 6" cyl, simple case, tune card, 12" long.*	750.00	1000.00
☐ *4 tune 7¾" cyl, key wind, sectional comb, single comb, simple case style.*	750.00	1500.00
☐ *4 tune 8" cyl, key wind, single comb, simple fruitwood box with some minor case decoration.*	500.00	1000.00
☐ *4 tune 8" cyl, key wind (Swiss), mahogany (or fruitwood) case with simple decoration, inner glass lid.*	1000.00	2200.00
☐ *4 tune 10¾" cyl, overture box, Swiss, c. 1850, brass plaque, tune sheet, key wind, rosewood case, boxwood brass and enamel inlay.*	2250.00	3500.00
☐ *4 tune 11" cyl, double spring, interchangeable cyls (3), inlay on lid, full inner glass lid, tune card, stop-start mechanism, base moulding on case.*	2500.00	3500.00
☐ *4 tune 11½" cyl, bells with butterfly strikers, simple wood case with painted decoration, ornate tune card.*	2500.00	4000.00
☐ *4 tune 12" cyl, keywind, case 20½", plain.*	2500.00	3000.00
☐ *6 tune 3½" cyl, simple painted wood case with decal decoration, tune card, stop/start and change levers, tune indicator.*	350.00	550.00
☐ *6 tune 3¼" cyl, zither attachment, Swiss made, spring lever movement, outside crank wind, inside glass cover, tune indicator, simple case style with some decoration.*	300.00	600.00
☐ *6 tune 4½" cyl, lever wind, grained case with inlaid decoration on lid.*	350.00	550.00
☐ *6 tune 5" cyl, inlay, painted grain, 14½" case.*	500.00	750.00
☐ *6 tune 6" cyl, 14" inlay case.*	450.00	750.00
☐ *6 tune 6" cyl, rosewood case, 16" long, some decoration.*	550.00	750.00
☐ *6 tune 6¼" cyl, simple case style with some inlaid decoration on lid, 3 bells.*	350.00	550.00
☐ *6 tune 8" cyl, plain case, 16" long, inner glass lid, floral inlay.*	550.00	850.00

	Price Range	
☐ 6 tune 8¼" cyl, simple case with inlaid decoration on lid, tune sheet, 3 bells.	600.00	1250.00
☐ 6 tune 8¼" cyl, c. 1900, zither attachment, stop/start and change levers, rosewood case, inlaid musical motif and other simple case decorations.	750.00	1000.00
☐ 6 tune 9" cyl, interchangeable cyls (2), painted wood grain, case decoration, zither attachment, speed control, tune indicator.	1750.00	2500.00
☐ 6 tune 9" cyl, inlay on lid, simple case, 17" long.	750.00	1000.00
☐ 6 tune 10¼" cyl, walnut case with bird and floral inlay on lid, tune card, stop/start, change and instant stop levers, hinged end flap for key wind.	650.00	1250.00
☐ 6 tune 10¾" cyl, lever wind, grained mahogany case with inlaid decoration on lid.	500.00	1200.00
☐ 6 tune 10⅝" cyl, c. 1860, single comb, side panel holds stop/start and instant stop levers, simple case style, key wind.	500.00	1500.00
☐ 6 tune 11" cyl, double comb, Sublime-Harmony, inlaid rosewood, 22" case.	1500.00	2000.00
☐ 6 tune 11" cyl, (102 teeth comb), 18" inlaid case, zither, tune card, rosewood.	1250.00	1500.00
☐ 6 tune 13" cyl, inlaid 21" case, tune card, brass bedplate.	1000.00	1500.00
☐ 6 tune 13" cyl, interchangeable cyls, piccolo attachment, double spring, walnut (burled) case, matching table with storage.	3000.00	4500.00
☐ 6 tune 13" cyl, double comb, Sublime-Harmony, key wind, simple case.	1800.00	2500.00
☐ 6 tune 13" cyl, with castanet and bells, floral inlay, inner glass lid, tune card, lever wind.	1500.00	2500.00
☐ 6 tune 13½" cyl, Swiss, c. 1885, burl walnut and ebony case with inlaid brass and mother-of-pearl, inner glass lid, tune sheet interchangeable cyls (4), rachet wind, carrying handles.	2000.00	3000.00
☐ 6 tune 16" cyl, walnut inlay case with base moulding, Sublime-Harmony combs, tune indicator, inner glass lid.	1450.00	1750.00
☐ 6 tune 19" cyl, interchangeable cyls (3 fat cyls), sublime harmony piccolo, figured walnut, ornate brass handles.	2750.00	4000.00
☐ 8 tune 6" cyl, decorative inlay on lid, inner glass lid, tune card, tune indicator, 18" case.	300.00	850.00
☐ 8 tune 5" cyl, simple case style, some decoration, zither attachment, tune indicator, inner glass lid, outside crank, Swiss made.	250.00	750.00
☐ 8 tune 6" cyl, 3 saucer bells, walnut case with floral inlay, decorated tune card, inside glass lid.	500.00	1000.00
☐ 8 tune 7" cyl, inlay, simple case, 17" long, inner glass lid.	500.00	1000.00
☐ 8 tune 8" cyl, floral inlay case, 17" long.	600.00	1000.00
☐ 8 tune 8" cyl, burled walnut, decorated case, inner glass lid.	600.00	1000.00
☐ 8 tune 8" cyl, 6 bells, single comb, floral inlay, inner glass lid.	1250.00	2750.00
☐ 8 tune 9" cyl, inlaid rosewood 20" case.	600.00	1000.00
☐ 8 tune 10⅜" cyl, 3" wide diameter ("fat") cylinder, side panel reveals stop/start and change levers, single comb with 147 teeth, c. 1860.	2000.00	2500.00
☐ 8 tune 10¾" cyl, key wind, simple rosewood case with inlaid decoration on lid, border decorated tune sheet.	650.00	1200.00

	Price Range	
☐ *8 tune 11″ cyl, walnut case with floral inlay, long play.*	750.00	1500.00
☐ *8 tune 11″ cyl, 24″ rosewood case, tune indicator, inlay.*	600.00	1200.00
☐ *8 tune 11″ cyl, c. 1880, Guitar-tremolo, walnut case with ebony decoration, tune sheet.*	500.00	750.00
☐ *8 tune 11″ cyl, 6 bells, insect strikers, tune card, inlaid decorative case, inner glass lid.*	2000.00	2500.00
☐ *8 tune 11″ cyl, tune indicator, double spring, interchangeable cyls (3), floral inlay on cover, carrying handles, 35″ long, heavy base moulding hides drawer holding extra cylinders.*	2000.00	2750.00
☐ *8 tune 12½″ cyl, c. 1865, rachet wind, start/stop and repeat/change levers, mahogany case, tune sheet.*	750.00	1500.00
☐ *8 tune 13″ cyl, lever wind, tune card, 20½″ case, inlay on lid.*	1000.00	1500.00
☐ *8 tune 13″ cyl, 6 bells with bee strikers, inlay on front and cover of case, tune card.*	1250.00	2250.00
☐ *8 tune 13″ cyl, interchangeable cyls (3), burled walnut, matching table with storage drawer.*	2500.00	3000.00
☐ *8 tune 13″ cyl, interchangeable cyls (3), double spring barrel, stop/start and change levers, burled walnut case with fruitwood and ebony decoration, also brass, mother-of-pearl inlay, bottom half of front of box is storage space for extra cylinders.*	2000.00	3000.00
☐ *8 tune 13″ cyl, 6 bells, burled walnut, zither attachment.*	1300.00	2500.00
☐ *8 tune 13″ cyl, organ box (with bellows).*	1500.00	2500.00
☐ *8 tune 13″ cyl, 3″ diameter wide ("fat") cylinder, 26 key organ, rosewood veneer case with heavy base molding, multiple combs, inner glass lid, tune sheet, inlaid motifs on lid and front, side handles.*	2000.00	2500.00
☐ *8 tune 13½″ cyl, sublime harmony combs, rosewood case with floral marquetry, tune sheet inside lid, stop/start and repeat levers, innerglass lid, tune indicator.*	1000.00	1500.00
☐ *8 tune 15″ cyl, two part comb, piccolo expression, 25″ case.*	1000.00	1500.00
☐ *8 tune 15″ cyl, 9 bells with bird and bee strikers, burled walnut case with simple decoration and base molding, ornate side handles, stop/start and change levers, single comb, inner glass lid.*	1500.00	2700.00
☐ *8 tune 17″ cyl, 3″ diameter cyl, case decoration on front and lid, double comb, tune card, inner glass lid.*	1900.00	2500.00
☐ *8 tune 17½″ cyl, "Forte-Piano", operatic tunes, simple grained case with inlaid lid, single comb, tune sheet, inner glass lid.*	1500.00	3000.00
☐ *8 tune 18″ cyl, 4 combs, highly decorated lid, tune indicator, tune card, 30″ case, fancy handles on sides.*	1500.00	2100.00
☐ *10 tune 6″ cyl, bells with butterfly strikers, simple wood case with painted decoration, ornate tune card.*	750.00	1250.00
☐ *10 tune 6¼″ cyl, stencil decorated simple wood case, tune indicator, ornate tune card, single comb, inner glass lid, late 19th century.*	250.00	750.00
☐ *10 tune 6¼″ cyl, simple wood case, three bells with butterfly strikers, 18″ wide case.*	350.00	1000.00
☐ *10 tune 7½″ cyl, zither attachment, ebony finish, gold painted decoration, tune card, tune indicator.*	750.00	1000.00
☐ *10 tune 8″ cyl, 16″ mahogany case, tune card.*	500.00	1000.00

	Price Range	
☐ 10 tune 9" cyl, rosewood box, drum, 4 bells, butterfly strikers, tune indicator, some inlay decoration	1100.00	1500.00
☐ 10 tune 9¼" cyl, 3" wide ("fat") diameter cylinder, simple fruitwood case with some decoration, key wind side panel flap, tune sheet, single comb	1000.00	2000.00
☐ 10 tune 11" cyl, inlaid case, zither, tune indicator	500.00	650.00
☐ 10 tune 13" cyl, rosewood case with inlay, 23" case, tune card	1000.00	1500.00
☐ 10 tune 13" cyl, 6 bells with bird strikers, floral inlay front and top of case 23"	2750.00	4000.00
☐ 10 tune with bells, butterfly strikers, some inlay	1000.00	1500.00
☐ 12 tune 6" cyl, c. 1860, lever wind, rosewood with inlay decoration	500.00	1250.00
☐ 12 tune 8" cyl, zither attachment, plain case, some decorative details, inner glass lid, outside crank, tune indicator	600.00	1200.00
☐ 12 tune 8" cyl, simple case	500.00	950.00
☐ 12 tune 9" cyl, nickel plated metal parts, speed regulator, zither attachment, simple case style with some decorative details, inner glass lid, outside crank, tune indicator, tune sheet	750.00	1300.00
☐ 12 tune 11" cyl, zither attachment, inlay decorations, tune indicator, tune card	750.00	1100.00
☐ 12 tune 13" cyl, zither attachment, inlay case decoration, tune indicator, tune card	400.00	1000.00
☐ 12 tune 13" cyl, 6 bells, floral inlay case 25" long, zither, tune indicator	1250.00	1750.00
☐ 12 tune 13⅛" cyl, 3⅛" wide diameter ("fat") cylinder, simple mahogany case with minor decoration, single comb, tune card, stop/start and change levers, single spring barrel, late 19th century	1200.00	2000.00
☐ 12 tune 15" cyl, lever wind, rosewood with floral decoration	500.00	1600.00
☐ 12 tune 16" cyl, 3" diameter cyl, two part comb, figural inlay design on lid, 32" case, 6 bells, drum, tune indicator, full inner glass lid	1850.00	2750.00
☐ 12 tune 16¼" cyl, sublime harmony double combs, double spring, painted black case, lever wind, tune indicator, start/stop and repeat/change levers	300.00	750.00
☐ 12 tune 16⅜" cyl, rosewood case with inlay decoration, Swiss, sublime harmony combs, inner glass lid, tune indicator and changer, speed regulator, inner glass lid	1250.00	2250.00
☐ 12 tune 17" cyl, zither attachment, 20" long inlaid rosewood case, tune indicator	1750.00	2250.00
☐ 12 tune 20" cyl, 4 bells, butterfly strikers, tune indicator, plain case	2000.00	2500.00
☐ 20 tune 7½" cyl, (2 tunes per turn), simple case with gold decoration	750.00	1000.00
☐ 24 tune 13" cyl, zither attachment, double spring, inlay floral, decoration, tune indicator, tune card, 28" case	1000.00	1500.00
☐ 24 tune 17⅜" cyl, ("fat") cylinder, side panel reveals stop/start, change and instant stop levers, simple rosewood case, inlaid musical motif on lid	1250.00	2000.00
☐ 11½" cyl, c. 1850, French, keywind at side of case (side flips down), simple mahogany case	800.00	1000.00

	Price Range	
☐ *Musical photo album, 2 tune 2½" cyl, quarto plush ornamented album, tune plays when album is opened.*	50.00	150.00
☐ *Musical photo album, leather decorated cover, family photos, c. 1890's, 2 tune musical movement in back of album. (Many variations in photo album designs, music box essentially the same).*	75.00	200.00
☐ **SINGING BIRDS IN CAGE,** *One feathered bird on a branch, giltwood cage on square base 17" high.*	750.00	1250.00
☐ *Two feathered birds on a branch (one bird seated), domed gilt metal cage on a raised circular base, 20½" high.*	750.00	1750.00
☐ *Two feathered birds on a branch, gilt metal, domed cage on brass decorated base, 21" high.*	750.00	1100.00
☐ *Three painted mechanical birds, gilt metal domed cage, rectangular giltwood decorated base, 23" high.*	750.00	1200.00

ORCHESTRA AND ORGAN CYLINDER MUSIC BOXES—MAKERS UNKNOWN

☐ *4 tune 9¼" cyl, drum with ten beaters, three bells, stop/start, walnut case with simple decoration.*	1250.00	2250.00
☐ *6 tune 11 cyl, 6 bells, striking clock movement on outside front which plays music on the hour, burled walnut "serpentine" shaped case with inlay decoration and wide base moulding, inner glass lid.*	2500.00	3750.00
☐ *6 tune 11" cyl, interchangeable cyls (4), walnut decorated with inlay, corner moulding, drawer in base for extra cyls, drum, 6 bells, inner glass lid, tune cards.*	2500.00	3500.00
☐ *6 tune 11" cyl, Duplex cylinder box (plays both side by side cylinders at the same time), two combs, 8 bells, 8 drum beaters (one drum), decorative tune card, simple case style with minor decorative details.*	8000.00	10500.00
☐ *6 tune 11" cyl, interchangeable cyls (2), coin operated drum, zither attachment, 6 bells, tune indicator, 4 dancing dolls viewed from front glass panel, walnut case.*	2250.00	3250.00
☐ *6 tune 12" cyl, Swiss, c. 1870, lever wind spring movement, organ accompaniment, mahogany case, floral marquetry decoration on lid and front panel.*	600.00	900.00
☐ *6 tune 16¼" cyl, two drums with multiple beaters, 11 bells, castanets, flat top winding lever, rosewood veneer case with inlay decoration on lid and front, operatic selections, inner glass lid, tune sheet, single comb.*	2250.00	3000.00
☐ *8 tune 9¼" cyl, c. 1880, 4 saucer bells with butterfly strikers, drums, castanets, rosewood case with walnut and ebony details, floral decal on lid, tune sheet, inner glass lid, lever wind, start/stop and repeat/change levers.*	2000.00	2500.00
☐ *8 tune 10½" cyl, c. 1885, 6 saucer bells with bird and butterfly strikers, tune indicator, rosewood and ebony case with floral marquetry on lid, rachet wind movement, start/stop and repeat/wind levers.*	500.00	1500.00
☐ *8 tune 13" cyl (2¼" diameter fat cylinder), interchangeable cyls (3), walnut veneer, inlay rosewood and tulip, musical motif inlay on top and front.*	3000.00	4000.00

	Price Range	
☐ 8 tune 14" cyl, interchangeable cyls (4), bell, drum, castanet, bee strikers, burled walnut case 35" long, matching table with storage for extra cylinders.	3500.00	6500.00
☐ 10 tune 16" cyl, 6 bells, drum, castanet, 26" case, inlay, tune card.	2500.00	4000.00
☐ 10 tune 16" cyl, 17 key organ, 6 bells, burled walnut and ebony case with marquetry decoration, inner glass lid, tune sheet.	2250.00	3150.00
☐ 12 tune 13" cyl, drum with 5 bells, inlaid musical motifs on front and lid and other simple case decoration, burled walnut case, inner glass lid.	2000.00	2500.00
☐ 12 tune 14" cyl, with organ, 6 bells, drum, castanets, 30" burled walnut case, double spring, some inlay decoration, tune indicator.	2500.00	3500.00
☐ 12 tune 16" cyl, drum, 6 saucer bells, rosewood and ebony case with floral inlay decoration, tune sheet, lever wind start/stop and repeat/change levers.	2500.00	3000.00
☐ 12 tune 17" cyl, 6 bells, 9 beaters, 8 strikers, castanets, inlay decoration on front and top, 28" case.	2500.00	3500.00
☐ 12 tune 21" cyl, c. 1870, drum, hidden bells and castanets, divided comb, tune sheet, walnut case, floral inlay decoration, lever wind, start/stop and repeat change levers.	1650.00	3000.00
☐ 12 tune 21¼" cyl, 2 drums with multiple beaters, 6 bells, single comb, decorative inlay on case lid.	2750.00	4000.00
☐ 16 tune 13" cyl, (3⅜" diameter, fat cylinder), three governors, 41 key organ accompaniment, burl walnut with brass inlay decoration.	7500.00	10000.00
☐ "Dancing Doll" Orchestra box, organ, bells, drum, castanet, ornate inlaid case decoration.	2500.00	3500.00
☐ 6½" cyl, Swiss, interchangeable cyls, 6 saucer bells in view with strikers, rachet wind spring movement, stop/start control, rosewood and ebony case with marquetry decoration in floral motif, repeat/change lever, storage in drop front for extra cylinders.	700.00	1000.00
☐ 10" cyl, organ box, c. 1885, lever wind, divided comb, start/stop and repeat/change levers, rosewood and ebony case with floral inlay.	900.00	1400.00
☐ 12½" cyl, Swiss, c. 1880, reed organ, 9 saucer bells, bird strikers, lever wind, rosewood case with mother-of-pearl, ebony and mahogany decoration, carrying handles.	2500.00	3500.00
☐ 13" cyl, 6 bells, drum, castanets, inlay on lid, inside glass lid, tune card.	2400.00	2900.00
☐ 13" cyl, 6 bells, 8 beaters, bee strikers, floral inlay front and top, base moulding.	2500.00	3500.00
☐ 13" cyl, c. 1880, drum, 6 bells, bird flower and butterfly strikers, castanet, organ movement, walnut case with inlaid decoration (has fat cylinder).	3250.00	4000.00
☐ 15¼" cyl, Swiss, organ box, lever wind spring movement, start/stop and repeat/change levers, rosewood and ebony case, floral marquetry and inlay decoration.	500.00	1000.00
☐ 24 tune 16½" cyl, drum, castanet, 6 bells, butterfly strikers, double spring, zither attachment, tune indicator, wood box with some decoration, tune card.	2000.00	3000.00

METAL DISC MUSIC BOXES

	Price Range	
☐ **ADLER (J. H. Zimmermann, Leipzig, Germany)** *7" disc (Style #210, 18cm disc), small plain case, hand crank, 33 teeth comb, name on lid, with zither attachment (Style #210Z).*	375.00	800.00
☐ *7" disc (Style #220, 18cm disc), spring wind (lever on front), simple small case, name on lid, with zither (Style #220Z), 33 teeth comb.*	375.00	800.00

Adler Disc Music Box, table model.

☐ *14¾" disc (Style #250, 37cm), plain case, simple moulding on base and lid, ball feet, crank wind, spring with zither, walnut inlay case (Style #255Z), also inner glass lid, duplex comb, lithograph inside cover: Eagle and Cherubs.*	1500.00	2200.00
☐ *14¾" disc (Style #300Z), 77 teeth comb, upright (vertical) counter type, coin operated, zither attachment, walnut carved case, glass door, storage drawer just under mechanism (for discs).*	1400.00	1750.00
☐ *21¼" disc (54cm) large upright, walnut, highly decorated case, coin operated, double comb, zither attachment.*	1600.00	2650.00
☐ **BRITANNIA DISC MUSIC BOX** *9" disc, simple case, table model c. 1900.*	1000.00	1250.00
☐ *9" disc, upright (vertical) counter model, double comb, simple walnut case style with transfer and inlay decoration.*	1000.00	1500.00
☐ *11¾" disc, c. 1905, single comb, start/stop lever, 27" high counter top vertical style case, walnut with some case decoration, crank wind, mirrored solid front doors, (coin operated).*	1500.00	2000.00
☐ *17⅛" disc, upright, carved and fretwork decoration, duplex comb.*	3000.00	4000.00

	Price Range	
☐ **CAPITAL SELF PLAYING MUSIC BOXES (CUFF BOXES) F. G. OTTO & SONS, NJ** — *Use interchangeable steel tune cyls.*		
☐ *STYLE A c. 1895. Mahogany (oak), 44 teeth comb, winter scene inside lid, spring wind, simple cases, cylinders are 5½" long.*	**2000.00**	**3000.00**
☐ *STYLE B Mahogany (oak), 58 teeth comb, pastoral winter scene inside cover, zither attachment.*	**2250.00**	**3250.00**
☐ *STYLE C Mahogany (oak), 81 teeth, lithograph inside lid, simple case.*	**2500.00**	**3500.00**
☐ *STYLE D Same as style C, coin operated, Automatic "Penny" attachment.*	**2750.00**	**3250.00**
☐ *STYLE F Double comb (162 teeth), oak (mahogany), lithograph inside lid.*	**2500.00**	**3000.00**
☐ *STYLE G Same as style B with "Penny" attachment.*	**2500.00**	**3000.00**

Criterion Disc Music Box, table model.

	Price Range	
☐ **CELESTA** *8″ disc (21cm), simple box, lever wind on front.*	500.00	1000.00
☐ **CRITERION** *(Made c. 1900 by F. G. Otto & Sons, NJ), 8¾″ disc, table model, simple mahogany case with figural lithograph inside lid.*	500.00	750.00
☐ *11½″ disc, double comb, mahogany, lithograph inside cover, decorative moulding.*	1000.00	1750.00
☐ *15½″ disc, table model, mahogany case with some carved decoration, double comb.*	2000.00	2750.00
☐ *15¾″ disc, carved oak case, double comb, lithograph inside cover.*	1500.00	2000.00
☐ *15¾″ disc, mahogany simple case decoration, single comb, lithograph inside lid.*	1500.00	2500.00
☐ *15¾″ disc, table model, double comb, peripheral drive movement, stop/start and tempo controls, crank wind, carved (mahogany) walnut case, trademark lithograph inside lid, matching storage cabinet has open shelf on top and front door panel, also matching case decoration.*	1500.00	2500.00
☐ *20½″ disc, mahogany case, simple, lithograph inside lid.*	2000.00	2600.00
☐ **EDELWEISS** *4½″ disc, table model, hand crank, simple case with decoration inside lid.*	185.00	400.00
☐ *6½″ disc, table model, hand crank, simple beechwood case with decoration inside lid.*	250.00	500.00
☐ **EMPRESS (SEE MIRA, STYLE #290)**		
☐ **EUPHONIA** *15¾″ disc, large mahogany case, decorative metal corners on case, lithograph inside cover (female figure).*	1000.00	1250.00
☐ **EUTERPEPHON** *12″ disc (30.8cm), simple box, lithograph inside cover: "Goddess Euterpe", Polyphone and Regina discs will play on this music box.*	500.00	1500.00
☐ **FORTUNA (J. H. ZIMMERMANN, Leipzig, Germany)** *8¼″ disc, walnut simple case, ratchet wind.*	500.00	750.00
☐ *10¾″ disc, simple case.*	1250.00	1600.00
☐ *16″ disc, simple case.*	1500.00	1850.00
☐ **HARMONIA** *16¼″ disc, table model, single comb, burled walnut (mahogany) veneered case, decorative moldings and brass and ivory inlay on lid, zinc discs.*	1250.00	2250.00
☐ *20½″ disc table model, single comb, burled walnut case with brass and ivory inlay, zinc discs, carved corner columns.*	1850.00	2250.00
☐ **HELVETIA DISC** *8″ disc, 2 bells, black painted case, metal trim.*	1000.00	1250.00
☐ *8″ disc, transfer decorated case with handles, plays polyphone discs.*	250.00	450.00
☐ **KALLIOPE MUSIKWERKE (Leipzig, Germany)** *7″ disc (18cm), walnut case, simple case, design etched on lid, lithograph inside cover, spring wind.*	500.00	1000.00

	Price Range	
☐ 7" disc (18cm), 4 bells, walnut, simple case, lithograph inside lid, zither attachment, 36 teeth comb.	900.00	1250.00
☐ 7¾" disc (19.5cm), simple case, lithograph inside cover.	700.00	900.00
☐ 8" disc, table model with 6 bells, simple case style.	350.00	750.00
☐ 9¼" disc (23.5cm), plain case, lithograph inside cover, 49 teeth in comb.	500.00	850.00
☐ 9¼" disc with 6 bells, walnut case with floral inlay on lid, figural lithograph inside cover.	750.00	1250.00
☐ 9½" disc, table model, crank wind from center, single comb, mahogany case, simple case.	500.00	1000.00
☐ 9¾" disc (25cm), simple case, lithograph inside cover, single comb (42 teeth).	650.00	800.00
☐ 13½" disc (34cm), table model, simple case, zither attachment, lithograph of lady inside cover, 61 teeth in comb.	1250.00	1500.00
☐ 13½" disc with 10 bells, walnut case, decorated, "Kalliope" inside lid, (could have lithograph).	1000.00	2000.00
☐ 13½" disc (vertical) hanging case, walnut highly decorated with gallery, glass front, coin operated, 61 teeth in comb.	2000.00	2500.00
☐ 17¾" disc (45cm), carved upright case, counter top type, glass front, 106 extra wide teeth.	2500.00	3000.00
☐ 17¾" disc, with 10 bells, otherwise same as above.	3000.00	3500.00
☐ 17¾" disc, wall hanging, glass front, walnut case, coin operated, 82 teeth in comb.	2750.00	3250.00
☐ 17¾" disc, table model, deluxe walnut case, carving on base moulding, 82 teeth in comb, zither attachment.	1500.00	2500.00
☐ 17¾" disc, table model, walnut case, double comb (164 teeth) with 10 bells, zither attachment.	2750.00	3250.00
☐ 17¾" disc, "PANORAMA", upright (vertical) type, decorative moldings and columns on rosewood and walnut case, double comb, 53½" high, moving scene, glass door to view disc.	4500.00	6500.00
☐ 20½" (52.5cm) disc, upright on storage base, walnut with decorative carving and gallery, 12 saucer bells, 120 "extra wide" teeth.	3500.00	5500.00
☐ 20⅝" disc, upright (vertical) model on feet with matching storage unit, 74" high simple walnut veneer case with decorative columns, glass door to view disc, double combs.	3750.00	6250.00
☐ 22¾" (58cm) disc, counter top type with carved gallery, glass door, zither, 145 extra wide teeth.	2500.00	3000.00
☐ 25" disc, hanging vertical model with 12 saucer bells, some case decoration.	4000.00	6000.00
☐ **KOMET (Weissbach & Co., Leipzig, Germany)** 6¾" disc (17cm) walnut, decorative inlay, figural inlay inside lid.	500.00	850.00
☐ 8¾" disc, table model, simple walnut case.	500.00	1000.00
☐ 10¼" disc (126cm) simple case, some decoration, figural lithograph inside lid.	650.00	800.00
☐ 20½" disc (52cm), upright case on feet (3'3½" high) small storage drawer just under glass door, sits on base, "KOMET" etched on glass.	2000.00	3000.00
☐ 20½" disc, upright counter (vertical) model, coin operated, parallel twin combs, walnut case with decorative moldings and front glass door, top wind motor.	2500.00	3500.00
☐ 24½" disc, upright floor model, highly decorated case.	7000.00	8000.00

	Price Range	
☐ **LOCHMANN (Leipzig, Germany)** *10″ disc, "Original", table model, plain case.*	600.00	750.00
☐ *15″ disc, "Original", table model, scenic lithograph inside lid, simple case.*	1000.00	1250.00
☐ *24½″ disc, upright case, counter model, coin operated, tubular bells, curved glass over motor, oak case, some carving, gold decoration on glass front says "Original", 45½″ high, c. 1901.*	4500.00	7500.00
☐ *24½″ disc, c. 1905, upright floor model, 86″ high, double comb, 12 bells, coin operated (slot in front), crank wind, glass door, walnut case, storage for discs in base.*	7500.00	9500.00
☐ *25¾″ disc, (Model 200) weight driven motor, strings, tubular bells, walnut case with fretwork pediment, glass door, 66½″ high.*	5000.00	7500.00
☐ **MIRA (MERMOD FRÉRES)** *6¾″ disc, hand crank (manivelle), mahogany case, c. 1900.*	500.00	1250.00
☐ *7″ disc (Style #36), straight simple lines, single comb, 34 teeth, oak (mahogany), "Mira" inside cover.*	750.00	1000.00

Mira Disc Music Box, table model.

Mira Disc Music Box, style #132, table model, mahogany.

Mira Disc Music Box, 15¾″, disc console model, storage in base.

	Price Range	
☐ 9½" disc (Style #50), single comb, 48 teeth, oak (mahogany), zither attachment, simple case, "Mira" or lithograph inside cover.	800.00	1250.00
☐ 9½" disc (Style #100), oak (mahogany) with case moulding, duplex comb, 96 teeth, zither attachment, simple case.	1250.00	1600.00
☐ 12" disc, table model, center drive movement, zither attachment, tempo control, single comb, top wind, crank inside box, mahogany case with base molding.	1500.00	2000.00
☐ 12" disc (Style #132), oak (or mahogany), simple case with moulding on base and cover, duplex comb, 128 teeth, table model, "Mira" inside cover.	1500.00	1750.00

Miraphone Disc Music Box, console style #258.

☐ 12" disc (Style #66), 64 teeth in comb, oak (mahogany), moulding on base and cover, "Mira" inside cover, zither attachment.	1500.00	2000.00
☐ 15½" disc (Style #79), simple oak case, moulding on base and cover, zither long running movement, single comb, 79 teeth.	1750.00	2000.00
☐ 15½" disc (Style #158), Duplex comb, 158 teeth, long running movement, oak or mahogany, zither, case moulding, "Mira" on inside of lid.	2250.00	2750.00
☐ 15½" disc Miraphone, table model, music box/outside horn phonograph combination, double comb, mahogany.	4500.00	6000.00
☐ 15½" disc (Style #258), floor model with storage for discs, decorative moulding.	2500.00	3500.00
☐ 15¾" disc, console (floor) model, lid lifts up to reveal horizontal music box, storage for discs in base, mahogany case, also made with color decal decoration on case.	3000.00	4500.00
☐ 18½" disc (Style #190), simple oak or mahogany case, duplex comb, long running movement, zither.	3000.00	3500.00

	Price Range	
☐ *18½" disc (Style #290), floor model with storage, console style (sold under "EMPRESS" label).*	5000.00	7500.00
☐ *18½" disc, "Orchestral Grand", console (floor model) style, horizontal music box, lid lifts up with disc storage compartment underneath, simple mahogany case with inlay and colored decoration, 41½" high.*	4000.00	6000.00
☐ *18½" disc, MIRAPHONE, music box/phonograph combination, floor model with storage for discs and records.*	5000.00	7000.00
☐ **MONOPOL (Leipzig, Germany)** *6" disc, plain case, lithograph inside lid.*	400.00	600.00
☐ *7½" disc, hand crank, walnut with transfer decoration on lid.*	450.00	650.00
☐ *8¼" (8¾") disc, walnut, plain case, "MONOPOL" lithograph inside lid.*	500.00	700.00
☐ *12" disc, plain mahogany case, can play Symphonion discs.*	600.00	700.00
☐ *13⅝" disc, plain case, lithograph inside lid.*	650.00	1250.00

Olympia Disc Music Box,
table model,
with drawer for extra discs.

☐ *14" disc, walnut with decorative columns, lithograph inside lid, ornamented bedplate, will play Symphonion discs.*	750.00	1000.00
☐ *17¼" disc, upright counter model, carved decoration, single comb.*	1500.00	2000.00
☐ **NEW CENTURY (MERMOD FRERES)** *11½" disc, table model, mahogany (or oak), simple case style, duplex comb.*	2000.00	2500.00
☐ *15" disc, table model, mahogany (or oak), plain case with thin moulding around edges, double comb.*	2250.00	3250.00
☐ *18½" disc, "Soprano", double revolution movement, duplex comb, long running on one wind, oak (or mahogany).*	5000.00	7500.00

	Price Range	
☐ **OLYMPIA (F. OTTO AND SONS, NJ)** *"Princess", duplex comb, winter scene lithograph, highly ornate carving all over.*	1000.00	1500.00
☐ *8¾" disc, c. 1905, center drive movement with single comb, crank wind at side, oak case.*	400.00	900.00
☐ *14" disc, single comb, simple case, storage drawer for discs.*	1500.00	2100.00
☐ *15½" disc, single comb, coin operated, scenic lithograph inside lid, mahogany (cherry), carved decoration.*	1500.00	2750.00
☐ *15½" disc, highly carved decorated case, scenic lithograph inside lid, double comb.*	1500.00	2200.00
☐ *15¾" disc, table model, mahogany, some case decoration...*	1750.00	2500.00
☐ *20" disc, upright, carved decorated case with storage base.*	4500.00	5500.00
☐ *27" disc, upright floor model, mahogany, decorative moulding in columns along front sides of case, double doors top and bottom, 6' tall.*	5000.00	5500.00
☐ **ORPHENION** *8½" disc, table model, walnut case with simple decoration, single comb.*	750.00	1500.00
☐ *16¼" disc, c. 1877, simple case style, burl walnut, crank wind, exposed spring barrel.*	2500.00	3500.00
☐ **ORPHEUS** *18¼" disc, table model, multiple combs (3), decorative case and corner mouldings, "Orpheus" trademark lithograph inside lid.*	1500.00	2250.00
☐ **OTTO & SONS (SEE "OLYMPIA")**		
☐ **PERFECTION** *10½" disc, table model, simple mahogany case, scenic lithograph inside lid, zinc discs.*	1000.00	1500.00
☐ **POLYPHON MUSIKWERKE (Leipzig, Germany)** *6½" disc, simple case, 30 teeth in comb, walnut, lithograph inside cover.*	350.00	450.00
☐ *6½" disc, with 4 bells, spring driven, lithograph inside cover, wood case plain, decal "POLYPHONE" on lid, 30 teeth in comb.*	450.00	650.00
☐ *8-8¼" disc, hand crank, walnut case, decal design on lid, lithograph, inside crank, 41 teeth in comb.*	450.00	750.00
☐ *8-8¼" disc, with 4 saucer bells, lever spring wind, plain wood case, 30 teeth in music comb.*	500.00	800.00
☐ *8-8¼" disc, serpentine style case, walnut, color lithograph on inside front cover, spring wind via front lever outside case, 41 teeth in comb.*	550.00	750.00
☐ *9½" disc, table model, simple case style.*	300.00	500.00
☐ *9½" disc, front lever, spring wind, 6 bells, simple case, 46 teeth in comb.*	750.00	1500.00
☐ *9¾" disc, 6 saucer bells, some decoration simple case, pictorial lithograph inside cover, spring wind via front lever, 41 teeth in comb.*	500.00	900.00
☐ *9⅝" disc, single comb, 6 bells, ratchet wind, grained wood case, transfer decorated lid.*	500.00	900.00
☐ *11" disc, table model, 6 bells, simple walnut case, outside front ratchet wind, print inside lid, single comb.*	750.00	1250.00

Polyphon Disc Music Box, walnut floor model, with storage in base.

	Price Range	
☐ *11¼" disc, walnut, some floral inlay on cover, decorative moulding, 54 teeth in comb, single comb, lithograph of cherubs inside lid, plays Regina discs also.*	**750.00**	**1250.00**
☐ *11¼" disc, duplex comb, 108 teeth, satinwood inlay case, decorative moulding.*	**1000.00**	**1500.00**
☐ *11¼" disc, with 8 bells, walnut case.*	**1250.00**	**1750.00**
☐ *14½" disc, with 12 bells, walnut, scenic lithograph inside lid, some inlay in cover, 112 notes.*	**1500.00**	**2000.00**
☐ *15½-¾" disc, coin operated, single comb, 78 teeth, walnut case with some moulding, lithograph inside cover, glass lid over mechanism.*	**1200.00**	**1750.00**
☐ *15½", peripheral drive movement, 1½ combs, start/stop control, floral marquetry decoration on case, table model.*	**1750.00**	**3750.00**
☐ *15½-¾" disc, single comb, 77 teeth, walnut simple case, some decoration.*	**1000.00**	**1750.00**

Polyphon Upright Disc Music Box, walnut storage base.

	Price Range	
☐ *15½" disc, Sublime-Harmonie Piccolo, duplex comb, 154 teeth in music comb, table model, walnut with elaborate carvng and inlay, will play Regina discs (storage drawer for discs)*	1225.00	2250.00
☐ *15½" disc, upright (vertical) counter model, double comb, peripheral drive movement, crank wind, walnut case with columns and deep moulding, front panel is pierced with lyre design in center, drawer in bottom for extra discs, coin operated*	2000.00	3000.00
☐ *15 ⁵/₈" disc, upright counter model, walnut, carved top gallery and front columns, 78 teeth music comb, coin operated, on feet, glass door to view disc mechanism*	2250.00	3250.00
☐ *15 ⁵/₈" disc, twin combs, veneer case, lithograph inside lid*	1000.00	1700.00
☐ *15 ⁵/₈" disc, Longcase Hall Clock, weight driven movement, walnut case with highly carved and turned ornaments, 91" high*	5000.00	7000.00

	Price Range	
☐ *17½" disc, table model, 12 bells, walnut case with inlay on lid, lithograph inside cover, 72 teeth.*	2000.00	2500.00
☐ *19⅝-20" disc, walnut case with inlay, decorative moulding, lithograph inside lid, 118 teeth, table model.*	3500.00	4500.00
☐ *19⅝" disc, floor model (one whole cabinet), highly carved case, glass front top door, motor mechanism in glass case, coin operated, fully carved free columns between top and bottom sections in front to form a shelf-like section in the middle, storage of discs in base.*	4800.00	6500.00
☐ *19⅝-20" disc, counter model, upright, front columns, glass door, coin operated, top gallery (clock), 118 teeth in music comb, walnut.*	2250.00	3500.00
☐ *19⅝" disc, floor model, carved walnut case, glass front, storage in base, glass panel over motor mechanism, 118 teeth in music comb.*	3750.00	4500.00
☐ *22½" disc, upright with 16 bells, on feet with storage base, decorative moulding, glass front, walnut (Glockenspiel).*	5000.00	7000.00
☐ *22½" disc upright (vertical) counter model, coin operated, glockenspiel accompaniment, glass front door, walnut case with some decorative moulding, columns and fretwork, sits on feet, 43½" high.*	3000.00	5000.00
☐ *24½" disc, upright floor model, carved walnut, very loud tone, large springs, 159 teeth, storage unit for discs in base, coin operated.*	4500.00	7000.00
☐ *24½" disc, upright automatic changer, floor model, holds 12 discs, selection indicator, ornate case and gallery, walnut, 159 notes.*	10000.00	22500.00
☐ *24⅝" disc, upright model on feet with base storage cabinet fretwork, gallery and finials, glass front door, zither attachment, side wind motor, walnut case, 92" high.*	4000.00	6000.00
☐ *25⅝" disc, upright coin operated, counter model, side wind motor, double combs, walnut case, glass door, on feet.*	4750.00	7000.00

REGINA MUSIC BOX COMPANY (Rahway, NJ) The Regina Boxes originally all had numerical style numbers. For easy reference they are arranged in this order, however, this is not necessarily the order in which they were made.

*Below are disc size and other reference guides to locating a particular box.

DISC SIZE	STYLE
8½" disc styles	*21, 22, 91*
11" disc styles	*19, 20*
12¼" disc styles	*16, 17, 17a, 29, 30, 41, 141, 42, 142, 71, 171, 72, 172, 81, 116, 129*
15½" disc styles	*1, 2, 3, 9-15, 35, 36 (Round and Flat), 40, 140, 240, 51, 251, 50, 151, 250, 55, 255, 155, 67, 113, 215, 216, 217, 246*
20¾" disc styles	*24, 25, 26 (Early and Late), 27 (Early and Late), 126, 226, 28, 31, 32, 37, 38 (Round and Flat), 39, 139, 239, 44, 144, 61*
27" disc styles	*4, 5, 6, 7, 8, 8a, 33, 34, 45, 145*

ACCORDIAN TOP STYLES

20¾"	*26*
27"	*6, 7*

Regina Music Box,
style #4,
Orchestral Regina,
plays 27″ discs.

Regina Disc Music Box,
style #6, oak.

AUTOMATIC CHANGERS

15½" 35, 36
20¾" 31, 32
27" 8, 8a, 33, 34
32" 300

CLOCKS

12¼" 81
15½" 3

COIN OPERATED STYLES

Table models: Style #
12¼" disc . . . . 17 (double comb), 30 (single comb)
15½" disc . . . . 2, 14, 217 (single comb), 15, 51 (double comb)
20¾" disc . . . . 27 (double comb)
27" disc . . . . 7 (double comb)

Upright Floor models:
15½" disc . . . . 1, 36 (double comb)
20¾" disc . . . . 25, 38 (double comb)
27" disc . . . . 5, 34, 8 (double comb)

Vertical Counter models:
12¼" disc . . . . 17a (double comb)
20¾" disc . . . . 32 (double comb)

Regina Music Box, oak accordion table model, style #6, mahogany.

CONSOLE (FLOOR) STYLES

12¼" 41, 42
15½" 40, 43, 67, 246
20¾" 44
27" 45

COUNTER TOP (VERTICAL) STYLES

12¼" disc ....17a (coin operated)
20¾" disc ....32 (coin operated)
Style 18: ....several disc sizes

DESK STYLE

20¾" disc ....61, Reginaphone 161

GUM VENDING MACHINE

Style 18 ....several disc sizes

REGINAPHONE: DISC MUSIC BOX/PHONOGRAPH COMBINATION

Table models: Outside Horn (for phonograph)
12¼" disc 129, 171, 172
15½" disc 113, 150, 155
20¾" disc 126, 139

Table models: Inside Horn
15½" disc 250, 251, 255
20¾" disc 226, 239

Regina Disc Music Box,
upright, style, #8, automatic changer.

Regina Disc Music Box,
style #10, oak.

Regina Disc Music Box,
style #10, mahogany.

Regina Disc Music Box,
table model, style #11.

Console (Floor) models: Outside Horn
12¼" disc 141, 142
15½" disc 140, 143
20¾" disc ....144, 161 (Desk style)
27" disc 145

Console (Floor) models: Inside Horn
15½" disc ....240 (Lions' heads)

TABLE STYLES
8½" disc 21, 22, 91
11" disc 19, 20
12¼" disc 16, 17, 29, 30, 71, 72
15½" disc 6, 7, 9, 10, 11, 11a, 12, 13, 14, 14a, 15, 50, 51, 55, 215, 216, 217
20¾" disc 26, 28, 27, 39

UPRIGHT (VERTICAL FLOOR) STYLES
15½" disc 1, 2, 35, 36
20¾" disc 24, 25, 31, 37, 38
27" disc 4, 5, 8, 8a, 33, 34

	Price Range	
☐ *STYLE #1 — 15½" upright coin operated, long play "Musical Automation", duplex comb, oak (mahogany).*	3000.00	4000.00
☐ *STYLE #2 — Same as above, single comb.*	3000.00	3500.00
☐ *STYLE #3 — 15⅓" disc movement musical clock (Seth Thomas), play hourly, or any time desired, grandfather style highly decorated (various case styles).*	3750.00	4750.00
☐ *STYLE #4 — 27" disc, ORCHESTRAL REGINA, oak (mahogany, walnut), large-for-home-use upright music box, storage bin in base for discs.*	5000.00	7000.00
☐ *STYLE #5 — Same as above, coin operated.*	5000.00	8000.00

	Price Range	
☐ *STYLE #6 — 27" disc, folding (Accordian top), oak (mahogany), table model, hinged cover opens so disc can lie flat, duplex comb, long running, 172 tongues.*	4000.00	6000.00
☐ *STYLE #7 — 27" disc, coin operated version Style #6.*	7000.00	7500.00
☐ *STYLE #8a — 27" disc automatic changer, 12 discs, ornate case, floor model, carved dragons, finials on gallery.*	6500.00	11,000.00
☐ *STYLE #8 — coin operated version Style #8a.*	6600.00	10,000.00
☐ *STYLE #9 — 15½" disc table model, duplex comb, ornately carved paneling, walnut (oak, mahogany).*	1750.00	2000.00
☐ *STYLE #10 — 15½" disc table model, long running movement, ornate case, oak (mahogany), duplex comb.*	2000.00	3500.00
☐ *STYLE #11 — 15½" disc table model, oak, long running movement, several case styles, some with storage drawer, basic plain straight case (see also Style #50).*	1900.00	2600.00

Regina Disc Music Box, oak accordion table model, style #26.

☐ *STYLE #11a — 15½" disc, regular movement, duplex comb, REGINA lithograph inside cover.*	1900.00	2200.00
☐ *STYLE #12 — 15½" disc, table model with storage drawer in case for discs, single comb.*	1500.00	2250.00
☐ *STYLE #13 — 15½" disc, table model, plain (and decorated case styles) oak case, regular movement, single comb.*	1250.00	2200.00
☐ *STYLE #113 — REGINAPHONE outside horn version #13.*	1750.00	2500.00
☐ *STYLE #14 — table model 15½" disc, coin operated, single comb.*	1500.00	2500.00

Regina Disc Music Box,
style #26, early,
table top model,
mahogany.

Regina Disc Music Box,
style #31,
automatic changer, oak.

Reginaphone Disc Music Box / Phonograph, style #255, table model, inside horn.

	Price Range	
☐ *STYLE #14a — duplex version #14.*	1600.00	2000.00
☐ *STYLE #15 — 15½" disc, coin operated (version #11), duplex comb, long running, oak (mahogany).*	1600.00	2600.00
☐ *STYLE #16 — 12¼" disc table model, double comb.*	1000.00	1250.00
☐ *STYLE #17 — 12¼" disc table model, double comb, coin operated.*	1000.00	1250.00
☐ *STYLE #17a — 12¼" disc, vertical counter style table model, double comb, coin operated.*	3000.00	3500.00
☐ *STYLE #18 — gum vending machine, "A Musical Salesman", vertical counter top style, glass front, examples, were made in 11", 12¼", 15½" disc styles. Coin operated, dispersed gum, played a tune.*	3500.00	4000.00

Regina Disc Music Box, style #35, coin-op #36, automatic changer, plays 15½" discs, leaded glass, mahogany.

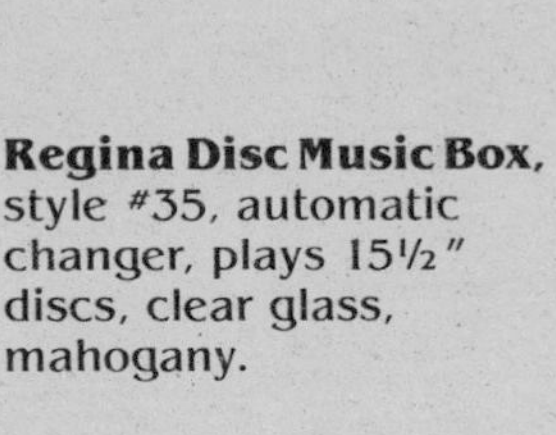

Regina Disc Music Box, style #35, automatic changer, plays 15½" discs, clear glass, mahogany.

Regina Disc Music Box, late, style #33, upright "Orchestral Corona," automatic changer.

Regina Automatic Disc Changer, mahogany, floor model, style #37.

	Price Range	
☐ STYLE #19 — 11″ disc, duplex comb, walnut with case decoration, 112 teeth comb.	1000.00	1250.00
☐ STYLE #20 — 11″ disc, single comb, lever wind on front of case, lithograph inside cover, plain case, oak or mahogany, center drive.	850.00	1250.00
☐ STYLE #21 — 8½″ disc, hand crank, single comb, oak or mahogany, 41 teeth, plain case.	500.00	750.00
☐ STYLE #22 — 8½″ disc, single comb, spring wind, plain oak (mahogany), lithograph inside cover.	500.00	750.00
☐ STYLE #24 — REGINA SUBLIMA, 20¾″ disc, Parlor upright long running, double comb, oak (mahogany), 71″ high, carved, flat rectangular case design, openwork gallery, round glass opening the size of disc.	6000.00	10,500.00
☐ STYLE #25 — coin operated version #24.	9000.00	11,000.00
☐ STYLE #26 early — folding top (Casket or accordion top), 20¾″ disc, hinged cover opens out to allow for disc to lie flat, oak (mahogany), long playing, two combs, table model.	4500.00	6250.00

Regina Disc Music Box,
Style #39, "Cupola"

	Price Range	
☐ *STYLE #26 late — 20¾" disc, standard straight sided case, duplex comb, banjo attachment, oak (mahogany), speed regulator.*	3000.00	4000.00
☐ *STYLE #126 — REGINAPHONE outside horn, nickel Morning Glory style "Cupola" top on lid on all models.*	4750.00	5250.00
☐ *STYLE #226 — REGINAPHONE with inside horn.*	3500.00	4000.00
☐ *STYLE #27 early — coin operated version #26.*	4500.00	6500.00
☐ *STYLE #27 late — coin operated version late #26.*	3250.00	4250.00
☐ *STYLE #29 — 12¼" disc, table model, single comb, (various case styles).*	1000.00	1500.00
☐ *STYLE #129 — outside horn REGINAPHONE, nickel Morning Glory horn.*	2000.00	2500.00
☐ *STYLE #30 — 12¼" disc, table model, single comb, coin operated.*	1000.00	1500.00
☐ *STYLE #31 — 20¾" disc, REGINA SUBLIMA CORONA, automatic disc changer, 64" high case, top half of upright floor model case is recessed to form a narrow shelf with bottom section, glass fronts top and bottom, decorative case, long running movement, two combs, oak (mahogany).*	9000.00	11,000.00
☐ *STYLE #32 — counter top version of #31, coin operated, 20¾" disc.*	6500.00	8500.00
☐ *STYLE #33 — 27" disc, REGINA ORCHESTRAL CORONA, automatic changer, two combs, oak (mahogany), 66" high, piano sounding board, long running, straight case, Style like #31, earlier examples more ornate case design.*	9000.00	11,000.00
☐ *STYLE #34 — 27" disc, coin operated version of Style #33, generally top section of case has two doors.*	8000.00	13,000.00
☐ *STYLE #35 — 15½" disc CORONA, Parlor model, automatic changer, 12 discs long play movement, oak (mahogany) turned wood columns on front of case, curved legs, gallery, 66" high, tempo regulator, tune selector, bow glass front (some with art glass), banjo attachment, (some have Seth Thomas clock in top gallery).*	8000.00	13,000.00
☐ *STYLE #36 round — coin operated, 15½" disc, 12 disc automatic tune changer, same style as #35 with coin mechanism.*	12,000.00	14,000.00
☐ *STYLE #36 flat — coin operated, 15½" disc, made for arcades on cast iron legs, flat style case design, piano sounding board, long running, duplex comb, oak (mahogany), 68" high.*	9000.00	11,000.00
☐ *STYLE #37 — 20¾" disc, REGINA SUBLIMA CORONA, automatic changer, long play, piano sounding board, 75" tall, two combs (130 Tongues), oak (mahogany) on curved legs, case decoration, (larger size version #35).*	13,000.00	15,000.00
☐ *STYLE #38 round — coin operated version of Style #37, 20¾" disc, REGINA SUBLIMA CORONA, automatic changer.*	12,500.00	15,000.00
☐ *STYLE #38 flat — REGINA SUBLIMA CORONA, coin operated, 20¾" disc, flat glass front, spiral columns on front, carved gallery, ornate legs, solid back, open sides and front on base (casters).*	12,500.00	15,000.00

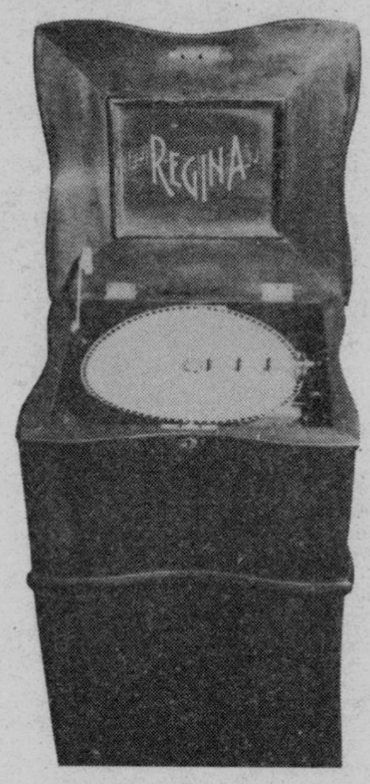

Regina Disc Music Box, style #41 or #42, console floor model.

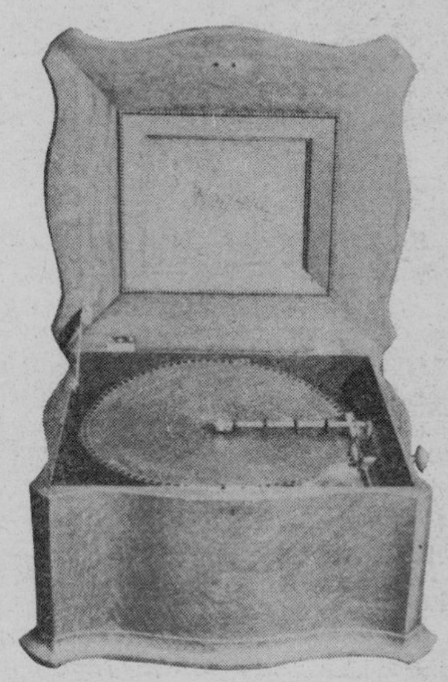

Regina Disc Music Box, style #50, table model, serpentine case, oak.

Reginaphone Disc Music Box / Phonograph Combination, style #240, inside horn, floor model. Left: oak. Right: mahogany.

	Price Range	
☐ STYLE #39 — table model, Serpentine style case, "Cupola" (raised ventilated section of the lid) cover, 20¾" disc.	2500.00	3500.00
☐ STYLE #139 — REGINAPHONE with outside horn (nickel, Morning Glory style).	2500.00	3000.00
☐ STYLE #239 — inside horn REGINAPHONE.	2250.00	2750.00
☐ STYLE #40 — 15½" disc, console floor model 40" high, duplex comb, cabinet in base for disc storage (150), oak (mahogany), Serpentine curved case style with carved lions' heads and paw columns on front sides, mandolin attachment.	3000.00	4000.00
☐ STYLE #140 — REGINAPHONE version with nickel Morning Glory horn, storage for discs and records.	4000.00	4500.00
☐ STYLE #240 — REGINAPHONE version with inside horn and carved lions' heads and paw columns on front sides, storage in base for discs and records.	4000.00	5800.00

Regina Disc Music Box, style #50, table model, serpentine case, mahogany.

	Price Range	
☐ *STYLE #41 — 12¼" disc, console floor model, duplex comb, storage base, Serpentine curved style, mahogany.*	3000.00	3500.00
☐ *STYLE #141 — REGINAPHONE version with outside horn, (Morning Glory, nickel) for phonograph, storage holds both discs and records.*	3500.00	4500.00
☐ *STYLE #42 — 12¼" disc, console floor model, single comb, Serpentine case style, mahogany, storage for discs.*	3000.00	3500.00
☐ *STYLE #142 — REGINAPHONE version with outside horn (Morning Glory, nickel), storage for discs and phonograph records.*	3500.00	4500.00
☐ *STYLE #43 — same as Style #40 but with storage base to the floor instead of sitting on legs (duplex comb).*	4000.00	4500.00
☐ *STYLE #143 — REGINAPHONE version of Style #43, outside horn.*	4250.00	4700.00
☐ *STYLE #44 — floor model, simple straight sided case, two doors in base open to store 200 discs, 20¾" disc, mahogany, 43" high.*	4250.00	4500.00
☐ *STYLE #144 — REGINAPHONE, outside horn, storage holds 100 discs, 200 phono records.*	4500.00	5000.00

Reginaphone Disc Music Box / Phonograph Combination, style #150, coin operated, outside horn.

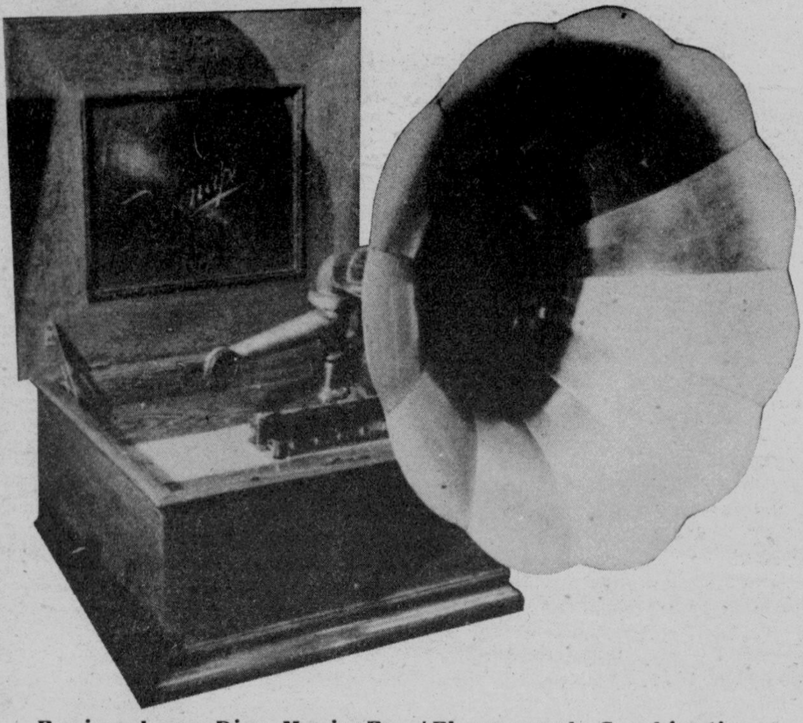

Reginaphone Disc Music Box / Phonograph Combination, style #155, outside horn.

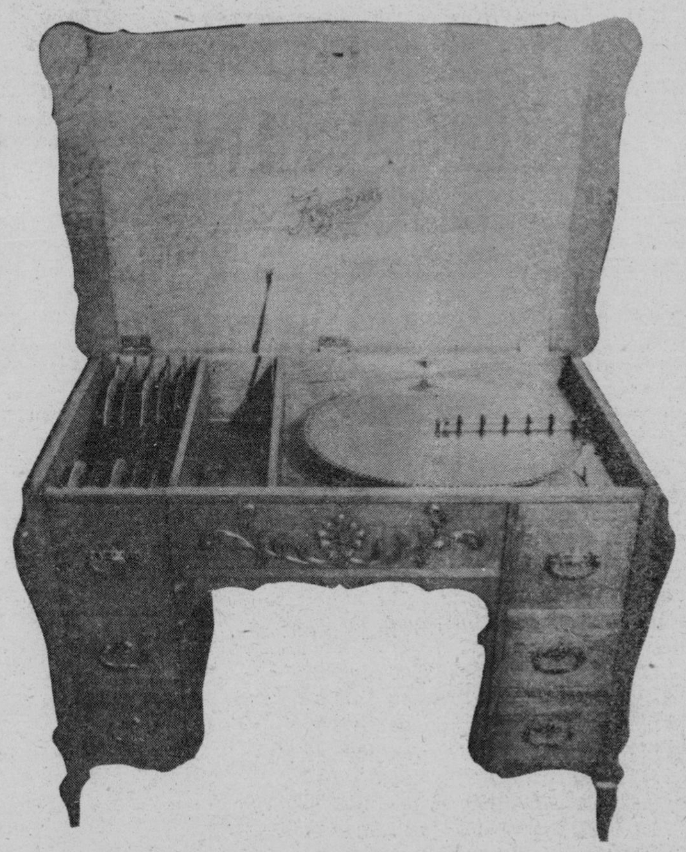

Regina Disc Music Box, style #61, "Musical Desk," oak.

	Price Range	
☐ *STYLE #45 — 27" disc, same as Style #44 cabinet, mahogany only.*	4250.00	4500.00
☐ *STYLE #145 — REGINAPHONE with outside horn and storage.*	4500.00	5000.00
☐ *STYLE #50 — table model 15½" disc, duplex comb, Serpentine curved case, banjo attachment, tempo regulator, long running movement, oak or mahogany. A matching table was made for this model with storage for discs.*	2800.00	3750.00
☐ *STYLE #150 — REGINAPHONE version of style #50, outside horn phonograph.*	4000.00	5000.00
☐ *STYLE #250 — Inside horn version REGINAPHONE, table model, duplex comb, Serpentine case, 15½" disc.*	2750.00	3500.00

	Price Range	
☐ *STYLE #51 — Table model, 15½" disc, duplex comb, coin operated, speed regulator, long running, plain case, short bed plate.*	2500.00	3600.00
☐ *STYLE #251 — REGINAPHONE, inside horn, duplex comb.*	2750.00	3250.00
☐ *STYLE #55 — 15½" disc, single comb, tempo regulator, banjo attachment, simple case oak (mahogany), REGINA Trademark inside cover.*	3250.00	3750.00
☐ *STYLE #155 — REGINAPHONE with outside horn.*	3000.00	4000.00
☐ *STYLE #255 — REGINAPHONE, inside horn.*	3500.00	4000.00
☐ *STYLE #61 — 20¾" disc, Regina Musical Desk, kneehole style with the appearance of drawers on each side, top lifts to reveal music box and storage of discs, oak (mahogany), some decorative moulding.*	8000.00	12,000.00
☐ *STYLE #161 — REGINAPHONE, outside horn.*	8500.00	9500.00
☐ *STYLE #67 — 15½" disc, highly decorated finish (ROOKWOOD) floor model, duplex comb, tempo regulator, upright arrangement of disc enclosed in case, two front doors open to reveal music box and storage bin.*	6000.00	6500.00
☐ *STYLE #71 — 12¼" disc, table model, duplex comb, curved Serpentine style case, banjo attachment, oak (mahogany).*	1750.00	2000.00
☐ *STYLE #171 — REGINAPHONE with outside horn.*	2000.00	2500.00
☐ *STYLE #72 — single comb version of Style #71, REGINA inside lid.*	1500.00	2000.00
☐ *STYLE #172 — REGINAPHONE version of #72, outside horn.*	2000.00	2500.00
☐ *STYLE #81 — REGINA CHIME CLOCK, 12¼" disc, Mission style case, oak, chiming bells activated by the disc. There are no combs.*	5000.00	7500.00
☐ *STYLE #91 — 8½" disc, single comb, oak (mahogany), some decorative moulding.*	500.00	750.00
☐ *STYLE #113 — REGINAPHONE (see Style #13)*		
☐ *STYLE #126 — REGINAPHONE (see Style #26)*		
☐ *STYLE #139 — REGINAPHONE (see Style #39)*		
☐ *STYLE #140 — REGINAPHONE (see Style #40)*		
☐ *STYLE #141 — REGINAPHONE (see Style #41)*		
☐ *STYLE #142 — REGINAPHONE (see Style #42)*		
☐ *STYLE #143 — REGINAPHONE (see Style #43)*		
☐ *STYLE #144 — REGINAPHONE (see Style #44)*		
☐ *STYLE #145 — REGINAPHONE (see Style #45)*		
☐ *STYLE #150 — REGINAPHONE (see Style #50)*		
☐ *STYLE #155 — REGINAPHONE (see Style #55)*		
☐ *STYLE #161 — REGINAPHONE (see Style #61)*		
☐ *STYLE #171 — REGINAPHONE (see Style #71)*		
☐ *STYLE #172 — REGINAPHONE (see Style #72)*		
☐ *STYLE #215 — with 12 bells, single comb, 15½" disc made for bell accompaniment, oak (mahogany).*	3500.00	4500.00
☐ *STYLE #216 — duplex comb version of Style #215.*	3750.00	4750.00
☐ *STYLE #217 — coin operated version of Style #216.*	3750.00	4750.00
☐ *STYLE #226 — REGINAPHONE (see Style #26)*		
☐ *STYLE #239 — REGINAPHONE (see Style #39)*		

	Price Range	
☐ *STYLE #240 — REGINAPHONE (see Style #40)*		
☐ *STYLE #246 — 15½" disc console floor model, rectangular cabinet style, duplex comb, two doors in storage section.*	3000.00	3500.00
☐ *STYLE #250 — REGINAPHONE (see Style #50)*		
☐ *STYLE #251 — REGINAPHONE (see Style #51)*		
☐ *STYLE #255 — REGINAPHONE (see Style #55)*		
☐ **SIRION** *14½" disc, shifting disc mechanism, table top style, walnut case with decoration, stop/start, coin operated.*	3000.00	4000.00
☐ *19" disc, table model, elaborate mouldings and inlay decoration on fruitwood case, double comb.*	2500.00	3750.00
☐ **STELLA (MADE BY MERMOD FRERES)** *9½" (10") disc, oak or mahogany, large spring motor, duplex comb, decorative moulding on case, disc centered in case.*	900.00	1000.00

Stella Disc Music Box, table model, mahogany.

☐ *14" disc, oak (mahogany), duplex comb, some case decoration, disc placed toward left side in case.*	1500.00	2000.00
☐ *15" disc, concert table model, double comb, oak (mahogany), some case decoration.*	2000.00	3000.00
☐ *15½" disc, oak (mahogany), duplex comb, moderator (tempo), large spring motor.*	2000.00	2500.00

Stella Disc Music Box, console model with storage in base, mahogany.

	Price Range	
☐ *17" disc, table model, peripheral drive movement, single comb tempo control, crank wind, mahogany case with carved floral decoration and base moulding, storage drawer in bottom of case for extra discs.*	2000.00	3000.00
☐ *17¼" disc, Stella Grand, duplex comb, carving in front panel of base, oak (mahogany), drawer in base for 100 discs (variations in case decoration).*	2500.00	3250.00
☐ *17¼" console floor model, 36" high, duplex comb, storage for discs, case decoration.*	3500.00	5000.00
☐ *17¼" disc, table model, mahogany, single comb, storage drawer for discs.*	1900.00	2100.00
☐ *25" disc, upright floor model, 8' tall, storage in base for extra discs, carved decoration and finials, glass doors.*	3500.00	5500.00
☐ *25½" disc, upright floor model, highly carved and decorated, walnut and rosewood case with floral marquetry front panel in base, storage base for discs, peripheral-drive movement, single comb, stop/start button, crank.*	4000.00	6500.00
☐ *26" (25 11/16") disc, orchestral grand (for home use), glass front doors, highly carved on top, storage in base, oak (mahogany), 6'3" high, (coin operated).*	4500.00	7000.00

Stella Disc Music Box, table model.

	Price Range	
☐ *26" disc, Orchestral Grand, console case model, case decoration (shell and ribbon pattern), two doors in base open to reveal storage for discs, oak or mahogany, loud volume, duplex combs (some models electrically powered (Electric Orchestral Grand).*	**5000.00**	**7000.00**
☐ *26" disc, upright floor model, 81" high, peripheral-drive wind movement, double comb, crank wind outside case, rosewood case with fluted columns, carved mouldings, round glass panel in top door, carved laurel wreath motif on front door of base cabinet.*	**4500.00**	**6500.00**
☐ **SYMPHONION (Leipzig, Germany)** *4 ⅝" disc, mantle clock, case decoration.*	**1750.00**	**2400.00**
☐ *5½" disc, table model, simple case style.*	**450.00**	**750.00**
☐ *5¾" disc, plain black case with decal decorations, hand cranked (Manivelle), 40 teeth in comb (14.5cm).*	**500.00**	**750.00**
☐ *6¼" disc, plain case, winding lever, "Symphonion" in script on cover, rosewood case, 4 bells.*	**400.00**	**600.00**
☐ *7½" disc, table model, simple maple case, pictorial lithograph inside lid, single comb.*	**600.00**	**1000.00**
☐ *7¾" disc, center drive movement, single comb, stop/start control, walnut case with some decoration, colored lithograph inside lid.*	**500.00**	**750.00**

	Price Range	
☐ 7 5/8" disc, simple grained case, colored lithograph inside lid, floral transfer decoration on lid.	500.00	750.00
☐ 7 11/16" (7¾") disc, walnut plain case, "Symphonion" decal on lid.	600.00	700.00
☐ 7 11/16" (7¾") disc, 3 saucer bells, zither attachment, "Symphonion" decal on lid, lithograph inside cover, crank.	650.00	800.00
☐ 8¼" disc, black plain wood case, decal design on lid, walnut, duplex Sublime-Harmonie combs, decorated card inside lid.	500.00	800.00
☐ 8 5/8" disc, Sublime-Harmonie, simple rectangular walnut case, monochrome print inside lid.	250.00	500.00
☐ 9½" disc, black polished plain case with decal decoration "Symphonion", 72 teeth comb, (case variation—walnut with base and lid moulding).	650.00	750.00
☐ 10" disc, walnut, lever wind on front, duplex comb, decorative moulding, lithograph inside cover, zither.	500.00	750.00
☐ 10" disc, 6 bells, walnut with case decoration, lithograph inside lid, duplex comb, Sublime-Harmonie.	1000.00	1500.00

Symphonion Upright Disc Music Box.

	Price Range	
☐ *10" disc, table model, lever wind, simple rosewood case, "Symphonion" trademark lithograph inside lid.*	650.00	1000.00
☐ *10½" disc, table model, spring wind movement, rachet lever, double comb, start/stop lever, black painted simple case.*	500.00	750.00
☐ *10¾" disc, Sublime-Harmonie combs, lithograph inside cover, walnut case with base moulding.*	500.00	1000.00
☐ *10⅝" disc, black polished wood plain case with decal decoration on lid, 84 teeth in comb (also walnut, decorative moulding on base and lid).*	900.00	1100.00
☐ *11¾" disc, Sublime-Harmonie combs, vertical cabinet counter model, walnut, gold ornamentation and lettering on glass front, coin operated, ornate carved case with gallery, (also with painted decoration on front door instead of glass), home use model not coin operated.*	1500.00	3000.00
☐ *11¾" disc, walnut case with moulding on lid and base, Sublime-Harmonie combs, carrying handles on side, lithograph inside cover, 84 teeth comb.*	1500.00	2000.00

Symphonian Twin-Disc Music Box, table model on storage base, plays two 11⅞" discs at the same time on separate combs, speed regulator, crank in center front of mahogany case, inlaid floral decoration on lid, carrying handles, very rare.

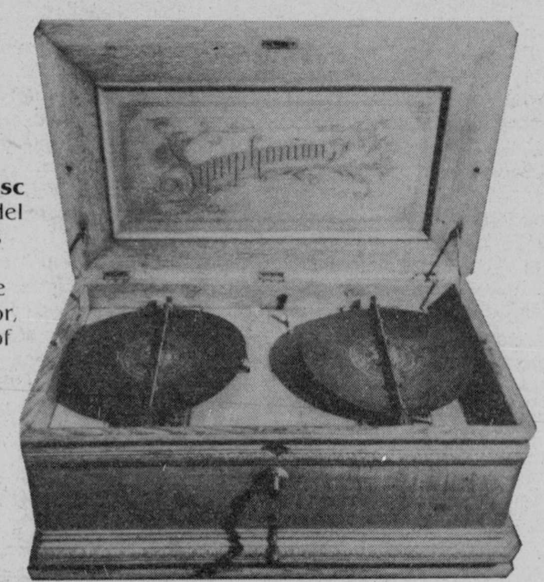

Symphonian Twin-Disc Music Box, table model on storage base, plays two 11⅞" discs at the same time on separate combs, speed regulator, crank in center front of case, inlaid floral decoration on lid, carrying handles, very rare.

Symphonion Disc Music Box, table model, plays 11¾" discs.

	Price Range	
☐ *11¾" disc, highly ornate case, walnut, carved corner columns, mouldings, brass handles, some inlay on lid, glass plate over mechanism, storage for discs, Sublime-Harmonie combs, 84 teeth comb.*	2500.00	4000.00
☐ *11 ⅞" disc, table model, coin operated, Sublime-Harmonie combs, simple walnut case, embossed name on lid.*	1200.00	2200.00
☐ *11 ⅞" disc, table model, Sublime-Harmonie combs, figural lithograph inside lid, decorative case moulding with matching storage cabinet, oak.*	1500.00	3500.00
☐ *11 ⅞" disc, c. 1900, center-drive movement, Sublime-Harmonie combs, stop/start knob, detachable handle, mahogany, figural lithograph inside lid, carved corner and base mouldings, inner glass lid, inlaid floral spray on lid.*	1500.00	2500.00
☐ *11 ⅞" disc, vertical counter model, coin operated, some case decoration.*	2000.00	3000.00
☐ *11 ⅞" disc table model, TWIN-DISCS: two discs play at the same time on separate combs, speed regulator, crank in center front of case, inlaid floral decoration on lid, carrying handles, mahogany (oak).*	5000.00	7000.00
☐ *11 ⅞" disc, Hall Clock, style 25, highly decorated with carved ornamentation, 79" high, walnut, storage in base for extra discs.*	5500.00	7500.00
☐ *12" disc, double comb (84 teeth), walnut cabinet, lithograph inside lid, table model, stop/start knob, inner glass lid, decorative corner and base moulding.*	1500.00	2000.00
☐ *13¼" disc, single comb, walnut case, decorative moulding, some inlay, 8 bells.*	1750.00	2250.00
☐ *13¼" disc, duplex combs, Sublime-Harmonie, walnut with base moulding, figural lithograph inside cover.*	1000.00	2500.00
☐ *13¼" disc, vertical upright counter type, ornate case, gallery (with clock), coin operated, duplex comb.*	2500.00	3000.00
☐ *13½" disc, double comb, mahogany case, carved decoration, 18½" long case, "Imperial Symphion", figural lithograph.*	1000.00	1750.00
☐ *13½" disc, center drive movement, table model, burled walnut case with base and corner mouldings, inner glass lid, lithograph inside lid.*	1000.00	1600.00
☐ *13⅝" disc, combs in Sublime-Harmonie, ornate walnut case, some inlay, glass plate over mechanism.*	1250.00	2000.00
☐ *13⅝" disc, Sublime-Harmonie Piccolo, floor model upright case, highly decorated, gallery, walnut (oak), disc storage in base (also: art glass front, or advertising on glass, or carved wood front), case variations, "HAYDN".*	3000.00	3750.00
☐ *13⅝" disc, vertical counter top model, Sublime-Harmonie combs, walnut case (clock in gallery), "METEOR".*	1500.00	2800.00
☐ *13 ⅝" disc, Musical Longcase Clock, "EROICA", highly decorated, ornately carved case.*	6500.00	8500.00
☐ *14" disc, "EROICA", upright floor model, sets of 3 discs (A, B, C) Play in Harmony, three separate movements, each with 100 teeth, two combs in Sublime-Harmonie arrangement, oak or walnut, front panel glass or wood (art glass, coin operated).*	8000.00	11,500.00
☐ *14¾" disc, table model, walnut, inlay lid, highly decorated carved panels and moulding, double comb.*	1600.00	2000.00

Symphonion Three-Disc Music Box, side-by-side format, plays 17⅝″ discs.

	Price Range	
☐ *14¾″ disc, table model, with 10 saucer bells, duplex comb, walnut case with decoration, "Cherub" lithograph inside lid. . .*	2500.00	3500.00
☐ *15″ disc, c. 1900, center drive movement, double comb, tempo control, crank wind, stop/start button outside front, mahogany case with matching storage cabinet on carved legs, beaded carved wood decoration on case and stand, trademark lithograph inside lid. . . . .*	3000.00	4750.00
☐ *15½″ disc, table model, simple case style, oak, some case moulding at base, double comb, slow/fast lever, stop/start knob at front. . . . .*	1500.00	2500.00
☐ *15¾″ disc, single comb, plain comb, moulding on base and cover. . . . .*	1500.00	2000.00
☐ *15¾″ disc, ornate walnut case, 10 bells, duplex comb (156 teeth). . . . .*	2500.00	3000.00
☐ *15¾″ disc, walnut case, some decoration, duplex comb, lithograph inside cover. . . . .*	1250.00	1650.00
☐ *15 ⅝″ disc, table model, single comb, zither attachment, large decorative bedplate, walnut case with simple moulding, lithograph inside lid, some decoration on lid. . . . .*	1250.00	2250.00

	Price Range	
☐ *17¾ (17⅝") disc, carved moulding, mahogany, "Cherub" lithograph inside lid.*	2500.00	3500.00
☐ *17⅝" disc, upright vertical (style 106), oak case with decorative moulding, storage for discs in base.*	3500.00	4500.00
☐ *17⅝" disc, 3-DISC upright floor model, A, B, C, discs arranged side-by-side in cabinet, play same tune but each disc slightly different, large oak case, simple decoration, three separate combs, one crank.*	11,000.00	15,000.00
☐ *18¼" disc, floor model, upright vertical disc arrangement, two combs, top section slightly recessed from bottom, storage bin in base, glass door, open work gallery.*	3500.00	4500.00
☐ *19⅛" disc, vertical upright disc arrangement, walnut ornate case on feet (no base), clock in gallery, two combs (106 teeth).*	3750.00	4750.00
☐ *19⅛" disc, floor model glass front, highly decorated, walnut case, pull-out storage bin for extra discs, double comb in Sublime-Harmonie arrangement.*	4500.00	5500.00
☐ *19⅛" (19") disc, counter top, upright model, coin operated, walnut, highly carved case decoration, glass door, on feet.*	2000.00	3000.00
☐ *19⅛" disc, two combs, grandfather hall clock, very ornate case, music plays hourly.*	4000.00	5000.00
☐ *19½" disc, double comb, coin operated (uses British pennies) carved walnut.*	2750.00	3750.00
☐ *21¼" disc, simple walnut case, 10 saucer bells, upright vertical disc arrangement on feet, gallery, double comb (120 teeth), coin operated. (also ornate case.)*	5000.00	7500.00
☐ *21¼" disc, 10 saucer bells, large upright automatic disc changer, tune selector crank, ornate walnut, fully carved front legs on base, "Symphonion" on glass door (Style 100). Several case variations with and without storage.*	15,000.00	17,000.00
☐ *25¼" disc, upright floor model, two combs in Sublime-Harmonie (192 teeth), sits on storage base, ornate gallery, glass front door on top, carved decoration, 7½' high, (also without storage cabinet, on feet).*	6000.00	8500.00
☐ *25¼" disc, upright floor model, coin operated, Sublime-Harmonie combs, walnut case with highly carved decoration, storage base.*	5750.00	6750.00
☐ *27½" disc, 12 saucer bells, walnut case, decoration and gallery, on feet counter top, upright model.*	6500.00	9000.00
☐ **TANNHAUSER** *table model, shifting disc mechanism, two tunes per disc, burled case with corner and base decorative moulding.*	3500.00	4000.00
☐ **TROUBADOUR (B. GROSZ & CO., Leipzig, Germany)** *8¾" disc (22cm), walnut, inlay on lid.*	600.00	800.00
☐ *8¾" disc, with 4 saucer bells, simple walnut case, figural lithograph inside lid.*	750.00	1250.00
☐ *9" disc (22.5cm), simple case with gold decoration, name on cover, outside crank wind (44 teeth).*	750.00	1000.00
☐ *9" disc (22.5cm), with 4 saucer bells, simple case, figural lithograph inside cover (scenic landscape).*	800.00	1500.00
☐ *11¾" disc (30cm), single comb, table model, decorative moulding on base and cover, lithograph inside cover with "TROUBADOUR", (56 teeth), walnut with floral inlay on cover.*	1000.00	1300.00

Troubadour Disc Music Box, table model.

MUSIC BOX DISCS

It is rare that one finds an interchangeable cylinder for sale (without the music box) that will fit into a box purchased at some other time and place.

Part of the great appeal of the disc music box was its capacity for almost unlimited tune choices through its interchangeable discs. The more popular disc sizes had the widest variety of tunes. Discs come up for sale all the time. "Auctions and Dealers" are a good source.

The size of the disc and comb determine the length and complexity of the musical arrangement.

Prices for discs are subject to variables like disc condition, maker, size, tunes, etc. Generally they average about $5-10.00 each. The more common the size, the lower the value. Of course, demand also plays a big part; for example, a Polyphone 6½" disc brings around $3.00 each while a 22" disc with bell accompaniment arrangement is worth around $20.00.

DISCS FOR MUSIC BOXES

Sampling of current prices for discs:

	Price Range	
ADLER:		
7" disc.	3.00	
8¼" disc.	3.00	
10½" disc.	4.00	
14¼(¾)" disc.	4.00	
BRITANNIA:		
17 ⅛" disc.	5.00	
CAPITOL:		
7¼" cuff.	15.00	25.00
CRITERION:		
15¾(½)" disc.	15.00	
20½" disc.	20.00	
EDELWEISS:		
4½" disc.	3.00	
6½" disc.	3.00	
KALLIOPE:		
7" disc.	3.00	
9¾" disc.	4.00	
17¾" disc.	4.00	
20½" disc.	5.00	
KOMET:		
10¼".	4.00	
LOCHMAN:		
25¾" disc.	10.00	
MIRA:		
12" disc.	10.00	15.00
15½" 2" disc.	12.50	15.00
MONOPOL:		
8¼(¾)" disc.	3.00	

	Price Range	
OLYMPIA:		
15¾" disc.	10.00	15.00
POLYPHONE:		
6½" disc.	2.50	
8(¼)" disc.	2.50	
9½" disc.	3.00	
11" disc.	3.50	
14¼(½)" disc.	5.00	
19 ⅝" disc.	10.00	13.00
REGINA:		
15½" disc.	5.50	7.50
20¾ disc.	8.00	10.00
27" disc.	15.00	30.00
STELLA:		
9¾" disc.	10.00	20.00
17¼" disc.	15.00	
25½" disc.	15.00	
SYMPHONION:		
5¾" disc.	2.50	
10" disc.	6.00	
10 ⅝" disc.	7.00	10.00
11¾" disc.	5.00	7.00
13½(¼)" disc.	6.00	
20" disc.	15.00	20.00
21¼(½)" disc.	15.00	17.00
Eroica 3-disc sets.	50.00	set
TROUBADOUR:		
8¾" disc.	3.00	
11¾" disc.	6.00	

ORGANETTES AND ROLLER ORGANS

The table model Organette industry was fully developed in the 19th-century, reaching its peak in the 1880's and 1890's. By the early 20th-century it had lost its popularity to other forms of mechanical music.

The organette mechanism is operated by hand cranking either a revolving wooden cob with protruding pins, paper roll (similar to a piano roll), or cardboard (sometimes metal) disc which activates organ reeds by the creation of a vacuum or wind pressure through internal bellows. There are many similar varieties of organettes.

Music for these organs ranged from patriotic to religious, with hymns being the most common. The cobs are not as difficult to locate as the paper rolls and discs. One must rely mainly upon mechanical musical auctions and dealer's inventories. Prices vary from $2.00 each and up. (See "Auctions and Dealers" section.)

	Price Range	
☐ **AMORETTE ORGANETTE** *Ebony finish case, some decoration, plays metal discs (22.5cm) 8¾".*	350.00	500.00
☐ **ARIOSA ORGANETTE (SCHMIDT & CO., Leipzig, Germany)** *Simple case style, ring or donut-like disc (metal or cardboard), 11¾", 18 brass reeds, disc placed off center and extends past case. (Other examples with centered disc, ebony finish cases.)*	275.00	600.00
☐ **ARISTON ORGANETTE** *Gold case decoration, carved corner decoration, 13" heavy cardboard disc, hand crank, 24 full size organ reeds.*	375.00	575.00

Ariston Organette.

☐ **ARISTON ORGANETTE** *22" x 22" case with some decoration, 36 reeds.*	500.00	1000.00
☐ **AUREPHONE** *"Casket" type case with cover, stencil decoration, 17 key, 9½" disc (similar to Tournaphone).*	575.00	750.00
☐ **AUTOPHONE** *Walnut case, bellows operated by hand, 22 reeds, music sheets.*	475.00	750.00
☐ **AUTOPHONE** *Paper Strips.*	5.00	8.00
☐ **BATES ORGANETTE,** *American, c. 1885, plays 14 note paper roll.*	500.00	1000.00

	Price Range	
☐ **BIJOU ORCHESTRONE** *Walnut case, top opens to reveal roll mechanism (similar to Celestina and others in appearance), 20 key 3³/₈" paper roll.*	275.00	575.00
☐ **CABINETTO ORGANETTE** *"Casket" style case (cover), gold stencil design, 25 reed, 13¾" paper roll.*	400.00	750.00
☐ **CELESTINA ORGANETTE (WILCOX AND WHITE, CT)** *Walnut case, doors on top fold back to reveal roll mechanism, also control volume, 20 reeds, 5½" wide paper roll.*	300.00	500.00
☐ **CHAUTAUQUA ROLLER ORGAN** *Walnut case with front glass lift-up door covering cob section (same as the Concert Roller Organ made by Autophone Co., NY), 6½" cob with metal pins.*	350.00	650.00
☐ **CHORDEPHON MECHANICAL ZITHER, #15A,** *German, plays 14" discs, flat rectangular base with metal strings in wooden frame on tiny turned legs, clockwork mechanism.*	1400.00	2400.00
☐ **CLARIONA ORGANETTE** *Walnut case 13" high, open roll assembly, reed pipe device attaches over the roll once it is put in place on top of the organ, it is then covering the roll across the middle, 14 note 8" wide paper roll.*	350.00	650.00
☐ **CONCERT ROLLER ORGAN** *Related to Gem but case style different, fully enclosed organ, glass door opens at front top to show cob section, walnut case, gold stencil decoration, 6½" cob with metal pins. (This organ was sold by many companies under many names, including Sears Roebuck).*	400.00	800.00
☐ **CORONET ORGAN** *Simple case, 7⁷/₈" paper roll.*	350.00	550.00

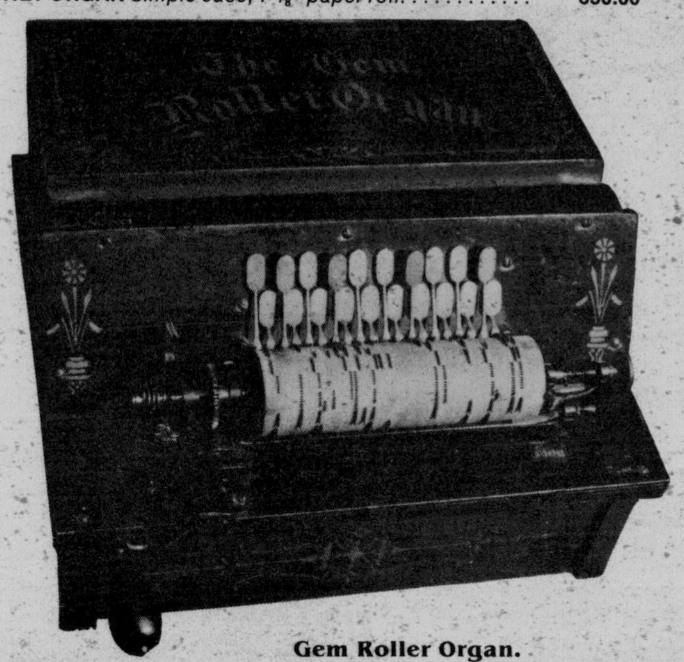

Gem Roller Organ.

	Price Range	
☐ **EUPHONIA ORGANETTE** *Wood base with open roll assembly on each side, valve mechanism in center, 16 key 5¾" paper roll.*	350.00	550.00
☐ **GATELY ORGAN** *Square "Casket" style case with expression opening down middle of cover, hand crank, 14 key 8" wide roll (similar to Aurephone), walnut, gold decoration.*	300.00	600.00
☐ **GEM ROLLER ORGAN (AUTOPHONE CO., Ithaca, NY)** *Walnut case, gold decoration, name on top, cob exposed with valves on one side, bellows on other side, 6½" long cob with metal pins, hand crank, 20 note organ.*	350.00	550.00

Guitarophone Mechanical Zither, table model, plays 14½" discs.

☐ **GEM ROLLER ORGAN** *Also black painted case, sold under other names, e.g. "HOME".*	250.00	600.00
☐ **GEM COBS,** *wood cylindrical shape with tiny metal pins protruding from surface.*	4.50	7.00
☐ **GRAND ROLLER ORGAN (AUTOPHONE CO.)** *Large oak case with lift up glass fronted hood on top to reveal 15" cob (with pins), wooden cylinder, 32 note scale.*	950.00	2500.00
☐ **GUITAROPHONE (U.S. Guitar Zither Co.)** *Mechanical zither plays 14½" metal discs, simple case style, c. 1890's, spring-wind, tiny hammers strike strings, (also came coin operated).*	1000.00	1500.00

	Price Range	
☐ **HARMONETTE ROLLER ORGAN**.	300.00	500.00
☐ **HELIKON ORGANETTE** *Polished black case, gold decoration, carved corner columns, square case, 16 reeds, hand crank (examples used metal or cardboard discs), similar in appearance to Ariston.*	300.00	500.00
☐ **HEROPHONE (EUPHONIKA, Leipzig, Germany)** *Black square case, corner decoration, name on side, 24 reeds, square disc (cardboard with metal edges), mechanism revolves under stationary disc.*	500.00	1000.00
☐ **HOME ROLLER ORGAN** *(see "GEM")*		
☐ **INTONA ORGANETTE (SCHMIDT & CO., Leipzig)** *Ebony finish case, "donut" style disc, 9" hard paper disc, 16 steel reeds. (Variations in case and disc placement).*	450.00	650.00
☐ **MANDOLINA ORGANETTE (MUNROE ORGAN REED CO.)** *Walnut case with gold decoration, lids on top fold out to reveal paper roll mechanism, 20 key, 5½" roll (very similar to Celestina.)*	375.00	575.00
☐ **MANOLINATA ORGANETTE** *24 reeds, metal disc, some case decoration, name on side of ebony finish case with gold decoration, crank wind.*	500.00	1000.00
☐ **MANOPAN ROLLER ORGAN (EUPHONIKA MUSIKWERKE)** *Black case with gold decoration, decorative moulding and corner columns, cardboard music strips attached to side mechanism.*	650.00	825.00
☐ **MASCOTTE ORGANETTE** *Walnut case, some decoration, roll mechanism in top under lid, 2½" wide roll, 14 keys.*	400.00	600.00
☐ **McTAMMANY ORGAN** *Walnut case, decoration 7¾" continuous "roll" strip is clamped down by top mechanism holding it in place as organ is hand cranked, rollers on each end.*	500.00	750.00
☐ **MECHANICAL ORGUINETTE** *Floor model, when shut looks like a lamp table with velvet top, 25" high, 20 note reed organ, plays 5½" wide paper roll.*	1000.00	1750.00
☐ **MECHANICAL ORGUINETTE,** *Floor model, desk shaped, walnut, decorative mouldings, 47" high, plays 21½" paper roll, foot pedals.*	1600.00	2600.00
☐ **MELODIA** *Walnut case, whole lid lifts up to reveal roll mechanism, 14 reed notes, 7⅞" (7¾") paper roll.*	350.00	550.00
☐ **MIGNON ORGANETTE** *"Casket" style box with lid, paper roll inside cover, walnut with stencil decoration, hand crank on front, 22 reeds, 5¼" paper roll.*	550.00	750.00
☐ **MUSETTE (MECHANICAL ORGUINETTE CO.)** *Walnut case with stencil decoration, 16 key 3½" wide paper roll (very similar to Celestina)*	400.00	600.00
☐ **MUSICAL CASKET ORGANETTE (MECHANICAL ORGUINETTE CO.)** *Decorated case, front lid lifts up to reveal paper roll mechanism, 14 key, 7¾" wide roll.*	300.00	500.00
☐ **ORCHESTRAL ORGANETTE** *Painted case decoration, button stops, 8" wide roll, 14 reeds.*	400.00	600.00
☐ **ORGANINA (MASSACHUSETTES ORGAN CO.)** *Rounded glass front, elaborate gold painted decoration all over walnut case, 11" high small box, 16 key 8¼" wide continuous paper strip.*	300.00	500.00

	Price Range	
☐ **ORGANITA ROLLER ORGAN** *Table model, walnut case with rounded segmented top, 14 note organ plays multiple tune paper strip, volume control button on top of case.*	350.00	500.00
☐ **ORGUINETTE PAPER ROLL ORGAN (MECHANICAL ORGUINETTE CO.)** *Long paper strips feed through a mechanism holding it in place (McTammany style), as it is cranked, there are rollers on each end.*	350.00	550.00
☐ **ORPHEUS MECHANICAL ZITHER** *Hand crank mechanism uses Ariston organette discs, ebony finish case in shape of miniature grand piano, 34″ long, 22 strings, plays 13″ cardboard disc (24 notes).*	2000.00	3500.00
☐ **PHOENIX ORGANETTE** *Decorated case with corner columns, "donut" ring type metal disc, 14½″, 24 reeds, hand crank.*	500.00	700.00
☐ **PIANOLODEON (Child's Toy).** *In the shape of a miniature upright player piano, 30 key, plays paper rolls, plastic case (gold decoration on either red mahogany or beige plastic).*	100.00	275.00
☐ **PIANO MELODICO ORGANETTE,** *German, string instrument, with hand crank, ebony case, plays music books.*	500.00	1000.00
☐ **PLA ROLA ORGAN (Pla Rola Manufacturing Co., Easton, PA)** *Red and gold painted metal, 5 ⅛″ long, plays paper rolls, 4¼″ wide.*	50.00	150.00
☐ **Q-R-S PLAY-A-SAX (CLAROLA)** *Shaped like a miniature saxophone, pot metal painted gold, sounds like a Harmonica, 16 note paper roll, one blows into mouth piece and cranks rolls at the same time.*	100.00	200.00
☐ **ROLMONICA** *Mouth organ in a bakelite case (various colors) with a paper roll mechanism, when one blows into mouthpiece and cranks roll, harmonica tunes are played, separate rewind crank, case is 4″ x 3⅝″.*	75.00	150.00
☐ **ROLMONICA** *paper rolls.*	5.00	7.50
☐ **SERAPHONE** *Cabinet base 11″ high, center top lid lifts up to reveal roll mechanism, 20 key, 3½″ paper roll.*	400.00	600.00
☐ **SONORA ORGANETTE (SCHMIDT & CO., Leipzig)** *Vertical case carved columns with finials and gallery, decorated, "donut" style ring discs, hand crank.*	700.00	900.00
☐ **SYMPHONIA (WILCOX AND WHITE)** *Walnut case lid opens to reveal roll mechanism, 20 key, 5⅛″ roll (similar in style to Celestina).*	300.00	600.00
☐ **TANZBAR PLAYER ACCORDION (PLAYER CONCERTINA)** *Square ebony finish case with decorative nickel trim (other case variations, some with inlay), 9″ x 11″ x 11″, concertina works manually, one end opens to reveal roll housing, plays 4¼″ wide paper rolls.*	425.00	750.00
☐ **TOURNAPHONE ORGAN** *"Casket" type case with expression shutter in cover, 25 reeds, 13¾″ paper roll.*	575.00	675.00
☐ **TOURNAPHONE CONSOLE** *With storage in bottom.*	775.00	875.00
☐ **TRIOLA (MECHANICAL ZITHER)** *Operates by a paper roll, manual bass accompaniment, some decoration on wood case.*	2000.00	3000.00

SMALL BARREL ORGANS

Small portable barrel organs were popular well into the 20th-century. They had, by that time, been around for over a century, though they did show signs of decline as early as 1900.

A barrel organ operates by means of a wooden cylinder with protruding metal pins (arranged for several tunes) by activating the bank of organ pipes as the mechanism is hand cranked. There are also special effects like "piccolos", "flutes", "trumpets", etc.

The organ is carried through the streets supported by a strong shoulder strap, center support post or moving stand.

One must rely mainly on special mechanical musical auctions and dealers as these organs are rare.

Bacigalupo Harmon Pan Barrel Organ.

	Price Range	
☐ **BACIGALUPO ORGAN** *Many case variations, painted decorations, grill and cloth variations, white case, red cloth, painted flowers, decorative grill.*	3500.00	6500.00
☐ **BACIGALUPO BARREL ORGAN** *47 key, 4 stops, plays 8 tunes, c. 1920's, ornately decorated.*	3750.00	5000.00
☐ **BACIGALUPO HARMON PAN BARREL ORGAN** *25 keys, 8 tunes, straight wood case painted with floral decorations, view pipes from top cut out, crank wind, 17" wide.*	4000.00	6000.00
☐ **E. BOECKER BARREL ORGAN** *Harmonipan, 33 key, 19 caned flutes on front, 8 tune barrel, decorated case, 27" long by 26" wide.*	4500.00	6500.00
☐ **BRODERIP & WILKINSON BARREL ORGAN** *c. 1825, Regency style mahogany case, simple lines, decoration on legs, 57" high, faux giltwood pipes on decorated front panel.*	700.00	1000.00
☐ **BRUDER BARREL ORGAN,** *48 key, 9 tun barrel (36" wide), trumpet pipes, case 58" high.*	4000.00	5750.00
☐ **BRUDER PORTABLE BARREL ORGAN** *26 note, 8 tune, 4 stops, Rosewood veneered case, inlaid decoration, floral marquetry, c. 1910.*	1250.00	2500.00
☐ **CHIAPPA & SONS BARREL ORGAN** *Table size, 36 key, 10 tune, 37" high, brass trumpets, piccolos, flutes.*	3000.00	4000.00
☐ **ENGLISH STREET PIANO** *Spring Barrel operated, maple case, one cent coin operated, c. 1915, 10 tune barrel.*	2000.00	2500.00
☐ **FRATI & CO. BARREL ORGAN (Berlin)** *Decorated case, mirror front, copper medallions, 24" high metal pipes, wooden roller cylinder.*	3000.00	4500.00
☐ **FRATI "MONKEY ORGAN"** *plays Mexican tunes.*	2500.00	3500.00
☐ **FRATI & CO., CORONETINA** *two foot square "monkey" organ, 10 exposed brass coronets, 61 pipes, 33 key, hand crank barrel movement, case decoration.*	7500.00	9500.00
☐ **FRENCH BARREL ORGAN** *15 key, 10 tune barrel (15" wide), walnut case 18½" high, 53 pipes, 4 ranks.*	1500.00	3000.00
☐ **GAVIOLI BARREL ORGAN** *Hurdy Gurdy type, highly decorated case with inlay.*	3000.00	4000.00
☐ **GAVIOLI & CIE (Paris) FLUTE ORGAN** *Portable barrel organ, 36 key mechanism, 9 tunes, rosewood veneer case, with inlaid floral and other marquetry and painted decoration, red cloth covered openings, hand crank.*	6500.00	8000.00
☐ **GERMAN BARREL ORGAN** *c. 1866, simple grained pine case, 6-tune barrel, plays reeds and pipes.*	750.00	1200.00
☐ **J. KAMENIK - PRAHA BARREL REED ORGAN** *Portable, simple wood case with fretwork panel, 17½" wide.*	1600.00	2000.00
☐ **G. MOLINARI & SONS (NY)** *c. 1898 — Flute hand organ, 23 key, 7 tune, small size carried with shoulder strap, fancy front panels, inlay decoration on black walnut case, (also 9 tune, 24 key with 10 tune).*	2500.00	3500.00
☐ **G. MOLINARI & SONS** *Flute and trumpet hand organ, flower and scroll case decoration, otherwise much like the above, 32 and 34 key, 8 tune, 8 trumpets (also 37 and 42 key, 8 tune, 12 trumpets), slightly larger case than above.*	4500.00	5500.00

	Price Range	
☐ **D. POIROT OF PARIS STREET BARREL ORGAN** *35 key, 65 flute pipes, 9 tunes, 35½" high.*	3250.00	4750.00
☐ **SPANISH BARREL PIANO** *18" high on two-wheeled cart, 6-tune 10" barrel, wood block, triangle, decorated case and cart, hand crank on front.*	500.00	750.00
☐ **WREDE VIOLINO - PAN BARREL ORGAN** *26 key, 8 tune barrel, 14 pipes in view, floral decoration, sits on corner mouldings (feet), metal trim, hand crank.*	5750.00	8000.00
☐ **ZIMMERMAN HURDY-GURDY (Leipzig)** *Some case decoration, shoulder strap, 11 brass piccolo pipes, small size.*	2750.00	3750.00
☐ **BARREL ORGAN** *Maker Unknown. 32 key portable, plays 8 tunes, green painted case, elaborate floral and musical decoration all over case, hand crank, 20 visible flutes, 24" wide.*	2000.00	3000.00

PHONOGRAPHS — CYLINDER AND DISC TYPE

The development of the tinfoil phonograph in the late 1870's by Thomas Edison was the beginning of what was to become a dynamic new home entertainment industry. It really got underway in the late 1890's. In the late '20's and '30's the radio, and, later, television made a real dent in its popularity. In spite of that the "record player" survives today and is a highly sophisticated machine. This guide covers the period from the 1890's to around 1930 when the phonograph was a beautiful, much simpler machine and leader in the home entertainment field.

The capacity of the phonograph and recorded sound to entertain were unlimited, unlike any other type of mechanical machine. Everything was recorded on records quite early on, from all kinds of music and singing to speeches, vaudeville sketches and language courses. Even blank cylinders were supplied to record your own performance.

It is a long, complex, fascinating history that requires volumes to tell. See "Further Reading", "Publications and Reprints", and "Mechanical Musical Societies" sections.

Phonographs can still be found at local sales, antique shops, flea markets, local auctions and shows. The rarer examples are sometimes advertised for sale in the phonograph publications. (See section on "Publications and Reprints"). Occasionally they will come up for sale at special auctions when a collector sells his treasures.

Note: Many descriptions of phonograph models indicate either a metal or wood horn. Unless otherwise noted, a wood horn will increase the value of a phonograph by $175-$300. The condition of the horn is very important, especially the veneer. (These are models that came originally with either type horn.)

AMERICAN GRAPHOPHONE CO. *See COLUMBIA PHONOGRAPH CO.*

	Price Range	
APOLLO		
☐ *APOLLO (Disc) — Table model, plain oak case, outside blue fluted metal (painted) horn, crank wind, plays 78rpm records, Apollo, Jr. reproducer (sound box) European maker.*	250.00	350.00
☐ *APOLLO FLOOR MODEL (Disc) — Highly styled fruitwood case, curved legs, storage for records, cover lifts to reveal turntable, nickel plated exposed parts, European maker.*	285.00	385.00
APOLLOPHONE *See Section on Player Pianos*		
ADLER		
☐ *ADLER (Disc) "Box Camera" style portable, tone arm fits into opening in cover, "horn" is drawer in the cover which opens out on one side to form a horn, turntable is three spokes which open out to hold record, hand crank, 7" x 4" x 7".*	125.00	200.00
ARETINO		
☐ *ARETINO (Disc), table model, rear mount horn bracket, 3" spindle, morning glory horn.*	250.00	500.00
AUX-E-TO-PHONE (Auxeto-Gramophone)		
☐ *AUX-E-TO-PHONE c. 1903 (Disc) — Sold in U.S. by Victor, mahogany floor cabinet with carved and gold decoration, uncovered 12" turntable on top with outside brass bell horn, operates on Electro-Pneumatic principle, reed sound box, motor drive, triple spring (simpler case variations).*	2500.00	3500.00
BEBE JUMEAU TALKING DOLL *(See "Lioret")*		
(EMILE) BERLINER GRAM-O-PHONES *(Canada) F.L.*		
☐ *BERLINER "STANDARD" GRAM-O-PHONE TYPE A (Disc). Simple oak case on wood base, top crank wind, 7" turntable, plays 7" and 10" Berliner records, brass bell horn 16" long, nickel plated metal parts, metal horn support with wood "tone arm", reproducer attached at end of tone arm and horn (Clark/Johnson Reproducer), very similar to Victor Type "B" Trademark machine.*	1500.00	2750.00
☐ *BERLINER "IDEAL" TYPE B (Disc). Oak case with heavy base and top moulding, side crank wind, double spring, 7" turntable, plays 7" and 10" records, 16" brass bell horn, nickel plated metal parts, wood and metal horn support and "tone arm".*	1000.00	1300.00
☐ *BERLINER "GRAND" TYPE C (Disc). Oak case with heavy base moulding, double spring, side crank wind, 10" turntable with nickel plated exposed metal parts, 21" brass bell horn, wood "tone arm" and metal horn support.*	1000.00	1350.00
☐ *BERLINER "BIJOU" TYPE E (Disc). Small oak case, base moulding, single spring, 7" turntable plays 7" and 10" records, 16" brass bell horn, nickel plated metal parts, metal horn support and wood "tone arm"*	750.00	1200.00

	Price Range	
BOSTON TALKING MACHINE CO.		
☐ *BOSTON TALKING MACHINE CO. (Disc) "Little Wonder Disc Phonograph", cast iron case and horn, tone arm comes out from center of 6 sided horn rests on rear mount bracket, 6½" turntable, single spring, records must have vertical cut grooves, plays "Little Wonder" discs, c. 1909-12.*	125.00	200.00
BRUNSWICK-BALKE-COLLENDER CO.		
☐ *BRUNSWICK c. 1921 (Disc). Mahogany table model, plain square sided case, rotating reproducer plays both lateral and vertical groove records. 11¾" turntable.*	100.00	200.00
☐ *BRUNSWICK MODEL 105 (Disc). Table model, c. 1921, mahogany case, 19½" high, two headed reproducer will play both lateral and vertical cut record, 11¾" turntable, simple rectangular case style with cover, oval fretwork grill, crank wind.*	150.00	250.00
☐ *BRUNSWICK (Disc). Upright Model 135, 49" high, mahogany (or walnut), decorative front grill, doors beneath phonograph contain storage for discs, hand crank. (There were several similar models with varying degrees of decorative details, in oak, black lacquer, mahogany and walnut).*	150.00	250.00
☐ *BRUNSWICK (Disc). Console floor model deluxe, "The Beaux Arts", walnut case, decorative moulding, 45" high, electrically powered, on legs, turntable on one side, storage for discs on the other. (Brunswick made many period cabinet styles).*	350.00	450.00
☐ *BRUNSWICK MODEL 200 c. 1923 (Disc). Floor model oak (mahogany) disc phonograph, oval shaped grill opening with fret work, storage in base for discs, 12" turntable, reproducer head rotates to play either lateral or vertical cut records (inside horn). Case variations in floor models.*	100.00	250.00
BUSY-BEE O'NEIL-JAMES *(Chicago).*		
☐ *BUSY-BEE "NEW" (Cylinder). Open works small cylinder machine on small metal base, 13½" horn with bell, key wind, plays Busy-Bee cylinder records (see also Columbia Type "Q" first series).*	200.00	350.00
☐ *BUSY-BEE GRAND c. 1905 (Disc). Oak, simple case table model with front mount horn support for large 8 petal Morning Glory horn (red or blue with gold), reproducer attached at end of horn (No "tone arm"), plays Busy-Bee records only. (Some variation in placement of horn and bracket and decal.)*	350.00	575.00
☐ *BUSY-BEE "QUEEN" c. 1906 (Cylinder). Oak case, plain, lyric reproducer, small ribbed horn (also: front crane supported ribbed horn), Busy-Bee decal on front, (see Columbia Jewel "Type BK").*	350.00	450.00
CAMERAPHONE		
☐ *CAMERAPHONE (Disc). Very small portable phonograph in the shape of an old box camera, leather covered case, simulated tortoise shell (resonator), horn, metal spoke turntable fold out, very compact, good volume (Variations in case, some wood, some covered in black material), plays 78 rpm discs.*	125.00	150.00

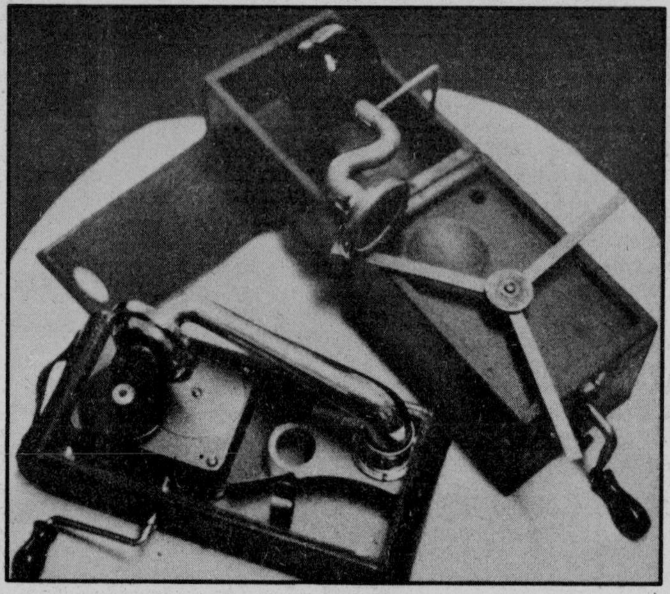

Left to Right: **Thorens Excelda Cameraphone.**

COLUMBIA DISC GRAPHOPHONE

THE TYPE YOU SEE ADVERTISED EVERYWHERE

The Columbia Disc Graphophone is an inexhaustible and universal entertainer which is particularly appropriate for

A HOLIDAY PRESENT

It will make home delightful and afford no end of pleasure, from the coming CHRISTMAS until the next one. It is always ready; does not get out of order, and the variety of records used on it is endless—songs, instrumental solos, orchestral and band pieces, amusing stories, etc.

Columbia Disc Graphophones are superior to all others. Our FLAT, INDESTRUCTIBLE RECORDS are composed of a material controlled EXCLUSIVELY by us. They are the sweetest, smoothest and most brilliant records ever heard. Until you listen to them you can form no accurate idea of the progress that has been made in bringing the disc records to the point of perfection. Their excellence is fully equaled by their durability.

The Disc Graphophone is made in three types, selling at $15, $20, and $30

7-inch Records, 50 cents each; $5 per dozen *10-inch Records, $1 each; $10 per dozen*

COLUMBIA HIGH SPEED MOULDED RECORDS fit all makes and all types of talking machines using cylindrical records and are superior to all others. Send for Catalogue. Sold by Dealers Everywhere and by the

COLUMBIA PHONOGRAPH COMPANY

Pioneers and Leaders in the Talking Machine Art

(GRAND PRIZE—PARIS, 1900)

NEW YORK: Wholesale and Retail, 93 Chambers St.; Retail only, 573 Fifth Ave.

BOSTON: 164 Tremont St.
MINNEAPOLIS: 13 Fourth St., S.
BALTIMORE: 110 E. Baltimore St.
PHILADELPHIA: 1609 Chestnut St.
PITTSBURG: 615 Penn Ave.

SAN FRANCISCO: 125 Geary St.
CHICAGO: 88 Wabash Ave.
DETROIT: 37 Grand River Ave.
WASHINGTON: 1212 F St., N. W.
ST. LOUIS: 709 Pine St.

BUFFALO: 645 Main St.
PARIS: 34 Boulevard des Italiens
LONDON: 122 Oxford St., W.
BERLIN: 65-A Friedrichstrasse

	Price Range	
CAPITOL PHONO LAMP		
☐ *CAPITOL PHONO LAMP (Disc). Metal base large table lamp, fringed shade opens up to reveal disc turntable and tone arm.*	500.00	1200.00
CARYOLA HAT BOX PHONOGRAPH		
☐ *CARYOLA HAT BOX PHONOGRAPH (Disc). Flat style rounded case portable disc phonograph.*	75.00	150.00
COLIBRE		
☐ *COLIBRE "BOX CAMERA" PORTABLE (Disc). Black metal case.*	100.00	150.00

COLUMBIA PHONOGRAPH COMPANY, NY *(Columbia Graphophones and Grafonolas)* *COLUMBIA MODELS* are listed alphabetically. If a model has a name and type designation then the name takes precedence over the "type". All entries have cross references; e.g.: Columbia Type BII (see Columbia Improved Sterling).

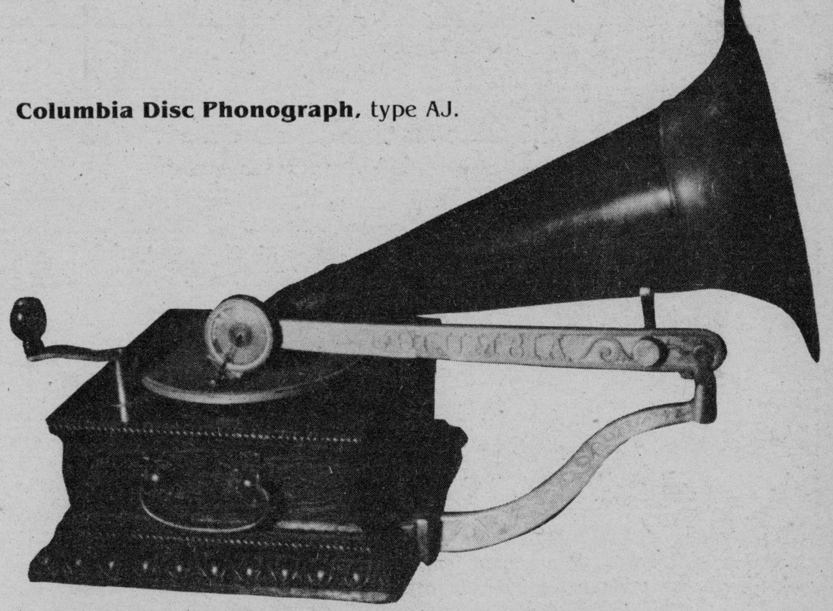

Columbia Disc Phonograph, type AJ.

☐ *COLUMBIA TYPE A c. 1897 (Cylinder). Oak case and cover (plain), nickel plated and black painted metal parts with gold and red decoration, open ended mandrel, small belled horn, plays 2-minute cylinder records, "Graphophone" decal, black reproducer, early version made in Washington, later in New York.*	**Washington** 400.00	600.00
	New York 300.00	425.00
☐ *COLUMBIA TYPE AA c. 1901 (Cylinder). Small case, ornate mouldings, oak, large ribbon decal, exposed mechanism nickel plated, horizontally placed reproducer, 14" horn with bell, Eagle reproducer.*	275.00	375.00

Columbia Business Cylinder Phonograph Dictaphone.

	Price Range	
☐ *COLUMBIA TYPE AB "McDonald Graphophone" (Cylinder). Open works, key wind, mounted on oak base (fancy moulding and decoration) plays regular 2-minute cylinders and 5" Grand cylinders, 5" mandrel fits over the smaller one, nickel plated works and belled horn, Heavy Eagle, (later Model "D" reproducer).*	750.00	1250.00
☐ *COLUMBIA TYPE AD c. 1901 (Cylinder). Oak "Home Grand" cabinet, plays regular 2-minute cylinders and Grand cylinders, 5" mandrel fits over 2" mandrel, nickel plated works, six spring motor (very, very rare), (see Columbia Home Grand for case description).*	1000.00	1500.00
☐ *COLUMBIA TYPE AF (Cylinder). Plays concert and regular cylinders.*	2000.00	3000.00
☐ *COLUMBIA TYPE AG (See Grand AG and Concert Grand AG)*		

	Price Range	
☐ *COLUMBIA TYPE AH (Disc). Highly decorative case design (mouldings top and bottom, corner columns, brass handles on sides), side mount detachable horn bracket, horn and reproducer attached at end of bracket, 22" brass bell horn, "analyzing" reproducer. ("Columbia" cut-out design in horn bracket.)*	600.00	950.00
☐ *COLUMBIA TYPE AJ. c. 1903-1905, (Disc). Fancy front mount aluminum tone arm/horn bracket, black horn with brass bell, oak case with highly decorative mouldings and rounded corner columns, side wind, carrying handles.*	450.00	750.00
☐ *COLUMBIA TYPE AK (Disc). Oak case, heavy moulding and decoration, ribbon decal, wood and metal horn bracket, reproducer and horn attached at end of bracket, 16" black bell horn, raised turntable, "analyzing" reproducer.*	400.00	750.00

Columbia "Baby Grand" Shaped Disc Phonograph, floor model.

	Price Range	
☐ COLUMBIA TYPE AN (Cylinder). Installed in a desk style cabinet with rounded top lid which opens to reveal the phonograph set into the surface of the desk, 8 storage drawers with pegs for cylinder records, (holds 200 cylinders).	2000.00	3000.00
☐ COLUMBIA TYPE AO c. 1902 (Cylinder). Highly ornate case, heavy carved mouldings, triple spring, "D" type reproducer (later case variations).	375.00	475.00
☐ COLUMBIA TYPE AQ Second Series c. 1903 (Cylinder). Long tapering trivet type base that also acts as part of horn support, small horn, key wind, simple mechanism plays 2-minute cylinders, Model "D" reproducer (Columbia produced this for Sears Roebuck called the "Oxford Junior").	285.00	385.00
☐ COLUMBIA TYPE AR (Disc). Similar to Columbia Type AY but with single spring motor.	375.00	475.00
☐ COLUMBIA TYPE AS Coin operated. (See Coin Operated Phonographs).		
☐ COLUMBIA TYPE AT c. 1898 (Cylinder). Oak case, decorative moulding along top edge, corner columns, ribbon decal, nickel plated mechanism (also black with gold decoration), double spring, Eagle Aluminum Reproducer, High Trunion Model c. 1903, oak case, decorative corner mouldings, new style "D" reproducer, 14" bell aluminum horn with bell, reproducer sits in horizontal position over cylinder.	325.00	600.00
☐ COLUMBIA TYPE AU c. 1903 (Disc). Open works mounted on base, 7" (6¾") turntable, 16" metal horn with bell, horn support and metal "tone arm", reproducer attached at end of horn (see also Standard Talking Machine).	300.00	400.00
☐ COLUMBIA TYPE AW c. 1903 (Cylinder). Triple spring, ornately decorated case with corner columns, 14" aluminum horn (bell), base moulding, Type AO and AW are essentially the same except the AW has a different reproducer (greater volume).	600.00	1400.00
☐ COLUMBIA TYPE AZ c. 1905 (Cylinder). Simple straight case style, plain base and top moulding, "Graphophone" decal, lyric reproducer, plays 2-minute cylinder records.	300.00	400.00
☐ COLUMBIA TYPE B c. 1894 (See Columbia Eagle).		
☐ COLUMBIA BABY GRAND (TYPE G) (Cylinder). Oak case, simple straight design, no decal, black reproducer attached from above facing down onto cylinder plays 2-minute cylinder records.	600.00	800.00
☐ COLUMBIA "BABY GRAND" SHAPED PHONOGRAPH (Disc). Floor model, mahogany, vertical louvered "speaker", curved Queen Anne type legs (3), lid lifts up to reveal turntable.	1850.00	2850.00
☐ COLUMBIA BABY REGENT (REGENT JR.) (Disc). Inside horn phonograph built into a squarish shaped mahogany table with four carved cabriole legs, drawer pulls out to reveal turntable, inside horn has louvered speaker.	600.00	1200.00
☐ COLUMBIA TYPE BC (See Columbia Twentieth Century).		
☐ COLUMBIA TYPE BD (See Columbia Majestic).		

	Price Range	
☐ *COLUMBIA TYPE BE (See Columbia Leader).*		
☐ *COLUMBIA TYPE BET (See Columbia New Invincible).*		
☐ *COLUMBIA TYPE BF (See Columbia Peerless).*		
☐ *COLUMBIA TYPE BFT (See Columbia New Peerless).*		
☐ *COLUMBIA TYPE BG (See Columbia Sovereign).*		
☐ *COLUMBIA TYPE BGT (See Columbia New Sovereign).*		
☐ *COLUMBIA TYPE BH (See Columbia Champion).*		
☐ *COLUMBIA TYPE BI (See Columbia Sterling).*		
☐ *COLUMBIA TYPE BII (See Columbia Improved Sterling).*		
☐ *COLUMBIA BIJOU (TYPE AN, N) c. 1895-97 (Cylinder). Simple case style, oak, large ribbon decal, nickel plated mechanism, black reproducer, plays 2-minute cylinders, small horn. . . . . .*	400.00	600.00
☐ *COLUMBIA TYPE BJ (See Columbia Imperial).*		
☐ *COLUMBIA TYPE BK (See Columbia Jewel).*		
☐ *COLUMBIA TYPE BKT (See Columbia New Leader).*		
☐ *COLUMBIA TYPE BM (See Columbia Home Premier).*		
☐ *COLUMBIA TYPE BN (See Columbia Improved Champion).*		

Columbia Disc Phonograph, "Baby Regent."

Price Range

- ☐ *COLUMBIA TYPE BNW (See Columbia Improved Royal).*
- ☐ *COLUMBIA TYPE BO (See Columbia Invincible).*
- ☐ *COLUMBIA TYPE BQ (See Columbia Rex).*
- ☐ *COLUMBIA TYPE BS Coin operated (See Coin Operated Phonographs).*
- ☐ *COLUMBIA BUSINESS Graphophones (See Columbia Universal Type C).*
- ☐ *COLUMBIA TYPE BV (See Columbia Royal).*
- ☐ *COLUMBIA TYPE BVT c. 1908 (Cylinder). Rear mount horn and tapering tone arm (aluminum) version of Type BV (Royal). See entry on the Columbia Royal for further description. Sears Roebuck sold a model like this under the name Oxford Talking Machine.* **750.00 900.00**
- ☐ *COLUMBIA TYPE BX (Cylinder). Keywind mechanism, open works, rectangular oak base, domed lid, black painted horn.* **500.00 1000.00**
- ☐ *COLUMBIA TYPE BY (See Columbia Improved Imperial).*
- ☐ *COLUMBIA TYPE C (See Columbia Universal).*
- ☐ *COLUMBIA "COLONIAL" ROUND TABLE DISC PHONOGRAPH. Floor model in the shape of a round center pedestal table, pull out drawer to reveal turntable, mahogany, c. 1912, hand crank.* **1000.00 1500.00**
- ☐ *COLUMBIA CONCERT GRAND TYPE AG (Cylinder). Oak case, decorative corners and top moulding, plays both regular and grand cylinders, 5" diameter mandrel fits over regular 2" mandrel, nickel plated mechanism, black and gold decorated parts, recorder. Some examples installed in desk style cabinet (See Columbia Type AN for full description).* **750.00 1350.00**
- ☐ *COLUMBIA DESK TABLE (See Columbia Regent).*
- ☐ *COLUMBIA DRUM TABLE (See Columbia Baby Regent).*
- ☐ *COLUMBIA EAGLE TYPE B c. 1897 Cylinder. Open works mounted on oak base with cover, nickel plated mechanism, "Graphophone" decal on cover, double spring, plays 2-minute wax cylinders, Aluminum Eagle Reproducer, small black horn (no bell) or ear tubes.* **250.00 500.00**
- ☐ *COLUMBIA ELITE (Disc). Table model mahogany square shaped inside horn style, front grill flaps forward for volume control, top cover, aluminum tone arm, plays 78rpm records.* **100.00 150.00**
- ☐ *COLUMBIA TYPE G (See Columbia Baby Grand).*
- ☐ *COLUMBIA TYPE GG (See Columbia Grand).*
- ☐ *COLUMBIA GRAFONOLA c. 1920's (Disc). "Jacobean style", floor model in antique oak finish, vertical louvered adjustable grill, record storage in base cabinet, decorative mouldings and finish, bulbous short legs and stretchers (many period style variations).* **170.00 270.00**
- ☐ *COLUMBIA GRAFONOLA c. mid 1920's (Disc). Table model inside horn, plain mahogany (oak) case, plays 78rpm discs, louvered grill volume control, nickel plated metal parts.* **100.00 200.00**

Columbia Grafonola Disc Phonograph, floor model.

	Price Range	
☐ *COLUMBIA GRAFONOLA DELUXE (Disc). Regina Music Box and Columbia Disc Phonograph combination (see also Reginaphone Style #240), floor model 48½" high, inside horn, mahogany disc phonograph with a 15½" disc music box mechanism, storage in base for discs and records, top front section is decorated with fully carved lions, head on claw feet columns, one on each side of speaker area, aluminum tone arm, Serpentine curved case style.*	**no music box**	
	1750.00	**2750.00**
	with music box	
	3750.00	**4750.00**
☐ *COLUMBIA GRAFONOLA FLOOR MODEL (Disc). Inside horn, floor model disc phonograph, plain case, oak (mahogany), storage for records in base, triple spring (many case variations).*	**100.00**	**200.00**
☐ *COLUMBIA GRAFONOLA REGENT (See Columbia Regent).*		

	Price Range	
☐ COLUMBIA GRAFONOLA TYPE A-2 (Disc). Table model, inside horn, horizontal louvers cover "Speaker grill" (control volume), no cover.	100.00	200.00
☐ COLUMBIA GRAFONOLA TYPE C-Z & D-Z (Disc). Table models similar to A-2 with covers.	100.00	200.00
☐ COLUMBIA GRAFONOLA TYPE L-2 (Disc). Upright floor model inside horn, door below turntable for record storage, mahogany (oak or walnut), record ejector system, vertical louvers over "speaker", plated metal parts, elaborate case decoration. Other Grafonola models in this series with varying degrees of case decoration and details, some without ejector system.	350.00	450.00
☐ COLUMBIA GRAFONOLA TYPE #22A (Disc). Table model, oak, triple spring, rectangular case style of simple lines, base moulding and horizontal louvered shutters over "speaker", hand crank.	75.00	100.00
☐ COLUMBIA GRAFONOLA TYPE #25A (Disc). c. 1920's, floor model, oak, 39½" high, triple spring, Garrand motor, 12" turntable, tone arm rotates on ball bearings, #7 reproducer, automatic brake, simple straight case lines, 5 shelf storage for discs, vertically louvered speaker grill.	125.00	250.00
☐ COLUMBIA GRAPHOPHONE MODEL B 1 (Disc). Rear mount outside horn table model, 8 petal morning glory horn, decorative corner and base mouldings, crank wind, nickel metal fittings and horn.	850.00	1000.00
☐ COLUMBIA GRAPHOPHONE MODEL Bn (Disc). Oak outside horn table model, 11 petal morning glory, simple case style, rear mount horn bracket and tone arm.	650.00	950.00
☐ COLUMBIA GRAND (TYPE AG) (Cylinder). Oak case (similar to Type AT) decorative top, corner and base mouldings, large ribbon decal, 5" diameter mandrel plays Grand cylinders, black painted exposed metal parts, gold decoration, type "D" reproducer (Heavy Eagle Reproducer).	1000.00	2000.00
☐ COLUMBIA GRAND (TYPE GG) c. 1898 (Cylinder). Oak, carved mouldings all over base, side and top of case and cover, plays 5" Grand cylinders, hinged front panel folds down, triple spring, black painted metal parts with gold decoration, Heavy Eagle Reproducer.	750.00	1500.00
☐ COLUMBIA TYPE HG (See Columbia Home Grand).		
☐ COLUMBIA HIGH TRUNION (TYPE AT) (See Type AT).		
☐ COLUMBIA HIGH GRAND (TYPE HG) c. 1899 (Cylinders). Highly decorated mouldings all over base, top and sides and cover, corner columns, plays 5" Grand cylinders, black metal exposed mechanism decorated with flowers, double spring, nickel plated metal parts, Heavy Eagle Reproducer (or Model "D" reproducer).	1000.00	2000.00
☐ COLUMBIA HOME PREMIER (TYPE BM) c. 1906 (Cylinder). In "Sovereign" mahogany case, 3" diameter Higham Reproducer, Quadruple spring.	1000.00	2000.00
☐ COLUMBIA IMPERIAL (TYPE BJ) (Disc). Single spring, 3 records on one winding. Otherwise same as Majestic Type BD.	500.00	1000.00

	Price Range	
☐ *COLUMBIA IMPROVED CHAMPION (TYPE BN) (Disc). Table model, simple lines, corners, base and top mouldings, rear mounted horn, ribbed "floral horn", black with gold lines (nickel or wood), double spring, 10" turntable, needle clamp, decal: profile of rear mount outside horn phonograph with the word "Columbia" inside it.*	575.00	900.00
☐ *COLUMBIA IMPROVED IMPERIAL (TYPE BY) (Disc). Mahogany case with curved sides and rounded corners and mouldings, Serpentine style four spring motor, 12" turntable with nickel trim edge, tone arm and elbow nickel plated, needle clamp, 23¾" long Morning Glory nickel plated (or mahogany) horn.*	1000.00	1950.00
☐ *COLUMBIA IMPROVED ROYAL (TYPE BNW) (Disc). Oak case with straight simple lines, heavy base with top mouldings, outside horn, table model, 78rpm disc phonograph, double spring, nickel plated tone arm, nine petal black ribbed Morning Glory horn, black ribbed floral horn with gold lines (or nickel or wood), 10" turntable, needle clamp, "silhouette" (profile) Columbia decal, rear mount horn.*	400.00	600.00
☐ *COLUMBIA IMPROVED STERLING (TYPE BII) (Disc). Table model, rear mount outside Morning Glory horn, 78rpm disc phonograph, oak case with heavy base and top mouldings, corner columns, tone arm, nine petal ribbed oak horn, 10" turntable, nickel plated exposed metal parts.*	400.00	600.00
☐ *COLUMBIA INVINCIBLE (TYPE BO) c. 1907 (Cylinder). Table model, oak, unusual case decoration (long oval cutouts in oak veneer on sides of case), ribbon "Graphophone" decal, rear mount Morning Glory horn with tapered aluminum tone arm, plays 2-minute cylinders, 6" long mandrel, triple spring, nickel plated mechanism, lyric reproducer in horizontal position.*	650.00	750.00
☐ *COLUMBIA JEWEL (TYPE BK) c. 1906 (Cylinder). Oak simple case, ribbon "Graphophone" decal, 14" horn with bell (or front crane with ribbed horn), crane screws to base of case, lyric reproducer for 2-minute cylinders, exposed metal parts are either nickel plated or black with gold decoration (also made as 2- and 4-minute combination with Columbia Indestructible Reproducer for the 4-minute cylinders).*	500.00	800.00
☐ *COLUMBIA TYPE K (Disc). Front mount outside horn, 10" turntable, brass belled horn.*	500.00	750.00
☐ *COLUMBIA LAMP TABLE (Disc) (See Columbia Baby Regent).*		
☐ *COLUMBIA LANGUAGE PHONE (Cylinder) (See Columbia "Q" Second Series).*		
☐ *COLUMBIA LEADER (TYPE BE) c. 1906 (Cylinder). Oak case, decorative corners, base and top mouldings, triple spring, 14" horn with brass bell, ribbon "GRAPHOPHONE" decal, lyric reproducer and recorder.*	250.00	500.00

Columbia Cylinder Phonograph, type BE, "Leader."

	Price Range	
☐ *COLUMBIA MAJESTIC (TYPE BD) (Disc). Solid mahogany table model, rounded smooth case style, moulding on top and base and corners, heavy duty spring motor, aluminum tone arm, 12" turntable, rear mounted 23¾" long Morning Glory horn (nickel plated), "analyzing" reproducer, automatic needle clamp.*	**400.00**	**750.00**
☐ *COLUMBIA - McDONALD GRAPHOPHONE (See Columbia Type AB).*		
☐ *COLUMBIA TYPE N (See Bijou).*		

	Price Range	
☐ *COLUMBIA NEW INVINCIBLE (TYPE BET) c. 1907 (Cylinder). Case style like the "Leader Type BE" with the addition of the rear mounted horn and tapering tone arm (aluminum), nickel plated and black with gold details, metal parts, nickel Morning Glory horn (or wood), plays 2- and 4-minute cylinders (Indestructible 4-minute cylinders played with the Indestructible Reproducer, lyric reproducer for the 2-minute wax cylinders.*	**375.00**	**600.00**

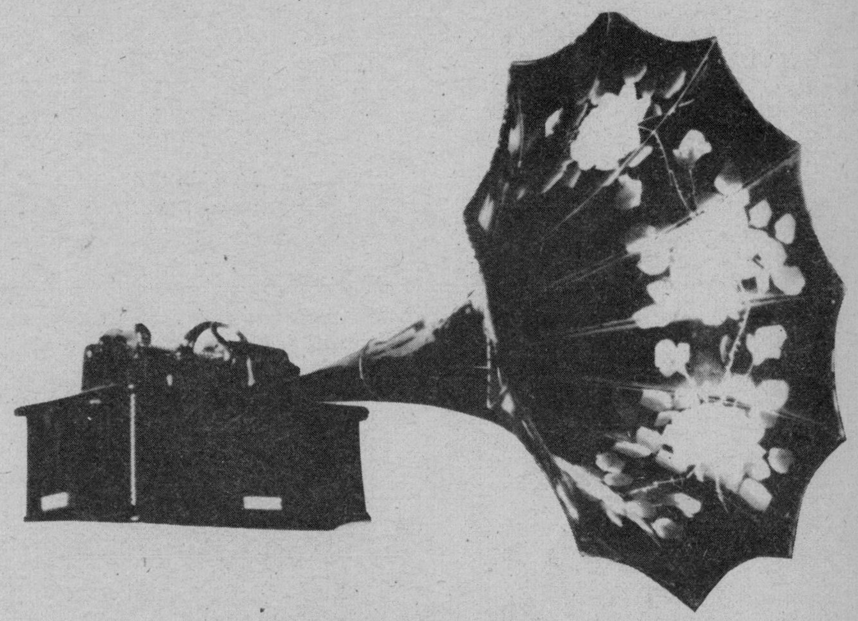

Columbia Cylinder Phonograph, type BET, with morning glory cylinder horn.

☐ *COLUMBIA NEW LEADER (TYPE BKT) c. 1907 (Cylinder). Case like the "Jewel" Type BK but with a rear mounted Morning Glory horn and tapered aluminum tone arm, double spring, plays 2- and 4-minute cylinder records, horn is black with gold lines, nickel or wood, ribbon decal, lyric reproducer for 2-minute wax cylinders.*	**500.00**	**750.00**
☐ *COLUMBIA NEW PEERLESS (TYPE BFT) c. 1907 (Cylinder). Case style like the "Peerless Type BF" but with the rear mounted Morning Glory horn and tone arm (aluminum), plays 2- and 4-minute cylinders (See Peerless for further description).*	**500.00**	**750.00**
☐ *COLUMBIA NEW SOVEREIGN (TYPE BGT) c. 1907 (Cylinder). Case style like the "Sovereign Type BG" mahogany case with hinged lid to reveal mechanism, quadruple spring, nickel plated exposed parts, rear mounted, 17½" long Morning*		

	Price Range	
Glory horn (nickel or wood) with tapered tone arm (aluminum), plays 2- and 4-minute cylinders with lyric and Indestructible reproducers.	500.00	750.00
☐ COLUMBIA PEERLESS (TYPE BF) c. 1906 (Cylinder). Oak case similar in style to the "Leader" but larger, quadruple spring, long play 6" mandrel to accommodate Twentieth Century (Type BC) cylinders as well as regular 2-minute cylinders, 14" brass bell horn, ribbon "Graphophone" decal, sapphire stylus lyric reproducer and recorder.	425.00	750.00
☐ COLUMBIA PREMIER (See Columbia Twentieth Century).		
☐ COLUMBIA "PRINCESS" UPRIGHT FLOOR MODEL c. 1912 (Disc). Square shaped case with lid over turntable, long curved legs, open storage shelf under machine, plated metal parts.	150.00	225.00
☐ COLUMBIA "Q" c. 1898 (Cylinder). Metal base plate, open works simple mechanism, single spring, key wind, aluminum Q reproducer, no wood base.	185.00	250.00
☐ COLUMBIA TYPE QC (Cylinder). Open works, small table model, oak cover and baseboard (works mounted to base), plays 2 minute cylinders.	200.00	275.00
☐ COLUMBIA TYPE QQ c. 1898-1902 (Cylinder). Keywind, exposed works, mounted on oak base, single spring, aluminum reproducer Type Q, belled horn with nickel finish, 'bent' wood oak cover with large "The Graphophone" decal.	220.00	260.00

Columbia Cylinder Phonograph.

☐ COLUMBIA "Q" SECOND SERIES c. 1903 (Cylinder). Black and gold base open works simple mechanism, plays 2-minute cylinders, key wind, type "D" reproducer.	185.00	250.00
☐ Also sold as the "Languagephone" with special language cylinders (Rosenthal).	200.00	275.00
☐ COLUMBIA REGENT or GRAFONOLA REGENT (Disc). Floor model, mahogany "desk" style, console case style (walnut, oak) some case decoration, carved claw feet, top drawer pulls out to reveal 78rpm phonograph, two storage compart-		

	Price Range	
ments for 200-12" records, small doors on one side near top open to reveal grilled speaker (electric).	750.00	1500.00
☐ COLUMBIA REGENT JR. (See Columbia Baby Regent).		
☐ COLUMBIA REX (TYPE BQ) c. 1907 (Cylinder). Similar case style to "Jewel" Type BK but with rear mounted Morning Glory horn and tapered aluminum tone arm (red horn with gold lines) plays 2-minute cylinder records with lyric reproducer, oak case.	500.00	750.00
☐ COLUMBIA ROYAL (TYPE BV) c. 1907 (Cylinder). Oak simple case, single spring, nickel plated mechanism, lyric reproducer, ribbon "Graphophone" decal, ribbed Morning Glory horn with front mounted horn crane. Sears Roebuck sold this model as the "Home Queen".	350.00	500.00
☐ COLUMBIA SOVEREIGN (TYPE BG) c. 1906 (Cylinder). Mahogany case and cover, heavy base and top mouldings, corner columns, nickel plated top mechanism, quadruple spring, 14" bell horn, long 6" mandrel for Twentieth Century cylinders, plays regular cylinders as well, ribbon "Graphophone" decal, Sapphire lyric reproducer and recorder.	350.00	600.00

Columbia Sovereign Gramaphone, type BG.

	Price Range	
☐ *COLUMBIA STERLING (TYPE BI) c. 1906 (Disc). Oak case with decorative corner columns, base moulding, aluminum tone arm, double spring, 10" turntable, ribbon "Graphophone" decal, "analyzing" reproducer, 17½" long Morning Glory horn, rear mounted.*	500.00	1000.00
☐ *COLUMBIA TWENTIETH CENTURY (TYPE BC) c. 1906 (Cylinder). Large oak case, hinged front panel, decorative corner columns and moulding, special 6" long mandrel for Twentieth Century cylinders, 4" diaphragm on reproducer, also plays regular cylinders, crank wind, motor driven (Universal electric motor runs on alternating or direct current), large ribbed horn with floor stand horn crane, high domed matching cover, carrying handles (also plays 4-minute Indestrucible records).*	crank 750.00	1250.00
	electric 1250.00	1750.00

Columbia 20th Century, table model, type BC.

☐ *COLUMBIA UNIVERSAL (TYPE C) c. 1897 (Cylinder). Oak case, front panel is hinged on the bottom, triple spring plays 6" long cylinders, ribbon decal "Graphophone". Designed as a business machine (plays regular 2" cylinders as well).*	400.00	650.00
☐ *UNIVERSAL (TYPE CE) (Operated on a 2-volt battery electric motor).*	500.00	1000.00
☐ *UNIVERSAL (TYPE CI) (Operated on 110-volt electric motor).*	525.00	600.00

COLUMBIA: MISCELLANEOUS ITEMS

☐ *COLUMBIA ALUMINUM HORN, 14" long.*	75.00	125.00
☐ *COLUMBIA FRONT MOUNT HORNS:*		

	Price Range	
☐ *19" long with 11" bell.*	50.00	75.00
☐ *21" long with 14" bell.*	75.00	125.00
☐ *COLUMBIA LYRIC REPRODUCER*	35.00	55.00

DAVIS CORNER PHONOGRAPH

☐ *DAVIS CORNER PHONOGRAPH (Disc). Mahogany finish triangular shaped floor model disc phonograph, on high legs, top cover, cloth covered speaker on one side, wood tone arm, 12" turntable.* **300.00 600.00**

DECCA JUNIOR PORTABLE

☐ *DECCA JUNIOR PORTABLE STYLE JC (Disc). Leather covered case with carrying handle, end of tone arm folds down from center of "Horn" in cover of case, 8" turntable, exposed metal parts nickel plated (many variations of portables by Decca and other companies).* **100.00 185.00**

DUPLEX PHONOGRAPH COMPANY *(Kalamazoo, MI)*

☐ *DUPLEX PHONOGRAPH COMPANY (Disc). Plain oak table model case style, corner columns, "Duplex" decal, two brass bell horns coupled to one reproducer, metal horn bracket, holds both horns, small turntable.* **1000.00 1750.00**

EDISON—THOMAS A. EDISON, INC., (ORANGE, NJ) (National Phonograph Co., Orange, NJ) There are so many models of Edison Phonographs that we have listed them alphabetically for easy access. This is not their order of production.

☐ *EDISON ACME (See Coin Operated Phonographs).*

☐ *EDISON ALVA (Cylinder). Mahogany table model with mahogany cygnet horn, "Edison" decal on front of wood case, Model "O" reproducer, Universal motor operates on direct or alternating current, exposed metal parts painted black with gilt decoration, Amberol and 2-minute cylinders. (Also Cygnet horn, black painted with gold trim or oak wood; gold plating, nickel plating or extra decoration on exposed mechanism was also used, Edison Recorder was also supplied.)* **2000.00 4000.00**

☐ *EDISON AMBEROLA MODEL 1A c. 1909 (Cylinder). 42" high floor model, 2-and 4-minute cylinder records, mahogany (walnut, oak) Diamond Model "M" reproducer (turn over type), exposed mechanism finished in oxidized copper gilt decoration, 4 drawers in base store 100 cylinder records, drawers hidden behind door, decorative front grill, plays 5 records on one winding of double spring, automatic stop, one of the best of the Amberola models, belt driven.* **2000.00 3000.00**

☐ *EDISON AMBEROLA MODEL 1B c. 1911 (Cylinder). Floor model, 4-minute cylinder records only, mahogany (walnut) case, Diamond Model "A" reproducer (Model "L"), "Opera" motor, exposed mechanism is dark red with gilt decoration, mandrel oxidized bronze, worm and gear driven Model 1B oak case mechanism is gun metal finish.* **1500.00 2500.00**

☐ *EDISON AMBEROLA MODEL III c. 1912 (Cylinder). 44" high floor model with open shelf underneath, 4-minute only, oak (mahogany), Diamond Model "A" reproducer (Model "L"), deep red finish on exposed mechanism, mandrel metal gray,*

Price Range

double spring, stationary reproducer, worm and gear drive (no belt), gilt and blue decoration on metal parts. **750.00 1400.00**

☐ *EDISON AMBEROLA MODEL IV c. 1913 (Cylinder). Floor model, Mission oak style, open shelf for storage under phonograph, single spring, traveling reproducer, belt driven, simple straight case and front grill. . . . .* **650.00 850.00**

☐ *EDISON AMBEROLA MODEL V c. 1912 (Cylinder). Table model with cover, simple case and grill, mahogany (oak), single spring, stationary mandrel, automatic stop, traveling reproducer connected to swivel arm, Diamond Model "B" reproducer, worm and gear driven. . . . .* **375.00 750.00**

☐ *EDISON AMBEROLA MODEL VI c. 1913 (Cylinder). Table model, simple case and grill, 4-minute cylinder records, Diamond Model "B" reproducer, single spring, stationary mandrel, traveling reproducer. . . . .* **350.00 550.00**

☐ *EDISON AMBEROLA MODEL VIII c. 1913 (Cylinder). Table model, simple case and grill, fireside style mechanism, "Popular Market Model", oak, single spring, swivel arm connects horn to reproducer, belt drive, Model "B" reproducer. . .* **300.00 450.00**

☐ *EDISON AMBEROLA X (Cylinder). Table model oak case, single spring, belt drive, diamond Reproducer: Model B, simple case style. . . . .* **275.00 450.00**

☐ *EDISON AMBEROLA FLOOR MODEL 30 (Cylinder). Floor floor model with cylinder record cabinet in base, table model set into a floor cabinet, front door in base opens to reveal pull-out shelves that hold cylinder records in the boxes. (See description of table model below). . . . .* **500.00 1000.00**

☐ *EDISON AMBEROLA MODEL 30 (Cylinder). Table model simple oak case, inside horn, front metal grill painted with wood grain, Diamond "C" reproducer, spring wind, 12¾" high, 3 cylinder records play on one winding, originally priced at $30.00 hence the model #30. . . . .* **275.00 325.00**

☐ *EDISON AMBEROLA MODEL 50 (Cylinder). Table model, mahogany (or oak), wooden front grill, 15" case, double spring, worm and gear driven, Diamond Model "C" reproducer. . . . .* **225.00 400.00**

☐ *EDISON AMBEROLA MODEL 75 (Cylinder). Floor model of #50, storage shelves for cylinders (84), feed screw drive moves the reproducer across the cylinder, Diamond "C" reproducer, mahogany (oak). . . . .* **300.00 450.00**

☐ *EDISON AMBEROLA MODEL 80 c. 1928 (Cylinder). 45" high floor model in Diamond Disc case, two drawers in base hold 72 cylinder records, Model "C" reproducer. . . . .* **425.00 525.00**

☐ *EDISON AUTOMATIC PHONOGRAPH MODEL "M" (See Edison Model "M" coin operated phonograph in the "Coin Operated Phonographs" section.).*

☐ *EDISON "BALMORAL" (Cylinder). Table model, oak (mahogany), battery operated electric motor (2 volts), Model "C" reproducer, recorder, shaving device (later version of the model "M" Victor), front mount 33" long black painted ribbed metal horn, exposed mechanism may be gold plated, plays 2-minute cylinder records. . . . .* **2500.00 3000.00**

☐ *EDISON "BIJOU" COIN OPERATED (See section on Coin Operated Phonographs).*

	Price Range	
☐ *EDISON BUSINESS MACHINE (Cylinder). Table model oak case and cover, wax cylinders, recorder, dictation horn (mouthpiece), playback horn, operated by direct current (110-120 volt) electric motor.*	300.00	600.00
☐ *EDISON "CLASS E" ELECTRIC (Cylinder). Early version of the Edison "Conquerer", electric motor operated, 110-120 volts.*	2250.00	3000.00
☐ *EDISON "CLASS M" ELECTRIC ("VICTOR") (Cylinder). Early version of the Edison "Balmoral". 2-volt battery operated, table model, oak case, exposed metal parts finished in black with gilt decoration and nickel Edison Automatic Reproducer, recorder, shaving device, 14" brass horn or two way hearing tube.*	2750.00	4000.00
☐ *EDISON CLIMAX Coin operated. (See section on Coin Operated Phonographs).*		
☐ *EDISON COIN OPERATED PHONOGRAPHS (See section on Coin Operated Phonographs).*		
☐ *EDISON "CONCERT" c. 1899-1908 (Cylinder). Plays 5" diameter (large) cylinder records, triple spring drive, plays 6-8 concert records on one winding, (case variations), early model, oak simple case with "square" corners, no decal, exposed mechanism painted black, some gilt decoration, front drawer, 24" brass belled horn with floor stand, shaving device, Automatic reproducer, recorder. Later models: Triumph type case, "Edison" decal (May have Model "D" reproducer and repeating device).*	1800.00	2500.00
☐ *EDISON CONCERT with Polyphone attachment (See Polyphone Talking Machines).*		
☐ *EDISON "E" CONCERT Operated by direct current electric motor (110-120 volts), otherwise same as "Concert" description above.*	2000.00	2500.00
☐ *EDISON "M" CONCERT c. 1900 (Cylinder). Battery operated (2 volts).*	2000.00	2500.00
☐ *EDISON CONQUERER (Cylinder). Table model (later version of the Model "E", see "Class E, Class M), oak (mahogany), operated by direct current (110-120 volt) electric motor, front mount horn crane, 33" long ribbed black horn, recorder, shaving device, Model "C" reproducer, plays 2-minute cylinder records, (also came with nickel or gold plated exposed mechanism).*	2500.00	3000.00
☐ *EDISON DIAMOND DISC MODEL A-80 c. 1913-15. Table model, oak (mahogany) simple case with cover, base moulding, 12" turntable, Diamond reproducer, nickel plated metal parts, turntable stop.*	200.00	300.00
☐ *EDISON DIAMOND DISC MODEL A-100 ("MODERNE") c. 1915-19. Floor model, mahogany, open storage shelf under phonograph, tapered legs, Sheraton style, 12" turntable, nickel plated parts, automatic stop Diamond reproducer.*	250.00	375.00
☐ *EDISON DIAMOND DISC MODEL A-150 c. 1915. Floor model, oak (mahogany), open shelf storage under phonograph, case decoration, tapered legs, shelf will hold 6 Edison record portfolios, 12" turntable, Diamond reproducer, metal parts oxidized bronze, automatic stop, 44" high.*	200.00	300.00

Edison Diamond Disc,
table model,
style #A-80.

Edison Diamond Disc,
floor model,
style #A-100,
"Moderne."

	Price Range	
☐ EDISON DIAMOND DISC MODEL A-200 c. 1915. Floor model, oak (mahogany), simple lines, curved legs (on wheels), large storage drawer under phonograph grill holds 36 discs, 12" turntable, automatic stop, gold plated exposed metal parts, 47" high.	250.00	350.00
☐ EDISON DIAMOND DISC MODEL A-250 c. 1915. Floor model, mahogany (oak), two large storage drawers behind a door hold 72 discs, decorative grill, 51½" high (Amberola IA case), gold plated exposed metal parts, volume control, Diamond reproducer, automatic stop.	375.00	500.00
☐ EDISON DIAMOND DISC MODEL A-290 Basically Model A-275 with marquetry decoration.	375.00	500.00
☐ EDISON DIAMOND DISC MODEL A-300 Same as Model A-250 in Circassian walnut.	400.00	600.00
☐ EDISON DIAMOND DISC MODEL A-375 c. 1912-14. Louis XV style case floor model, mahogany, highly decorative case, curved legs, ornate grill, case moulding, storage drawer for 36 discs, 12" turntable, Diamond reproducer, gold plated metal parts, automatic stop, 50" high.	400.00	650.00
☐ EDISON DIAMOND DISC MODEL A-400 c. 1912-14. Louis XVI style case, floor model, mahogany, highly stylized case decoration, decorative moulding, fluted decoration, tapered legs, storage drawer for 36 discs, 12" turntable, Diamond reproducer, gold plated exposed metal parts, automatic stop, 48" high.	400.00	650.00
☐ EDISON DIAMOND DISC MODEL A-425 Same style in Circassian walnut.	400.00	650.00
☐ EDISON DIAMOND DISC MODEL A-450 Same style in Circassian walnut as above.	400.00	650.00
☐ EDISON DIAMOND DISC MODEL B-60 c. 1913-14. Table model, oak simple case and grill, no cover, 12" turntable, nickel plated exposed parts (turntable, "arm" and reproducer head), single spring, turntable stop, plays Edison Diamond Disc records, Diamond reproducer.	200.00	250.00
☐ EDISON DIAMOND DISC MODEL B-80 (Disc). c. 1915. Table model, simple grill, mahogany case, 12" turntable, single spring.		
☐ EDISON DIAMOND DISC MODEL C-150 c. 1915-19. Floor model, straight lines, stylized grill design, storage for discs under grill, oak (mahogany), Diamond reproducer, automatic stop, 12" turntable.	200.00	350.00
☐ EDISON DIAMOND DISC MODEL C-200 c. 1915-19. Floor model, straight lines, decorative grill, storage drawer in base holds 36 discs, Diamond reproducer, mahogany, single spring, 12" turntable.	250.00	450.00
☐ EDISON DIAMOND DISC MODEL C250. "Official Laboratory Model" Chippendale style floor model, oak case with decorative "Speaker" grill and trim, gold metal fittings, storage in base for records, 49¾" high.	250.00	450.00
☐ EDISON DIAMOND DISC MODEL S19. Floor model, gold plated metal parts, oak case with fretwork grill, flap down bottom door conceals record storage space, 43½" high.	250.00	450.00

Edison Diamond Disc,
floor model,
style #C-250.

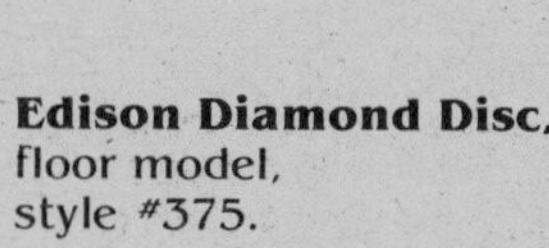

Edison Diamond Disc,
floor model,
style #375.

Edison Diamond Disc Phonograph, model #C-150, Sheraton style, upright floor model.

	Price Range	
☐ *EDISON DIAMOND DISC MODEL — ADAMS 18th Century English c. 1918-22. Console floor model cabinet, mahogany, decorative double grill front, on tapering legs, double spring, gold plated trim and hardware. By 1922 equipped for long playing records.*	350.00	500.00
☐ *EDISON DIAMOND DISC MODEL: CHALET Table model gum wood case, very simple design, lattice like grill design, nickel plated parts, single spring, automatic stop, 12" turntable, 20" high, (also called Bungalow, Style B-19).*	300.00	350.00
☐ *EDISON DIAMOND DISC MODEL: CHIPPENDALE (CC-32) c. 1922, console model disc phonograph, basically simple lines, two compartments for record storage (64 discs), grill same as C-19 and C-250) somewhat oriental) double spring, some decorative moulding along top and grill, 12" turntable.*	400.00	750.00
☐ *EDISON DIAMOND DISC MODEL: HEPPLEWHITE c. 1919-1926. Floor model, mahogany (oak), simple case style, highly carved grill, storage in base for discs, 12" turntable, tone modulator, Diamond reproducer, automatic stop, single spring, gold trim, 41½" high (MODEL H-19).*	400.00	550.00
☐ *EDISON DIAMOND DISC MODEL: JACOBEAN c. 1919-27. Floor model, oak, simple lines, some case decoration, decorative grill, horizontal supports between legs, storage*		

Edison Diamond Disc Phonograph "Chalet," also called Bungalow, style #B-19.

Edison Diamond Disc Phonograph, model #CC-32, Chippendale style console.

	Price Range	
beneath phonograph for discs, 12" turntable, Diamond reproducer, automatic stop, single spring. By 1927 equipped to play long playing discs.	375.00	500.00
☐ *EDISON DIAMOND DISC MODEL: LONDON NO. 1 (L35) c. 1922. Table model made for export market, equipped with reproducer to play 78rpm records as well.*	275.00	400.00
☐ *EDISON DIAMOND DISC MODEL: LONDON UPRIGHT (LU 37) Brown mahogany floor model, fretwork grill, simple case, storage for discs, 43½" high (export item).*	475.00	575.00

Edison Diamond Disc,
London upright model,
style #LU-37.

☐ *EDISON DIAMOND DISC MODEL LOUIS XIV c. 1919-27. Floor model, Louis XIV stylized case design, walnut, case moulding and decoration, rounded cover, 50" high, storage for discs, 12" turntable, tone modulator, Diamond reproducer, automatic stop, double spring, by 1927 equipped for long playing records.*	325.00	575.00
☐ *EDISON DIAMOND DISC MODEL: SHERATON. Floor model, oak, straight lines, decorative grill and moulding, gold plated metal parts, automatic stop, Diamond reproducer, storage in base.*	200.00	325.00
☐ *EDISON DIAMOND DISC MODEL: WILLIAM AND MARY, Period art case, floor model, gold plated metal parts, automatic stop, Diamond reproducer, disc storage in base.*	250.00	350.00

Edison Diamond Disc, oak, floor model, "Sheraton."

	Price Range	
☐ EDISON DISC Table model, outside horn disc phonograph, oak simple large case, rounded corners, base and top moulding, Morning Glory type horn, tapered end curves down and around to form tone arm in one piece, reproducer attached at end of it, rear mounted special horn support, plated metal parts.	400.00	550.00
☐ EDISON DISC: ARMY AND NAVY TABLE MODEL c. 1917. Single spring, painted wood case, metal grill inside protective front flap, reinforced case construction, storage for 10 discs.	1000.00	2000.00
☐ EDISON DOLL (See Edison Talking Doll).		
☐ EDISON DUPLEX (Cylinder). Table model simple oak case, plays regular cylinders and concert cylinders by means of a slip on concert mandrel and automatic reproducer.	750.00	900.00

Edison Disc Phonograph, "Army and Navy," table model, c. 1917.

	Price Range	
☐ *EDISON FIRESIDE MODEL A c. 1909 (Cylinder). Compact table model, oak cabinet, rounded corners and cover, "Edison" decal on front of case, single spring belt drive, 2- and 4-minute, Model "K" reproducer, 19" long two piece ribbed metal horn (maroon, blue or black).*	380.00	550.00
☐ *c. 1910. Cygnet horn also (black ribbed, mahogany, spruce, oak).*	450.00	650.00
☐ *MODEL B c. 1912-14. 4-minute only, improved spring motor, variety of horns: Cygnet wood or metal, blue flowered horn, two part Fireside Horn, Model "N" or Diamond "B" reproducer.*	500.00	750.00
☐ *EDISON GEM MODEL A c. 1898 (Cylinder). Table model, key wind, 2-minute wax cylinder records, metal case black with gold decoration, knob to control speed and moves in and out to stop or start, 10" black horn, (no bell), with gold band, single spring, one cylinder on one wind.*	225.00	375.00
☐ *EDISON GEM MODEL A c. 1901 (Cylinder). Table model, metal case on wooden base, gold painted decoration, improved stop and start mechanism and speed control, black horn (no bell), key wind.*	250.00	375.00
☐ *EDISON GEM MODEL B c. 1905 (Cylinder). Table model, black metal case on wooden base, gold painted decoration, 2-minute cylinder records, crank permanently placed in machine, slot in cover to accommodate crank, Model "C" reproducer, plain black horn.*	300.00	400.00
☐ *EDISON GEM MODEL D c. 1909 Maroon (Cylinder). Table model, metal case finished in maroon, gilt decoration, oak*		

Edison Gem Cylinder, phonograph.

Edison Gem Phonograph, model D.

	Price Range	
base and cover, 2- and 4-minute combination, single spring, Model "H", Model "R" reproducers, 2-piece crane (or Model "K" combination reproducer).	420.00	750.00
☐ *EDISON GEM MODEL E c. 1912 Maroon (Cylinder). Maroon finish metal case, maroon ribbed horn, 4-minute only, Model "N" reproducer, oak base and cover.*	1000.00	1400.00
☐ *EDISON GEM WITH POLYPHONE ATTACHMENT (See Polyphone Talking Machine).*		
☐ *EDISON HOME MODEL A c. 1896-1901 (Cylinder). Suitcase Model, clip type cover, oak case, ribbon decal on cover, black painted mechanism, single spring, starting lever, speed control, 14" brass bell horn, slotted crank, shaving device found on some early models.*	350.00	600.00
☐ *EDISON HOME MODEL A c. 1901 (Cylinder). Table model, rounded "new style" case and cover, ribbon decal on base, Model "C" reproducer, 2-minute cylinder records, 14" polished brass horn (also 30" ribbed horn, with rear mount crane) 18" case.*	275.00	375.00

Edison Home Cylinder Phonograph.

☐ *EDISON HOME MODEL B c. 1906 (Cylinder). Table model, oak "new style" case, shorter than Model "A", 16½" wide, single spring, Model "C" reproducer, threaded crank, 14" bell horn (brass), 19" ribbed black horn with front mount crane (repeat mechanism).*	250.00	400.00
☐ *EDISON HOME MODEL C c. 1908. Table model, oak, plain case, push button lift to carrier arm, Model C reproducer, plays 2 minute cylinders, 10 petal ribbed cygnet horn.*	350.00	475.00
☐ *EDISON HOME MODEL D c. 1908 (Cylinder). Table model, short oak case, 2- and 4-minute cylinder records, used Model "C" and "H" reproducers, 19" horn and crane, "Edison" decal on front of case (also: cygnet horn and crane in black metal or oak).*	300.00	400.00

	Price Range	
☐ EDISON HOME MODEL E c. 1911 (Cylinder). Oak case, plays 2- and 4-minute cylinder records, Model "O" reproducer, cygnet horn, open ended mandrel.	400.00	650.00
☐ EDISON HOME MODEL F c. 1911 (Cylinder). Very similar in all respects to Model "E" and "D".	295.00	375.00
☐ EDISON HOME MODEL G c. 1912 (Cylinder). Oak case table model, plays 4-minute cylinders only, Diamond Model "B" reproducer, metal cygnet horn (painted oak finish).	375.00	425.00

Edison Home Cylinder Phonograph, horizontally mounted reproducer for cygnet horn.

☐ EDISON HOME MODEL H Coin operated (See Coin Operated Phonographs).		
☐ EDISON HOME WITH POLYPHONE ATTACHMENT (See Polyphone).		
☐ EDISON IDEAL (See Edison Idelia).		
☐ EDISON IDELIA MODEL D1 c. 1907 (Cylinder). Originally called "Ideal" table model, mahogany case, heavy mouldings, rounded cover, decorative carrying handles on sides, 2-minute cylinders, triple spring, "Edison" decal on front of base, horn, crane, reproducer (Model "C") recorder, all oxidized bronze finish, also mahogany horn.	4000.00	6000.00
☐ EDISON IDELIA MODEL D2 c. 1908 (Cylinder). Table model, mahogany case, combination 2- and 4-minute, Model "C" and Model "H" reproducers, recorder, triple spring.	3750.00	5750.00
☐ Later Model c. 1910-11. Exposed metal parts enamelled maroon instead of oxidized, mahogany finish cygnet horn, nickel plated crane, Model "O" reproducer, double spring.		

	Price Range	
May be fitted with a repeating attachment which allowed a cylinder to be played over and over automatically (other Edison models could be fitted with this device).	3500.00	5000.00
☐ *EDISON "LANGUAGE" PHONOGRAPH (See Edison Standard Model "B").*		
☐ *EDISON LONG PLAYING CONSOLE, MODEL No. 1, c. 1920's (Disc). Two speed gearing for 12" long play discs and Diamond discs, two front doors on cabinet, one for record storage, one for speaker, turned legs, some applied case decoration on front doors.*	250.00	450.00
☐ *EDISON LONG PLAYING CONSOLE MODEL No. 2, 3, and 4 c. 1920's (Disc). Simple brown mahogany case with center grill, classical style decoration, turned legs, (all three models differ only slightly in size not style), two speed gearing for 12" long play and Diamond discs, double spring.*	275.00	525.00

Edison Long Playing Disc Console, model 2, 3 or 4.

	Price Range	
☐ *EDISON OPERA c. 1911-13 (Cylinder). Table model, mahogany case also in oak, exposed mechanism in enamelled maroon, sliding mandrel automatic stop, self-supporting cygnet type wood horn ("Music Master"), oxidized bronze crank, reproducer and carrying handles, Model "L" reproducer and Diamond Model "A" reproducer, 4-minute wax and blue Amberol Cylinder records.*	2600.00	3200.00

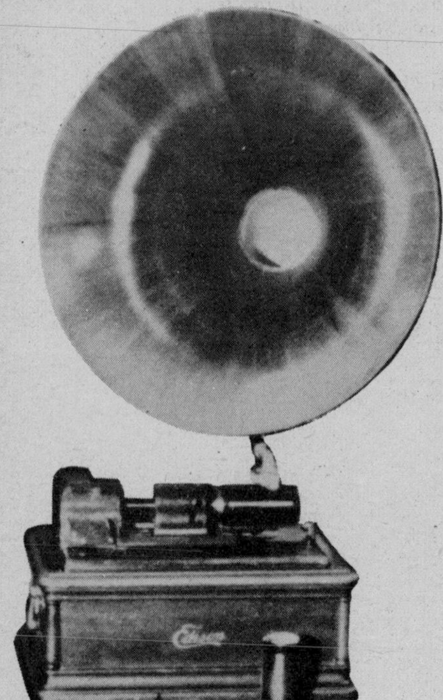

Edison Opera Cylinder Phonograph, with oak cygnet horn.

☐ *with matching cylinder cabinet.*	3200.00	4200.00
☐ *EDISON POLYPHONE CYL. PHONOGRAPH (See EDISON TRIUMPH Phonograph with Polyphone attachment).*		
☐ *EDISON SCHOOL PHONOGRAPH c. 1912 (Cylinder). Table model, metal case fits into metal floor stand, on wheels with four storage boxes for 96 cylinders (Blue Amberol), self-supporting cygnet type black metal horn, Diamond Model "A" reproducer (Opera mechanism).*	1500.00	2500.00
☐ *EDISON SPRING MOTOR PHONOGRAPH (See Edison Triumph Model "A").*		
☐ *EDISON STANDARD MODEL A c. 1897 (Cylinder). Oak case, "suitcase" style model with metal clips to hold cover, plays 2-minute cylinders, slotted crank, plays 3 cylinders on one winding, squared off corners on base of case, 14" brass belled horn, shaving device, single spring.*	350.00	450.00

	Price Range	
☐ *EDISON STANDARD MODEL B c. 1905 (Cylinder). Oak case and rounded cover, base moulding, mechanism screwed to lid of base, Model "C" reproducer, ribbon decal, speed control, screw on crank, single spring, plays 2-minute cylinder records (no shaving device), 14" brass belled horn, may be fitted with manual language repeater mechanism operated by pressing on lever attached to front of mechanism. The reproducer is set back several grooves to repeat last phrases, usually accompanied by a small plate on front of machine, e.g. "International Textbook Co." Special language cylinders were made with a whole course of instruction.*	**275.00**	**375.00**
☐ *With language repeat (International Correspondence School).*	**350.00**	**500.00**
☐ *EDISON STANDARD MODEL C (See Model "B").*		
☐ *EDISON STANDARD MODEL D c. 1908 (Cylinder). Oak case and cover, combination 2- and 4-minute gearing, single spring, Model "C" and Model "H" reproducers, flowered ribbed horn and crane, exposed metal parts black with gold decoration and nickel plated.*	**350.00**	**450.00**

Edison Triumph, with polyphone attachment.

Edison Triumph Cylinder Phonograph,
horizontally mounted reproducer for cygnet horn.

	Price Range	
☐ *EDISON STANDARD MODEL E c. 1911 (Cylinder). Oak case with cover, plays 2- and 4-minute cylinder records, reproducer carriage arranged horizontally to accommodate a cygnet horn (ribbed black metal with gold decoration), combination Model "S" or "O" reproducer (Model "C" and Model "H" reproducers).*	300.00	600.00
☐ *EDISON STANDARD MODEL G c. 1912 (Cylinder). Oak case and cover, plays Blue Amberol cylinders only (4-minute), cygnet horn, Diamond Model "B" reproducer, (flowered horn).*	360.00	550.00
☐ *EDISON STANDARD WITH POLYPHONE ATTACHMENT (See Polyphone).*		
☐ *EDISON TALKING DOLL c. 1890 (Edison Phonograph Toy Manufacturing Co.) Female doll with bisque head, wood and plaster limbs, metal body with grill holes in front for sound, back panel of body comes off to expose cylinder record mechanism, hand crank, cylinder was permanently placed in doll, 3" diameter cylinder plays ½-minute. There were a variety of tunes available. One tune per doll.*	1750.00	2500.00
☐ *EDISON TREADLE PHONOGRAPH. Foot powered cylinder phonograph mounted on a sewing machine base with drawers, originally conceived for both commercial and household use. RARE (confined mainly to Museum examples).*	5000.00	7000.00

	Price Range	
☐ *EDISON TRIUMPH MODEL A c. 1895-1900 (Cylinder). Edison spring motor, simple oak case with small front drawer, no decals, triple spring, 2-minute cylinder records, 14" brass horn, square winding crank, Edison Automatic Reproducer and Recorder (shaving device).*	500.00	1000.00
☐ *(Later Model) c. 1900. Oak "new style" case, case moulding, ribbon decal on front, exposed mechanism painted black with gold decoration, nickel plated, triple spring, 14" brass horn, Edison Automatic Reproducer and Recorder (Model "C" reproducer c. 1902, other horns of various sizes also supplied).*	600.00	800.00
☐ *EDISON TRIUMPH MODEL B c. 1906 (Cylinder). Oak case with raised panels on sides, "Edison" decal, triple spring, plays 2-minute cylinders, screw on crank, 14" brass horn, Model "C" reproducer (triumph horn).*	650.00	750.00

Edison Triumph Cylinder Phonograph.

	Price Range	
☐ EDISON TRIUMPH MODEL D c. 1908 (Cylinder). Oak (mahogany) case and cover, decorative base moulding and raised panels on all sides of base, "Edison" decal, plays 2-and 4-minute cylinder records, Model "C" and Model "H" reproducers, 33" long ribbed black horn, speed control, triple spring (cygnet horn).	700.00	1000.00
☐ EDISON TRIUMPH MODEL E c. 1910 (Cylinder). Oak (mahogany), triple spring, speed regulator, plays 2- and 4-minute cylinder records, Model "O" combination reproducer with sapphire stylus, cygnet or straight ribbed horn.	800.00	1250.00
☐ EDISON TRIUMPH MODEL F c. 1911 (Cylinder). Case style slightly different, corner columns, no raised panels. Otherwise description is same as Model "E", oak cygnet horn.	800.00	1250.00
☐ EDISON TRIUMPH MODEL G c. 1912 (Cylinder). Oak case, corner pillars, no raised panels, "Edison" decal, plays 4-minute cylinders only (Blue Amberol), Diamond Model "B" reproducer, oak cygnet horn.	800.00	900.00
☐ EDISON TRIUMPH CYLINDER PHONOGRAPH WITH POLYPHONE ATTACHMENT, machine has a special double reproducer which holds two small belled horns, this unit played on one cylinder. (Edison offered this attachment as an option).		
☐ EDISON WINDSOR Coin operated (See section on Coin Operated Phonographs).		

EDISON: MISCELLANEOUS PHONOGRAPH ITEMS

☐ EDISON AMBEROLA MODEL "B" REPRODUCER, 4-minute diamond stylus.	50.00	95.00
☐ EDISON BLUE AMBEROL 4-minute was		2.00 & up
☐ EDISON CONCERT CYLINDER RECORDS 5" diameter	10.00	25.00
☐ EDISON CYLINDER RECORDS 2-minute wax.		3.00 & up
☐ EDISON CYLINDER (AMBEROL) 4-minute wax.		3.00 & up
☐ EDISON DIAMOND DISCS.		1.00 & up
☐ EDISON FIRESIDE MORNING GLORY HORN, two-piece metal, painted.	150.00	225.00
☐ EDISON LONG PLAYING DISCS.		10.00 & up
☐ EDISON MODEL C REPRODUCER.	35.00	75.00
☐ EDISON MODEL H REPRODUCER.	45.00	75.00
☐ EDISON MODEL K REPRODUCER.	60.00	125.00
☐ EDISON MODEL N "RED GEM" REPRODUCER.	80.00	175.00
☐ EDISON MODEL O REPRODUCER.	75.00	95.00
☐ EDISON DIAMOND B REPRODUCER.	75.00	95.00
☐ EDISON DIAMOND DISC REPRODUCER.	25.00	50.00
☐ EDISON HOME SHAVER c. 1912. Oak case, shave off previous recordings on 4-minute wax cylinders, 4-minute recorder and blanks came with the shaver.	50.00	75.00
☐ EDISON FLOOR MODEL SHAVER Black metal.	35.00	65.00
☐ EDISON 78rpm PHONOGRAPH HEAD nickel plated.	45.00	65.00
☐ EDISON RECORD CABINET (Cylinder Records) Doors open to reveal five pull out shelves, simple case style, holds 75 cylinders.	175.00	350.00

	Price Range	
☐ *CYLINDER RECORD CABINET Oak, 5 drawers, holds 75 cylinders, decorative moulding, brass pulls (many variations, some holding well over 100 cylinders).*	200.00	400.00
☐ *EDISON 4-minute recorder.*	50.00	65.00
☐ *EDISON Mahogany cygnet horn.*	100.00	200.00

EXCELDA *(See Thorens "Excelda"*

EXCELSIOR

☐ *EXCELSIOR (Cylinder). Key wind motor, vertical crank wind, aluminum reproducer and belled horn (one piece horn), machine mounted on oak base, curved cover with Excelsior decal.*	300.00	450.00

FAIRY PHONOGRAPH LAMP

☐ *FAIRY PHONOGRAPH LAMP c. late 1930's (Disc). "Copper" metal base, wood grain finish, cloth shade (quite elaborately decorated), 35" high, center section of lamp base holds turntable, Eagle on cover of phonograph section, plays 78rpm records.*	500.00	1000.00

Fairy Phono Lamp, plays disc records.

	Price Range	
FERN-O-GRAND PHONOGRAPH		
☐ *FERN-O-GRAND PHONOGRAPH (Disc) Small "Baby Grand" Piano style floor model phonograph case, lid lifts to reveal turntable, tone arm, etc. Plays 78rpm records (See Phonogrand).*	600.00	775.00

GRAM-O-PHONES *(See Berliner Gram-O-Phones).*

GUITAROPHONE *(See Organettes and Roller Organs).*

HARMONY		
☐ *HARMONY c. 1906 (Disc). Rear mount outside horn, painted Morning Glory horn (blue, 8 petals), oak case some decoration, rounded column at corner, single spring motor, plays large holed records.*	500.00	600.00
☐ *HARMONY (Disc). Front mount outside horn, painted Morning Glory horn, large spindle.*	350.00	450.00

HIS MASTER'S VOICE GRAMOPHONE CO. *(British Company related to the Victor Talking Machine Co.). ("H.M.V.")*

☐ *H.M.V. JUNIOR GRAND c. 1910 (Disc). Oak floor model, inside horn, exhibition reproducer, gooseneck tone arm, two front doors open to reveal "Speaker Horn", grill, storage in base for disc records, 45¾" high.*	175.00	225.00
☐ *H.M.V. LUMIERE PHONOGRAPH MODEL #460 c. 1924-26 (Disc). Plain large rectangular table model case with cover, oak veneer, 14" pleated gold paper diaphragm which folds down parallel to the turntable when not in use. (Louis Lumiere Patent), gold plated exposed metal parts and trim, double spring, 12" turntable.*	850.00	1250.00
☐ *H.M.V. LUMIERE CABINET GRAND MODEL #510 c. 1926 (Disc). Floor model, straight case style with storage for discs, mahogany (oak), curved legs, 14" pleated gold paper diaphragm (See last entry for further description), Quadruple Spring Motor.*	1250.00	1750.00
☐ *H.M.V. MODEL 32 c. 1927 (Disc). Table model, outside horn, mahogany case, some decoration, quadruple-spring motor, black ribbed Morning Glory horn.*	200.00	300.00
☐ *H.M.V. MODEL 102C PORTABLE (Disc). Blackcloth covered carrying case, suitcase style, #5B reproducer (also came in blue leather-like cloth, with #5A reproducer, storage for records).*	75.00	125.00
☐ *H.M.V. MODEL 110 (Disc). Inside horn table model, oak, gooseneck tone arm, door covered louvered horn grill.*	75.00	125.00
☐ *H.M.V. MODEL 126 c. 1925-26 (Disc). Inside horn table model, #4 Reproducer, louvered grill over horn with doors, shaped bracket feet, oak.*	75.00	125.00

HOME QUEEN

☐ *HOME QUEEN (Sears Roebuck) (See Columbia Royal).*

ELDRIDGE JOHNSON GRAM-O-PHONES

☐ *ELDRIDGE JOHNSON GRAM-O-PHONES (See Victor Type A, B, C).*

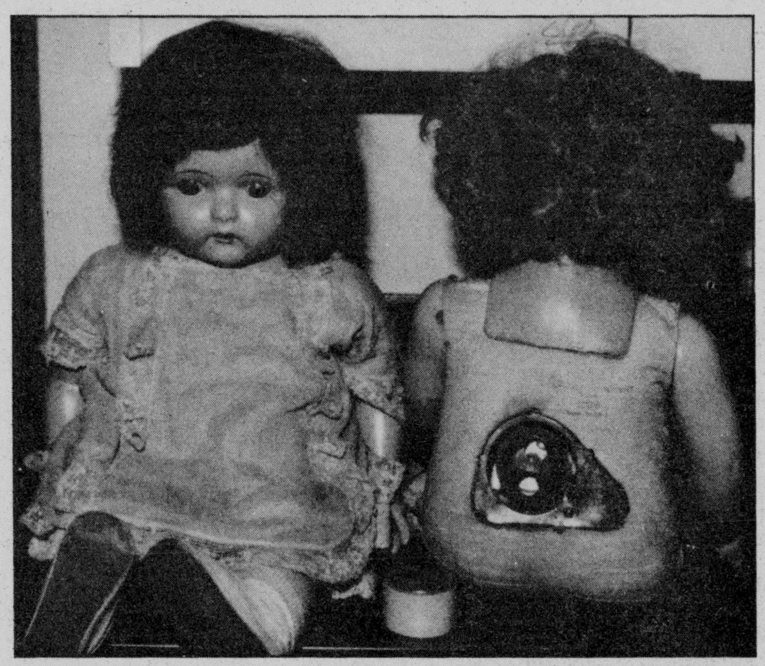

Madame Hendren Talking Doll.

	Price Range	
JUNOPHONE		
☐ *JUNOPHONE (Disc). Table model, outside horn, disc phonograph, oak plain case, rear mount metal horn in simulated wood grain finish, Junophone Reproducer (case variations and different horns, e.g. red fluted metal horn with pressed design).*	200.00	275.00
KAMERAPHONE		
☐ *KAMERAPHONE PORTABLE DE LUX (Disc). "Box Camera" style, 5" x 6" x 7", 5" turntable, tone arm fits into a ring inside the lid, crank wind.*	125.00	175.00
KLINGSOR		
☐ *KLINGSOR TABLE MODEL (Disc). Simple rectangular case style with cover, small front doors open to reveal horn (speaker) opening, crank wind.*	200.00	285.00
☐ *KLINGSOR TABLE MODEL WITH "ZITHER" STRINGS c. 1908 (Disc). 38" high case contains two leaded glass doors on top which open to reveal internal horn with zither like piano strings on a metal frame, turntable located beneath this section, acoustic reproducer.*	1500.00	2000.00
☐ *KLINGSOR PHONOGRAPH WITH ZITHER STRINGS. Upright floor model, storage cabinet for disc records in base, 60" high (phonograph sits on storage cabinet).*	1750.00	2500.00

	Price Range	
LAKESIDE PHONOGRAPH		
☐ *LAKESIDE PHONOGRAPH (Cylinder). Sold by Montgomery Ward, oak case, plain style, plays 2- and 4-minute cylinder records, 14" horn with brass bell, rear horn crane.*	150.00	300.00
☐ *LAKESIDE PHONOGRAPH (Cylinder). Table model, inside horn.*	125.00	250.00
LANGUAGE PHONE		
☐ *LANGUAGE PHONE (See Columbia "Q" second series).*		
LANGUAGE PHONE COMPANY		
☐ *LANGUAGE PHONE COMPANY (Disc). Table model outside horn, rear mount horn bracket and tone arm, 8 petal Morning Glory horn, decal on front of case.*	750.00	1000.00
LARK PORTABLE		
☐ *LARK PORTABLE (Disc). Wood case, nickel plated metal parts.*	75.00	150.00
LIORET'S		
☐ *LIORET'S BEBE JUMEAU TALKING DOLL (Cylinder), c. 1897, celluloid on brass mandrel.*	275.00	475.00
MADAME HENDREN		
☐ *MADAME HENDREN TALKING DOLL (Cylinder). Child's Doll 26" long, stuffed cloth body, metal horn in chest is open and goes through to mechanism in back where cylinder record is placed, crank on right side of body, light blue celluloid type cylinders are 2" diameter by 1½" long and are interchangeable, name stamped on metal end of cylinder: "Averill Manufacturing Company, N.Y." Variety of children's tunes and verses were available all sounding like a little girl, e.g. "Mary Had a Little Lamb", "Now I Lay Me Down to Sleep".*	150.00	225.00
MAE STARR		
☐ *MAE STARR TALKING DOLL c. 1930's (Cylinder). Child's doll 29" long, 2" (2⅛") diameter celluloid cylinders, phonograph in the doll's back, horn grill in chest, wound with a handle, plays nursery rhymes.*	250.00	400.00
MARKSMAN PHONOGRAPH		
☐ *MARKSMAN PHONOGRAPH (Disc). Rear mount disc phonograph with cygnet type horn and Marksman Reproducer (European).*	300.00	400.00
McDONALD GRAPHOPHONE		
☐ *McDONALD GRAPHOPHONE (See Columbia Type AB).*		
MIGNONPHONE (Paris)		
☐ *MIGNONPHONE PORTABLE (Disc). Flat "box camera" type case, 8¾" x 5½" x 2¾", collapsible hexagonal cardboard horn, cloth covered octagonal reproducer will play both lateral and vertical cut records, 4⅜" turntable, crank wind.*	125.00	200.00

	Price Range	
MIKIPHONE		
☐ *MIKIPHONE POCKET PORTABLE c. 1924-25 (Disc). "Pocket Watch" style phonograph, black (celluloid) composition resonator, "Mikiphone" sound box, 4" diameter turntable, metal tone arm plays 1½" to 10" records, key wind.*	200.00	300.00
MIRAPHONE (Germany)		
☐ *MIRAPHONE (Disc). Outside horn phonograph, c. 1905, oak case, 7" turntable, green painted flowered horn, Exhibition reproducer (See also "Mira" listing in "Metal Disc Music Box" section).*	500.00	1000.00
MODERNOLA		
☐ *MODERNOLA PHONOGRAPH LAMP (Disc). Floor model disc phonograph with a fringed lamp coming out of the top of the console cabinet, walnut, decorated grill, highly embellished lampshade.*	750.00	1600.00
MUSIC MASTER		
☐ *MUSIC MASTER HORN. Mahogany, Morning Glory style, used on outside horn disc phonographs.*	200.00	300.00
ODEON TALKING MACHINE CO. (London, England)		
☐ *ODEON TALKING MACHINE CO. (Disc). Table model, simple case lines, base moulding, crank wind, brass belled horn, straight tone arm.*	400.00	500.00
OXFORD		
☐ *OXFORD JR. (See Columbia Type AQ Second Series).*		
OXFORD		
☐ *OXFORD TALKING MACHINE (Sears Roebuck) (See Columbia Type BVT).*		
PAILLARD PORTABLE		
☐ *PAILLARD PORTABLE c. 1920's (Disc). "Suitcase" style, spring wind, thin rectangular case.*	100.00	200.00
PARLOGRAPH		
☐ *PARLOGRAPH (Cylinder). Black metal painted case, 14" brass bell horn, name in large script gold letters on side of case.*	175.00	225.00
PARLOPHON (German)		
☐ *PARLOPHON (Disc). Table model outside horn, oak case, rear mounted horn bracket and tone arm, 30" long brass bell horn with 17½" bell, free standing column at the four corners of the case, wide column at the four corners of the case, wide base moulding, straight tone arm, crank wind, large single spring, 11¾" turntable.*	350.00	450.00
☐ *PARLOPHON (Disc). Table model, outside horn, Morning Glory horn (fluted, painted), rear mounted horn bracket and tone arm, crank wind, simple plain case style with wide base moulding, oak, 10" turntable.*	350.00	450.00

	Price Range	
☐ *PARLOPHON (Disc). Inside horn table model, simple straight case with cover over turntable, horizontal grill louvers, crank wind, mahogany, 11¼" turntable.*	**50.00**	**100.00**

PATHE (Paris, France).

☐ *PATHE (Disc Phonograph). Outside horn oak, (mahogany) table model, rear mount Morning Glory type ribbed horn painted, some case decoration (many variations), single spring, metal tone arm, 11" turntable.*	**400.00**	**750.00**
☐ *PATHE (Disc Phonograph). Inside horn, table model, simple case with cover, some decoration (many variations), metal tone arm, simple front grill, 11" turntable.*	**200.00**	**300.00**
☐ *PATHE ACTUELLE (Disc). Outside horn, disc table model, rear mount, tapering tone arm, simple case with some corner decoration, Morning Glory horn with gold decoration.*	**300.00**	**500.00**
☐ *PATHE "AIGLON" (Cylinder). Open works on flat metal base, "bent" wood oak cover with large decal, plays 2-minute was cylinders, key wind on right side, curved bell horn 27" long with 10" bell, table model.*	**225.00**	**325.00**
☐ *PATHE "CONCERT A" c. 1908-11 (Disc). Outside horn table model, single spring, speed regulator, brake lever, rear mounted horn support and tone arm connection, 11¼" turntable, highly decorated case and moulding, 12 petal (ribbed) Morning Glory horn (later known as "Majestik").*	**400.00**	**500.00**
☐ *PATHE COQUET (Cylinder). Simple walnut case, Orpheus attachment, bakelite reproducer and recorder, slip on Salon mandrel, aluminum horn, plays both 2" diameter and 4" diameter Salon cylinders, shallow cover.*	**450.00**	**650.00**
☐ *PATHE "DUPLEX" GRAND CONCERT (Cylinder). Simple oak case, carrying handles, small aluminum bell horn, plays both regular and Salon size cylinders, slightly smaller than the Concert Cylinder, Orpheus attachment.*	**225.00**	**450.00**
☐ *PATHE "ELF" c. 1915 (Disc). Table model, "horn" built into the cover of the machine and finished to match the oak case, the tone arm comes down from the center of the "horn", hand crank wind, simple lines.*	**225.00**	**325.00**
☐ *PATHE MODEL B (Disc). Table model, outside horn, simple case with base and top moulding, Reproducer attached to end of horn, 9¾" turntable, single spring, small ribbed horn supported by rod type horn support.*	**350.00**	**500.00**
☐ *PATHE "EXCELSIOR" (Cylinder). Walnut case and cover, double spring, slip on Salon mandrel.*	**275.00**	**350.00**
☐ *PATHE "REFLEX" c. 1912 (Disc). Oak table model, inside horn, disc phonograph, tone arm folds down from center of cover, the horn is in the cover as well, speed control (case variations, e.g. wood base with metal cover painted to simulate wood base).*	**250.00**	**300.00**
☐ *PATHE MODEL 175 (Disc). Inside horn, upright floor model, 12" turntable, turn over diaphram reproducer, mahogany, record storage compartment in base, 47½" high.*	**275.00**	**350.00**

Price Range

PETER PAN CAMERAPHONE

☐ *PETER PAN CAMERAPHONE c. 1924 (Disc). "Box Camera" style portable disc phonograph, goose neck tone arm, bellows horn in lid, leather covered case (variations in case covering).* **100.00 200.00**

PET-O-FONE

☐ *PET-O-FONE (Disc). "Box Camera" portable style.* **100.00 200.00**

PHONOGRAND

☐ *PHONOGRAND PHONOGRAPH c. 1920's (Disc). Floor model in shape of Baby Grand Piano, lid lifts up to reveal turntable, crank wind, case is almost 3' deep, 35" high.* **750.00 1250.00**

PHONOGRAPH DOLLS *(See Edison Talking Doll, Lioret's Bebe Jumeau, Madame Hendren).*

POLLY PHONOGRAPH CO. (New York)

☐ *POLLY PHONOGRAPH CO. c. 1922 (Disc). Flat portable with cover, paper folding horn, 9" turntable, tone arm, crank wind.* **50.00 125.00**

POLYPHONE TALKING MACHINE CO.

☐ *POLYPHONE CYLINDER PHONOGRAPH c. 1898 Simple oak case, cylinder phonograph with polyphone special attachment that allowed two reproducers each with their own small bell horn playing at the same time on one cylinder record. This produced an echo effect with a louder tone than one reproducer.* **750.00 1500.00**

T. Edison Co., Orange, NJ advertised this attachment with some of their models:

☐ *EDISON GEM with Polyphone attachment.* **400.00 600.00**

☐ *EDISON HOME with Polyphone attachment.* **475.00 675.00**

☐ *EDISON STANDARD with Polyphone attachment.* **450.00 650.00**

☐ *EDISON CONCERT with Polyphone attachment.* **2000.00 2750.00**

REGINA HEXAPHONE *(See Coin Operated Phonographs).*

REGINAPHONE

☐ *REGINAPHONE (Disc). Many outside and inside horn styles with disc music box and disc phonograph combination mechanisms. (See Disc Music Boxes - Regina for descriptions).*

SILVERTONE (Sears Roebuck Co.)

☐ *SILVERTONE c. 1914 (Disc). Table model, serpentine style case, oak, interesting fretwork grill, 10" turntable, two reproducers for lateral and vertical cut records.* **100.00 200.00**

SONORA DISC CONSOLE PHONOGRAPHS *c. 1920's.* Many period style variations were made and were quite expensive at the time.

☐ *"CANTERBURY", walnut or mahogany, nickel plated exposed parts, double spring, auto stop, storage for 60 records.* **150.00 250.00**

☐ *ISLINGTON disc floor model phonograph similar in style to the above but has no disc storage.* **100.00 200.00**

Talk-O-Phone,
"The Herbert," disc.

Sonora Inside Horn Console Disc Phonograph, with record storage.

	Price Range	
☐ *"LUZERNE", without storage, otherwise companion style case (English Renaissance case style quite similar with storage for 80 records).*	125.00	175.00
☐ *"NOTRE DAME" style, no storage for discs.*	175.00	225.00
☐ *SONORA DUNCAN PHYFE DELUXE "FULTON" style, mahogany (oak), triple spring, gold plated, tone modifier, automatic stop, stores 100 records, simple case lines with delicate trim decoration.*	200.00	300.00
☐ *SONORA GOTHIC DELUXE c. 1920's. "NORMANDY" console case style, walnut, triple spring, gold plated metal parts, automatic stop, storage for 80 records, gothic junior*	200.00	350.00
☐ *SONORA HEPPLEWHITE DELUXE "TRAYMORE", mahogany console with graceful delicate case decoration, basically simple case style, gold trim automatic stop, storage for 80 records.*	200.00	300.00
☐ *SONORA INVINCIBLE (Disc). Floor model, mahogany (or walnut) cabinet, 50" high, gold plated exposed metal parts and trim, 12" turntable, triple spring, plays 45 minutes on one winding, automatic stop, holds 80 records in base, curved (bowed) case lines, decorative corner details, fancy front speaker grill, front doors open to reveal record storage.*	275.00	350.00
☐ *SONORA ITALIAN RENAISSANCE "MILANO" style walnut case, turned legs, some case decoration, triple spring, gold plated, automatic stop, storage for 100 discs.*	275.00	400.00
☐ *SONORA MELODIE (Disc). Table model, 16" high, straight simple case style and grill, nickel plated trim, double spring, automatic stop, separate record cabinet with slightly curving corner decoration on legs, front doors open to reveal storage for 80 discs.*	75.00	125.00

SPRANGOPHONE (German)

☐ *SPRANGOPHONE PORTABLE (Disc). "Box Camera" style, oak case, 6½" x 5" x 7¼", telescopic tone arm, fixed into the lid, 4½" diameter turntable, crank wind.*	125.00	200.00

STANDARD TALKING MACHINE CO. (Related to Columbia Phonograph Co.)

☐ *STANDARD TALKING MACHINE c. 1903-05 (Disc). Small metal open works machine on wood base, 6¾" (7") turntable, all black bell horn, large spindle (9/16") requires special disc records with large hole made by Standard, metal front "tone arm" and horn brackets. (See also Columbia Type "AU").*	250.00	400.00
☐ *STANDARD TALKING MACHINE MODEL A c. 1902-05 (Disc). Oak table model, outside horn, disc phonograph, rear mount Morning Glory horn (red with gold lines), ½" (9/16") spindle for special standard discs, some case decoration.*	350.00	500.00
☐ *STANDARD TALKING MACHINE MODEL X c. 1902-10 (Disc). Outside horn, table model, disc phonograph, front mount Morning Glory style horn, 10" turntable, oak case, ½" (9/16") wide spindle for special standard discs. (Nickel ribbed horn).*	450.00	750.00

STUART PHONOGRAPH

☐ *STUART PHONOGRAPH (Disc). Table model, inside horn, round metal small case style with grill in base.*	75.00	125.00

Price Range

TALKING DOLLS *(See Edison Talking Doll, Lioret's Bebe Jumeau, Madame Hendren.)*

TALK-O-PHONE COMPANY *(Toledo, Ohio)*

☐ *TALK-O-PHONE "THE BROOKE" c. 1904 (Disc) Table model, oak case with decorative base moulding, nickel plated exposed metal parts, front mount brass bell horn (16" long), single spring, 10" turntable, exhibition concert TALK-O-PHONE reproducer, metal detachable front mount bracket, metal horn support "tone arm", brake and speed regulator. . .* **425.00** **575.00**

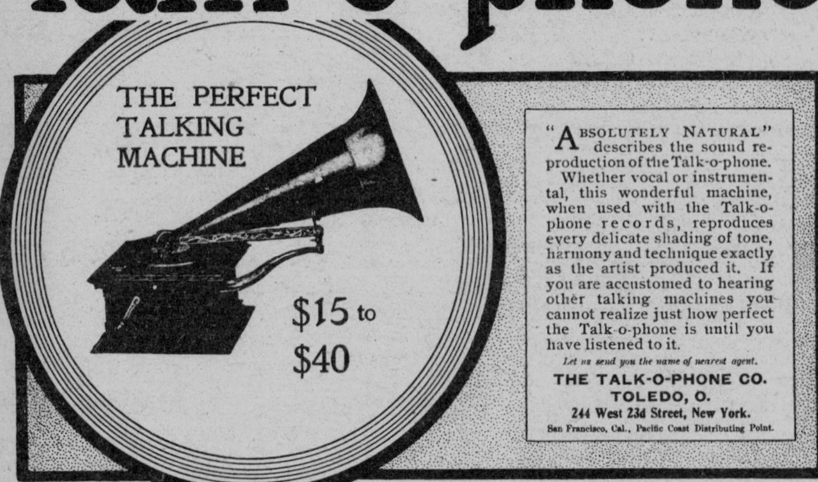

☐ *TALK-O-PHONE "THE CLARK" c. 1904 (Disc). Oak table model with beading decoration along top, bottom and sides of case, triple spring, 10" turntable, detachable metal front mount horn bracket and "tone arm" horn support for 30" steel horn with brass bell, Talk-O-Phone Exhibition Concert Reproducer, combination brake and speed regulator. . . . .* **425.00** **575.00**

☐ *TALK-O-PHONE "THE ENNIS" c. 1904 (Disc). Oak table model with base moulding and decorative corner carving, nickel plated exposed parts, double spring, 10" turntable, Talk-O-Phone Exhibition Concert Reproducer, 21" front mount horn with brass bell detachable metal front mount horn bracket and "tone arm" horn support, combination brake and speed regulator. . . . .* **425.00** **575.00**

Price Range

☐ *TALK-O-PHONE "THE HERBERT" c. 1904 (Disc). Simple oak case style, base moulding, front mount 16" horn with brass bell, detachable metal horn bracket and support, Talk-O-Phone Exhibition Concert Reproducer, single spring, 9" turntable, combination speed and brake regulator.* **425.00 525.00**

☐ *TALK-O-PHONE "THE SOUSA" c. 1904 (Disc). Oak table model, highly carved decoration on sides, nickel or gold plated exposed metal parts, triple spring, 10" turntable, Talk-O-Phone Exhibition Concert Reproducer, 30" horn with bell (all brass) detachable metal horn bracket and support, combination brake and speed regulator.* **500.00 650.00**

THORENS

☐ *THORENS "EXCELDA" c. 1930's (Disc). Portable phonograph in metal case made to look like Kodak Folding Camera, nickel plated metal parts, screw on nut holds disc in place (tiny turntable). Case comes in several colors: red, green, brown and black.* **150.00 275.00**

☐ *THORENS PORTABLE (Disc). Small rectangular box (somewhat like "box camera") 8¼" x 6" x 4", 6½" tone arm attaches inside of lid, trademark inside lid, 4¾" turntable, (another model with slightly larger model 8 ⅝" x 6½" x 5½").* **75.00 125.00**

☐ **THORNWARD CYLINDER PHONOGRAPH** *c. 1895 (Cylinder). Sold by Montgomery Ward, Made by Columbia.* **275.00 325.00**

VICTOR TALKING MACHINE CO. (Camden, NJ) *All Victor models were disc machines.*

☐ *VICTOR c. 1900 Eldridge R. Johnson (Toy). Hand crank, open works, simple mechanism, mounted on wood base, 7" turntable, top wind, small horn 10" metal no bell, horn rests on horn support, no "tone arm", reproducer attached at end of horn. Made for children with special 7" discs with children's tunes.* **250.00 350.00**

☐ *VICTOR TYPE A c. 1900 Eldridge Johnson. Simple metal mechanism mounted on wood base, spring wind top crank wind, 16" black metal bell horn, small turntable plays 7" and 10" discs, uses the Victor Standard (or Victor Concert) sound box reproducer, changeable steel needles, reproducer attached to horn at horn support bracket, wood and metal horn support.* **375.00 500.00**

☐ *VICTOR AUX-E-TO-PHONE (See Aux-E-To-Phone).*

☐ *VICTOR TYPE B c. 1900 Eldridge Johnson ("Trademark"). Oak case table model with some decorative trim moulding, top wind crank, metal and wood horn support, metal bell horn, Victor Standard (or Victor Concert) Reproducer (Eldridge Johnson Reproducer). This model was used in the "HIS MASTER'S VOICE" Trademark with the dog "Nipper". It is also like the Berliner Type A Gram-O-Phone. Plays 7" discs.* **1500.00 3000.00**

	Price Range	
☐ *VICTOR TYPE C c. 1900 Eldridge Johnson. Oak case, table model, decorative fluted corner columns, base and top mouldings, wood "tone arm", wood and metal horn support, reproducer attached to the end of the horn, Victor Standard (or Victor Concert) Reproducer, brass bell horn, crank on side, plays 7" and 10" discs. Another case design also identified as an Eldridge Johnson Model "C" has what appears to be a "Royal Type R" case with metal corner decorations but with a horn bracket support like the above Victor Model "C" c. 1900.*	**500.00**	**1500.00**
☐ *VICTOR TYPE D (Disc). c. 1893-1907. Table model, rear mount horn bracket, large oak case with decorative corner columns and base, 12" turntable, triple spring, tapering metal tone arm, Concert reproducer.*	**1500.00**	**1800.00**
☐ *VICTOR TYPE E c. 1901 (Monarch Junior). Oak case with fluted corner columns, metal horn bracket, belled horn, 7" turntable, slotted crank, Concert or Exhibition reproducer.*	**385.00**	**700.00**
☐ *Front mount horn bracket.*	**600.00**	**800.00**
☐ *Rear mount horn bracket.*	**475.00**	**675.00**
☐ *VICTOR JUNIOR c. 1910-11 (Toy). Oak case with simple moulding top and base, front mount Morning Glory horn (dark red with gold trim), decorative horn bracket support, combination brake and speed regulator, 8" turntable, plays all sizes of records.*	**285.00**	**385.00**
☐ *VICTOR MONARCH c. 1901. Table model with heavy base moulding, corner columns, 21" brass bell horn, 7" turntable, wood "tone arm", horn support and metal bracket, "Concert" reproducer attached at end of horn, plays 10" Monarch discs.*	**700.00**	**1500.00**
☐ *VICTOR "IMPROVED" MONARCH c. 1902. Oak table model with heavy base moulding, corner columns, 10" turntable, larger case than the "Special", brass bell horn, metal "tone arm".*	**450.00**	**600.00**
☐ *VICTOR MONARCH JUNIOR (See Victor Type E)*		
☐ *VICTOR MONARCH M c. 1902-03. Rear mount table model, oak case, fluted corner columns, decorative mouldings, slotted crank, double spring, black metal horn with brass bell, tapered tone arm.*	**700.00**	**1250.00**
☐ *VICTOR MONARCH SPECIAL TYPE MS c. 1901. Highly decorated table model, corner columns, 10" turntable, heavy spring motor, wood tone arm on metal front mount bracket, black metal brass bell horn, reproducer attached on end of horn.*	**750.00**	**1750.00**
☐ *VICTOR TYPE O c. 1907-08. Rear mount, plain case, threaded crank, 8" turntable, Morning Glory type horn, mahogany case, tapering tone arm, brake, speed regulator, single spring, Exhibition Reproducer, horn painted in amber shading 16" long.*	**450.00**	**675.00**
☐ *VICTOR TYPE P (Disc). c. 1902-1906. Table model, front mount horn bracket, hinged to wood tone arm, Concert reproducer, 10" turntable, single spring, oxidized copper hardware, 18" black horn with brass bell, simple oak case style.*	**550.00**	**750.00**

	Price Range	
☐ *VICTOR TYPE R c. 1901-02 ("ROYAL"). Front mount table model, black horn with brass bell, 7" turntable, wood "tone arm" support with metal bracket, simple case design with metal corner decoration, Exhibition or Concert Reproducer, 7" discs.*	**500.00**	**700.00**
☐ *VICTOR SCHOOL HOUSE VV — XXV Floor model, outside horn, golden oak case and horn, straight simple case design, nickel plated exposed metal parts, phonograph has a top cover and storage shelf underneath that folds up to make space to store horn, pull out writing tray, triple spring Exhibition Reproducer.*	**1250.00**	**1800.00**

Victor School House Disc Phonograph, floor model VV-XXV.

☐ *VICTOR I c. 1902-08. Plain oak case, 8" turntable, slotted crank, rear mount, Exhibition Reproducer, heavy base moulding, tapering arm, brake, speed control, fluted black horn with gold decoration (20" brass bell horn, oak horn) also Concert Reproducer (later examples had 10" turntable, Exhibition reproducer.*	**400.00**	**600.00**

	Price Range	
☐ *VICTOR II Plain oak case with heavy base moulding, rear mount ribbed horn (black with gold decoration) 23" long, Exhibition Reproducer, tapering tone arm, brake speed regulator, 10" turntable, single spring (also brass belled horn or oak wood horn).*	400.00	600.00
☐ *VICTOR III Oak case, fluted corner columns, heavy base moulding, Exhibition Reproducer, tapering tone arm, brake, speed regulator, 10" turntable, double spring, 23" long ribbed horn (black metal with gold decoration) rear mount. (Also brass belled horn, oak wood horn or flowered horn).*	650.00	1200.00
☐ *VICTOR IV Mahogany case with rounded corner columns, base and top moulding, rear mount 24" ribbed horn (black metal with gold decoration), tapering tone arm, brake, speed control, 10" turntable, heavy double spring, Exhibition Reproducer (also black tapered horn with brass bell, flowered horn or mahogany horn).*	750.00	1400.00
☐ *VICTOR V Oak case with corner columns, heavy base and top moulding, 12" turntable, triple spring, tapering tone arm, brake, speed control, Exhibition Reproducer, 26" black ribbed horn (flowered or oak horn).*	900.00	1500.00
☐ *VICTOR VI c. 1906. Mahogany case with fluted Corinthian corner columns, with carved capitals, gold decoration on columns, 14 karat triple gold plated Exhibition or Concert reproducer and tone arm, triple spring, 24" bell brass Morning Glory horn or mahogany horn, 12" turntable.*	1800.00	2700.00
☐ *VICTOR XXV (See Victor School House VV-XXV).*		
☐ *VICTOR VICTROLA (Disc). Floor model, inside horn, straight style case lines, storage for 10 albums arranged on each side and below centered speaker doors (doors are cut out forming an "L" shape around speaker doors, no grill over speaker, storage drawer in center bottom of cabinet, triple spring, gold plated exposed metal parts, Exhibition or Concert reproducer, 12" turntable, mahogany, maroon cloth covered record albums, 48" high, speed regulator (also came in several case finishes including painted decoration).*	200.00	250.00
☐ *VICTOR VICTROLA (VV-IV) Oak inside horn, table model, plain case, two front doors open to reveal louvered speaker, rear mount tone arm, Exhibition sound box (no cover), 10" turntable, single spring, metal parts nickel plated, brake, speed control.*	75.00	125.00
☐ *VICTROLA VI Oak, inside horn, table model, case essentially the same as IV, slightly larger with double spring.*	100.00	150.00
☐ *VICTROLA VIII Oak, inside horn, table model with cover and two doors in front covering louvered speaker, 10" turntable, Exhibition Reproducer, double spring, nickel plated metal parts.*	75.00	125.00
☐ *VICTROLA IX (VV-IX) Mahogany (oak), inside horn, table model with cover, two doors over speaker, double spring, 12" turntable, nickel plated Exhibition Reproducer (case variations).*	75.00	125.00

	Price Range	
☐ *VICTROLA X Mahogany, inside horn, table model (oak), with cover, some case decoration, tapered nickel plated tone arm, Exhibition Reproducer, two doors in front cover speaker, 12" turntable.*	**75.00**	**150.00**
☐ *VICTROLA X (Floor model). Mahogany (oak), inside horn, floor model on slightly curved legs with shelf for storage underneath, two doors cover speaker, nickel plated Exhibition Reproducer, double spring, all metal parts nickel plated, brake, speed regulator and indicator.*	**100.00**	**200.00**
☐ *VICTROLA XI Mahogany (oak), inside horn, table model with cover, decorative gold decoration on case, gold plated tone arm, reproducer and metal trim, heavy double spring, two doors in front cover louvered speaker, lock for cover.*	**75.00**	**150.00**

Victrola Disc Queen Anne Console, floor model.

	Price Range	
☐ *VICTROLA XI (Floor model). Mahogany (oak) floor model, inside horn with cover, plain case, 43" high, slightly curving corner mouldings down to legs, two doors over speaker, storage in base for records, nickel plated metal parts, Exhibition Reproducer, brake, speed regulator and indicator, double spring.*	100.00	200.00
☐ *VICTROLA XII Mahogany, inside horn, table model with cover, two small doors on front open to reveal louvered speaker, gold plated metal parts.*	75.00	125.00
☐ *VICTROLA XIV Mahogany (oak), inside horn, floor model, simple case lines, curved legs, gold plated (nickel plated) exposed metal parts, tapered tone arm, Exhibition Reproducer, trim, storage in base for 6 record albums holding 102 records, triple spring, 45" high, two doors cover front speaker.*	125.00	225.00
☐ *VICTROLA XVI (Floor model). Mahogany (oak, walnut) 50" high floor model, inside horn, cabinet with some case decoration along front corners (slightly carved with gold decoration), two doors cover speaker, storage in base for 14 Victor record albums for a total of 231 records, gold plated exposed metal parts, Exhibition Reproducer, triple spring, many case finishes including painted decorations.*	150.00	250.00
☐ *VICTROLA XVII (Disc) c. 1916. Floor model, triple spring motor, gold plated exposed metal parts, automatic speed indicator, Exhibition (Victor #2) reproducer, storage in base for 16 record albums (160 records), mahogany (oak painted, or walnut), slightly curved case lines, some decorative details.*	100.00	200.00
☐ *VICTROLA XVIII (Disc) c. 1915. Floor model, bowed front and sides, mahogany (walnut), triple spring (also electrified), fancy veneer work and decorative details, Exhibition reproducer, speed indicator, semiautomatic stop, 12" turntable, gold plated exposed metal parts, 48" high.*	150.00	250.00
☐ *VICTROLA XX (Disc) c. 1908. Floor model, very similar to Victor Victrola with additional elaborate case decoration, mahogany veneers with gilded applied decoration.*	250.00	325.00
☐ *VICTROLA MODEL #1-1 (Disc). Table model, inside horn, open turntable (no cover), mahogany case, very simple grill work over "horn", crank wind.*	75.00	150.00
☐ *VICTROLA MODEL #1-2 (Disc). Same as Victrola #1-1 except case painted with color decorations for children.*	85.00	150.00
☐ *VICTROLA MODEL #1-70 (Disc). Table model, inside horn rectangular cabinet 12½" high x 17½" wide x 14" deep, grill cloth over speaker ("horn"), mahogany with maple inlay, No. 4 reproducer, spring motor, crank wind.*	150.00	200.00
☐ *VICTROLA PORTABLE MODEL #2-30 (Disc). Rectangular "suitcase" style straight case, black cloth with nickel fittings, 7¾" high x 11¾" wide x 14" deep, storage for six 10" disc records, No. 4 reproducer, crank wind.*	75.00	125.00
☐ *VICTROLA PORTABLE MODEL #2-60 (Disc). Slightly larger case than #2-30 with "safety" record holder inside lid for 12 records, gold finished fittings inside and out, dark blue or brown textured cloth covered case.*	100.00	125.00

Victrola (X, XI, XII) Table Model inside Horn Disc Phonographs on record storage cabinets.

Victrola Model #300 Console Disc Phonograph with record storage.

	Price Range	
☐ *VICTROLA 125 (Disc). Floor model, inside horn, disc storage in base under phonograph, graceful case style and decorative details, two doors cover speaker ("horn"), mahogany (walnut), crank or electric. There were several models of similar case style.*	200.00	285.00
☐ *VICTROLA 130 Oak (mahogany), painted decoration, inside horn, floor model, Serpentine curved case style, some corner decorations, gold plated metal parts, storage in base, two doors cover speaker.*	300.00	400.00
☐ *VICTROLA 215 (Disc). Console floor model, mahogany case, turntable on right side, storage for record discs on left, Victrola #2 reproducer, replaceable needles, automatic brake, crank wind.*	150.00	200.00
☐ *VICTROLA 220 (Disc). Console floor model, lid on right lifts to reveal turntable, left side holds disc records, mahogany (oak, walnut) crank or electric.*	150.00	200.00
☐ *VICTROLA 300 (Disc). Console floor model, lid covering turntable in center of cabinet, center front doors open for speaker (inside "horn"), storage on each side of speaker, some case decoration, mahogany (also oak, walnut), crank or electric. There were several models similar in style to the Model 300.*	200.00	350.00
☐ *VICTROLA PERIOD CASE STYLE: Queen Anne stye, (Disc). Console cabinet, phonograph set in center of case, small double doors open to reveal louvered inside horn, long doors on right and left and compartment under phonograph allow for storage of many albums, "pear drop door pulls, cabriole leg" (many period styles similar to this with minor case variations).*	250.00	300.00

VICTOR ORTHOPHONIC PHONOGRAPH *was an acoustic system with improved tonal quality.*

☐ *ORTHOPHONIC VICTROLA 1-90 (Disc). Portable mahogany veneer with overlay rectangular mahogany table cabinet, grill cloth over speaker (inside "horn"), automatic stop without pre-setting, similar in appearance to the Victrola #1-70.*	200.00	250.00
☐ *ORTHOPHONIC VICTROLA 4-3 Console "Hepplewhite Colonial" style mahogany veneer, straight lines, some maple overlay, 36½" high and 19⅛" wide, automatic stop, holds 24 discs, plays 10 minutes on one winding of spring motor (also, Induction Disc or Universal Electric Motor).*	250.00	500.00
☐ *ORTHOPHONIC VICTROLA 4-7 Simple mahogany veneer console case in "Italian Renaissance" style, 38" high and 21¾" wide, automatic stop, holds 30 records, spring motor runs 10 minutes on one wind (also Induction Disc or Universal Electric Motor).*	225.00	325.00
☐ *ORTHOPHONIC VICTROLA 4-40 Console cabinet, simple case lines, mahogany veneer, raised panels, 37¾" high and 37" wide, tapered legs with stretchers, automatic stop, plays 10 minutes on one wind, holds 72 records (also Induction Disc or Universal Electric Motor).*	400.00	575.00

	Price Range	
☐ *ORTHOPHONIC VICTROLA 8-12 Console walnut veneer case on curved legs in "French Renaissance" style, 45" high and 30½" wide, some case decoration, automatic stop, holds 96 records, spring motor plays 20 minutes on one winding (also Induction Disc or Universal Electric Motor).*	400.00	550.00
☐ *ORTHOPHONIC VICTROLA 8-30 Console type cabinet in walnut (mahogany), Italian Renaissance decoration on low round feet, 46" high and 31" wide automatic stop, spring motor runs 20 minutes on one winding, storage for 80 records (also Induction Disc or Universal Electric Motor). Case variation came with tooled leather paneling.*	500.00	700.00
☐ *AUTOMATIC ORTHOPHONIC VICTROLA 1050 "French Renaissance" cabinet style in walnut veneer, highly decorative carving, gold plated, 48" wide and 49" high, changes its own records (12), automatic stop. Induction Disc or Universal Electric Motor.*	750.00	1500.00

WIZARD PHONOGRAPH

☐ *WIZARD PHONOGRAPH (Cylinder). Oak table model, plain case, the mechanism is attached to the underside of the cover, when flipped over and clamped down the whole mechanism is exposed, a horn elbow holds the Morning Glory horn in position. (Other examples have been identified by labels "Champion" and "Ellisdon").*	500.00	1000.00

ZON-O-PHONE *(Universal Talking Machine Co., NY)*

☐ *ZON-O-PHONE TYPE A c. 1899 (Disc). Table model, outside horn, oak case, corner columns, beveled glass sides on case, black metal horn with brass bell (or all brass horn), metal horn bracket support and "tone arm", front mounted horn.*	750.00	2000.00
☐ *ZON-O-PHONE TYPE B (Disc). Oak case table model with raised decorated side panels, corner columns, brass bell horn, metal horn bracket and "tone arm" horn support, "V" sound box, reproducer.*	400.00	800.00
☐ *ZON-O-PHONE TYPE C (Disc). Oak table model, some decoration, small raised turntable, base moulding, front horn bracket and support, "V" sound box, reproducer.*	400.00	750.00
☐ *ZON-O-PHONE TYPE D (Disc). Oak table model, simple case, front horn bracket and support, small turntable, "V" reproducer.*	400.00	750.00
☐ *ZON-O-PHONE "CHAMPION" c. 1910 (Disc). Table model, rear mount, oak case, double spring, tapering tone arm, ribbed brass horn.*	400.00	750.00
☐ *ZON-O-PHONE "CONCERT" (Disc). Table model, oak case, simple lines, tapering tone arm, 9" turntable, 27" Morning Glory horn (red, blue or green), double spring, rear mount.*	500.00	1000.00
☐ *ZON-O-PHONE "CONCERT GRAND" c. 1901-04 (Disc). Oak case, ornate front mount horn support, all brass belled horn, reproducer attached to horn at tapered end, 10" turntable.*	750.00	1250.00
☐ *ZON-O-PHONE "GRAND OPERA" (Disc). Table model oak case, rounded corner columns and heavy base moulding, triple spring, tapering tone arm (nickel plated), rear mount 27" wood ribbed horn, Morning Glory painted horn or brass horn, 10" turntable.*	650.00	1250.00

COIN OPERATED PHONOGRAPHS

CYLINDER AND MULTIRECORD PHONOGRAPHS

The "One-Record" coin operated cylinder phonograph was the first attempt at charging the public to hear a recorded voice. They were found largely in arcades and similar places. Later came multi-tune cylinder mechanisms, the Multiphone being a real forerunner of the jukebox.

Jukeboxes are coin operated disc phonographs with elaborate record changing devices that allow the listener to choose from several selections. Several companies made many case variations culminating in what was the "Classic Period" in case styles from 1939-1950. Few jukeboxes are still made today.

For information and history see "Further Reading" section. For sources see "Dealers and Restorers" and "Publications and Reprints" sections.

	Price Range	
☐ **AUTOPHONE** *c. 1912. Floor model 200, holds 12 Edison Blue Amberol records on a large wheel, one full winding will play all 12, console mahogany cabinet, front top panel folds down to expose the whole wheel mechanism, decorative grill in front under mechanism on curved legs.*	3500.00	4750.00

Columbia, Type BS, cylinder

	Price Range	
☐ **COLUMBIA TYPE AS** *c. 1897. Coin operated cylinder phonograph, one 2-minute cylinder plays on machine at a time, basically type "A" machine with curved glass top, hand crank, bottom of case drops down to reveal inner mechanism.*	1500.00	2500.00
☐ **COLUMBIA TYPE BS** *c. 1898. Coin operated "Eagle", with curved glass top, mechanism mounted on a board, horn attached at top outside, oak, ribbon decal, 2-minute cylinder record.*	1800.00	2500.00
☐ **COLUMBIA TYPE S** *(Cylinder). Table model phonograph, curved glass top cover, motor in cabinet below.*	2000.00	2500.00
☐ **COLUMBIA TYPE SG** *(Cylinder). Coin operated, curved glass cover on top, oak case, listening tubes, electrified.*	2250.00	3000.00
☐ **EDISON ACME** *Coin operated floor model cylinder phonograph, 46" high (with advertising sign, 72" high) operating on alternating electric current, oak, cabinet, square top fitted with beveled glass, top and three sides, mirror in back section, rubber hearing tubes or 24" horn with crane, some case decoration, Model "B" reproducer, Model "D" return attachment.*	2000.00	3250.00
☐ **EDISON AUTOMATIC PHONOGRAPH MODEL M** *(See Edison Model "M").*		
☐ **EDISON BIJOU** *c. 1901-08. Table model, plain Edison phonograph base cabinet with curved glass top cover over phonograph, coin operated, spring wind once coin is inserted, plays one 2-minute cylinder, Gem mechanism, 14" black bell horn attached outside top of glass, Model "B" reproducer, oak, "Bijou" decal on front base.*	1500.00	2000.00
☐ **EDISON CLASS M ELECTRIC** *(See Edison Model M).*		
☐ **EDISON CLIMAX** *c. 1901-03. Floor model with curved glass top covering phonograph mechanism, oak case, door in bottom, plays large Concert cylinder record, 24" brass horn and crane attached at top of glass cover, coin operated, hand crank, Model "B" reproducer (There are battery operated and electically wound versions, too).*	3000.00	4750.00
☐ **EDISON ECLIPSE** *Operates on 125 volt direct current, electrically controlled governor, otherwise description the same as for the "Acme".*	2500.00	3700.00
☐ **EDISON EXCELSIOR** *c. 1901-08. Table model, oak base cabinet with high curved glass cover over phonograph (Edison Standard mechanism), coin operated, 14" brass bell horn attached at top of glass cover, plays 2-minute cylinder record, spring wind after coin is inserted, "Excelsior" decal on base front of case, Model "B" reproducer, Model "D" return attachment.*	2750.00	3750.00
☐ **EDISON MODEL H ("Domestic")** *Table model coin operated phonograph (uses Edison "Home" mechanism), oak base with decorative moulding with a curved glass cover, plays 2-minute cylinder record, automatic reproducer.*	1250.00	1750.00

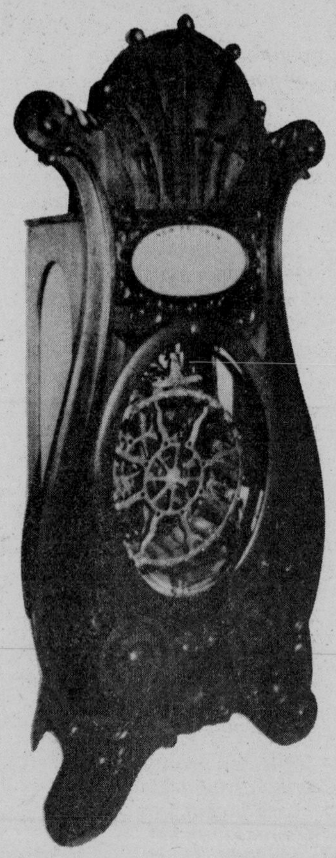

Multiphone Lyre, floor model.

	Price Range	
☐ **EDISON MODEL M COIN SLOT PHONOGRAPH** *Floor model 53" high, automatic reproducer plays 2-minute cylinder records, automatic coin slot, 2-volt battery operated, no winding necessary, oak case, curved glass top section, case decoration, 24" brass horn attached by elbow and support on the top of glass top.*	2250.00	4250.00
☐ **EDISON MODEL E COIN SLOT PHONOGRAPH** *The same as above only electric motor wound on direct current — 110-120 volt.*	2500.00	5000.00
☐ **EDISON MODEL M CONCERT COIN OPERATED PHONOGRAPH** *Same as model "M" above but plays 5" diameter concert cylinder records. (Model "E" Concert same difference as above).*	3500.00	6000.00
☐ **EDISON STANDARD,** *Suitcase style, mahogany table model with curved glass cover, coin operated.*	1500.00	2500.00

	Price Range	
☐ **EDISON WINDSOR** *Operates on a two-volt battery, governor electrically controlled, otherwise description is the same as for the "Acme".*	2500.00	3700.00
☐ **MANHATTAN PHONOGRAPH CO., (NY)** *Coin operated one cylinder phonograph (similar to Edison Excelsior), oak case on cast iron curved legs, sign on top.*	2750.00	3250.00
☐ **MULTIPHONE (Kalamazoo, MI)** *c. 1900. Tall rectangular case of simple lines with large brass horn extending out of top, on legs, oak case, 24 2-minute cylinders on a wheel, hand crank tune selector, coin operated, large glass front exposing record, some case decoration, fluted columns on sides (Case variations).*	4000.00	6000.00
☐ **MULTIPHONE "LYRE"** *c. 1905-08. Large floor model, decorative lyre shaped case, speaker on top, carvings and mouldings (very impressive appearance), 24 cylinders on a large wheel, large oval glass front panel to view the wheel, coin operated, spring motor crank.*	6000.00	8900.00
☐ **MULTIPHONE** *c. 1913. Tall thin basically rectangular case 6'2½" high, plays 12 cylinders on a revolving mechanism (4-minute cylinders), coin operated, long glass viewing panels, some decorative fretwork and moulding on case top.*	5000.00	10,000.00
☐ **REGINA HEXAPHONE** *c. 1909-21. Console cabinet, oak, wood horn in front section of cabinet open, tilted glass top covering phonograph mechanism, large mandrel 6 selections, 4-minute cylinder records, coin operated, diamond stylus reproducer (several case style variations over a 10-year period).*	4500.00	6500.00
☐ **ROSENFIELD AUTOMATIC TALKING MACHINE** *Columbia "AZ" works, simple rectangular case on feet, square glass top and sides cover the phonograph mechanism, electric motor winds the main spring after each play, one 2-minute cylinder, lyric reproducer, nickel play.*	2000.00	3500.00

JUKEBOXES

AUTOMATIC MUSICAL INSTRUMENT CO.

☐ *AMI MODEL A c. 1946-8. 40 tune selections, large case with a lot of plastic, "Mother of Plastic", window in center front to view record mechanism, grill on top lights up different colors, "jewels" in metal sitting down front.*	1250.00	2500.00
☐ *AMI MODEL B c. 1947-49. 40 tune selections, large case, grill front, tune card in top front panel, large crown top plastic, plastic side panels, metal trim, simple lines, actually holds 20 records but has flipping device so both sides can be played, color wheel in upper case.*	900.00	1800.00
☐ *AMI MODEL C.*	800.00	1400.00

	Price Range	
☐ *AMI MODEL FR c. 1932. Simple wood case in an art deco style, 20 tunes, top glass panel is record mechanism and tune cards.*	300.00	400.00
☐ *AMI "SINGING TOWER" c. 1941. 10 tunes, 78rpm, 6' high, looks like an art deco skyscraper, colored panels with pressed designs, lights behind.*	2500.00	3000.00
☐ *AMI "STREAMLINER" c. late 1930's. 20 tune selections, narrow glass panel near top to view mechanism, colored plastic along corners and top, decorative metal grill, lights up.*	350.00	500.00
☐ *AMI "TOP FLIGHT" c. 1936. 20 tune selections, straight rectangular case, metal trim, rounded speaker opening, lights up.*	400.00	750.00
CAPEHART		
☐ *CAPEHART DELUXE c. 1930's. Two horizontal record stacks, automatic changer.*	500.00	1000.00
☐ *CAPEHART JUKEBOX Early example, oak rectangular cabinet, some decoration but basically simple case, large three part glass panel in top speaker with decorative grill in base.*	500.00	750.00
CARRYOLA *(Allen H. Carryola Co., Milwaukee, WI)*		
☐ *CARRYOLA "CABARET" JUKEBOX c. 1930's. Coin operated, electrically amplified, 3'6½" high wood case, large front grill, top lifts to reveal turntable.*	700.00	1000.00
FILBEN		
☐ *FILBEN "MAESTRO" c. 1940's. 30 tune selections, push buttons, very space age design, long front aluminum metal grill looks like a locomotive, orange plastic top, front panels, metal trim.*	1000.00	1500.00
GABEL'S		
☐ *GABEL'S CHARME c. 1936. All wood rectangular case, 18 tune selections, selection dial, some case decoration, tune cards inside clear glass window.*	275.00	500.00
☐ *GABEL'S JR. Simple rectangular case, case decoration, beveled glass panels on top to view mechanism, grill in front.*	250.00	500.00
MILLS NOVELTY CO.		
☐ *MILLS AUTOMATIC PHONOGRAPH 12 disc "Ferris Wheel" record changer mechanism (10" size disc), 61" high burled walnut case, simple rectangular case, some decorative case details on legs, two glass panels in top front to view "Ferris Wheel", selector dial tune cards.*	650.00	1300.00
☐ *MILLS "EMPRESS" MODEL 910 c. 1939. 20 tune selections, push buttons, small glass panel to view tune cards, large decorative metal front section, large rounded case corners, orange plastic panels, mechanism unusual in that the rack moves to the record position but the changer remains stationary, lights up.*	1250.00	1750.00

	Price Range	
☐ *MILLS JUKEBOX early 1930's. 12 selections (78rpm), arranged in a "Ferris Wheel" effect, wood case, some decoration, fluted columns on sides, dial tune selector, volume control, doors open on front top of case, speaker grill in bottom. (Many case variations).*	500.00	1250.00
☐ *MILLS "THRONE OF MUSIC" 20 tune selections, push buttons, large orange plastic panels, wood trim and base (similar in appearance to "Empress"), tune selections behind small glass panel in front top, lights up.*	1000.00	1500.00

PACKARD

☐ *PACKARD "MANHATTAN" c. 1946. Burled wood cabinet, "cylinder" front edged window, glass window panel, 24 tunes, chromed mechanism, large front open grill design. Tune selection cards on revolving wheel on top, open fretwork decoration.*	750.00	1250.00
☐ *PACKARD PLA-MOR (CAPEHART) 24 selections, plastic and wood, large viewing window in top front to view mechanism, decorative grill in base, tune selection cards on top on a wheel, plastic on top and sides, coin mechanism in top center.*	750.00	1500.00

ROCK-OLA *(Arranged Alphabetically by Model Name)*

☐ *ROCK-OLA "COMET" c. 1953. 120 selections, modern case design, curved glass top section, multi colored base side panels, compact console model.*	1000.00	1500.00
☐ *ROCK-OLA "COMMANDO c. 1942. High wood case, no viewing window, large glass panels along sides and top, 20 tune selections, smaller panels (plastic) in base.*	1000.00	1500.00
☐ *ROCK-OLA "FIREBALL" MODEL 1436 c. 1950's. 120 selections, push button, wood case, dome glass top, colored plastic panels on front corners.*	1000.00	1500.00
☐ *ROCK-OLA "LUXURY LIGHT-UP" 20 tune selections, large rounded corners case, orange and green plastic panels throughout front of case, push button tune selector in center of front, tune cards just under the plastic panel, decorative grill panel and trim.*	2000.00	2500.00
☐ *ROCK-OLA "LUXURY LIGHT-UP SUPER" c. 1939. 20 tune selections, simpler case style than "Luxury Light-up", large plastic panels, rounded case, metal grill in center, two vertical panels, tune selections and push buttons, mechanism cannot be seen.*	1850.00	2750.00
☐ *ROCK-OLA "MONARCH" c. 1938. 20 tune selections, push button panel in center of case, clear viewing window to see record mechanism, two-tone wood case, metal grill.*	500.00	750.00
☐ *ROCK-OLA "MULTI-SELECTOR" c. 1935. 12 tune selections, clear glass, top front panel to view mechanism, push button tune selection, simple wood case and front grill (walnut).*	400.00	750.00
☐ *ROCK-OLA "RHYTHM KING" c. 1937. 12 tune selections, wood case (walnut), simple style, decorative grill, push buttons, viewing window.*	720.00	1250.00

Rock-Ola,
style #1422,
"Magic Glo,"
c. 1946.

Rock-Ola,
style #1426,
"Classic Style,"
c. 1947.

	Price Range	
☐ *ROCK-OLA "ROCKET" MODEL 1434 early 1950's. 50 tune selections, push button, simple grill, colored panels, dome top covers record mechanism, colored corner panels.*	**500.00**	**1250.00**
☐ *ROCK-OLA "COMMANDO", c. 1942. High wood case, no viewing window, large glass panels along sides and top, 20 tune selections, smaller panels (plastic) in base.*	**1000.00**	**1500.00**
☐ *ROCK-OLA "SPECTRAVOX", 1941. 7' high, golden bowl on top with lights.*	**1000.00**	**2000.00**
☐ *ROCK-OLA STYLE 1422, "MAGIC GLO" c 1946. Center front grill of wood, fluted plastic panels on sides and top, multi-colored, first in the series, see also 422 and 1426.*	**1200.00**	**2000.00**
☐ *ROCK-OLA STYLE 1426 c. 1947. 20 tune, "Classic Style", push buttons, revolving lights, large front metal grill work, plastic behind grill and around top and sides, speaker in bottom, viewing window, wood case (1422).*	**1600.00**	**2250.00**
☐ *ROCK-OLA STYLE 1428. Same basic lines of 1422 and 1426. Fluted side and center plastic panels with raised patterns, decorative chrome trim, patterned front grill, wood case, viewing window.*	**1700.00**	**2250.00**

SEEBURG *(Arranged Alphabetically)*

☐ *SEEBURG early model c. 1934. 10 tune selections, very simple rectangular case, clear glass panel to view records, tune cards, selector dial.*	**350.00**	**500.00**
☐ *SEEBURG AUDIOPHONE c. 1928. 8 disc records, plain rectangular case, oval glass opening on top front to view mechanism and discs, "Ferris Wheel" type mechanism with 8 turntables (one for each disc as it comes into play), speaker on door in front.*	**400.00**	**750.00**
☐ *SEEBURG AUDIOPHONE MODEL E c. 1931. Wood case with decorative grill over speaker in base, selector dial, tune cards inside glass panel.*	**350.00**	**500.00**
☐ *SEEBURG AUDIOPHONE SENIOR c. 1928. 8 disc selections, rectangular wood case, decorative grills over speakers on either side of glass panel on top, mouldings on bottom of case, small glass panel on top front to view records, tune cards over panel, selector dial.*	**350.00**	**500.00**
☐ *SEEBURG "COMMANDER" c. 1940. 20 selections, "Space Age" 1930's look, plastic front, sides, top, decorative trim mouldings, button next to each tune card.*	**750.00**	**1500.00**
☐ *SEEBURG "ENVOY" c. 1940's. Hidden mechanism, large red panels at sides and top, alot of wood trim, decorated panels, 20 tune selections.*	**1000.00**	**1250.00**
☐ *SEEBURG "HI TONE" WW II Unusual case style, rounded simple lines, tune card selection area slopes down, rounded speaker enclosure above, mechanism in base, lighted columns, revolving color wheel, science fiction robot shape and appearance, wood and plastic.*	**400.00**	**800.00**
☐ *SEEBURG P146.*	**800.00**	**1200.00**

	Price Range	
☐ *SEEBURG P147 P148 c. 1947. 20 tune selections, "Washing Machine" rounded shape, tapering slightly down, plastic top, wood with plastic panels on sides, large decorative grill on front.*	750.00	1200.00
☐ *SEEBURG SYMPHONOLA c. 1936. 12 tune selections, selector dial, (case variations), decorative grill, rectangular wood case, simple lines, glass window to view mechanism.*	500.00	1250.00
☐ *SEEBURG "SYMPHONOLA CLASSIC" c. 1938. 20 tune selections, push button, mainly wood and red plastic panels in front and top corners, decorative trim, lights up.*	500.00	1000.00
☐ *SEEBURG "SYMPHONOLA REGAL" c. 1940. 20 tune selections with push buttons, rounded sides and top, orange plastic panels along corners and top, tune cards in top, (no viewing of mechanism), wood case and trim, green plastic on front grill area.*	1000.00	1500.00
☐ *SEEBURG MODEL 9800, c. 1940's. Rounded shape with "tower" effect on top, plastic panels, front panel lighted to give multi color effect, hidden mechanism.*	750.00	1000.00
WURLITZER *(Arranged by Model Number)*		
☐ *WURLITZER MODEL P 10 c. 1934. 10 selections, rectangular wooden case, simple lines, glass window to view record changer mechanism, tune selector dial, simple front grill on bottom, early version of "Simplex".*	250.00	500.00
☐ *WURLITZER MODEL P 12 c. 1935. 12 tunes, similar to style P 10, front speaker grill larger with decorative fretwork, tune selector dial.*	250.00	500.00
☐ *WURLITZER MODEL P 20 c. 1934. 10 selections, slight case difference, otherwise very like P 12.*	250.00	500.00
☐ *WURLITZER MODEL 24 c. 1938. 24 tunes, floor model, art deco style, tune selector dial in center with tune cards on either side under glass viewing panel.*	250.00	500.00
☐ *WURLITZER MODEL P 30 c. 1935. 12 tune selections, simple wood case, art deco lines, decorative grill, tune selector dial.*	300.00	400.00
☐ *WURLITZER MODEL 35 c. 1930's. 12 tune selections, more elaborate walnut case, art deco style, clear glass front window to view mechanism.*	350.00	500.00
☐ *WURLITZER COUNTER MODEL 41 c. 1940. 12 tune selections, metal and wood veneer trim, rounded case style, plastic sides, some on top front, small open window to view record.*	1000.00	2250.00
☐ *WURLITZER MODEL 50 c. 1937. 12 tune selections, floor model, simple rectangular lines, wood case, glass window to view mechanism (changer), oval shaped grill in base with decorative fretwork, push button tune selector.*	300.00	475.00
☐ *WURLITZER COUNTER MODEL 51 c. 1937. 12 tune selections, push buttons, very modernistic wood case, rectangular with speaker on left side and small glass panel on right.*	500.00	750.00
☐ *WURLITZER COUNTER MODEL 61 c. 1938-39. 12 tune selection, wood base and sides, some plastic and metal decoration (came with matching floor stand).*	1000.00	2000.00

	Price Range	
☐ *WURLITZER COUNTER MODEL 71 c. 1940-41. 12 tune selections, graceful decoration of metal and plastic sides, front and top, larger than Style 41, wood areas.*	**1250.00**	**3000.00**
☐ *WURLITZER COUNTER MODEL 81 c. 1940's. 12 tune selections, wood base and sides, curving plastic panels, graceful front grill, small viewing window with tune selection cards, push buttons directly under window.*	**1000.00**	**2000.00**
☐ *WURLITZER MODEL 312 c. 1936. 12 tune selections, early.*	**275.00**	**400.00**
☐ *WURLITZER SIMPLEX "MODERNISTIC" 316 c. late 1930's. 16 tune selections, case mainly wood with fluted plastic front-side panels, tune selection dial, clear glass front panel to view record mechanism.*	**500.00**	**750.00**
☐ *WURLITZER (P) 400 c. 1935-36. Similar in design to the P-12, rectangular wood case, simple lines, dial indicator, glass viewing window, tune cards inside window, simple decorative grill over speaker.*	**275.00**	**400.00**
☐ *WURLITZER MODEL 412 c. 1936. 12 tune selections 78rpm, early.*	**750.00**	**1600.00**
☐ *WURLITZER MODEL 416 mid 1930's. 16 tune selections, simple wood case, tune selector dial, rounded front corner columns, decorative front grill over speaker.*	**350.00**	**450.00**
☐ *WURLITZER MODEL 500 c. 1938-39. 24 selections, very similar case design to Model 600, plastic panels on corners, front and along sides of grill, decorative grill, push buttons, wood case.*	**750.00**	**1750.00**
☐ *WURLITZER MODEL 600 c. 1938-39. 24 selections, rectangular case, plastic panels, top, front corners, sides and on either side of metal grill, wood case, tune indicator dial in center front, clear glass front panel to view tune cards and record mechanism.*	**1000.00**	**2000.00**
☐ *WURLITZER MODEL 616 SIMPLEX c. late 1930's. 16 tune selections, wood case, rounded rectangular style, simple lines, clear glass top front viewing panel, tune selector dial, decorative grill, tune cards on top of case above viewing window.*	**750.00**	**1750.00**
☐ *WURLITZER MODEL 616A c. late 1930's. 12 tune, walnut case, rounded simple lines, art deco feeling, viewing window tune cards on top above window, tune selector dial.*	**250.00**	**450.00**
☐ *WURLITZER MODEL 700 c. 1940. 24 selections, wood case, plastic panels on front corners and top, push button tune selections, decorative metal grill.*	**1000.00**	**2500.00**
☐ *WURLITZER SIMPLEX "MODERNISTIC" 716 c. 1937. 16 tune selections, multi color wood case, simple lines in art deco style, tune selector dial, clear glass viewing window to see record mechanism (some variation in case design).*	**400.00**	**600.00**
☐ *WURLITZER MODEL 750 c. 1937-40's. "Classic Style" 24 tune selections, large rounded case style, plastic panels down sides, up and around front top of case, large oval center section of case contains half circle glass panel on top to view record mechanism and tune cards, push buttons directly under viewing panel, coin mechanism in center of case, decorative speaker grill in base.*	**2000.00**	**3250.00**

	Price Range	
☐ *WURLITZER MODEL 780 c. 1941. 24 tune selections, "Colonial Style" model, decorative moulding on side (corner), front panels and grill, push button tune selector, viewing windows.*	500.00	700.00
☐ *WURLITZER MODEL 800 c. 1940. 24 selections, wood trim and base, large orange and red plastic corner sides and top panels, decorative grill, clear glass panel to view mechanism and tune selections, lights up, wood case.*	1500.00	3000.00
☐ *WURLITZER MODEL 840 "PEACOCK" c. 1941. "Classic Style", 24 tune selections, highly styled case, large plastic panel along rounded side corners and up around top front of case, center panel "peacock" design, stylized grill section U-shaped around "peacock" panel, half circle glass viewing panel on top, tune selector cards in rows under glass panel, push buttons, lights up, wood case.*	5000.00	7000.00
☐ *WURLITZER MODEL 850, "PEACOCK". Polarized film unit created prism effect behind plastic panels (looks like Model 840).*	4750.00	6750.00
☐ *WURLITZER MODEL 850A c. 1941.*	4750.00	6750.00
☐ *WURLITZER MODEL 950 c. 1942. "Classic Model", 24 tune selections, curved top, large corner plastic panels, also on top front and sides of speaker, grill decorated with art deco motifs of animals and satyrs, half circle glass panel on top to view record mechanism, tune cards and buttons just below window, wood sides and base.*	7000.00	11,000.00
☐ *WURLITZER "VICTORY" c. 1942-43. 24 selections, distinctive design, wood case with angular straight lines on top, decorated multi-colored glass panels along front top and down front sides with musical instruments, harlequins, etc., small half circle viewing window, push buttons, decorative grill with colored panels behind.*	2000.00	2750.00
☐ *WURLITZER MODEL 1015 c. 1946-47. 24 tune selections, "Classic Style", revolving lights in plastic "bubble tubes" all around top front and down front sides of case, U-shaped plastic tubes in middle around decorative grill half circle viewing window in top front of case, tune cards with push buttons just under glass viewing window, metal trim.*	3500.00	6500.00
☐ *WURLITZER MODEL 1050 c. 1974. Nostalgia model, 100 tune selections, similar in style to the 1015 "Classic Style", this model turns up in sales with older models but it does not really compare in design quality at all.*	2000.00	4000.00
☐ *WURLITZER MODEL 1080 c. 1947-49. 24 tune selections, "Classic Model", graceful curving contours with decorated mirrored panels along front sides and around top, large lyre shaped grill, glass panel to view mechanism, tune selection cards in front above speaker grill.*	4000.00	5750.00
☐ *WURLITZER MODEL 1080A c. 1946. "Colonial", lyre grill.*	3000.00	4000.00

	Price Range	
☐ *WURLITZER MODEL 1100 c. 1948-49. 24 tune selections, space age look, large pointed half dome top provides full view of record mechanism, tune selection push buttons, tune cards are on a roller type mechanism with 8 cards showing at one time, swirl design large front side panels with multi-colors, metal grill with decorative grate on bottom.*	2250.00	3500.00
☐ *WURLITZER MODEL 1200 (See Model 1100).*		
☐ *WURLITZER MODEL 1250 c. 1950. 48 tune selections, wood case rounded top clear plastic dome, decorative multi-colored panels along front sides of speaker, metal grill, push buttons.*	1000.00	1750.00
☐ *WURLITZER MODEL 1400 c. 1951-52. 48 selections, can play 45, 78 and 33⅓rpm discs, see also Model 1450.*	750.00	1750.00
☐ *WURLITZER MODEL 1450 c. 1951-52. 48 tune selections, push buttons, dome top to view mechanism, wood case, multi-colored front panels, decorative metal grill.*	500.00	1000.00
☐ *WURLITZER MODEL 1500 c. 1952. 104 tune selections, wood case, rounded top to view mechanism, colored corner front panels, push buttons, twin stacks of discs, either 78, 45 or 33⅓rpm.*	400.00	750.00
☐ *WURLITZER MODEL 1600. 48 selections, simple lines, large dome top, push buttons, 78rpm (Model 1650 looks the same).*	500.00	750.00
☐ *WURLITZER MODEL 1700.*	750.00	1100.00
☐ *WURLITZER MODEL 1800.*	750.00	1100.00
☐ *WURLITZER MODEL 1900.*	750.00	1100.00
☐ *WURLITZER "AMBASSADOR" c. 1947. Cosmetic change in Model 1015. No bubble tubes, large red curved top plastic multi-tone side panels, red U-shaped center panels, window to view mechanism, 24 tune selections.*	2000.00	3000.00

PIANOS (SELF PLAYING)

The Push-Up Piano Player came into general prominence in the 1890's. By the early 1900's the Player Piano (inner player) took over the industry. Between the turn of the century and the early 1930's there were literally hundreds if not thousands of piano companies in this country. Quite a number of them ventured into the player piano field. Some companies made their own player mechanism for their own pianos exclusively. Most used player mechanism for their own pianos exclusively. Most used player mechanisms made by companies specializing in the field. The Standard Pneumatic Action Co. and The Simplex Player Action Co. are two well-known examples.

The player piano is a self-playing piano that uses suction which is controlled by a paper roll passing over a tracker bar to activate valves and then pneumatics (little bellows), which operate on the piano action, cause the notes to play. This type of mechanism was made by many companies. The original concept was made in a separate cabinet unit. The push-up piano player mechanism was housed in a free-standing floor cabinet which sat in front of the keyboard of a regular piano and when a roll was inserted and the player was foot pumped, the mechanism acted upon the tops of the keys like little fingers.

While the regular player piano produces its music with basically the same degree of force and volume, the reproducing expression piano has a much more elaborate mechanism which produces a human-like master performance, by varying the amount of suction and thereby causing the notes to play louder and softer.

The three reproducing mechanism which dominated the field through the 1930's are: Welte-Mignon, Duo-Art and Ampico. Welte produced push-up players as well.

Except for early foot pumped transitional models, the reproducing players were built with electric motors.

When sales in pianos and players began to decline in the 1920's, companies were bought up and consolidated into other companies. This has led to some confusion over the years. Needless to say only a handful of companies still exist from those days.

THE FOLLOWING COMPILATION IS AN EFFORT TO IDENTIFY SOME OF THE BETTER KNOWN COMPANY NAMES AND INDICATE WHAT TYPE OF PLAYER MECHANISM WAS USED IN THEIR PIANOS.

WHEN EVALUATING A PLAYER OR REPRODUCING EXPRESSION PIANO THE MAIN POINTS ARE:

1. The overall reputation of the piano company.
2. The type of player mechanism used in the piano.
3. Related to #2 is whether the piano and player mechanism have been expertly restored and how well it plays.

It must be noted here that it is quite rare that one comes upon a player in "original unrestored" condition, that is to say, playing as it was meant to. Time and temperature have dried and worn it out. Most require restoration.

4. Case styles — while most players, especially upright models, are basically straight simple styles in mahogany or oak, there are many exceptions. When a piano has an "art case", it is decorated with fancy mouldings, carvings, inlay or veneer work, or all of these. The more elaborate, the more valuable There are more examples of this in the reproducing pianos than the reguar players. (For specific examples see "Reproducing Expression Pianos".)

For history and detailed information see "Further Reading" section.

In some parts of the U.S.A. more than others, players are still quite common. House sales, antique shops, local auctions are all good sources. (See "Dealers and Restorers".)

PUSH-UP PIANO PLAYERS

	Unrestored	Restored
☐ **AEOLIAN** *65-note Push-Up Player, some case decoration.*	250.00	1000.00
☐ **AEOLIAN METROSTYLE PIANOLA** *65-note Push-Up Player.*	150.00	1250.00
☐ **AEOLIAN METROSTYLE-THEMODIST** *Push-Up Piano, 65-note and 88-note combination player.*	750.00	1500.00-2500.00
☐ **AEOLIAN STECK** *65-note Push-Up Player.*	250.00	1000.00
☐ **ANGELUS** *Push-Up Player, 65-note, some case decoration.*	250.00-500.00	1750.00-2750.00
☐ **ANGELUS REED ORGAN** *Push-Up Player.*	300.00	1000.00
☐ **APPOLLO** *58-note, auto rewind, made by Clark.*	250.00	1000.00
☐ **ARTEMIS (Krell)** *65-note Push-Up Player.*	275.00	1250.00

	Unrestored	Restored
☐ **CECILLIAN Push-Up Player,** *65-note, paneled case in ebony finish, foot pump, plays Cecillian rolls and has an adaptor for regular 65-note rolls.*	200.00-250.00	1350.00-2000.00
☐ **CHASE AND BAKER** *65-note Push-Up Player.*	250.00	1000.00
☐ **HUPFELD** *65-note Push-Up Player.*	500.00	1250.00
☐ **KRELL,** *Auto Push-Up Player, 65-note, foot pump, simple case decoration, c. 1900-05.*	225.00-300.00	1250.00-2000.00
☐ **ROTH AND ENGLEHARDT** *Piano Player, mahogany case with some decoration, 35" high.*	200.00-250.00	1350.00-1950.00
☐ **SIMPLEX** *(early) Push-Up Player, rosewood, fluted legs.*	250.00	1250.00
☐ **STERLING CABINET PLAYER** *oak console.*	250.00	1250.00
☐ **WELTE-MIGNON VORSETZER,** *Push-Up Player, Cabinet on legs.*	1200.00	2750.00
☐ **WELTE-MIGNON VORSETZER** *Push-Up Player, console, "Red" Welte Rolls.*	1500.00	2750.00
☐ **WELTE VORSETZER** *"Red Welte", push-up player, simple cabinet, style down to floor, factory painted, raised border panel decoration.*	1000.00-1500.00	2500.00-3000.00
☐ **WILCOX & WHITE, ANGELUS** *65-note (with reeds), Push-Up Player.*	300.00	1000.00
☐ **WILCOX & WHITE** *Push-Up Player, 65-note, with two ranks of organ reeds.*	200.00-350.00	1000.00-2250.00

Many 65-note push-up players use special 65-note player rolls (with pin ends). These rolls were made by Aeolian, Angelus, Universal, Connorized, Chase and Baker, and others. The musical selections were somewhat limited and they cannot be played on regular 88-note players.

PLAYER PIANOS

Unless otherwise described the values given are for upright regular player pianos.

	Unrestored	Restored
☐ **ACKERMAN AND LOWE PIANO CO. (OH)** *Used foot pump regular player mechanism made by AMPHION.*	250.00	2500.00

ADAPTO *Player mechanism used in upright pianos made by the LINDENBERG PIANO CO. (Columbus, OH).*

	Unrestored	Restored
☐ **ADLER MANUFACTURING CO. (Louisville, KY)** *Used the Amphion Player mechanism.*	250.00	2500.00-3000.00

☐ **AEOLIAN COMPANY (NY) and the AEOLIAN WEBER PIANO & PIANOLA CO. (NY)** *Controlled the production of the Pianola Players, Duo Art Reproducing Player mechanism and the following piano companies: Weber, George Steck & Co., Wheelock, Stuyvesant, Chilton, Technola and others. They produced players known as the Weber Pianola, George Steck*

	Unrestored	Restored
Pianola, Wheelock Pianola, Stuyvesant Pianola, and Stroud Pianola. They also manufactured the Aeolian Orchestrelle and the Aeolian Pipe Organ, and controlled the Melodee and Universal Music Companies which produced piano rolls. The Aeolian Player mechanism is identified by a name plate above the tracker bar. (See "Reproducing Expression Pianos" section for examples, and see individual listings for values.) Regular Pinaolas.	**250.00-400.00**	**2250.00-2750.00**
☐ **AERIOLA PLAYERS** *Made by Aeolian.*	**150.00-250.00**	**2500.00-2750.00**
☐ **ALDRICH PIANO CO.** *Used the Aeolian Player mechanism or the Simplex Player mechanism.*	**250.00**	**2000.00**

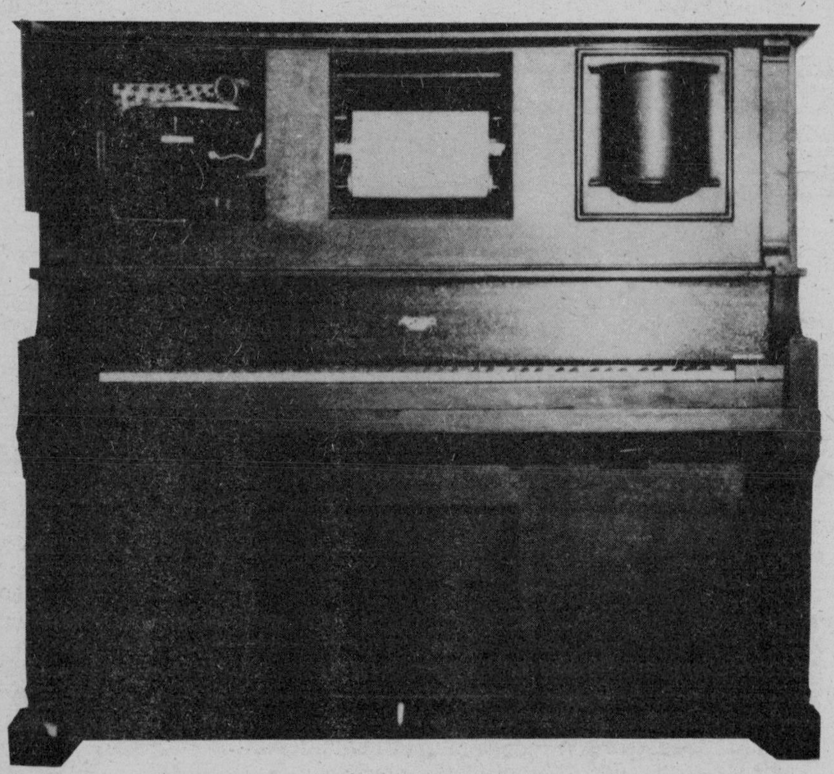

Apollophone Upright Player, with built in disc phonograph.

	Unrestored	Restored
☐ **AMERICAN PIANO CO. (NY)** *By the mid 1920's this company was the affiliation of several well established piano companies: Chickering and Sons (Boston), William Knabe and Co. (Baltimore, MD), Mason and Hamlin Co. (Boston), Foster-Armstrong (Rochester, NY), Haines Bros., Marshall and Wendell Piano Co., Franklin Piano Co., Brewster Piano Co., The Ampico Co., Armstrong Piano Co., The Amphion Co. (See "Reproducing Expression Pianos" section for examples, and see individual listing for values.)*		
☐ **AMERICAN PLAYER PIANO** *(See Bjur Bros. of N.Y.)*		
☐ **AMPHION PIANO PLAYER CO. (Syracuse, NY)** *Maker of regular player actions found in numerous pianos, e.g. Ackerman and Lowe, Adler, Baumeister, Claredon, Emerson, R. S. Howard, Krakauer, Laffargue and others. (See also American Piano Company and see individual listings for values.)*		
☐ **AMPICO** *(AMERICAN PIANO CO., NY) Maker of reproducing expression player actions found in many good pianos, e.g. Chickering, Marshall & Wendell, Fischer, Knabe, Steck, Franklin, Haines Bros., Steinway and others. The Ampico mechanism can be identified in many ways, the most obvious is a name plate. (For examples and values see section on "Reproducing Expression Pianos".)*		
☐ **ANGELUS** *Player action affiliated with the Premier Grand Piano Corp. It used what was called the "Artistyle" system of expression and is found in many pianos, e.g. Wilcox and White, Emerson, Lindemann, George Norris. Early examples were push-up players. (See sections on "Reproducing Expression Pianos" and "Push-Up Players" for examples, and see individual listings for values.)*		
☐ **APOLLO PIANO CO. (IL)** *Used foot pump player actions made by Melville and Simplex in their pianos.*	**200.00-275.00**	**2000.00-2500.00**
☐ **APOLLOPHONE** *Upright player piano, foot pump, with built in disc phonograph inside front left panel next to paper roll assembly.*	**1200.00-2500.00**	**3500.00-5000.00**
☐ **AUTO ART PIANO CO. (NY)** *Used Standard player mechanism.*	**150.00-250.00**	**2500.00-2750.00**

AUTO PLAYER *(See Werner Industries)*

AUTO PNEUMATIC PLAYER *Regular player mechanism used in Kohler Pianos, NY. (See Horace Waters.)*

	Unrestored	Restored
☐ **ARTEMIS (KRELL)** *Player action used in Thompson, Steger, Reid and Sons, Krell and other pianos.*	**250.00**	**1500.00-2000.00**

ARIA DIVINA *Reproducing player mechanism by M. Schulz (See M. Schulz Co.)*

ARTISTANO *Player pianos made by A. B. Chase Co. (See A. B. Chase Co.)*

ARTISTYLE *Player system (See Angelus).*

ARTRONOME *Made by Straube Piano Co. (Hammond, IN). Player mechanism which had a "Penulum Valve" (See Straube Piano Co.)*

AUTOLA *Trade name for players made by the Horace Waters Co. Piano Company of NY. (See Horace Walters).*

	Unrestored	Restored
☐ **AUTOPIANO COMPANY (NY)** *Maker of a player piano mechanism used in many pianos, e.g. Symphotone, Peck & Sons, Jacob Bros., Cunningham and others. Also produced the Autopiano Grand, Welte-Mignon, The Autopiano Electric Self-Expression Piano and the Pianista Player.*	250.00	1500.00-2500.00
☐ *WELTE.*	500.00-1000.00	2750.00-3000.00

AUTOSTYLE *Player affiliated with John Church Company Cincinnati, OH. (See John Church Co.)*

	Unrestored	Restored
☐ **AUTOTONE PIANO CO.** *Used the Hardman Peck Player mechanism, it was also used in Harrington Pianos (Made by Hardman Peck).*	250.00	2000.00-2500.00
☐ **FRANCIS BACON PIANOS (NY)** *Used the Standard Player mechanism.*	250.00-400.00	2000.00-2500.00
☐ **BACHMAN PIANO COMPANY** *Used the Standard Player mechanism.*	200.00	2250.00
☐ **BAILEY PIANO COMPANY (NY)** *Used the Bjur Bros. Player mechanism.*	200.00	2150.00
☐ **BALDWIN PIANO MANUFACTURING CO. (Cincinnati, OH)** *Controlled the manufacture of the following piano companies: Ellington, Hamilton, Howard, Monarch, St. Regis. They produced the Manualo Player for their pianos, also used the Welte-Mignon Reproducing Player mechanism. (See "Reproducing Expression Pianos-Welte" for examples).*	250.00-350.00	2250.00-2750.00
☐ **BARKLAY PIANO** *Used the Aeolian Pianola mechanism.*	200.00	2000.00-2500.00
☐ **BAUMEISTER PIANO** *Used the Amphion Player mechanism.*	200.00-250.00	2000.00-2500.00
☐ **BAUS PIANO CO. (NY)** *Controlled by and used the Jacob Doll Player mechanism.*	200.00-250.00	1500.00-2500.00
☐ **H. C. BAY (Chicago, IL and Bluffton, IN)** *Made their own player action, also used in other pianos, e.g. Harmony, Strauss, Walters, Wegman.*	200.00-250.00	1750.00 2500.00
☐ **BECHWITH PIANOS** *Sold by Sears Roebuck only; used the Standard, Simplex and Beckwith's own player mechanisms.*	200.00-250.00	2000.00 2500.00
☐ **BECKER BROS. (NY)** *Standard or Amphion Player mechanisms were used in their pianos. They also produced the Bennington, Playernola and Mell-O-Tone Pianos and players.*	200.00-250.00	2000.00-2250.00
☐ **BEHNING & SONS PIANOS CO. (NY)** *Used the Behning or Standard Player mechanisms.*	225.00-275.00	2250.00-2750.00

	Unrestored	Restored
☐ **BEHR BROS. AND CO. (NY)** *Used their own player mechanism, also the Standard Player mechanism and the Auto deluxe Welte-Mignon Reproducing mechanism.*	200.00-500.00	2000.00-3000.00
☐ *With Welte mechanism.*	400.00-600.00	2750.00-4000.00
☐ **BENNINGTON PIANOS** *Made by Becker Bros., NY with a Standard Player mechanism.*	250.00	2000.00-2500.00
☐ **BILLINGS AND CO.** *Used the Standard Player mechanism.*	200.00-250.00	1950.00-2500.00
☐ **BJUR BROS. CO.** *Made their own player mechanism and Bjur mechanism was also used in Bailey, Craighead, Stultz & Co. Pianos.*	200.00-250.00	1750.00-2500.00
☐ **BLASIUS AND SONS** *Used the Pratt & Read Player mechanism in their pianos.*	250.00	2250.00
☐ **BOARDMAN AND GRAY** *Used the Standard Player action in their pianos.*	200.00-250.00	2000.00-2500.00
☐ **BOUDOIR PIANO COMPANY** *Used the Amphion Player action in their pianos.*	200.00	2000.00-2500.00
☐ **BRADLEY PIANO COMPANY (MA)** *Used the Simplex Player action.*	200.00-250.00	2000.00-2500.00
☐ **BRAMBACH PIANO CO. (NY)** *Used the Standard Player action, also the Auto deLuxe Welte-Mignon in their Grand Pianos.*	250.00	2000.00-2750.00
☐ *With Welte mechanism.*	500.00-750.00	3000.00-4500.00
☐ **BREWSTER PIANOS** *Used the Standard Player action in their pianos.*	250.00	2500.00
☐ **BRIGGS PIANO CO. (Boston, MA)** *Used the Simplex or National Air-O-Player mechanisms in their pianos.*	300.00	2500.00
☐ **BRINKERHOFF PIANO CO. (Chicago, IL)** *Used the Schulz Player action. This company also made the Schriver & Sons piano.*	200.00	2500.00
☐ **BUSH AND GERTS PIANOS (Chicago, IL)** *Used Simplex, Standard, Amphion, Gulbransen, Pratt Read, Autopiano, and Otto Higel player mechanisms.*	250.00-400.00	2750.00-4000.00
☐ **BUSH AND LANE (MI)** *Manufacturer of the Cecilian Player action mechanism. The Welte-Mignon Reproducing mechanism was used in upright and grand models as well.*	250.00	2500.00-2750.00
☐ *WELTE.*	500.00-1500.00	2500.00-4000.00
☐ **BUTLER BROS. (Cincinnati, OH)** *Used the H. C. Bay, Simplex and Gulbransen Player mechanisms in their pianos.*	200.00-250.00	2500.00-3000.00

	Unrestored	Restored
☐ **CABLE CO. PIANOS (Chicago, IL)** *Made their own regular player action (usually trademark found on harp of piano), this mechanism was used in other Cable Company Pianos, Conover, Kingsbury and Wellington Pianos.*	250.00	2000.00-2500.00
☐ **HOBART M. CABLE (IN)** *Associated with Story and Clark Co., used player actions made by Standard, Simplex, Amphion, Pratt and Read, Stauch Bros.*	250.00-300.00	2500.00-3000.00
☐ **CABLE-NELSON (MI)** *Used several different player mechanisms in their pianos, e.g.: Standard, Simplex, Amphion mechanisms. They also made the Radcliff Piano (Boston).*	250.00-300.00	2500.00-3500.00
☐ **CAMBRIDGE PIANO CO. (NY)** *Made small players, e.g. Style "O" is 3'9", Style "F" is 4'3".*	500.00-1000.00	2750.00-3750.00
☐ **CAMP AND CO. PIANOS** *Made by Henry G. Johnson Piano Manufacturing Co. (Bellevue, IA) made a line of players.*	200.00-250.00	2000.00-2750.00

CAROLA INNER PLAYER *Player mechanism used in Cable Co. Pianos, e.g. Conover.*

	Unrestored	Restored
☐ **CECILIAN PLAYER ACTION by FARRAND (MI)** *Pianos are usually marked "Cecilian", some grands are labeled "Farrand".*	200.00-300.00	2500.00-3500.00
☐ **CELLOTONE PIANOS** *Sold by S. A. Hawke & Co. (Mass.) A line of players were sold under the name Cellotone.*	250.00-275.00	2500.00
☐ **A. B. CHASE (ALLEN B. CHASE, OH)** *Used Chase's own player mechanism, also the Standard and Amphion.*	250.00	2500.00-3000.00
☐ **CHASE AND HACKLEY CO. (Michigan)** *Used Standard and Otto Higel player mechanisms.*	175.00-300.00	2500.00-3000.00
☐ **CHICKERING AND SONS (NY)** *Used a regular Gulbransen player mechanism, also the Ampico Reproducing Player mechanism. (See "Reproducing Expression Pianos-Ampico" section for examples).*	300.00-500.00	2500.00-5000.00
☐ **CHRISTMAN PIANO CO. (NY)** *Used their own player mechanism and the Welte-Mignon reproducing player mechanism.*	250.00	2250.00
☐ *With Welte mechanism.*	500.00-1000.00	3000.00-5000.00
☐ **JOHN CHURCH CO.** *Made player mechanisms found in the Everett and Dayton Pianos.*		
☐ **CHUTE AND BATLER (IN)** *Used the Standard Player mechanism.*	200.00-250.00	1750.00-2500.00
☐ **CLARENDON PIANO CO. (Rockford, IL)** *Used the Amphion and Pratt and Read Player mechanism.*	250.00	2500.00
☐ **MELVILLE CLARK (Chicago, IL)** *Used their own player action, also used in Appollo Pianos.*	250.00	2500.00

	Unrestored	Restored
☐ **CONCERTONE** *Player made by Mansfield Piano Co. (NY) for their pianos.*	250.00	2500.00
☐ **CONOVER CABLE CO.** *Used the Cable Co. Player mechanism and the Welte-Mignon Reproducing mechanism. (See "Reproducing Expression Pianos" section for examples).*	250.00-300.00	2500.00-3000.00
☐ *With Welte mechanism.*	500.00-1000.00	
☐ **CONREID (KOHLER & CAMPBELL)** *Used the Standard Player mechanism.*	250.00	
☐ **CONWAY (Boston, MA)** *Used the Simplex Player mechanism and Angelus Reproducing Grands.*	200.00-500.00-	2000.00-4000.00-
☐ **COPLEY PIANOS (Chicago, IL)** *Made a line of players.*	225.00-250.00	2500.00-2750.00
☐ **CUNNINGHAM PIANO CO. (Philadelphia, PA)** *Used the Standard and Autopiano Player mechanisms.*	250.00	2000.00-2500.00
☐ **DAVENPORT AND TREACY (NY)** *Used the Standard Player mechanism and the Welte Reproducing mechanism.*	250.00	2500.00
☐ *With Welte mechanism.*	500.00-1000.00	3000.00-5000.00
☐ **DERIVAS AND HARRIS (NY)** *Used Standard and Simples player mechanisms.*	150.00-250.00	2500.00-2750.00
☐ **DETMER, HENRY (Chicago, IL)** *Used the Amphion Action.*	250.00	2500.00-2750.00
☐ **JACOB DOLL & SONS (NY)** *Used their own player mechanism. This mechanism was also used in the Gabler, Hudson, Lakewood, Mason, Stodart, Victor and Wellsmore Pianos. Doll pianos also used the Welte Reproducing mechanism.*	350.00	2500.00-3500.00
☐ *With Welte mechanism.*	500.00-1000.00	3000.00-5000.00
☐ **DOLL AND SON** *(See also Jacob Doll). Used Standard, Simplex, and Jacob Doll mechanisms.*	175.00-300.00	2500.00-3250.00
DRACHMAN PLAYER PIANO *Made by H. C. Bay.*		
☐ **DUCHESS PIANOS** *Trade name of line of players by Werner Industries Corp.*	250.00	2500.00
☐ **DUNBAR PIANOS** *Used the Kimball Player mechanism.*	250.00	2500.00
☐ **DUO ART** *Reproducing player action made by Aeolian (NY) used in many makes of pianos. (See "Reproducing Expression Pianos" section for examples)*		
DYNACORD *Trademark name used by the Amphion Piano Player Co.*		
☐ **EBERSOLE PIANO** *Made by Smith & Nixon (Cincinnati). Used Standard, H. C. Bay, and Krell player mechanisms.*	150.00-250.00	2500.00-2750.00
☐ **ELBURN MUSIC CO. (Kansas City, MO)** *Used the Aeolian Player mechanism.*	250.00	2500.00-2750.00

	Unrestored	Restored
☐ **ELECTROVA CO. (NY)** *Controlled by Jacob Doll & Sons. This company made automatic electric instruments (coin operated).*		
☐ **ELLINGTON PIANO CO. (Cincinnati, OH)** *Used the Baldwin Player mechanism*	250.00-300.00	2500.00-3000.00
☐ **EMERSON PIANO CO. (Boston, MA)** *Used the Standard, Simplex, Amphion and Angelus Player mechanisms.*	250.00-500.00	2500.00-5000.00
☐ **ESTEY PIANO CO. (NY and Bluffton, IN)** *Made a line of upright and grand pianos, also used the Welte Reproducing mechanism. (See "Reproducing Expression Pianos" for examples).*	250.00	3000.00-6000.00
EUPHONA REPRODUCING INNER PLAYER *Mechanism made by Cable Co.*		
☐ **EUPHONOLA (Jesse French)** *Used the Amphion Player mechanism*	250.00-300.00	2000.00-2500.00
☐ **EVERETT PIANO CO.** *Used the John Church Player mechanism*	200.00	1650.00-2250.00
☐ **EXCELTONE PLAYER PIANO** *Manufactured by Chase-Hackley Piano Co. (Muskegon, MI).*	200.00-250.00	2000.00-2500.00
☐ **FABER PIANO CO. (NY)** *Controlled by Jacob Doll (also used Welte Reproducing mechanism).*	250.00-300.00	2500.00-3000.00
☐ *With Welte mechanism*	500.00-750.00	2750.00-4000.00
☐ **FARRAND PIANO CO. (Holland, MI)** *Maker of the Cecilian Player mechanism, also made Farrand Reproducing Grands.*	250.00-300.00	2500.00-3000.00
☐ **J & C FISCHER (NY)** *Used the Standard and Amphion Player mechanisms. Also used the Ampico Reproducing Player mechanism. (See "Reproducing Expression Pianos" for examples).*	500.00	3000.00-5000.00
☐ **FOSTER-ARMSTRONG (Rochester, NY)** *Affiliated with the American Piano Co. (NY).*	200.00-250.00	2250.00-2500.00
☐ **FRANKE PIANOS (NY)** *Made by Baldwin. Used Autopiano and Baldwin player mechanisms.*	250.00-350.00	2500.00-3500.00
☐ **FRANKLIN PIANO CO. (NY)** *Used the Ampico Reproducing Player mechanism. (See "Reproducing Expression Pianos" for examples).*	250.00-500.00	3000.00-5500.00
☐ **JESSE FRENCH & SONS** *Used the Standard, Simplex and Amphion Player mechanisms.*	250.00-500.00	2500.00-3000.00
☐ **E. GABLER BROS.** *Used the Jacob Doll Player mechanism.*	250.00	2500.00-3000.00

	Unrestored	Restored
☐ **A. B. GARDNER (Los Angeles, CA)** *Used the Amphion Player mechanism*	250.00	2500.00-3000.00
☐ **GODFREY PIANOS (New York)** *Melodic upright, 88-note regular players*	250.00	2500.00-2750.00
☐ **GORDON & SONS (KOHLER & CAMPBELL)** *Used the Standard and Pratt and Read Player mechanisms.*	250.00	2500.00 2750.00
☐ **GRINNELL BROS. (Detroit, MI)** *Used the Aeolian and Lester Player mechanisms*	250.00-300.00	2500.00-3000.00
☐ **GRUNET-HUPFELD SOLOPHONOLA.** *Regular upright player, foot pump (see also Hupfeld, Ludwig)*	350.00-450.00	3500.00-4500.00
☐ **GUEST PIANO CO. (Burlington, IA)** *Made a line of Players*	250.00	2500.00
☐ **GULBRANSEN (Chicago, IL)** *Made their own player mechanisms. They made what they called a "Registering Piano" Player mechanism. Early model was screwed together, later the stack was glued together and is much more difficult to restore. Gulbransen Player mechanisms found in many pianos*	200.00-250.00	2500.00
☐ **GULBRANSEN-DICKINSON (Chicago, IL)** *Used their own player mechanism*	250.00	2500.00-2750.00
☐ **HADDORF PIANO CO. (Rockford, IL)** *Used the Amphion Player mechanism*	250.00	2500.00-3000.00
☐ **HAINES BROS. (NY)** *Used the Pratt and Read Player mechanism and also used the Ampico Reproducing mechanism*	250.00	2500.00
☐ **HALLET AND DAVIS (Boston, MA)** *Used the Simplex Player mechanism and Angelus Reproducing Grand.*	250.00-350.00	2500.00-3500.00
☐ **HAMILTON PIANO CO. (IL)** *Used the Baldwin Player mechanism.*	250.00	2500.00-3000.00
☐ **HAMMOND PIANOS** *Made by Straube (Indiana). Used the Standard, Simplex, Pratt-Read and Straube player mechanisms*	250.00-350.00	2500.00-3500.00

HARDMAN *Autotone and Playotone mechanisms found in Harrington, Hensel, Minipiano and Playotone Pianos and others.*

	Unrestored	Restored
☐ **HARDMAN PECK CO. (NY)** *Made their own player mechanism. It was used in other pianos as well. (See "Reproducing Expression Pianos" for examples).*	300.00-500.00	3000.00-5000.00
☐ **HARMONIST PLAYERS** *Made by the Peerless Player Co.*		
☐ **E. G. HARRINGTON AND CO. (NY)** *Used the Hardman Player mechanism*	250.00-300.00	2250.00-2750.00

	Unrestored	Restored
☐ **HARRISON PIANO** *Used the Kimball Regular Player mechanism.*	250.00	2000.00-2500.00
☐ **HAYES PIANO** *Used the Lester Player mechanism.*	200.00-250.00	2500.00-2750.00
☐ **HAZELTON BROS. (KOHLER & CAMPBELL, NY)** *Used the Standard Player mechanism and the Welte-Mignon Reproducing Player mechanism.*	250.00	2500.00
☐ *With Welte mechanism*	500.00-1000.00	3000.00-4000.00
☐ **HEINTZMAN AND CO. (Toronto, Canada)** *Used the Otto Higel Player mechanism.*	250.00	2000.00-3000.00
☐ **HENSEL PIANOS** *Made by Hardman, Peck and Co. Used regular and Welte Reproducing Player mechanisms.*	250.00	2500.00
☐ *With Welte mechanism*	500.00-1000.00	3000.00-4000.00
☐ **OTTO HIGEL PLAYER ACTION** *Used in Bond, Lindsay and Worthington Pianos and others.*	250.00	2500.00-2750.00
☐ **HINZE PIANO (Chicago, IL)** *Made by Kimball with Kimball Player mechanism.*	250.00	2500.00
☐ **HOLLAND PIANO CO.** *Used the Simplex Player mechanism.*	350.00	3500.00
☐ **HOWARD PIANO CO. (Cincinnati, OH)** *Made by Baldwin with Baldwin Player mechanism (Manualo).*	250.00	2500.00
☐ **R. S. HOWARD (NY)** *Used the Amphion and Pratt and Read Player mechanism.*	250.00	2500.00
HUMANA *(See Lauter)*		
☐ **HUNTINGTON PIANOS (CT)** *Made by Sterling. Used Standard or Sterling Player mechanisms.*	250.00	2500.00-2750.00
☐ **HUPFELD, LUDWIG INC.** *BLUTHNER-HUPFELD SOLOPHONOLA. Regular upright and grand player foot pump piano.*	350.00-450.00	3500.00-4500.00
☐ *GRUNET-HUPFELD SOLOPHONOLA. Regular upright player foot pump.*	350.00-450.00	3500.00-4500.00
☐ *LANGHAM-HUPFELD SOLOPHONOLA. Upright foot pump player piano.*	350.00-450.00	3500.00-4500.00
☐ *RONISCH-HUPFELD SOLOPHONOLA. Upright foot pump player piano.*	350.00-450.00	3500.00-4500.00
☐ *HUPFELD GOTHA SOLOPHONOLA. Upright foot pump player piano.*	350.00-450.00	3500.00-4500.00
INVISIBLE PLAYER PIANOS *Name used by the Milton Piano Co. (NY)*		
☐ **IRVING PIANOS** *Made by the M. Schulz Co. (Chicago). Used the Schulz Player mechanism.*	200.00-300.00	2500.00-3000.00

	Unrestored	Restored
☐ **IRVINGTON PIANOS** *Made by Story and Clark (Chicago). Used their own player mechanism*	200.00-300.00	2500.00-3000.00
☐ **IVERS AND POND (MA)** *Made a line of players.*	200.00-300.00	2500.00-3000.00
☐ **JAMES AND HOLSTROM (NY)** *Used Standard and Autopiano player mechanisms.*	175.00-300.00	2500.00-3200.00
☐ **JANSSEN PIANO CO. (NY)** *Made a line of players*	200.00-300.00	2500.00-3000.00
☐ **JARRETT PIANOS** *Used the Lester player mechanism*	200.00-300.00	2500.00-3000.00
☐ **E. P. JOHNSON (IL)** *Used the Standard, Simplex, Pratt and Read Player mechanisms.*	200.00-250.00	2500.00-3000.00
☐ **HENRY G. JOHNSON (Bellevue, IA)** *Player De Luxe Piano Co.*	250.00-300.00	2000.00-3000.00
☐ **GEORGE F. KELLER PLAYER PIANOS** *Made by Laffargue Co. (NY).*	200.00-250.00	2000.00-2500.00
☐ **W. W. KIMBALL CO. (Chicago, IL)** *Made several variations in their player mechanism. Used in the following pianos: Kimball, Hinze, Whitney, Harrison, Dunbar. Also used Welte Reproducing mechanism.*	250.00	2500.00
☐ **KINGSBURY (CABLE PIANO CO.) (Chicago, IL)** *Used the Cable Player mechanism.*	250.00	2500.00-3000.00
☐ **KINGSTON PIANOS** *Made by Wurlitzer. Used Wurlitzer, Simplex, H. C. Bay and Standard player mechanisms.*	150.00-250.00	2500.00-2750.00
☐ **WM. KNABLE & CO. (Baltimore, MD)** *Used the Standard and Angelus player mechanisms and the Ampico Reproducing Player mechanism. (See "Reproducing Expression Pianos" section for examples).*	400.00-750.00	3000.00-7000.00
☐ **KNIGHT-BRINKERHOFF (IN)** *Used the Standard Player mechanism*	250.00	2500.00-2750.00
☐ **KOHLER & CAMPBELL (NY)** *Used the Standard Player mechanism and the Welte Reproducing Player mechanism. This company made many pianos notably: The Autopiano, Artistyle, Peterpan, Soloist, Solostyle, Symphonia, Symphotone, Tom Thumb, Waldorf. (See "Reproducing Expression Pianos" section for examples).*	250.00-350.00	2500.00-3500.00
☐ **KRAKAUER BROS. (NY)** *Used the Amphion Player mechanism.*	250.00-300.00	2500.00-3500.00

	Unrestored	Restored
☐ **KRANICH AND BACH (NY)** *Used their own regular player mechanism and the Welte Reproducing Player mechanism. (See "Reproducing Expression Pianos" section for examples).*	250.00-350.00	2500.00-3500.00
☐ **KRELL AUTO-GRAND PIANO CO. (IN) (ARTEMIS-KRELL)** *Used their own player mechanism.*	200.00-300.00	2500.00-3000.00
☐ **KROEGER PIANO CO. (CT)** *Used the Otto Higel Player mechanism.*	250.00-275.00	2500.00
☐ **KURTZMANN (Buffalo, NY)** *Used the Standard or Pratt and Read Player mechanism, also the Welte.*	250.00	2500.00
☐ *With Welte mechanism.*	500.00-1000.00	3000.00-5000.00
LAFAYETTE *Trade name used by H. Lehr & Co. (Eastern, PA) Players.*		
☐ *LAFFARGUE PIANO CO. (NY) Used the Amphion Player mechanism.*	250.00	2500.00
☐ **LAGONDA PIANO CO. (IN)** *Made by Krell-French and Jesse French. Used Simplex and Amphion player mechanisms.*	150.00-250.00	2500.00-2750.00
☐ **LAKESIDE PIANOS** *Made by Cable Nelson (Chicago). Made a line of players.*	250.00	2500.00
☐ **LAUTER-HUMANA CO. (Newark, NJ)** *Used their own player mechanism.*	250.00-350.00	2750.00-3500.00
☐ **LAWRENCE PIANO** *Used the Lester Player mechanism.*	250.00	2500.00
☐ **LEITER PIANOS** *Used the Aeolian Player mechanism.*	250.00	2500.00-2750.00
☐ **LENOX PIANO MANUFACTURING CO.** *Made by and used the Lauter Player mechanism.*	250.00	2500.00
☐ **LEONARD & CO. (LESTER)** *Used the Standard, Simplex and Lester Player mechanisms.*	250.00	2500.00
☐ **LESTER PIANO CO. (Philadelphia, PA)** *Used their own and the Standard, and Simplex Player mechanisms. The Lester mechanism was also used in the Hayes, Jarrett, Lawrence, Leonard and other pianos.*	250.00	2500.00-3000.00
☐ **LEXINGTON PIANO CO. (Boston, MA)** *Used the Simplex Player mechanism.*	250.00	2500.00-2750.00
☐ **LINDEMAN PIANO CO. (NY)** *Used the Standard and Amphion Player mechanisms.*	250.00-300.00	2500.00-2750.00
☐ **LINDEMANN AND SONS** *Used the Angelus Player mechanism.*	250.00-350.00	2500.00-3500.00
☐ **LINGARD PLAYER PIANO** *Made by Rudolf Wurlitzer Co.*	250.00	2500.00-2700.00
LINK PIANO CO. *(See section on "Nickelodeons")*		
☐ **LIVINGSTON PIANOS** *Controlled by Weaver Piano Co. (York, PA). Made a line of players.*	250.00	2500.00-2700.00

	Unrestored	Restored
☐ **LORRAINE PIANOS** *Made for the Field-Lippman Piano Stores (St. Louis, MO). Sold a line of popular priced player pianos.*	250.00	2500.00
☐ **LUDWIG AND CO. (NY)** *Used the Standard Player mechanism.*	200.00-250.00	2500.00-3000.00
☐ **LYON AND HEALY PIANO CO. (Chicago)** *Used the Amphion Player mechanism in their players. (See also "Nickelodeon" section).*	250.00-350.00	2500.00-3500.00

MANUALO *Player mechanism made by Baldwin (See "Baldwin" for further information)*

	Unrestored	Restored
☐ **MARQUETTE PIANO CO. (Milwaukee, WI)** *Made player mechanism for their own pianos. (See also "Nickelodeon" section).*	250.00	2500.00-3500.00
☐ **MARSHALL AND WENDELL PIANO CO. (NY)** *Used the Standard and Aeolian Player mechanisms and also the Ampico Reproducing Player mechanism. (For example see the section on "Reproducing Expression Pianos-Ampico").*	250.00-500.00	3500.00-5000.00
☐ **MASON AND HAMLIN PIANO CO. (NY)** *Used the Aeolian Player and Ampico Reproducing Player mechanisms. (See section on "Reproducing Expression Pianos-Ampico" for examples).*	350.00-1000.00	3250.00-6000.00
☐ **MASON AND RISCH (Toronto, Canada)** *Used their own player mechanism.*	200.00-250.00	2500.00
☐ **MASTER PLAYER PIANO** *Made by Winter & Co. (NY).*	250.00	2500.00
☐ **MATHUSHEK PIANO CO. (NY)** *Used the Auto Piano Player mechanism, also Welte Reproducing Player mechanism.*	250.00	2500.00
☐ *With Welte mechanism.*	350.00-750.00	3500.00-5500.00
☐ **MEHLIN AND SONS (NY)** *Used the Standard Player mechanism and the Welte-Mignon Reproducing Player mechanism. (See section on "Reproducing Expression Pianos-Welte").*	250.00	2500.00-3000.00
☐ **MELBOURNE PIANO** *Used the Baldwin Player mechanism.*	250.00	2500.00
☐ **MELODIGRAND** *Made by Lindeman. Used Standard and Otto Higel player mechanisms.*	200.00-275.00	2500.00-3250.00
☐ **MELOSTRELLE PIANOS** *Made by Steger and Sons Piano Manufacturing Co. (Chicago).*	200.00-250.00	2500.00-2750.00
☐ **MENDELSSOHN PIANOS** *Made by Winter later Aeolian. Used Simplex, Pratt-Read, Standard, Higel and Sterling Player mechanisms.*	225.00-300.00	2500.00-3500.00

	Unrestored	Restored
☐ **MERCER PLAYER PIANOS** *Controlled by Weaver Co. (York, PA).*	250.00	2500.00-2750.00
☐ **MERRILL PIANO MANUFACTURING CO. (MA)** *Used several player mechanisms in their pianos: The Simplex, Jacob Doll, Angelus, "Reproducing" Grand and National Air-O-Player.*	250.00	2500.00-2750.00
METROSTYLE PIANOLA *Made by Aeolian. This mechanism also found in early 65-note push-up players.*		
☐ **MIESSNER PIANO CO. (Milwaukee, WI)** *Made small upright players less than 4' high.*	750.00-1250.00	3000.00-4750.00
☐ **HENRY F. MILLER (MA)** *Made their own player mechanism.*	250.00	2500.00-2750.00
☐ **MILTON PIANO CO. (NY)** *Used the Standard Player mechanism.*	250.00	2500.00-2750.00
☐ **MODELLO PLAYER PIANO** *Made by Baldwin and used the Manualo Player mechanism.*	250.00	2500.00
☐ **MONARCH PIANO CO. (IL)** *Used the Baldwin Manualo Player mechanism.*	250.00	2500.00
☐ **NATIONAL AIR-O-PLAYER** *Player mechanism used in the Merrill, Briggs, Norris and Hyde Pianos.*	250.00	2500.00
☐ **H. P. NELSON (Chicago, IL)** *Used their own player mechanism. It was also used in the Stanley & Sons, and Weiler Pianos.*	250.00	2500.00
☐ **NETZOW PIANO CO. (Milwaukee, WI)** *Used the Simplex and Gulbransen Player mechanisms.*	200.00-300.00	2500.00
☐ **NEWBY AND EVANS (NY)** *Used the Simplex, Standard, Amphion, and Pratt and Read Player mechanisms.*	250.00-300.00	2500.00-3000.00
☐ **NORRIS AND HYDE** *Used the National Air-O-Player mechanism.*	250.00	2500.00
OPERATORS' PIANO CO. (Chicago, IL) *(See section on "Nickelodeons")*		
☐ **PACKARD PIANO CO. (IN)** *Used the Standard, Simplex, Pratt and Read Player mechanisms and the Welte-Mignon Reproducing Player mechanism. (See also section on "Reproducing Expression Pianos-Welte").*	250.00-350.00	2500.00-4250.00
☐ **PEASE PIANO CO. (NY)** *Used the Standard Player mechanism.*	250.00	2500.00
☐ **PERRYOLA PLAYER PIANOS** *Made by Ludwig & Co., NY.*	250.00	2500.00
☐ **PHILHARMONIC PLAYER PIANOS** *Affiliated with Paul G. Mehlin & Sons.*	250.00	2500.00
☐ **H. L. PHILLIPS PIANOS** *Made for Knight-Campbell Music Co., Denver, CO by Cable-Nelson Piano Co.*	250.00-350.00	2500.00-3500.00
☐ **PIANISTA PLAYER PIANO (NY)** *Made by Auto Piano later Kohler and Campbell. Used Autopiano Standard player mechanism.*	200.00-300.00	2500.00-3250.00

	Unrestored	Restored
☐ **PIANOLA** *Trademark name used by Aeolian for their Player Pianos*	200.00-250.00	2500.00-2750.00
☐ **PLAYERNOLA** *Player made by Becker Bros.*	250.00	2500.00
☐ **PLAYOTONE** *Player made by Autotone of Hardman Peck.*	250.00	2750.00-3000.00
☐ **PLAYTONA** *Player made by Grinnell Bros.*	250.00	2500.00

PRATT AND READ *Player mechanism used in many pianos. Many examples have a nameplate with a "9R" trademark in tracker bar area.*

	Unrestored	Restored
☐ **PREMIER GRAND PIANO CORP. (NY & Los Angeles, CA)** *Maker of the Premiera "Reproducing" Grand. They also used the Welte Reproducing Player mechanism in many different case styles.*	750.00-1500.00	3750.00-4500.00
☐ **PRICE AND TEEPLE (Kankakee, IL)** *Used their own player mechanism and the Standard Player mechanism.*	250.00	2500.00
☐ **PRIMATONE** *Small players made by Foster-Armstrong (NY)*	250.00-300.00	2500.00-3000.00
☐ **PUTNAM PIANOS** *Made by Wissner & Sons (NY).*	250.00	2500.00
☐ **F. RADLE CO. (NY)** *Used the Auto Piano Player mechanism.*	250.00	2500.00-2750.00
☐ **REGAL PIANOS (NY)** *Used the Standard Player mechanism.*	250.00	2500.00
☐ **REMINGTON** *Made by Starr with the Starr Player mechanism.*	250.00	2500.00

REPRO-PHRASO *Player mechanism made by Story and Clark.*

	Unrestored	Restored
☐ **RICCA & SON (NY)** *Used the Standard Player mechanism.*	250.00	2500.00-2750.00
☐ **RICHMOND** *Made by Starr with the Starr Player mechanism.*	250.00	2500.00
☐ **RIDGEWAY PLAYERS** *Made by O. K. Houck Piano Co. (Memphis, TN).*	200.00-250.00	2500.00
☐ **ROTHCHILD OR ROTHSCHILD PIANOS (Chicago)** *Used Simplex and Amphion player mechanisms.*	200.00-300.00	2500.00-3250.00
☐ **ROYAL PIANOS** *Made by Krell and used the Artemis (Krell) Player mechanism.*	200.00	2500.00
☐ **RUDOLF PIANO CO. (NY)** *Used the Winter and Co. Player mechanism.*	250.00	2500.00
☐ **SALYER AND SALYER** *Used the Amphion Player mechanism.*	250.00	2500.00-2750.00
☐ **SARGEANT PIANOS** *Used the Baldwin Manualo Player mechanism.*	250.00	2500.00
☐ **ADAM SCHAAF (Chicago, IL)** *Used the Simplex and Amphion Player mechanisms.*	250.00-300.00	2500.00-3500.00
☐ **SCHOMAKER PIANO CO. (Philadelphia, PA)** *Used the Angelus Player mechanism.*	250.00-350.00	2500.00-4000.00
☐ **SCHROEDER PIANO** *Used the Baldwin Manualo Player mechanism.*	300.00	3000.00

	Unrestored	Restored
☐ **SCHUBERT PIANO CO. (NY)** *Used the Schumann Player mechanism.*	250.00	2500.00
☐ **M. SCHULZ CO. (Chicago, IL)** *Used their own regular player mechanism. In Grand Models their "Aria-Divina" mechanism and also the Welte-Mignon Reproducing Player mechanism was used. Their regular player mechanism is also found in the Irving, Griggs, Bradford, Walworth, Werner, Meyers, Brinkerhoff and George Allen pianos. (See "Reproducing Expression Pianos" section for specific examples).*	250.00	2500.00
☐ *ARIA-DIVINA.*	500.00	5000.00
☐ **SCHUMANN PIANO (Chicago, IL)** *Used their own player mechanism, also found in other pianos.*	250.00	2500.00

J. P. SEEBURG PIANO CO. (Chicago, IL) *(See section on "Nickelodeons").*

☐ *SHERMAN CLAY CO. (San Francisco, CA) Used the Aeolian and Amphion Player mechanisms.*	250.00-300.00	2500.00-3000.00
☐ **SHERMAN CLAY CO. (San Francisco, CA)** *Used Amphion and Aeolian player mechanisms.*	250.00-350.00	2750.00-3500.00

SIMPLEX PLAYER ACTION COMPANY (Worcester, MA) *Very popular player mechanism used in many pianos.*

☐ **SOHMER AND CO., INC. (NY)** *Made a line of upright players and used the Welte-Mignon Reproducing Player mechanism in their player Grands. (See "Reproducing Expression Pianos" section).*	250.00-400.00	2500.00-5000.00
☐ **SMITH AND BARNES (Chicago, IL)** *Installed Standard 88-note player action.*	250.00	2500.00

STANDARD PNEUMATIC ACTION CO. (NY) *Maker of one of the most popular regular player mechanisms found in many pianos.*

☐ **P. A. STARCK (Chicago, IL)** *Used the Standard and Simplex player mechanisms.*	275.00	2750.00
☐ **STARR PIANO CO. (IN)** *Made many variations of their own Starr Player mechanism, also found in other pianos, e.g. The Remington, Maxwell, Zimmermann and others.*	200.00-250.00	2500.00

GEORGE STECK & CO. (NY) *Related to the Aeolian Co. Used the Duo-Art Reproducing Player mechanism. (See section on "Reproducing Expression Pianos-Duo-Art").*

☐ **STEGER AND SONS (Chicago, IL)** *Made a line of player pianos.*	250.00	2500.00-3000.00
☐ **M. STEINERT (GA)** *Used the Simplex Player mechanism.*	250.00	2500.00-2750.00

STEINWAY & SONS (NY) *Used the Welte, Duo-Art and Ampico Reproducing Player mechanisms in upright and grand models. (See "Reproducing Expression Pianos" section for numerous examples).*

☐ *Some Upright examples had Aeolian Themodist 65/68-note foot pump mechanisms.*	500.00-1000.00	3500.00-4750.00

	Unrestored	Restored
☐ **STERLING PIANO CO. (CT)** *Used their own and the Standard Player mechanisms. The Sterling mechanism also found in Harvey, Huntington, Mendelssohn and other pianos.*	**250.00**	**2500.00-3250.00**
☐ **STORY AND CLARK PIANO CO. (Chicago, IL)** *Used their own player mechanism. Also made miniature upright players. Their mechanism also used in Gibbs, Irvington, Iverson and other pianos.*	**275.00-325.00**	**2500.00-3000.00**
☐ **STRAUBE PIANO CO. (Chicago, IL)** *Made their own player mechanism and also used the Standard mechanism. Straube mechanism also used in Woodward, Hammond and Gilmore Pianos.*	**250.00**	**2500.00-2750.00**
☐ **STROUD PIANOS (AEOLIAN)** *Used the Aeolian and Duo-Art Reproducing Player mechanism. (See "Reproducing Expression Pianos-Duo-Art").*	**350.00**	**3500.00**
☐ **STULTZ AND BAUER (NY)** *Used the Standard Player mechanism.*	**250.00**	**2500.00**
☐ **STUTZ AND CO. (NY)** *Used the Bjur Bros. Player mechanism.*	**200.00-250.00**	**2500.00-2750.00**
☐ **STUYVESANT PIANOS (NY)** *Used the Aeolian Player mechanism.*	**250.00**	**2500.00**
☐ **SYMPHONOLA PLAYER PIANO** *Made by Price and Teeple Piano Co.*	**275.00**	**2750.00**
☐ **SYMPHONY PLAYER** *Made by Paul G. Mehlin & Sons.*	**275.00**	**2750.00**
☐ **TECHNOLA PLAYER PIANO** *Made by Aeolian.*	**250.00-275.00**	**2500.00-2750.00**
☐ **TEMPLE PIANO** *Used Simplex and Aeolian Player mechanism.*	**250.00-300.00**	**2500.00-3000.00**
☐ **WILLIAM TONK & BRO. INC. (NY)** *Maker of players, Triplex Electric Player and Reproducing Uprights and Grands.*	**250.00**	**2500.00**
☐ **GEORGE TRAYSER (IN)** *Used the Starr Player mechanism.*	**200.00-250.00**	**2500.00-2750.00**
☐ **VAN DYCK PIANO CO. (Scranton, PA)** *Made a line of players.*	**250.00**	**2500.00**
☐ **VICTOR PIANO & ORGAN CO. (Chicago, IL)** *Used the Bush and Lane (Cecilian) player mechanism.*	**250.00-350.00**	**2500.00-2750.00**
☐ **VIRTUOLO PLAYER** *Made by Hallet and Davis Piano Co., later affiliated with Jacob Doll and Premier Grand Piano Co.*	**300.00-400.00**	**2500.00-4000.00**
☐ **VOSE AND SONS (Boston, MA)** *Used their own player mechanism.*	**250.00-300.00**	**2500.00-3000.00**
☐ **WALDORF PIANO CO.** *Controlled by Autopiano Co. Made a line of players.*	**250.00-275.00**	**2500.00-3000.00**
☐ **WALTERS PIANO CO. (Long Island, NY)** *Made pianos under several names among them Bloomingdale Bros. Used Standard, H. C. Bay and Strauch Bros. player mechanisms.*	**250.00-350.00**	**2750.00-3500.00**

	Unrestored	Restored
☐ **WASHBURN (LYON AND HEALY) (Chicago, IL)** *Used the Amphion Player mechanism.*	325.00	2750.00-3000.00
☐ **HORACE WATERS & CO. (NY)** *Made the Autola Player and also used the Pratt and Read Player mechanism.*	250.00-300.00	2500.00-3000.00
☐ **WEAVER PIANO CO. (York, PA)** *Used the Standard Player mechanism.*	250.00-350.00	2500.00-3500.00
☐ *With Welte mechanism.*	500.00-1000.00	3500.00-4500.00
☐ **WEBER & CO. (NY)** *Used the Aeolian and the Duo-Art Reproducing Player mechanism. (See "Reproducing Expression Pianos-Duo-Art" section). Regular Player*	300.00-600.00	3000.00-5500.00
☐ **WEBSTER PIANO CO. (MA)** *Used the Pratt and Read Player mechanism.*	250.00	2500.00-3250.00
☐ **WEGMAN PIANOS (NY)** *Used the Standard and H. C. Bay Player mechanisms.*	250.00-300.00	2500.00-3000.00
☐ **WELLSMORE PIANO CO. (NY)** *Used the Simplex and Jacob Doll Player mechanisms.*	250.00	2500.00
☐ **WERNER INDUSTRIES CO. (Chicago, IL)** *Affiliated with Krell, Auto-Player, Royal and Duchess Pianos. Made their own player mechanism.*	250.00	2750.00
☐ **WESER BROS. (NY)** *Used their own player mechanism.*	250.00-400.00	2500.00-3750.00
☐ **WESER PIANO CO.** *(Also Weser Bros., NY) Used the Standard, Simplex, Amphion, Aeolian and their own player mechanisms.*	250.00-400.00	2750.00-3750.00
☐ **CALVIN WESER MONARCH UPRIGHT SELF PLAYING PIANO,** *oak, some case decoration.*	750.00-1250.00	2750.00-4500.00
☐ **WEYDIG PIANO CORP. (NY)** *Used the Standard and Simplex Player mechanisms.*	250.00-350.00	2500.00-3500.00
☐ **WHEELOCK PIANO CO. (NY)** *Used the Aeolian and Duo-Art Reproducing Player mechanism. (See "Reproducing Expression Pianos" section). Regular Player*	250.00-350.00	2500.00-3750.00
☐ **WILCOX AND WHITE (CT)** *Used the Angelus mechanism.*	350.00	3750.00
☐ **WINTER AND CO. (NY)** *Used their own player mechanism. Winter mechanism also found in Heller & Co., Andrus, Rudolf, Reinhardt and other pianos.*	350.00	3500.00

	Unrestored	Restored
☐ **WISSNER AND SONS (NY)** *Used the Stauch Bros. Player mechanism.*	275.00	2750.00
☐ **WONDERTON PLAYER PIANOS** *Made by Lindenberg Piano Co. (Columbus, OH).*	250.00	2500.00
☐ **WOODBURY PIANOS** *Used the Simplex and Pratt and Read Player mechanisms.*	250.00	2750.00
☐ **WRIGHT AND SONS CO.** *Used their own player mechanism.*	250.00-275.00	2500.00-3000.00

RUDOLF WURLITZER CO. (IL) *Used the Apollo Reproducing mechanism (See "Nickelodeon" section).*

☐ **YORK PLAYER PIANOS (York, PA)** *Made by Weaver Piano Co.*	250.00	2500.00-2750.00

PLAYER ORGANS AND ORCHESTRELLES

The rise in popularity of the player piano directly related to the short lived market for player organs for home use. In America their popularity spanned from the mid 1880's to the first decade of the 20th-century.

These organs look like large upright keyboard pianos with highly ornate fretwork decoration.

A paper roll activated by foot pumping operates the mechanism, there are many manually controlled stops which create special effects: harp, oboe, viola, flute, etc. Knee operated swell levers control the volume. Their popularity peaked in the 1890's.

These machines are difficult to find and are most commonly seen for sale in dealer catalogues. (See "Dealers and Restorers" section.)

☐ **AEOLIAN DUO ART PLAYER AND PIPE ORGAN,** *13 ranks.*	1000.00-2500.00	5500.00-7500.00
☐ **AEOLIAN DUO ART ORCHESTRELLE PLAYER REED ORGAN** *Breakfront style when closed, keyboard folds down when in use, mahogany cabinet, uses Duo Art organ rolls.*	1500.00-3000.00	8000.00-12000.00
☐ **AEOLIAN GRAND PLAYER ORGAN** *c. 1900-1910. 58-note, 73 keys, 20 stops red mahogany, 5 fretwork panels, carved columns high back keyboard upright piano style foot pump, 60" high.*	750.00-1750.00	2250.00-4500.00
☐ **AEOLIAN HAMMAND PLAYER ORGAN** *Walnut case, plays Aeolian-Skinner Duo-Art Semi Automatic Player Organ Rolls.*	750.00-1500.00	3000.00-4000.00
☐ **AEOLIAN-SKINNER DUO-ART** *semi-automatic player organ rolls.*	20.00	27.00
☐ **AEOLIAN ORCHESTRELLE** *18 stops, mahogany, upright style, 58-note.*	500.00-1000.00	2500.00-4500.00

	Unrestored	Restored
☐ **AEOLIAN ORCHESTRELLE STYLE F** *116-note, mahogany case, electric or foot pump, plays 116-note solo and 58-note rolls interchangeably.*	2250.00-3250.00	12500.00-20000.00
☐ **AEOLIAN ORCHESTRELLE STYLE V** *5'6" high, fretwork panels, decorative mouldings, upright piano style.*	1500.00-3000.00	7500.00-10000.00
☐ **AEOLIAN ORCHESTRELLE STYLE Y** *58-note player organ, golden oak case, plays Aeolian Grand Rolls, 8'4".*	1500.00-3000.00	8000.00-10000.00
☐ **AEOLIAN PLAYER ORGAN** *5' high, 5'2" wide upright, 3 panels of fretwork on front, roll in center just above keyboard, front legs fully carved, foot pump, 46-note 9½" (9⅝") music roll, 17 stops. Rolls $8.00 and up.*	500.00-1500.00	2750.00-4500.00
☐ **AEOLIAN ORGAN STYLE 1500** *Ebony finish upright piano style, three fretwork panels, plays Aeolian 46-note organ rolls.*	1000.00-1600.00	3750.00-5000.00
☐ **AEOLIAN SOLO ORCHESTRELLE** *Mahogany, 6'7" high upright style, plays Aeolian Grand 58-note rolls and Aeolian pipe organ 116-note rolls. Rolls: $5.00 and up.*	2000.00-3000.00	7000.00-9000.00
☐ **AEOLIAN STYLE 1050 PLAYER REED ORGAN** *12 stops.*	1250.00-1500.00	3000.00-4500.00
☐ **ANGELUS ORCHESTRAL PLAYER ORGAN** *58-note organ piano, mahogany, 7 stops.*	500.00-850.00	2000.00-3500.00
☐ **C.A.V. LUNDHOLM (Stockholm) REED ORGAN** *Upright piano style, 51½" high, bellows pumped by piano type pedals, knee swells, ebony finished case, plays Ariston organette discs, mechanism is situated on outside side end of case.*	500.00-1000.00	2400.00-4000.00
☐ **ORCHESTRONE STYLE 441 B PAPER ROLL ORGAN** *c. 1880's, 55" high, (made by Munroe Organ Reed Co.), ornately carved walnut case with fretwork decoration, bowed front section houses roll assembly, storage for extra rolls on either side.*	3000.00-4000.00	8000.00-12000.00
☐ **ORCHESTRONE PAPER ROLL ORGAN** *47" high, walnut case, carved decoration, foot pedals create vacuum, roll operates by hand crank, 48 note organ, 8½" wide paper roll.*	750.00-1500.00	2750.00-4000.00
☐ **REPRODUCO (OPERATOR'S PIANO CO.) PIPE ORGAN** *Three ranks of pipes, coin operated, combination mechanism plays 88-note piano rolls as well as "OS" and "NOS" rolls.*	3000.00 4000.00	6500.00-7500.00
☐ **REPRODUCO PIANO PIPE ORGAN** *Made by Operator's Piano Co., Chicago, double keyboard upright piano style, mahogany, rank of pipes, uses "OS" and "NOS" rolls.*	2000.00-3000.00	6000.00-7500.00

	Unrestored	Restored
☐ **SEEBURG MORTUARY ORGAN MODEL H-O** *61-note, all pipes, plays H-O rolls also Seeburg XP and regular 88-note piano rolls, double keyboard, simple lines, case cabinet comes up and around keyboard and pipes leaving a wide curved opening in front.*	3500.00-4500.00	7500.00-9500.00
☐ **SEEBURG THEATER PIANO/ORGAN** *4'10½" high upright keyboard piano style, simple case with candle holders on front side panels, mahogany, blower, pseudo organ pipes.*	3750.00-4500.00	7500.00-9500.00
☐ **STORY AND CLARK "ORPHEUS" PARLOR PLAYER ORGAN** *c. 1898. Single keyboard, 61-note, two sets of reeds, plays 58-note rolls, decorative embossed and colored panels on top front, middle panel contains roll box, 9 stops, walnut case, plays "Orpheus" grand 10 7/16" rolls.*	1500.00-2000.00	3000.00-5000.00
☐ **VICTOLIAN PLAYER ORGAN** *46-note, oak plain case, tempo and re-roll stops, knee swells, 59-key, roll placed just above keyboard in center.*	1600.00-2000.00	3000.00-5000.00
☐ **WELTE PHILHARMONIC PIPE ORGAN** *8 ranks, fully automatic roll playing mechanism, harp and chimes.*	3000.00-4000.00	6500.00-9500.00
☐ **WELTE PLAYER ORGAN** *8 Rank Organ, player cabinet, harp, chimes.*	1500.00-2000.00	6500.00
☐ **WILCOX AND WHITE PLAYER ORGAN** *44 note piano keyboard style, three elaborately designed front panels (pressed wood), roll assembly just above keyboard, foot pedals, 57½" high.*	500.00-900.00	2250.00-3750.00
☐ **WILCOX AND WHITE PNEUMATIC SYMPHONY** *Reed Organ, upright piano style, oak, fretwork center panel, some case decoration, roll mechanism just above keyboard, 22 stops.*	1000.00-1500.00	2500.00-4000.00
☐ **WURLITZER RESIDENCE (OR MORTUARY) ORGAN** *c. 1930. 4'11" high, double keyboard, "Gothic" style case decoration, 4 ranks of pipes, one metal, swell shutters, 61-note organ, 88-note piano, remote suction motor, walnut case.*	4000.00-4500.00	10000.00-13000.00
☐ **WURLITZER THEATER PIPE ORGAN STYLE 135** *Console piano style, twin roll player, 88-note rolls, two keyboards, 5 ranks of pipes, drums, xylophone, bells.*	3000.00-4000.00	8000.00-10000.00

REPRODUCING AND EXPRESSION PIANOS

See introduction to Player Piano section for brief history and description. Welte-Mignon was the first well-known reproducing and expression system in the United States though it originated in Germany, Duo-Art and Ampico developed their mechanisms here.

Reproducing and expression mechanisms were installed in the usual upright piano styles most people associate with the player piano. They were also installed in many sizes and makes of baby and full grand pianos. The Ampico system was installed in a "drawer" horizontally placed beneath the keyboard. One pulls the drawer outward to reveal the tracker bar/roll assembly with the tempo, play/rewind and other controls. The Ampico "B" system is later than the "A" system. In the open drawer position there are dials instead of sliding controls for the tempo, etc.

In grand style pianos, the Duo Art piano roll housing is located above the Keyboard, just below and slightly in front of the music desk. The center section lifts up to reveal the tracker bar. The tempo, play/rewind, etc. controls are located in the key slip in front of the keys. In later examples the controls are up near the tracker bar.

The Welte piano roll housing is placed like the Duo Art above the keyboard. The Welte Liscensee system is in a drawer beneath the keyboard like the Ampico.

The Recordo system is housed in a drawer beneath the keyboard also.

Except for early examples most Reproducing pianos were originally powered electrically. This is true of the upright models as well.

All reproducing mechanisms require especially arranged piano rolls to produce the proper "expressive" performance desired. Each company made rolls for their mechanism that would not work on any other make.

Regular 88-note rolls will play on these pianos, however, they will sound much as they do on a regular player piano.

Reproducing Expression mechanisms were made for all types and sizes of pianos, from a tiny Kohler and Campbell Tom Thumb Recordo upright with 61 notes to the large Steinway Duo-Art Grands.

(See "Piano Rolls" section for further information about reproducing rolls. Also "Dealers and Restorers—Piano Roll Dealers".)

Unlike the previous section, the following values are for specific piano styles in either restored or unrestored condition: Unrestored (complete but not working), Restored (completely, inside and out to "original working condition").

These values are subject to the variables described in the introduction to the "Player Piano" section and the "Determining Values" explanation in the front of the book.

	Unrestored	Restored
AMPICO "A"		
☐ *CHICKERING AMPICO "A" Upright, simple lines.*	1000.00-2000.00	4000.00-7000.00
☐ *CHICKERING AMPICO "A" GRAND Art case, Italian Renaissance, ornately carved, matching bench.*	4200.00	10000.00-15000.00
☐ *CHICKERING AMPICO "A" GRAND, c. 1930. Simple case style in mahogany, 5′2″.*	1600.00-2000.00	5000.00-8000.00
☐ *CHICKERING AMPICO "A" GRAND, c. 1927. Painted art case with floral and figural decoration, triple legs with fancy mouldings, 5′2″.*	2000.00-3500.00	10000.00-15000.00

	Unrestored	Restored
☐ *CHICKERING AMPICO "A" GRAND Art case, William and Mary case style, 5′3½″, mahogany (walnut) bulbous legs, scalloped moulding.*	**4500.00**	**8000.00-12000.00**
☐ *CHICKERING AMPICO "A" GRAND 5′4″, c. 1924, walnut with maple burr decoration.*	**2000.00-3500.00**	**10000.00-15000.00**
☐ *CHICKERING AMPICO "A" GRAND, c. 1925. Simple mahogany case style, 5′4″.*	**1500.00-3000.00**	**8000.00-11000.00**
☐ *CHICKERING AMPICO "A" GRAND Art case style decoration, Louis XVI 5′4″.*	**1500.00-3000.00**	**8000.00-10000.00**
☐ *CHICKERING AMPICO "A" GRAND Art case, Louis XV 5′8″, carved legs and trim.*	**5000.00**	**13500.00-15000.00**
☐ *CHICKERING AMPICO "A" GRAND Simple style, 5′9″, ebony case finish.*	**1500.00-2000.00**	**5000.00-7000.00**
☐ *CHICKERING AMPICO "A" GRAND Simple lines (Style #65), 6′5″, mahogany or walnut.*	**3500.00**	**8000.00-12000.00**
☐ *CHICKERING AMPICO "A" GRAND (Style #52), simple case, double legs.*	**1500.00-3000.00**	**8000.00**
☐ *CHICKERING AMPICO "A" GRAND (Style #58), straight lines, double legs, 5′8″ Grand.*	**2500.00-3500.00**	**7000.00-11000.00**

	Unrestored	Restored
☐ CHICKERING AMPICO "A" GRAND Art case, florentine, walnut with gold decoration especially on fluted legs, 5'3½"	5000.00-7000.00	13000.00-15000.00
☐ CHICKERING AMPICO "A" GRAND Simple mahogany case style, 6'0"	2000.00	7000.00
☐ CHICKERING AMPICO "A" GRAND 9', simple lines, mahogany	8500.00-10000.00	20000.00
☐ CHICKERING AMPICO "A" GRAND 5'4", simple case, fruitwood	2500.00-3500.00	6500.00-7000.00
☐ CHICKERING AMPICO STUDIO CABINET PIANO, keyboardless, carved walnut case in Italian Renaissance style, very rare, c. 1927	2500.00-3500.00	10000.00-14000.00
☐ CHICKERING AMPICO "A", SQUARED OFF GRAND Cabinet style ("coffin case", 8 legs, Jacobean style decoration	3000.00-5000.00	8000.00-12000.00
☐ FISCHER SPINET AMPICO "A" c. late 1930's. Top loading	1500.00-2000.00	3500.00-4000.00
☐ FISCHER AMPICO "A" GRAND 5'2", simple case style	1500.00-2000.00	8000.00-9000.00
☐ FISCHER AMPICO "A" GRAND 5'3", mahogany, Louis XV art case, single legs, matching bench	2500.00-3500.00	8500.00-9500.00
☐ FISCHER AMPICO "A" GRAND 5'4", simple case, mahogany, matching bench	2000.00-3000.00	7500.00-9000.00
☐ FISCHER AMPICO "A" GRAND Louis XV, walnut art case, decorative mouldings	1500.00-3000.00	8000.00-12000.00
☐ FISCHER AMPICO A/B GRAND, c. 1929. Rosewood case, 5'7", some decoration	1500.00-1750.00	7500.00-10000.00
☐ FISCHER STUDIO UPRIGHT c. 1930's. Top loading, Ampico "A", 3'10"	2000.00-3000.00	3500.00-7000.00
☐ FISCHER AMPICO "A" GRAND c. 1923, simple case style	1500.00-1750.00	6500.00-10000.00
☐ FRANKLIN AMPICO "A" GRAND c. 1923. 5', simple case style	1500.00-2000.00	5000.00-7000.00
☐ FRANKLIN AMPICO "A" Upright, simple case, mahogany	1000.00-2000.00	4000.00-5000.00
☐ FRANKLIN MARGUE AMPICO UPRIGHT c. 1923. Simple mahogany case style, foot pump	750.00-1500.00	3500.00-4500.00
☐ HAINES BROS. Upright Ampico "A"	700.00-1200.00	3750.00-4750.00
☐ HAINES BROS. MARQUE AMPICO UPRIGHT c. 1920. Mahogany case, simple straight style, foot pump	1000.00-1500.00	3000.00-4000.00

	Unrestored	Restored
☐ HAINES BROS. AMPICO "A" GRAND 5'1", c. 1925, mahogany simple case.	1750.00-2500.00	6000.00-8000.00
☐ HAINES BROS. AMPICO "A" GRAND c. 1922. Louis XV mahogany art case, 5'4".	2500.00-3500.00	8500.00-9500.00
☐ HAINES BROS. AMPICO "A" EXPRESSION (Model "B" Drawer) c. 1930. Semi-art case.	3500.00-4000.00	7500.00-8500.00
☐ KNABE AMPICO PARLOR GRAND 6'5", c. 1928, black walnut, cabriole legs with carving.	2500.00-3500.00	7000.00-9000.00
☐ KNABE AMPICO "A" GRAND 5'2", simple case style.	1500.00-2500.00	6500.00-10000.00
☐ KNABE AMPICO "A" GRAND 5'3", walnut art case (style A-GE).	2600.00-4600.00	6750.00-8200.00
☐ KNABE AMPICO "A" GRAND 5'4", plain case.	2600.00 3400.00	6700.00 8500.00
☐ KNABE AMPICO "A" GRAND 5"4" Louis XVI art case style, 9 legs, with stretchers, decorative mouldings.	3000.00-5000.00	8000.00-12000.00
☐ KNABE AMPICO "A" GRAND 5'8", simple case, heavy legs.	3000.00 3900.00	10000.00 12500.00
☐ KNABE AMPICO "A" GRAND c. 1921. 5'8", Louis XV case style, graceful curved legs with decoration, mahogany.	3000.00-5000.00	8000.00-12000.00
☐ KNABE AMPICO "A" GRAND 6', c. 1925, Louis XV style case, walnut, cabriole legs.	3500.00-4500.00	8000.00-10000.00
☐ KNABE AMPICO "A" Upright, 4'8¾", plain case.	750.00-1750.00	4500.00-6000.00
☐ KNABE AMPICO "A" Upright, 4'4¼", plain case.	750.00-1750.00	4500.00-6000.00
☐ KNABE AMPICO "A" SPINET c. late 1930's. Top loading.	2500.00	5000.00 6000.00
☐ KNABE AMPICO "A" GRAND 7"7½", three sets of double width legs, ornate decoration, gilded painted panels and carved mouldings.	7500.00-10000.00	20000.00-30000.00
☐ KNABE AMPICO "A" GRAND 9', rosewood, decorative music stand and trim.	3500.00-4500.00	10000.00-12000.00
☐ MARSHALL AND WENDELL AMPICO "A" 4'8", mahogany Grand.	2500.00-3500.00	6500.00-7500.00
☐ MARSHALL AND WENDELL APMICO "A" GRAND 5'0", c. 1930, simple mahogany.	2500.00-3000.00	6500.00-8000.00
☐ MARSHALL AND WENDELL AMPICO "A" GRAND c. 1925. 5", Louis XVI art case style.	2000.00-3000.00	6500.00-7500.00

	Unrestored	Restored
☐ *MARSHALL AND WENDELL AMPICO "A" GRAND c. 1924. 5′1″, mahogany simple case.*	2500.00-3500.00	7000.00-8500.00
☐ *MARSHALL AND WENDELL AMPICO "A" GRAND 5′, walnut.*	2000.00-3000.00	7000.00-8000.00
☐ *MARSHALL AND WENDELL AMPICO "A" GRAND c. 1927. 5′4″, Spanish style art case, wrought iron decoration (also called "Mediterranean" style).*	3000.00-5000.00	8600.00-12000.00
☐ *MARSHALL AND WENDELL AMPICO "A" GRAND 5′5″, mahogany art case, carved floral mouldings, 3 "triple" legs with carved fretwork (center leg), stretchers connecting legs.*	3000.00-5000.00	10000.00-15000.00
☐ *MARSHALL AND WENDELL Upright, 46″, mahogany.*	1500.00-2250.00	4000.00-6000.00
☐ *MARSHALL AND WENDELL AMPICO "A" Upright, 55″ high, c. 1922, Circassian walnut.*	1750.00-2250.00-3000.00	4500.00-6500.00-6500.00
☐ *MARSHALL AND WENDELL AMPICO "A" Upright, 5′3″, mahogany, simple case style.*	1000.00-1500.00	3000.00-4000.00
☐ *MARSHALL AND WENDELL Studio upright, Ampico "A", simple case.*	1250.00-2250.00	5000.00-6500.00
☐ *MARSHALL AND WENDELL AMPICO "A" SPINET (BABY AMPICO) 37″.*	2000.00-2500.00	6750.00-8200.00
☐ *MASON AND HAMLIN AMPICO "A" GRAND 5′4″, plain mahogany case.*	4500.00	8500.00
☐ *MASON AND HAMLIN AMPICO "A" GRAND 6′4″, c. 1928, simple mahogany case.*	3000.00-4000.00	9000.00-12000.00
☐ *MASON AND HAMLIN AMPICO "A" GRAND 5′9″, Style AR, simple mahogany case.*	3500.00	8500.00-10000.00
☐ *MASON AND HAMLIN AMPICO "A" GRAND 6′2″, figural walnut.*	3500.00-5000.00	14000.00-18500.00
☐ *MASON AND HAMLIN AMPICO "A" GRAND c. 1926. 6′2″, "Colonial" style art case.*	3500.00-5000.00	8000.00-12000.00
☐ *MASON AND HAMLIN AMPICO "A" GRAND 7′, c. 1925, plain case.*	4000.00-7500.00	15000.00-25000.00
☐ *MASON AND HAMLIN AMPICO "A" GRAND, Style AA, ebony finish, simple case style.*	2750.00-4500.00	7500.00-9000.00
☐ *STECK AMPICO "A" SPINET c. late 1930's. Top loading roll mechanism.*	2500.00	6000.00

	Unrestored	Restored
AMPICO "B"		
☐ CHICKERING AMPICO "B" GRAND Walnut case with some maple decoration	3000.00-4500.00	10000.00-15000.00
☐ CHICKERING AMPICO "B" GRAND c. 1940. 5', mahogany.	4000.00	10500.00
☐ CHICKERING AMPICO "B" GRAND c. 1930. 5'4", Sheraton art case style.	2750.00-4000.00	7500.00-9500.00
☐ CHICKERING AMPICO "B" GRAND c. 1934. 5'10", walnut.	5000.00	12500.00
☐ FISCHER AMPICO "B" SPINET STYLE c. 1930's. Some case moulding and decoration.	1500.00 2500.00	4000.00 6000.00
☐ FISCHER AMPICO "B" GRAND 4'10". Walnut case finish with single "french" leg.	2000.00-2750.00	5500.00-7500.00
☐ FISCHER AMPICO "B" GRAND 5'4", c. 1930, mahogany, simple case style.	2500.00-3250.00	7000.00-9000.00
☐ HAINES BROS. AMPICO "A/B" GRAND 4'8", Louis XV art case.	2000.00-3000.00	5500.00-7500.00
☐ HAINES BROS. AMPICO "B" GRAND 4'8", simple case, turned legs.	2000.00-3000.00	7500.00-8500.00
☐ HAINES BROS. AMPICO "B" GRAND 5', art case.	2000.00-3000.00	5500.00-7500.00
☐ KNABE AMPICO "B" GRAND c. 1926. 5', simple case style.	1750.00-2000.00	7000.00-8000.00
☐ KNABE AMPICO "B" GRAND 5'4", Queen Anne single leg, figured walnut with decorative details.	3000.00-6000.00	13500.00-17000.00
☐ KNABE AMPICO "B" GRAND Style #406, 5'8", mahogany, with Ampichron unit.	5000.00-6000.00	12000.00-15000.00
☐ KNABE AMPICO "B" GRAND 5'3", Louis XV art case, walnut.	4000.00	8000.00-10000.00
☐ KNABE AMPICO "B" GRAND c. 1933. Walnut, 5'4", simple case.	3000.00	8500.00-9500.00
☐ KNABE AMPICO "B" GRAND c. 1941.	2000.00-3000.00	14000.00-16900.00
☐ MARSHALL AND WENDELL AMPICO "B" GRAND c. 1931. 5'2", mahogany, simple case style.	2500.00	8500.00
☐ MARSHALL AND WENDELL AMPICO "B" GRAND 5'2", Mediterranian art case style.	2000.00-3000.00	9000.00-11000.00
☐ MARSHALL AND WENDELL AMPICO "B" GRAND 4'8", simple mahogany case.	2500.00-3500.00	7500.00-9500.00

	Unrestored	Restored
☐ *MARSHALL AND WENDELL AMPICO "B" GRAND c. 1931. 4'8", William and Mary art case style.*	2000.00-3000.00	7500.00-8500.00
☐ *MARSHALL AND WENDELL AMPICO "B" GRAND c. 1930's. 4'10".*	2500.00	7500.00-9500.00
☐ *MASON AND HAMLIN AMPICO "B" GRAND c. 1933, plain case.*	2500.00-3000.00	5000.00-7000.00
☐ *MASON AND HAMLIN AMPICO "B" Louis XV art case, painted decoration.*	5000.00-7000.00	13500.00-17500.00
☐ *MASON AND HAMLIN AMPICO "B" GRAND c. 1930. 5'8", Florentine art case, walnut.*	5000.00-7000.00	25000.00-35000.00
☐ *MASON AND HAMLIN AMPICO "B" GRAND c. 1942. 5'8", art case.*	5000.00-7000.00	25000.00-35000.00
☐ *MASON AND HAMLIN AMPICO "B" GRAND c. 1930. 5'8", brown mahogany, simple style.*	3000.00-5000.00-	15000.00-20000.00
☐ *MASON AND HAMLIN AMPICO "B" GRAND 7', simple case style.*	3000.00-5000.00	15000.00-20000.00
☐ *STECK AMPICO "B" GRAND 5', mahogany, matching bench, jumbo rolls.*	2500.00-3500.00	6000.00-8500.00
☐ *STEINWAY AMPICO "B" GRAND c. 1930's. Simple case, pull out drawer.*	10000.00	20000.00

ANGELUS EXPRESSION PIANOS

	Unrestored	Restored
☐ *CHICKERING ANGELUS GRAND 6'6", foot pump, simple mahogany case style.*	1000.00-1500.00	4000.00-6000.00
☐ *EMERSON ANGELUS 65-note player.*	750.00-1500.00	3500.00-5000.00

APOLLO EXPRESSION PIANOS

	Unrestored	Restored
☐ *APOLLOPHONE UPRIGHT PLAYER/PHONOGRAPH COMBINATION 57½", simple case style phonograph installed on upper left side of piano above keyboard.*	2000.00-2500.00	5000.00-7500.00
☐ *MELVILLE CLARK APOLLO GRAND Simple case style.*	1000.00-1500.00	5000.00-7000.00
☐ *WURLITZER APOLLO GRAND 4'9", mahogany, simple case style.*	1500.00-2000.00	4500.00-6500.00

DUO-ART

	Unrestored	Restored
☐ *AEOLIAN DUO-ART GRAND Style RR, 5'2½", mahogany.*	3000.00	8000.00
☐ *AEOLIAN DUO-ART GRAND 5'6", mahogany case, simple style.*	1500.00-2000.00	5000.00-7000.00

	Unrestored	Restored
☐ LYON AND HEALY DUO-ART GRAND 5'4", c. 1928, simple case style.	1500.00-2000.00	5000.00-7000.00
☐ MASON AND RISCH DUO-ART GRAND c. 1930. 6'1", mahogany.	5000.00	10000.00
☐ GEORGE STECK DUO-ART GRAND 5', plain case.	1500.00-2500.00	4500.00-5500.00
☐ GEORGE STECK DUO-ART GRAND 5'4", c. 1920's, plain mahogany case.	2000.00-3000.00	5000.00-7500.00
☐ GEORGE STECK DUO-ART GRAND 5'7", walnut.	1000.00-2000.00	6000.00-7500.00
☐ GEORGE STECK DUO-ART GRAND c. 1922. 5'8", mahogany.	1000.00-2000.00	6000.00-8000.00
☐ GEORGE STECK DUO-ART GRAND Style HR.	1000.00-2000.00	6000.00-7500.00
☐ GEORGE STECK DUO-ART GRAND Style MM, 6'½", mahogany plain.	1000.00-2000.00	7000.00-8500.00
☐ GEORGE STECK DUO-ART c. 1922. Upright, walnut.	750.00-1000.00	4000.00-5000.00
☐ GEORGE STECK DUO-ART Upright, 4'4¾", mahogany (oak), foot pump, early.	500.00-1000.00	3500.00-4500.00
☐ STECK-GOTHA DUO-ART GRAND, pump pedals enclosed in case under keyboard at pedal lyre, triple legs, inlaid garlands, oval scenes in medallions along body of case (art case) early Duo-Art.	2250.00-3250.00	8000.00-12000.00
☐ STEINWAY DUO-ART GRAND 6'1", c. 1920, walnut case.	3500.00-4500.00	10500.00-15000.00
☐ STEINWAY DUO-ART Style XR, 6'1", mahogany.	5000.00-7000.00	13000.00-15000.00
☐ STEINWAY DUO-ART GRAND, Model OR, Italian Renaissance art case style, c. 1929.	8500.00-10500.00	15000.00-20000.00
☐ STEINWAY DUO-ART c. 1922. Style OR, 6'6", turned double legs, matching bench.	6000.00-7000.00	13000.00-16000.00
☐ STEINWAY DUO-ART Upright, Style "S", c. 1920. mahogany case.	2500.00-3000.00	5500.00-6500.00
☐ STEINWAY UPRIGHT DUO-ART Simple case.	3000.00	8000.00
☐ STEINWAY DUO-ART GRAND Style AR, 6'11½", mahogany.	5000.00-6000.00	13000.00-15000.00
☐ STEINWAY DUO-ART GRAND Art case, "Italian" style fluted, tapered double legs, decorative mouldings.	10000.00	20000.00
☐ STEINWAY DUO-ART MODEL SALON GRAND 6'6", Spanish Renaissance, highly carved, turned legs.	10000.00	20000.00
☐ STEINWAY DUO-ART GRAND Model OR, mahogany.	4000.00	10000.00-15000.00

	Unrestored	Restored
☐ STEINWAY DUO-ART GRAND Model OR, art case, Louis XVI, fluted carved legs, 6'5"	10000.00	20000.00
☐ STEINWAY VERTIGRAND, c. 1911, Aeolian Player	1500.00-2000.00	4000.00-5000.00
☐ STEINWAY DUO-ART GRAND Style XR, Louis XV art case, 6'2", matching bench	4000.00-5000.00	15000.00-20000.00
☐ STEINWAY DUO-ART GRAND c. 1918. Ebony, 6'4"	4000.00-5000.00	10000.00
☐ STEINWAY DUO-ART GRAND Model D, 9'6", extra braced double legs	4500.00-5500.00	20000.00-30000.00
☐ STROUD DUO-ART GRAND c. 1932, 5", walnut case	1500.00-2500.00	5250.00-6000.00
☐ STROUD UPRIGHT DUO-ART c. 1928	1000.00-1500.00	3000.00-4500.00
☐ STROUD UPRIGHT DUO-ART 4'7", mahogany	1000.00-1500.00	3000.00-4500.00
☐ STROUD DUO-ART UPRIGHT Foot pump, 4'6", early	750.00-1500.00	3750.00-5000.00
☐ STROUD DUO ART GRAND 5'2", simple case style, some decoration	3000.00-4000.00	6000.00-7500.00
☐ STROUD DUO ART GRAND 5'3", art case style, decorative details and moulding	3000.00-4000.00	6000.00-7500.00
☐ STROUD DUO-ART c. 1932. 5'4", fruitwood, (brown mahogany)	3000.00-4000.00	6000.00-8000.00
☐ STROUD DUO ART GRAND c. 1928. 5'8", gold and white painted case decoration	3000.00-4000.00	6500.00-8000.00
☐ WEBER DUO-ART GRAND 5'9"	3000.00	6500.00-9000.00
☐ WEBER DUO-ART GRAND Style FR, 5'11½", mahogany	4000.00	8000.00-9000.00
☐ WEBER DUO-ART GRAND 5'8", inlaid art case	6000.00	10000.00-12000.00
☐ WEBER DUO-ART GRAND 5'8", walnut art case	4000.00-5000.00	8000.00-10000.00
☐ WEBER DUO-ART GRAND Fruitwood finish, 5'8", matching bench and roll cabinet	3000.00	8500.00-12000.00
☐ WEBER DUO-ART GRAND 5'8", burled oak, gothic style case, 10 legs	6000.00-8000.00	15000.00-17500.00
☐ WEBER DUO-ART GRAND 6'1", painted case	4000.00	8000.00
☐ WEBER DUO-ART GRAND c. 1921. 6'3", walnut	3500.00-4500.00	7500.00-9500.00
☐ WEBER DUO-ART GRAND c. 1924. 6'2", walnut case with some simple decoration	3500.00-4500.00	7500.00-9000.00

	Unrestored	Restored
☐ *WEBER DUO-ART GRAND c. 1920. 5'10", Style WR, brown mahogany*	3000.00-3400.00	6000.00-8000.00
☐ *WEBER DUO-ART GRAND c. 1929. 5'6", inlaid medallions on case, bench.*	1500.00-3000.00	9000.00-12000.00
☐ *WEBER DUO-ART GRAND c. late 1920's. Louis XVI art case, scroll details.*	4000.00-5000.00	8000.00-12000.00
☐ *WEBER DUO-ART UPRIGHT c. 1915, Flame grain mahogany.*	1500.00-2000.00	4000.00-5000.00
☐ *WEBER UPRIGHT DUO-ART Foot pump (and electric), 4'5", plain case, mahogany*	750.00-1250.00	3500.00-4500.00
☐ *WEBER UPRIGHT DUO-ART Oak, 4'5", plain case.*	1000.00-1500.00	3750.00-5000.00
☐ *WHEELOCK DUO-ART UPRIGHT Early, 4'6¾", mahogany case, foot pump*	750.00-1000.00	3250.00-4500.00

HUPFELD EXPRESSION PIANOS

	Unrestored	Restored
☐ *HUPFELD (BLUTHNER) THIPHONOLA GRAND 6'3", rosewood, foot pump with electric expression, simple case lines, double leg*	5000.00-6000.00	10000.00-12000.00
☐ *HUPFELD-DEA GRAND 6'1", ebony finish, foot pump and electric expression, simple case lines, double leg*	4500.00-5000.00	7500.00-10000.00
☐ *HUPFELD-DEA (RONISH) UPRIGHT c. 1905. Mahogany with some case decoration, electric drive*	2500.00-3500.00	6000.00-7000.00
☐ *HUPFELD PHONOLA UPRIGHT 65-note, foot pump, ebony case finish, mother-of-pearl decoration.*	1200.00-1500.00	6000.00-7000.00
☐ *HUPFELD PHONOLA UPRIGHT 73-note, pedal operated, decorated walnut case with brass and mother-of-pearl inlays, candle holders on sides of top front panels.*	1200.00-1500.00	6000.00-7000.00
☐ *HUPFELD (RONISCH) TRIPHONOLA UPRIGHT 4'4", mahogany case, foot pump and electric expression mechanism, simple case style*	2500.00-3500.00	6000.00-7000.00

RECORDO

	Unrestored	Restored
☐ *APOLLO RECORDO GRAND Simple case style*	750.00-1250.00	3750.00-5000.00
☐ *H. C. BAY 5'3", Baby Grand with bench.*	500.00-1000.00	3500.00-4750.00
☐ *BRINKERHOFF RECORDO Small Grand.*	750.00-1100.00	3500.00-5000.00

	Unrestored	Restored
☐ *BUSH AND LANE RECORDO GRAND c. 1924. 5", simple case style.*	1000.00	3500.00-4750.00
☐ *CABLE-NELSON RECORDO Upright, 4'10" high, plain case.*	2000.00-3000.00	5500.00-7500.00
☐ *CHOPIN RECORDO GRAND c. mid 1920's. 5'2", mahogany, simple case style.*	500.00-1000.00	3500.00-5000.00
☐ *CUNNINGHAM RECORDER GRAND c. 1927. 5', Auto De Luxe, Circassian walnut, single cabriole legs.*	750.00-1250.00	3500.00-5500.00
☐ *JACOB DOLL c. 1928. 4'8", Baby Grand, drawer under keyboard.*	500.00-1000.00	3000.00-3500.00
☐ *KOHLER & CAMPBELL "TOM THUMB" c. 1926, 61-note upright Chinese art case and bench, rare.*	1500.00-2500.00	4000.00-4500.00
☐ *LINGARD (WURLITZER) RECORDO GRAND 5', "A" expression mechanism, mahogany case.*	1800.00-2500.00	4500.00-5500.00
☐ *MEHLIN & SONS, c. 1934. 4'9", Baby Grand, walnut.*	1500.00-2000.00	4000.00-4500.00
☐ *RECORDO PIXIE-DAVENPORT & TREACY PIANO CO. 41", 40½" wide, 61-note, mahogany, matching bench.*	750.00-1500.00	3000.00-4000.00
☐ *STUYVESANT UPRIGHT Simple case, mahogany.*	500.00-1000.00	3500.00-4000.00
☐ *WALTHAM GRAND 5'1", mahogany.*	1000.00-1500.00	3000.00-4000.00
☐ *WURLITZER 4'10", mahogany, art case, (9 legs).*	1500.00-2000.00	4000.00-5750.00

WELTE, WELTE-MIGNON, WELTE LICENSEE

	Unrestored	Restored
☐ *BALDWIN WELTE GRAND Art case, Louis XIV.*	2500.00-3500.00	7000.00-9000.00
☐ *BALDWIN WELTE GRAND Art case, Louis XVI.*	2500.00-3500.00	7000.00-9000.00
☐ *BALDWIN WELTE GRAND Art case, Jacobean.*	2500.00-3500.00	7000.00-9000.00
☐ *BECHSTEIN WELTE GRAND 7', Ebony finish.*	3500.00-4500.00	10000.00-15000.00
☐ *BECHSTEIN WELTE MIGNON GRAND Model 98, plays green Welte rolls, simple case style.*	1000.00-2000.00	7000.00-9000.00
☐ *BRAMBACH WELTE LICENSEE GRAND 4'10", brown mahogany, simple case style.*	1000.00-1750.00	3500.00-5000.00
☐ *BUSH AND LANE WELTE GRAND c. 1923. 6', art case style with decorative mouldings.*	1000.00-1500.00	5000.00-6500.00

	Unrestored	Restored
☐ *BUSH AND LANE WELTE GRAND 6′6″, walnut art case*	1250.00-1750.00	6000.00-7000.00
☐ *CABLE (HOBART M.) WELTE GRAND 4′10″, mahogany, simple case.*	1000.00-1500.00	5500.00-7500.00
☐ *CABLE NELSON WELTE LICENSEE Art case upright, turned front legs, decorative moulding, inlay.*	1500.00-2000.00	4500.00-5000.00
☐ *CHICKERING WELTE ACOUSTIGRANDE.*	1500.00-2000.00	7000.00
☐ *CONOVER WELTE UPRIGHT Simple case.*	500.00-1000.00	3500.00-4750.00
☐ *ELLINGTON WELTE MIGNON LICENSEE GRAND c. 1914. 5′6″, brown mahogany.*	1000.00-1500.00	5000.00-7000.00
☐ *ESTEY WELTE-MIGNON 5′3″, Grand, walnut.*	1500.00	5000.00-6500.00
☐ *ESTEY WELTY MIGNON GRAND 5′7″, burled mahogany case, some decoration.*	1000.00-1250.00	4500.00-6500.00
☐ *FARRAND WELTE GRAND c. 1926. 5′2″, Jacobean case style, decorative mouldings.*	500.00-1000.00	3000.00-4000.00
☐ *FEURICH WELTE UPRIGHT Mahogany, 5′ high.*	1850.00-2250.00	4500.00-5500.00
☐ *FEURICH WHITE CABINET KEYBOARDLESS UPRIGHT PIANO (Oak) mahogany, "RED" Welte System, 5′.*	2000.00-3000.00	7000.00-10500.00
☐ *HARDMAN WELTE-MIGNON 5′10″, Grand, Jacobean art case, mahogany with burled walnut inlay, matching bench.*	1500.00-2000.00	7500.00-9500.00
☐ *HARDMAN WELTE UPRIGHT Simple lines, mahogany.*	750.00-1000.00	3500.00-4750.00
☐ *HOWARD (BALDWIN) WELTE GRAND Simple case.*	750.00-1000.00	3000.00-4000.00
☐ *KIMBALL WHITE GRAND 5′9″, simple case style.*	500.00-1250.00	4500.00-5500.00
☐ *KIMBALL WELTE GRAND 6′, simple case.*	500.00-1250.00	4500.00-5500.00
☐ *KRANICH AND BACH BABY GRAND c. 1924. Welte-Mignon, 5′, Grand.*	2000.00-2500.00	3500.00-4500.00
☐ *KRANICH AND BACH WELTE c. 1928. Art case, Louis XV, walnut.*	4000.00	10000.00
☐ *LESTER WELTE GRAND 5′7″, simple case style.*	1500.00-2000.00	4500.00-6500.00
☐ *MASON AND HAMLIN WELTE UPRIGHT c. 1913. Simple case style.*	1000.00-2000.00	7500.00-9500.00
☐ *MATHUSHEK WELTE GRAND c. 1935. 5′3″, action in drawer.*	2000.00	5000.00

	Unrestored	Restored
☐ *MEHLIN AND SONS, WELTE UPRIGHT Simple case style, mahogany*	500.00-1000.00	3000.00-4750.00
☐ *PACKARD WELTE UPRIGHT Plain case style, mahogany*	500.00-1000.00	3000.00-4750.00
☐ *SCHULZ WELTE GRAND 5'1", plain case*	1000.00-2500.00	4500.00-6500.00
☐ *SCHULZ WELTE Art case, Bardini Italian Renaissance, carved double legs, decorative moulding, action in drawer*	1500.00-2500.00	4000.00-6500.00
☐ *SCHULZ WELTE Art case, "French" style (also Spanish style), action in drawer*	1500.00-2500.00	4000.00-5000.00
☐ *SOHMER WELTE UPRIGHT Simple case*	500.00-1000.00	2000.00-2500.00
☐ *SOHMER WELTE Art case, Queen Anne style*	750.00-1500.00	4000.00-6000.00
☐ *SOHMER WELTE GRAND Art case, Jacobean*	1000.00-2500.00	4000.00-6000.00
☐ *SOHMER WELTE GRAND Art case, Italian Renaissance style*	1500.00-3500.00	6000.00-8500.00
☐ *SOHMER WELTE GRAND 6', walnut case, simple lines*	2000.00-3000.00	5500.00-7500.00
☐ *STEINWAY WELTE GRAND Simple case style with large single leg supports, top front roll loading mechanism (13½" roll)*	2000.00-4000.00	8000.00-12000.00
☐ *STEINWAY WELTE MIGNON GRAND Model 100, 6'10", plays Red Welte rolls, simple case style in ebony finish*	3500.00-4500.00	9000.00-11000.00
☐ *STEINWAY WELTE UPRIGHT c. 1910. 13½" roll, play action in top only, 6', upright*	4000.00	9000.00-11000.00
☐ *STEINWAY WELTE GRAND (Red and Green Rolls) c. 1913. 6'11", (German), inlaid case decoration, remote pump*	4000.00-6000.00	9000.00-12000.00
☐ *STEINWAY "RED" WELTE VERTIGRAND c. 1908. 6', upright style, Birdseye Maple*	6000.00 7000.00	9000.00-12000.00
☐ *STEINWAY GREEN WELTE UPRIGHT Ebony finish, large simple case, (German made)*	4000.00-6000.00	9000.00-11000.00
☐ *(CHARLES M.) STIEFF WELTE LICENSEE GRAND 4'8", (drawer), dark mahogany, delicate case decoration*	500.00-1000.00	3500.00-6500.00
☐ *STIEFF WELTE MIGNON GRAND c. 1928. 5', walnut case, graceful Louis XV art case style, curved legs with carved decoration (drawer)*	750.00-1250.00	4000.00-6500.00

	Unrestored	Restored
☐ *WEISER & SONS WELTE GRAND 5'4", walnut, some simple case decoration.*	750.00-1500.00	4000.00-6500.00
☐ *WELTE LICENSEE GRAND Louis XV art case.*	2500.00-3500.00	7000.00-10000.00
☐ *WELTE GRAND 5'3", mahogany, some case decoration.*	1500.00-2500.00	7000.00-8000.00
☐ *WELTE UPRIGHT (with Red Welte Mechanism), simple case style.*	500.00-1250.00	3750.00-6500.00
☐ *"RED" WELTE Cabinet style keyboardless upright piano, oak, 5'3".*	2500.00-3500.00	7000.00-9000.00
☐ *"RED" WELTE GRAND 6'4", ebony finish.*	2000.00-2500.00	9000.00-10000.00

MISCELLANEOUS EXPRESSION PLAYER PIANOS

	Unrestored	Restored
☐ *A. B. CHASE ARTECHO GRAND c. 1921. 5'8", ebony finish, simple case style.*	1000.00-2000.00	4500.00-6500.00
☐ *EMERSON ANGELUS 65 note player.*	750.00-1000.00	3500.00-5000.00
☐ *MERRILL ARTRIO-ANGELUS c. 1928.*	750.00-1500.00	3500.00-5000.00
☐ *J. D. PHILLIPS & SONS DUCA GRAND c. 1923. (German), 7'10", some case decoration.*	2500.00-3500.00	12000.00-15000.00
☐ *SCHULTZ MARIONETTE ARIA DIVINA GRAND, miniature 3'8" size, walnut art case, 73 note.*	1500.00-2500.00	5500.00-7000.00
☐ *SHIEDMAYER-PHONOLA UPRIGHT c. 1912. 73-note player, walnut, inlaid decorative panels, (German).*	2000.00-2500.00	4750.00-5500.00
☐ *WILCOX AND WHITE ANGELUS UPRIGHT "Artistyle" expression system, 88-note player, could also play 65-note Angelus rolls.*	1500.00-2000.00	3750.00-5000.00

PIANO ROLLS PRODUCERS

During the height of the Player Piano's popularity there were hundreds of companies producing rolls. Some of the better known and easier to find labels are as follows:

AMPICO CORP. *(American Piano Co., NY)*
ARTEMPO WORD ROLLS *(Bennett & White, Buffalo)*
ARTISTYLE MUSIC ROLL *(Wilcox & White, CT)*
ATLAS WORD ROLL *(Newark, NJ)*
CAPITOL ROLL & RECORD CO. *(Chicago)*
CECILIAN PIANO ROLL (The) *(Detroit)*
CHASE AND BAKER MUSIC ROLLS *(Buffalo)*
COLUMBIA WORD ROLL CO. *(Chicago)*
CONNVORIZED PLAYER ROLL CO. *(NY)*

DELUXE (WELTE) REPRODUCING PLAYER ROLL CORP. *(NY)*
DUO-ART *(Aeolian Company, NY)*
ELECTRA MUSIC ROLLS *(Standard Music Roll Co., NY)*
GLOBE MUSIC ROLLS *(Phila.)*
IDEAL MUSIC ROLLS *(Rose Valley Co., Media, PA)*
IMPERIAL PLAYER ROLL CO. *(Chicago)*
INTERNATIONAL PLAYER ROLL CO. *(NY and Phila.)*
KEYNOTE SONG ROLLS *(Music Note Roll Co., Illinois)*
KIBBEY MUSIC ROLLS *(Chicago)*
LANDAY WORD ROLL *(Atlas Player Roll Co., Newark, NJ)*
MEL-O-ART *(Baltimore)*
MEL-O-DEE MUSIC CO. *(Chicago)*
MELOGRAPHIC ROLL CO. *(Buffalo)*
MENDELSSOHN PERFORATED MUSIC ROLL *(Boston)*
PARAMOUNT MUSIC ROLL *(NY)*
PERFECTION MUSIC ROLL *(NY)*
PIANOSTYLE WORD ROLL *(Brooklyn, NY)*
Q. R. S. *(Buffalo)*
REPUBLIC PLAYER ROLLS *(NY)*
ROYAL MUSIC ROLLS *(Buffalo)*
RYTHMODIK RECORD MUSIC ROLLS *(Belleville, NJ)*
STANDARD MUSIC ROLL *(Orange, NJ)*
UNITED STATES MUSIC CO. *(Chicago)*
UNIVERSAL MUSIC ROLL *(Chicago)*
VOCALSTYLE MUSIC CO. *(Cincinnati, OH)*
WELTE-MIGNON REPRODUCING *(RECORD) (NY)*

As in all things, condition of roll and box, rarity of music and artist govern value. Most of the above piano roll companies made 88-note regular rolls which play on any regular player action piano. (See section on "Dealers and Restorers — Piano Roll Dealers".)

Reproducing Rolls (Ampico, Duo-Art, Welte-DeLuxe) express only on the piano equipped with that particular reproducing mechanism. These pianos can also play regular 88-note rolls.

PLAYER PIANO ROLLS

Sampling of current prices for Reproducing and Expression Piano Rolls.

	Price Range	
☐ **AEOLIAN GRAND ROLLS**	**4.00**	**6.00**
☐ **AMPICO "A" ROLLS**	**3.00**	**8.00**
☐ **AMPICO "B" ROLLS**	**5.00**	**12.00**
☐ **AMPICO JUMBO ROLLS**	**10.00**	**25.00**
☐ **ANGELUS ROLLS**	**3.00**	**5.00**
☐ **APOLLO CONCERT GRAND ROLLS**	**2.00**	**3.50**
☐ **APOLLO SOLO ROLLS**	**2.00**	**3.50**
☐ **ART-ECHO ROLLS**	**10.00**	**15.00**
☐ **CECILIAN 65-NOTE ROLLS**	**2.00**	**3.00**
☐ **DE LUXE** *(for use on Welte)*	**3.00**	**6.50**
☐ **DUO ART ROLLS**	**3.00**	**6.00**

	Price Range	
☐ **DUO ART AUDIOGRAPHIC**	15.00	20.00
☐ **ELECTROVA ROLLS** *(88-note)*	3.00	6.00
☐ **HUPFELD DEA ROLLS**	10.00	14.00
☐ **HUPFELD "T" ROLLS** *(for Tri-Phonola)*	8.00	10.00
☐ **HUPFELD 73-NOTE ROLLS**	8.00	10.00
☐ **RECORDO ROLLS**	3.00	5.00
☐ **SIMPLEX ROLLS**	2.00	3.00
☐ **WELTE MIGNON ("RED") ROLLS**	12.50	20.00
☐ **WELTE MIGNON ("GREEN") ROLLS**	15.00	25.00
☐ **WELTE LICENSEE ("PURPLE")**	10.00	12.00
☐ **WELTE LICENSEE**	3.00	7.00
☐ **WURLITZER AUTOMATIC PLAYER ROLLS**	15.00	20.00
☐ **58-NOTE ROLLS**	2.00	4.00
☐ **65-NOTE ROLLS**	1.00	3.00

NICKELODEONS AND SMALL ORCHESTRIONS

A coin operated piano can simply be defined as basically an upright player piano which is electrically activated by the insertion of a coin. There are differences from the home player piano however. Generally the roll mechanism is a larger multi-tune system which rewinds automatically after the last tune on the roll is played. It is then ready to begin again. Depending on the maker there are many places the "roll" may be located inside and outside the piano. Most coin operated pianos were originally designed for public places and the cases may be elaborate with clear, leaded or art glass panels. They usually had a mandolin attachment if nothing else.

The term nickelodeon in this instance can be defined as a coin operated piano as described above though it might have one or two more instruments in addition to the piano. Basically it is a semantic difference used by the makers.

Orchestrions go back to the 19th-century in Europe. Their production there and in America essentially came to an end with the depression in 1930. Orchestrions (sometimes referred to as Nickelodeons, as well) are coin operated upright piano or cabinet case mechanisms with a piano sounding board and other instruments and effects. Cases can be quite large and elaborate with highly decorative art glass panels.

All of the above described types are basically related to the player piano in their pneumatically operated mechanisms. When pipes are part of the instrumentation, they work on wind pressure.

These machines are the most difficult to come by. (See sections on "Auctions", "Dealers and Restorers" and "Mechanical Musical Societies".)

	Price Range	
AMERICAN PIANO PLAYER		
☐ *UPRIGHT PIANO, plays 5-tune Wurlitzer paper rolls, coin operated.*	4000.00	4500.00
BERRY-WOOD PIANO PLAYER CO. (Kansas City, MO)		
☐ *BERRY-WOOD AUTO ELECTRIC PIANO PLAYER Upright keyboard piano case style, endless roll mechanism (large container attached to rear of piano to catch "Roll"), 88-note and 65-note mechanism, vacuum pump, coin operated, examples have large oval or rectangular clear glass panel in top front section of piano (art glass, also), oak case, plain.*	5000.00	7500.00
☐ *BERRY-WOOD STYLE AOH ORCHESTRION, "High Back" Upright piano style, leaded art glass panels, case decoration, hanging lamps, front top panels open to reveal mechanism, 88-note player action, violin, flute pipes, bass and snare drums, cymbal, triangle (Variations in instrumentation: mandolin attachment, tympani, wood block tambourine, xylophone), endless roll (also came in rewind roll type: AOHR).*	10000.00	20000.00
☐ *BERRY-WOOD STYLE AOE: AUTO ORCHESTRA ORCHESTRION High upright piano style, art glass, hanging lamps, 88-note player, flute or violin pipes, bass and snare drum, cymbal, triangle, 5-tune endless roll, coin operated (Style AOSR: rewind roll with 8 tunes).*	10000.00	20000.00
☐ *BERRY-WOOD STYLE C-B Upright keyboard piano with art glass front panels, 25 orchestra bells, endless roll.*	5000.00	10000.00
☐ *BERRY-WOOD STYLE A.O.W. (Auto Orchestra, Style W) High back upright keyboard style, art glass panels, lamps, piano, flute, pipes, violin pipes, orchestra bells, xylophone, snare, kettle and bass drums, castanets, crash cymbal, tambourine and mandolin, rewind roll.*	7500.00	15000.00
☐ *BERRY-WOOD STYLE F Upright piano style, teakwood finish, art glass leaded panels (three), violin and flute pipes, 88-note player action, coin operated.*	7500.00	10000.00
☐ *BERRY-WOOD STYLE 15 Upright piano style with high back, flute pipes, mandolin attachment, art glass, front panels, mission oak case style, hanging lamps on front side panels.*	7500.00	12500.00
CAPITOL PIANO AND ORGAN CO. (North Tonawanda Musical Instrument Works, NY)		
☐ *CAPITOL NICKELODEON Oak upright piano style case, simple lines, three art glass panels on top front, center panel is clear glass (shows roll mechanism). Piano, mandolin attachment, xylophone (usually has violin or flute pipes), A-roll: 10 tunes. (Variations in number and design of art glass panels).*	4000.00	8000.00
CHICAGO ELECTRIC PIANOS		
☐ *CHICAGO ELECTRIC PIANO Upright piano model, art glass panels, coin operated, regular A-roll (10 tunes), mandolin attachment, 4'7" high.*	6000.00	8000.00
☐ *CHICAGO ELECTRIC PIANO WITH XYLOPHONE Coin operated, rectangular case style, art glass, mandolin attachment, A-roll.*	5000.00	10000.00

	Price Range	
COINOLA (OPERATORS' PIANO COMPANY, Chicago, IL)		
☐ *COINOLA MIDGET STYLE A Console style case, 5'4" high, leaded art glass panel in top, coin operated, piano, mandolin, plays 65-note rolls, piano action on top, motor and roll mechanism on bottom.*	3750.00	5500.00
☐ *COINOLA MIDGET ORCHESTRION STYLE K Cabinet style, small art glass panel in center top, coin operated, instruments in top, roll mechanism in bottom, volume control behind cloth covered grill in bottom (louvered shutters), metal violin and wood flute pipes, oak case, Style O roll (all models have piano, mandolin attachment).*	4000.00	6000.00
☐ *COINOLA MIDGET ORCHESTRION STYLE F Same description as Style K but only flute pipes.*	3750.00	4750.00
☐ *COINOLA MIDGET ORCHESTRION STYLE O c. 1920's. Cabinet style, grill work, bottom doors, 10 tune "O" roll, piano mandolin effect, orchestra bells and drums.*	4000.00	6000.00
☐ *COINOLA MIDGET ORCHESTRION STYLE V Same description as Style K but with violin pipes.*	4000.00	6000.00
☐ *COINOLA MIDGET ORCHESTRION STYLE X Same description as Style K but with xylophone or bells.*	4000.00	6000.00
☐ *COINOLA "CUPID" (DUPLEX) Cabinet style, 4½' high, piano, mandolin (xylophone), two 10-tune A-roll mechanisms side by side in top section of cabinet, glass panel.*	4500.00	6500.00
☐ *COINOLA STYLE C Upright piano style, mandolin attachment, A-roll 10 tunes, 65-note, art glass, case decoration, oak, high front posts.*	3500.00	4750.00
☐ *COINOLA STYLE C REPRODUCING Piano, mandolin, use 88-note expression rolls.*	3250.00	4500.00
☐ *COINOLA STYLE CF Description same as Style C with flute pipes, O-roll.*	3750.00	5000.00
☐ *COINOLA STYLE CX Description same as Style C but with xylophone mechanism, O-roll.*	3750.00	5000.00
☐ *COINOLA STYLE CK Upright piano style similar to other Style C Models but with solo violin pipes and flute pipes, O-roll.*	3900.00	6500.00
☐ *COINOLA STYLE C2 Upright piano style, leaded art glass, oak, mandolin attachment, bass and snare drums, cymbal.*	5500.00	8500.00
☐ *COINOLA STYLE CO High upright keyboard piano style, 3 art glass panels, hanging lamps, instruments in top section of case, tambourine, mandolin attachment, bass and snare drums, tympani, cymbal, xylophone, flute pipes, Indian block triangle.*	7000.00	10000.00
☐ *COINOLA STYLE J Upright piano style, simple lines, small leaded glass panel in top front center section, hanging lamps, coin operated, 65-note player piano with mandolin attachment, A-roll.*	4000.00	6500.00
☐ *COINOLA STYLE JF Same description as Style J but with flute pipes added, O-roll.*	4750.00	7000.00
☐ *COINOLA STYLE JK Same description as Style J but with violin pipes added, O-roll.*	4750.00	8000.00
☐ *COINOLA STYLE JX Same description as Style J but with xylophone added, O-roll.*	4750.00	7000.00

	Price Range	
☐ *COINOLA STYLE X Upright piano style case, high front posts, rounded glass sections in front top section, instruments in base, O-roll, oak, instrumentation: piano, mandolin attachment, xylophone, bass, plus snare drums, tympani, cymbal, triangle, wood block.*	7500.00	15000.00
☐ *COINOLA PUSH-UP ORCHESTRA Cabinet style (full height of an upright piano) when pushed up against front of piano keyboard plays piano with instrument accompaniment (Style X instruments).*	5000.00	7500.00

CREMONA (MARQUETTE PIANO COMPANY, Chicago, IL)

☐ *CREMONA STYLE 2 Upright piano style, art glass panels in top front section, oak simple lines, 57" high, coin operated, mandolin attachment, 10-tune rolls.*	4500.00	6750.00
☐ *CREMONA STYLE 3 Upright piano style, clear glass panels on top front (art glass examples), A-roll. Reginapiano same model made by Marquette.*	3000.00	4500.00
☐ *CREMONA STYLE 4 and STYLE 5 Upright piano style, oak (mahogany, walnut), art glass, coin operated, A-roll.*	3750.00	5750.00
☐ *CREMONA STYLE 20, 30 Upright piano style, art glass, hanging lamps, oak, coin operated, tune selector device, M-roll (allowed patron to choose the tune he wanted, otherwise the tunes played in order) paper M-roll, mandolin attachment, 88-note roll.*	5000.00	7500.00
☐ *CREMONA STYLE A Upright piano style, 57" high, large art glass panels across front top section, hanging lamps, coin operated, 10-tune roll, oak.*	6000.00	9000.00
☐ *CREMONA STYLE G WITH FLUTE PIPES High back upright piano, art glass panels, hanging lamps, oak (walnut) 10-tune A-roll piano, mandolin, flute or violin pipes.*	7500.00	13000.00
☐ *CREMONA STYLE J 80" high upright piano style, art glass panels (case variations), piano, mandolin, flute (violin), bass and snare drums, cymbal, triangle, xylophone, tympani, coin operated, special 88-note (M-roll) orchestral music roll.*	10000.00	20000.00
☐ *CREMONA STYLE K 67" high upright piano style, "Grecian" design case, oak, front legs extend up from floor to top of piano and form a narrow open archway on each side for hanging lamps, 4 large leaded glass panels in front, flute pipes, piccolo, violin pipes, piano, mandolin, triangle, tambourine, castanets. 88-note orchestral music rolls (M-roll).*	15000.00	20000.00
☐ **EMPRESS ELECTRIC PIANO (Sold by Lyon and Healy)** *Keyboard upright piano style, small art glass panel in top front section, coin operated, piano, mandolin attachment, xylophone (or bell unit), O-roll. (Coinola mechanism made by Operators Piano Co.).*	3900.00	6250.00

☐ **ENCORE AUTOMATIC BANJO** *Coin operated automatic 4-string banjo (plays by means of tiny hook-like steel fingers through pneumatically operated fret buttons activated by a paper roll mechanism. Case resembles an upright disc music box. Display case type top section houses the banjo, roll in*

Encore Automatic Banjo.

	Price Range	
bottom section. Oak simple case (must be restored, tuned and regulated expertly to be appreciated). (Some case variations). Plays 5-tune endless roll.	8000.00	15000.00

ENGELHARDT & SONS PIANO CO., (ST. JOHNSVILLE, NY) (Peerless Piano Player Co.)

☐ *ENGELHARDT CABINET NICKELODEON (Peerless) 4'10" high plain cabinet style case, large art glass panel in front section, oak, piano, mandolin attachment, A-roll.*	5000.00	7500.00
☐ *ENGELHARDT NICKELODEON (Peerless) Upright piano style case, with xylophone, mahogany finish, coin operated.*	6000.00	8000.00
☐ *ENGELHARDT NICKELODEON (Peerless) With flute pipes, upright piano case, large art glass panel, piano, mandolin, flute pipes in top section, roll and motor mechanisms in bottom, coin operated.*	5750.00	8500.00

LUDWIG HUPFELD, INC. (Leipzig, Germany)

☐ *HUPFELD CLAVIMONIUM Upright piano with harmonium effects, walnut case, 4'7" high, two glass windows on top front.*	3750.00	5900.00
☐ *HUPFELD CLAVITIST UNIVERSAL Piano, mandolin, xylophone.*	6000.00	7500.00

	Price Range	
☐ *HUPFELD KONZERTIST UNIVERSAL ORCHESTRION Upright keyboard piano style, 8′ high, painted scene on three large glass panels, piano, mandolin, bass and snare drum, xylophone, crash cymbal.*	8500.00	14000.00
☐ *HUPFELD ANIMATIC CLAVITIST PIANO Upright piano, light walnut, 4′5″ high, electric.*	2850.00	4250.00
☐ *HUPFELD HELIOS ORCHESTRION Keyboardless style piano mandolin, bass and snare drums, violin and cello pipes, cymball, bells.*	14500.00	47500.00
☐ *HUPFELD PHONOLISZT VIOLINA, MODEL A Duplex 6 roll automatic changer.*	65000.00	95000.00
☐ *HUPFELD PHONOLIZST VIOLINA, MODEL B Upright expression autograph piano, hanging lamps on front of piano, three violins placed vertically in section above piano, rotating circular bow (many case variations).*	25000.00	30000.00

IMHOF AND MUKLE (Germany)

☐ *IMHOF AND MUKLE "LUCIA" ORCHESTRION c. 1900, 10′7″ high, three large floral art glass front panels, violin and cello pipes, orchestra bells, bass and snare drums, tympani, cymbals, mandolin accompaniment, keyboardless piano, elaborate case decoration.*	12500.00	23000.00
☐ *IMHOF AND MUKLE ORCHESTRION c. 1908-14. Keyboard style, louvered swell shutters, pipes high back upright style, pictorial scene, hanging glass lamps.*	10000.00	20000.00
☐ *IMHOF AND MUKLE "RAMONA" VIOLIN PIANO Upright keyboard piano case with high back (6′ high), oak case, mandolin, violin pipes, plays 88-note rolls and Imhof and Mukle rolls.*	7500.00	15000.00

KREITER NICKELODEON

☐ *KREITER NICKELODEON PIANO Oak keyboard style, coin operated, three glass panels on top front, 10 tune roll mechanism in base.*	7500.00	15000.00

LINK PIANO CO., INC. (Binghamton, NY)

☐ *LINK STYLE A ORCHESTRION Large keyboard type piano case, 6′ high, art glass front panels, (Chaddorff Piano), mandolin attachment, metal violin, wood flute pipes, wood block, snare drum, triangle, tom tom, tambourine, continuous roll on top.*	6500.00	12000.00
☐ *LINK STYLE C c. 1915-20. High back upright keyboard style case, 28 flute pipes, oak, several art glass panels, coin operated lamps, RX endless rolls.*	15000.00	20000.00
☐ *LINK STYLE E Upright keyboard piano style, high back, art glass panels and lamps, mandolin, xylophone, oak.*	10000.00	15000.00
☐ *LINK STYLE 2E Cabinet style (plain, rectangular case), clear glass panels on top and bottom for viewing "continuous" endless roll, coin operated, xylophone.*	5500.00	7500.00

	Price Range	
☐ *LINK STYLE R Upright keyboard style piano with art glass panels, and hanging lamp, piano, mandolin, violin or flute pipes, continuous roll.*	4000.00	7500.00
☐ *LINK RELIABLE Upright piano style, coin operated, mandolin attachment, continuous roll feed into a bin attached to the front under the keyboard but outside the case, beveled oval mirror in top section, bin slides out to change roll. The model sold under other company names, e.g. Majestic by Lyon and Healy.*	4500.00	6900.00
☐ *LINK NICKELODEON Upright keyboard style, 6'5" high, simple oak case lines with hanging lights, four large leaded glass panels with folding doors covering top glass panels.*	4500.00	6500.00.00

PAUL LOSCHE (Leipzig Orchestrion Works)

☐ *LOSCHE "JAZZBAND" ORCHESTRION c. 1920's. Piano, mandolin attachment, 4 beater bass drum, triangle, 3 beater wood block, 3 beater cymbal, snare drum.*	10000.00	15000.00
☐ *LOSCHE NICKELODEONS Upright keyboard piano style, plain case, roll in center, mandolin attachment, oak case.*	3500.00	6000.00
☐ *LOSCHE ORCHESTRION (FLUTE AND VIOLIN SOLO PIANO) High keyboard style, 7½' high, beveled mirrors and hanging lamps, oak case, flute and violin pipes, piano, mandolin attachment (also xylophone and clarinet pipes).*	4500.00	7500.00

LYON AND HEALY (Chicago, IL) *Sold machines made by other companies.*

☐ *LYON AND HEALY EMPRESS ELECTRIC PIANO (See Empress Electric Piano)*		
☐ *LYON AND HEALY LITTLE EMPRESS ELECTRIC CABINET PLAYER (Made by Operators' Piano Co.) Coin operated cabinet style case sits on or up against keys, plain case (Also came fitted with all the instruments of a COINOLA X).*	4000.00	6500.00
☐ *LYON AND HEALY MAJESTIC (See Link Reliable)*		
☐ *LYON AND HEALY MAJESTIC JUNIOR Cabinet style, glass top, 44-note piano, coin operated, endless roll in bottom section.*	4000.00	6250.00
☐ *LYON AND HEALY PIANETTE (Made by F. G. Otto & Sons, NJ) Cabinet style piano operated by a metal disc, 39 notes, long running, 75" high, coin operated, oak (mahogany), glass panels in front doors.*	5000.00	6750.00

MARQUETTE PIANO CO. (See Cremona)

MILLS NOVELTY CO. (Chicago, IL)

☐ *MILLS VIOLANO VIRTUOSO-GRAND MODEL "Single Mills", roll activated mechanism plays real violin mechanically, straight rectangular floor console case, 5'4" high, mahogany (oak), 4 glass paneled doors fold open to view violin, 5-tune roll, coin operated, 44-note piano.*	7900.00	12500.00
☐ *MILLS VIOLANO VIRTUOSO—CONCERT GRAND Just slightly larger cabinet size.*	7000.00	10000.00
☐ *MILLS VIOLANO VIRTUOSO—DELUXE MODEL "Double Mills", two violins, 5'9", otherwise same as "Grand" model.*	12500.00	25000.00

	Price Range	
☐ *MILLS VIOLANO VIRTUOSO—EARLY COMMERCIAL MODEL "Art Nouveau" style curved case, bowed with carving and decoration, single violin, piano action, glass front and side panels on top.*	7000.00	12500.00
☐ *MILLS AUTOMATIC PIANO (LINK) Upright piano keyboard style, large beveled glass panel in top front of piano, coin operated, endless roll in bin at front of piano under keyboard, oak.*	3750.00	6500.00
☐ *MILLS MAGNETIC EXPRESSION PIANO Straight plain rectangular cabinet style, oak (mahogany), 65-note piano, 5'5" high, whole front opens like a door, piano action attached to the door, also pneumatic action (very compact), roll mechanism in base of cabinet, plays Mills Electric Piano Rolls, art glass panels.*	4000.00	6000.00

NATIONAL AUTOMATIC MUSIC CO. *(See NATIONAL PIANO MANUFACTURING CO.)*
NATIONAL PEERLESS PIANOS. *(See PEERLESS PIANO PLAYER CO.)*
NATIONAL PIANO MANUFACTURING CO. (Grand Rapids, Michigan, MI)

☐ *NATIONAL NICKELODEON PIANO Upright piano style, mandolin, large rectangular glass panel in top front, oak case, 10-tune A-roll.*	3750.00	6250.00
☐ *NATIONAL NICKELODEON PIANO WITH AUTOMATIC CHANGER Upright piano style case (keyboardless), coin operated, clear glass top front panel, 8-roll automatic changer, tune selector, one tune per roll, roll assembly housed in wooden case below "keyboard" area.*	4000.00	8000.00

NELSON WIGGIN PIANO CO. (Chicago, IL)

☐ *NELSON-WIGGIN BANJ-O-GRAND Cabinet style, art or clear glass, mandolin attachment, A-roll (Gambling devices on this model).*	5000.00	7000.00
☐ *NELSON-WIGGIN CASINO X 5½' high cabinet style, simple case, glass panel on top, piano, coin operated, A-roll (Gambling devices added).*	3700.00	6700.00
☐ *NELSON-WIGGIN STYLE 3 PIANOGRAND Coin operated keyboard piano style, 4'6" high, mandolin, xylophone, walnut case, three art glass panels.*	6000.00	8500.00
☐ *NELSON-WIGGIN STYLE 4 Cabinet style, contains the following instrumentation; piano, mandolin, xylophone, snare drum, triangle, cymbal.*	6000.00	12000.00
☐ *NELSON-WIGGIN STYLE 4X Cabinet style, three glass sections on top, decorative columns on corners, two doors in base, piano, mandolin trap effects, G and 4X rolls, 10 tunes.*	5000.00	7000.00
☐ *NELSON-WIGGIN STYLE 5X 5½' high cabinet style, three glass panels in top front (art or clear glass), walnut (mahogany), contains piano, banjo (mandolin) attachment, set of marimbas, snare drum, triangle, plays standard orchestral 10-tune roll, G-rolls, 4X rolls, xylophone.*	10000.00	15000.00

☐ *NELSON-WIGGIN STYLE 6 ORCHESTRA Cabinet style, columns on front, simple console case, glass section on top, curtains behind, double doors on bottom, roll mechanism in*

Mills Violano Virtuoso Grand Model, doors open to reveal roll mechanism in base.

	Price Range	
bottom, piano, mandolin, xylophone, bass plus snare drum, cymbal, triangle, tympani, castanets, wood block, tambourine, 5½' high, walnut, 10-tune 4X and G-roll.	**12000.00**	**20000.00**
☐ *NELSON-WIGGIN STYLE 7 FULL ORCHESTRA KEYBOARD PIANO Upright piano style, art glass in top front section, walnut, roll mechanism in top, piano, xylophone, banjo (mandolin), bass and snare drum, tympani, cymbal, triangle, castanets, Indian block.*	**15000.00**	**20000.00**

	Price Range	
☐ *NELSON-WIGGIN STYLE 8 Cabinet style, some decoration, art glass panels, oak, mahogany, walnut, 4½' high, roll in base section, piano, mandolin, xylophone, bells, special "G" roll.*	5000.00	8000.00
☐ *NELSON-WIGGIN SELECTOR DUPLEX (DUAL KEYBOARD) PIANO ORGAN Upright piano style, full piano, organ 10-tune roll, mechanism plays 5 tunes forward then 5 tunes in rewind position.*	5000.00	9000.00

NORTH TONAWANDA MUSICAL INSTRUMENT WORKS, (NY)

☐ *NORTH TONAWANDA PIANOLIN Cabinet style, beveled glass top section, protruding base section holds endless roll mechanism, 44-note piano action, violin and flute pipes, coin operated.*	5000.00	9500.00
☐ *NORTH TONAWANDA AUTOMATIC KEYBOARD PIANO STYLE L Upright keyboard style, two art glass panels in top front, hanging lamps, oak 4½' high piano, mandolin attachment, violin or flute pipes, coin operated, roll in top center, 14-tune L-roll, later 10-tune A-roll.*	5000.00	8500.00

OPERATORS' PIANO CO. *(See COINOLA).*

PEERLESS PIANO PLAYER CO. (NATIONAL "PEERLESS" PIANOS)

☐ *PEERLESS "ARCADIAN" ORCHESTRION STYLE O High upright keyboard piano style, high front posts with globes on top, leaded glass front and panels.*	6500.00	12500.00
☐ *PEERLESS ART CABARET STYLE A Upright piano keyboard case, art glass panel in top front, piano, mandolin, roll on top.*	3000.00	5000.00
☐ *PEERLESS ART CABARET STYLE B 5'1" high, oak upright keyboard case, 24 flute pipes, large art glass panel in top front, lamps on either side of front.*	5000.00	7500.00
☐ *PEERLESS ART CABARET STYLE C Instrumentation: piano, mandolin, bass and snare drums, cymbal, triangle (semi-orchestrion).*	6000.00	8000.00
☐ *PEERLESS ART CABARET STYLE D Instrumentation: piano, mandolin, bass and snare drums, cymbals, triangle, violin and flute pipes (called Theatre or Peerless Orchestrion).*	7000.00	9000.00
☐ *PEERLESS STYLE D NICKELODEON PIANO Keyboard upright style, oval beveled glass in top section, endless roll mechanism in cabinet in back of piano, coin operated, oak...*	2750.00	5000.00
☐ *PEERLESS STYLE 44 Cabinet style, clear beveled glass top section (oval or scalloped), endless roll, 44-note piano, coin operated.*	3000.00	5000.00
☐ *PEERLESS NICKELODEON PIANO Upright keyboard style, three art glass panels in front, oak, coin operated, 10-tune A-roll.*	3000.00	6000.00

PHILIPPS AND SONS (Frankfurt, Germany)

☐ *PHILIPPS DUCA PIANO REPRODUCING High back upright reproducing piano, with (or without) roll changer, coin operated, simple case, some decoration.*	3750.00	6000.00

	Price Range	
☐ *PHILIPPS PIANELLA NICKELODEON STYLE C Upright keyboard piano style, mandolin attachment, oak case, coin operated.*	**3000.00**	**5750.00**
☐ *PHILIPPS PIANELLA PIANO STYLE PC 3 Upright piano style with hanging lamps, piano, mandolin (roll changer) type PM rolls, 4 tunes.*	**4000.00**	**6750.00**
☐ *PHILIPPS PIANELLA MODEL #15 Upright cabinet, keyboardless style cabinet, elaborate case decoration including three large art glass panels, 6 hanging lamps, instrumentation includes; piano, mandolin, xylophone, bell, bass and snare drums, tambourine, cymbal, castanettes, triangle, automatic six roll changer mechanism.*	**50000.00**	**75000.00**
☐ *PHILIPPS STYLE PC-7 Ornate decorated high back upright piano turned front legs and other case decoration, also large top panel with scenic panel "motion picture". Uses Philipps PM rolls.*	**9000.00**	**13000.00**
☐ *PHILIPPS STYLE PC-10 ORCHESTRION Upright keyboard style high back (7½' high), beveled mirror and some case decoration, piano, mandolin, violin pipes, snare and bass drums, xylophone, crash cymbal.*	**9000.00**	**13000.00**

POLYPHONE COIN PIANOS (Leipzig, Germany)

☐ *POLYPHONA I Keyboard style case, high upright, hanging lamps, case decoration, pneumatically operated, piano, mandolin, xylophone, bells.*	**4000.00**	**6250.00**
☐ *POLYPHONA II Upright keyboard style, high back, hanging lamps, decoration, piano, mandolin attachment.*	**4000.00**	**6000.00**
☐ *POLYPHONA IV—DUX High upright piano case, art glass lamps on high front posts, piano, mandolin, xylophone.*	**4500.00**	**7000.00**

POPPER AND CO. (Leipzig, Germany)

☐ *POPPER "HAPPY JAZZBAND" Upright piano orchestrion, 6' high, drums, wood block, triangle, cymbal, mandolin attachment, oak case, bracket lamps, circular "jazzband" painted picture on drum, coin operated.*	**7500.00**	**15000.00**
☐ *POPPER JAZZ BAND Upright keyboard piano, high back, some case decoration, instrumentation in top section. Piano, mandolin, bass and snare drums, tympani, wood block, triangle.*	**5000.00**	**7500.00**
☐ *POPPER REPRODUCING PIANO Upright, "Stella" (many case variations), hanging lamps, leaded glass panels, coin operated (wall boxes).*	**3700.00**	**5000.00**
☐ *POPPER NICKELODEON Upright keyboard piano, simple lines, hanging lamps, mandolin attachment, 5' high, coin operated.*	**3750.00**	**5500.00**
☐ *POPPER "ROLAND" (WITH SWANEE WHISTLE) ORCHESTRION Tall case upright keyboard style, simple lines (art deco style) with Swanee whistle attachment.*	**15000.00**	**18500.00**
☐ *POPPER "WELT" PIANO Upright high back piano case, art glass, hanging lamps, case decoration (variations in case design), coin operated, piano, mandolin, xylophone, drums.*	**3500.00**	**6000.00**

	Price Range	
☐ **REGINAPIANO** *(See Cremona, Style #3) Upright keyboard piano, three glass panels, mandolin attachment, 10-tune A-roll (made by MARQUETTE).*	3500.00	5750.00
☐ **REGINA SUBLIMA PIANO STYLE 302** *Cabinet style over 7′ high, oak, mandolin attachment, coin operated.*	3500.00	7500.00
☐ **ROLAND BARREL ORCHESTRION** *c. 1900. 7′6″ high rectangular case style, some decoration, two front doors, glass windows reveal barrel (8-tune) and other instruments, piano, bass and snare drums, crash cymbal.*	5500.00	7500.00
J. P. SEEBURG PIANO CO. (Chicago, IL)		
☐ *SEEBURG STYLE A NICKELODEON Upright keyboard piano, simple lines, coin operated, art and clear glass, front panel, mandolin attachment, plays A-roll, 10 tunes, 65-note piano, automatic rewind, oak (mahogany) case and glass variations.*	3750.00	7500.00
☐ *SEEBURG STYLE B More elaborate art glass and case details.*	4500.00	6500.00
☐ *SEEBURG STYLE C Upright keyboard style, five arched sections in top front of piano with a continuous scene in leaded art glass, lamps on front posts, A-roll coin operated.*	5000.00	8000.00
☐ *SEEBURG STYLE E Keyboard piano, oak, art glass on top front doors, hanging lamps, 65-note, 10-tune selections, automatic rewind, violin or flute pipes, mandolin attachment, coin operated.*	6500.00	8500.00
☐ *SEEBURG STYLE E SPECIAL Same case style with piano, mandolin, xylophone, bass and snare drum, tympani, cymbal, triangle, castanets, tambourine, Chinese block, coin operated.*	6750.00	22000.00
☐ *SEEBURG STYLE G High back upright keyboard piano style (6′7½″ high), 4 large art glass panels, oak case, violin and flute pipes, mandolin attachment, bass and snare drum, tympani, cymbal, triangle, 65-note, 10-tune rolls, coin operated.*	15000.00	25000.00
☐ *SEEBURG STYLE H SOLO ORCHESTRION High keyboard upright piano style, two fully carved figures on side posts, three leaded art glass shades along top front of case, 4 large art glass panels in front top section, piano, flute, violin pipes, piccolo and clarinet, mandolin attachment, bass and snare drums, tympani, cymbal, triangle, castanets, oak case, H-roll, instruments in top section, coin operated.*	30000.00	40000.00
☐ *SEEBURG STYLE J SOLO ORCHESTRION Upright keyboard style case, high back, large elaborate art glass, decorated case, walnut (mahogany), 6′ high, piano, mandolin attachment, pipes for flute, violin, oboe, clarinet, triangle, castanets, xylophone, coin operated, H-roll.*	17500.00	22500.00
☐ *SEEBURG STYLE K "MIDGET" ORCHESTRION "EAGLE" Cabinet style case, 5′2″ high, simple style, some case decoration, gold trimming, oak, art glass panel in top section, half circle with "Eagle" design (other designs used). Piano, mandolin, xylophone, coin operated, 65-note, 10 tune selection.*	9000.00	12500.00

	Price Range	
☐ *SEEBURG STYLE KT ORCHESTRION "EAGLE" Same description with added instrumentation: castanets, triangle, tambourine, G-roll.*	9000.00	15000.00
☐ *SEEBURG STYLE KT SPECIAL Cabinet style case, 5'5½" high, simple lines, "Oriental" design art glass panel on top, oak with gold trim, piano, mandolin attachment, xylophone, bass and snare drums, tympani, cymbal, triangle, castanets, tambourine, Chinese block, G-roll, 10-tune, rewind device to shut off all instruments but piano, coin operated.*	12500.00	17500.00
☐ *SEEBURG KT SPECIAL (EDGERTON REPLICA).*	12500.00	15000.00
☐ *SEEBURG STYLE L NICKELODEON "SEEBURG JUNIOR" Cabinet style, art glass panels on top, piano, mandolin, mahogany (oak), 51½" high, roll in top center of cabinet, A-roll, 10-tune, 65-note (also known as "LILLIPUTIAN"), coin operated.*	4000.00	7000.00
☐ *SEEBURG STYLE L ORCHESTRION Oak case, 10-tune "G" rolls, piano, mandolin, flute pipes, bass and snare drums, tympani, triangle, cymbal, art glass.*	25000.00	40000.00
☐ *SEEBURG STYLE P-G-A Console style, leaded art glass top front panel, coin operated, 10-tune A-roll.*	4500.00	7000.00
☐ *SEEBURG STYLE X ELECTRIC EXPRESSION PIANO Upright piano, reproducing expression mechanism, coin operated, (oak) mahogany plain case, X-P roll (4-6 selections per roll), 88-note roll also plays, 4'9½" high.*	4500.00	6500.00

VIOLANO VIRTUOSO *(See MILLS NOVELTY CO.)*

WEBER (GEBRUDER WEBER)

☐ *WEBER MAESTRO ORCHESTRION c. 1920's. Oak case, 9'3" high, piano, mandolin, xylophone, violin, cello, flute, saxophone, clarinet, oboe, trumpet, drums, castanets, full rounded columns on front, other case decoration mirrors, hanging lamps, expression devices.*	50000.00	85000.00
☐ *WEBER "UNIKA" PIANO ORCHESTRA c. 1920's. High back keyboard style, approximately 6½' high, mandolin, violin pipes, oak case, mirrored doors, two double brass lamps on each side front panel, some case decoration, roll is housed behind mirrored doors well above keyboard.*	8000.00	12000.00

WESTERN ELECTRIC PIANO CO. (J. P. SEEBURG)

☐ *WESTERN ELECTRIC SELECTRA MODEL B Console cabinet style, 5'2" tall, oak, simple case, simple decorative glass panels in top section, piano, mandolin, xylophone, selectra tune selecting mechanism, tune card, indicator dial, coin operated.*	4500.00	8000.00
☐ *WESTERN ELECTRIC STYLE X Cabinet style, doors on top and bottom, simple case, glass panels in top, roll mechanism in top, piano, mandolin, xylophone, oak.*	3000.00	6000.00
☐ *WESTERN ELECTRIC "DERBY" RACE HORSE PIANO Console cabinet, oak, simple case, glass front on top to view diorama of racing horses, coin operated, A-roll, piano (mandolin attachment).*	7000.00	9000.00

	Price Range	
RUDOLPH WURLITZER CO. (North Tonawanda, NY)		
☐ *WURLITZER AUTOMATIC PLAYER PIANO Upright piano case style, 65-note player, mandolin attachment, three beveled glass panels in top front, case decoration, oak, coin operated (early example c. 1907), plays 10-tune A-roll.*	2700.00	4500.00
☐ *WURLITZER STYLE A AUTOMATIC PLAYER PIANO Upright piano case style, 65-note, one rank of pipes violin or flute, mandolin attachment, 4'10" high, electric, 5-tune roll, beveled clear (or art) glass panel in top front of piano, oak.*	3750.00	6500.00
☐ *WURLITZER STYLE AX c. 1920. 5' high, oak case, 6-roll mechanism.*	7500.00	12000.00
☐ *WURLITZER STYLE AX AUTOMATIC PLAYER PIANO Upright piano, 65-note, mandolin attachment, flute or violin pipes, art glass panels in top front, automatic roll changer plays 65-tune rolls.*	3500.00	6500.00
☐ *WURLITZER STYLE B ORCHESTRION High back upright piano case style, three art glass panels, piano, mandolin, flute pipes, bass and snare drum, cymbal, triangle, panel just above center of keyboard for roll: Wurlitzer automatic player piano 10-tune rolls, coin operated.*	10000.00	19500.00
☐ *WURLITZER STYLE BX ORCHESTRION WITH "WONDER LIGHT" High back upright piano case, three large art glass panels, case decoration (many variations in case and glass designs), violin or flute pipes, automatic roll changer, "wonder" light in top gallery (rotating "Jeweled" light).*	15000.00	25000.00
☐ *WURLITZER STYLE BX 7' high, plays six 5-tune rolls, bass and snare drums, triangle, 38 flute pipes.*	15000.00	21000.00
☐ *WURLITZER STYLE CX ORCHESTRION Automatic Roll Changer (similar to Style BX), high back oak case, several art glass panels, keyboard style, instruments, flute pipes.*	15000.00	28500.00
☐ *WURLITZER BIJOU ORCHESTRA Large 8½' tall cabinet, galleries, lamps, art glass panels, roll in center front section, automatic roll changer, 44-note piano, mandolin attachment, violin pipes, xylophone, snare drum, pianino roll.*	13000.00	17000.00
☐ *WURLITZER AUTOMATIC HARP (J. W. Whitlock & Co., Rising Sun, IN) Style A straight rectangular case 6'6" high, automatically activated by a 8½" wide perforated paper roll, 6 tunes per roll, automatic rewind, coin operated.*	7500.00	17500.00
☐ *STYLE B decorative case design, curved top section and carved post (looked more like a harp)*		
☐ *WURLITZER STYLE LX ORCHESTRION High back upright piano style, leaded art glass panels, oak, 2 ranks of pipes, bells, 2 drums, triangle, instruments in top section, roll changer over keyboard, 7½' high.*	17000.00	22000.00

Wurlitzer Automatic Roll Changer Mechanism

	Price Range	
☐ *WURLITZER ELECTRIC PIANO AUTOGRAPH STYLE Upright keyboard piano, 4'9" high, plain simple case, coin operated, automatic roll changer, plays special expression rolls: autograph reproducing piano rolls.*	**2500.00**	**5750.00**
☐ *WURLITZER ELECTRIC PIANO STYLE IXB Upright keyboard style, three art glass front panels, mandolin attachment, automatic roll changer, 65-tune rolls, coin operated (orchestra bells).*	**6000.00**	**8500.00**
☐ *WURLITZER MANDOLIN QUARTETTE 5' high rectangular case, some decoration, beveled glass sections in top, oak (mahogany, many finishes), 34-note piano and 27-note mandolin attachment, 5-tune rolls, coin operated, roll mechanism in top middle section behind glass door.*	**5000.00**	**10000.00**
☐ *WURLITZER PHOTOPLAYER PIANO STYLE G Upright piano case, 4'10" simple case, double roll mechanism, (automatic player piano rolls) 65-note Wurlitzer rolls, piano, mandolin attachment, storage chest situated next to piano held instrumentation: violin, flute pipes, drums, sound effects.*	**6000.00**	**9000.00**

	Price Range	
☐ *WURLITZER PIANINO Console case style, 5′ high, 44-note electric piano, protruding middle section for roll mechanism, leaded art glass on top front, oak case, coin operated, mandolin attachment. (Late models, case variations).*	4000.00	8000.00
☐ *WURLITZER SOLO VIOLIN PIANO Upright keyboard piano, plain case, 88-note player, violin pipes, automatic roll changer ("violin" can play solo), 4′10½″ high.*	5000.00	8000.00
☐ *WURLITZER TONOPHONE Upright piano case style, large oval beveled glass panel in top front, with or without keyboard, coin operated, 10-tune wooden cylinder.*	3500.00	6000.00
☐ *WURLITZER STYLE W ORGANETTE Upright piano style, two keyboards, pipe organ, walnut, two roll mechanisms side by side in top front.*	4000.00	6000.00
☐ *WURLITZER VIOLIN-FLUTE PIANINO Keyboardless cabinet, 4′8″ high, fancy decorative details, 21 flute pipes and violin pipes.*	9500.00	12500.00
☐ *WURLITZER #146 BAND ORGAN "Carouselle Organ", simple case ivory painted trimmed in black and gold, three front panels (painted silk), 6′7″ high, drums mounted outside, cymbal on top, pipes on center front panel, plays paper roll, instrumentation effects: trombones, basses, trumpets, flute pipes, violin pipes.*	8000.00	15000.00
☐ *WURLITZER #148 MILITARY BAND ORGAN Duplex roll mechanism, exposed belled horns (18), drums and cymbal mounted at sides on top, plays paper rolls.*	6500.00	9500.00

NICKELODEON, ORCHESTRION, AND BAND ORGAN ROLLS

☐ **NORTH TONAWANDA,** *one tune endless roll.*	8.00	10.00
☐ **NICKELODEON "A" ROLLS,** *recuts.*	10.00	20.00
☐ **PEERLESS** *65-note endless roll, multitone.*	7.50	15.00
☐ **PEERLESS** *44-note endless roll.*	7.50	15.00
☐ **PIANOLIN** *6-tune endless roll.*	12.00	17.00
☐ **WURLITZER CONCERT PIANO ORCHESTRA ROLLS.**	10.00	20.00
☐ **WURLITZER BAND ORGAN ROLLS.**	7.50	15.00

MUSICAL INSTRUMENTS

Musical instruments, being native to nearly all races and societies and having primitive origins dating to prehistoric times, exist in vast varieties and offer the collector wide choice. It would be very mistaken to believe, however, that all classes of instruments are to be found in profuse quantities on the antique market, or that the finest examples of noted instrument manufacturers can be easily obtained. The sort of instruments available in the greatest quantity as antiques are those which enjoyed extensive popularity in the age of classical instrument making, especially violins and pianos. Antique wind instruments are somewhat less common, if one speaks of specimens of 200 or 300 years ago.

The approach to collecting antique instruments may be either from a musical point of view, or with regard to styling and ornamentation or, in the case of very early specimens, as historical pieces. A **specialized** collection may deal with instruments of one given sort, such as mandolins or flutes or harps. But, as even this is rather broad territory, the collector is likely to specialize still further, confining himself to German flutes of the 19th-century or Italian harps of the 18th or, very likely, examples of the work of a single manufacturer. In violin collecting, the traditional approach has long been to concentrate on the work of one craftsman or family of craftsmen. As instruments are not the sort of articles of which large collections can be easily made, this is probably the wisest course to follow.

It is not only the collector who seeks out antique instruments, however. There are other buyers and potential buyers, whose activities in the market have an influence both on the availability of specimens and their price. First is the musician. It is difficult to state what proportion of antique instruments that pass through the hands of dealers, auctioneers, etc., are purchased by musicians, but it is unquestionably a fact that sales of antique instruments to musicians have increased over the past 10-15 years. Violins and stringed instruments in general head the list; there are others sought by musicians, too, who are of the opinion (rightly or wrongly) that a certain manufacturer, perhaps long deceased, made his instruments to a standard not found in current examples. The musician is a powerful force in the market, as he buys perhaps one instrument to last a lifetime and thus can expend a great amount of money on it, rather than making the frequent purchases of a collector.

Investors also account for a certain measure of sales. As with any commodity that shows a history of gaining steadily in value, there will be individuals who may have little love or knowledge of the item, but will buy on speculation. This is all the more true of instruments than many other articles, as they have some decorative appeal for the home, and no excuse need be made for owning or displaying them.

So far as the advisability of investing in musical instruments is concerned, this is a complex matter. Certain instruments gain more steadily in value than others, depending on the strength of demand. Usually — but not mandatorily — the more suitable the instrument is for modern use, especially concert use, the more even will be the demand and the more steadily will be its rise in value. Museum-type instruments that have no place in the modern concert hall, such as the spinet or certain kinds of obsolete horns, may be quite valuable but the demand over a long period of time is difficult to forecast. Auctioneers, who have the task of estimating prices only two or three months in the future, are hard pressed on occasion when faced with the task of evaluating "offbeat" instruments or unusual models of standard instruments, and frequently guess wrong. Instruments are one class of collectors' item for which past sales records cannot be relied upon too faithfully in determining what the next sale will bring. Obviously, there will always be buyers for $20,000 antique harpsichords, even should the bottom totally fall out of the instrument market; but at what prices, nobody could hope to know.

The investor who purchases only "top of the market" items may be interested to know that instruments of somewhat less reputation, but of nearly as fine quality, have advanced more sharply in price over a period of years. It is really not difficult to see why. The world supply of fine instruments is not inexhaustible, and while some reach peaks of price, going beyond range of all but the wealthiest buyers, others suddenly become attractive. The musician of 1900 who saved or borrowed to buy a genuine Amati or Stradivari violin, stubbornly believing these the only violins of worthy quality, now contents himself with a 17th or 18th-century instrument by a lesser-known maker. The fact that Strads and Amatis are out of reach for most buyers has opened up demand for the works of many other makers, which, in due time, will probably also become prohibitively costly. Then buyers will turn to still lesser-known names, and so on, until (though this should be a long distance off) every violin dated before 1800 is cherished and fought over in the salesrooms.

The following may better illustrate this point.

	Average price, 1930	Average price, Mid 1980's	% of increase
Stradivarius	$10,000	$55-125,000	550-1,250%
Fabris	600	3,500-4,500	c. 600-750%
Meloni	480	4,000-6,000	c. 800-1,200%

For an instrument to be a good investment, it must be a good instrument. It must be identifiable to a maker. It must have a reputation, even if only locally. It must be an instrument that a musician could play and would not be ashamed to play. And it should, preferably, be representative of the better class of work produced by its maker. Factory products, as opposed to instruments made and signed by craftsmen, are generally not as good investments.

After all this talk of "antique instruments," it may be well to define or attempt to define what is meant by this expression. Technically, there is no satisfactory definition which can be applied to all classes (or even to most classes) of instruments. The usual standard for antiques — anything 100 or more years old — does not suit instruments, as some instruments have much earlier origins than others, and some fell into the class of factory or commercial work earlier than others. It might, for example, be proper to term a Sears Roebuck violin of 1895 an antique, but it is neither desirable nor valuable on that account. Nor is it entirely proper to class a 1720 and an 1890 piano under the heading of "antique" without making any further distinction. This is why the term (loose though it may be) "classical instruments" has been adopted, to signify instruments which, in addition to merely being old, are noteworthy on other grounds; or, if merely old, are sufficiently old to be valuable for that reason alone.

BUYING ANTIQUE MUSICAL INSTRUMENTS

A number of possible sources of supply exist for the collector, the principal ones being: retail dealers who make a specialty of musical instruments; auction houses; musicians; private parties; exchange clubs; advertisements in collector magazines; and various others. It is impossible to state that any single source is preferable to others, as this depends very much on the individual collector and his circumstances. First (and foremost) it should be borne in mind that a buyer who is not an authority on the material he buys leaves himself at the seller's mercy, and really has no alternative — unless he enjoys risks — but to rely on competent dealers.

BUYING FROM DEALERS SPECIALIZING IN ANTIQUE INSTRUMENTS

There are a fair number of full-time dealers both here and abroad (more in Europe than the U.S.) who make a specialty of antique musical instruments. Some of them deal in just one variety of instrument, others in miscellaneous instruments, while still others also sell general musicana as well (sheet music, phono records, record players and the like). Some issue catalogues or price listings. Others do not prepare lists, stating as their reason for not doing so the fact that merchandise moves too quickly and prices rapidly become outdated. Most do, however, sell by mail in addition to making shop sales. The usual method in selling by mail is either through advertisements in the collector press or individual quotations to interested parties. The collector should be aware that items offered to him by mail are seldom held in reserve pending a reply, but have been (or will be) offered to others as well, on a first-come basis.

Are dealers' prices fair? This is a question that could be discussed at great length. Because the musical instrument market is not regulated by standard catalogue prices — such as exist for stamps, coins, and many kinds of collectors' items — there is opportunity for the dealer to make somewhat freer evaluations. However, it is not in the best interest of any dealer to attempt selling a $200 instrument for $1,000, or to overprice at all, as most of his customers are well aware of values and an overpriced item is not likely to sell. The fact that dealers' prices run higher on average than auction sale prices is undeniable, but this is likewise true of most kinds of antiques. The dealers do a great deal of their buying at auctions, and when you buy from them you must pay the auction price plus their margin of profit. There is really no substitute for buying from an experienced, responsible professional dealer, however. You have the option of keeping or returning the item (within a specified time limit), personal attention, and someone to ask questions of and obtain advice from. Not every dealer is in this lofty category but we do have in this country a number of professionals in whom the trade can take pride, and without whom the activities of collectors might not be so successful.

When buying by mail, it is wise to ask that a photograph be sent of any item that you seriously contemplate buying. A slight charge might be made for this, as the dealer is not likely to have photos on hand unless he issues catalogues and has to take the picture especially for you. It will most likely be a Polaroid in color.

BUYING FROM AUCTIONS

Good buys can be made at auctions, but there is somewhat more uncertainty than in purchasing through retail channels. Auctions are not advisable as a source of supply for the beginning collector, unless he has an agent to advise and act for him.

Antique instruments turn up at all classes of auctions, from those conducted by prestigious international houses to local estate sales. Sometimes the larger galleries hold sales devoted entirely to instruments, but such sales are rare, especially in the U.S., as few private collections of instruments are large enough to warrant an auction of their own. More commonly, instruments are included in general sales of "western art" or "European art." In an estate sale there may be just a single instrument among 400 or 500 miscellaneous lots, but this is where some of the best opportunities occur. At the average estate sale, there are few bidders who have knowledge of antique instruments and, usually, no dealers who specialize in them. Therefore, an informed buyer is likely to have the chance at purchasing material well below its actual value. The problem is that many estate sales are unaccompanied by catalogues or listings, and the majority of those issuing catalogues provide inadequate information; it is impossible to know from their descriptions whether an instrument being sold is modern or old. Unless one attends the sale, it is very difficult to make intelligent purchases.

A certain share of open-mindedness is necessary at country or estate auctions. Do not pre-judge the quality of instruments being sold by the quality of other items in the sale. An estate may consist of mediocre furnishings, pictures, etc., but contain a really good antique guitar, mandolin, or other instrument. The item itself must be examined before reaching any conclusion.

ANTIQUE SHOPS AND OTHER NON-SPECIALIST DEALERS

Musical instruments are very frequently offered by general dealers in antiques. A non-specialist dealer will not often place a large investment in valuable instruments, but specimens of ordinary variety are acquired in the normal course of business, from estate purchases and the like. These are more likely to be smaller wind instruments and guitars rather than anything of substantial proportions. Sometimes violins will turn up, and a good quantity of harmonicas, accordions, and banjos. The dealer's geographical location plays some part in the sort of instruments he is apt to acquire, certain instruments being more popular in one part of the country than another (banjos in the southern states, for example).

There is no harm in buying antique instruments from antique shops, if you have a fair knowledge of the material purchased and an eye for quality. To build a collection via such purchases is difficult, though, because of the uncertainty of what will be available from one shop to another and from one moment to the next. Usually, the instruments sold in American antique shops are of late 19th- or 20th-century manufacture, the kind sold by mail-order firms or otherwise widely produced and distributed and not too highly respected as antiques. They are apt to be in somewhat less than good condition and on occasion are badly damaged, as antique dealers are not, on the whole, as discriminating in their acquisitions as are the specialist dealers in antique instruments. They will buy an old banjo with a string missing for $5 or

$6, feeling that some customer capable of making the necessary repair will be willing to buy it for $10. On occasion an 18th-century violin or something similar will turn up, but this is far more likely to occur in foreign shops.

BUYING FROM PRIVATE COLLECTORS

This is not a bad source, if the seller is a responsible party and a fair price can be agreed upon. Often, however, private owners over-value their instruments, and do not back up the sale with a guarantee of satisfaction. When private owners ask for "offers" on instruments they have for sale, this can be taken as an indication that they have little or no knowledge of values, and probably also have little knowledge of instruments. What they are selling is, most likely, some item discovered in the attic, which may generously be worth $40 or $50 but which they fondly hope will bring them untold riches.

GARAGE SALES, FLEA MARKETS, ETC.

Well worth looking into, if just for entertainment. A chance of finding desirable instruments, but a slim one.

VALUES OF ANTIQUE MUSICAL INSTRUMENTS

There are no hard fast rules about the values of instruments. The prices presented in this section are merely a guide to general values. Any given instrument may sell higher or lower, depending on quality and circumstances of sale. Naturally, there is a greater variation in values of the more costly specimens than of modestly priced items. A Stradivari violin that might normally carry an evaluation of $75,000 could easily fetch double that amount in a hotly contested international sale, especially if such a sale occurs during a market peak. Also, it should be understood that these prices do not represent forecasts or predictions of future values, but rather the values current at the time of compiling. Conditions change, sometimes rapidly, and demand for instruments of any given type could force prices beyond the levels shown here. Barring events of a very extreme nature, however, we feel that these prices should be valid for at least one year following publication.

The prices stated are retail selling prices, not wholesale prices or prices at which a dealer would buy from a private owner. We have not attempted to give "average buying prices," in the belief this would only lead to confusion. But it can be pretty safely assumed that the average or fair buying price on most instruments will run from 40 to 50 percent of the sums indicated, for specimens in good playable condition.

BOOKS ON INSTRUMENTS

ACOUSTICS	Price Range	
☐ **CULVER, C. A.** *Musical Acoustics, Philadelphia, 1947.*	9.00	12.00
☐ **LLOYD, L. S.** *Music and Sound, London, 1937.*	10.00	14.00
☐ **MILLER, C. D.** *The Science of Musical Sounds, New York, 1922.*	15.00	20.00
☐ **OLSON, HARRY F.** *Musical Engineering, New York, 1952.* . . .	9.00	12.00
☐ **SEASHORE, C.** *The Psychology of Music, New York, 1938.* . . .	13.00	18.00

	Price Range	
☐ **VON HELMHOLTZ, H.** *The Sensations of Tone, London, 1875.*	18.00	24.00
☐ **WOOD, ALEXANDER.** *The Physics of Music, London, 1944...*	10.00	14.00

ANCIENT AND FOLK

☐ **ANDERSSON, O.** *The Bowed Harp, London, 1930.*	15.00	20.00
☐ **BAINES, A.** *Bagpipes, Oxford, 1960.*	7.00	10.00
☐ **FARMER, H. G.** *The Minstrelsy of the Arabian Nights, Glasgow, 1945.*	10.00	14.00
☐ **PANUM, H.** *Stringed Instruments of the Middle Ages, London, 1940.*	11.00	15.00
☐ **SACHS, CURT.** *The Rise of Music in the Ancient World, New York, 1943.*	10.00	14.00

CLAVICHORDS

☐ **NEUPERT, H.** *Das Klavichord, Kassel, Germany, 1950.*	11.00	15.00

ELECTRONIC

☐ **DORF, R. H.** *Electronic Musical Instruments, New York, 1954.*	15.00	20.00
☐ **DOUGLAS, ALAN.** *The Electronic Musical Instrument Manual, London, 1949.*	25.00	32.00

GENERAL

☐ **BESSARABOFF, N.** *Ancient European Musical Instruments, Cambridge, 1941.*	15.00	20.00
☐ **BUCHNER, A.** *Musical Instruments Through the Ages, London, 1956.*	13.00	18.00
☐ **CARSE, ADAM,** *The Orchestra in the 18th-Century, Cambridge, 1940.*	15.00	20.00
☐ **CARSE, ADAM,** *The Orchestra from Beethoven to Berlioz, London, 1948.*	11.00	15.00
☐ **DONINGTON, R.** *The Instruments of Music, London, 1949....*	14.00	19.00
☐ **GALPIN, F. W.** *Old English Instruments of Music, London, 1910.*	40.00	55.00
☐ **GEIRINGER, K.** *Musical Instruments, London, 1943.*	15.00	20.00
☐ **HIPKINS, A. J. and GIBB, W.** *Musical Instruments, Historic, Rare and Unique, Edinburgh, 1888.*	185.00	230.00
☐ **KINSKY, G.** *History of Music in Pictures, Leipzig, 1929.*	30.00	40.00
☐ **SACHS, CURT.** *The History of Musical Instruments, New York, 1940.*	8.00	11.00
☐ **TERRY, C. S.** *Bach's Orchestra, London, 1932.*	13.00	17.00

HARPSICHORD AND RELATED

☐ **BOALCH, DONALD.** *Makers of the Harpsichord and Clavichord, 1440-1840, London, 1956.*	23.00	30.00
☐ **RUSSELL, RAYMOND.** *The Harpsichord and Clavichord, London, 1959.*	10.00	14.00

HORNS (BRASS)

☐ **COAR, B.** *The French Horn, Ann Arbor, MI, 1947.*	17.00	23.00
☐ **FARKAS, P.** *The Art of French Horn Playing, Chicago, 1956.* .	13.00	18.00
☐ **MORLEY-PEGGE, R.** *The French Horn, London, 1960.*	11.00	15.00

	Price Range	
LUTES		
☐ **BOETTICHER, W.** *Studien zur soloistischen Lautenpraxis der 16ten und 17ten Jahrhunderte, Berlin, 1943.*	15.00	20.00
PIANOFORTES		
☐ **HARDING, ROSAMUND.** *The Pianoforte, Its History Traced to the Great Exhibition, 1851, Cambridge, 1933.*	30.00	40.00
☐ **HIPKINS, A. J.** *The Story of the Pianoforte, London, 1896.*	7.00	10.00
☐ **HIPKINS, E.** *How Chopin Played, London, 1937.*	9.00	12.00
PRIMITIVE		
☐ **IZIKOWITZ, K. G.** *Muical and Other Sound Instruments of the South American Indians, Goteborg, 1935.*	22.00	30.00
☐ **KIRBY, P. R.** *The Musical Instruments of the Native Races of South Africa, London, 1934.*	35.00	45.00
VIOLINS		
☐ **BACHMANN, ALBERTO.** *An Encyclopedia of the Violin, New York, 1929.*	15.00	20.00
☐ **DUBORG, G.** *The Violin, London, 1836.*	55.00	70.00
☐ **HART, G.** *The Violin, London, 1875.*	40.00	55.00
☐ **HERON-ALLEN, E.** *Violin Making As It Is, London, 1884.*	60.00	75.00
☐ **OTTO, J. A.** *Treatise on the Structure and Preservation of the Violin, London, 1848.*	80.00	100.00
☐ **SAINT-GEORGE, HENRY.** *The Bow, London, 1896.*	35.00	45.00
☐ **SANDYS, W. and FORSTER, S. A.** *History of the Violin, London, 1864.*	55.00	70.00
☐ **VAN DER STRAETEN, E.** *The History of the Violin, two volumes, London, 1933.*	70.00	90.00
WOODWINDS		
☐ **BAINES, A.** *Woodwind Instruments and Their History, London, 1957.*	18.00	23.00
☐ **BATES, P. A.** *The Oboe, London, 1956.*	9.00	12.00
☐ **BOEHM, THEOBALD.** *The Flute and Flute-Playing, Cleveland, 1922.*	14.00	19.00
☐ **CARSE, ADAM.** *Musical Wind Instruments, London, 1939.*	17.00	13.00
☐ **CHAPMAN, F. B.** *Flute Technique, London, 1936.*	11.00	15.00
☐ **LANGWILL, L. G.** *The Bassoon and Double Bassoon, London, 1948.*	10.00	14.00
☐ **LORENZO, L. DE.** *My Complete Story of the Flute, New York, 1951.*	12.00	17.00
☐ **RENDALL, F. G.** *The Clarinet, London, 1954.*	12.00	17.00
☐ **ROCKSTRO, R. S.** *A Treatise on the Flute, London, 1890.*	23.00	30.00
☐ **ROTHWELL, E.** *Oboe Technique, London, 1953.*	12.00	17.00
☐ **THURSTON, F.** *Clarinet Technique, London, 1955.*	12.00	17.00
☐ **WELCH, C.** *History of the Boehm Flute, London, 1883.*	16.00	22.00
☐ **WILLAMAN, R.** *The Clarinet and Clarinet Playing, New York, 1949.*	10.00	14.00

AMERICAN FOLK

American folk instruments comprise a race unto themselves. In many instances it is difficult to draw a clear distinction between folk and nonfolk work but even when instruments of this class are put aside, a great deal remains which can unquestionably be labeled "native art".

What is a folk instrument? The best and most universally understood definition is: an instrument not commercially produced but made for use by its manufacturer, his family or someone in the local community. The term "commercially produced" should not be interpreted too literally, however. It is certainly conceivable that some folk instruments were made with the intent of selling them, but they were not made by persons who manufactured instruments as a livelihood and therein lies the difference.

Why were folk instruments made in America? A good question. It is readily understandable why Africans, South Sea Islanders, South American Indians, etc., made their own instruments — because no other source of supply was available. In America where professionally manufactured instruments could be purchased, why did some persons take the trouble of making them? For several reasons. In the first place, "store-bought" instruments were not accessible in some parts of the country until the late 19th-century mail-order boom. Where they were available, they were often more expensive than common persons could afford. Also, in many areas, especially "backwoods", there was a taste for certain varieties of instruments that factories did not offer. Then, too, local craftsmen prized their efforts (rightly or wrongly) well above the esteem in which they regarded commercial output.

The 19th-century was the prime era for American folk instruments, though a good many were produced beforehand and after — and continue to be today. They were of many sorts, some in imitation of standard instruments, others bearing no resemblance to them. Many were made of odd materials and were played in ways that could only be termed bizarre. Their designation as musical instruments might well be challenged by some persons, on the basis that anything which makes noises could be termed an instrument — even beating on a table with a hammer. However, folk instruments seldom originated out of a quest for novelty. Strange though some may be, they were designed and created to be used either as part of a band or by a lone performer, and this would seem sufficient to declare them instruments.

The study of American folk instruments is no cake walk. Dates and points of origin are rarely known for sure and must be estimated. Often this is difficult. Just because a particular sort of instrument was common to a given locality is no reason to conclude that every specimen originated there. Values are equally hard to fix. They depend on a variety of considerations, including (but not necessarily in this order) age, type of instrument, styles, quality, decoration, materials and state of preservation. Rarity, of course, enters the picture but is not generally the deciding factor. A freak instrument may be very rare insofar as few or no others quite like it are known to exist, but it will not necessarily realize a high price.

Some folk instruments — it is not easy to estimate the proportion — are unquestionably within the class of "tramp art", i.e., items fashioned out of driftwood and throw-away materials by itinerants, who sought to exchange them for food or drink. These can reasonably be dated in the 1870-1930 era.

Others are the work of children. They are no less highly regarded on this account, assuming they meet the standards of desirability that would be applied to any folk instruments.

A few words to the prospective buyer of folk instruments. This is a "collectible" found in diverse places, to put it mildly. Some of the best specimens have come to light in junkshops, at rummage sales, and, literally, in garbage dumps. The proportion handled by recognized dealers is very small, compared to those changing hands "at the source". Not too many persons can recognize the value of a folk instrument or distinguish between old and new. A great deal of personal initiative is necessary in this hobby as well as a level of expertise that might not be required when collecting certain types of commercially made instruments. Inspect all components. A genuinely old instrument is not made partially from old and partially from recent materials.

NOTE: Many folk instruments do not have accepted names. In these cases we have described the instrument rather than attempting to name it.

BANJO	**Price Range**	
☐ *Made from a tambourine to which a length of mahogany is attached, backed in sheet tin, painted, damaged, Southern U.S., pre-Civil War.*	210.00	250.00
☐ *Made from a barrel stave with skin stretched over, hardwood neck, strings missing, skin broken, probably Arkansas or Kentucky, c. 1870.*	125.00	150.00
☐ *Made from sheet zinc, 28" long, maple neck, eastern U.S., c. 1890.*	65.00	80.00

FLUTE

☐ *Carved from a solid piece of walnut, 16½" long, probably Pennsylvania, c. 1780.*	575.00	650.00
☐ *Carved from a solid piece of ebony wood, whalebone mouthpiece, possibly sailor-made, thought to be of New England origin, early c. 1800's.*	480.00	535.00
☐ *Carved from maple, 12⅝" long, five holes, mouthpiece broken, place of origin not known, early 19th-century.*	210.00	250.00
☐ *Carved from whalebone, silver mouthpiece and decoration, size not stated, Massachusetts(?), c. 1840.*	1750.00	2250.00
☐ *Carved from pine, 13¼" long, eastern U.S., c. 1850.*	250.00	275.00
☐ *Carved from rosewood, 18" long, mouthpiece missing, eastern U.S. or possibly foreign (England or Wales), c. 1950.*	315.00	350.00
☐ *Carved from white ash, painted (paint decayed), 15" long, possibly Pennsylvania, c. 1850-70.*	315.00	350.00
☐ *Carved from elephant tusk, 11½" long, several cracks, ivory discolored, eastern U.S., third quarter of the 19th-century.*	1400.00	1800.00
☐ *Carved from cedar, boxwood mouthpiece, 21½" long, seven holes, place of origin unknown, name "K. Brown" carved in wood, c. 1880.*	400.00	450.00
☐ *Carved from oak, 15¼" long, nickel mouthpiece, place of origin unknown, possibly foreign, c. late 1800's.*	250.00	300.00
☐ *Made from bronze plumbing pipe with holes bored in, size not stated, possible Southern U.S., c. early 1900's.*	85.00	100.00

	Price Range	
☐ *Made from galvanized steel tubing, 20" long, place of origin unknown, c. early 1900's.*	60.00	80.00
☐ *Made from heavy rolled cardboard, painted, 19" long, possibly New England, age uncertain.*	65.00	80.00

ONE-MAN BAND

☐ *Contraption containing a harmonica, zither, small trumpet, ocarina, chimes, bells and other instruments, attached to several leather-covered lengths of wood, straps broken, used by a vaudeville performer who did a one-man act, Eastern U.S., c. 1900.*	210.00	240.00

STRINGED INSTRUMENT

☐ *Wooden cigar box attached to broom handle, 37" long, three strings, painted, Southern U.S.(?), second half of the 19th-century.*	55.00	70.00
☐ *Sawn barrel bottom with hardwood neck, repaired, two strings (three others missing), eastern U.S., second half of the 19th-century.*	70.00	90.00
☐ *Instrument resembling mandolin, oval shaped body carved from sandalwood, walnut neck, strings missing, decorated with shallow line incising, traces of old paint, Virginia or Kentucky, late 19th-century.*	285.00	350.00
☐ *Instrument constructed from flat wooden board, 12"x16", oval cut in center, eight strings running across from top to bottom, board painted with floral design, worn, Pennsylvania(?), late 19th-century.*	150.00	175.00

WASHBOARD INSTRUMENT

☐ *Metal washboard, wooden frame, mounted on a larger wooden plank measuring overall 22"x34", painted dark brown with eagle head and other decorations, name "L. Cotter" painted at foot, rusted, worn, Appalachia, c. 1870-1890.*	95.00	110.00
☐ *Metal washboard, wooden frame (broken), size not stated, to one side is attached a length of thin chain with a wooden stick at the end, Appalachia, c. 1890.*	80.00	100.00
☐ *Metal, washboard, 29"x41", narrow homemade wooden frame, two bells attached, Southern or Southeast U.S., c. 1880-1900.*	80.00	100.00
☐ *Metal washboard with pine frame, 32"x51", with a leather strap attached so musician could wear it over his body, painted dull green, name "Mulvey's Minstrels" in silver letters, worn, partially damaged, probably eastern U.S., c. 1880-1900.*	200.00	240.00

INDIVIDUAL INSTRUMENTS

ACCORDIONS

The most popular of the bellows-type instruments, in which sound is produced by aspiration and expiration (sucking in and pushing out of wind), the accordion is of rather modern invention. It was developed in 1822 by a German named Friedrich Buschmann, who also invented — the previous year — the mouth organ. It was termed the Ziehharmonika. The earliest models not only operated on the bellows principle but closely resembled a bellows. The accordion gained almost instant acceptance, though its use was restricted mainly to folk and popular music. Rarely was it used as a classical orchestral instrument. Later it saw even wider use in vaudeville and music halls, both in Europe and America. Improvements in design were made throughout the 19th and into the 20th-century. By the late 19th-century, accordions were being manufactured in a number of localities in Europe, though Germany held the lead in production and German accordions were considered the most desirable.

Accordions were manufactured in a great variety of styles, sizes and quality of materials. There were cheap models imported from Europe into the American market which retailed at as little as $2.25 around 1900. At the same time, a top-quality accordion could be had for $10 to $15. Retail prices rose sharply during the 1920's.

	Price Range	
☐ **"Accordeon"** *(so marked), molded frame, enameled cloth trimmed bellows, nickel key cover, 10 keys, one stop, two sets of reeds, American, c. 1895.*	150.00	175.00
☐ *American, 1906.*	375.00	425.00
☐ **Concertone,** *marked "Nicolo Salanti", 21 pearl keys, 12 basses, four sets of steel reeds, 18-fold bellows, leather covered, rosewood finish frames, made in Italy for sale in U.S. by Montgomery Ward, c. early 1920's.*	250.00	300.00
☐ **Concertone,** *10 keys, two long spoon basses, 10-fold bellows, nickel corner protectors, enameled, mahogany finish pearls, ebonized moldings, size 10¼"x5½" (closed).*	120.00	150.00

Accordion Italian, c. 20th century. *Courtesy: The Metropolitan Museum of Art, gift of Mrs. Margaret Gatz Werner, 1969.*

	Price Range	
☐ **Concertone,** *10 keys, four basses, metal valves and two sets of steel bronze reeds, rosewood finish with white enameled pressed borders, 14-fold bellows, 10"x5½".*	135.00	170.00
☐ **Concertone,** *31 pearl keys, 12 basses, metal valves, six sets of steel reeds, 18-fold cloth-covered leather bellows, rosewood finish frames, inlaid fingerboard and front edge, 12½"x8¾".*	275.00	335.00
☐ **Concertone,** *two stops, two sets of reeds, 10 keys, gilt valves, 9-fold bellows, ebonized panels and frames, 12"x6".*	100.00	125.00
☐ **Concertone,** *German model, 10 keys, two basses, three sets of reeds, three ebonized wooden stops, gilt valves with brass basses, 8-fold bellows with three middle partitions, 11⅛"x6".*	130.00	150.00
☐ **Concertone,** *10 keys, gilt valves, four sets of steel bronze reeds, four enameled wooden stops, ebonized enamel woodwork, gilt embossing, 12⅞"x7".*	150.00	175.00
☐ **Concertone,** *marked "Corelli", 21 keys, metal valves, four sets of steel bronze reeds set on lead plates, 14-fold bellows, rosewood finish frame, enameled embossings, oak finish panels, 11"x5¾".*	185.00	225.00
☐ *Ebonized molding, nickel edges, open keyboard, 10 nickel keys ornamented with gilt stars, panels, corners and clasps bronzed, two stops, two sets of reeds, double bellows, c. 1890's.*	185.00	225.00
☐ *German, c. 1860.*	725.00	1100.00
☐ *Imitation oak, hand carved molding, corners and clasps heavily nickel-plated, double bellows, 10 keys, two stops, two sets of reeds, late 19th-century.*	210.00	250.00
☐ *Imitation oak, open keyboard, corners and clasps nickel-plated, double bellows, 10 keys, two stops, two sets of reeds, German-made (marketed in America), c. 1890.*	210.00	240.00
☐ *Italian, third quarter of the 19th-century.*	750.00	1000.00
☐ *Italian, 1891.*	650.00	850.00
☐ **Kalbe Imperial,** *ebonized moldings, sunken panels, twin bellows, nickel-plated clasps and corners, 10 nickel-plated keys, two stops, two sets of reeds.*	425.00	550.00
☐ **Kalbe Imperial,** *medium size, bellows frame silver-stamped, corners and clasps nickel-plated, 10 keys, two basses, two stops, two sets of broad reeds.*	475.00	600.00
☐ **Kalbe Imperial,** *ebonized moldings, gilt-stamped panels, ten nickel-plated keys and two basses, leather-bound bellows with nickel protectors, bellows frame silver-stamped, two stops, two reed sets.*	500.00	650.00
☐ **Kalbe's Improved Accordion,** *12 keys, ebonized moldings, hand-painted bellows frame, open keyboard, nickel-plated corners and clasps, double leather bound bellows, two stops, two sets of reeds, c. late 1800's.*	375.00	450.00
☐ *Miniature accordion, hand-painted, panels and moldings ebonized, 10 nickel-plated keys, clasps and corners nickel-plated, double bellows, two stops, two sets of reeds, about ¾ full size, c. 1890-1900.*	375.00	450.00

	Price Range	
☐ *Molded frame, open keyboard, 10 nickel-plated keys, double bellows, two stops, two sets of reeds, made in Germany for the American market, c. 1890-1900.*	250.00	300.00
☐ *Molded frames, panels nickel-ornamented, mirrored nickel round rings, double leather-bound bellows, 17 keys, two stops, four sets of reeds.*	475.00	600.00
☐ **Pitzchier Accordion,** *fluted moldings in imitation mahogany, mahogany panels, sunken open-action keyboard, 19 nickel keys, heavy twin bellows with nickel protectors, nickel-plated corners and clasps, four stops, four sets of reeds, made in Germany (sold in America), c. late 1800's.*	550.00	700.00
☐ **Pitzschier Accordion,** *identical to above except has 21 keys instead of 19.*	600.00	750.00
☐ *10 nickel-plated keys, nickel-plated corners and clasps, ornamented panels, 16 trumpets in molding and 10 trumpets in key cover, triple bellows, two stops and two sets of reeds.*	425.00	475.00
☐ **"Tuxedo", with "Vox Humana" or Tremola attachment,** *may be Kalbe, ebonized moldings and panels, open keyboard with 10 nickel-plated keys and two basses, leather-bound twin bellows, two stops, two sets of reeds.*	440.00	490.00

APOLLO HARPS

The Apollo Harp was a harp with a keyboard; or, it might be better put, an instrument with a keyboard, as it bore only slight resemblance to a harp. It originated in the late 1800's, at a time when instrument manufacturers (and novelty manufacturers) strove to place on the market a variety of musical devices that could be played with little practice or talent — items whose appeal would not be to the serious musician but the public.

☐ *Imitation rosewood, 33 strings, sliding four-bar keyed bridge, produces 32 chords.*	100.00	125.00
☐ *Imitation rosewood, 34 strings, five-bar sliding keyed bridge which produces five chords in every key, overall size 12½"x21".*	130.00	160.00
☐ *Imitation rosewood, 36 strings, six-bar sliding keyed bridge, American, c. 1890's.*	170.00	210.00
☐ *Imitation rosewood, six-bar sliding keyed bridge.*	215.00	300.00
☐ *33 strings, three-bar keyed sliding bridge, bridge can be adjusted to play in keys of C, C sharp, D, E flat, E or F, produces 18 chords, American, c. 1890's.*	60.00	80.00

BAGPIPES

The principle of the bagpipe is simple. Air is blown into a large bladder, then forced out through pipes. As it passes through the pipes, it creates various musical tones which can be shortened or lengthened depending on the rate of air-escape. The bagpipe is among the most historically important of instruments and surely one of the most varied, if one takes into account the geographical area in which it has been produced and the many designs of bagpipes. It might also be mentioned that the bagpipe is one instrument, one of a relatively few, that can have considerable value as a collector's item even in deteriorated condition.

Bagpipe **collecting,** as opposed to the purchase of a single secondhand instrument to play, is a complex endeavor whose techniques we could hardly hope to explore here at any length. The advanced specialist seeks not only the earliest obtainable examples but those of specially fine workmanship, or from territories that have yielded few antique bagpipes. As the manufacturers of early bagpipes have left behind far scantier records of their activities than makers of, say, violins or pianos, it is often difficult or impossible to determine the origin of any given specimen.

Bagpipes of a primitive form were in use by the 3rd or 4th-century A.D. in the Near East, from whence they appeared in Europe, but it was not until late in the Middle Ages that the instrument became really widespread. Scotland has had a reputation for bagpipe-making (and playing) from at least as early as the 15th-century. Contrary to general belief among the public, however, many other nations and peoples have adopted bagpipes as a national instrument, including the Irish, Slavic and Turkish.

	Price Range	
☐ *French, early 18th-century.*	3000.00	5000.00
☐ *French, Louis XV.*	2800.00	4500.00
☐ *Scottish, walnut chaunters, 16th-century.*	6200.00	10500.00
☐ *Scottish, early 17th-century.*	4800.00	7200.00
☐ *Scottish, c. 1630.*	4500.00	6500.00
☐ *Scottish, rosewood chaunters, late 17th-century.*	3700.00	5700.00
☐ *Scottish, c. 1710.*	3500.00	5000.00
☐ *Scottish, mid 18th-century.*	2900.00	4000.00

Bagpipe, Italian, c. 19th century. *Courtesy: The Metropolitan Museum of Art, gift of Burt Ives, 1963*

BANJOS

The banjo is most familiar as the chief instrument of old-time minstrel shows. It has had a revival today in the folk music field where it is almost as widely used as the guitar. Its origins are obscure. Apparently, a primitive type of banjo was played in Africa in the 17th and 18th-centuries and was taken to America by slaves. Much easier to construct and to play than most other stringed instruments, it became a favorite in this country. By the time of the Civil War, the banjo was clearly the leading "folk" instrument of the southern and southwest states. Though not extensively used north of Virginia, its influence extended into New England and even Canada.

	Price Range	
☐ *American, wooden shell covered in goatskin, hardwood neck, 41" overall, c. 1840*	550.00	750.00
☐ *American, boxwood shell covered in calfskin, hardwood neck, 39", Civil War era*	450.00	550.00
☐ *American, maple shell with nickel band, neck finished in imitation cherry, 10" calfskin head with six screw brackets, c. 1895-1905*	200.00	250.00
☐ *American, nickel shell, wood lined, neck stained in imitation cherry, with seven nickel-plated hexagon brackets, calfskin head, c. 1895-1905*	210.00	260.00
☐ *American, imitation mahogany head, raised frets, nine nickel-plated hexagon brackets, calfskin head, c.1895-1905*	225.00	300.00
☐ *American, calfskin head, heavy strainer hoop, 21 nickel-plated brackets with protection nuts, polished cherry neck, ebony fingerboard inlaid with pearl position dots, ebony pegs, c. 1900*	325.00	400.00
☐ *American, nickel shell, maple rim, wired edges, 25 nickel-plated brackets with rabbeted stainer hoop, solid birch neck, ebony fingerboard inlaid with pearl and metal, ebony pegs, c. 1900*	375.00	450.00
☐ *Banjo mandolin, used mainly in bands playing European folk dances, 11" maple rim, 20 nickel-plated brackets, birch neck, calfskin head, c. 1920's*	100.00	125.00

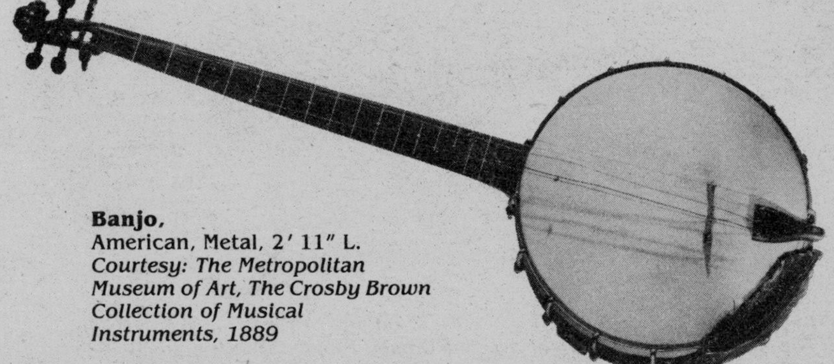

Banjo,
American, Metal, 2' 11" L.
Courtesy: The Metropolitan Museum of Art, The Crosby Brown Collection of Musical Instruments, 1889

	Price Range	
☐ **"Bird's-Eye"**, *maple rim, five strings, 11" rim, 20 nickel-plated brackets.*	85.00	115.00
☐ **Edgemere Banjo,** *nickel shell, wood-lined, 17 nickel-plated hexagon brackets, raised frets, birch neck finished in imitation mahogany, c. 1900.*	260.00	320.00
☐ *Five-string, wood rim, 11" rim, 12 nickel-plated brackets, birch neck, three pearl position dots, celluloid pegs, c. 1920's.*	70.00	90.00
☐ **Leader Banjo,** *nickel shell, calfskin head, wired edges, nickel-plated strainer hoops, 21 nickel-plated brackets, fretted fingerboard, raised frets, inlaid with pearl position dots, birch neck.*	275.00	350.00
☐ *Tenor banjo, maple rim, four strings (A, D, G, C), 20 nickel-plated brackets, pearl position dots.*	120.00	160.00

BASSOONS

The bassoon, firmly entrenched in orchestras since the Baroque age though never a truly popular instrument, underwent major alterations in the 19th-century to arrive at its present design and performance. Early bassoons were attacked for unevenness of notes. In the 1820's Carl Almenraeder designed a new bassoon with realigned fingerholes and keys. Though a substantial technical improvement which rendered the bassoon easier and more practical to play, Almenraeder's instrument was greeted with reservations by purists, who felt the tone was not equal to that of old bassoons. Later in the same century, another German, Wilhelm Heckel, succeeded in producing a bassoon that combined the best features of the old and new types. Bassoons manufactured today are essentially identical to Heckel's.

☐ **Buffet-Crampon** *model, Paris, 20th-century.*	1600.00	2100.00
☐ *Four keys, brass mouthpiece, preserved in a fleece-lined walnut box with clasps and lock, late 17th-century.*	4200.00	5700.00
☐ **Heckel** *model, Biebrich, 20th-century.*	1500.00	1850.00
☐ *Six keys, made by Wrede, London, c. 1795.*	3500.00	4500.00

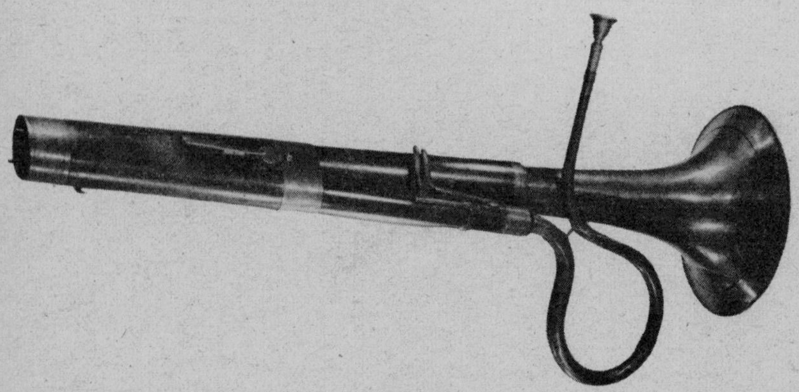

Bassoon in B Flat, French, c. 1800, wood and brass, 3' 3" L. *Courtesy: The Metropolitan Museum of Art, The Crosby Brown Collection of Musical Instruments, 1889*

BONES

Bones, normally made of wood, derive their name from the practice in primitive cultures of making clappers from actual bone. It is quite likely that bones are the oldest of all musical instruments; their use may well date before recorded history. Nor could it be claimed to be stretching things too far to call them instruments. The principle by which they produce sound — one object striking another — is not unlike the drum's. They are, even today, an integral ingredient in the native folk music of many lands. Their popularity in America occurred in the late 1800's and early 1900's, when vaudeville and sideshow entertainers employed them. They have never served as a band instrument in the western world.

	Price Range	
☐ *Ebony, 5½", set of four.*	20.00	25.00
☐ *Ebony, large size, 7", set of four.*	22.00	30.00
☐ *Hardwood, 5½", set of four, American made, sold in the period c. 1890-1900.*	18.00	23.00
☐ *Ivory, 5½", set of four, carved decor, c. 1910.*	65.00	95.00
☐ *Ivory, 6", set of four, etched designs, probably New England.*	200.00	250.00
☐ *Rosewood, 5½", set of four.*	20.00	25.00
☐ *Rosewood, large size, 7", set of four, c. late 1800's.*	23.00	30.00

BOWS

It is hardly surprising that the bows made for playing certain stringed instruments (violin, viola, cello, etc.) have become collectible in themselves. For centuries the art of bow making has been an important phase of the musical instruments trade. It was well known even before the days of Stradavari and Amati that the best violin would not perform up to its potential if played with a less than perfect bow. Of course this is true of all other instruments employing a bow, too. Not only has technical precision gone into the crafting of fine bows over the years, but lavish materials including gold, silver, ivory, tortoiseshell, pearls and occasionally even platinum. The finest bows are acknowledged to be works of art, and a selection of them is generally included in every major sale of collectible musical instruments. Prices have advanced steadily to the point where, today, it is by no means easy to purchase a high quality antique bow for less than four figures. Some are commanding as much as $5000 and occasional specimens go even higher. Of course the collecting appeal of bows is quite obvious, insofar as they display magnificently and consume very little space compared to most instruments. They were made all over the world, with Europe reigning as the chief production center. While most of the fine violins on the antiques market are Italian, this is not the situation with bows, where one finds a predominance of French specimens along with many of English, German and miscellaneous origins. The American makers did not really compete on a level with those of Europe but some domestic manufacturers did gain a reputation for their bows, notably John Norwood Lee of Chicago.

In purchasing antique bows it is advisable to make a thorough examination, or have this done by a competent expert if you are not confident of your own skills. Some have replacement parts.

	Price Range	
☐ Cello, English by James Tubbs of London, round stick mounted with silver, ebony frog, pearl dots, ebony adjuster.	2500.00	3300.00
☐ Cello, English by John Dodd of London, round stick mounted with nickel, ebony frog, pearl dots, ebony adjuster.	700.00	850.00
☐ Cello, French by Adam of Paris, octagonal stick mounted with silver, ebony frog, pearl dots, ebony adjuster.	2100.00	2450.00
☐ Cello, French by Francois Lupot of Paris, octagonal stick mounted with silver, ebony frog, pearl dots, bone adjuster, c. 1810.	5250.00	6500.00
☐ Cello, French by Christian Schaeffer of Paris, round stick mounted with ivory and silver, ivory frog, ivory adjuster with silver rings.	1600.00	1900.00
☐ Cello, French by an unidentified maker, round stick mounted with silver, ebony frog, pearl dots, ebony adjuster, c.1840-1860.	3200.00	3700.00
☐ Cello, French by Fand Freres of Paris, round stick mounted with silver, ebony frog, pearl dots, ebony adjuster, c. 1860-1880.	2275.00	3000.00
☐ Cello, French by Jean Dominique Adam of Paris, octagonal stick mounted with gold, ebony frog, pearl dots, ebony adjuster, c. 1830-1840.	6200.00	7500.00
☐ Cello, French by Charles Jean Baptise Collin-Mezin of Paris, round stick mounted with silver, ebony frog, pearl dots, ebony adjuster.	1700.00	2200.00
☐ Cello, French by Gand of Paris, round stick mounted with silver, ebony frog, pearl dots, ebony adjuster.	2100.00	2375.00
☐ Cello, French by Eugene Sartory of Paris, octagonal stick mounted with silver, ebony frog, pearl dots, ebony adjuster.	3800.00	4600.00
☐ Cello, German by Sigfried Finkel with no place of residence given, octagonal stick mounted with gold and ivory, ivory frog, pearl dots, ivory adjuster.	1600.00	1900.00
☐ Viola, American by John Norwood Lee of Chicago, round stick mounted with gold, ebony frog, pearl dots, gold rings, ebony adjuster.	1600.00	1875.00
☐ Viola, American by Emile A. Ouchard of New York, round stick mounted with silver, ebony frog, pearl dots, ebony adjuster mounted in silver.	2100.00	2350.00
☐ Viola, English by William Watson of London, octagonal stick mounted with silver and tortoiseshell, tortoiseshell frog, pearl dots, ebony adjuster.	2000.00	2450.00
☐ Viola, English by Stephen Bristow of London, round stick mounted with silver, ebony frog, pearl dots, ebony adjuster.	700.00	850.00
☐ Viola, French by Roger Gerome, octagonal stick mounted with gold, ebony frog, pearl dots, ebony adjuster.	2250.00	2875.00
☐ Viola, French by Roger Gerome, octagonal stick mounted with gold, ebony frog, pearl dots, ebony adjuster.	1600.00	1900.00
☐ Viola, Swiss by Bernard Ouchard of Geneva, octagonal stick mounted with gold and ebony, ebony frog, pearl dots, ebony adjuster.	1600.00	1850.00
☐ Violin, American by John Norwood Lee of Chicago, round stick mounted with gold and tortoiseshell, tortoiseshell frog, pearl dots, ebony adjuster.	2200.00	2850.00

	Price Range	
☐ *Violin, American by John Norwood Lee of Chicago, octagonal stick mounted with gold and tortoiseshell, tortoiseshell frog, pearl dots, ebony adjuster.*	2200.00	2850.00
☐ *Violin, English by C. E. Tubbs of London, round stick mounted with silver, ebony frog, pearl dots, ebony adjuster.*	1600.00	1800.00
☐ *Violin, English by W. E. Hill of London, octagonal stick mounted with silver, ebony frog, pearl dots, ebony adjuster.*	1575.00	1850.00
☐ *Violin, English by Hart of London, round stick mounted with silver, ebony frog, pearl dots, ebony and silver adjuster.*	900.00	1200.00
☐ *Violin, English by Arthur Bultitude of London, octagonal stick mounted with gold and tortoiseshell, tortoiseshell frog, gold flower ornaments.*	2100.00	2450.00
☐ *Violin, English by W. E. Hill of London, octagonal stick mounted with silver and tortoiseshell, tortoiseshell frog with silver decorations, tortoiseshell adjuster.*	1750.00	2175.00
☐ *Violin, English by W. E. Hill of London, round stick mounted with silver, ebony frog, pearl dots, ebony adjuster.*	1100.00	1350.00
☐ *Violin, French by F. N. Voirin of Paris, octagonal stick mounted with gold, ebony frog, pearl dots, ebony adjuster, c. 1850.*	4300.00	5600.00
☐ *Violin, French by Francois Tourte, round stick mounted with silver, ebony frog, pearl dots, ebony adjuster.*	6000.00	7500.00
☐ *Violin, French by Eugene Sartory of Paris, round stick mounted with silver, ebony frog, pearl dots, ebony adjuster.*	3200.00	3675.00
☐ *Violin, French by J. B. Vuillaume with no place of residence given, round stick mounted with silver, ebony frog, pearl dots, ebony adjuster.*	2600.00	2850.00
☐ *Violin, French by an unidentified maker, round stick mounted with silver, ebony frog, pearl dots, ebony adjuster.*	2250.00	2750.00
☐ *Violin, French by Emile A. Ouchard with no place of residence given, round stick mounted with silver and tortoiseshell, tortoiseshell frog, pearl dots, silver capped adjuster.*	1400.00	1700.00
☐ *Violin, French by Alfred Lamy of Paris, octagonal stick mounted with engraved silver, ebony frog, pearl dots, ebony adjuster capped in silver.*	1900.00	2375.00
☐ *Violin, French by Charles Peccatte of Paris, round stick mounted with silver, ebony frog, pearl dots, ebony adjuster, c. 1860-1880.*	2100.00	2375.00
☐ *Violin, French by Alfred Lamy of Paris, round stick mounted with silver, ebony frog, pearl dots, ebony adjuster.*	1800.00	2150.00
☐ *Violin, French by an unidentified maker, round stick mounted with ivory, ivory frog, ivory adjuster, c. 1820.*	900.00	1150.00
☐ *Violin, French by Alfred Lamy of Paris, round stick mounted with silver, ebony frog, pearl dots, ebony adjuster.*	2300.00	2800.00
☐ *Violin, French by Paul Simon of Paris, octagonal stick mounted with silver, ebony frog, pearl dots, ebony adjuster, c. 1840-1860.*	4200.00	5500.00
☐ *Violin, French by Claude Thomassin of Paris, octagonal stick mounted with silver, ebony frog, pearl dots, ebony adjuster.*	1800.00	2250.00
☐ *Violin, French by Marcel Lapierre, round stick mounted with gold and ivory, ivory frog, pearl dots, gold rings, ivory adjuster.*	1175.00	1400.00

	Price Range	
☐ Violin, French by Joseph Henry of Paris, round stick mounted with gold and tortoiseshell, tortoiseshell frog, pearl dots, ebony adjuster, c. 1850.	3200.00	3750.00
☐ Violin, French by Guillaume Maline of Paris, round stick mounted with silver, ebony frog, pearl dots, ebony adjuster, c. 1830-1840.	4300.00	5600.00
☐ Violin, German by Ludwig Bausch, round stick mounted with silver, ebony frog, pearl dots, ebony adjuster.	1100.00	1425.00

BUGLES

☐ American, c. 1878.	160.00	200.00
☐ American, Artillery Bugle, brass, c. 1900.	130.00	160.00
☐ American, Artillery Bugle, nickel-plated, c. 1900.	185.00	225.00
☐ American, Cavalry Bugle, brass, c. 1900.	150.00	185.00
☐ American, Cavalry Bugle, nickel-plated, c.1900.	160.00	200.00
☐ American, Civil War.	325.00	450.00
☐ American, Infantry Bugle, brass, c. 1900.	125.00	175.00
☐ American, Infantry Bugle, nickel-plated, c. 1900.	160.00	190.00
☐ American, Officer's Bugle, c. 1900.	80.00	110.00
☐ American, Officer's Bugle, nickel-plated, c. 1900.	100.00	130.00
☐ English, by Metzler of London, six keys, copper mounted with brass, white metal keys, 16¼", c. 1840-1850.	800.00	1000.00

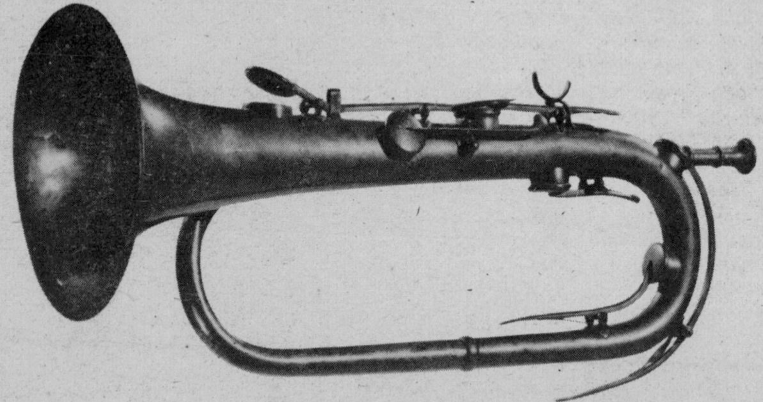

Bugle, keyed, Belgium, c. 19th century, brass, 1′ 9″ L. *Courtesy: The Metropolitan Museum of Art, The Crosby Brown Collection of Musical Instruments, 1889*

CASTINETS *(also spelled Castanets)*

Castinets are known as a Spanish or Latin-American instrument only because the Latin peoples have preserved its use in their folk music. It was not their invention or exclusive property, as castinet-type instruments (consisting of two lengths of wood, bone or other material clapped together to produce clicking sounds) are both ancient and universal. Castinets are ideal collectors' items; old specimens do not get "out of order", and often are splendidly decorated or made from exotic materials. Unfortunately, not too many good specimens are available on the American market. The traveler in Mexico, Brazil, Argentina or Spain stands a better chance of encountering fine examples, if he hunts the music shops and secondhand markets.

	Price	Range
☐ *American, early 20th-century.*	35.00	40.00
☐ *Argentinian, early 19th-century.*	170.00	215.00
☐ *Mexican, 1890.*	70.00	90.00
☐ *Portuguese, c. 1830.*	150.00	185.00
☐ *Spanish, late 18th-century.*	200.00	250.00
☐ *Spanish, c, 1810.*	160.00	200.00
☐ *Spanish, mid 19th-century.*	140.00	175.00
☐ *Spanish, c. 1860.*	80.00	110.00

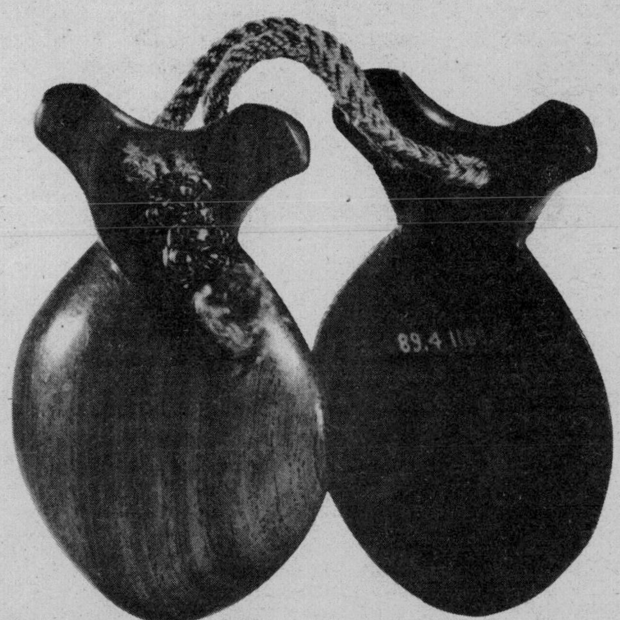

Castinets, Spanish, c. 19th century, hardwood, 2″ x 2¾″. *Courtesy: The Metropolitan Museum of Art, The Crosby Brown Collection of Musical Instruments, 1889*

CELLOS

The cello, or violoncello as it was originally and still correctly called, has long been an important orchestral and solo instrument, first in classical music and more recently in jazz, rhythm and blues and rock. The cello provided the "beat" on rock recordings of the 1950's. But there is considerable difference in the manner of play between classical and rock cello, one played with a bow, the other with fingers.

The cello became a standard orchestra instrument in the 17th-century, though developed earlier. The first solo pieces for cello were composed by an Italian named Gabrielli (1659-1690), who is generally credited with bringing it to a level of attention it had not previously attained. Various modifications and improvements were made to the cello in the following century and a half.

Cellos of the 17th-century are rarely on the market. When sold, their price is well into the four-figure and often five-figure range, if the specimen is decently preserved. Those of the 18th-century are more plentiful but, still, fine ones are very expensive.

	Price Range	
☐ *American made, "Patent Head" cello, c. 1900.*	340.00	420.00
☐ *American, inlaid edges, sold by Sears Roebuck, c. 1900.*	420.00	525.00
☐ *American, peg head, pegs and fingerboard of ebony, c. 1895-1900.*	475.00	600.00
☐ *American, brass plate "Patent Head", turn of the century.*	525.00	650.00
☐ *American, ebony fingerboard, ebony tailpiece, solid ebony trimmings.*	610.00	760.00
☐ *Double Bass, half-size, dark red wood, American, c. 1900.*	630.00	800.00
☐ *Four String Bass, American, iron head, c. 1895-1905.*	700.00	800.00
☐ *Three-Quarter Size Double Bass, four strings, iron head, American, c. 1900.*	850.00	1100.00
☐ *Three-Quarter Size, four strings, ebony fingerboard, American, c. 1895-1905.*	900.00	1250.00
☐ *Czech, violoncello by Bohuslav Lantner of Prague, back in two sections, broad grain table, burnt orange varnish, back measures 29¼", c. 1920.*	3275.00	3850.00
☐ *English, violoncello by unidentified maker, back in two sections, fine grain table, burnt orange varnish, back measures 27¼", c. 1820.*	2700.00	3250.00
☐ *French, maker and city of origin unidentified, single piece back, medium grain table, burnt orange varnish, back measures 29½", c. 1820-1840.*	1750.00	2250.00
☐ *German, violoncello by Leopold Widhalm of Nuremberg, single piece back, fine grain table, burnt rust-red varnish, back measures 29½", dated 1768.*	1100.00	1425.00
☐ *German, violoncello, maker and city of origin unidentified, back in two sections, broad grain table, red brown varnish, back measures 27½", undated.*	1000.00	1450.00
☐ *German, violoncello by Johann Lippold of Neukirchen, back in two sections, medium grain table, burnt orange varnish, back measures 29⅞", dated 1823.*	2175.00	2825.00
☐ *Italian, violoncello by Fratelli Sirleto of Naples, back in two sections, broad grain table, reddish brown varnish, back measures 29¼", dated 1983.*	6200.00	5150.00

	Price Range	
☐ *Italian, violoncello by Ettore Soffritti of Ferrera, back in two sections, medium grain table, pale orange hued varnish, back measures 29¾", dated 1923.*	7500.00	10000.00
☐ *Italian, violoncello, believed to be made by Carlo Antonio Testore but unconfirmed, back in two sections, medium grain table, honey brown varnish, back measures 28", date undetermined.*	5000.00	6000.00
☐ *Italian, violoncello by Niccolo Gagliano of Naples, back in two sections, plain head, medium grain table, inlaid with gold leaf, orange brown varnish, back measures 29¼", dated 1774.*	65000.00	75000.00
☐ *Japanese, violoncello by Hajime Nakamura of Tokyo, back in two sections, fine grain table, red brown varnish, back measures 29½", dated 1981.*	3500.00	4500.00
☐ *Swiss, violoncello, maker and city of origin unidentified, back in two sections, broad grain table, reddish brown varnish, back measures 28½", date undetermined.*	900.00	1150.00

CLARINETS

Laube clarinets, *13 keys, two rings, Grenadilla wood, nickel silver keys and trimmings, cork joints, graduated bore, c. 1920.*

☐ *B-flat, low pitch.*	300.00	375.00
☐ *A, low pitch.*	300.00	375.00
☐ *C, low pitch.*	300.00	375.00
☐ *E-flat, low pitch.*	300.00	375.00
☐ **Laube clarinet,** *B-flat, low pitch, 15 keys, four rings, four rollers.*	450.00	600.00
☐ *A, low pitch, 15 keys.*	450.00	600.00
☐ *C, low pitch, 15 keys.*	450.00	600.00
☐ *E-flat, low pitch, 15 keys.*	450.00	600.00

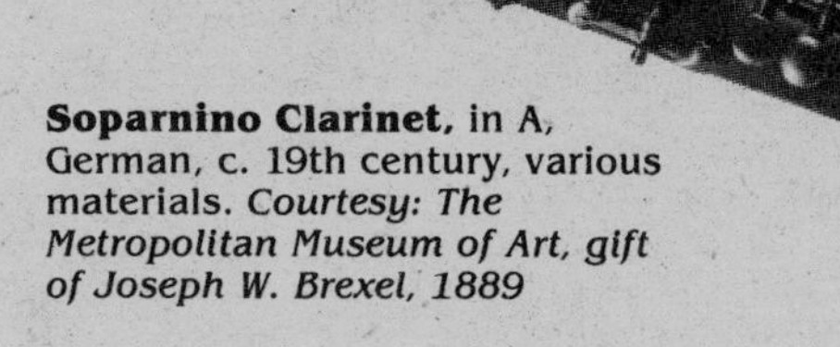

Soparnino Clarinet, in A, German, c. 19th century, various materials. *Courtesy: The Metropolitan Museum of Art, gift of Joseph W. Brexel, 1889*

CONCERTINAS

	Price Range	
☐ *American, late 19th-century.*	135.00	175.00
☐ *American, child's toy, c. 1900.*	100.00	130.00
☐ *American, child's toy, c. 1920.*	70.00	90.00
☐ *American, child's toy, c. 1940's.*	35.00	50.00
☐ *French, c. 1830.*	400.00	500.00
☐ *French, mid 19th-century.*	375.00	475.00
☐ *French, c. 1871.*	275.00	360.00
☐ *Mahogany tops, decorated with German-silver edges and inlaying, double bellows.*	85.00	110.00
☐ *Mahogany tops, 20 keys, nickel ornaments and sound rings, large bellows, c. 1890-1900.*	100.00	130.00
☐ *Mahogany with German-silver inlayings, leather bound bellows, 20 keys, broad reeds, figure of dog on top.*	150.00	175.00
☐ *Mahogany, 20 keys, leather bound bellows with five folds, made in England, in the original wooden case, 1897.*	225.00	300.00
☐ *Mahogany, 20 keys, bone buttons, nickel sound rings, c. 1895.*	75.00	100.00
☐ *Rosewood tops, figured moldings, 20 bone keys, large bellows.*	140.00	170.00

CORNETS

☐ **Artists' B Flat,** *brass, polished, before 1910.*	235.00	280.00
☐ **Artists' B Flat,** *nickel-plated.*	275.00	335.00

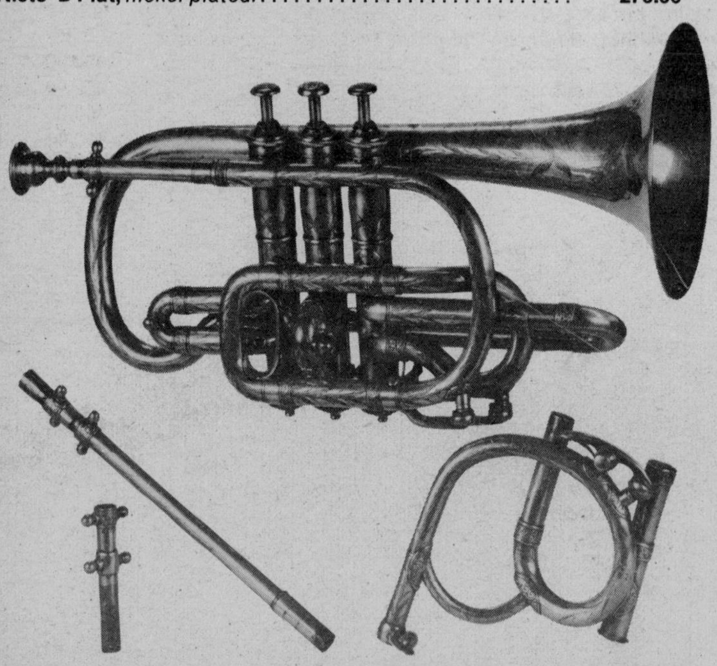

Cornet In B Flat, American, 20th century, silverplated brass. *Courtesy: The Metropolitan Museum of Art, The Crosby Brown Collection of Musical Instruments, 1889*

	Price Range	
☐ **Artists' B Flat,** *silver-plated, satin finish, gold lined bell.*	325.00	425.00
☐ **Artists' B Flat,** *silver-plated, polished, gold lined bell.*	350.00	450.00
☐ **Concertone,** *one water key, pearl buttons, nickel silver mouthpiece, 16½" long, brass, c. 1920's.*	125.00	175.00
☐ **Concertone,** *as above, nickel-plated.*	130.00	180.00
☐ **Concertone,** *as above, silver-plated, satin finish, gold plated bell.*	200.00	250.00
☐ **Dupont B Flat,** *single water key, brass finish.*	120.00	150.00
☐ **Dupont B Flat,** *single water key, burnished nickel plate.*	130.00	160.00
☐ **Dupont B Flat,** *single water key, triple silver plate, satin finish.*	160.00	200.00
☐ **Dupont B Flat,** *single water key, triple silver plate, burnished.*	200.00	250.00
☐ **Dupont B Flat,** *double water key, highly polished brass.*	150.00	185.00
☐ **Dupont B Flat,** *double water key, burnished nickel plate.*	175.00	225.00
☐ **Dupont B Flat,** *double water key, triple silver plate.*	225.00	275.00
☐ **Dupont B Flat,** *double water key, triple silver plate, burnished.*	285.00	350.00
☐ **Dupont B Flat,** *double water key, ornamental trimmings, heavily braced, highly polished brass.*	210.00	250.00
☐ **Dupont B Flat,** *double water key, ornamental trimmings, heavily braced, burnished nickel plate.*	210.00	250.00
☐ **Dupont B Flat,** *double water key, ornamental trimmings, heavily braced, triple silver plate, satin finish.*	250.00	320.00
☐ **Dupont B Flat,** *double water key, ornamental trimmings, heavily braced, triple silver finish, burnished.*	300.00	350.00
☐ **Dupont C,** *highly polished brass.*	125.00	160.00
☐ **Dupont C,** *burnished nickel plate.*	135.00	170.00
☐ **Dupont C,** *triple silver plate, satin finish.*	160.00	210.00
☐ **Dupont C,** *triple silver plate, burnished.*	180.00	230.00
☐ **Dupont E Flat,** *highly polished brass finish.*	100.00	140.00
☐ **Dupont E Flat,** *burnished nickel plate.*	125.00	160.00
☐ **Dupont E Flat,** *triple silver plate, satin finish.*	145.00	170.00
☐ **Dupont E Flat,** *triple silver plate, burnished.*	160.00	200.00
☐ **Leaders' B Flat,** *double water key, brass, polished, c. 1905-1910.*	225.00	280.00
☐ **Leaders' B Flat,** *double water key, nickel-plated.*	250.00	320.00
☐ **Leaders' B Flat,** *silver-plated, satin finish.*	285.00	350.00
☐ **Leaders' B Flat,** *silver-plated, polished.*	300.00	400.00
☐ **Marceau B Flat,** *brass, highly polished.*	85.00	115.00
☐ **Marceau B Flat,** *nickel-plated.*	100.00	125.00
☐ **Marceau B Flat,** *double water key, brass, highly polished.*	140.00	180.00
☐ **Marceau B Flat,** *double water key, nickel-plated.*	150.00	190.00
☐ **Marceau C,** *brass.*	100.00	125.00
☐ **Marceau C,** *nickel-plated.*	110.00	140.00
☐ **Marceau E Flat,** *brass, highly polished, c. 1905-1910.*	80.00	110.00
☐ **Marceau E Flat,** *nickel-plated.*	95.00	120.00

CYMBALETS

The cymbalet was a novelty instrument never really taken seriously and rarely if ever, to my knowledge, played professionally. It made a moderate splash on the American market late in the 1800's, about the time that many other novelty music-making contrivances were put out. The public of that era had a remarkable appetite for small instruments which, according to the ads, could be played by young and old with little practice or skill. The cymbalet was something in the nature of a tambourine.

	Price Range	
☐ *Made of two pieces of bent wood, fastened together, with two loose brass jingles at each end, c. 1897*	12.00	16.00

CYMBALS

Cymbals are concussion instruments; that is, they produce sound not by being struck by something (as with **per**cussion instruments), but by being struck against each other. The cymbal's heritage is Near Eastern and it remains today more popular and widely produced in that part of the world than the west. Cymbals have made themselves known in Europe and America, however, in classical, swing, jazz and rock music — in fact in nearly all forms of music with the exception of country and western.

Turkey has been headquarters of the cymbal for well over a century, supplying this instrument to distributors in all corners of the globe. Cymbals have been made elsewhere, including America, but the reputation for Turkish-made specimens has been such that others, no matter of what quality, receive little notice. It is believed that cymbals were first used in a presentation of western classical music in Germany in 1680, in a not-too-well-remembered opera entitled "Esther" by Nicolaus Strungk. From Germany the employment as an orchestral accessory spread into neighboring lands. The big wave of commercial success came in the American marching band era (1880-World War I). Since then they have been included in nearly every street parade, football "half-time" show and other public amusements.

☐ *American, 10", leather handles, c. 1900.*	80.00	110.00
☐ *American, 11", leather handles, c. 1900.*	95.00	120.00
☐ *American, 12", leather handles, c. 1900.*	110.00	145.00
☐ *American, 13", leather handles, c. 1900.*	130.00	160.00
☐ *Chinese, late 19th-century.*	80.00	110.00
☐ *Dutch, late 19th-century.*	95.00	120.00
☐ *English, c. 1800.*	140.00	175.00
☐ *French, late 18th-century.*	200.00	250.00
☐ *French, c. 1800.*	160.00	215.00

Cymbals, European, brass, 1′ 3″. *Courtesy: The Metropolitan Museum of Art, The Crosby Brown Collection of Musical Instruments, 1889*

	Price Range	
☐ *French, first quarter 19th-century.*	150.00	200.00
☐ *Italian, brass mid 19th-century.*	120.00	160.00
☐ *Turkish, 10″, leather handles, c. 1900.*	100.00	135.00

DRUMS

Drums are of ancient origins and are to be found among the native culture of almost all peoples. Their variety — in size, design and materials — is undoubtedly greater than of any other instrument.

Primitive drums are known to have been made and used as long ago as 1,500-2,000 B.C. by the Mesopotamians and were likely in use by other ancient civilizations at this same time. To place a date on the invention of drums, or even to name their place of origin, is impossible, as the first drums or drum-like instruments were hollow logs of wood on which prehistoric men beat with their fists or sticks.

One type of Mesopotamian drum is known today as a friction drum. It differs from the traditional variety in that it was not struck to produce sound. Instead, it consisted of a bowl with animal hide stretched across the top, with a stick running up through the bottom. Upon rubbing the stick, the instrument gave forth a sort of groan. Needless to say, these specimens are not available to collectors.

By the 4th or 5th-century B.C., drums of one kind or other were known to the Persians, Asian Indians, Greeks and probably Chinese. The Romans used drums extensively at a somewhat later period. It was during the Middle Ages that the kettledrum was introduced into Europe. Returning Crusaders brought specimens back from the eastern battlefronts, probably just as curiosities at first, but the kettledrum became popular in the west. The English named it "nakers", a not-too-successful attempt to phonetically translate its Arabic name, **naqqara**. From the kettledrum evolved all subsequent European (and American) drums though later models bore little resemblance to the naqqara.

Antique and semi-antique percussion instruments are found on the market in enormous quantity and variety. Many were not designed as orchestral instruments but for marching bands, fife and drum corps, etc. Their military connection lends value to certain specimens over and above their interest as antique instruments. Normal signs of use are to be expected on the skins of early drums; this does not detract from the value. However, drums on which the skin is split or otherwise defective, or the stringing damaged, are worth considerably less than the prices indicated here.

	Price Range	
☐ **Acme Professional Bass,** *24″ diameter, c. 1900*	175.00	200.00
☐ **Acme Professional Bass,** *26″ diameter, c. 1900*	200.00	250.00
☐ **Acme Professional Bass,** *28″ diameter, c. 1900*	200.00	270.00
☐ **Acme Professional Bass,** *30″ diameter, c. 1900*	220.00	275.00
☐ **Acme Professional Snare,** *14″ diameter, c. 1900*	160.00	200.00
☐ **Acme Professional Snare,** *16″ diameter, c. 1900*	170.00	220.00
☐ **Acme Professional Snare,** *16″ diameter, 8 rawhide snares, c. 1900*	185.00	240.00

Bass Drum, American, double head, wood, parchment, leather, brass. *Courtesy: The Metropolitan Museum of Art, The Crosby Brown Collection of Musical Instruments, 1889*

	Price Range	
☐ *American, painted with scenes of fire-fighting, inscribed "32nd Battalion", some damage, early 19th-century*	1100.00	1500.00
☐ *American, War of 1812 vintage, 16" diameter.*	1000.00	1400.00
☐ *American, 15½" diameter, c. 1788.*	850.00	1100.00
☐ *American Revolutionary field drum*	1300.00	2000.00
☐ *American, mounted on wooden trestle, 29" diameter, second quarter of the 19th-century*	1400.00	2100.00
☐ *American, painted with stars and stripes, perhaps New England origin, c. 1820*	1100.00	1400.00
☐ *American, band instrument, second quarter of the 19th-century.*	900.00	1175.00
☐ *American Civil War military drum, c. 1860's.*	800.00	1050.00
☐ *American toy, 12½" diameter, c. 1850's.*	475.00	625.00
☐ *American toy, 14" diameter, c. 1860.*	475.00	625.00
☐ *American toy, painted with figures of wild animals, paint chipped, c. 1860-70.*	500.00	650.00
☐ *American toy, 11¾" diameter, leather strap, c. 1870's.*	400.00	500.00
☐ *American toy, c. 1890's.*	160.00	210.00
☐ *American toy, tin, cord strap, c. 1920's.*	75.00	100.00
☐ *American toy, Mickey Mouse, c. 1930's.*	300.00	375.00
☐ *American toy, the Beatles, c. 1960's.*	80.00	110.00
☐ *Bass, American, c. 1900.*	300.00	375.00
☐ *Bass, English, mid 19th-century.*	350.00	460.00
☐ *Bass, English, late 19th-century.*	230.00	300.00
☐ *Bass, French, c. 1790.*	1250.00	1600.00
☐ *Bass, German, silver mountings, early 19th-century.*	725.00	900.00
☐ *Bass, German, c. 1830.*	550.00	700.00
☐ *Bass, German, foot pedal, c. 1860.*	500.00	650.00
☐ *Bass, German, third quarter of the 19th-century.*	450.00	600.00
☐ *Bass, Italian, wooden mountings, 18th-century.*	900.00	1200.00
☐ *Bass, Italian, Roman, 1791.*	800.00	1100.00
☐ *Bass, Portuguese, purple membranes, silver chased, c. 1810.*	1200.00	1600.00
☐ *Bass, Russian, 19th-century.*	550.00	750.00
☐ *Bass, Swiss, ivory inlays, early 19th-century.*	700.00	900.00
☐ *English, 13½" diameter, leather straps, 18th-century.*	625.00	800.00
☐ *English, 14" diameter, painted with figural subjects, c. 1760.*	700.00	900.00
☐ *English, 16½" diameter, restored, leather straps renewed, c. 1800.*	500.00	600.00

FANFARES

This was a name applied to a special kind of brass horn, similar to a bugle. It was supposedly easier to play than either a bugle or trumpet. But, alas, it never attained much popularity.

☐ *Eight reed valves, c. 1890-1900.*	40.00	45.00
☐ *Six reed valves, c. 1890-1900.*	30.00	35.00
☐ *10 reed valves, c. 1890-1900.*	45.00	55.00

FIFES

☐ **"Acme Hand Made"**, *metal, nickel-plated, c. 1900.*	150.00	200.00
☐ *American, early 19th-century.*	475.00	600.00

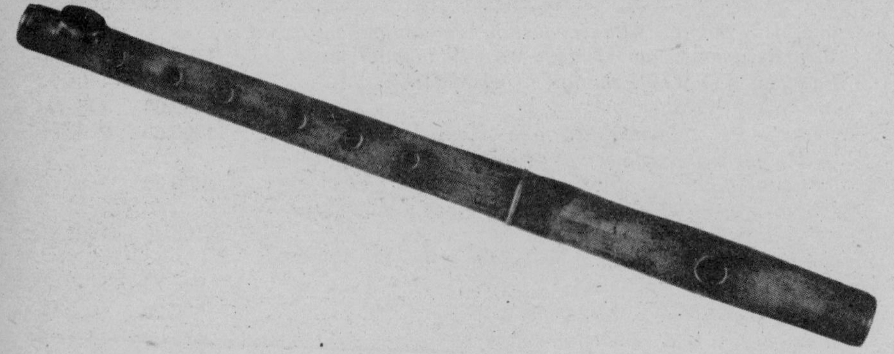

Fife In B Flat, Austria, c. 1880, light wood, 1′ 1¼″ L. *Courtesy: The Metropolitan Museum of Art, The Crosby Brown Collection of Musical Instruments, 1889*

	Price Range	
☐ *Cocoa wood, c. 1900.*	50.00	70.00
☐ **"Crosby Model",** *ebony, c. 1900.*	110.00	150.00
☐ *Ebony, nickel-plated ferrules, c. 1900.*	90.00	120.00
☐ *French, "Atlas", cast metal, nickel-plated, c. 1900.*	45.00	60.00
☐ *Irish, c. 1725.*	450.00	600.00
☐ *Irish, c. 1820.*	300.00	400.00
☐ *Rosewood, brass ferrules, c. 1900.*	50.00	65.00
☐ *Scottish, c. 1680.*	600.00	750.00
☐ *Scottish, c. 1710.*	550.00	700.00
☐ *Scottish, ivory, silver mountings, c. 1740.*	550.00	700.00
☐ *Scottish, last quarter of the 18th-century.*	400.00	525.00

FLUTES

☐ *American, 8-keyed, c. 1920's.*	125.00	150.00
☐ *Bavarian, c. 1805.*	5200.00	7000.00
☐ *Cherrywood, American, first quarter 19th-century.*	3000.00	3200.00
☐ *Ebony, Italian, length 27″, in a leather covered fleece-lined case, 18th-century.*	4600.00	5500.00
☐ *Ebony, Prussian, length 26¼″, c. 1800.*	2000.00	2400.00
☐ *Ebony, Scottish, late 18th-century.*	2600.00	3700.00
☐ *Ebony, two keys, mid 18th-century.* **This specimen had been in the collection of Frederick II of Prussia and its value is somewhat higher on that account.**	24000.00	35000.00
☐ *English, by Thomas Stanesby, Jr. of London, ivory with silver mountings, silver key, 21½″, c. 1740.*	3475.00	4600.00
☐ *Flemish, walnut, 18th-century.*	2000.00	2600.00
☐ *French, one-keyed, ivory, 22⅜″, mid 18th-century.*	6500.00	8000.00
☐ *French, ivory, one-keyed, c. 1800.*	3000.00	3600.00
☐ *French, by Claude Laurent of Paris, glass with silver mountings, silver keys and key covers, 24½″, dated 1838.*	4650.00	5450.00
☐ *German, mid 18th-century.*	6250.00	7500.00
☐ *German, cocoa wood, silver-trimmed, one-keyed, late 19th/early 20th-century.*	55.00	75.00

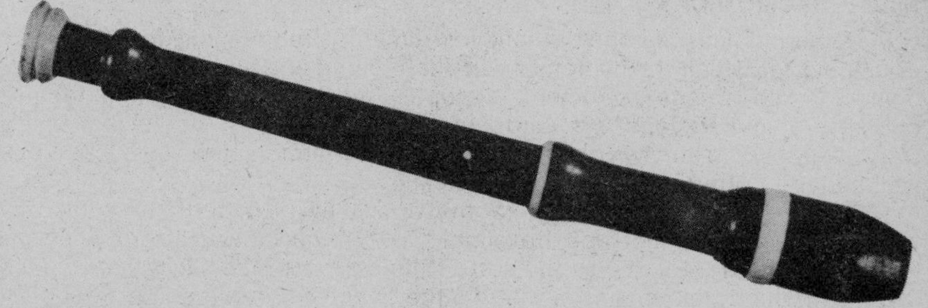

Flute, German, c. 18th century, wood, 10″ L. *Courtesy: The Metropolitan Museum of Art, The Crosby Brown Collection of Musical Instruments, 1889*

	Price Range	
☐ *German, grenadilla wood, silver-trimmed, 4-keyed, late 19th/early 20th-century*	85.00	110.00
☐ *Grenadilla wood, 8-keyed, tuning slide, c. 1900.*	100.00	130.00
☐ *Hardwood, English, early 19th-century*	1000.00	1300.00
☐ **Henry Hill,** *carved ivory, six-keyed*	550.00	700.00
☐ *Italian, length 25¾″, c. 1781.*	3000.00	4000.00
☐ *Italian, Milan, in carry box, c. 1786*	3300.00	4500.00
☐ *Ivory, seven-keyed, by Goulding & Co., London, silver mounts and keys, long "F" with pewter plugs, 23³/₁₆″, c. 1800*	2600.00	3150.00
☐ **Meyer Model,** *8-keyed, c. 1900.*	175.00	210.00
☐ **Meyer Model,** *10-keyed, c. 1900.*	250.00	325.00
☐ *One-keyed, by Thomas Stanesby, Jr., London, 24″, headcap bearing an inscription presenting the flute from H. R. H. the Prince of Wales to T. Wackett, 1738.*	7500.00	10000.00
At least half the price of this specimen rests with the inscription and association interest. But it is, nevertheless, a fine flute.		
☐ *Rosewood, Italian, late 18th-century*	3475.00	4250.00
☐ *Russian, silver mountings, in case, c. 1790.*	6200.00	9000.00
☐ *Russian, silver mountings, c. 1807.*	6000.00	8000.00
☐ *Six-keyed, ivory, Goulding & Co., London, silver mounts and keys, c. 1815.*	800.00	1100.00
☐ *Spanish, ebony with silver, early 19th-century*	950.00	1200.00

FLUTE ACCORDIONS

Flute accordions are a novelty instrument played mostly by amateurs and manufactured mainly in the late 1800's and early 1900's.

☐ *Nickel-trimmed, ten keys, two basses*	32.00	42.00
☐ *10 bone keys, nickel-covered case, projecting metal bell, American made.*	35.00	45.00
☐ *10 bone keys, two basses, reeds, with original wooden case, c. 1895*	40.00	55.00
☐ *10 patent nickel keys, two basses, ebonized sides and keyboard with gilt ornaments, nickel-plated corners, trumpet and mouthpiece*	65.00	85.00

FLUTE HARMONICAS

Flute harmonicas are one of those instruments pretty readily found as antiques but for which the customer will search long and hard in the shops of dealers in newly-made instruments. A popular novelty for awhile, its time ran out several generations ago, probably all for the best. If one believes Darwin's theory of survival of the fittest, the flute harmonica was a hybrid not well suited to other members of the species.

The flute harmonica belongs to the era (1880-1920 or thereabout) of vaudeville entertainment and traveling shows, when many bizarre instruments came and went. It was the sort of thing a "one-man-band" performer used, and which children got — whether they wanted one or not, the latter being probably the more usual case — at Christmas. A cross between flute and harmonica, is was musically inferior to both, in addition to being weird-looking. But it was fun to fool with, and to pretend to oneself that you were playing music, and this undoubtedly accounted for its brief success.

	Price Range	
☐ *Eight long keys, gilt trumpets, gilt mouthpiece, sold by mail-order houses in the 1890-1900 era.*	**13.00**	**18.00**
☐ *Nickel-plated frame with 10 keys, two basses and bell.*	**15.00**	**20.00**
☐ *Wooden case with nickel and paper cover, eight round keys.*	**10.00**	**15.00**

GUITARS

The guitar is one of those instruments of vast antiquity whose history is enveloped with much legend and whose actual inventor is unknown. That it had an inventor cannot even be stated with certainty. Like man himself, the guitar very likely evolved gradually from lower forms, changing a bit here and there as it passed through the hands of various ethnic groups. It is without argument one of the most universal of instruments, having achieved popularity on all continents and among musicians of all sorts from classical to folk to rock.

Guitars, or their close ancestors, are definitely known to have existed in Spain in the 12th-century A.D., to which they had apparently come via Asia. They became widely used in late medieval Europe by court musicians, troubadors, wandering minstrels and balladists. The poems of Chaucer and other early poets were originally recited to music and, frequently, guitarists and other independent musicians contrived their own lyrics. By the 15th-century, guitars were being manufactured not only in Spain but France, Portugal and elsewhere. They became extremely widespread in the 16th-century. Henry VIII of England, who died in 1547, owned 21 guitars (which he did not play; he was a collector of instruments and boasted some 381 of various types).

The six-string or standard guitar familiar today belongs to the late 18th-century. It is now known who made the first "modern" six-string guitar nor where it originated. It might possibly have been an Italian innovation. This advance brought the instrument even greater popularity. Soon afterward, guitar makers sprung up in many areas where none had previously been active, including a number of U.S. towns.

☐ *American, Civil War era.*	**2000.00**	**2800.00**
☐ *American, "The Troubadour", c. 1900.*	**95.00**	**115.00**
☐ *American, "The Edgemere", c. 1900.*	**120.00**	**160.00**

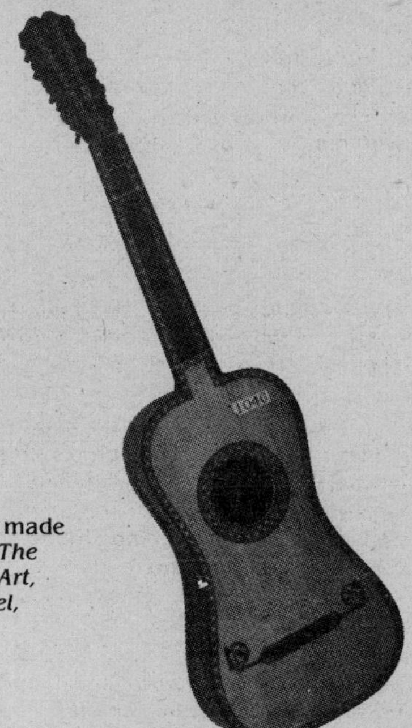

Guitar, French, c. 1770, made by Guillaume. *Courtesy: The Metropolitan Museum of Art, Gift of Mrs. Lucy W. Drexel, 1889.*

	Price Range	
☐ *American, "The Marlowe", c. 1900.*	140.00	180.00
☐ *American, "The Acme", c. 1900.*	150.00	200.00
☐ *American, "The Kenmore", c. 1900.*	160.00	210.00
☐ *American, "The Aron", c. 1900.*	160.00	220.00
☐ *American, "The Julien", c. 1900.*	185.00	240.00
☐ *American, "The Richard", standard size, c. 1900.*	235.00	300.00
☐ *American, "The Richard", concert size.*	265.00	350.00
☐ *American, "The Richard", grand concert size.*	275.00	375.00
Construction of "The Richard": mahogany neck, rosewood veneer on front and back, convex ebony fingerboard, inlaid with pearl position marks. Bone nut and saddle.		
☐ *American, "The Seroco", standard size, c. 1900.*	300.00	400.00
☐ *American, "The Seroco", concert size.*	325.00	425.00
☐ *American, "The Seroco", grand concert size.*	375.00	500.00
☐ **"The Cambridge",** *rosewood back and sides, spruce top, inlaid around sound hole with colored wood and celluloid, ebony fingerboard, nickel-plated head, c. 1905-1910.*	130.00	160.00
☐ **"The Columbia",** *back and sides made of quarter-sawn oak, inlaid with vari-colored woods, spruce top, inlaid around sound hole with colored woods and celluloid, c. 1905-1910.*	100.00	130.00
☐ **"The Cornell",** *rosewood sides and back, spruce top, sound hole inlaid with vari-colored woods and celluloid, mother-of-pearl inlays on front.*	175.00	220.00
☐ *English, maple, early 19th-century.*	1600.00	2000.00

	Price Range	
☐ *English, mid 19th-century.*	1500.00	1900.00
☐ *English, third quarter of the 19th-century.*	1000.00	1300.00
☐ **"The Harvard"**, *rosewood back and sides, back inlaid down the center with mother-of-pearl, spruce top, mahogany neck, brass head, c. 1905-1910.*	250.00	310.00
☐ *Hawaiian Guitar, spruce top, basswood neck, celluloid bound ebonized fingerboard, colored cut-block inlay around sound hole and top edge, white celluloid binding around top edge, six strings.*	150.00	200.00
☐ *Italian, by Matteo Sellas of Venice, five course, arched back, lavishly decorated with ivory, overall 38", c. 1620-1640.*	11000.00	14250.00
☐ *Italian, c. 1800.*	2100.00	2500.00
☐ *Italian, c. 1840.*	1600.00	2000.00
☐ *Koa wood, birch top, back and sides, metal tailpiece, steel strings. (This was an inexpensively produced guitar sold on the American market for under $5 in the 1920's).*	50.00	65.00
☐ *Mahogany back and sides, spruce top, imitation pearl and cut block inlay with celluloid binding around sound hole and top edge, pearl inlaid fingerboard, ebonized pin bridge, steel strings.*	135.00	170.00
☐ *Mexican, c. 1880.*	475.00	600.00
☐ *Mexican, early 20th-century.*	235.00	300.00
☐ **"The Oakwood"**, *imitation quarter-sawn oak, spruce top, edges inlaid with wood of varying shades, bound with white celluloid, brass head, metallic frets, nickel-plated tailpiece, c. 1905-1910.*	50.00	65.00
☐ **"The Oxford"**, *back and sides mahogany, spruce top, colored woods inlaid around sound hole, head inlaid with rosewood, metallic frets on fingerboard, c. 1905-1910.*	125.00	160.00
☐ *Portuguese, c. 1860.*	1100.00	1500.00
☐ **"The Princeton"**, *rosewood back and sides, inlaid down the middle with colored wood, spruce top, head inlaid on front and back with rosewood, raised frets, pearl position dots, c. 1905-1910.*	170.00	225.00
☐ *Rosewood, birch back and sides, vertical grained spruce top, inlays around sound hole, consisting partly of celluloid, basswood neck, ebonized bridge, c. 1920.*	80.00	100.00
☐ *Spanish, mid 16th-century.*	20000.00	30000.00
☐ *Spanish, late 16th-century.*	16000.00	30000.00
☐ *Spanish, early 17th-century.*	9000.00	22000.00
☐ *Spanish, mid 17th-century.*	7500.00	16000.00
☐ *Spanish, early 18th-century.*	4000.00	11000.00
☐ *Spanish, c. 1740.*	3350.00	8500.00
☐ *Spanish, late 18th-century.*	2300.00	5000.00
☐ *Spanish, c. 1800.*	2075.00	4500.00
☐ *Spanish, mid 19th-century.*	2000.00	3000.00
☐ *Spanish, by Antonio de Torres of Seville, rosewood back composed of triple sections, rose hole, mahogany neck, back measures approximately 19", c. 1860.*	3500.00	4500.00

	Price Range	
☐ **"The Stanford"**, *hardwood sides and back, finished in imitation rosewood, spruce top, brass head, rosewood fingerboard, nickel-plated tailpiece*	85.00	110.00
☐ **"The University"**, *rosewood back and sides, heavily ornamented with vine and leaf patterns, spruce top, ebony guard plate, mahogany neck, trimmed in mother-of-pearl, c. 1905-1910.*	225.00	300.00

HARMONICAS

Though it would appear from their vastly dissimilar size and design that no connection could exist between the organ and harmonica, the latter came into being as an attempt (not overly successful, but that's another story) to create a small, easily handled, cheaply produced instrument that would approximate the musical virtuosity of an organ.

Harmonicas have received, over the years, what might be termed a "bad press", to the degree that many histories of musical instruments fail even to take any note of them — as if they do not deserve classification as true instruments but rather as novelties or curiosities. This results from (a) their modern origin; (b) lack of use in performance of classical music; (c) the great proliferation of badly-made, near-worthless models that have flooded the market. From as long ago as the late 1800's, cheap harmonicas — and there is no reason to presume that an **old** bad harmonica is better than a **new** bad harmonica — were being given away as prizes at amusement parks and sold as souvenirs at seaside resorts. Today there are conservatively a thousand poorly made harmonicas on the market for every one that could be said to claim some musical quality. In the face of these odds, it should not be surprising that the instrument has gained a less-than-enviable reputation. But decent harmonicas are to be found. They will never, perhaps, end up playing Bach, but are far from toys or junk.

☐ **Angel's Clarion,** *made by Weiss, 28 holes, brass reed plates, c. 1900.*	35.00	50.00

Mouth Harmonica, Germany, 19th century, 4½" x 1¼". *Courtesy: The Metropolitan Museum of Art, The Crosby Brown Collection of Musical Instruments, 1889*

	Price Range	
☐ **"Baseball Club Band Mouth Organ",** *32 bell metal reeds, two sound horns, c. 1920's.*	12.00	17.00
☐ **Bell Harmonica (Richter),** *10 single holes, brass reed plates, German-silver covers, extended ends, one bell.*	30.00	40.00
☐ *As above, with two bells.*	35.00	45.00
☐ **Bohm's Professional Harmonica,** *10 single holes, 20 brass reeds, c. 1890's.*	25.00	35.00
☐ **Bohm's Jubilee Harmonica,** *10 single holes, 20 brass reeds, brass reed plates, c. 1900.*	22.00	28.00
☐ **Bohm's Sovereign,** *5½"x1½", 16 double holes, 32 steel reeds, nickel covers.*	22.00	28.00
☐ **The Brass Band Clarion,** *by Weiss, 10 single holes, 20 reeds, c. 1900.*	25.00	35.00
☐ **Columbian Exhibition Harmonica,** *10 single holes, nickel reed plates and covers, bronzed wood.*	65.00	80.00
NOTE: The value is a bit higher than it might be otherwise, as this model is collected as a World's Fair item. Actually it was extensively retailed in the 1890's, not sold just at the fair, if indeed it was sold at the fair at all.		
☐ *Concert harmonica with two bells, 10 double holes with 40 reeds, brass reed plates, engraved German-silver covers.*	50.00	65.00
Bell harmonicas are collected as interesting fossils of the music instrument world; they are seldom played any longer.		
☐ **Doerfel's International,** *made of celluloid, 10 double holes, 40 reeds, brass reed plates.*	55.00	70.00
☐ **Doerfel's New Best-Quality Harmonika,** *48 steel-bronze reeds, brass reed plates, in original box. (Also known as "Nero Mouth-Organ".).*	12.00	17.00
☐ **Doerfel's Patent Universal Harp,** *made of celluloid, 10 single holes, 20 reeds, brass reed plates, one of the earliest celluloid harmonicas (introduced 1890's).*	40.00	55.00
☐ **Duss Band Harmonica,** *14 double holes, 28 metal reeds set on brass plates, nickel covers, 4¾" long, c. 1920's.*	15.00	20.00
☐ **Duss Band Tremelo,** *three-in-one harmonica, each tuned to a different key (the instrument was rotated, as if the player were eating an ear of corn). 32 double holes, 96 reeds, brass plates, nickel covers, 8¾" long, post-World War I.*	20.00	25.00
☐ **Duss Full Concert Harmonica,** *10 double holes, 40 reeds on brass plates, nickel covers, 4½" long.*	12.00	16.00
☐ **Carl Essbach's French Harp #44,** *10 single holes, 20 German-silver reeds, brass reed plates, nickel covers.*	14.00	20.00
☐ **Carl Essbach's Richter Harmonica,** *10 single holes, 20 reeds, brass reed plates, nickel cover, marked "French Harp #22".*	12.00	16.00
☐ *European, "Brass Band Harmonica", 10 double holes, 40 reeds, brass reed plates.*	45.00	60.00
☐ *European, 10 single holes, white metal reed plates with steel reeds, c. 1890's.*	20.00	25.00
☐ **"High Art",** *16 double holes, 32 reeds, brass plates, curved mouthpiece, nickel covers, 4" long.*	10.00	15.00
☐ **Hohner Auto Harmonica,** *shaped like auto (late version, sold in 1920's), 14 double holes, 28 reeds, metal cover.*	25.00	35.00

	Price Range	
☐ **Hohner,** *Concert harmonica, marked "Ulm 1871-Philadelphia 1873", actually made in c. 1890's, 20 double holes, 80 reeds, brass reed plates, nickel covers*	225.00	300.00
☐ **Hohner Double Side Harmonica,** *64 reeds, brass plates, steel covers, nickel-plated, turned-in ends, made in c. 1920's*	25.00	35.00
☐ **Hohner,** *"Grand Auditorium", 16 double holes, 32 reeds, brass reed plates, nickel covers*	130.00	200.00
☐ **M. Hohner Harmonica,** *10 single holes, brass reed plates, c. 1900*	20.00	30.00
☐ **Hohner Harmonica,** *20 double holes, 80 reeds, brass reed plates, nickel covers, c. 1900*	75.00	100.00
☐ **Hohner,** *harp-shaped, 14 double holes, 28 tremolo reeds, brass plates, nickel-plated covers, 4⅝" long*	20.00	30.00
☐ **M. Hohner's Newest and Best Full Concert Harmonica,** *10 double holes, 40 reeds, brass reed plates, nickel covers.*	45.00	60.00
☐ **Hohner,** *10 double holes, 40 reeds, brass reed plates, nickel covers*	75.00	100.00
☐ **"The Improved Emmet",** *10 single holes, brass reed plates, nickel-plated covers, c. 1890's*	35.00	45.00
☐ **Ludwig Harmonica,** *double sided with 10 holes and 20 reeds on each side, c. 1890's.*	60.00	80.00
☐ **Ludwig Harmonica,** *Richter Pattern, 10 single holes, 20 reeds, c. 1890's*	30.00	40.00
☐ **Ludwig Harmonica,** *20 double holes, 40 brass reeds, heavy brass reed plates and nickel covers, c. 1900*	70.00	95.00
☐ **Gebruder Ludwig's "Professional Concert (mouth) Organ",** *10 double holes, 40 reeds, brass reed plates, German-silver covers*	65.00	85.00
☐ **"The New Troubador",** *20 single holes, ten on each side, c. 1897*	25.00	35.00
☐ **"The Prairie Queen",** *10 single holes, steel-bronze reeds, nickel-plated reed plates and covers*	45.00	60.00
☐ **"The Quadruple Reed Mouth Organ",** *160 reeds, 7¼" long, inscribed "House Music, Best Harp for Artists from Ocean to Ocean"*	15.00	20.00
☐ **"Radio Band" Harmonica,** *two sets of reeds, pitched in different keys, in the original hinged box, c. 1920's*	10.00	15.00
☐ **"Radio Band Jazz Mouth Organ",** *novelty harmonica in shape of flashlight with horn at end, 11" long, sold in U.S., 1929*	15.00	20.00
☐ **"Reveille Mouth Organ",** *nickel-plated covers, c. 1925.*	7.00	10.00
☐ **Richter "C",** *10 single holes, brass reed plates, nickel covers.*	15.00	20.00
☐ **"The Silver-Tongued Richter",** *10 double holes, brass reed plates, nickel covers.*	45.00	60.00
☐ **Sousa's Band Harmonica,** *4x1", 10 holes, 20 brass reeds, c. 1900*	25.00	35.00
☐ **Sousa's Band Harmonica,** *4¾"x1¼", 20 holes, 40 brass reeds, c. 1900.*	35.00	50.00

	Price Range	
☐ *Wilhelm Thie, four harmonicas in box, all identical with 10 single holes, brass reed plates, nickel covers, but in different keys. This set was made in the c. 1890's in Germany for exportation and sale in America, price given is for a set in the original box.*	55.00	75.00
☐ **"World's Fame"**, *10 single holes, 20 reeds, brass plates, nickel covers, 4" long.*	7.00	10.00

HARPS

Harps have been in use since as early as 3,000 B.C. They were played in Egypt at the time of the Pharaohs, in Mesopotamia, Babylonia and throughout most of the ancient world. Harp playing was popular even in India, in Alexander the Great's time. Each nation designed its harps somewhat differently, as we know from representation in art (sadly, few ancient specimens themselves survive), and styles changed periodically within given localities. Basically, though, the ancient-world harp was a much smaller instrument than its modern descendant, some small enough to be easily carried about and played in the road by itinerant musicians. China had harps at least as early as the 4th-century A.D.; how much earlier it is impossible on strength of present evidence to speculate. The harp was one of the few popular classical instruments that remained in use throughout the European Middle Ages though, of course, it like others became more or less limited to the realm of church music. It is believed that harps were played in England from the time of the Conquest (1066) or before. Their use in Ireland is probably of earlier beginnings. Irish harps were generally regarded as superior to the English. They were mostly made of willow and would often be richly ornamented with carving.

During the European Renaissance, with its revival of secular interest in music, harps regained the prominence they had enjoyed in Greek and Roman times. A number of fine specimens from this era and shortly afterward survive today, the majority in museums or churches. Only a small percent of European harps made before 1650 have reached the American trade. They are held in high regard and seldom have any difficulty realizing prices of five digits.

☐ *English, maple base, 4'7", c. 1650.*	1200.00	1500.00
☐ *English, three strings lacking, wood split, Restoration.*	1100.00	1400.00
☐ *English, 6'5", mid 18th-century.*	1900.00	2750.00
☐ *English, polished walnut, late 18th-century.*	1150.00	1500.00
☐ *French, by Cousineau of Paris, painted and gilded with a pattern of floralwork and insects, 64", c. French revolutionary era.*	2300.00	2750.00
☐ *Italian, Renaissance, polychromed wood with cherubic figures, carved acanthus leaf designs at base, portions of original gilding with red paint showing through, partially restored, restrung, 6'7" tall, c. 1580.*	5500.00	7000.00
☐ *Italian, walnut, carved base, traces of old gilding, partially restored base, restrung, c. 1620.*	3175.00	3750.00
☐ *Italian, carved rosewood, 5'2½" tall, possibly Naples, third quarter of the 17th-century.*	3175.00	3750.00

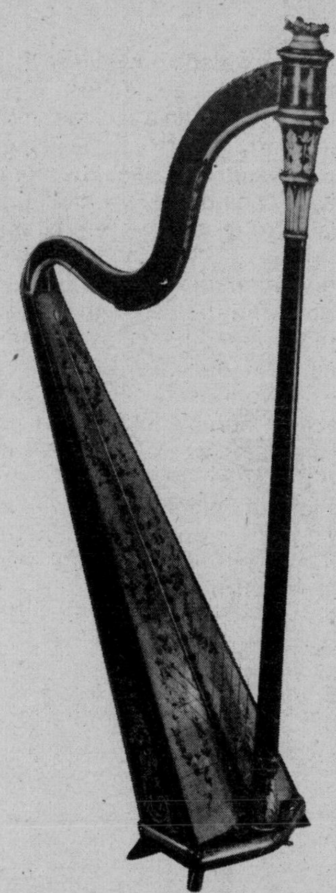

Harp, c. 1750, Portable Minstrel Harp, wood. *Courtesy: The Metropolitan Museum of Art, The Crosby Brown Collection of Musical Instruments, 1889.*

	Price Range	
☐ *Italian, gilded and polychromed wood, base replaced in the 19th-century, restrung, 6' tall, c. 1680.*	**2600.00**	**3000.00**
☐ *Italian, Milan, late 17th-century.*	**1500.00**	**2000.00**
☐ *Italian, Turin, 7'8", c. 1700.*	**2150.00**	**2700.00**
☐ *Italian, mahogany, 2'11", early 18th-century.*	**1650.00**	**1875.00**

HURDY GURDY

☐ *French, maker unidentified, guitar shape, maple, stamped pegbox, black painted wheel cover, iron handle, 25", c. 1790-1810.*	**2200.00**	**2750.00**

JEWS' HARP

The Jews' Harp, also known as jaws-harp or juice-harp, is strictly an instrument for close-range audiences. It produces a sound that can be heard distinctly no further than a few feet from the performer. Thus, it is unsuitable for orchestral or concert use, if indeed anyone would conceive of using a Jews' Harp for such purposes. But for this serious minus it can offer several major plusses, being easily handled, mastered without painstaking effort and adaptable to music of every kind — as well as to improvisational creations.

It is a very small instrument held to the mouth while playing, but is not a wind instrument in the sense of a harmonica or flute. Rather it is played by plucking and vibrates between the player's teeth. Among the most primitive of instruments, its close relatives or ancestors can be found in use by primitive peoples in various parts of the world. The belief that it originated in ancient Israel and thereby obtained its name is probably incorrect; in fact, it is likely that the name was at first jaws-harp, which eventually came to be corrupted into the present form thanks to cheap versions being sold by street peddlers, most of whom were Jewish.

The Jew's Harp is an excellent instrument to collect as antiques because of the many types that can be found and their relative cheapness compared to many other instruments.

	Price Range	
☐ *American, 2" frame, c. 1900.*	**9.00**	**12.00**
☐ *American, 2¼" frame, c. 1900.*	**12.00**	**17.00**
☐ *American, 2½" frame, c. 1900.*	**12.00**	**17.00**
☐ *American, 2¾" frame, c. 1900.*	**73.00**	**18.00**
☐ *American, 3¼" frame, c. 1900.*	**15.00**	**20.00**
☐ *American, 3½" frame, c. 1900.*	**17.00**	**23.00**
☐ *American, 3¾" frame, c. 1900.*	**20.00**	**25.00**
☐ *American, 4¼" frame, c. 1900.*	**30.00**	**40.00**

"KAZOO BAND" INSTRUMENTS

"Kazoo Band" instruments are a class of small-size versions of (in most cases) standard band instruments, designed for use in a "kazoo" or mini-orchestra. They were sold extensively in the 1920's and '30's and aimed partly to juveniles and partly to persons who had musical ambitions but could not afford or could not perform on instruments of full size. They have some appeal today as collectors' items; as musical instruments, not much can be said of the majority of them.

☐ *Baby Jazz Kazoo Clarinet, 6½", brass finish.*	**5.50**	**7.50**
☐ *Baby Jazz Kazoo Saxophone, 6½", brass finish.*	**5.50**	**7.50**
☐ *Bugle, 20" long, brass finish, combination bugle, kazoo and blow-horn, (sold in large numbers to Boy Scout troops).*	**7.00**	**10.00**
☐ *Clarinet, 18", brass finish, 8 plungers.*	**11.00**	**15.00**
☐ *Cornet, 15", 3 plungers.*	**9.00**	**12.00**
☐ *Cornet, 11", 3 plungers.*	**5.50**	**8.50**
☐ *Cornet, 12", flaring bell end, (a real "piece of tin" that gave a sound no better than a party noisemaker).*	**7.50**	**6.00**
☐ *Saxophone, 20", brass finish, 8 plungers.*	**11.00**	**15.00**

	Price Range	
☐ *Saxophone, 9"*	7.00	10.00
☐ *Trombone, 27" closed, about 38" extended.*	10.00	15.00
☐ *Trombone, 11" closed, 15" extended.*	5.00	7.00
☐ *Trumpet, also called "musical submarine", c. 1920's.*	3.50	5.00

LUTES

If the lute was not the first stringed instrument of the western world, it was certainly one of the first, and became the inspiration for many related instruments that followed. It was known in a primitive forms by 2,000 B.C., perhaps as early as 2,500 B.C. Its use in the ancient world extended into Persia, Mesopotamia, India, China and elsewhere. Surprisingly, it never became popular in the two chief centers of European culture, Greece and Rome, for reasons that have yet to be explained. There is no doubt that the Greeks and Romans knew of lutes, however. In India the lute developed into the modern **sitar.**

Widespread use of the lute in Europe dates from the 13th-century A.D., when Crusaders introduced it (reintroduced might be a better word) from the East. It soon became one of the favorite instruments of the time and is represented in numerous drawings, sculpture and other art of the late Middle Ages. Very few lutes of this era still exist but they do occasionally turn up.

Lutes were manufactured in a range of sizes and many kinds of wood, according to local taste or the availability of materials. During the 16-century, a time of immense popularity for this instrument, the favorite woods were cypress, sandalwood and sycamore, with the "belly" made of common pine. There is every reason to believe that good lutes cost a rather substantial sum of money then, more so, proportionately, than the price later became. Decoration at this period was minimal in most specimens. Lutes continued in favor until well into the 18th-century. They were especially well suited as accompaniment instruments for madrigal singers.

☐ *Balkan, early 19th-century*	1000.00	1300.00
☐ *English, Tudor*	11000.00	15000.00
☐ *English, late 17th-century*	6500.00	8200.00
☐ *English, Restoration*	4000.00	7000.00
☐ *English, Georgian*	1800.00	4000.00
☐ *Flemish, c. 1470*	20000.00	25000.00
☐ *Flemish, mid 16th-century*	16000.00	21000.00
☐ *French, c. 1350*	27500.00	37500.00
☐ *French, c. 1480*	21000.00	25000.00
☐ *French, early 16th-century*	16000.00	21000.00
☐ *French, c. 1570*	15000.00	20000.00
☐ *French, mid 17th-century*	13000.00	17000.00
☐ *French, Louis XIV*	12500.00	16500.00
☐ *French, Louis XV*	8000.00	11000.00
☐ *French, Louis XVI*	5200.00	7200.00
☐ *Genoese, early 18th-century*	5000.00	7000.00
☐ *Hungarian, c. 1800*	1100.00	1400.00
☐ *Italian, 15th-century*	30000.00	35000.00
☐ *Italian, mid 16th-century*	15000.00	20000.00

Lute, European, 2′ 11″ x 11″
Courtesy: The Metropolitan Museum of Art, The Crosby Brown Collection of Musical Instruments, 1889

	Price Range	
☐ *Italian, mid 1700's*	2600.00	3500.00
☐ *Italian, c. 1800*	1500.00	2000.00
☐ *Spanish, first quarter 17th-century*	10000.00	14000.00
☐ *Spanish, late 17th-century*	6000.00	9000.00
☐ *Swiss, c. 1750*	3150.00	3750.00

MANDOLINS

☐ **"Ballinger"**, *nine ribs of alternating mahogany and maple with strips of black wood between, rosewood cap, imitation tortoise shell guard plate, c. 1905-1910*	45.00	60.00
☐ **"Challenge"**, *15 ribs of mahogany with strips of black wood between, rosewood cap, sound hole inlaid with ring of colored wood, imitation tortoise shell guard plate*	65.00	80.00
☐ **"Competition"**, *nine ribs of alternating mahogany and maple with strips of black wood between, rosewood cap and top of silver spruce, mahogany neck, rosewood fingerboard*	45.00	60.00
☐ **"Concertone"**, *flat back (similar to guitar), birch back and sides, spruce top, basswood neck, ebonized fingerboard, black and white inlay around sound hole, tortoise celluloid guard plate, c. 1920*	65.00	80.00

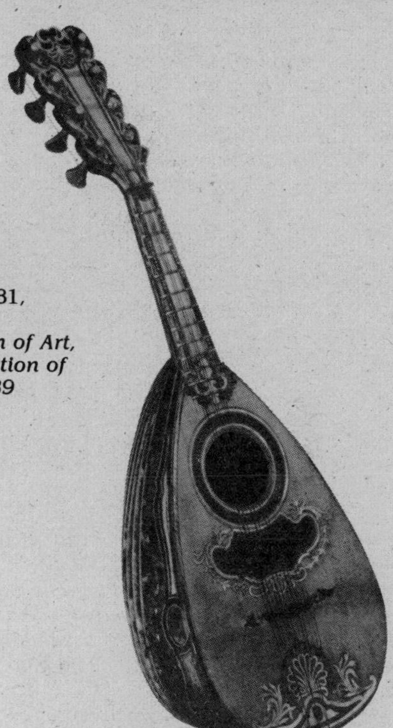

Mandolin, Italian, c. 1781, 1′ 11″ x 7½″. *Courtesy: The Metropolitan Museum of Art, The Crosby Brown Collection of Musical Instruments, 1889*

	Price Range	
☐ **The Edgemere,** *13 ribs of mahogany with black inlay between the, rosewood cap, edges bound with celluloid and wood inlaying, imitation tortoise shell guardpiece, nickel-plated tailpiece.*	**275.00**	**325.00**
☐ *English, medieval.*	**31000.00**	**42000.00**
☐ *English, c. 1650.*	**14000.00**	**19000.00**
☐ *English, early 18th-century.*	**6100.00**	**9000.00**
☐ *English, mid 1700's.*	**3200.00**	**4800.00**
☐ *English, c. 1800.*	**1400.00**	**1800.00**
☐ *Flemish, c. 1500.*	**40000.00**	**50000.00**
☐ *French, 14th-century.*	**45000.00**	**70000.00**
☐ *French, first quarter of the 16th-century.*	**32000.00**	**52000.00**
☐ *French, c. 1550.*	**27000.00**	**42000.00**
☐ *French, late 16th-century.*	**22000.00**	**40000.00**
☐ *French, early 17th-century.*	**15000.00**	**26000.00**
☐ *French, Louis XIV.*	**7500.00**	**14000.00**
☐ *French, Louis XV.*	**3200.00**	**8500.00**
☐ *French, Louis XVI.*	**3000.00**	**6000.00**
☐ *French, early 19th-century.*	**2000.00**	**3200.00**

	Price Range	
☐ **The Glencoe,** *13 ribs of rosewood and mahogany, redwood strips inlaid between, rosewood cap and sides, spruce top, celluloid imitation tortoise shell guardplate, c. 1900.*	300.00	375.00
☐ **The Illinois,** *nine mahogany ribs, alternating with maple, rosewood fingerboard with inlaid position dots, fretted with raised frets, imitation mahogany neck, c. 1900.*	200.00	250.00
☐ *Italian, Renaissnce.*	35000.00	50000.00
☐ *Italian, first quarter of the 17th-century.*	27500.00	42000.00
☐ *Italian, mid 1600's.*	20000.00	35000.00
☐ *Italian, c. 1700.*	10000.00	20000.00
☐ *Italian, first quarter 18th-century.*	8000.00	17000.00
☐ *Italian, third quarter of the 18th-century.*	3300.00	8500.00
☐ **"New Departure",** *13 ribs of rosewood with white holly between, rosewood cap, inlaid with vari-colored woods, c. 1905-1910.*	80.00	125.00
☐ *Nine figured hardwood ribs, hardwood top, basswood neck, ebonized fingerboard, black celluloid binding around top edge, c. 1920's.*	85.00	125.00
☐ *Rosewood, 16 ribs, inlaid white lines between, mahogany finished neck, tortoise celluloid side quard plate, colored block inlay around top and edge.*	150.00	200.00
☐ **The Royal,** *11 ribs of rosewood with white holly inlaid between strips, inlaid guard plate, c. early 1900's.*	400.00	500.00
☐ **The Senora,** *15 ribs of rosewood with white holly between strips, rosewood cap and sides, celluloid binding, American made, c. 1900.*	475.00	575.00
☐ **"20th-Century",** *21 ribs of rosewood, spruce top inlaid with pearl, mahogany neck, rosewood veneered head, c. 1900.*	425.00	500.00

MIDWAY MUSETTE

The Columbian Exposition of 1892-93 featured Oriental music played at the Midway. New at the time to most Americans visiting the fair, it caused a temporary fad for instruments that could produce Oriental-sounding tones. The Midway Musette was heralded by its manufacturers and retailers as the perfect instrument for this purpose. It looked something like the long narrow tin horns used as noisemakers at parties. The assertion that "anyone can play it" was true insofar as everyone, whether musically skilled or not, got about the same results — disappointing. As an example of musical instrument fadism, it rates high.

☐ *Nickel-plated, with reed, manufactured shortly after the Columbian Exposition.*	55.00	75.00

MUSICAL SLEIGH BELLS

The playing of bells as musical instruments originated in ancient times. It is beyond the scope of this book to enter into bells and their musical properties, but we have included Musical Sleigh Bells on grounds that they were retailed strictly as musical instruments with no other purpose. They consisted of a set of bells attached to straps, the straps being strung on a vertical frame. Though never really popular, musical sleigh bells reached the point of being featured in a number of dealer catalogues of the late 19th-and early 20th-centuries. They have more interest as a curiosity than an instrument.

Colonial Sleigh Bell, American, 2″ Dia. *Courtesy: The Metropolitan Museum of Art, The Crosby Brown Collection, of Musical Instruments, 1889*

	Price Range	
☐ *Mounted on frame made of oak, measuring 30″x24″, eight straps with six bells attached, keys represented are B flat, C, D, E flat, F, G, A and B flat in that order, American made, c. 1890's.*	95.00	120.00

NOSE FLUTES

The lowly nose flute probably rates as the least glamorous of musical instruments. Whether it can properly be termed an instrument is open to debate; but a great many were manufactured and sold in the U.S., especially during the period 1920-1940. A contemporary advertisement stated "the tone is very musical and flute-like. It is capable of the most charming modulations, and the most popular melody or the most elaborate operatic air can be played . . ." It was a small metal object shaped roughly as a figure eight, with a wind-hole and air passage similar to a whistle. It was played by holding it to the nose and exhaling.

☐ **"The Magic Nose Flute",** *1920's.*	3.00	5.00

OBOES

☐ *English, early 18th-century*	8000.00	10000.00
☐ *English, third quarter of the 18th-century*	5000.00	7000.00
☐ *English, first quarter of the 19th-century*	4375.00	6000.00
☐ *English, early Victorian*	1100.00	1500.00
☐ *English, late Victorian*	700.00	900.00
☐ *German, 17th-century*	22000.00	30000.00
☐ *German, first quarter of the 18th-century*	5000.00	7000.00

Oboe, French, c. 20th century.
Courtesy: The Metropolitan Museum of Art, Funds from various donors, 1976

	Price Range	
☐ *German, mid 18th-century.*	4250.00	6000.00
☐ *German, c. 1770.*	3175.00	4000.00
☐ *Italian, mid 18th-century.*	1600.00	2000.00
☐ *Italian, c. 1790.*	1600.00	2000.00
☐ *Italian, c. 1840.*	550.00	700.00
☐ *Italian, third quarter of the 19th-century.*	500.00	650.00
☐ *Three-keyed, by Thomas Stanesby, Sr., London, 23$^{3}/_{16}$" long, c. 1700.*	17500.00	22500.00

OCARINAS

These small instruments, never highly regarded by professional musicians, were sold in great quantities to the American public in the period from about 1880 to 1930. They were advertised in nearly every mail-order catalogue, including the famous Johnson Smith, as well as in comic books. Most sold originally for under $1 or could be obtained free by sending in coupons or cereal boxlids. The majority of purchasers were children, or parents who fondly hoped (not often successfully) that by introducing their child to the ocarina, he might develop a taste for music. In the early days of vaudeville they became a standard in music shows, especially minstrel shows, along with various other nonconcert instruments. They were used even by country and western artists occasionally.

☐ *European, A, Alto, c. 1900.*	28.00	35.00
☐ *European, A, Bass, c. 1900.*	55.00	80.00
☐ *European, A flat, Alto, c. 1900.*	30.00	40.00
☐ *European, A flat, Bass, c. 1900.*	75.00	95.00
☐ *European, A, Soprano, c. 1900.*	15.00	20.00
☐ *European, B flat, Alto, c. 1900.*	25.00	35.00
☐ *European, B flat, Bass, c. 1900.*	60.00	80.00
☐ *European, B flat, Soprano, c. 1900.*	15.00	20.00
☐ *European, C, Alto, c. 1900.*	25.00	35.00
☐ *European, C, Bass, c. 1900.*	50.00	70.00
☐ *European, C, Soprano, c. 1900.*	15.00	20.00
☐ *European, D, Bass, c. 1900.*	42.00	55.00
☐ *European, E, Alto, c. 1900.*	42.00	55.00
☐ *European, E, Soprano, c. 1900.*	22.00	33.00

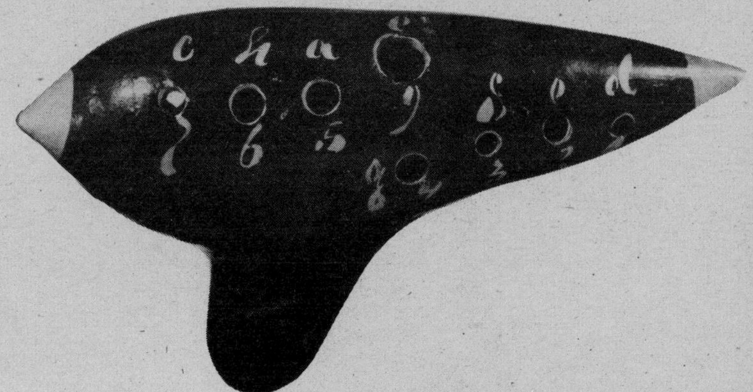

Ocarnia, Austrian, c. 19th or 20th century, clay. *Courtesy: The Metropolitan Museum of Art, The Crosby Brown Collection of Musical Instruments, 1889*

	Price Range	
☐ *European, E flat, Alto, c. 1900*	**42.00**	**55.00**
☐ *European, E flat, Soprano, c. 1900.*	**22.00**	**32.00**
☐ *European, F, Alto, c. 1900.*	**40.00**	**55.00**
☐ *European, F, Soprano, c. 1900.*	**20.00**	**25.00**
☐ *European, G, Alto, c. 1900.*	**40.00**	**55.00**
☐ *European, G, Bass, c. 1900.*	**90.00**	**175.00**

PANDORA OR BANDORA

The pandora, also called bandora, was an instrument of the late Middle Ages/Renaissance. Similar in design to a lute, it could be played solo but was used mainly by groups of instrumentalists to supply bass notes to complement the lute, mandolin or guitar. There are no modern examples of it and the possibilities of a collector ever possessing a specimen are quite slim. A splendid pandora with elaborately decorated body was manufactured by John Rose of London in 1580, during the reign of Elizabeth I. This instrument, if it reached the market, would be worth a great sum of money. Few other specimens are known.

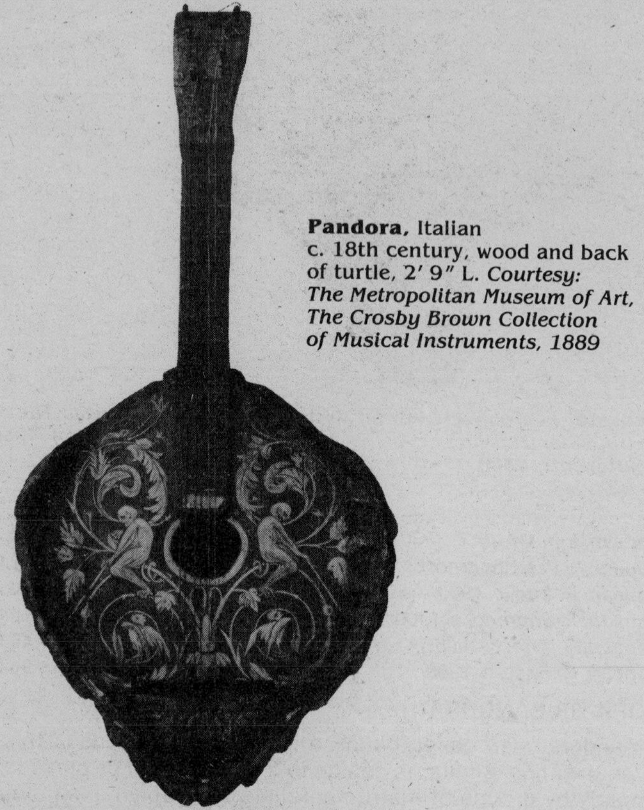

Pandora, Italian
c. 18th century, wood and back of turtle, 2′ 9″ L. *Courtesy: The Metropolitan Museum of Art, The Crosby Brown Collection of Musical Instruments, 1889*

PIANOS

Private collections of pianos are few, not so much because of their price, (antique violins, which fall more or less within a comparable price range, are collected) but the space necessary for storage. Nevertheless there are many devotees of antique pianos, who, even though they may wish to own just one single specimen, will pay dearly for the piano that appeals most to them. In fact it is collectors — or, maybe more accurate to say, those who take an interest in pianos from a historical and artistic point of view — who account for the majority of sales, as few musicians seek out antique pianos. This is quite a different situation than with violins.

The musical merits of antique pianos is a subject too complex to enter into in this book. The claim of some experts is that old pianos, especially those of noted manufacturers, produce a finer tone than any currently offered. Others feel quite the opposite, that antique pianos are splendid museum pieces but not so desirable from a musician's point of view. Probably, the real answer lies in the sort of music being played. French harpsicords and pianos of the later 17th and 18th centuries, with their sweet sugary tones, are not likely to be matched by modern instruments for playing French compositions of that area. Ditto for Wagnerian scores played on old German pianos. Today's pianos are, if not so perfectly suited to any one type of music, at least more versatile.

Of course, it must be understood that any piano of 200 years age has been restrung, retuned, and otherwise serviced innumerable times, so that its performance may no longer be an exact duplication of the original, even though it appears "like new" visually. The tonal character of a piano is subject to all manner of influences, from heat, cold, being moved about, carelessly played, improperly cleaned, etc. If maintained at regular intervals from time of manufacture to the present, its sound may approximate the original; but any piano neglected for 20, 50, or more years, then serviced, is apt to end up sounding very different (though perhaps just as good) as it once did. Thus, by playing an antique piano you do not necessarily hear 200 year old scores "just as the composer intended them to be heard". The odds that they will sound as the composer intended, even with a $100,000 instrument, are not too great.

The survival rate of antique pianos is not especially high. It would be expected, by someone unaware of all circumstances involved, that old pianos should exist today in numbers close to the original output. Representing sizable investments, they were well cared for by the original purchasers. However, being difficult to move about, pianos were frequently abandoned when fires broke out, and left behind when European towns had to be evacuated during time of war. Rather than being taken as war spoils, as were valuable small articles, they were generally destroyed by the enemy. The number of pianos that perished during the Napoleonic Wars (to name one of many) must have been enormous. Thus the present-day existing totals of pianos once manufactured are roughly as follows:

16th-century, 5-8%, of which 70% or more are in museums
17th-century, 10-15%, of which 50-70% are in museums
18th-century, 25-40%, of which less than 50% are in museums
19th-century, 40-60%, of which less than 20% are in museums

Of very early pianos which do exist, many are no longer in a condition approximating the original, either structurally or musically.

Piano making (and we are talking of all piano-like instruments collectively, as the first true piano was not brought out until 1709) did not become an industry in the accepted sense of the term until the last quarter of the 18th-century. Prior to that time, piano-making studios were small, on the same order as violin shops, and, because of the greater length of time needed to produce each specimen, turned out fewer instruments than violin makers. Production was stepped up around 1780, to satisfy a more affluent ready market, but still the output lingered well behind that of most smaller instruments. "A piano in every home" became a popular advertising slogan of three generations ago, but not only was this far from realized then, it certainly did not reflect the situation of 1700 or 1800. European noble families were the chief owners of piano-like instruments up to about 1720. Private ownership was uncommon in the 17th-century. In America there were very few pianos in the colonial era, though the proportion owned by private individuals, per capita, was probably as great as in Europe. During the first and second quarters of the 19th-century many French and English pianos we imported into this country. The second half of the 19th-century witnessed e tensive piano manufacture in the U.S.

Buying Antique Pianos. While the reputation of manufacturers may mea less with pianos than violins, the careful buyer will generally seek out respected name and purchase the best piano by that manufacturer he can a ford. Unfortunately, much antique piano-buying is done for the wron reasons, by persons who, though wealthy enough to afford fine material, a not equipped with the knowledge or connoisseurship to buy intelligently.

Antique pianos may be acquired through instrument dealers, auctions, c from private parties. Unless you have the knowledge to make accurate o the-spot appraisals, buying from private sources is the least favorable. Man estate sales include pianos. They are well worth watching, as good-qualit antique pianos can often be bought at these sales at prices under the mark value.

When buying from foreign dealers or auctioneers, keep in mind that th cost of transporting a piano overseas is very high, and that there is risk of arriving damaged. The auctioneers will not perform the actual crating; this i done by private contractors, who charge for their service in addition t transportation.

Values of Antique Pianos. The value of any antique piano, whether mad by a celebrated manufacturer or a second-rater, depends very much on de sign and casework. Almost every manufacturer offered various grades c pianos, from rather plain and inexpensive to "art grands" that were lavishl sculptured, painted, or otherwise decorated. The artwork on art grands of th 17th- and 18th- centuries is often remarkable, and would be worth fair sum in itself beyond the value of the instrument.

Listed below are representative examples of pianos of various ages an grades, ranging from highly desirable to quite ordinary. This is but a mer sampling of the available specimens that pass through the market; man others are to be found, in all ranges of price.

	Price Range	
☐ **Baldwin Art Grand,** *Cincinnati, painted scenes on sides, otherwise modest design, c. 1900.* ***The Baldwin factory, not as renowned as Steinway, produced some exceptional work.***	11000.00	16500.0
☐ **Baldwin Baby Grand,** *5'3", c. early 1900's.*	500.00	700.0
☐ **Baldwin Concert Grand,** *Cincinnati, 9'.*	9100.00	14000.0
☐ **Baldwin Upright,** *rebuilt, c. early 1900's.*	550.00	750.0
☐ **Beckwith Acme Cabinet Grand,** *upright model.*	775.00	1175.0
☐ **Beckwith Artists' Cabinet Grand.**	700.00	1100.0
☐ **Beckwith Cabinet Grand,** *upright model, c. early 1900's.*	1100.00	1600.0
☐ **Beckwith Home Favorite,** *upright model.*	550.00	700.0
☐ **Beckwith Palace Grand,** *upright model.*	700.00	1000.0
☐ **Blasser, Thomas, Harpsichord,** *London, two manual, inscribed on name board "Thomas Blasser fecit Londini 1744", 8'1½", 1744.*	22000.00	28750.0

	Price Range	
☐ **Bluthner, Julius, Art Grand,** *Leipzig, Egyptian motifs, late 19th-century.*	25000.00	30000.00
The styling of piano cases to suit contemporary fads of interior decor was common throughout almost the whole history of piano making. As styles changed so rapidly during the Victorian era, many variations of piano cases are to be found from that period. The Egyptian style is not one of the more heralded today.		
☐ **Bosendorfer, Ludwig, Art Grand,** *Vienna, second quarter of the 19th-century.*	33000.00	40000.00
☐ **Broadwood, John, and Sons, Art Grand,** *featuring various colored inlays, late 18th-century.*	70000.00	90000.00
☐ **Broadwood Grand,** *7½'.*	2750.00	3775.00
☐ **Broadwood Grand, Pianoforte,** *marquetry by A. Morris & Company, 7'6", late 19th-century.*	15000.00	20000.00
☐ **"Chang",** *made in Korea, 6'2".*	6000.00	7500.00
☐ **Chickering Ampico-A Grand,** *5'4".*	5750.00	7500.00
☐ **Emerson Oak Grand,** *new strings and hammers.*	5000.00	6250.00
☐ **Erard, Sebastian, Art Grand,** *London, exquisitely decorated with carved and gilded cherubs in the Louis XVI fashion (Erard was a Frenchman), c. 1800.*	35000.00	45500.00

Honduras Mahogany Piano, Mason & Hamlin

	Price Range	
☐ **Fisher Grand,** *5'1", ebony.*	4000.00	4500.00
☐ **Fritz, Johann, square,** *Vienna, 65½".*	2750.00	3500.00
☐ **Ganer, Christopher, square,** *London, 59½", c. 1781.*	2000.00	2750.00
☐ **Hallet and Davis Baby Grand,** *5'2".*	4200.00	5200.00
☐ **Kimball Grand,** *5'3", mahogany.*	3950.00	4575.00
☐ **Kimball Grand,** *5'8", walnut.*	4800.00	5600.00
☐ **Kirkman, Jacob, Harpsichord,** *London, two manual, c. 1760.*	2500.00	3200.00
☐ **Kirkman, Jacob, Harpsichord,** *London, two manual, inscribed "Jacobus Kirckman Londini fecit 1767", mahogany case, 7'9", c. 1767.*	40000.00	50000.00
The difference in value between these two specimens from the same studio is attributable mostly to case decoration. Kirkman's name is often spelled Kirckman.		
☐ **Kirkman, Jacob and Abraham, Harpsichord,** *London, single manual, inscribed "Jacobus and Abraham Kirckman Londini fecerunt 1774", 7'3", c. 1774.*	20000.00	23750.00
☐ **Kirkman, Jacob and Abraham, square,** *London, 4'8¾", c. 1775.*	4500.00	6000.00
The Kirkmans were the most prolific English piano and related-instrument makers of their time. Their pianos are still rather common on the market, even at a distance of 200 years. Their musical quality is considered less than brilliant.		
☐ **Player, John, Spinet,** *London, inscribed "Johannes Player, Londini, fecit", walnut body on oak trestle stand, 5'1½", undated, third quarter of the 17th-century.*	22000.00	27500.00
This fine spinet dates from the time of Samuel Pepys and the Restoration. At about this time, "popular" music — that is, ballads and poems that could be set to simple music — was gaining great favor in Britain. There were music masters who could be hired to teach spinet playing, singing, etc. The spinet was often called a virginal. Pepys owned one of these instruments; his would be worth at least five times the value shown, for association interest.		
☐ **Pleyell-Lyon Gothic Upright,** *Paris, c. 1900.*	11500.00	14000.00
A well-designed case with motifs borrowed from gothic choir stalls of the 15th-century. In workmanship it was perhaps the finest piano that could be bought at the time; but gothic design soon fell out of favor in pianos, tallcase clocks and just about everything else.		
☐ **Pleyell-Lyon Renaissance Art Grand,** *Paris, an admixture of styles (really more Louis XIV) that would not readily be recognized as Renaissance by most persons, c. 1900.*	20000.00	25000.00
The Pleyell-Lyon factory was the French equivalent of Steinway. It turned out some very handsome pianos that won high favor among French musicians. Its instruments gained only limited popularity elsewhere in Europe.		
☐ **Rucker, Hans, Double Spinet,** *Antwerp, Flanders, a specimen designed to suit the decor of a lavish 16th-century interior, well carved and featuring a large mural painting on the underside of lid, c. 1560.*	165000.00	225000.00
The double spinet was a variety of harpsichord in use before introduction of the piano. It remained popular thereafter but gradually lost favor during the latter part of the 18th-century.		

	Price Range	
☐ **Schiller Cabinet Grand,** *upright model, c. 1890's.*	1500.00	2000.00
☐ **Schiller,** *seven and one-third octaves, double veneered case, double roll fall-board, ivory keys, ebony sharps, double repeating action, Sostenuto pedal, upright model.*	1650.00	2000.00
☐ **Schiller,** *seven and one-third octaves, iron frames and continuous hinge on fall-board, ivory keys, ebony sharps, double repeating action, nickel-plated rail, upright model.*	1275.00	1800.00
☐ **Schmahl Portable Pianoforte,** *Ulm, Germany, case painted with vines and rose, 46¾", probably third quarter of the 18th-century.*	11500.00	16000.00
☐ **Sears Roebuck American Home Parlor Grand,** *upright piano measuring 4'7" tall, 61" wide, 2'3" deep, mahogany finish.*	1500.00	2000.00
☐ **Sears Roebuck Home Favorite piano-organ,** *upright, 4'10½" long, 4'7½" high, 2'1½" deep, seven and one-third octaves of keys and four sets of reeds, 176 reeds in all, walnut, c. 1900.*	750.00	975.00
☐ **Sears Roebuck Home Favorite,** *as above, mahogany.*	725.00	950.00
☐ **Sears Roebuck Home Favorite,** *an improved version of the above with 214 reeds, walnut case.*	750.00	1100.00
☐ *As above, 214 reeds, mahogany case.*	950.00	1400.00

Steinway Grand Piano, rosewood, 1973

	Price Range	
☐ **Sears Roebuck New American Home,** *upright grand piano, 4'7" high, 61" long, maple with walnut finish, c. 1900.*	1000.00	1300.00
☐ **Steinway and Sons Art Grand,** *New York, a massive and richly ornamented instrument, manufactured at an original cost of $40,000 as a "special order", late 19th-century.*	65000.00	87500.00
The American Art Grand of this era sometimes became very grand indeed, as American millionaires wished to own pianos that equaled the finest obtainable in Europe. Tonally they were superior to the average run of instruments but their huge prices went mostly for casework. Collectors view them with mixed feelings.		
☐ **Steinway Grand,** *Model "L", 5'10½", ebony body, c. 1935.*	7000.00	9000.00
☐ **Trasunti, Allessandro, Art Harpsichord,** *Italy, an elaborate early specimen, probably commission work for the apartment of a nobleman, decorated with a series of inset paintings, c. 1531.*	165000.00	190000.00
Harpsichords of this age, well over 400 years old, are very uncommon. Not made for general sale, they were almost exclusively commissioned work. Those who have the commissions were as concerned with the instrument's decor as with its musical qualities, perhaps more so. They generally reach the market only through the sale of old European estates.		

Harpischord, Italian, c. 17th century. *Courtesy: The Metropolitan Museum of Art, The Crosby Brown Collection of Musical Instruments, 1889*

	Price Range	
☐ **Waverly,** *burled walnut, seven and one-third octaves, double roll fall-board, ivory or celluloid keys (found with either; does not affect value), carved trusses, upright model, mode in Oregon, Illinois, c. 1890-1900.*	900.00	1200.00
☐ **Weber Louis XIV Art Grand,** *New York, sculptured, gilded case, late 19th-century.*	8000.00	9500.00

PICCOLOS

The piccolo is a close relative to, and offshoot of, the flute. It is in reality a small flute and plays at one octave higher than do most flutes. It is not an instrument to which great attention has been given by composers but it has, gradually but firmly, become accepted in the world of classical music. It is also used by jazz musicians. Because of its ease of handling, compared to a standard flute, and its lower price, piccolos became quite popular as an instrument by which children could be introduced to music. Many students primed for an eventual career as flutists were started off on the piccolo.

☐ **"Atlas Piccolo",** *cast metal, c. 1900.*	40.00	55.00
☐ *Cocoa wood, one key, c. 1900.*	65.00	85.00
☐ *Cocoa wood, one key and tuning slide, c. 1900.*	85.00	110.00

Piccolo In E Flat, German, c. 19th or 20th century. *Courtesy: The Metropolitan Museum of Art, gift of Hugh W. Conlon, 1975*

☐ *Grenadilla wood, four keys and tuning slide, c. 1900.*	120.00	150.00
☐ *Grenadilla wood, six keys, c. 1900.*	160.00	200.00
☐ *Italian, c. 1730.*	675.00	850.00
☐ *Italian, hardwood with silver trimming, enclosed in a finely decorated walnut box lined with plush, c. 1742.*	800.00	1100.00
☐ *Italian, c. 1761.*	475.00	625.00
☐ *Italian, c. 1800.*	365.00	450.00
☐ *Italian, early 19th-century.*	325.00	400.00
☐ *Meyer, grenadilla wood, ivory head, six keys, c. 1900.*	250.00	300.00
☐ **Piccolo-Flageolet** *(combination), boxwood, c. 1900.*	110.00	135.00
☐ **Piccolo-FFlageolet,** *grenadilla wood, c. 1900.*	125.00	150.00

SAXOPHONES

☐ **Bantone,** *bell front, three valves, lacquer bore.*	1000.00	1350.00
☐ **Bantone,** *same as above, upright bell.*	950.00	1250.00
☐ **Dupont Alto - Solo,** *bell front, highly polished brass.*	150.00	200.00
☐ **Dupont Alto - Solo,** *bell front, burnished nickel plate.*	150.00	200.00
☐ **Dupont Alto - Solo,** *bell front, triple silver plate, satin finish.*	200.00	250.00

Saxophones, French, c. 1867. *Courtesy: The Metropolitan Museum of Art, The Crosby Brown Collection of Musical Instruments, 1889*

	Price Range	
☐ **Dupont Alto - Solo,** *bell front, triple silver plate, burnished.*	265.00	315.00
☐ **Dupont Alto - Solo,** *bell upright, highly polished brass.*	150.00	185.00
☐ **Dupont Alto - Solo,** *bell upright, burnished nickel plate.*	160.00	210.00
☐ **Dupont Alto - Solo,** *bell upright, triple silver plate, satin finish.*	180.00	225.00
☐ **Dupont Alto - Solo,** *bell upright, triple silver plate, burnished.*	200.00	250.00
☐ **Dupont Alto,** *French Horn model, highly polished brass.*	275.00	350.00
☐ **Dupont Alto,** *French Horn model, burnished nickel plate.*	325.00	400.00
☐ **Dupont Alto,** *French Horn model, triple silver plate, satin finish.*	400.00	500.00
☐ **Dupont Alto,** *French Horn model, triple silver plate, burnished.*	450.00	600.00
☐ **Dupont B Flat Tenor,** *highly polished brass.*	190.00	240.00
☐ **Dupont B Flat Tenor,** *burnished nickel plate.*	225.00	275.00
☐ **Dupont B Flat Tenor,** *triple silver plate, satin finish.*	225.00	300.00
☐ **Dupont B Flat Tenor,** *triple silver plate, burnished.*	275.00	350.00
☐ **Dupont B Flat Baritone,** *highly polished brass.*	300.00	400.00

	Price Range	
☐ **Dupont B Flat Baritone,** *burnished nickel plate.*	325.00	425.00
☐ **Dupont B Flat Baritone,** *triple silver plate, satin finish.*	375.00	475.00
☐ **Dupont B Flat Baritone,** *triple silver plate, burnished.*	400.00	500.00
☐ *Double French Horn, mechanical valve linkage, ball-bearing suspension, bronze bell.*	3000.00	3600.00
☐ **Holton,** *Double French Horn, lacquer bore.*	1400.00	2000.00
☐ **Holton,** *Double "Farkas", nickel silver.*	1500.00	1800.00
☐ **Holton,** *Double "Farkas", nickel silver, screw bell.*	2150.00	2675.00
☐ **Holton,** *Double "Farkas", brass, screw bell.*	2150.00	2675.00
☐ **Holton,** *Double "Farkas", lightweight brass.*	2150.00	2675.00
☐ **Holton,** *"Hand horn".*	2300.00	2800.00
☐ **Holton,** *Double "Farkas" hand horn, lightweight brass, screw bell.*	2200.00	3000.00
☐ **Marceau E Flat** *Alto, brass, polished, c. early 1900's.*	110.00	150.00
☐ **Marceau E Flat** *Alto, nickel, polished.*	125.00	160.00
☐ **Marceau E Flat** *Alto, silver-plated, satin finish.*	150.00	200.00
☐ **Marceau B Flat** *tenor, brass, polished.*	125.00	160.00
☐ **Marceau B Flat** *Tenor, nickel, polished.*	130.00	170.00
☐ **Mellophonium,** *bell forward, lacquer bore.*	1100.00	1400.00
☐ *Single French Horn in key of F.*	900.00	1150.00
☐ *Single French Horn, B Flat.*	1000.00	1500.00
☐ **Tourville & Co.** *Alto, brass, polished, c. early 1900's.*	200.00	265.00
☐ **Tourville & Co.** *Alto, nickel-plated.*	175.00	225.00
☐ **Tourville & Co.** *Alto, silver, satin finish.*	225.00	280.00
☐ **Tourville & Co.** *Alto, silver, polished.*	250.00	350.00
☐ **Tourville & Co.** *B Flat Baritone, brass, polished.*	225.00	280.00
☐ **Tourville & Co.** *B Flat Baritone, nickel-plated.*	250.00	330.00
☐ **Tourville & Co.** *B Flat Baritone, silver-plated, satin finish.*	325.00	425.00
☐ **Tourville & Co.** *B Flat Baritone, silver-plated, polished.*	325.00	425.00
☐ **Tourville & Co.** *Tenor, nickel-plated.*	275.00	350.00
☐ **Tourville & Co.** *Tenor, silver, satin finish.*	275.00	350.00
☐ **Tourville & Co.** *Tenor, silver, polished.*	300.00	375.00

SERPENT

☐ *English, by Thomas Key, London, c. 1820. Leather-bound wood tube, brass and nickel mountings, four brass keys, brass crook and bit with ivory mouthpiece. Length of tube 7'11½".*	1900.00	2400.00

(On strength of rarity, this imposing wind instrument, an ancestor of the tube, deserves a higher price. Its value is low because it is not suitable either as a concert or orchestral instrument, and is really only in the category of a museum piece.)

Serpent In C, English, c. 1820, wood and leather, 2' 4" L. - *Courtesy: The Metropolitan Museum of Art, The Crosby Brown Collection of Musical Instruments, 1889*

TAMBOURINES

	Price Range	
☐ *Albanian, c. 1860.*	70.00	100.00
☐ *Albanian, silver jingles, third quarter of the 19th-century.*	100.00	125.00
☐ *Brazilian, second quarter of the 19th-century.*	125.00	180.00
☐ *Czech, 19th-century.*	110.00	150.00
☐ *English, 1860.*	115.00	160.00
☐ *English, third quarter of the 19th-century.*	90.00	120.00
☐ *English, c. 1895.*	75.00	100.00
☐ *Irish, 19th-century.*	95.00	125.00
☐ *Italian, mid 19th-century.*	100.00	125.00
☐ *Mexican, c. 1890-1900.*	70.00	100.00
☐ *Polish, early 19th-century.*	165.00	215.00
☐ *Polish, c. 1840.*	150.00	225.00
☐ *Polish, third quarter of the 19th-century.*	90.00	125.00
☐ *"Salvation Army" model, c. 1900.*	60.00	90.00
☐ *"Salvation Army" model with 32 sets of jingles, c. 1900.*	60.00	100.00
☐ *Spanish, c. 1870.*	85.00	110.00
☐ *Spanish, late 19th-century.*	70.00	100.00

TRIANGLES

It is very likely that the average public estimation of the triangle is no higher than of the kazoo or Jews' harp, that it represents someone's perverted notion of what ought to be included in an orchestra. But the simple little triangle — just a length of bent metal — is a bonafide instrument with a long, well-documented history in the performance of classical and semi-classical music. It would be impossible without the triangle to produce certain notes necessary for the correct rendering of many scores. They vary quite a bit in quality, too, and it would not be an exaggeration to state that a triangle player values a fine instrument almost to the degree that a violinist does, despite its lesser versatility.

	Price Range	
☐ *Four inches, nickeled steel, with hammer, c. 1890's.*	8.00	11.00
☐ *Six inches, nickeled steel, with hammer.*	9.00	13.00
☐ *Seven inches, nickeled steel, with hammer, American made, c. 1890-1900.*	10.00	15.00
☐ *Eight inches, nickeled steel, with hammer.*	12.00	17.00
☐ *10 inches, nickeled steel, with hammer.*	15.00	20.00
☐ *12 inches, nickeled steel, with hammer.*	22.00	30.00

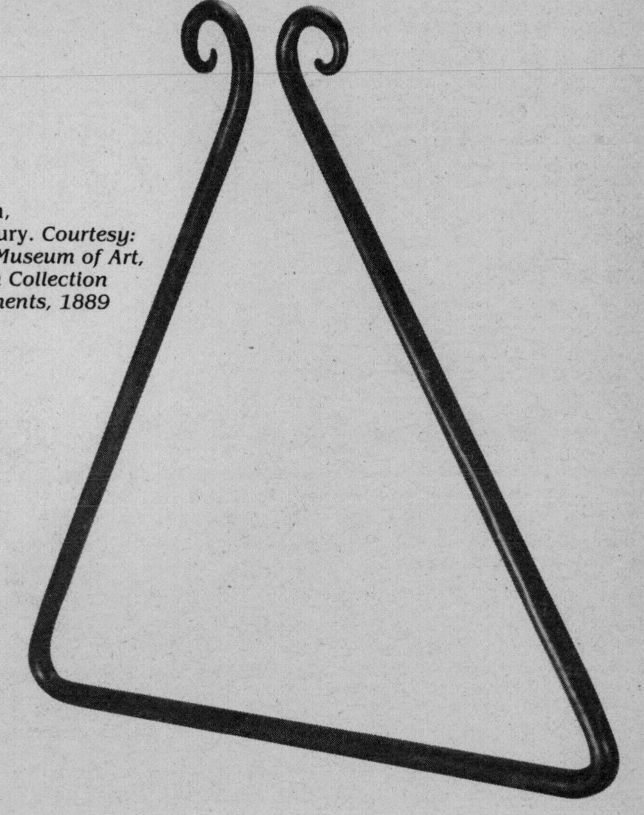

Triangle, German, c. early 19th century. *Courtesy: The Metropolitan Museum of Art, The Crosby Brown Collection of Musical Instruments, 1889*

TROMBONES

	Price Range	
☐ **Concertone B Flat Tenor Slide,** *low pitch, nickel silver mouthpiece and music rack, 42½" long, c. early 1920's.*	200.00	265.00
☐ **Concertone,** *as above, nickel-plated.*	210.00	270.00
☐ **Concertone,** *as above, silver-plated, satin finish, gold plated bell.*	275.00	335.00
☐ **Dupont B Flat Baritone Valve,** *highly polished brass.*	500.00	625.00
☐ **Dupont B Flat Baritone Valve,** *burnished nickel plate.*	625.00	750.00
☐ **Dupont B Flat Baritone Valve,** *triple silver plate, satin finish.*	750.00	950.00
☐ **Dupont B Flat Bairtone Valve,** *triple silver plate, burnished.*	800.00	1000.00
☐ **Dupont B Flat Tenor Slide,** *highly polished brass.*	400.00	500.00
☐ **Dupont B Flat Tenor Slide,** *burnished nickel plate.*	425.00	550.00
☐ **Dupont B Flat Tenor Slide,** *triple silver plate, satin finish.*	600.00	725.00
☐ **Dupont B Flat Tenor Slide,** *triple silver plate, burnished.*	750.00	1000.00
☐ **Dupont B Flat Tenor Valve,** *burnished nickel plate.*	550.00	625.00
☐ **Dupont B Flat Tenor Valve,** *triple silver plate, satin finish.*	575.00	650.00
☐ **Dupont B Flat Tenor Valve,** *triple silver plate, burnished.*	600.00	775.00
☐ **Dupont B Flat Tenor Valve,** *highly polished brass.*	525.00	650.00
☐ **Dupont E Flat Alto Slide,** *highly polished brass.*	525.00	650.00
☐ **Dupont E Flat Alto Slide,** *burnished nickel plate.*	525.00	650.00
☐ **Dupont E Flat Alto Slide,** *triple silver plate, satin finish.*	600.00	775.00

Trombone, American, c. 19th century, brass, 3′ 10½″ L. *Courtesy: The Metropolitan Museum of Art, The Crosby Brown Collection of Musical Instruments, 1889*

	Price Range	
☐ **Dupont E Flat Alto Slide,** *triple silver plate, burnished.*	700.00	900.00
☐ **Dupont E Flat Alto Valve,** *highly polished brass.*	300.00	375.00
☐ **Dupont E Flat Alto Valve,** *burnished nickel plate.*	325.00	400.00
☐ **Dupont E Flat Alto Valve,** *triple silver plate, satin finish.*	400.00	525.00
☐ **Dupont E Flat Alto Valve,** *triple silver plate, burnished.*	400.00	525.00
☐ **Lamoreaux Freres Slide,** *ornamented bell, brass, polished, c. 1905.*	250.00	300.00
☐ **Lamoreaux Freres,** *nickel-plated.*	325.00	425.00
☐ **Lamoreaux Freres,** *silver-plated, satin finish.*	325.00	425.00
☐ **Lamoreaux Freres,** *silver-plated, polished.*	300.00	375.00
☐ **Marceau Slide,** *leaf-work ornament, brass, polished, c. 1905.*	200.00	250.00
☐ **Marceau,** *nickel-plated, polished.*	275.00	350.00
☐ **Marceau,** *silver-plated, satin finish, gold lined bell.*	300.00	370.00
☐ **Marceau,** *silver-plated, burnished gold lined bell.*	260.00	300.00

TRUMPETS

☐ **Concertone B Flat,** *high pitch with low pitch slide, quick change slide to A, medium bore and bell, one water key, nickel silver mouthpiece, pearl buttons, 20⅝" long, 4¾" bell, brass, sold in the 1920's.*	160.00	200.00
☐ **Concertone,** *as above, nickel-plated.*	175.00	225.00
☐ **Concertone,** *as above, silver-plated, satin finish, gold plated-bell.*	250.00	300.00

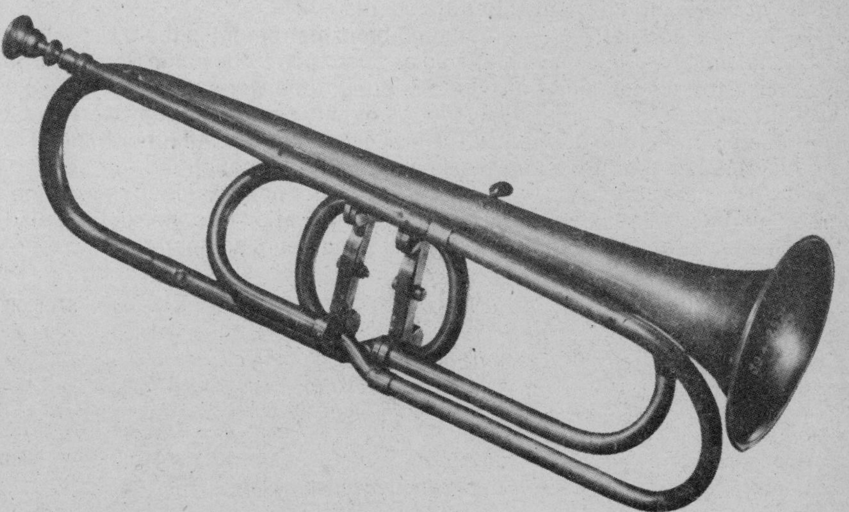

Trumpet In E Flat, English, c. 19th century, brass. *Courtesy: The Metropolitan Museum of Art, The Crosby Brown Collection of Musical Instruments, 1889*

	Price Range	
☐ **Holton B Flat Bass,** *lacquer.*	1200.00	1400.00
☐ **Holton B Flat,** *"Maynard Ferguson Firebird", slide valve combination, lacquer.*	1600.00	1850.00
☐ **Holton B Flat,** *lacquer bore.*	300.00	400.00
☐ **Holton B Flat,** *red brass bell, "U" hook third valve.*	375.00	450.00
☐ **Holton B Flat,** *nickel finish.*	500.00	625.00
☐ **Holton B Flat,** *"Al Hirt Special", lacquer.*	750.00	900.00
☐ **Holton B Flat,** *"Maynard Ferguson".*	1000.00	1200.00
☐ **Holton E Flat/D.**	950.00	1200.00
☐ **Holton E Alto,** *with E Flat slide.*	1500.00	1800.00
☐ **Holton,** *four valve trumpet.*	1400.00	1700.00
☐ *English, slide trumpet by Richard J. Bilton of London, foliage decoration and spiral twisting, slide operates by clockwork spring, 23", c. 1840-1850.*	750.00	975.00

TUBAS

The tuba, the largest brass in general use as an orchestral instrument, is closely related to the cornet and the old European "post horn", a horn of circular body sounded by post riders. Because of its difficulty of handling and the lung power necessary to play it properly, it has become the dread of young music students. Compared to many other instruments, it is of rather modern origin, the first tuba having been constructed in 1835. It is seldom used in solo recitals, being of limited musical flexibility, but is indispensable to the orchestration of many operatic scores.

Tubas were popularized as a marching-band instrument in the U.S. by John P. Sousa and are still widely employed as such today. The name Sousaphone is applied to a special kind of tuba designed to be worn about the player's neck. Cheap commercial versions of good-quality orchestra tubas were widely marketed in the U.S. during the World War I-1930's era. All other things being equal, tubas tend to be more expensive, whether bought new or secondhand, than other brasses. A "cheap" tuba is normally as costly as a fine-grade clarinet. This is due to its size and complication of construction, also because tubas are made in relatively limited numbers compared to the more popular instruments.

☐ **Holton BB Flat,** *four valves, lacquer bore.*	4475.00	5700.00
☐ *BB Flat, upright bell, lacquered bore.*	1700.00	2200.00
☐ *CC, upright bell, four valves, lacquer bore.*	5500.00	7000.00
☐ **Concertone,** *one water key, pearl buttons, nickel silver mouthpiece, music rack, engraved bell, 28" long, 14" bell, brass.*	210.00	260.00
☐ **Concertone,** *as above, nickel-plated.*	240.00	310.00
☐ **Concertone,** *as above, silver-plated, satin finish, gold-plated bell.*	360.00	425.00
☐ **Dupont B Flat Bass,** *highly polished brass.*	385.00	450.00
☐ **Dupont B Flat Bass,** *burnished nickel plate.*	415.00	500.00
☐ **Dupont B Flat Bass,** *triple silver plate, satin finish.*	465.00	575.00
☐ **Dupont B Flat Bass,** *triple silver plate, burnished.*	520.00	625.00
☐ **Dupont E Flat Bass,** *highly polished brass.*	415.00	500.00
☐ **Dupont E Flat Bass,** *burnished nickel plate.*	435.00	525.00

	Price Range	
☐ **Dupont E Flat Bass,** *triple silver plate, satin finish.*	490.00	575.00
☐ **Dupont E Flat Bass,** *triple silver plate, burnished.*	540.00	650.00
☐ **Dupont E Flat Contra Bass,** *highly polished brass.*	435.00	525.00
☐ **Dupont E Flat Contra Bass,** *burnished nickel plate.*	445.00	500.00
☐ **Dupont E Flat Contra Bass,** *triple silver plate, satin finish.*	560.00	700.00
☐ **Dupont E Flat Contra Bass,** *triple silver plate, burnished.*	575.00	725.00
☐ *E Flat, upright bell, lacquered bore.*	1675.00	2000.00
☐ **Marceau B Flat Bass,** *brass, polished, pre-World War I.*	220.00	300.00
☐ **Marceau B Flat Bass,** *nickel-plated, polished.*	195.00	250.00
☐ **Marceau E Flat Bass,** *brass, polished.*	230.00	275.00
☐ **Marceau E Flat Bass,** *nickel-plated, polished.*	250.00	300.00
☐ **Marceau E Flat Bass,** *brass, polished.*	275.00	350.00
☐ **Marceau E Flat Bass,** *nickel-plated, polished.*	325.00	400.00
☐ *Recording model, BB Flat, three valves.*	5000.00	7000.00
☐ *As above, four valves.*	5500.00	7500.00
☐ **Sousaphone, BB Flat,** *fiberglass white bore.*	1750.00	2200.00
☐ *BB Flat, upright bell, four valves, lacquer bore.*	2300.00	3000.00
☐ **Sousaphone BB Flat,** *brass, lacquer bore.*	2500.00	3100.00
☐ *BB Flat, upright bell, three valves.*	4000.00	5500.00
☐ **Tourville & Co. B Flat Bass,** *brass, polished.*	300.00	400.00
☐ **Tourville & Co. B Flat Bass,** *nickel-plated.*	325.00	425.00
☐ **Tourville & Co. B Flat Bass,** *silver-plated, satin finish.*	350.00	450.00
☐ **Tourville & Co. B Flat Bass,** *silver-plated, polished.*	430.00	525.00
☐ **Tourville & Co. E Flat Bass,** *brass, polished.*	410.00	475.00
☐ **Tourville & Co. E Flat Bass,** *nickel-plated.*	400.00	500.00
☐ **Tourville & Co. E Flat Bass,** *silver-plated, satin finish.*	525.00	650.00
☐ **Tourville & Co. E Flat Bass,** *silver-plated, polished.*	550.00	700.00

UKELELES

☐ *Banjo, 7" maple shell, birch neck, rosewood fingerboard, nickel-plated straining hoop and tailpiece, three pearl position dots.*	80.00	115.00
☐ *Birch body, black rings around sound hole, white celluloid binding, c. 1920's.*	35.00	50.00
☐ *Koa wood, black and white inlay around sound hole, brass pegs, violin gut strings, koa wood bridge.*	80.00	100.00
☐ *Mahogany body, brass peds, block inlay around sound hole.*	50.00	65.00

VIOLINS

In terms of their antiquity, craftsmanship and reputation for musical quality, old violins are unquestionably the premier collectors' items among instruments. It is impossible in the limited space available here to enter fully into the background of violin making or collecting, or to render extensive advice on the purchase of antique violins. A few words only for the beginner can be given, summed up with this standard but still wise advice: entrust your purchasing to an expert, and go to the experts for answers to any questions or problems you have. Antique violins are a very complex "collectible". To know them thoroughly and buy them intelligently, one must have some knowledge of (or at least an ear for) tonal quality, coupled with the experienced collector's instinct for fine workmanship.

Why an Old Violin? Why indeed? Why are antique violins so highly respected by musicians? It is natural enough that collectors, museums and others whose interest lay with historical objects prefer early violins to those manufactured recently. Buy why does a violinist prefer to play a 250-year-old Stradivarius rather than the best current models?

First, it should be understood that violins are not automatically valuable or desirable (either as antiques or instruments) merely on grounds of being old. Any skilled violinist will agree that the **majority** of antique specimens, even those dating back 200 or more years, are in no way superior to the best modern violins. Many are inferior, in fact; not because of decay or damage but simply were not first-rate when manufactured. The violin-maker geniuses of olden days were comparatively few, matched against the thousands (yes, thousands) of independent violin makers who flourished in the 17th, 18th and 19th centuries. But there **were** geniuses, here and there, who produced instruments that no modern artisan has been successful in duplicating. It is these instruments — not "old violins" as a lot — which are sought by concert musicians and which sell for high sums on the antiques market. If one wishes simply to own a product of 18th-century violin making, it can be had pretty cheaply (they turn up in antique shops that do not even specialize in instruments), but for a "Strad" or an Amati you will be asked to pay a sum of at least five and possibly six figures.

Whether or not a fine old violin, like wine, improves with age is a point on which the authorities do not agree; but it certainly loses nothing with age, and properly cared for will retain its tonal qualities for an indefinite period of time, very likely a thousand years or more.

Values. Violins are really the only antique musical instruments in which the maker's fame or reputation serves as the basis for price. Yes, it is true that a piano by Erard will be worth more than another made at approximately the same time by a less celebrated manufacturer but the difference in price is not so great. An "Art Grand" piano of 1800, well preserved, cannot help but be expensive, no matter its maker. With violins you have a situation where the best are valued 20 or 30 times higher than the run-of-mill.

The best antique violins are costly for a variety of reasons. Rarity in itself is not a prime factor. One often reads, in the comments of uninformed writers, of "rare Stradivarius". In fact the products of this extremely long-lived manufacturer (93 years) are among the most plentiful violins of their time. Somewhere between 500 and 600 original "Strads" exist, or about ⅓rd the total that left his factory. This is a very hefty supply, compared to the existent number of other costly collectors' pieces: the 1856 British Guiana one cent postage stamp, 1804 silver dollar, Gutenberg Bible. Of course, many are in museums, but several hundred remain "in circulation", that is, in the hands of musicians, collectors, dealers and (increasingly these days) investors. They are well distributed, too, thoughout many parts of the world, with U.S. owners possessing their share of Strads.

One thing to realize is that good violins were expensive from the beginning. The 1856 postage stamp mentioned above cost its original purchaser a penny. Volume one, number one of "Action Comics" — now worth many thousands — cost just a dime when issued. But violin makers, especially those of reputation, did not give away their products. Even during Stradivari's lifetime, owners of violins made by him 20 or 30 years earlier were selling them for considerable prices. They were not collectors' items or museum pieces, but musicians knew their worth and paid dearly for them.

Also, the collecting of violins as a hobby is quite old, going back at least to 1800. As soon as collectors entered the market, competing against musicians for the better examples, prices rose sharply, and continued more or less to rise ever since. As a "blue-chip" collectible, one with a good long track-record of increased valuations and demand, violins have few equals. Even during the depression of 1930-38, Strads were fetching in the neighborhood of $10,000; cheap compared to their present prices, but very strong for a buyer's market.

Some Hints for Violin Buyers. As stated earlier, trust the experts rather than your own taste or judgment unless you have more than a basic knowledge of violins. There are no "bargains" to be had, except for the occasional (now almost unheard-of) discovery of valuable violins in junk shops, etc. It is very rare for any dealer or private party who does not know the value of antique violins to come into possession of a valuable specimen, more rare for it to be offered for sale. You may, sometimes, get a slight price-break on violins by makers whose names are not known to the general public, but whose instruments might be worth more than the lowest garden-variety violins of their time. Some antiques dealers, if they do not find the name Stradivari or Amati or something else they recognize in a violin, price the item by age or appearance. This of course is very foolish, as the violins of one maker can be worth much more than of another, even if both worked at the same time, the same place, and turned out instruments similar in appearance.

Normally, it is more sensible for the collector to purchase from dealers or auction houses than from musicians. The relationship between collectors and musicians has never been the best, from the earliest days of violin collecting. It is undeniable that musicians often place a higher cash value on their instruments than they would actually be worth on the market. It has been suggested that the reason for this may be the fact that a musician thinks in terms of the profits (from performing) that an instrument earns him.

Do not buy violins on the basis of beauty of design. Some manufacturers who produced handsome cases did not take such care with the tonal quality of their instruments.

A violin must be played (not necessarily by yourself, but by a skilled musician in your presence) before purchase. No amount of visual examination can take the place of hearing the instrument being played.

Fakes and counterfeits (and "ghosts"). Faked specimens of violins by most of the celebrated makers exist and are a plague to the market. They do not often fool the experts, but unwary buyers frequently purchase them, in the belief they are "getting the best of the seller" by paying 30 percent or 40 percent less than the market price.

Fakes are produced in various fashions, by manufacturing violins in the style of old masters, by taking unimportant old violins and changing varnish, label, etc., to give the impression that they were made by noted craftsmen, and in other ways. Labels are easy to fake, for someone expert in the practice.

"Ghosts" are violins bearing labels of makers who never existed. This is not a study for the amateur. It is sometimes impossible, because of lack of evidence, to prove whether a particular maker actually existed. The fact that one violin bearing his label has been found is not proof of a "ghost", nor even reason to suspect one; there are many instances of manufacturers leaving behind just one specimen.

Care of Violins. It should be needless to point out that violins, whether antique or modern, should not be subjected to sudden changes in temperature or humidity if possible; should be kept in a proper case, made for a violin; and should be attended to by a competent restorer when in need of repair.

* * *

The following pages give approximate values for violins by manufacturer. When dealing with violins made before 1900, and especially before 1800, this is the chief point on which values are based and the only way in which values can be sensibly arrived at. **It must be understood,** however, that values vary from one specimen to another even on violins made by the same hand, depending on when it was made and other considerations. For examples the products of Stradivari dating after 1700 are considered superior to his earlier efforts.

The **place of sale** plays a part in price. Generally, fine violins (say those in the $10,000-up category) fetch higher sums in the salesrooms of New York and London than elsewhere. It should also be taken into account that **advertised prices** at which dealers are offering antique violins are not necessarily the figures at which sales are finally made.

Prices of antique violins do fluctuate. Though the overall trend is up (by about 8-10% per year in a normal non-recession year), you cannot take a list of prices from ten years ago, multiply them by a certain figure, and hope to arrive at figures that would be fair in today's market. The violins of some makers rise in price and demand faster than others. There are fads in this field, though nobody cares to admit it (classical violins are supposed to be above fads). The fact is that violin collectors are very much influenced by circumstances and opinion. When a book is published praising the violins of a given maker, his work is sure to increase pretty rapidly in price; while a sour word from an expert (or supposed expert) can damage the market for violins of any but the most outstanding names. Perhaps this should not be, especially as opinion varies from one book to another and one expert to another, but it is. Investors are constantly watchful for things of this sort.

In the following list, the arrangement is: name of maker; city of occupation (which may or may not be birthplace); years of life or activity; value. Date of birth and death are stated **when known;** otherwise the dates of those during which the maker was active.

It is **important to note** that the range of prices has nothing to do with condition, unlike the situation with price ranges in most sections of this book. Rather, it reflects the scope of values for different violins by the same maker, and for identical violins sold under different sale conditions.

	Price Range	
☐ **Abbati, Giambattista.** *Modena, 1755-1795*	7500.00	10500.00
☐ **Adani, Pancrazio.** *Modena, 1770-1830*	6500.00	8500.00
☐ **Albanesi, Sebastiano.** *Cremona, 1720-1762*	4000.00	5500.00
☐ **Albani, Paolo.** *Various cities, 1630-1695*	7000.00	10000.00
☐ **Amati, Jerome.** *Cremona, 1649-1740*	25000.00	37000.00
☐ **Amati, Nicolo.** *Cremona, 1596-1684*	55000.00	80000.00

Nicolo Amati was the teacher of Stradivari. It is not for this reason that his violins are highly prized, but on their own merit. He was indisputably the supreme violin maker of the middle part of the 17th-century.

☐ **Baldantoni, Guiseppi.** *Ancona, 1784-1873*	4000.00	5200.00

Baldantoni, a not-very-remarkable artisan, made violins of average quality for their time. He had a habit of using old labels, thus fooling purchasers into believing his violins are rather more antique than they really are.

Violin, Italian c. 1691, various woods, 23¼" x 7¾". *Courtesy: The Metropolitan Museum of Art, gift of George Gould, 1955*

	Price Range	
☐ **Balestrieri, Pietro.** *Cremona, 1725-1740*	9500.00	120000.00
Balestrieri was active at Cremona at the same time as Stradivari, the "golden age" of Italian violin making.		
☐ **Balestrieri, Tommaso.** *Mantua, 1720-1795*	25000.00	34000.00
☐ **Barbanti, Silvio.** *Corregio, mid 1800's*	3000.00	4000.00
☐ **Barnia, Fedele.** *Venice, 1745-1780*	5500.00	7500.00
☐ **Barzellini, Aegidius.** *Cremona, 1670-1720*	4750.00	6000.00
☐ **Belveglieri, Gregorio.** *Bologna, 1742-1772*	5750.00	8000.00
☐ **Benedetti, Giuseppi.** *Piacenza, early 18th-century*	3700.00	5000.00
☐ **Bergonzi, Carlo.** *Cremona, 1676-1747*	55000.00	76000.00
Bergonzi, a contemporary of Stradivari, was thought by some to be, at least if not the equal of the maestro, next to him in skill among makers of that time. His instruments have exceptional tonal quality and deserve, perhaps, to sell for even higher prices; they bring on average only half the sums of Stradivari's and are certainly better than half as good.		
☐ **Bergonzi.** *In addition to the above-named Carlo, at least a dozen members of this family were active as violin makers from the 17th to 19th centuries. Their instruments are generally of above average quality, with prices ranging from $10,000 to $50,000.*		
☐ **Bertolotti, Gasparo.** *Brescia, 1540-1609*	40000.00	55000.00
The instruments of this pioneer violin maker are well-respected and rare. Brescia was an important center of violin making for about 200 years, gaining a reputation for its violins before Cremona.		
☐ **Cabroli, Lorenzo.** *Milan, 1716-1720*	4000.00	5375.00
Cabroli's violins are not the best musically but very handsomely finished.		
☐ **Camilli, Camillus.** *Mantua, 1704-1754*	19000.00	24000.00
☐ **Casini, A.** *Modena, 1630-1710*	6500.00	8000.00
☐ **Cosetto, Guiseppi.** *Venice, 1760-1790*	5750.00	7500.00
☐ **Danieli, Giovanni.** *Padua, 1745-1785*	4000.00	5000.00
☐ **Eberle, Tommaso.** *Naples, 1760-1792*	15000.00	20000.00
☐ **Emiliani, Francesco.** *Rome, 1704-1736*	16500.00	22000.00
Rome was significant as a center for violin production only for a brief time in the 18th-century. Even then, it boasted no makers to equal those of Cremona, a much smaller town.		
☐ **Fabris, Luigi.** *Venice, 1838-1873*	4750.00	6000.00
One of the outstanding makers of the 19th-century, whose violins would undoubtedly bring higher prices if there was greater collecting enthusiasm for instruments of the mid to later 19th-century.		
☐ **Farinato, Paola.** *Venice, 1695-1725*	5000.00	6500.00
☐ **Filano, Donato.** *Naples, 1763-1783*	3600.00	4200.00
☐ **Gabrielli, Giovanni.** *Florence, 1739-1770*	15000.00	20000.00
☐ **Gagliano, Alessandro.** *Naples, 1660-1725*	37000.00	45000.00
One of the foremost Neapolitan violin makers.		
☐ **Gibertini, Antonio.** *Parma, Genoa, 1797-1866*	4150.00	5300.00
☐ **Gigli, Giulio.** *Rome, 1721-1762*	19000.00	25000.00
☐ **Jorio, Vincenzio.** *Naples, c. 1780-1849*	4500.00	6000.00

	Price Range	
☐ **Landolfi, Carlo.** *Milan, 1714-1787*	28000.00	32500.00
☐ **Lanza, Antonio.** *Brescia, 1650-1715*	6500.00	8500.00
☐ **Leb, Matthias.** *Piacenza, third quarter of the 18th-century*	9500.00	13000.00
☐ **Maggini, Giovanni.** *Brescia, 1580-1632.* ***A legendary violin maker, who gave Brescia a reputation for fine instruments nearly a century before Cremona attained one.***	60000.00	85000.00
☐ **Mantegazza, Pietro.** *Milan, 1750-1760*	9750.00	12500.00
☐ **Meloni, Antonio.** *Milan, late 17th-century*	5750.00	7750.00
☐ **Montaganna, Domenico.** *Venice, 1690-1750* ***The greatest Venetian violin maker. Also spelled Montagnana.***	67000.00	130000.00
☐ **Nadotti, Joseph (Guiseppi).** *Piacenza, 1757-1789*	10000.00	12500.00
☐ **Pazzini, Giovanni.** *Brescia, Florence, 1630-1666*	7000.00	10000.00
☐ **Pressenda, Gian.** *Various cities, 1777-1854*	24000.00	30000.00
☐ **Rinaldi, Gofredo.** *Turin, 1850-1888*	4000.00	5000.00
☐ **Rogeri, Giovanni.** *Brescia, 1650-1730*	16000.00	20000.00
☐ **Ruggeri, Francesco.** *Cremona, 1645-1700*	45000.00	60000.00
☐ **Soliani, Angelo.** *Modena, 1752-1810*	19500.00	25000.00
☐ **Stradivari, Antonio.** *Cremona, 1644-1737*	125000.00	200000.00
☐ **Tanegia, Carlo.** *Milan, 1725-1731*	4000.00	5000.00
☐ **Tassini, Bartolomeo.** *Venice, 1740-1756*	12000.00	16000.00
☐ **Valenzano, Giovanni.** *Various cities, 1771-1825*	7500.00	10000.00
☐ **Zanotti, Antonio.** *Lodi and Mantua, 1709-1745*	12000.00	15000.00

Examples of Values of Individual Specimens

The following is a brief presentation of the value ranges of antique violins based on individual specimens, rather than the ranges given above for makers.

☐ *Czech, viola by Bohuslav Lantner of Prague, back in two sections, medium grain table, orange brown varnish, back measures 15⅞", dated 1882.*	3300.00	3750.00
☐ *Czech, viola d'amore by Joannes Guidantus of Prague, back in two sections, pegbox topped by carving of female masque, back measures 15½", dated 1740.*	5300.00	6700.00
☐ *Czech, by Caspar Strnad of Prague, single piece back, broad grain table, slightly curved ribs, back measures 17", Napoleonic era.*	3200.00	3750.00
☐ *English, viola by John Betts of London, back in two sections, maple with geometrical motif, maple ribs, broad grain table, reddish maroon varnish, back measures 15½", c. 1780-1790.* ***English musicians of that era were well acquainted with the superiority of Italian violins. However the cost of Italian violins plus their importation made them very expensive on the London market and gave an incentive for local makers to compete.***	3300.00	3775.00

	Price Range	
☐ *English, by Joshua Hill of Westminster, single piece back, fine grain table, burnt orange varnish, back measures 14", dated 1750.*	2700.00	3300.00
Joshua Hill gave his address as "Angel Court, Westminster." Actually Westminster was not a city in itself but a neighborhood of London.		
☐ *English, by Norman Duke of London, back in two sections, medium grain table, honey brown varnish, back measures 14", c. 1770.*	2175.00	2800.00
☐ *English, by John Johnson of London, back in two sections, fine grain table, burnt orange varnish, back measures 14", dated 1753.*	900.00	1100.00
☐ *Flemish, by Ambroise DeComble of Tournai, back in two sections, medium grain table, reddish brown varnish, back measures 14¼", dated 1772.*	2500.00	3375.00
☐ *French, by Nicolas Chappuy of Paris, back in two sections, medium grain table, pale honey brown varnish, back measures 14", c. 1770.*	6000.00	7250.00
☐ *French, by Paul Bailly, single piece back, broad grain table, reddish brown varnish, back measures 14", c. 1860-1880.*	3200.00	3750.00
☐ *French, by Charles Jean B. Collin-Mezin of Paris, back in two sections, medium grain table, honey brown varnish, back measures 14", dated 1887.*	2600.00	3350.00
☐ *French, copy of a Stradivarius, unknown maker, back in two sections, medium grain table, reddish brown varnish, back measures 14¼", c. 1870.*	1600.00	1850.00
If today's collector thinks he has problems with reproductions, think of the musicians who have been confronted for 300 years with reproductions of Stradivarius violins. Most of these copies, like the one listed here, bore Stradivari's name, and it was by no means easy to tell the difference unless one had intimate knowledge of violins.		
☐ *French, by J. Baptiste Vuillaume of Paris, single piece back, medium grain table, burnt orange varnish, back measures 14¼", dated 1844.*	3300.00	4375.00
☐ *Italian, viola by Umberto Lanaro of Padua, single piece back, medium grain table, yellowish varnish, back measures 16⅝", dated 1967.*	2200.00	2750.00
☐ *Italian, viola by Vincenzo Cavani of Modena, single piece back, medium grain table, pale golden honey varnish, back measured 16½", dated 1958.*	3800.00	4700.00
No, a fine violin need not be an antique to command a price in this range. When sold to a musician (rather than a collector) it is the musical capability of the instrument which sets the price. A new or recent violin may well be on a par musically with one of two centuries earlier.		
☐ *Italian, viola by Enzo Barbieri of Mantua, single piece back, medium curl ribs, yellow beige varnish, back measures 16½", dated 1983.*	3000.00	3750.00

	Price Range	
☐ *Italian, viola, maker and city of origin unidentified, single piece back, broad grain table, golden brown varnish, back measures 15½", c. late 1700s.*	2250.00	2750.00
Unidentified violins were seldom issued anonymously. In most instances it is simply a case of the maker's label becoming detached and lost.		
☐ *Italian, viola by Guiseppi Borona of Bologna, back in two sections, medium grain table, burnt orange varnish, back measures 16½", dated 1896.*	4500.00	5450.00
☐ *Italian, viola by Ferandino Ferroni of Florence, back in two sections, medium grain table, orange hued varnish, back measures 16½", c. 1920-1930.*	3650.00	4650.00
☐ *Italian, viola by Loveri Fratelli of Naples, back in two sections, maple, medium grain table, burnt orange varnish, back measures 15¾", c. World War II era.*	2250.00	2800.00
☐ *Italian, viola d'amore by Leandro Bisiach of Milan, single piece arched back, cupid head, ivory inlaid tuning pegs, back measures approximately 14¼", dated 1904.*	3500.00	4500.00
☐ *Italian, by Lorenzo Ventapane of Naples, back in two sections, medium grain table, golden brown varnish, back measures 14", c. 1820.*	4300.00	5650.00
☐ *Italian, by Francesco Ruggieri of Cremona, back in two sections, medium grain table, reddish brown varnish, back measures 14", dated 1696.*	25000.00	30000.00
☐ *Italian, br Francesco Grancino of Milan, back in two sections, medium grain table, honey brown varnish, back measures 14", dated 1740.*	6200.00	7750.00
☐ *Italian, by Antonio Pedrinelli of Crespano, back in two sections, fine grain table, reddish brown varnish, back measures 14", dated 1828.*	5375.00	6750.00
☐ *Italian, by Antonio Stradivari of Cremona, back in two sections, medium grain table, burnt orange varnish, back measures 14", dated 1712.*	150000.00	180000.00
☐ *Italian, by Lorenzo and Tomasso Carcassi of Florence, back in two sections, fine grain table, honey brown varnish, back measures 14", c. 1770.*	4250.00	5675.00
☐ *Italian, by Joannes F. Pressenda of Torino, single piece back, medium grain table, burnt orange varnish, back measures 14", c. 1835-1845.*	32000.00	36000.00
☐ *Italian, by Gioffredo Cappa of Saluzzo, back in two sections, medium grain table, burnt orange varnish, back measures 14", dated 1695.*	20000.00	25000.00
☐ *Italian, by Gasparo de Salo of Brescia, back in two sections, broad grain table, burnt orange and red varnish, back measures 14", c. 1580.*	25000.00	30000.00
Specimens this early are very scarce on the market, yet they generally fall far short in price of the Cremona masterpieces of the 1700s.		
☐ *Italian, by Bernardo Calcani of Genoa, back in two sections, medium grain table, honey brown varnish, back measures 14¼", dated 1744.*	6500.00	7750.00

	Price Range	
☐ *Italian, by Gennaro Gagliano of Naples, back in two sections, medium grain table, burnt orange varnish, back measures 13⅞", mid 1700s.*	37000.00	46000.00
☐ *Italian, by Antonio and Hieronymus Amati of Cremona, single piece back, medium grain table, burnt orange varnish, back measures 13⅞", dated 1626.*	18000.00	23000.00
☐ *Italian, by Lorenzo Vangelisti, back in two sections, fine grain table, honey brown varnish, back measures 14", dated 1648.*	2600.00	3350.00
☐ *Italian, by Tommaso Carcassi of Florence, back in two sections, fine grain table, burnt orange varnish, back measures 14", dated 1749.*	9000.00	11500.00
☐ *Italian, by Enrico Rossi of Pavia, back in two sections, fine grain table, burnt orange varnish, back measures 14¼", dated 1884.*	3800.00	4700.00
☐ *Italian, by Camillus Camilla of Mantua, single piece back, fine graine table, honey brown varnish, back measures 13⅞", dated 1730.*	850.00	1075.00
☐ *Italian, by Alessandro d'Espine of Torino, single piece back, fine grain table, honey brown varnish, back measures 14", c. 1830.*	16000.00	18500.00

Semi-Antique Commercially Made Violins

Beginning in the later 19th-century, cheap violins made for sale to students, amateur musicians, and others who could not afford (or who perhaps did not appreciate) the work of masters came on the market in very large numbers. They were sold by variety houses, department stores, music shops and by mail order. Numerous different models were offered, mostly named after noted makers, but bearing little resemblance (especially in tonal quality) to the originals. They were advertised in such a fashion as to suggest that, by spending just a few dollars (some cost as little as $2.50), the purchaser could have an instrument equal or nearly equal to the antique. But they did serve a purpose; they encouraged violin practice and, undoubtedly, some of their purchasers went on to bigger and better things.

These violins, like their more illustrious predecessors, were "hand made", the difference being that they were produced in large commercial factories in a sort of assembly-line process rather than in the studio of a master craftsman who gave each instrument his personal attention.

Semi-antique violins are not usually sought by musicians, but they do have a modest collector appeal. Prices given are for specimens in good condition, but without carrying cases. They were not usually sold with cases.

☐ **Amati Model,** *curly maple back and sides, maple neck and scroll, the top was said to be made from old wood*	125.00	150.00
☐ **Amati Model,** *maple (grained) back, spruce top, ebony pegs with gold mountings, ebony fingerboard, c. early 1920's.*	285.00	375.00
☐ **Caspar DaSalo Model,** *reputedly made from choice old wood, European manufacture, sold for $14.25*	150.00	200.00
☐ **Concert Strad,** *spruce top, full-lined shell, ebony pegs.*	200.00	250.00
☐ **Conservatory Model,** *Reddish brown, with ebony fingerboard and tailpiece, original price $3.45*	100.00	125.00

	Price Range	
☐ **Duerer Model,** *these violins were bought in wholesale quantities for the American mail-order market from the Duerer factory of Germany. They were facsimiles of Stradivari.*	175.00	225.00
☐ **"Genuine" Stradivarius Model,** *European, somewhat superior to the $2.45 model, maple, spruce and ebony, this sold originally for $6.95*	125.00	175.00
☐ **Guarnerius Model,** *grained maple back and sides, spruce top, full-lined shell, first quarter of the 20th-century.*	140.00	175.00
☐ **Guarnerius Model,** *Amber varnish, ebony trimmed*	150.00	190.00
☐ **Imperial Amati,** *one of the better semi-antique violins, made by Wilhelm Duerer*	170.00	210.00
☐ **Maggini Model,** *advertised as "a direct copy of violins by that great maker". It was, in fact, a fair visual facsimile; its tone was another matter*	100.00	125.00
☐ **Paganini Model,** *made by Lowendall (Germany), amber varnish, label with signature of Louis Lowendall, original price $19.95.*	195.00	240.00
☐ **Stainer Model,** *maple (grained), name "Stainer" stamped on back, ebony fingerboard and tailpiece.*	200.00	230.00
☐ **Stainer Model,** *mediocre tone, ebony trimmings, original price $5.65*	110.00	135.00
☐ **Stainer Model,** *mediocre tone, this Stainer Model was supplied with a case*	150.00	200.00
☐ *Spruce back, full-lined shell, maple neck, ebonized fingerboard, tailpiece and pegs, c. 1920.*	125.00	160.00
☐ **Stradivarius Model,** *briar brown finish, maple back, spruce top, ebony pegs and fingerboard, c. 1920's.*	250.00	300.00
☐ **Stradivarius Model,** *"specially selected wood, beautifully varnished, reddish color, highly finished", manufactured in the tens of thousands and sold originally for $2.45*	65.00	90.00
☐ **Stradivarius Model,** *two-piece maple back, spruce top, ebonized fingerboard, post-World War I.*	160.00	200.00

Violin Outfits

Department stores and mail-order houses did a brisk business in "violin outfits" in the 1890-1910 era. The outfits consisted of (usually), a carrying case, instructional book, rosin, strings, fingerboard chart and a very cheap violin. Occasionally these outfits are still found with the original accessories. Prices are for complete outfits.

☐ **Sears Roebuck Violin Outfit #12R300,** *Stradivarius model violin, Brazil wood bow, case, set of strings, piece of rosin, instruction book, lettered fingerboard chart*	100.00	125.00
☐ **Sears Roebuck Violin Outfit #12R304,** *Maggini model violin, Brazil wood bow, case, set of strings, piece of rosin, instruction book, fingerboard chart*	140.00	175.00
☐ **Sears Roebuck Violin Outfit #12R308,** *Stradivarius model violin (better grade), Brazil wood bow, case made of wood, strings, rosin, instruction book, fingerboard chart, tuning pipe*	150.00	200.00

	Price Range	
☐ **Sears Roebuck Violin Outfit #12R316,** *Stradivarius violin, "Vuillaume" model bow, wood case, rosin, instruction book (a better one than provided with the above sets), strings, fingerboard chart, tuning pipes, book of "choice violin music", sold originally for $15*	250.00	325.00
☐ **Sears Roebuck Violin Outfit #12R318,** *Lowendall violin, "Tourte" bow, wood case, rosin, instruction book, strings, chin rest, fingerboard chart, tuning pipes, violin mute, book of violin music*	250.00	325.00

XYLOPHONES

The modern xylophone evolved slowly during a period of many centuries from an instrument which, though played in essentially the same fashion, bore only slight resemblance to its present physical state. It won favor only after a very lengthy trial during which time its enthusiasts had no success convincing professional musicians, composers or critics of its musical possibilities. Perhaps the simplicity of its appearance counts against it as it has all the look of a plaything for children to bang on. It is, in fact, while perhaps not a sophisticated apparatus, an instrument which can produce very effective and pleasing music in the hands of a skill performer. Because of its close similarity to primitive and native instruments of various parts of the world, it can be adapted to music of many diverse kinds and is equally at home in a classical as a jazz orchestra.

Xylophones are of Asian origin and have been played there, in one form or another, since days of vast antiquity. The earliest European or western xylophones date from the late 15th- or beginning of the 16-th century. At this time it was merely a curiosity in the West and retained that status for quite a long while. Records of xylophone makers (or players, or owners) during the 16th-, 17th- and even the 18th-century, are scant and the likelihood is that few specimens were produced. It was in the class of a gypsy instrument during that time, played by persons who learned it as children but were otherwise musically uneducated. During the 19th-century its fortunes improved considerably. Felix Mendelssohn witnessed the concert of a xylophonist in 1836 and was struck with the instrument's capabilities and the performer's virtuosity (the musician was a Russian named Gusikov). He wrote favorably of it and this brought it to attention. By the third quarter of the 19th-century it was firmly entrenched as a concert instrument and was being used in orchestras — something that would not have been believed a hundred years earlier. Around 1900 it was riding a super crest of popularity, with xylophones in the tens of thousands being manufactured annually by commercial factories and sold to the public as well as to musicians. Since then its appeal has waned somewhat — probably because of the introduction of electronic instruments, which have turned attention away from many standard nonelectric instruments.

☐ *American, 15 maple bars, c. 1900*	90.00	115.00
☐ *American, 25 maple bars, c. 1900*	275.00	335.00
☐ *Eastern European, c. 1830*	225.00	300.00
☐ *German, mid 1800's*	275.00	375.00
☐ *German, c. 1870*	230.00	295.00

	Price Range	
☐ *Italian, c. 1810.*	300.00	395.00
☐ *Italian, mid 19th-century.*	240.00	325.00
☐ *Polish, late 19th-century.*	175.00	225.00

ZITHERS

The Egyptians, Greeks and other early civilizations had zithers among their ample storehouses of musical instruments — a supply which, even matched against the variety available in today's market, was formidable indeed. Two types of zithers came from the ancient world — the plucked and struck varieties. Both spread out over the European continent in the Middle Ages and were firmly established in most countries of the west by 1500. Since then the zither's popularity has risen and fallen in stages but it has never, despite the many improvements made upon it in the way of more advanced instruments of a similar kind, been exterminated nor is it ever likely to be. Zithers were known by different terminology in different areas of Europe and generally each nation or region had its favorite design. Plucked zithers were traditionally, at least in early times, the general choice in southern Europe. Cheap zithers of various sizes, often stunted, poured upon the American market in the late 19th-century and continued to be sold in remarkable numbers well into the 20th. It was considered (not wisely) an instrument that anyone, with or without musical aptitude, could learn to play as well as a professional. This resulted in many zithers landing in the hands of not-very-musically-inclined children, who played them to the utter distraction of everyone within earshot. But anyone who has heard a zither played well could hardly fail to agree that it is a worthy instrument.

☐ *Autoharp, 20 strings, three bars, pre-World War I.*	25.00	32.00
☐ *Autoharp, 23 strings, five bars.*	37.00	45.00
☐ *Autoharp, 32 strings, eight bars.*	50.00	65.00
☐ *Autoharp, 37 strings, 12 bars.*	60.00	75.00
☐ *Autoharp, six bars, 16 chords, pine sounding board, edges inlaid with white marble, bars and supporters enameled in black, celluloid finger buttons.*	70.00	90.00
☐ **Columbia,** *19½", maple, c. 1900.*	135.00	175.00
☐ **Columbia,** *same as above but imitation ebony, 31 strings, c. 1900.*	175.00	225.00
☐ **Columbia,** *14"x20", 38 strings, c. 1900.*	190.00	235.00
☐ **Columbia,** *16"x21½", 47 strings, c. 1900.*	265.00	350.00
☐ **Deweylin Harp,** *three instruments in one, 31 strings, four chords, c. 1900.*	165.00	210.00
The Deweylin Harp never achieved much popularity. Its interest today is basically as a curiosity.		
☐ *Guitar, 31 strings, four chords, c. 1905-1910.*	22.00	30.00
☐ *Guitar, 31 strings, four chords, maple body, ebonized, sound hole ornamented.*	35.00	45.00
☐ *Guitar, 41 strings, five chords.*	40.00	55.00

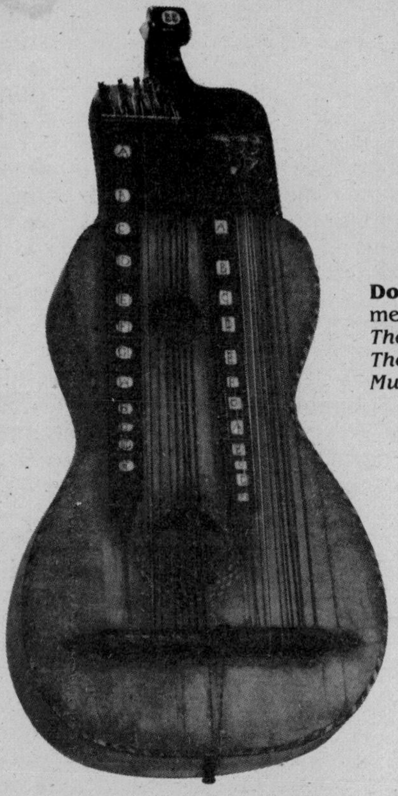

Double Zither, German, wood, metal, bone. *Courtesy: The Metropolitan Museum of Art, The Crosby Brown Collection of Musical Instruments, 1889*

	Price Range	
☐ *Guitar, 51 strings, six chords.*	55.00	70.00
☐ *Harp, 21 melody strings, five groups of chords, size 25"x23".*	45.00	65.00
☐ **Marx Harp Piano,** *23 strings, seven hammers, 11"x20".*	35.00	45.00

MUSIC RACKS

Racks or holders are designed to hold music scores so they can be referred to by the musician. They are not to be confused with music **stands,** which are mounted generally on tripod legs and rest upon the floor. Racks are normally attached to the instrument itself or, in cases where this is not practical, to the musician's arm or other part of his body. Music racks had their beginnings with marching bands which could not, for obvious reasons, employ stands. Since then they have also been used by jazz, swing and various orchestral musicians.

The following racks are all of American manufacture and date from 1890 to the early 1900's. They are quite easy to find, not only in music shops but wherever antiques are sold.

	Price Range	
☐ *Brass, square wire shank, three separate prongs, for band instruments.*	15.00	20.00
☐ *Brass, three separate prongs, with plate for bass drums.*	20.00	25.00
☐ *Brass, three separate prongs, with plate for snare drums.*	25.00	33.00
☐ *Brass, three separate prongs, with arm-strap (for use when playing instruments to which rack cannot be mounted).*	22.00	30.00
☐ *Brass, similar to above but with long shank for trombones.*	25.00	35.00
☐ *Nickel-plated, adjustable ring, for clarinets.*	20.00	25.00
☐ *Nickel-plated, three separate prongs, for trombones.*	30.00	40.00
☐ *Nickel-plated, square wire shank, three separate prongs, for band instruments.*	20.00	25.00

MUSIC STANDS

Music stands are one of the few items in this book collected by persons with no special interest in music; they appeal to antique lovers because of their designing, which often is very attractive, their age and other factors. Over the years, they have been fashioned of almost every conceivable variety of wood, as well as other materials, and have been styled to suit various decors. The handsomest ones likely to be encountered by the average collector are of Victorian origin. These, while factory products, are still held in high regard. Earlier examples tend to be costly. Places of origin of early music stands are often difficult to judge with accuracy.

It should be pointed out to buyers that so-called "classic" designs of early periods were frequently imitated at later dates (many Victorian stands are in Louis XIV to Louis XVI style), often very convincingly, and if one is not well versed in antiques, it is quite easy to be confused. Music stands in styles of 100-200 years ago are still in fact being produced, mainly in France and Italy.

Restorations and repairs. As with the purchase of any antiques, potential buyers should take care to note whether restorations or repairs have been made and, if so, whether this is reflected in the price. Minor repairs have little effect on value, especially in a very rare or elegant stand. But occasionally examples will be found in which the neck, feet or other components are modern replacements, and in this instance the value is considerably reduced. In the cases of painted, gessoed or gilded stands, the paint or other surface coating should be original or at least closely contemporary with the date of manufacture. A modern refinishing job ruins, or at the least seriously reduces, the desirability of a fine old specimen.

☐ *English, rosewood with mahogany legs, pearl inlaying along music rest, height 38½", early 19th-century.*	800.00	1075.00
☐ *French, mid-height, bronze, tapered neck, last quarter of the 18th-century.*	3000.00	4200.00
☐ *Italian, carved walnut, finished with gesso and gilt (peeling), the legs in the form of cherubs, one with head missing, late 16th/early 17th-century.*	3200.00	4500.00
☐ *Italian, maple with bronze and marble inset base, height 3'11½", acanthus leaf carving with repetitive scrollwork, mid 17th-century.*	2850.00	3975.00
☐ *Umbrella pattern, made of iron, japanned, folds up, American, c. 1890's.*	9.00	12.00
☐ *Same as above, nickel-plated.*	15.00	20.00

ACCESSORIES

In the early days of musical instruments (European Renaissance/Baroque eras) it was usually necessary, when one needed a certain attachment or accessory, to have it custom manufactured. When large-scale commercialization of instruments began, factories produced accessories to be sold separately. By the mid-1800's it was possible to buy ready-made accessories of all types for every kind of instrument, just as today.

While old accessories are not necessarily collectors' items in themselves (though they could possibly be), they are frequently sought by owners of antique instruments in cases where replacements or alterations must be made.

BANJO

	Price Range	
☐ *Bag, canvas, fleece-lined, for 10-13" banjo*	11.00	14.00
☐ *Bag, green cloth, buttoned, for 10-13" banjo.*	8.00	11.00
☐ *Bracket, globe pattern, brass, polished, bolt and nut.*	7.00	9.00
☐ *As above, nickel-plated*	9.00	12.00
☐ *Bracket, hexagon pattern, brass, turned and polished, with bolt and nut.*	9.00	12.00
☐ *As above, nickel-plated*	11.00	14.00
☐ *Bracket, leaf pattern, brass, cast with bolt and nut, c. 1890-1900.*	9.00	12.00
☐ *As above, nickel-plated, c. 1890-1900.*	12.00	15.00
☐ *Bridge, celluloid, "professional model", imitation tortoise shell.*	6.00	8.00
☐ *Bridge, ebony, American made.*	5.00	7.00
☐ *Bridge, maple, American made, c. late 1800's/early 1900's.*	5.00	7.00
☐ *Case, brown canvas, edges leather-bound, flannel-lined.*	14.00	19.00
☐ *Case, russet leather, embossed, flannel-lined, with strap and buckle, for 10 or 11" instrument, c. 1900.*	28.00	35.00
☐ *As above, for 12-13" instrument*	30.00	40.00
☐ *Case, wood, black varnished, flannel-lined, lock and hooks, for 11" banjo, late 1800's.*	18.00	24.00
☐ *Head, nickel-plated, engraved sides, bone buttons, good quality, c. 1895.*	9.00	12.00
☐ *Peg, celluloid, imitation amber, Greek cross design.*	5.00	7.00
☐ *Peg, celluloid, imitation ebony, nickel-mounted, "Champion" patent.*	5.00	7.00
☐ *As above, white, nickel-mounted.*	5.00	7.00
☐ *Peg, ebony, hollow shape, pearl dot in each end.*	3.00	5.00
☐ *Peg, imitation ebony, hollow shape, pearl dot on handle, American made.*	2.50	4.00
☐ *As above, w th side pegs.*	2.50	4.00
☐ *Peg, same as above but side peg.*	3.00	5.00
☐ *Tailpiece, brass, nickel-plated.*	5.00	7.00
☐ *Tailpiece, celluloid, imitation ivory, solid heel piece.*	5.00	7.00
☐ *Tailpiece, ebony, c. late 1800's.*	3.00	5.00
☐ *Tailpiece, walrus ivory, engraved, "Artist model".*	10.00	13.00
☐ *Thimble, made of German silver, c. 1890's.*	3.00	5.00
☐ *Wrench, brass, key shape, nickel-plated.*	5.00	7.00
☐ *Wrench, cast brass, ground and lacquered, for ¼" or 5/16" nut.*	7.00	10.00

GUITAR	Price Range	
☐ Bag, cloth, with buttons, late 19-century.	9.00	12.00
☐ Bag, canvas, fleece-lined.	11.00	14.00
☐ Bridge, celluloid, imitation amber.	6.00	8.00
☐ Bridge, ebony, American made, late 1800's.	6.00	8.00
☐ Bridge, ebony, pearl inlaying, American made, c. 1895.	12.00	14.00
☐ Bridge, pearl inlaid at each end, c. 1890-1900.	8.00	11.00
☐ Bridge-pin, celluloid, imitation amber.	2.50	4.00
☐ Bridge-pin, celluloid, imitation tortoise shell.	2.50	4.00
☐ Bridge-pin, ebony, polished pearl inlaying.	4.00	6.00
☐ Bridge-pin, ivory, polished pearl inlaying, c. 1895.	6.00	8.00
☐ Bridge-pin, maple, black finish, polished head, c. 1890-1900.	2.50	4.00
☐ Capo d'Astro, brass, nickel-plated, rubber covered clamps, vest pocket model.	6.00	8.00
☐ Capo d'Astro, brass, lacquered, cork lined clamps.	6.00	8.00
☐ As above, nickel-plated.	8.00	11.00
☐ Capo d'Astro, nickel-plated, spring action, felt covered clamps.	8.00	11.00
☐ As above but made of aluminim, c. 1895.	9.00	12.00
☐ Case, American made, wood, half-lined, with lock, handle and hooks, c. 1890's.	25.00	32.00
☐ Case, brown canvas, leather bound edges, open end, with strap, buckle and handle, c. 1890-1900.	14.00	18.00
☐ Same as above, larger size (for concert model guitar).	20.00	25.00
☐ Case, hand-sewn leather, embossed, sold by Sears Roebuck in c. 1890's.	42.00	55.00
☐ As above, concert size.	55.00	70.00
☐ End-pin, ebony, polished head, American made, late 19th-century.	3.50	5.00
☐ End-pin, ebony, pearl dot inlaid.	5.00	8.00
☐ Fingerboard, ebony, plain (without frets), American, c. 1895.	12.00	17.00
☐ Fingerboard, ebony, with frets, c. 1895.	14.00	19.00
☐ Fret, brass, c. 1895.	2.50	4.00
☐ Patent head, brass, engraving on sides, bone buttons, c. 1895.	14.00	19.00
☐ Patent head, nickel-plated, engraved, bone buttons.	16.00	20.00
☐ Patent head, polished and lacquered, while celluloid buttons.	22.00	25.00
☐ Tailpiece, celluloid, imitation ivory, c. 1890's.	8.00	11.00
☐ Tailpiece, nickel-plated brass.	10.00	14.00

MANDOLIN		
☐ Bag, canvas, fleece-lined, c. 1890's.	14.00	18.00
☐ Bag, green cloth, buttons, American made.	15.00	17.00
☐ Bridge, ebony, ivory inlaid.	7.00	10.00
☐ Bridge, ebony, plain finish.	5.00	8.00
☐ Case, black leather, hand-sewn, flannel-lined, leather carrying strap.	55.00	70.00
☐ Case, brown canvas, leather bound edges, flannel-lined, sold by Sears Roebuck in c. 1890's.	24.00	33.00
NOTE: Prices on cases that are defective in any respect, such as having the carry-strap missing, are considerably lower. It is to be expected, however, that specimens of 75-100 years age will show moderate wear.		
☐ Head, brass, nickel-plated, white celluloid buttons.	20.00	25.00
☐ Head, German-silver, full plate style, engraved.	27.00	35.00

	Price Range	
☐ *Pick, gutta-percha, oval shape.*	3.50	4.50
☐ *Pick, similar to above but large size.*	3.50	4.50
☐ *Pick, tortoise shell, oval shape, c. 1895.*	3.50	4.50
☐ *Pick, tortoise shell, triangular shape, c. 1890-1900.*	3.50	4.50
☐ *Tailpiece, brass, nickel-plated, c. 1890's.*	8.00	11.00

VIOLIN

☐ *Becker's chin rest, ebonite and nickel, pre-1900.*	22.00	28.00
☐ *Bridge, "Panpi" model, maple, three scrolls, c. 1895.*	5.00	8.00
☐ *Bridge, "Vuillaum" model, maple, three scrolls.*	8.00	11.00
☐ *Case, papier-mache, "French" shape, lines with baize, nickeled lock.*	40.00	50.00
☐ *Case, varnished black wood, "exposition" shape, flannel-lined, with nickeled lock, handle and spring clasps, American, c. 1890's.*	42.00	53.00
☐ *Case, varnished wood, flannel-lined, nickel-plated lock, hook clasps.*	37.00	45.00
☐ *Case, varnished wood, half-lined with flannel, turn of the century.*	28.00	35.00
☐ *Case, varnished wood, half-lined with flannel, without lock.*	26.00	30.00
☐ *Case, wood covered in leather, velvet-lined, leather handles, plated lock.*	70.00	90.00
☐ *Chin rest, ebony, nickel-plated double screw fastenings.*	12.00	16.00
☐ *Chin rest, gutta-percha, nickel-lated mountings.*	20.00	25.00
☐ *Chin rest, velvet covered, German-silver double screw fastening.*	20.00	25.00
☐ *Fingerboard, ebony, c. 1890's.*	8.00	11.00
☐ *Fingerboard, maple, imitation ebony finish.*	6.00	8.00
☐ *Head, nickel-plated, engraved sides, bone buttons.*	14.00	18.00
☐ *Head, solid brass, engraved on sides, bone buttons, c. 1895.*	9.00	12.00
☐ *Mute, ebony, c. 1890-1900.*	5.00	8.00
☐ *Mute, German-silver, c. late 1800's.*	5.00	8.00
☐ *Mute, German-silver, with tuning pipe.*	9.00	12.00
☐ *Screw, ebony and German-silver button, octagon shape, inlaying in end.*	5.00	7.00
☐ *Tailpiece, celluloid, imitation amber, decorated in relief.*	16.00	20.00
☐ *Tailpiece, ebony, inlaid with colored pearl flower and two leaves.*	14.00	18.00
☐ *Tailpiece, imitation ebony finish, inlaid with fancy colored pearl flowers and leaves.*	6.00	8.00
☐ *Tailpiece, maple, black stained, plain pearl inlaying.*	3.00	4.00
☐ *Tailpiece, solid ebony, c. 1890-1900.*	6.00	8.00

ZITHER

☐ *Brush, bone handle, 19th-century.*	6.00	8.00
☐ *Case, wood, black varnish, flannel-lined, with lock.*	20.00	25.00
☐ *Duster, bone handle, American made, late 19th-century.*	8.00	11.00
☐ *Head, nickel-plated, engraved.*	20.00	25.00
☐ *Ring, made of German silver.*	1.00	3.00
☐ *Ring, made of horn.*	2.50	4.00
☐ *Ring, nickel-plated steel.*	2.50	4.00
☐ *Tunning hammer, black handle, c. 1890's.*	2.50	4.00
☐ *Tunning hammer, ivory handle, early 1900's.*	7.00	10.00

The quantity of old zither accessories found on the market bears testimony to the popularlity this instrument once enjoyed.

BOOKS AND SHEET MUSIC

BOOKS ON MUSIC

Music literature is a huge and varied subject for the collector, ranging from choir books of the middle ages to books of psalms published in colonial America to a vast array of semi-modern and modern works on every field of music. In this section of "Books on Music", we have included general reference titles as well as a number of rare works that fetch rather high prices.

COLLECTING MUSIC LITERATURE

Generally, the approach is to specialize in some way or other, either by author, date, place of origin or (more usually) the specific field of music to which the book relates. The possibilities are limitless, the only restriction being those imposed by the collector's budget. Even a relatively obscure topic, such as the history of a given instrument, could be the basis for a library of several hundred titles, with rarities included.

The prime sources for rare and out-of-print musicana are specialist dealers. These are antiquarian booksellers, some with shops and some who deal out of their homes (usually through postal box addresses), who normally offer not only books but music memorabilia, posters, sometimes autographs and other matérial. Desirable items are also likely to be found on the shelves of general "used" bookshops, at prices lower than the specialists charge. Music books also turn up in antiques shops, at auctions, garage sales and the like. Collectors make a practice of following the auction schedules and attending sales in which an array of musical instruments are offered, on the chance that anyone who had owned instruments might also have possessed a reference library of musical literature. Usually the auction lists are not very thorough in giving titles or other information, so a trip to the sale (or the presale exhibition) is mandatory to really discover what is being offered.

VALUES

The cash value of out-of-print musical literature is set on the same basis as that of other collector's items: supply and demand. Age alone is not the determining factor, though any book strictly on music (as opposed to an encyclopedia with just a section on the subject) that is over 100 years old will have some collector value. **Song** books tend not to be as valuable as works on instruments, music history, opera librettos and the like. This is largely because early song books carried only lyrics without musical notations; therefore, they are considered by many collectors, to be in the category of poem books. Even where noted authors are involved, the value can be rather low.

Any title may be scarce or even rare without having more than a minimal value, if not in demand. On the other hand, a much-sought work will carry a high price even if in more or less plentiful supply. The more desirable early histories of music, such as Hawkins' **A General History of the Science and Practice of Music** (London, 1776), five volumes, sells in the neighborhood of $750 for a decently-preserved set, yet is far from a "hard to get" item. Most specialist dealers sell several copies of Hawkins every year, but the price is high because of the work's reputation and its appeal to buyers.

CHOIR BOOKS

We have not listed choir books within the main listings because, as manuscripts, no two are quite alike and it is, therefore, impossible to arrive at standard values. A few words on the subject here might not, however, be out of place.

There are few collectors of choir books or hymnals; that is, few persons who make a specialty of collecting them to the exclusion of other musical literature, but a number of collectors, especially those whose interests run to the history of music, choose to purchase one or two specimens of these impressive volumes just as examples of their species. It could almost be said that no library of music history is complete without at least one good choir book, regardless its age or origin or even (if you can't afford a really prime specimen) condition. Failing this, individual leaves can be easily had, at prices ranging from $3 upwards, which make excellent decorations when matted and framed. These can be bought from dealers in prints as well as from specialists in musical literature, as well as, sometimes, general dealers in rare books.

Choir books were those large, usually ponderously large, collections of chants or other works sung at church service. Beginning collectors often wonder about their huge sizes; why was it necessary to design them so large? For the simple reason that the entire choir, which might have comprised 50 or more voices, all read from the same book, which stood open on a lecturn across the choir stall. Some members of the choir might be 20 or 30 feet from the book and could not easily read it if the writing were small. Thus you have leaves of double folio or elephant folio size — sometimes even larger (the Escorial in Spain has choir books five feet high). Each letter is usually about the size of an egg. There are, however, smaller choir books to be found, often referred to as antiphonals.

The range in price of early choir books is just as varied as their size and composition. Contrary to the belief of some beginners, they are not uniformly expensive. Many can be had at rather reasonable prices, in light of their age, history, and workmanship. A good price break can be had, too, on specimens that are handsome and essentially complete but have several leaves lacking and/or a defective binding.

Manuscript choir books were almost always (and, in the case of specimens dating to the 16th-century and earlier, without exception) written on vellum rather than paper, not because paper was unobtainable but vellum afforded more durability. Choir books received a lot of heavy handling. For this reason, even though vellum was used and stout sturdy bindings applied, it is not to be expected that their present-day condition be as fresh and blemish-free as a book designed for occasional use.

The average choir book consisted of no more than 100 leaves, often much fewer, but this was sufficient, with the thickness of vellum as opposed to paper, to make a book of considerable width. Their bindings were sometimes elegant and highly decorated, but more often designed to withstand wear and tear rather than for visual attractiveness. The usual binding consisted first of wooden planks or boards of ¼- to ½-inch thickness, oak being the preferred variety. These were sanded, then covered over in a good strong leather, such as calf or pigskin; for a volume of major proportions, a whole animal hide was used. Then, various metal attachments would be added:

clasps (two for smaller volumes, four for larger — two at the fore-edge and one each at top and bottom) to keep the volume tightly shut while not in use and prevent the vellum from curling or becoming unduly soiled; brass or iron cornerpieces to keep the corners from bruising; centerpieces so the leather at the sides of the binding would not be scratched or torn; and, sometimes, a chain and staple to keep the book attached to its stand and reduce the risk of theft (this being, of course, a problem as choir books, like most manuscript volumes, had a rather high value and were subject to theft). It is not often, however, that copies are discovered with all these accessories still intact, nor does it detract very much from their value when any are missing.

Most choir books found on the antiquarian market (as opposed to those in European national libraries or churches) are not as early as might be believed. The popular concept is that choir books, being manuscripts, antedate the invention of printing in c. 1450 A.D. Some of them, of course, do but these are rarely offered for sale and, when found, are in the upper price bracket ($1,000 and upwards, with prices of $50,000 not unusual for brilliantly decorated examples). Those on the market are basically of Spanish or Italian origin and date from the 16th, 17th, and 18th-centuries. It may seem odd that manuscript choir books were still in production as late as the 1700's, with printing 300 years old by then, but this was done simply because the scribe, using a brush, could draw letters much larger than a printer could print with the equipment then available.

PRICES OF CHOIR BOOKS

The values hinge on size, age, place of origin (where known, which it frequently is not; the language is not a clue, this being always in Latin), decoration and various other considerations. A specimen of Spanish origin, dating from 1650-1750, measuring 14x20 inches and containing 75 leaves, would have a retail value of from $500 to $750. With a really handsome binding, and if the volume could be reasonably shown to be complete (it is not always easy to prove a choir book either complete or incomplete), the figure might be pushed up to $1,000. On the other hand, this same volume, with somewhat smaller measurements, and containing 50 instead of 75 leaves, would fall in the $250-$400 territory. The leaf count is important because many choir books, especially those which are incomplete or have a damaged binding, **are bought by dealers for the purpose of breaking them up and selling the leaves individually.** As leaves will retail usually for $3-$5, a dealer will seldom pay more than $2 per leaf for a choir book unless the leaves are exceptionally large or very well decorated.

Choir books of English origin are not frequently found on the market. They are worth more than continental specimens, all other things being equal. Many English churches apparently imported their service books from abroad.

BUYING TIPS FOR OUT-OF-PRINT AND RARE MUSICAL LITERATURE

First of all, know what you're buying! A set of three volumes worth $100 may be worth only $30 if a volume is missing. A book normally valued at $75 could bring just $20 or even less if several text or illustration pages are lacking. A $200 first edition might be worth $50 or $20 or less in a second or later edition. You must be aware of these things to buy intelligently, and you must know enough of the physical anatomy of books, especially old ones, to determine their condition. Normally, when buying from specialist dealers through catalogues or price listings, a full description will be provided for each item, giving the condition, etc., and the price will be adjusted accordingly. This is not the case when making purchases from the shelves of bookshops, however. It is uncommon for a bookseller to make a notation of defects in his books, and in fact he may be unaware of defects until brought to his attention by a customer. You cannot just assume that because a volume is being offered by a reputable bookseller, it must be complete and in good condition. Every bookshop has among its stock a certain number of volumes that are defective in some way or other; this is not considered a black blot on the shop, because these books, even while defective, do have **some** value and are desirable to persons who cannot afford better.

When inspecting an old book, it will (or should) be obvious whether the binding is well or poorly preserved. Volumes bound in calf — those dating from the early 19th-century and before — will sometimes show peeling or, if dry, flaking of leather at the sides or spine. The spine labels, if any, may be missing. Check the hinges — the juncture at which the covers meet the spine — for possible wear. They may be weak or even completely broken, in which case the cover(s) will be detached or on the verge of becoming detached. It is not too expensive a task for a professional binder to reattach the covers, but on a book worth only $10 or $15 this is hardly worthwhile. Are the blank endleaves present? Very often on old books they are not. Their lack is not a matter of great concern, certainly not so important as if text leaves are missing, but the value may be brought down by 10 percent or so. Inspect the title page. Are corners torn away? Is it wrinkled or otherwise damaged? Moreover, is it present at all? Nearly all books published from the mid 16th-century onward have a title page. When no title page is present, it can be assumed that this is missing, and that the volume is worth **considerably less** than if intact. A missing title page will normally result in a price reduction of at least 30 percent and up to 50 percent. In a cheap book it will entirely destroy the value. A $5 book without title page is usually placed in the bookseller's "grab-'em" tray at 25¢ or 35¢ each.

Determining whether **plates of illustration are lacking,** in illustrated books, can be difficult if no list of plates is provided. This can be accomplished easily if the plates are numbered in series; all you need do is check the numbers to see if they run consecutively. It will **not** tell you, however, if additional plates should be present **after** those found in the book. A clue can possibly be found by carefully running through the text for references to plates. The matter of missing plates is of no small consequence in early books, especially those with colored or steel engraved plates, as the original owners quite often subjected these books to cutting and framing the plates.

VALUES OF SPECIAL COPIES

Just as defective copies are worth less than the normal prices, there are many situations in which a book, by virtue of a fine binding or otherwise, carries a value higher than is normal for that particular edition. In the case of books dating from the era of cloth bindings (the third quarter of the 19th-century to today), most copies that exist will be in similar bindings — those applied by the publisher — except those in which the binding became so damaged that a rebinding was necessary. However, early books which did not carry cloth bindings, may be found in a variety of coverings. It was usual in the pre-cloth era to issue books in a very cheap unsubstantial kind of binding, such as strawboards backed with leather or merely paper, so that the book would be inexpensive enough to market to a wide audience. Some buyers chose to leave them "as they came", but others preferred to ship them off to a bindery to be encased in leather, half-leather, or whatever appealed to them. The fashion in some countries, at certain times, was for the owners of fine libraries to have their initials or heraldic shield appear in gold gilt on the upper cover of each volume. Other book collectors had very elaborate gold or silver tooling applied to the covers and spines of their books. Some had the covers set with ivory miniatures, etc. These special copies, when found, are naturally in a different category than ordinary specimens and generally command much higher prices. A really exquisite binding on a $50 book can result in a $200 or $300 price — more for binding than contents. Old music books are sometimes found with gilt stampings of instruments on the covers, or figures of nymphs playing harps. These are desirable copies. It is impossible to set price guidelines because every "deluxe" binding is different than others and must be appraised in light of the age, workmanship, originality, and the quality of leather. Full morocco is the most respected and in most circumstances most valuable of binding leathers. Books bound in full morocco will normally carry the title and author in gilt on labels attached to the spine, and the spine will be "compartmented", that is, divided up into sections via raised bands.

TERMINOLOGY

The terms used in book collecting are far more numerous to attempt listing here in anything approaching completeness, but we herewith present a brief sampling of some of the more oft-encountered words and expressions. (For further information, consult "The Official Guide to Old Books", published by The House of Collectibles.)

ANONYMOUS. This can mean either of two things, that the author is not named in the book but his identity is known, or the author is unnamed and unknown. When the former is the case, a catalogue will state "ANONYMOUS (Bartolin, Edward)", or simply "(BARTOLIN, Edward)". Whenever anything appears in brackets in a bookseller's catalogue, this means the information is deduced rather than stated in the book. The same is true of a date. "(1769)" means the work is known to have been published then, but is undated. If the cataloguer is simply making an estimate, it appears as "(c. 1769)" or "(1769 ?)". The authorship of anonymous books is sometimes guessed at, too.

ASSOCIATION COPY. A book that once belonged to someone noteworthy, often a relative or close associate of the author, and bears evidence of having done so. The most valuable association copies are those which belonged to the author and carry his corrections or other notations.

BINDER'S CLOTH. A cloth binding that was not applied by the publisher when the book was issued, but by a bindery at a later date. It is always worth less than a copy in the publisher's binding. Nor can you tell, from a catalogue description which merely states "binder's cloth", whether the volume was bound recently or ages ago.

BOARDS. This can mean wooden boards, stiff paper, strawboards, or boards covered in linen, buckram, canvas, etc. Generally, though, when a book is said to be bound in boards, paper boards — either bare or covered in thin paper — can be expected. Boarded books date mostly from 1750-1820, the era just before cloth bindings.

CALF. A leather used in binding. The natural color is light tan to medium brown. It is rarely dyed. Calf is a good-quality leather, durable if properly cared for, but not as good-looking (in traditional opinion) as morocco.

CHEAP COPY. A defective book, which the bookseller is offering at a discount and wants to be sure everybody realizes it.

COLLATED PERFECT. The volume has been inspected page by page and come through with flying colors — everything supposed to be present is. However, the book could still be stained, mutilated, foxed or otherwise undesirable.

CONTEMPORARY BINDING. Not the original binding probably, but one applied before the book got very old. When used on books printed before 1700, it can be taken to mean no more than 25 years after publication. But, of course, it represents only an estimate, as the exact dating of bindings, in the absense of real evidence, is impossible.

CROPPED. Margins cut so close by the binder that text or illustrations are shaved. This occurs mostly in old books that have been rebound several times.

CUTS. Illustrations of any kind, including photographic.

DECKLE EDGES. Rough page-ends, untrimmed.

DISBOUND. This does not mean a volume lacking its binding, but rather an unbound pamphlet or other brief work that once was part of a larger one. Values are hard to fix.

DUST JACKET (or WRAPPER). Experiments with dust jackets began in the early 1800's but they did not become common until around 1910. Even then, many volumes were without them. Their importance is greater with first editions of novels than with music books or most non-fiction.

FIRST EDITION. Ideally, the first appearance of that book. But it isn't always so simple. When a book has been published in England and America in the same year, it can be difficult or impossible to tell which came first. Also, there are many instances of writings serialized in newspapers or periodicals before appearing in book form. The term "first collected edition" refers to matter published in dribs and dribbles over the years, in various periodicals or even other books, before collected into a book of its own.

FOLIO. A book of large size, ranging from about 12 inches up. A royal folio stands about 18 inches, an atlas folio 24, an elephant folio 30, a double elephant folio 36.

FOXED. Brownish spots on old (sometimes not so old) paper are known as foxing. It's caused by lice, which have a particular craving for moist paper. When light it can be overlooked, but heavy foxing is a defect in most books, unless printed on paper of such poor grade that heavy foxing was inevitable. It tends to be strongest on endleaves and plates of illustrations.

HALF MOROCCO (or HALF CALF, VELLUM, etc.). A binding in which the spine and an inch or two of the sides are leather, the remainder of the covers buckram or plain boards. In a quarter binding only the spine is leather, and in a three-quarter binding the corners are also leather.

HALF TITLE. The page before the actual title page, which states the book's title but nothing else. Sometimes the reverse side of the half title carries the dedication. The lack of a half title, if the book was published with one, is a serious defect (deduct about 20 percent from the value).

IMPERFECT. A defective book, which could be missing just one leaf or a hundred (and the binding, too).

LARGE-PAPER COPY. Large-paper copies had their origins in the 18th-century, as a way of satisfying collectors and ordinary readers. When issuing a book of some importance, publishers were torn between putting out a really deluxe edition or keeping the price low enough to attract a wide circle of buyers. This was solved by issuing a part of the edition on small paper in a cheap binding, and a limited number on large paper in a better binding. Usually the text was identical and printed from the same type. The only difference was that large paper copies had wider margins. Additional illustrations were sometimes included, or impressions of the plates in two states. They always command a higher price than small-paper copies, sometimes much higher depending on circumstances.

LIBRARY (or EX-LIBRARY) COPY. Books that have been in **public** libraries are considered less desirable by collectors than those which haven't, up to about 50 percent less desirable. Exceptions are made in the case of rare volumes.

LIMITED EDITION. A book issued in a certain number of copies and no more, after which the type is broken up and illustration plates destroyed. To be recognized as bona fide, the number of copies must be stated in the book and each copy numbered. This is the only guarantee against the limitation number being overstepped.

MOROCCO. The most luxurious leather used in bookbinding. It is known in a variety of types: niger, levant, straight-grained, etc. and is made from goathide. Morocco takes a fine polish, has a wonderfully mellow glow, but does not always hold its color well. Green morocco fades to purple, and purple morocco deteriorates into a sort of mud color.

N.D. No date.

N.P. No place (of publication).

OCTAVO. The size of standard-format books, about 8½x6 inches. Abbreviated as 8vo.

OUT OF PRINT. No longer obtainable from the publisher. It is not so cut-and-dried as that seems to suggest, though. An edition can be out of print without a book being out of print.

PRIVATELY PRINTED. Financed by the author, as in subsidy publishing. Some privately printed books are offered for sale, others are just given away by the author to his friends or to libraries (which usually toss them into waste cans).

PROVENANCE. The history of a book's ownership; a kind of family tree of the book's past owners. A book owned by famous collectors tends to be more respected than an identical copy with unpedigreed background.

PUBLISHER'S CLOTH. Cloth binding (or buckram) applied by the publisher to a trade edition.

QUARTO. A book format in which the size varies from 8x10 to 7x9 inches. A "small quarto" is around 6½x8.

READING COPY. A damaged book suitable only for reading.

REMAINDER. When a book seems to have run its course on the market and sales are dwindling down, the publisher may dispose of unsold copies in his warehouse at a sharply reduced price. These are sold as "remainders".

ROAN. A cheap grade of leather that looks like imitation leather.

RUBBED. Leather bindings on which the surface is worn or scratched are said to be rubbed. Any book handled often over a long stretch of time is sure to get rubbed.

SHAKEN. The book is pulling loose from the spine.

SPINE. The backstrip or shelfback of a binding.

TRADE BINDING. A binding applied by the publisher to a trade edition, usually in cloth or buckram on books dating from the mid-1800's onward.

UNBOUND. Properly, this means a book issued in a binding but now lacking it. A work issued in wrappers is described as "softbound" or "stitched" or simply "wrappered".

UNCUT. The edges of the leaves are untrimmed.

UNOPENED. The leaves have not been cut apart — sure proof the book was never read.

VELLUM. Degreased calfskin, sometimes called parchment. Being white or yellowish, vellum bindings do not take gilding too well but can be decorated by blind stamping or in other fashions.

THE CARE AND REPAIR OF BOOKS

Books are not really difficult to care for. They tend to suffer more from improper handling and storage, not to mention simple neglect, than accidents. A normal book, printed on decent paper with rag content, will survive in good condition for hundreds of years if properly looked after. Proper care means shelving in a case which is not so overcrowded that the books must be squeezed in tightly; not leaving books lying about in heaps; dusting them periodically with a feather-duster; not taking books out of doors on rainy days; holding them carefully while reading, especially books with valuable or delicate bindings. Books bound in leather, with the exception of vellum, should be dressed with an oil preparation twice a year. This is very simple to do. Most bookbinders sell leather dressing. A small amount on a swab of cotton, worked into the leather with a circular motion, does the trick. This renews the natural grease content of the skin, which dries out in the same fashion as does a leather handbag or pair of shoes (but do not polish books with shoepolish, unless nothing better is available).

Repairs to valuable books should not be attempted by an amateur. With inexpensive books, there is no reason why a collector cannot do the job himself. Paste does the job nicely in most cases; always use either standard library paste or a polyvinyl acetate, such as "Elmer's Glue-all", rather than a clear glue. Use less than seems to be necessary; an excess of paste can cause soiling or other problems.

If you own valuable books in a delicate condition, or fine bindings that should not be subjected to rubbing against neighboring volumes on the shelf, you may want to consider having slipcases or boxes made for them. This is, however, rather costly.

VALUES

So far as the values stated in the following pages are concerned, it should be borne in mind that, because of the many varied factors involved, old books are among the most difficult of collectors' items to place price guidelines upon. Aside from differences in binding, condition and the like, one must take into account regional price differences. These do not come into play so much with the prices charged by catalogue-issuing dealers, who distribute their catalogues nationwide and make sales around the country, but are definitely a factor when buying off the shelf from local bookshops. Prices are higher in New York and Los Angeles because more book collectors are located in these cities; also, there are many dealers, and the dealers have each other as potential customers, whereas in a smaller town there are few secondhand bookshops and not too many local collectors. A $20 book in New York may be a $10 one in Kansas or Colorado.

BOOKS	Price Range	
☐ **AITKEN, ANNA LAETITIA.** *Poems, including Poem to the Origin of Song. London, 1773.*	20.00	25.00
☐ **AITKEN, JOHN.** *Essays on Song-Writing with a collection of such English Songs as are most eminent for poetical merit, to which are added some original pieces. London, n.d. c. 1770.*	30.00	37.00
☐ **ALBYN'S ANTHOLOGY** *or a Select Collection of the Melodies and Vocal Poetry Peculiar to Scotland and the Isles hitherto unpublished. Volume One only, Edinburgh, 1816.*	37.00	45.00
☐ **ALCOCK, JOHN.** *Harmonia Festi, or a collection of canons; cheerful and serious glees and catches . . . Oblong folio, 59 pp, privately printed. Lichfield, 1791.*	145.00	180.00
☐ **ARNOLD, BARTHELEMON, CARTER & SHIELD.** *A Selection of the most favorite Scots Songs chiefly pastoral adapted for the harpsichord with an accompaniment for a violin by masters. London, n.d. c. 1780.*	120.00	150.00
☐ **ATHOLE COLLECTION** *of Dance Music of Scotland Compiled and Arranged by James Stewart-Robertson. Two volumes, London, 1883.*	23.00	30.00
☐ **ATTWOOD . . .** *The Curfew. A Glee for three voices. London, n.d. c. 1810.*	110.00	135.00

	Price Range	
☐ **AYRES & SONGS, CHOICE.** *To Sing to the Theorbo, Lute or Bass . . . Composed by several Gentlemen of His Majesty's Musick and others. The Fourth Book, London, 1683.*	375.00	450.00
☐ **BATEMAN, S.** *The Strange evolution of our illiterate National Anthem from a Rebel Song. London, 1902.*	8.00	11.00
☐ **BEAUTIES OF MELODY, The.** *A collection of the most popular Airs, Duets, Glees, etc., of the most esteemed authors, also a selection of the most admired Irish melodies. London, 1827.*	12.00	15.00
☐ **BELLAMY, T.** *Lyric Poetry of Glees, Madrigals, Catches, Rounds. Performed in the Noblemen's and Gentlemen's Catch Club. London, 1840.*	9.00	12.00
☐ **BORREN, C. VAN DEN.** *The Sources of Keyboard Music in England. London, 1914.*	13.00	17.00
☐ **BOSSI, C.** *Irza. A Favourite Ballet as performed at the Kings Theatre, Haymarket. London, n.d. c. 1805.*	10.00	14.00
☐ **BOULTON, H.** *Songs of the Four Nations; England, Scotland, Ireland, Wales. For the most part never before published with complete words. London, 1893.*	13.00	17.00
☐ **BREMNER, ROBERT.** *Thirty Scots Songs. Adapted for a voice and harpsichord. The words by Allen Ramsey. London, n.d. c. 1770.*	60.00	80.00
☐ **BRITISH ORPHEUS, The.** *Being a selection of 270 Songs and Airs adapted for the Voice, Violin, German Flutes, Flageolet, etc., with Jigs, Dances. London, n.d. c. 1805.*	20.00	25.00
☐ **BULL, HENRY L.** *Dr. John Bull, the Queen's Master of Musicke. London, 1937.*	20.00	25.00
☐ **BUNTING . . .** *A General Collection of the Ancient Music of Ireland arranged for the Piano-forte. London, 1809.*	90.00	120.00
☐ **BURGH, A.** *Anecdotes of Music, historical and biographical in a series of letters. Three volumes, London, 1814.*	80.00	110.00
☐ **BURNS, ROBERT.** *The Songs of Robert Burns. Now first printed with the melodies for which they were written. Edited by J. C. Dick. Glasgow, 1903.*	20.00	25.00
☐ **BUTLER, T. H.** *A Select Collection of original Scottish Airs arranged for one and two voices with Introductory and Concluding Symphonies. Glasgow, 1790.*	25.00	32.00
☐ **CALLCOTT, J. W.** *A Musical Grammar. London, 1806.*	100.00	130.00
☐ **CHETHAM, JOHN.** *A Book of Psalmody. Leeds, 1787.*	60.00	80.00
☐ **CHRISTIE, W.** *Traditional Ballad Airs arranged and harmonized for the Piano-forte, from copies procured in the counties of Aberdeen, Banff and Moray, with illustrative notes. Edinburgh, 1876-81.*	110.00	145.00
☐ **CLARK, R.** *God Save the King. An account of the National Anthem entitled "God Save the King". Folding plates, London, 1822.*	30.00	40.00
☐ **CLIFFORD, JAMES.** *The Divine Services and Anthems usually sung in His Majesties Chapell. London, 1664.*	100.00	130.00
☐ **COX, JOHN EDMUND.** *Musical Recollections of the Last Half-Century. Two volumes, London, 1872.*	100.00	125.00

	Price Range	
☐ **CROSBY . . .** *English Musical Repository. A choice selection of esteemed English Songs adapted for the Voice, Violin and German Flute. Edinburgh, 1811.*	20.00	25.00
☐ **CROWEST, F.** *The Story of British Music from the earliest times to the Tudor Period. London, 1896.*	23.00	30.00
☐ **CUMMINGS, W.** *God Save the King, origin and history of the music and words. London, 1902.*	10.00	13.00
☐ **CURWEN, J. S.** *Music at the Queen's Accession. A paper read before the Society of Arts. London, 1897.*	6.00	9.00
☐ **DAVEY . . .** *History of English Music. London, 1895.*	10.00	13.00
☐ **D'EGVILLE . . .** *Barbara and Allen. A Favourite Ballet including the Celebrated Pas Seul. London, n.d. c. 1800.*	10.00	13.00
☐ **DERMODY, T.** *The Harp of Erin. Two volumes, London, 1807.*	15.00	20.00
☐ **DIBDIN, CHARLES.** *Six Songs written and Composed by the Late Celebrated Mr. Dibdin of Sans Souci, Strand and Leicester Place. Published by subscription for the benefit of his Widow and Daughter. 18 pp., London, 1816.*	13.00	18.00
☐ **DIBDIN, CHARLES.** *The Songs of Charles Dibdin chronologically arranged with notes, biographical and critical, and the music for the best and most popular of the melodies, with new pianoforte accompaniments. Two volumes, London, 1842*	30.00	38.00
☐ **D'URFEY . . .** *Wit and Mirth or Pills to Purge Melancholy. Songs Compleat, Pleasant and Diverting, set to Musick by Dr. John Blow, Mr. Henry Purcell and other excellent Masters of the Town. Three volumes. Facsimile of an 1876 facsimile of a work originally published in London, 1719-20. New York, 1959.*	55.00	75.00
☐ **ENGEL, CARL.** *The Music of the most Ancient Nations, particularly the Assyrian, Egyptian and Hebrew. London, n.d. 1909.*	45.00	60.00
☐ **FAIRBURN'S EVERLASTING SONGSTER,** *being an Extensive Collection of One Thousand Naval, Love, Comic, Hunting, Bacchanalian, etc. Songs. London, n.d. early 1800's.*	100.00	130.00
☐ **FITZGERALD, S. J. A.** *Stories of Famous Songs. The History of such well-known songs as Home Sweet Home, Auld Lang Syne, Yankee Doodle. London, 1898.*	20.00	25.00
☐ *Foundling Hymns, Psalters, Hymns and Anthems for the Foundling Chapel. London, 1809.*	50.00	65.00
☐ **FRAZER, CAPT. SIMON.** *The Airs and Melodies peculiar to the Highlands of Scotland and the Isles, communicated in an unusual pleasing familiar state. London, 1874.*	50.00	65.00
☐ **FULL & BY.** *Being a Collection of Verses by Persons of quality in Praise of drinking here. London, 1920.*	13.00	18.00
☐ **GAY . . .** *Polly, with the music prefixed to the songs. Limited to 350 copies. London, 1923.*	13.00	18.00
☐ **GIBBON, J. M.** *Melody and the Lyric from Chaucer to the Cavaliers. London, 1930.*	20.00	25.00
☐ **GILLMAN, F.** *Evolution of the English Hymn. An historical survey of the origins and development of the hymns of the Christian Church. London, 1927.*	13.00	18.00
☐ **GOW . . .** *The Vocal Melodies of Scotland arranged for the Pianoforte or Harp, Violin and Violincello by Nathaniel Gow. Folio, Edinburgh, 1822.*	45.00	60.00

	Price Range	
☐ **GRAVES, A. P.** *The Celtic Song Book. Representative folk songs of the six Celtic Nations. London, 1928.*	15.00	20.00
☐ **HAGUE, CHARLES.** *A Collection of Songs, Moral, Sentimental, Instructive and Amusing. The words selected and revised by Rev. James Plumptree. The music adapted and composed by Charles Hague. London and Cambridge, 1805.*	25.00	32.00
☐ **HANDEL, GEORGE FREDERIC.** *Flavius an Opera, as it was Perform'd at the Kings Theatre for the Royal Academy. London, n.d. 1723.*	450.00	600.00
☐ **HANDEL, GEORGE FREDERIC.** *Six Concertos for the Harpsichord or Organ (Opus 4). London, n.d. 1738.*	130.00	165.00
☐ **HANDEL, GEORGE FREDERIC.** *The Occasional Oratorio as it was Perform'd at Theatre Royal in Covent Garden. Second edition, London, n.d. c. 1747.*	200.00	250.00
☐ **HANDEL, GEORGE FREDERIC.** *Israel in Egypt An Oratoria, in Score, as it was Originally Composed by Mr. Handel. Large folio, London, n.d. 1771.*	325.00	425.00
☐ **HANDEL, GEORGE FREDERIC.** *Messiah An Oratorio in Score as it was Originally Perform'd. London, n.d. c. 1803.*	210.00	265.00
☐ **HANNAGAN, M. and CLANDILLON, S.** *Songs of the Irish Gaels with the Music and English Metrical translation. London, 1927.*	15.00	20.00
☐ **HAWKINS, JOHN.** *A General History of the Science and Practice of Music. Five volumes, originally bound in calf. The most comprehensive history of music published in the English language up to that time, and the most historically valuable sourcebook of 17th- and 18th-century English music history. London, 1776.*	1100.00	1500.00
☐ *Bound in full gilt morocco.*	1650.00	2000.00
☐ **HAYDN and MOZART.** *The Lives of Haydn and Mozart, translated from the French. Second edition, London, 1818.*	60.00	80.00
☐ **HIPKINS, A. J.** *Musical Instruments, Historic, Rare and Unique. Illustrated by a Series of 50 plates in colours, by William Gibb. Atlas folio, Artist's proof copy, one of 50. Edinburgh, 1888.*	1600.00	2150.00
☐ **HONNEYMAN, WILLIAM C.** *The Violin: How to Master It. Boston, n.d. c. 1895.*	50.00	65.00
☐ **HULLAH, JOHN.** *The History of Modern Music. London, 1896.*	55.00	70.00
☐ **JACKSON, V.** *English Melodies from the 13th to the 18th Centuries. London, 1910.*	20.00	25.00
☐ **JACOBS, B.** *National Psalmody. A collection of tunes with appropriate symphonies set to a course of Psalms selected from the new version by J. T. Barrett for the services of the United Church of England and Ireland. London, 1819.*	25.00	33.00
☐ **JEBOULT, H.** *Somerset Composers, Musicians and Music. London, 1923.*	4.00	6.00
☐ **JENKINS, JOHN.** *Fancies and Ayres. For 4 or 5 Viols, two trebles and bass violin. Wellesley, 1950.*	20.00	25.00
☐ **JONES, EDWARD.** *Musical and Poetical Relicks of the Welsh Bards preserved by Tradition and authentic manuscripts from very remote antiquity to the bardic times. London, 1805.*	100.00	130.00
☐ **KIDSON . . .** *Old English Country Dances. London, 1890.*	18.00	23.00

	Price Range	
☐ **LEVERIDGE, RICHARD.** *A Collection of Songs, with the Musick. Two volumes, London, 1727.*	425.00	550.00
☐ **LOGIER, J. B.** *A System of the Science of Music and Practical Composition. London, 1827.*	120.00	150.00
☐ **MAITLAND, J. FULLER.** *English Music in the 19th Century. London, 1902.*	15.00	20.00
☐ **MAY, PHIL.** *Songs and their Singers from "Punch". London, 1898.*	13.00	18.00
☐ **MEE, J.** *The Oldest Music Room in Europe. The Oxford Music Room, its history and that of the Society, with list of music in the library. London, 1911.*	13.00	18.00
☐ **MEYER, E.** *English Chamber Music, the history of a great art from the Middle Ages to Purcell. London, 1946.*	12.00	16.00
☐ **MUSICAL CABINET.** *The New Musical and Vocal Cabinet comprising a selection of the most favourite English, Scotch and Irish melodies. Volume one only. London, 1820.*	13.00	18.00
☐ **MUSICAL GOLCONDA, The.** *Or Beauties of Melody. A Collection of the most popular Airs, Duets, Glees of the most esteemed author ancient and modern, comprising those of Arne, Handel, Mozart, Winter... to which is prefixed observations and instructions on music. London, 1827.*	15.00	20.00
☐ **NAYLOR, E. W.** *An Elizabethan Virginal Book. Being a critical essay on the contents of a MS. in the Fitzwilliam Museum. London, 1905.*	20.00	25.00
☐ **NAYLOR, E. W.** *The Poets and Music. London, 1928.*	12.00	16.00
☐ **NEALE, RICHARD.** *A Pocket Companion for Gentlemen and Ladies' being a Collection of the finest Opera Songs and Airs in English and Italian. Two volumes, London, n.d. 1724.*	375.00	475.00
☐ **NIGHTINGALE, The.** *A Collection of Songs set to Music. London, n.d. c. 1825.*	9.00	12.00
☐ **PALGRAVE, F. T.** *The Treasury of Sacred Song. Limited to 600 copies, Oxford, 1889.*	9.00	12.00
☐ **PURCELL.** *The Beauties of Purcell Dedicated by Permission to Miss Susan Beckford in Two Volumes Consisting of the most favourite Songs, Duets, Trios, etc., selected from the various works of the Great Master. Two volumes, London, 1819.*	35.00	45.00

SHEET MUSIC

One of the most popular fields of music-related collectibles, sheet music — or "song sheets" — offer limitless possibilities. While space prohibits us from listing the very earliest specimens, music sheets as old as 200 years and even older exist. Probably close to a million have been published. They can be collected by song type, by composer, by era (such as swing-age sheets), or by the cover art. Those carrying photos of top celebrities on the cover are always worth a premium. If the star is someone like Al Jolson and the sheet dates to the early part of his career (say before 1920), you have a very in-demand item. Many hobbyists like to frame their song sheets. For a large collection, storage in file folders or boxes is most logical. Valuable specimens can be stored in mylar envelopes to guard against deterioration, and an indexing system set up to help you find any desired sheet.

As with paper collectibles in general, those with frayed edges, staining or other damage have less value than well-preserved examples. Reprints — which are common — are also of less value. Some reprints are included below to give an idea of their value — they are clearly indicated in the listings. But please note that a reprint is different than a facsimile or reproduction. A reprint of a song sheet was issued by a music publisher and sold in the same fashion as any other song sheet. Therefore, it certainly ranks as "collectible", even though its value is not as high as the original's. A facsimile is a reprint made by someone other than a music publisher, and is not desirable to collectors.

	Price Range	
☐ **After I've Called You Sweetheart (How Can I Call You Friend),** *words by Bernie Grossman, music by Little Jack Little, pub. Milton Weil, inset Little Jack Little, c. 1927.*	3.00	5.00
☐ **Alexander's Ragtime Band,** *by Irving Berlin, pub. Standard Music (reprint).*	2.25	3.00
☐ **All I Want Is You,** *lyric and music by Benny Davis, Harry Akst and Sidney Clare, Starmer cover, inset Corinne Arbuckle, c. 1927.*	3.00	5.00
☐ **Among My Souvenirs,** *words by Edgar Leslie, music by Horatio Nicholls, c. 1927.*	2.25	3.00
☐ **Annie Doesn't Live Here Anymore,** *lyric by Joe Young and Johnny Burke, music by Harold Spina, inset Guy Lombardo, c. 1933.*	2.25	3.00
☐ **Arm in Arm,** *words by Ned Washington, music by Frances Zinman and Victor Young, inset Arthur Tracy, the Street Singer, c. 1932.*	2.25	3.00
☐ **The Army Air Corps,** *words and music by Robert Crawford, pub. Carl Fischer, 1942 edition.*	2.25	3.00
☐ **As You Desire Me,** *words and music by Allie Wruble, inset Morton Downey, pub. Keit Engel, c. 1932.*	3.00	4.00
☐ **Away Down South in Heaven,** *words by Bud Green, music by Harry Warren, Barbelle cover, c. 1927.*	2.00	3.00
☐ **(Dance) Ballerina (Dance),** *lyric by Bob Russell, music by Carl Sigman, inset Vaughn Monroe, pub. Jefferson Music, c. 1947.*	2.00	3.00
☐ **Bebe,** *lyric by Sam Coslow, music by Abner Silver, pub. W, inset Bebe Daniels, c. 1923.*	2.25	4.00
☐ **Because I Love You,** *by Irving Berlin, Leff cover, c. 1926.*	2.25	3.00
☐ **Because of You,** *lyric by Walter Hirsch, music by Ted Fiorito, pub. Feist, c. 1925.*	3.00	4.00
☐ **Beside a Babbling Brook,** *lyric by Gus Kahn, music by Walter Donaldson, inset Karyl Norman, c. 1923.*	2.25	3.00
☐ **Blue Flame,** *lyric by Leo Corday, music by James Noble and Joe Bishop, nice photo Woody Herman, His theme song, recorded on Decca Record No. 3643, pub. Charling Music, blue printing of cover shows through on inside pages, c. 1943.*	3.50	5.00
☐ **Blue Grass,** *by B. G. DeSylva, Lew Brown and Ray Henderson, cl 1928.*	2.25	4.00
☐ **(I've Got The) Blue Ridge Blues,** *lyric by Chas. A. Mason, music by Chas. S. Cooke and Richard Whiting.*	2.25	4.00

All the King's Horses,
A Little White Gardenia,
words and music by Sam Coslow,
pub. Famous Music Corp.,
$3.00-$5.00.

Artists and Models,
Whispers in the Dark,
words and music by Leo Robin
and Frederick Hollander,
pub. Famous Music Corp.,
$2.50-$5.00.

	Price Range	
☐ **Breeze (Blow My Baby Back to Me),** *by Ballard MacDonald, Joe Goodwin and James F. Hanley, small inset Owsley and O'Day, black face, c. 1919.*	3.50	5.00
☐ **Broken Blossoms,** *lyric by Ballard MacDonald, music by A. Robert King, c. 1919.*	3.50	5.00
☐ **Burgundy,** *by Tommy Malie, Jimmy Steiger, Jimmy Steiger and Harry Richman, inset Albert E. Short, Musical Director Capitol Theatre, Chicago, pub. Frank Clark, Inc., Barbelle cover, c. 1925.*	2.25	3.00
☐ **Bye Lo,** *words and music by Ray Perkins, c. 1919.*	2.25	3.00
☐ **By the Campfire,** *lyric by Mary Elizabeth Girling, music by Percy Wenrich, pub. Feist, c. 1919.*	2.25	3.00
☐ **Carolina in the Morning,** *lyric by Gus Kahn, music by Walter Donaldson, inset Mildred Patrick, pencilled number on cover, c. 1922.*	2.25	3.00
☐ *As above, inset Maurice Sherman.*	2.25	3.00
☐ **(I Am Always Building) Castles in the Air,** *words by Ted Garton, music by A. Fred Phillips, pub. Garton music, M. M. Fisher cover, c. 1919.*	4.50	6.00
☐ **Catch a Falling Star,** *words and music by Paul Vance and Lee Pockriss, photo Perry Como, c. 1954.*	2.25	3.00
☐ **Cinna Mon Sinner (Selling Lollipop Lies),** *inset Tony Bennett, pub. Raleigh Music, c. 1954.*	2.25	3.00
☐ **Collegiate,** *words and music by Moe Jaffee and Nat Bonx, pub. SB, inset Fred Damons Greenwich Villagers, c. 1925.*	3.00	4.00
☐ **The Creaking Old Mill on the Creek,** *by Al Lewis, Larry Stock and Vincent Rose, nice photo Sammy Kaye, c. 1940.*	2.25	3.00
☐ **Croon a Little Lullaby,** *lyric by Harry D. Kerr, music by Chris Schonberg and Clyde Baker, pub. Sherman Clay, inset Jack Coakley and his Cabirians, c. 1925.*	2.25	3.00
☐ **Crying For You,** *by Ned Miller and Chester Cohn, inset Moher and Eldridge, pub. Feist, c. 1923.*	2.25	3.00
☐ **Danube Waves,** *by J. Ivonovici, pub. Morris, Key of "C" EXC.*	1.25	2.00
☐ **The Dardanella Blues,** *words by Fred Fisher, music by Johnny Black, Wohlman cover, pub. Fred Fisher, c. 1920.*	3.00	4.00
☐ **Dawn of Tomorrow,** *words by Jeanne Gravelle, music by Joe Green, pub. Henry Waterson, c. 1927.*	1.25	2.00
☐ **Dear Heart,** *words by Jean LeFavre, music by W. C. Polla, beautiful colored cover, pub. by Church, c. 1919.*	3.00	4.00
☐ **Dearie,** *by Bob Hilliard and Dave Mann, pub. Laurel, c. 1950.*	3.00	4.00
☐ **Don't Go To Sleep,** *lyric by Arthur Freed, music by Oscar Levant, inset John L. Fogarty, c. 1932.*	2.25	3.00
☐ **Down By the Meadow Brook,** *words by Edgar Leslie, music by Pete Wendling, Barbelle cover, c. 1919.*	2.25	3.00
☐ **Don't Let the Stars Get in Your Eyes,** *by Alan Qillwt, star Sales, inset Perry Como, inked and pencilled instructions inside, c. 1952.*	1.50	2.50
☐ **Do You Ever Think of Me,** *lyric by Harry D. Kerr, music by Earl Burtnett, c. 1920.*	2.00	3.00
☐ **Down the Trail to Home Sweet Home,** *by Ernest R. Ball, c. 1920.*	2.00	3.00

Broadway Rhythm,
Irresistible You,
words and music by Don Raye and Gene DePaul,
pub. Leo Feist, Inc.,
$1.50-$3.00.

Carefree,
I Used to be Color Blind,
words and music by Irving Berlin,
pub. Irving Berlin, Inc.,
$3.00-$5.00.

	Price Range	
☐ **Dream Train,** *words by Charles Newman, music by Billy Baskette, photo Guy Lombardo, pub. M. Weil, c. 1928.*	2.00	3.00
☐ **Dreamy Melody,** *words and music by Ted Koehler, Frank Magine and C. Naset, inset The Misses Dennis: Ruth, Ann and Cherie, c. 1922.*	2.50	3.50
☐ **(You Know-I Know) Ev'rything's Made for Love,** *by Howard Johnson, Charles Tobias and Al Sherman, Aileen Stanley photo on cover, c. 1926.*	2.75	3.50
☐ **Falling in Love With You,** *lyrics by Benny Davis, music by Joseph Meyer, c. 1926.*	2.75	3.50
☐ **Feather Your Nest,** *by Kendis and Brockman and Howard Johnson, inset Anna Chandler, pub. Feist, c. 1920.*	2.75	3.50
☐ **(That's Just My Way of) Forgetting You,** *by DeSylva, Brown and Henderson, Pud Lane cover, c. 1928.*	2.75	3.50
☐ **Forgive Me,** *words by Jack Yellen, music by Milton Ager, inset Grace Hayes, Barbelle cover, c. 1927.*	3.00	4.00
☐ **(On The) 'Gin 'Gin 'Ginny Shore,** *words by Edgar Leslie, music by Walter Donaldson, pub. SB, inset Adele Rowland, cover is southern scene with river boat, c. 1922.*	3.00	4.00
☐ **Girls,** *lyric by Alfred Bryan, music by Harry Carroll, Starmer cover, photos Five Geo White Girls, c. 1919.*	4.00	6.00
☐ **Give Me a Ukelele (And a Ukelele Baby),** *by Lew Brown and Gene Williams, Starmer cover, c. 1926.*	2.25	3.25
☐ **Give My Regards to Broadway,** *by George M. Cohan, reprint.*	2.25	3.25
☐ **Good Night, Wherever You Are,** *photo Ginny Sims on cover, S-VG, c. 1944.*	2.25	3.25
☐ **Granny,** *words by L. Wolfe Gilbert, music by Alex Belledna, pub. Gilbert & Freidland, DeTacaks cover, c. 1929.*	2.25	4.00
☐ **Granny (You're My Mammy's Mammy),** *music by Harry Akst, c. 1921.*	3.00	6.00
☐ **The Gypsy,** *words and music by Billy Reid, pub. Leeds, c. 1946.*	2.50	4.00
☐ **Hands Across the Table,** *lyrics by Mitchell Parish, music by Dean DeLettre, photo Lucienne Boyer, pub. Mill, c. 1934.*	2.50	4.00
☐ **Happiness (Where Are You),** *by L. Wolfe Gilbert and Leon Flatow, pub. Gilbert & Friedland, c. 1919.*	4.50	6.00
☐ **(There's A) Harbor of Dream Boats (Anchored on Moonlight Bay,** *by Nat Burton, Al Sherman and Arthur Altman, inset "The Townsmen", c. 1943.*	2.00	3.00
☐ **He,** *lyric by Richard Mullan, music by Jack Richards, inset McGuire Sisters, pub. Avas, c. 1954.*	3.00	4.00
☐ **Heaven's Artillery,** *March and Two-Step, by Harry J. Lincoln, W. J. Dittmar (?) cover, pub. Vandersloot, c. 1904.*	5.00	7.00
☐ **He's My Uncle,** *lyric by Charles Newman, music by Lew Pollack, introduced by Dick Powell on the "Maxwell House Coffee Time" with special version for school children, c. 1940.*	4.00	5.50
☐ **He She and Me,** *by Carmen Lombardo and Charles Newman, inset "Cookie" and his Ginger Snaps, pub. M. Weil, c. 1929.*	3.00	4.00
☐ **Hillbilly Fever,** *by George Vaughn, inset Kenny Roberts, pub. Forrest Music, c. 1950.*	2.25	3.00
☐ **Home Again Blues,** *by Irving Berlin and Harry Akst, c. 1920.*	2.25	3.00

The Dolly Sisters,
I Can't Begin to Tell You,
words by Mack Gordon,
music by James Monaco,
pub. BVC, Inc.,
$3.00-$7.00.

The Gay Bride,
Mississippi Honeymoon,
words by Gus Kahn,
music by Walter Donaldson,
pub. by Robbins Music Corp.,
$2.50-$4.50.

	Price Range	
☐ **Home Sweet Home Polka,** *words by Leni Mason, Melody by Arthur Berman, pub. Central Music, inset Texas Jim Robertson, c. 1948.*	3.00	4.00
☐ **Honey Hula,** *Hawaiian Waltz Song, words and music by Fred Fisher, pub. Fred Fisher, c. 1921.*	3.00	4.00
☐ **Hop Scotch Polka,** *words and music by William Whitlock, Carl Sigman and Gene Rayburn, inset Gene Rayburn and Dee Finch with mike from WNEW, pub. Cromwell Music, c. 1949.*	3.00	4.00
☐ **Hot Lips,** *words and music by Henry Busse, Henry Lange and Lou Davis, photo Henry Busse, pub. Feist, pencilled numbers on cover, c. 1922.*	3.00	4.00
☐ **How Do You Do,** *as introduced by Phil Fleming, Harry Geise and Vernon Rick, inset Carl Caul, special verses by Charlie Harrison and Cal De Voll, pub. Ted Browne, c. 1924.*	2.25	3.00
☐ **(I'm Tellin' the Birds - Tellin' the Bees) How I Love You,** *by Cliff Friend and Lew Brown, c. 1926.*	2.25	3.00
☐ **Hummingbird,** *words and music by Don Robertson, photo Les Paul and Mary Ford, pub. Ross Jungnickel, c. 1955.*	2.25	3.00
☐ **I Ain't Nobody's Darling,** *words by Elmer Hughes, music by Robert King, Wohlman cover, pub. Skidmore Music, c. 1921.*	2.25	3.00
☐ **I Love You All the More,** *words by Darl MacBoyle, music by Nat Vincent, E. E. Walton cover, pub. George T. Worth, c. 1919.*	4.00	5.50
☐ **I Love You So,** *lyric by Gus Kahn, music by Ted Fiorito, pub. Feist, c. 1930.*	3.00	4.00
☐ **I Said My Pajamas (And Put On My Prayers),** *words and music by Eddie Pola and Geo. Wyle, insets Fran Warren and Ton Marin, pub. Leeds, c. 1950.*	3.00	4.00
☐ **I Wanna Go Home (With You),** *words and music by Jack Joyce and Joe Cancullo, pub. Paxton, inset Perry Como, c. 1945.*	3.00	4.00
☐ **I Wouldn't Change You For the World,** *words by Charles Newman, music by Isham Jones, inset Tom Brown, pub. Olman, c. 1931.*	2.25	3.00
☐ **Ida I Do,** *words by Gus Kahn, music by Isham Jones, pub. IB, Perret cover, c. 1925.*	3.00	4.00
☐ **I Love to Fall Asleep and Wake Up in My Mammy's Arms,** *wods by Sam Lewis and Joe Young, music by Fred E. Ahlert, c. 1920.*	2.25	3.00
☐ **(I'd Climb the Highest Mountain) If I Knew I'd Find You,** *words and music by Lew Brown and Sidney Clare, inset Grace Aldrich, Leff cover, c. 1926.*	2.25	3.00
☐ **I'll Be Happy When the Preacher Makes You Mine,** *words by Sam M. Lewis and Joe Young, music by Walter Donaldson, c. 1919.*	3.00	4.00
☐ **I'll Be With You When the Clouds Roll By,** *by the Three White Kuhns: Robert, Paul and Charles, inset Joe Whitehear "A Fool There Was", Starmer cover, c. 1922.*	3.00	4.00
☐ **I'm A Dreamer That's Chasing Bubbles,** *words by Geo. A. Little, music by Frank Magine, Wohlman cover, pub. Jack Mills, c. 1919.*	2.25	3.00

It's Love Again,
I Nearly Let Love Go
Slipping Through My Fingers,
words and music by Harry Woods,
pub. Chappell & Co.,
$1.50-$3.00.

Johnny Doughboy
Found a Rose in Ireland,
words and music by Kay Twomey
and Al Goodhart,
pub. Crawford Music Corp.,
$2.00-$3.50.

	Price Range	
☐ **I'm Glad There Is You,** *words and music by Paul Madeira and Jimmy Dorsey, inset Dorsey, pub. Mayfair, c. 1942.*	2.25	3.00
☐ **I'm In Heaven (When I'm In My Mother's Arms),** *by Howard Johnson, Cliff Hess and Milton Ager, pub. Feist, c. 1920.*	3.00	4.00
☐ **I'm On My Way Home,** *by Irving Berlin, Leff cover, c. 1926.*	2.25	3.00
☐ **I'm Sorry Sally,** *words by Gus Kahn, music by Ted Fiorito, pub. Feist, c. 1928.*	2.25	3.00
☐ **In a Shanty in Old Shanty Town,** *words and music by Joe Young, John Siras and Little Jack Little, inset Abe Lyman, c. 1932.*	2.25	3.00
☐ **In a Little Garden (You Made Paradise),** *words by Earl Whittemore, music by Felice S. Iula, Starmer cover, c. 1926.*	2.25	3.00
☐ **I Found a Rose (In the Devil's Garden),** *words and music by Willie Raskin and Fred Fisher, pub. Fisher, Goldbeck cover, c. 1921.*	2.25	3.00
☐ **Indian Dawn,** *poem by Charles O. Roos, music by J. S. Zamecnik, pub. Fox, c. 1924.*	2.25	3.00
☐ **Indianola,** *by S. R. Henry and D. Onivas, pub. Jos. Stern, Starmer cover (Indian with head dress, blue and white), c. 1918.*	2.00	3.00
☐ **It Is No Secret (What God Can Do),** *words and music by Stuart Hamblen, pub. Duchess, c. 1950.*	2.00	3.00
☐ **It's All Over Now,** *words and music by Sunny Skylar and Don Marcotte, photos 12 recording artists, c. 1946.*	4.00	5.50
☐ **It's Been a Long Long Time,** *lyric by Sammy Cahn, music by Jule Styne, photo Stan Kenton, pub. Morris, c. 1945.*	2.25	3.00
☐ **It's Never Too Late To Be Sorry,** *words by J. E. Dempsy, music by Jos. A. Burke, pub. Stasney, c. 1918.*	2.25	3.00
☐ **I've Made Up My Mind to Forget You (But I Can't Let You Out of My Heart),** *words and music by May Tully and Martin Broones, Perret cover, c. 1923.*	2.25	3.00
☐ **Ivory Tower,** *words and music by Jack Fulton and Lois Steele, inset Cathy Carr, pub. Melrose, c. 1956.*	2.25	3.00
☐ **Johnny is the Boy for Me,** *lyrics by Marcel Stillman and Paddy Roberts, music by Les Paul, photos Les Paul and Mary Ford, pub. Iris Music, c. 1953.*	2.25	3.00
☐ **Just a Little Drink,** *words and music by Byron Gay, comical cover, c. 1925.*	2.25	3.00
☐ **Just a Little Fond Affection,** *by Elton Box, Desmond Cox and Lewis Ilda, pub. Skidmore, c. 1944.*	2.25	3.00
☐ **Just a Little Longer,** *by Irving Berlin, Leff cover, pub. IB, c. 1926.*	2.25	3.00
☐ **Just Around the Corner (May Be Sunshine For You),** *lyric by Dolph Singer, music by Harry Von Tilzer, inset Ted Lewis, c. 1925.*	2.25	3.00
☐ **Just a Prayer Away,** *words by Charles Tobias, music by David Kap, inset Mel Cooper, c. 1944.*	2.25	3.00
☐ **Just Between Friends,** *words and music by Robert Mellin and Gerald Rogers, pub. Mellin, c. 1955.*	3.25	4.50
☐ **Just Say I Love Her,** *(Dicitencello Fuie), lyric by Martin Kalmanoff and San Ward, music by Jack Val and Jimmy Dale, pub. Larry Spier, c. 1950.*	3.25	4.50

	Price Range	
☐ **Keep It a Secret,** *by Jessie May Robinson, inset Jo Stafford, Nick cover.*	2.00	3.00
☐ **Kiki,** *words and music by George A. Little, Paul Hosang and Art Sizemore, pub. Harold Rossiter, c. 1928.*	2.00	3.00
☐ **Kiss Me Goodnight,** *words by Archie Gottler, music by Horatio Nicholls, photo Morton Downey, c. 1931.*	3.00	4.00
☐ **La Cucarachua,** *English text by Stanley Adams, with guitar chords, inset Don Pedro, pub. Calumet.*	2.25	3.00
☐ **The Lady from 29 Palms,** *words and music by Allie Wrubel, pub. Martin Music, c. 1947.*	2.25	3.00
☐ **Lady of Spain,** *words by Erell Reaves, music by Tolchard Evans, photo Eddie Fisher, pub. Fox, c. 1944.*	2.25	3.00
☐ **Land of Dreams,** *lyrics by Norman Gimbel, music by Eddie Heywood, inset Hugo Winterhalter, pub. Meridian, c. 1954.*	2.25	3.00
☐ **Last Night I Dreamed You Kissed Me,** *lyric by Gus Kahn, music by Carmen Lombardo, pub. Feist, c. 1928.*	2.25	3.00
☐ **Laughing at Life,** *lyric by Nick and Chas. Kenny, music by Cornell and Bob Todd, inset Bert Lown, c. 1930.*	3.00	4.00
☐ **Laura,** *lyric by Johnny Mercer, music by David Raksin, c. 1945.*	2.25	3.00
☐ **Lay My Head Beneath a Rose,** *words by W. Madison, music by G. Falkenstein, Cameron covern, inset Ernest Morrison.*	2.25	3.00
☐ **Let Me Know,** *words and music by Slim Willet, inset Willet, pub. 4 Star Sales, c. 1953.*	2.25	3.00
☐ **Let the Rest of the World Go By,** *lyric by J. Kiern Brennan music by Ernest R. Ball.*	2.25	3.00
☐ **Lisbon Antigua (In Old Lisbon),** *lyric by Harry Dupreee, music by Raul Portela, J. Galhardo and A. do Vale, pub. Southern Music, inset Nelson Riddle, c. 1954 reprint.*	2.25	3.00
☐ **Little Crumbs of Happiness,** *lyric by J. Kiern Brennan, music by Ernest R. Ball, c. 1920.*	2.25	3.00
☐ **Little Curly Hair In a High Chair,** *words by Charles Tobias, music by Nat Simon, pub. Leo Feist, c. 1940 reprint.*	2.25	3.00
☐ **(Watch, Hope and Wait) Little Girl (I'm Coming Back to You),** *words by Lew Brown, music by Will Clayton, c. 1918 near mint.*	2.25	3.00
☐ **Little Grass Shack (In Kealakekua),** *words and music by by Bill Cogswell and Johnny Noble, inset Ted Fiorito, c. 1934.*	3.00	4.00
☐ **Little Log Cabin of Dreams,** *words and music by James F. Hanley and Eddie Dowling, c. 1927.*	2.25	3.00
☐ **A Little on the Lonely Side,** *music and lyric by Dick Robertdon, James Cavanaugh, Frank Weldon, inset George Olsen, pub. Advanced, c. 1944.*	2.50	3.75
☐ **Little White Lies,** *by Walter Donaldson, inset red photo Rudy Vallee, pub. W. Donaldson, c. 1930.*	2.50	3.75
☐ **Lonely Eyes,** *by Benny Davis and Harry Akst, c. 1926.*	2.50	3.75
☐ **Lonesome and Sorry,** *by Benny Davis and Con Conrad, pub. Henry Waterson, inset Lou Raderman, Barbelle cover, c. 1926.*	2.50	3.75
☐ **Those Lonesome Nights,** *by Gus Kahn, Harry Akst and Richard Whiting, c. 1931.*	2.50	3.75

The Little Cherub,
My Irish Rosie,
words by W.M. Jerome,
music by Jean Schwartz,
$3.50-$5.00.

Marianne,
Hang On to Me,
words by Raymond Klages,
music by Jesse Greek,
pub. Robbins Music Corp.,
$2.50-$4.00.

	Price Range	
☐ **Looking at the World (Thru Rose Colored Glasses),** *by Tommie Malie and Jimmy Steiger, inset Jack Osterman, pub. Weil, c. 1926.*	2.25	3.00
☐ **Lost (A Wonderful Girl),** *words by Benny Davis, music by James Hanley.*	2.25	3.00
☐ **The Love Bug Will Bite You (If You Don't Watch Out),** *words and music by Pinky Tomlin, photo Pinky Tomlin, c. 1937.*	2.25	3.00
☐ **Love Every Moment You Live,** *by Bennie Lowe, Kal Mann and Art Singer, inset June Valli, pub. Meridian, c. 1953.*	2.25	3.00
☐ **Love is a Melody,** *words and music by David Sokoloff and Charles F. Shisler, photo Patti Clayton, pub. J. W. Pepper, c. 1947.*	2.25	3.00
☐ **Mama Don't Want No Peas an' Rice an' Coconut Oil,** *by L. Wolfe Gilbert and L. Charles, pub. Marks, c. 1931.*	3.00	4.00
☐ **Mambo Italiano,** *by Bob Merrill, inset Rosemary Clooney, pub. Ryan Music, c. 1954.*	2.25	3.00
☐ **The Man Upstairs,** *by Dorinda Morgan, Harold Stanley and Gerry Manners, inset Kay Starr, pub. Vesta Music, c. 1954.*	2.25	3.00
☐ **Managua Nicargua,** *lyric by Albert Gamse, music by Irving Fields, photo Guy Lombardo, pub. Encore, c. 1946.*	2.25	3.00
☐ **Manhattan Serenade,** *music by Louis Alter, lyric by Harold Adamson, photo Guy Lombardo.*	2.25	3.00
☐ **Many Happy Returns of the Day,** *lyric by Al Dubin, music by Joe Burke, inset Russ Columbo, c. 1931.*	2.25	3.00
☐ **Masquerade,** *lyric by Paul Francis Webster, music by John Jacob Loeb, pub. Feist.*	2.25	3.00
☐ **Maybe It's Because,** *lyric by Harry Ruby, music by Johnny Scott, inset Andy and Della Russell, c. 1949.*	2.25	3.00
☐ **Meadow-Lark,** *by Ted Fiorito and Hal Keidel, c. 1926.*	2.25	3.00
☐ **Mellow Mountain Moon,** *by Fred Howard and Nat Vincent, pub. Calument, inset Herbie Kay, c. 1930.*	1.50	2.00
☐ **The Melody That Made You Mine,** *words by Cliff Friend, music by W. C. Polla, inset Vincent Lopez, c. 1925.*	2.25	3.00
☐ **Memories of France,** *words by Al Dubin, music by Russel Robinson, pub. WBS, c. 1928.*	2.25	3.00
☐ **Memories of Virginia,** *pub. Weile Pub. St. Louis, MO., c. 1918.*	2.25	3.00
☐ **The Merry-Go-Round Broke Down,** *words and music by Cliff Friend and Dave Franklin, inset Guy Lombardo, c. 1937.*	2.25	3.00
☐ **The Midnight Fire Alarm,** *by Harry J. Lincoln, arr. by E. T. Paul (colored litho).*	30.00	40.00
☐ **Midnight Rose,** *lyric by Sidney Mitchell, music by Lew Pollack, inset Friend and Sparling, Barbelle cover, c. 1923.*	2.25	3.00
☐ **Midnight Waltz,** *lyric by Gus Kahn, music by Walter Donaldson, inset Bernie Cumming's Recording Orchestra, pub. Feist, c. 1925.*	2.25	3.00
☐ **Moments to Remember,** *lyric by Al Stillman, music by Robert Allwn, insets Four Lads, pub. Beaver Music, c. 1955.*	2.25	3.00
☐ **Moonbeam Kiss Her for Me,** *lyric by Mort Dixon, music by Harry Woods, inset Geo. Lipschultz, Leff cover, c. 1927.*	2.25	3.00
☐ **Moonlight and Roses,** *by Edwin H. Lemare and Neil Moret, pub. Moret, B&W, inset Nell Gwynn, c. 1925.*	2.25	3.00

	Price Range	
☐ **Moonlight Down in Lover's Lane,** *words by George Pitman and Bartley Costello, music by Max Kortlander, pub. Joe Davis, c. 1933.*	2.25	3.00
☐ **Moonlight on the Ganges,** *words by Chester Wallace, music by Sherman Myers.*	2.25	3.00
☐ **Moon Love,** *by Mack David, Mac Davis and Andre Kostelanetz, Glenn Miller with trombone on back cover, c. 1939 near mint.*	5.00	7.00
☐ **Moon Melody,** *by Martin Broones, pub. Schirmer, c. 1935.*	2.25	3.00
☐ **Muddy Water (A Mississippi Moan),** *words by "Jo" Trent, music by Peter DeRose and Harry Richman, inset Nora Bayes.*	2.25	3.00
☐ **(Put Another Nickel In) Music! Music! Music!,** *words and music by Stephan Weiss and Bernie Baum, inset Teresa Brewer, pub. Cromwell, c. 1950.*	2.25	3.00
☐ **My Blue Heaven,** *words by George Whiting, music by Walter Donaldson, pub. Feist, c. 1927 reprint.*	2.25	3.00
☐ **My Blue Ridge Mountain Home,** *words and music by Carson Robison featured by Vernon Dahlhart, both photos on cover, pub. Triangle Music, c. 1927.*	2.25	3.00
☐ **My Cabin of Dreams,** *by Nick Kenny, Al Frazzini and Nat Madison, inset Nano Rodrigo, c. 1937.*	2.25	3.00
☐ **My Castles in the Air Are Tumbling Down,** *words by Arthur J. Lamb, music by W. C. Polla, pub. Church, beautiful colored litho by The Knapp Co., c. 1919.*	2.25	3.00
☐ **My Dream Christmas,** *by Nancy North and Stan Hadley, pub. Life Music, Barbelle cover, nice winter scene, c. 1950.*	2.25	3.00
☐ **My Dreams Are Getting Better All the Time,** *lyrics by Mann Curtis, music by Vic Mizzy, inset Marion Hutton, pub. SJ.*	2.25	3.00
☐ **My Heart Cries For You,** *by Carl Sigman and Percy Faith, inset Dinah Shore, pub. Massy, c. 1950.*	2.25	3.00
☐ **My Hindoo Queen,** *by Frederick Seymour and Fred W. Pike, pub. Waldorf, P. Hubbard cover, c. 1920.*	2.25	3.00
☐ **My Ohio Home,** *lyric by Gus Kahn, music by Walter Donaldson, pub. Feist, c. 1927.*	1.75	2.50
☐ **My Mammy Knows,** *by Harry DeCosta and M. K. Jerome, shows steam train.*	2.00	3.00
☐ **My Mother's Evening Prayer,** *by Bud Green, Charlie Pierce and Al Dubin, c. 1920.*	2.00	3.00
☐ **My Sin,** *by DeSylva, Brown and Henderson, inset Jack Osterman, c. 1929.*	2.00	3.00
☐ **My Sister and I,** *by Hy Zaret, Joan Whitney and Alex Kramer, Im-Ho cover, c. 1941.*	2.00	3.00
☐ **My Thoughts Are You,** *words by John Steel, music by Charles Wakefield Cadman, pub. Harold Flammer, c. 1923.*	1.50	2.00
☐ **My Twilight Dream,** *lyric and adaption by Lew Sherwood and Eddie Duchin, (based on Chopin's Nocturne in E Flat), photo Duchin, c. 1939.*	2.25	3.00
☐ **My Wishing Song,** *lyric by Irving Kahal, music by Joe Burke, inset Mark Fisher.*	2.25	3.00
☐ **Naturally,** *words and music by George and Bert Clarke and Ben Kruger, inset Guy Lombardo, pub. Olman, c. 1934.*	2.00	3.00

	Price Range	
☐ **The Naughty Lady of Shady Lane,** *by Sid Tepper and Roy C. Bennet, inset the Ames Bros., pub. Paxton, c. 1954.*	2.25	3.00
☐ **Nestle in Your Daddy's Arms,** *by Lou Herscher and Joe Burke, pub. Feist, c. 1921.*	2.25	3.00
☐ **Never a Day Goes By,** *words and music by Walter Donaldson, Peter De Rose and Mitchell Parish, inset Guy Lombardo, pub. Miller, c. 1943.*	2.25	3.00
☐ **Night and Day,** *words and music by Cole Porter, inset Frank Sinatra, pub. Harms, c. 1932.*	3.25	5.00
☐ **(Give Me) A Night In June,** *by Cliff Friend, Starmer cover, c. 1927.*	2.00	3.00
☐ **No! No! A Thousand Times NO!,** *by Al Sherman, Al Lewis and Abner Silver, pub. Feist, inset Milton Ebbins, c. 1934.*	1.75	2.50
☐ **Normandy,** *by Nelson Ingham, Frank Kienzle and Charles Smith, inset Sophia Kassmit, pub. Mills, Barbelle cover, c. 1920.*	1.50	2.50
☐ **Normancy,** *by Russell Robinson, Jack Little and Addy Britt, pub. Henry Waterson, c. 1925.*	2.00	2.75
☐ **No Stone Unturned,** *photo June Hutton, pub. Miller, c. 1953.*	1.50	2.50
☐ **Now and Then,** *lyric by Joe McKiernan, melody by Norman Spencer, pub. Richmond, c. 1920.*	2.00	2.75
☐ **Now-I-Know,** *music by S. R. Henry and D. Onivas, lyric by H. Warren, pub. Stern, colored litho cover by Knapp, c. 1919.*	1.75	2.50
☐ **Oceana Roll,** *words by Roger Lewis, music by Lucien Denni, pub. Jerry Vogel, reprint, c. 1938.*	1.50	2.00
☐ **O Dio Mio,** *words and music by Al Hoffman and Dick Manning, large photo Annette, pub. Topper, c. 1959.*	2.00	3.00
☐ **Oh, How I Love You,** *words by Joe Larkin, music by Ted Johnson, pub. Spitzer, inset Evelyn Knight, c. 1951.*	3.00	4.25
☐ **Oh! How I Wish I Could Sleep Until My Daddy Comes Home,** *words by Sam M. Lewis and Joe Young, music by Pete Wendling, inset Al Jolson, Barbelle cover, c. 1918.*	3.00	4.25
☐ **An Old Guitar and an Old Refrain,** *words and music by Gus Kahn, Ben Black and Neil Moret, pub. Villa Moret, c. 1927.*	2.25	3.00
☐ **The Old Master Painter,** *lyric by Haven Gillespie, music by Beasley Smith, inset Richard Hayes, c. 1949.*	2.25	3.00
☐ **Old Pal,** *lyric by Gus Kahn, music Egbert Van Alsyne, Med. Key of "F".*	2.25	3.00
☐ **The Old Refrain,** *words by Alice Mattullath, Viennese popular song, arr. Fritz Kreisler, pub. Fischer, key of "F".*	2.25	3.00
☐ **On a Dreamy Night,** *by Walter Smith, Stainford cover, c. 1920.*	2.25	3.00
☐ **On the Campus,** *from "Memories of Mt. Gallitzin", composed by a Sister of St. Joseph (Baden, PA).*	2.25	3.00
☐ **On Treasure Island,** *by Edgar Leslie and Joe Burke, pub. Morris, Cliff Miska cover, c. 1935.*	1.50	2.00
☐ **One Minute to One,** *words by Sam M. Lewis, music by Fred Coots, inset Ted Fiorito, pub. Feist, c. 1933.*	2.00	2.50
☐ **Only You,** *by A. H. Eastman and Fred Heltman, pub. Heltman, c. 1919.*	1.75	2.50
☐ **The Oregon Trail,** *words by Billy Hill, music by Peter DeRose, photo Fred Waring, c. 1935.*	2.25	3.00

	Price Range	
☐ **Our Bungalow of Dreams,** *by Tommie Malie, Charlie Newman and Joe Verges, pub. Ted Browne, inset Baby Dorothy Johnson, c. 1927.*	1.25	1.75
☐ *As above, inset Norma Leslie and Monte Vandergrift, (The California Poppy and the Sap).*	2.25	3.00
☐ **Our Love,** *words and music by Larry Clinton, Buddy Bernier and Bob Emmerich, pub. Chappe, c. 1929.*	1.50	2.00
☐ **Out of Nowhere,** *lyric by Edward Heyman, music by John W. Green, inset Seger Ellis, pub. Famous, c. 1931.*	2.00	3.00
☐ **Out Where the West Begins,** *words by Arthur Chapman, music by Estelle Philleo, c. 1917.*	2.00	3.00
☐ **Pagan Moon,** *by Al Bryan, Al Dubin and Joe Burke, c. 1931.*	2.00	3.00
☐ **Pale Moon (Indian Love Song),** *lyric by Jesse M. Glick, music by Frederic Knight Logan.*	1.50	2.00
☐ **Pal of My Cradle Days,** *lyric by Marshall Montgomery, music by Al Piantadosi, inset Franklyn Baur, pub. Feist.*	2.25	3.00
☐ **Pals,** *lyric by Gilbert Wells, music by Lynn Cowan, c. 1919.*	2.25	3.00
☐ **Paradise Lane,** *words and music by Charles O'Flynn, Charlie McCarthy and Mickey Addy, inset Frankie Master, pub. Feist, c. 1933.*	2.50	3.50
☐ **Paper Doll,** *by Johnny Black, inset Bing Crosby, pub. Marks, c. 1943.*	2.50	3.50
☐ **Paradise Isle,** *words by Ray Klages, music by Al Goering and Jack Pettin, pub. Harms, c. 1927.*	2.25	3.00
☐ **Parlez Moi d'Amour (Speak to Me of Love),** *words and music by Jean Lenoir, American version by Bruce Siever, pub. Harms.*	1.50	2.00
☐ **Patsy,** *lyric by Dick Coburn, music by Earl Burtnett and Dick Winfree, inset Art Landry and his Orchestra, Griffith cover, c. 1924.*	1.25	1.75
☐ **Peace of Mind,** *lyric by James Dyrenforth, music by Carrill Gibbons, pub. Gene Austin, c. 1929.*	2.25	3.00
☐ **Penny Serenade,** *words by Hal Hallifax, music by Melle Weersma, inset Guy Lombardo, c. 1938.*	2.25	3.00
☐ **Play to Me, Gypsy (The Song I Love),** *English version by Jimmy Kennedy, original lyrics by Beda, music by Karel Vacek, c. 1934.*	2.00	3.00
☐ **Poor Little Butterfly is a Fly Girl Now,** *lyric by Sam M. Lewis and Joe Young, music by M. K. Jerome, c. 1919.*	2.00	3.00
☐ **The Poor People of Paris,** *by Marguerite Monnot, pub. Reg Connelly, c. 1954.*	3.00	4.00
☐ **Poor Papa (He's Got Nothing at All),** *words by Billy Rose, music by Harry Woods, inset Bob Cause and his Collegians, c. 1926.*	3.00	4.00
☐ **Poppy,** *words by Phil Roy, music by Isabel Mayer, pub. Mayer, Portland, OR, inset Mildred Fields (The Texas Belle), c. 1947.*	2.00	3.00
☐ **Powder Your Face with Sunshine, Smile! Smile! Smile!,** *words and music by Carmon Lombardo and Stanley Rochinski, inset Lebert, Carmen and Guy Lombardo, pub. Lombardo Music, c. 1948.*	3.00	4.00

	Price Range	
☐ **Practice Makes Perfect,** *by Don Roberts and Ernest Gold, c. 1940*	2.25	3.00
☐ **Praise the Lord and Pass the Ammunition,** *words and music by Frank Loesser, pub. Famous, c. 1942*	3.00	4.00
☐ **Precious,** *words by Raymond B. Egan, music by Stephen Pasternacki and Richard Whiting, pub. Feist, c. 1926*	3.00	4.00
☐ **Pretend,** *by Lew Douglas, Cliff Parman and Frank Lavere, inset Ralph Marterie, pub. Brandom, c. 1952*	1.50	2.00
☐ *As above, inset Nat "King" Cole*	3.00	4.00
☐ **Pretending,** *words by Marty Symes, music by Al Sherman, inset Andy Russell, pub. Capitol, c. 1946*	1.50	2.00
☐ *As above, Bing Crosby on cover*	3.00	4.00
☐ **Pretty Baby,** *words by Gus Kahn, music by Tony Jackson and Egbert Van Alstyne, c. 1916*	2.25	4.00
☐ **Pretty Cinderella,** *words and music by Will J. Harris, pub. IB, Leff cover, c. 1926*	2.25	4.00
☐ **Pretty Kitty Blue Eyes,** *lyrics by Mann Curtis, music by Vic Mizzy, inset Joan Brooks, c. 1944*	1.50	2.00
☐ **Pretty Kitty Kelly,** *words by Harry Pease, music by Ed Nelson, pub. A. J. Stasney, colored litho cover, c. 1920*	2.00	2.75
☐ **Pretty Little Thing,** *words and music by Tommy Malie and Little Jack Little, pub. Feist, inset Evelyn Wilson*	3.00	5.00
☐ **Prisoner of Love,** *words and music by Leo Robin, Clarence Gaskill and Russ Columbo, inset Perry Como, pub. Mayfair, c. 1931*	2.25	3.00
☐ **The Prisoner's Song,** *words and music by Guy Massey*	2.25	3.00
☐ **Profecia (Bolero),** *(Cuban) words by Francisco Llorens, music by Rodriguez Fiffe, pub. Pan American, c. 1941*	2.25	3.00
☐ **Pua Kona,** *in C Sharp Minor, professional arr. for Hawaiian guitar, inset Sol Hoopii, pub. Ball Music, c. 1940*	2.50	3.50
☐ **Pucker Up and Whistle ('Til the Clouds Roll By),** *words and music by Blanche Franklyn and Nat Vincent, inset Yvette Rugel, Barbelle cover, pub. Fred Fisher, c. 1921*	2.25	3.00
☐ **Puddin' Head Jones,** *lyric by Al Bryan, music by Lou Handman, inset Ozzie Nelson, Harris cover, c. 1933*	3.00	4.25
☐ **Pu-Leeze! Mister Hemingway!,** *words and music by Milton Drake, Walter Kent and Abner Silver, inset Guy Lombardo, pub. Olman, c. 1932*	3.00	4.25
☐ **Put Away a Little Ray of Golden Sunshine,** *words by Sam M. Lewis and Joe Young, music by Fred E. Ahlert, pub. Waterson, inset Underhill Macy and J. William Scott, c. 1924*	2.25	3.00
☐ **Put On an Old Pair of Shoes,** *by Mr. and Mrs. Billy Hill, inset Ozzie Nelson and Harriet Hilliard, c. 1935*	4.00	6.00
☐ **Put Your Arms Where They Belong (For They Belong to Me),** *words and music by Lou Davis, Henry Santly and Herman Ackman, inset Nick Lucas, c. 1926*	2.25	3.00
☐ **Put Your Hand in the Hand,** *words and music by Gene MacLellan, pub. Beechwood, inset Anne Murray, c. 1970*	2.25	3.00
☐ **Rain,** *words by Billy Hill, music by Peter DeRose, inset Henry King*	1.75	2.50
☐ **Rain,** *lyrics and music by Eugene Ford, inset Brooke Jones, c. 1927*	2.25	3.00

Red River Valley,
Red River Valley,
insets of Gene Autry,
pub. Calumet Music Co.,
1935, **$3.00-$5.00.**

Revenge,
Revenge,
words by Lewis and Young,
music by Harry Akst,
pub. by Remick Music Corp.,
$3.00-$6.00.

	Price Range	
☐ **Red Sails in the Sunset,** *lyric by Jimmy Kennedy, music by Hugh Williams, inset Fred Waring, Barbelle cover, pub. SB, from Prindetown Follies, c. 1935.*	2.00	3.00
☐ **Remember,** *by Irving Berlin, pub. IB, Leff cover, c. 1925.*	2.00	3.00
☐ **Rio Nights,** *words and music by Elmer Vincent and Fisher Thompson, pub. Fisher Thompson, c. 1920.*	2.00	3.00
☐ **Rock-A-Bye Land,** *words and music by W. C. Weasner, pub. Weasner, c. 1921.*	2.00	3.00
☐ **Rock-A-Bye to Sleep in Dixie,** *words and music by Sylvester L. Cross, inset Clyde Kittell, WGY's Singing Announcer, pub. S. L. Cross, c. 1929.*	2.00	3.00
☐ **Roll Along Prairie Moon,** *by Ted Fiorito, Harry MacPherson and Albert Von Tilzer, photo Ted Fiorito, c. 1935.*	2.00	3.00
☐ **Rolling the Moon,** *words by Donald Hutton and Rholin Cooley, music by Vernon Suckow, pub. Madrona Music, Portland, OR, c. 1920.*	2.00	3.00
☐ **Rose O'Day (The Filla-ga-du-sha Song),** *by Charlie Tobias and Al Lewis, pub. Tobias-Lewis, c. 1941.*	1.50	2.25
☐ **Roses of Picardy,** *words by Fred E. Weatherly, music by Haydn Wood, pub. Chappell Harms, Medium in "C", c. 1916.*	1.75	2.75
☐ **Rosette,** *lyric by Charles Newman, music by Carmen Lombardo, Ransley Studio cover, pub. M. Weil, c. 1928.*	2.25	3.00
☐ **Rudolph the Red Nosed Reindeer,** *lyric and music by Johnny Marks, pub. St. Nickolas Music, c. 1949.*	2.00	3.00
☐ **Rumors Are Flying,** *words and music by Bennie Benjamin and George Weiss, inset Perry Como, c. 1946.*	2.25	3.00
☐ *As above, inset Margie Hughes, pub. Oxford.*	2.25	3.00
☐ **Russian Lullaby,** *by Irving Berlin, c. 1927.*	2.25	3.00
☐ **Sam the Old Accordion Man,** *words and music by Walter Donaldson, inset Joe Mace.*	1.50	2.00
☐ **Santa Claus Is Comin' to Town,** *words by Haven Gillespie, music by Fred Coots, pub. Feist, c. 1934.*	2.50	3.50
☐ **Satisfied With You,** *words by Harold Dixon, music by Sam H. Stept, inset The Record Boys: Sammy Stept, Si Bernard and Frank Kamplain, pub. Jack Mills, c. 1926.*	2.25	3.00
☐ **Scatter Brain,** *lyric by Johnny Burke, music by Keen-Bean and Frankie Masters, inset Masters.*	1.25	1.75
☐ **Sentimental Journey,** *by Bud Green, Les Brown and Ben Homer, inset Les Brown, pub. E. H. Morris, c. 1944.*	2.25	3.00
☐ **(When You and I Were) Seventeen,** *words by Gus Kahn, music by Chas Rosoff, Shea's Hippodrome Symphony Orchestra, c. 1924.*	2.50	3.50
☐ *As above, inset Mack Davis and his Paradise Orchestra.*	2.50	3.50
☐ **Shadows of Love,** *lyric by Annelu Burns, music by Madelyn Sheppard, pub. Geo Friedman, c. 1920.*	2.25	3.00
☐ **Shanghai Dream Man,** *by Benny Davis and Harry Akst.*	1.50	2.00
☐ **She's a Cornfed Indiana Girl,** *lyric and music by Fran Frey, Eddie Killfeather and George Olsen, pub. Feist, inset Geo. Olsen, c. 1926.*	2.25	3.00

1935 Scandals,
It's an Old Southern Custom,
words by Jack Yellen, Cliff Friend and Herb Magidson,
music by Joseph Meyer,
pub. Movietone,
$3.00-$5.00.

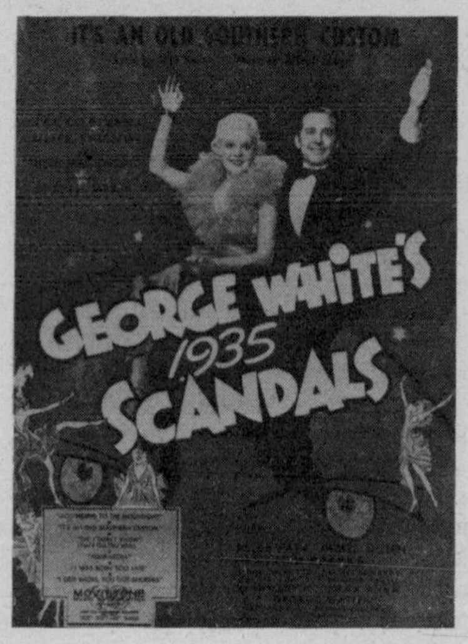

Oklahoma,
The Surrey With the Fringe On Top,
words by Oscar Hammerstein,
music by Richard Rodgers,
pub. Williamson Music, Inc.,
$2.50-$5.00.

	Price Range	
☐ **Shine on Harvest Moon,** *words and music by Nora Bayes and Jack Norworth.*	2.25	3.00
☐ **The Shrine of St. Cecilia,** *words by Carroll Loveday, music by Jokern, pub. Braun, c. 1940.*	2.50	3.00
☐ **The Singing Hills,** *by Mack David, Dick Sanford and Sammy Mysels, inset Blue Barron, c. 1940.*	2.25	3.00
☐ **Sing Me a Baby Song,** *words by Gus Kahn, music by Walter Donaldson, pub. Feist, c. 1927.*	2.25	3.00
☐ **Sing Me "O Sole Mio",** *lyrics by Gus Kahn, music by Egbert VanAlstyne, c. 1924.*	3.00	4.00
☐ **Sing Me to Sleep,** *words by Clifton Bingham, music by Edwin Greene, pub. Boston Music, c. 1902.*	2.25	3.00
☐ **Siren of a Southern Sea,** *by Abe Brashen and Harold Weeks, c. 1920.*	2.25	3.00
☐ **Sitting By the Window,** *by Paul Insetta, c. 1949.*	2.25	3.00
☐ **Sleepy Bye,** *A Lullaby Waltz, words and music by Carl Winge, pub. Weeks and Winge, inset Francesco Longo, c. 1925.*	1.00	1.50
☐ **Sleepy Head,** *words and music by Benny Davus and Jesse Greer, c. 1926.*	2.50	3.00
☐ **Smilin' Through,** *lyric and music by Arthur A. Penn, c. 1918.*	1.00	1.50
☐ **So Blue,** *by B. G. DeSylva, Lew Brown, Ray Henderson, based on a theme by Mrs. Jesse Crawford, inset Henri Garden, c. 1927.*	2.50	3.50
☐ **Soldier's Chorus from the Opera "Faust",** *by Charles Gounod, pub. Jack Mills.*	1.00	1.50
☐ **Somebody Else is Taking My Place,** *by Dick Howard, Bob Ellsworth and Russ Morgan, inset Vaughn Monroe, c. 1937.*	3.00	4.25
☐ **Some Day You'll Want Me Back (Maybe I Won't Want You),** *by Carey Morgan and Wel Retrop (Lew Porter?), pub. Stern, inset Fred Freddy, Gus Hill's Minstrels, c. 1919.*	2.25	3.00
☐ **Some Day (You'll Want Me To Want You),** *words and music by Jimmy Hodges, inset Vaughn Monroe, pub. Duchess, c. 1940.*	2.25	3.00
☐ **Somewhere,** *lyric and music by L. Earl Abel, Barbelle cover, c. 1922.*	2.25	3.00
☐ **Songs My Mother Taught Me,** *by Anton Dvorak, inset Gale Page, pub. Calumet.*	1.00	1.50
☐ **The Song of Songs,** *words by Clarence Lucas, music by Moya, c. 1914.*	2.25	3.00
☐ **Southern Dreams,** *slow melody waltz, words by Charles L. Browne, music by Geo Hamilton Green, pub. Daniels & Wilson, WR Campbell cover, c. 1919.*	2.25	3.00
☐ **Someone is Losin' Susan,** *by Roy Turk, Geo W. Meyer and Paul Ash, inset Bob Blake, pub. H. Waterson, Barbelle cover, c. 1926.*	2.00	3.00
☐ **Springtime,** *lyric by Gus Kahn, music by Anatol Friedland, c. 1920.*	2.00	3.00
☐ **(When It's) Springtime in the Rockies,** *by Mary Woolsey, Robert Sauer and Milt Taggart, inset Rudy Vallee, c. 1929.*	2.00	3.00
☐ **Star Dust,** *words by Mitchell Parish, music by Hoagy Carmichael, pub. Mills, c. 1929.*	3.00	4.00

	Price Range	
☐ **A Star Fell Out of Heaven,** *words and music by Mack Gordon and Harry Revel, inset Johnny Johnson, pub. Crawford, c. 1936.*	2.50	3.50
☐ **The Stars and Stripes Forever,** *by John Phillip Sousa, pub. Church, c. 1897.*	2.25	3.00
☐ **The Statue of Liberty is Smiling,** *words by Jack Mahoney, music by Halsey K. Mohn, c. 1918.*	2.25	3.00
☐ **Stolen Kisses,** *words by Francis Wheeler, music by Ted Snyder, Barbelle cover, c. 1921.*	2.25	3.00
☐ **Stumbling,** *words and music by "Zez" Confrey, pub. Feist, c. 1922.*	2.25	3.00
☐ **Suez,** *words by Will Pancoast, music by Ferdie Grofe and Peter DeRose, inset Waring's Pennsylvanians, pub. Triangle, c. 1922.*	2.25	3.00
☐ **Sunshine Rose,** *words by Jean Lefavre, music by W. C. Polla, Rolf Armstrong cover, pub. Church, c. 1920.*	2.50	3.50
☐ **Sweet and Low,** *words by Stanley Royce, music by Charles L. Johnson, pub. Forster, c. 1919.*	2.00	2.75
☐ **Sweet Child (I'm Wild About You),** *by Richard A. Whiting, Al Lewis and Howard Simon, inset Boyd Senter, c. 1935.*	2.00	2.75
☐ **The Sweetest Story Ever Told (Tell Me Do You Love Me),** *by R. M. Stults, pub. Ditson, c. 1920.*	2.00	2.75
☐ **Sweetheart,** *words by Benny Davis, music by Arnold Johnson, pub. Feist, c. 1921.*	2.25	3.00
☐ **(I Love You - I Love You) Sweetheart of All My Dreams,** *by Art Fitch, Kay Fitch and Bert Lowe, inset Wm. Stamm with the Kit Kat Boys, c. 1928.*	2.25	3.00
☐ **Sweetheart of My Dreams,** *by Al Jacobs and Al Pearce, photo Al Pearce and his Gang, c. 1933.*	2.00	2.75
☐ **Sweethearts on Parade,** *words by Charles Newman, music by Carmen Lombardo, c. 1928.*	2.00	2.75
☐ **Sweetie Please Tell Me,** *by Will R. McDowell, pub. McDowell, cover with apple blossoms and bluebirds, mint, c. 1921.*	2.50	3.50
☐ **Sweetness,** *lyric by Gus Kahn, music by Marie Dodge, B&W, c. 1920.*	1.50	2.00
☐ **Sweet Indiana Home,** *lyric and music by Walter Donaldson, inset Aileen Stanley, c. 1922.*	2.25	3.00
☐ **Sweet Jennie Lee,** *by Walter Donaldson, photo Guy Lombardo, pub. Donaldson, c. 1930.*	2.25	3.00
☐ **Sweet Little You,** *by Irving M. Bibo, pub. Maurice Abrahams.*	1.75	2.75
☐ **Sweet Violets,** *by Cy Coben and Charles Grean, photo Dinah Shore.*	1.25	1.75
☐ **Sweet Violets,** *novelty song by Benny Samberg, pub. Southern, inset Gene Kardos, c. 1932.*	1.75	2.25
☐ **The Sweetest Rose of All,** *lyric by O. Abbey, music by Wm. Witol, pub. American Music Pub., Leff cover, c. 1923.*	2.00	3.00
☐ **The Sweetheart of Sigma Chi,** *lyric by Byron Stokes, music by Dudleigh Vernor, pub. Melrose Bros., 28th ed., c. 1927.*	3.00	4.00
☐ **Swinging Down the Lane,** *lyric by Gus Kahn, music by Isham Jones, pub. Feist, inset Isham Jones, c. 1923.*	2.25	3.00
☐ **Swingin' in a Hammock,** *words by Tot Seymour and Chas O'Flynn, music by Pete Wendling, inset Eddie Lane, c. 1930.*	2.25	3.00

Second Fiddle,
Back to Back,
words and music by Irving Berlin,
pub. Irving Berlin, Inc.,
$3.00-$6.00.

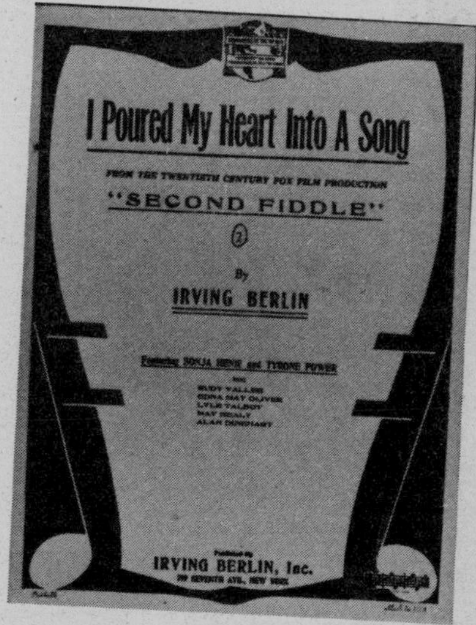

Second Fiddle,
I Poured My Heart Into a Song,
words and music by Irving Berlin,
pub. Irving Berlin, Inc.,
$3.00-$6.00.

	Price Range	
☐ **Symphony,** *words by Andre Tabet and Roger Bernstein, American version by Jack Lawrence, music by Alstone, inset Johnny Desmond, c. 1945.*	2.25	3.00
☐ **Syncopated Clock,** *words by Mitchell Parish, music by Leroy Anderson, pub. Mills, c. 1950.*	2.25	3.50
☐ **Take It Easy,** *words and music by Albert De Bru, Irving Taylor and Vic Mizzy, c. 1943.*	2.25	3.50
☐ **Take Me Back to My Boots and Saddle,** *words and music by Walter Samuels, Leonard Whitcup and Teddy Powell, inset Buddy Clark, pub. Schuster & Miller, c. 1935.*	2.50	3.50
☐ *As above, inset Dick Gasparre.*	2.25	3.00
☐ **Take Me Back to Your Heart,** *lyric by Billy Rose, music by George W. Meyer, inset Harry Meyer, conductor, Stanton Symphony Orchestra, Philadelphia, PA, Starmer cover, c. 1924.*	3.00	4.00
☐ **Take Me to the Land of Jazz,** *words by Bert Kalmar and Edgar Leslie, music by Pete Wendling, c. 1919.*	3.00	4.00
☐ **A Taste of Honey,** *words by Ric Marlow, music by Bobby Scott, pub. Songfest Music, c. 1962.*	2.25	3.00
☐ **Tea Leaves,** *by Morty Berk, Frank Capano and Mac C. Freedman, inset Geo. Olsen, c. 1948.*	1.75	2.50
☐ **Teddy Bear's Picnic,** *words by Jimmy Kennedy, music by John W. Bratton, c. 1947.*	2.00	3.00
☐ **Tell Me,** *lyric by J. Will Callahan, music by Max Kortlander, c. 1919.*	2.00	3.00
☐ **Tell Me Why,** *lyric by Richard Coburn, music by Vincent Rose, c. 1919.*	2.00	3.00
☐ **Temptation,** *lyric by Arthur Freed, music by Nacio Herb Brown, c. 1933.*	2.00	3.00
☐ **Ten Little Miles From Town,** *words by Gus Kahn, music by Elmer Schoebel, c. 1928.*	2.50	3.50
☐ **Tennessee Waltz,** *by Redd Stewart and Pee Wee King, inset Patti Page, pub. Acuff Rose.*	2.50	3.50
☐ **(Down Among the Sleepy Hills of) Ten-Ten-Tennessee,** *words by Joe Young and Sam M. Lewis, music by Geo W. Meyer, Perret cover, c. 1923.*	2.25	3.00
☐ **(Did You Ever Get) That Feeling in the Moonlight,** *by James Cavanaugh, Larry Stock and Ira Schuster, inset Gene Krupa..*	1.50	2.00
☐ **(You're the Only Girl) That Made Me Cry,** *words and music by Fred Fisher, pub. Fisher, Wohlman cover, c. 1920.*	2.25	3.00
☐ **That Naughty Waltz,** *lyric by Edwin Stanley, music by Sol. P. Levy, c. 1920.*	2.25	3.00
☐ **That Old Fashioned Mother of Mine (An Old Fashioned Lady),** *words by Worton David, music by Horatio Nicholls, medium in A Flat.*	1.50	2.50
☐ **That Old Irish Mother of Mine,** *lyric by Wm. Jerome, music by Harry VonTilzer, c. 1920.*	1.50	2.50
☐ **That Old Gang of Mine,** *words by Billy Rose, music by Ray Henderson, blue and white, reprint.*	2.50	3.50
☐ **That's How I Believe in You,** *lyric by Al. Dubin and Paul Cunninghamm, music by Bert Rule, c. 1921.*	2.25	3.00

Swing Symphony,
Cow Cow Boogie,
pub. Leeds Music,
$1.00-$2.50.

The Time,
the Place and the Girl,
Oh, But I Do,
words by Leo Robin,
music by Arthur Schwartz,
pub. M. Witmark & Sons,
$3.00-$7.00.

Original Manuscript Of "Dixie", by its composer Daniel D. Emmett

	Price Range	
☐ **That's My Desire,** *words by Carroll Loveday, music by Helmy Kresa, inset Alvino Rey, pub. Mills, c. 1931*	2.25	3.00
☐ **That's My Mammy,** *words by Harry Pease, music by Abel Baer and Ed Nelson, pub. Feist, inset Harry Richman, c. 1928.*	3.00	4.00
☐ **That's the Way I've Missed You,** *lyric by Gus Kahn, music by Egbert VanAlstyne, inset Mabel Juliene Scott, Lumiere Studios, photo*	2.50	3.50
☐ **That's Why I Love You,** *words and music by Walter Donaldson and Paul Ash, photo Paul Ash, pub. Feist, c. 1926.*	2.25	3.00
☐ **That's Your Mistake,** *words and music by Rudy Toombs, inset The Crew Cut, c. 1955.*	2.50	4.00
☐ **(I Wanna Go Where You Go - Do What You Do) Then I'll Be Happy,** *words by Sidney Clare and Lew Brown, music Cliff Friend, inset Crafts and Sheehan, Leff cover, c. 1925.*	2.50	4.00
☐ **There I Go,** *words by Hy Zaret, music by Irving Weiser, pub. BMI, c. 1940.*	2.25	3.00
☐ **There Must Be a Way,** *lyric and music by Sammy Gallop, Davis Saxon and Robert Cook, inset Charlie Spivak, pub. Stevens Music, c. 1945.*	2.25	3.00
☐ **There's a Star Spangled Banner Waving Somewhere,** *by Paul Roberts and Shelby Darnell, pub. Bob Miller, Barbelle cover, c. 1942*	1.75	2.50
☐ **There's Something Nice About Everyone "But" There's Everything Nice About You,** *words by Alfred Bryan, Arthur Terker, music by Pete Wendling, Barbelle cover, inset Lou Calabrese*	1.75	2.50
☐ **There's No You,** *lyric by Tom Adair, music by Hap Hopper, pub. Barton, inset Eileen Barton.*	2.25	3.00
☐ *As above, inset Frank Sinatra.*	3.00	4.25
☐ **There's Something About a Rose (That Reminds Me of You),** *words by Irving Kahal and Francis Wheeler, music by Sammy Fain, inset Nick Romano, c. 1928*	2.25	3.00
☐ **These Things I Offer You (For a Lifetime),** *words and music by Mort Nevins, Bennie Benjamin and George Weiss.*	2.50	3.50
☐ **They Were Doin' the Mambo,** *words and music by Sonny Burke and Don Ray, pub. Mayfair, inset Vaughn Monroe, c. 1954*	2.25	3.00
☐ **The Thing,** *words and music by Charles R. Grean, inset Phil Harris, pub. Hollis Music, c. 1950*	2.25	3.00
☐ **The Things I Love,** *words and music by Harold Barlow-Lewis Harris, inset Jimmy Dorsey, pub. Campbell, c. 1941.*	2.50	3.50
☐ **The Things We Did Last Summer,** *words by Sammy Cahn, music by Jule Styne, inset Joe Stafford, pub. Ed Morris, c. 1946*	2.50	3.50
☐ **The Things You Left in My Heart,** *by Buddy Kaye, Hugo Taiani and Herb Leighton, photo Freddy Martin, pub. Lewis, c. 1947*	2.50	3.50
☐ **This is No Laughing Matter,** *lyric by Van Loman and Martin Block, music by Al. Frisch, pub. Martin Block, c. 1941.*	2.25	3.00
☐ **This is Worth Fighting For,** *words and music by Edgar DeLange and Sam H. Stept, c. 1942*	2.25	3.00

	Price Range	
☐ **(Somewhere) This Side of Heaven,** *words and music by Chick Adams and Bert Reisfeld, pub. Yankee Music, Barbelle cover, c. 1943*	2.25	3.00
☐ **A Thousand Good Nights,** *by Walter Donaldson, inset Lebert Lombardo, c. 1934*	2.25	3.00
☐ **The Three Bells** *(The Jimmy Brown Song), inset The Browns, pub. Southern Music, c. 1945*	2.50	3.50
☐ **The Little Fishies (Itty Bitty Poo),** *by Saxie Dowell, c. 1939*	2.50	3.50
☐ **Three Little Sisters,** *lyric by Irving Taylor, music by Vic Mizzy, c. 1942*	2.50	3.50
☐ **Three O'Clock in the Morning,** *words by Dorothy Teriss, music by Julian Bobledo, c. 1922*	2.25	3.00
☐ **Three Little Maids From School,** *from "The Mikado", by Gilbert & Sullivan, pub. Calumet*	1.25	2.00
☐ **Three on a Match,** *words by Raymond B. Egan, music by Ted Fiorito, photo Fiorito, c. 1932*	2.25	3.00
☐ **Through the Years,** *words by Edward Heyman, music by Vincent Youmans, medium in E Flat, c. 1931*	1.50	2.00
☐ **Throw Another Log on the Fire,** *by Charles Tobias, Jack Scholl, Murray Mencher, inset Sam Robbins, pub. Feist, c. 1933*	2.25	3.00
☐ **Throwing Stones at the Sun,** *by Nat Simon, Billy Hueston and Sammy Mysels, inset Larry Siry, c. 1934*	2.50	3.00
☐ **Thru the Night,** *words by Virginia K. Logan, music by Frederic Knight Logan, Van Doorn cover, c. 1922*	1.25	1.75
☐ **Tie Me to Your Apron Strings Again,** *words by Joe Goodwin, music by Larry Shay, pub. M. Weill, c. 1925*	2.00	3.00
☐ **Till,** *words by Carl Sigman, music by Charles Danvers, inset Tony Bennett*	2.25	3.00
☐ **Till the End of Time,** *based on Chopin's "Polonaise", by Buddy Kayw and Ted Mossman, c. 1945*	1.50	2.25
☐ **Till the Heavens Roll Away,** *words and music by John R. Nelson, pub. Seliladean*	2.00	3.00
☐ **Till Then,** *words and music by Eddie Seiler, Sol Marcus and Guy Wood, pub. Sun, sung by the Mills Bros. on Decca Record #18599, c. 1944*	1.50	2.25
☐ **The Shadows Have Flown,** *lyric by Haven Gillespie and Lee Onidas, music by Egbert VanAlstyne, pub. VanAlstyne & Curtis, cover by C. T. Agnew, c. 1919*	1.50	1.75
☐ **Till We Meet Again,** *lyric by Raymond B. Egan, music by Richard Whiting*	1.50	2.00
☐ **'Til Reveille,** *words and music by Stanley Cowand and Bobby Worth, inset Rudy Vallee, pub. Melody Lane, c. 1941*	2.50	4.00
☐ *As above, inset Diane Courtney with large NBC mike*	2.50	4.00
☐ **Time on My Hands,** *words by Harold Adamson and Mack Gordon, music by Vincent Youmans, pub. Miller, c. 1930*	2.00	3.00
☐ **Ti-Pi-Tin,** *music and Spanish lyrics by Maria Grever, English lyrics by Raymond Leveen, photo Horace Heidt, pub. Feist, c. 1938*	2.00	3.00
☐ **To Be Worthy of You,** *words by Benny Davis, music by J. Fred Coots*	2.00	3.00

	Price Range	
☐ **Tomorrow Begins Another Year,** *by Webb Pierce and Harmie Smith, pub. Leeds, photo Smith, c. 1945.*	2.50	3.50
☐ **Tomorrow Land,** *by H. J. Tandler, Griffith cover, c. 1921.*	2.25	3.00
☐ **Too Many Kisses in the Summer (Bring too Many Tears in the Fall),** *words by Billy Rose and Al Dubin, music by Harry Warren, Barbelle cover.*	1.50	3.00
☐ **The Touch of Your Lips,** *by Ray Noble, Leff cover, c. 1936.*	2.25	3.00
☐ **To You,** *words and music by Benny Davis, Tommy Dorsey and Ted Shapiro, inset Harry Richman, c. 1939.*	2.25	3.00
☐ **Tricks,** *by "ZEZ" Confrey, pub. Feist, c. 1922.*	2.50	3.50
☐ **Trust in Me,** *by Ned Wever, Jean Schwartz and Milton Ager, inset Pete Pontrelli, c. 1936.*	2.50	3.50
☐ **(Tuck Me to Sleep in my Old) 'Tucky Home,** *words by Joe Young and Sam M. Lewis, music by Geo W. Meyer, c. 1921.*	2.00	2.75
☐ **Two in a Dream,** *by Al Sherman, Al Lewis and Abner Silver, inset Wayne King, pub. Feist, c. 1934.*	2.50	3.50
☐ **Underneath the Arches,** *by Bud Flanagan, inset Sammy Kaye, c. 1932.*	2.00	2.75
☐ **Under Western Skies,** *by James W. Casey, Harold Weeks and Henry Murtagh, inset Monte Austin, pub. Echo, c. 1920.*	1.75	2.50
☐ **Ukelele Lady,** *words by Gus Kahn, music by Richard A Whiting, inset Gendron Orchestra, c. 1925.*	1.75	2.50
☐ **We Three (My Echo, My Shadow and Me),** *by Dick Robertson, Nelson Cogane and Sammy Mysels, pub. Mercer & Mercer, Im-Ho cover, c. 1940.*	2.50	3.50
☐ **We'll Gather Lilacs,** *words and music by Ivor Novello, c. 1945.*	2.00	3.00
☐ **Were You Sincere,** *lyrics by Jack Meskill, music by Vincent Rose, inset Leo Reisman, c. 1931.*	2.25	3.00
☐ **The West a Nest and You,** *by Larry Yoell and Billy Hill, Griffith cover, c. 1923.*	2.25	3.00
☐ **We've Come a Long Way Together,** *lyric by Ted Koehler, music by Sam H. Stept, pub. Feist, c. 1939.*	2.00	2.75
☐ **What Could Be Sweeter Than You?,** *lyric by Lew Brown, music by Cliff Friend, inset Stanley Cable, Leff cover, c. 1925.*	2.00	2.75
☐ **What Do We Do On a Dew-Dew-Dewy Day,** *by Howard Johnson, Charles Tobias and Al Sherman, c. 1927.*	2.00	3.00
☐ **What'll We Do On a Saturday Night (When the Town Goes Dry),** *by Harry Ruby, Barbelle cover, c. 1919.*	3.00	4.00
☐ **What's the Use of Crying,** *lyric by Verdi Kindel, music by Lou Forbes, inset Lou Forbes, pub. Jenkins, c. 1926.*	2.00	3.00
☐ **The Wheel of the Wagon is Broken,** *words and music by Box & Cox and Michael Car, pub. Feist, c. 1935.*	2.25	3.00
☐ **When a Gypsy Makes His Violin Cry,** *words by Dick Smith and Jimmy Rogan, music by Emery Deutsch, inset Emery Deutsch, pub. Donaldson, Douglas & Gumble, c. 1935.*	1.75	2.50
☐ **When Did You Leave Heaven?,** *lyric by Walter Bullock, melody by Richard A. Whiting, photo Tony Martin, from "Sing Baby Sing", c. 1936.*	5.00	7.00
☐ **When Ireland Comes Into Her Own,** *words by Jeff Branen, music by Jack Stanley, c. 1919.*	3.00	4.00
☐ **When It's Sunset in Sweden,** *lyric by Dave Morrison, music by Earl Burtnett, c. 1919.*	3.00	4.00

	Price Range	
☐ **When My Ships Come Sailing Home,** *words by Reginald Steward, music by Francis Dorel, pub. Boosey, c. 1903.*	2.25	3.00
☐ **When the Autumn Leaves Begin to Fail,** *words by Neville Fleeson, music by Albert Von Tilzer, c. 1920.*	2.25	3.00
☐ **When the Dew is Falling,** *words by Fiona MacLeod, music by Edwin Schneider, pub. Boosey, c. 1915.*	2.25	3.00
☐ **When the Leaves Bid the Trees Goodbye,** *lyric by Tot Seymour, music by Vee Lawnhurst, c. 1935.*	2.25	3.00
☐ **When the Leaves Come Tumbling Down,** *words and music by Richard Howard, pub. Feist, c. 1922.*	1.75	2.25
☐ **When the Lights Are Low,** *words by Gerald M. Lane, music by Burton Arant, inset Avalon Male Quartet, pub. Arant Music, c. 1924.*	2.50	3.50
☐ **When the Lights Go On Again (All Over the World),** *by Eddie Seiler, Sol Marcus, Bennie Benjemen, c. 1942.*	2.00	3.00
☐ **When the Morning Glories Wake Up In the Morning (Then I'll Kiss Your Two Lips Good-Night),** *words by Billy Rose, music by Fred Fisher, pub. Weill, c. 1927.*	2.25	3.50
☐ **When They Ask About You,** *words and music by Sam H. Stept, inset Joan Brooks, c. 1943.*	2.25	3.50
☐ **When They Played the Polka,** *words by Lou Holzer, music by Fabian Andre, inset Ozzie Nelson, Sorokin cover, c. 1938.*	3.50	5.50
☐ **When Times Get Better,** *lyric by Irving Kahal, music by Sammy Fain, c. 1932.*	2.50	3.50
☐ **When Will the Sun Shine For Me,** *lyric by Benny Davis, music by Abner Silver, c. 1923.*	1.75	2.50
☐ **When You Come Back to Me,** *music by Neil Moret, words by Harry Williams, pub. Daniels and Wilson, c. 1919.*	1.25	1.75
☐ **When You Look in the Heart of a Rose,** *lyric by Marian Gillespie, music by Florence Methven, pub. Feist, c. 1918.*	2.00	3.00
☐ **When Your Lover Has Gone,** *words and music by E. A. Swan, Ben Harris cover, c. 1931.*	2.50	3.50
☐ **Where the Lazy Daisies Grow,** *by Cliff Friend, inset The Ross Girls, c. 1924.*	2.50	3.50
☐ **The Umbrella Man,** *words and music by James Cavanaugh, Larry Stock and Vincent Rose, inset Dorothy Rochelle.*	2.50	3.50
☐ **Undecided,** *words by Sid Robin, music by Charles Shavers, inset Ames Bros., pub. Leeds, c. 1939.*	2.25	3.00
☐ **Underneath Hawaiian Skies,** *lyrics by Fred Rose, music by Ernie Erdman, pub. Feist, c. 1920.*	2.50	4.00
☐ **Underneath the Stars with You,** *words and music by Sam Stept and Nick Lucas, early B&W printing, c. 1927.*	2.25	3.00
☐ **Under the Willow Tree,** *words and music by Billy Reid, pub. Peter Maurice Music, c. 1945.*	2.25	3.00
☐ **(It Will Have To Do) Until the Real Thing Comes Along,** *words and music by Mann Holiner, Alberta Nichols, Sammy Cahn, Saul Chaplin and L. E. Freeman, c. 1936.*	5.00	7.00
☐ **(Wait Till You Get Them) UP In the Air Boys,** *words by Lew Brown, music by Albert Von Tilzer, pub. BDW, c. 1919.*	5.00	7.00
☐ **The Utah Trail,** *words and music by "Bob" Palmer, pub. Palmer, c. 1928.*	2.25	3.00

	Price Range	
☐ **Valley of Broken Dreams,** *poem by Baron Keyes, music by Leigh Harline, pub. Campbell, c. 1930.*	2.25	3.00
☐ **Velvetone,** *The Heart of the Radio, pub. Velvetone Corp., inset Elinor Fairfax, "The Original Velvetone Girl", lyric by Fred D. Moore, music by Chas. Caldwell.*	2.50	3.50
☐ **Venetian Love Boat,** *by Frank Magine and Ted Koehler, pub. Feist, c. 1922.*	2.50	3.50
☐ **Vict'ry Polka,** *words by Samuel Cahn, music by Jule Styne, c. 1943.*	2.50	3.50
☐ **The Voice in the Old Village Choir,** *words by Gus Kahn, music by Harry Woods, inset Ted Fiorito.*	2.25	3.00
☐ **Wait For Me Mary,** *by Charlie Tobias, Nat Simon and Harry Tobia, Harris cover, pub. RE, c. 1942.*	2.50	3.50
☐ **Waitin' For the Train to Come In,** *by Sunny Skylar and Martin Block, insets Jo Stafford, Johnny Johnson, pub. Martin Block Music, c. 1945.*	2.50	3.50
☐ **Waiting,** *by Harold Lawrence, Jay Milton and Carl Ravazza, Barbelle cover, c. 1944.*	2.50	3.50
☐ **Waiting (When I Hear the Gate A-Swinging),** *words by Reginald Rigby, music by Leo C. Croke.*	1.75	2.25
☐ **Waiting at the End of the Road,** *by Irving Berlin, photo Kate Smith, from movie "Hallelujah", c. 1929.*	4.50	6.50
☐ **Waiting for the Rainbow,** *words by Billy Rose and Benny Davis, music by Harry Akst, pub. M. Weill, c. 1927.*	2.50	3.50

RECORDINGS AND MEMORABILIA

CLASSICAL

COMPOSER MEMORABILIA

Thanks to at least 200 years of active collecting, memorabilia relating to most composers of classical and semi-classical music is well preserved. It tends, however, to be more expensive than memorabilia of jazz, pop, country and other types of music, because of heavy institutional buying and the fact that classic music collectors are found throughout the world, whereas most collecting of other forms of music is limited to America.

One generally thinks, first in terms of autographs and these, of course, are highly desirable, but many other varieties of "collectible" items can be found, including (in the case of composers who lived from the mid 19th-century onward) photographs, personal items, posters, etc. The fame or importance of the composer has very little relation to the cash value of his memorabilia. It is mainly a question of what has been preserved, and the significance of the individual item. Verdi, perhaps the most celebrated operatic composer, lived a long life and was a voluminous letter-writer, hence his letters, excepting those of really worthy content, sell rather cheaply. Handwritten letters in this section are designated by the heading AL. The manner in which an item has been preserved also enters into the picture. An autograph that has been framed along with a photo, which is often done with composers' autographs, is sure to bring a higher price than if unframed.

The European dealers are the best sources for memorabilia of European composers. However, their prices are frequently higher than those charged by U.S. dealers, because of the overwhelming foreign demand for composers' autographs and other items. Auction sales both here and abroad are another prime source for this material.

	ALs	Signed Photo	Plain Signature
☐ **Albeniz, Isaac**	**40.00-50.00**	**75.00-100.00**	**5.00-8.00**
☐ **Bach, C. P. E.**	**1100.00-2200.00**		**120.00-150.00**
☐ **Bach, Johannes Sebastian**	**12000.00-16000.00**		**1100.00-1300.00**
☐ **Barber, Samuel.**	**100.00-125.00**	**50.00-70.00**	**7.00-12.00**
☐ **Bartok, Bella**	**180.00-265.00**	**100.00-135.00**	**7.00-12.00**
☐ **Beethoven, Ludwig von**	**11750.00-15500.00**		**1100.00-1300.00**
☐ **Bellini, Vincenzo.**	**505.00-800.00**		**20.00-25.00**
☐ **Berg, Alban**	**200.00-265.00**	**75.00-100.00**	**7.00-12.00**
☐ **Berlioz, Hector.**	**355.00-600.00**	**450.00-750.00**	**15.00-20.00**
☐ **Bernstein, Leonard.**	**25.00-40.00**	**6.00-9.00**	**3.00-4.00**

	ALs	Signed Photo	Plain Signature
☐ **Bizet, Georges.**	305.00- 450.00	375.00- 550.00	15.00- 20.00
☐ **Bloch, Ernest.**	120.00- 175.00	65.00- 85.00	7.00- 10.00
☐ **Boieldieu, Francois**	38.00- 45.00		
☐ **Boito, Arrigo**	50.00- 70.00	55.00- 75.00	4.00- 7.00
☐ **Borodin, Alexander**	450.00- 600.00	300.00- 400.00	13.00- 17.00
☐ **Brahms, Johannes**	325.00- 500.00	450.00- 600.00	45.00- 65.00
☐ **Britten, Benjamin.**	40.00- 60.00	43.00- 60.00	4.00- 6.00
☐ **Bruch, Max**	67.00- 110.00	35.00- 50.00	4.00- 6.00
☐ **Bruckner, Anton.**	93.00- 158.00	105.00- 165.00	6.00- 10.00
☐ **Busoni, Ferruccio.**	67.00- 93.00	60.00- 80.00	4.00- 7.00
☐ **Cage, John**	97.00- 155.00		4.00- 6.00
☐ **Chabrier, Alexis.**	67.00- 105.00	100.00- 150.00	4.00- 7.00
☐ **Charpentier, Gustave.**	37.00- 53.00	53.00- 75.00	3.00- 5.00
☐ **Chopin, Frederic**	2000.00- 2600.00		70.00- 100.00
☐ **Copland, Aaron.**	27.00- 43.00	15.00- 20.00	3.00- 4.00
☐ **Debussy, Claude.**	300.00- 370.00	195.00- 270.00	13.00- 20.00
☐ **Delibes, Leo.**	250.00- 315.00	275.00- 335.00	12.00- 17.00
☐ **Dello Joio, Norman.**	15.00- 20.00	6.00- 9.00	3.00- 4.00
☐ **Donizetti, Gaetano**	300.00- 400.00		15.00- 23.00
☐ **Dukas, Paul.**	25.00- 35.00	24.00- 35.00	4.00- 6.00
☐ **Dvorak, Antonin.**	125.00- 165.00	155.00- 225.00	6.00- 9.00
☐ **Elgar, Sir Edward**	155.00- 215.00	95.00- 135.00	6.00- 9.00
☐ **Falla, Manuel de.**	45.00- 60.00	65.00- 85.00	5.00- 6.00
☐ **Faure, Gabriel**	40.00- 55.00	50.00- 75.00	4.00- 6.00
☐ **Flotow, F. von.**	120.00- 165.00	300.00- 425.00	6.00- 9.00
☐ **Franck, Cesar**	105.00- 145.00	115.00- 160.00	5.00- 8.00
☐ **Gershwin, George**	600.00- 850.00	105.00- 105.00	6.00- 9.00

	ALs	Signed Photo	Plain Signature
☐ Giordano, Umberto	35.00-50.00	33.00-43.00	3.00-5.00
☐ Glazunov, Alexander	95.00-135.00	105.00-150.00	6.00-9.00
☐ Glinka, Mikhail	75.00-115.00	115.00-165.00	6.00-9.00
☐ Gounod, Charles	60.00-90.00	105.00-150.00	4.00-6.00
☐ Grieg, Edvard	175.00-250.00	190.00-235.00	6.00-9.00
☐ Handel, Georg F.	8000.00-12000.00		400.00-555.00
☐ Hanson, Howard	27.00-35.00	27.00-35.00	3.00-4.00
☐ Harris, Roy	20.00-28.00	20.00-28.00	3.00-4.00
☐ Haydn, Joseph	3000.00-4000.00		80.00-120.00
☐ Hindemith, Paul	25.00-34.00	28.00-35.00	3.00-4.00
☐ Holst, Gustav	70.00-100.00	75.00-120.00	4.00-6.00
☐ Honegger, Arthur	32.00-40.00	43.00-55.00	3.00-4.00
☐ Hovhannes, Alan	11.00-17.00	9.00-13.00	2.00-3.00
☐ Humperdinck, Engelbert	120.00-150.00	155.00-200.00	7.00-10.00
☐ Ives, Charles	95.00-125.00	35.00-55.00	7.00-10.00
☐ Khachaturian, Aram	70.00-115.00	60.00-85.00	5.00-7.00
☐ Kodaly, Zoltan	75.00-120.00	40.00-60.00	5.00-7.00
☐ Kreisler, Fritz	50.00-75.00	50.00-75.00	3.00-4.00
☐ Kreutzer, Rudolphe	140.00-215.00		8.00-12.00
☐ Lalo, Edouard	75.00-115.00	160.00-225.00-	5.00-7.00
☐ Leoncavallo, R.	75.00-115.00	90.00-120.00	5.00-7.00
☐ Liszt, Franz	350.00-525.00	350.00-470.00	8.00-13.00
☐ MacDowell, Edward	115.00-160.00	85.00-120.00	4.00-6.00
☐ Mahler, Gustav	500.00-700.00	250.00-320.00-	8.00-12.00
☐ Mascagni, Pietro	60.00-80.00	35.00-48.00	3.00-4.00
☐ Massenet, Jules	75.00-120.00	100.00-130.00	5.00-7.00
☐ Mendelssohn-Bartholdy	300.00-400.00		8.00-12.00

	ALs	Signed Photo	Plain Signature
☐ Menotti, G. C.	35.00-50.00	26.00-35.00	3.00-4.00
☐ Monteverdi, Claudio.	6750.00-11000.00		450.00-650.00
☐ Mozart, Wolfgang A.	17500.00-25000.00		1250.00-1600.00
☐ Offenbach, Jacques	160.00-220.00	335.00-420.00	7.00-10.00
☐ Orff, Karl.	25.00-35.00	20.00-26.00	3.00-4.00
☐ Paderewski, Ignace	70.00-110.00	55.00-70.00	4.00-6.00
☐ Paganini, Niccolo	320.00-460.00		7.00-10.00
☐ Palestrina, G. P.	4000.00-5500.00		175.00-230.00
☐ Ponchielli, A.	225.00-280.00	250.00-320.00	7.00-10.00
☐ Poulenc, Francis	32.00-40.00	30.00-38.00	3.00-4.00
☐ Prokofieff, Serge	320.00-420.00	110.00-155.00	7.00-10.00
☐ Puccini, Giacomo.	300.00-400.00	170.00-230.00	7.00-10.00
☐ Rachmaninoff, Sergei	160.00-200.00	200.00-250.00	5.00-8.00
☐ Ravel, Maurice	300.00-400.00	180.00-245.00-	5.00-8.00
☐ Rimsky-Korsakov, Nikolai	600.00-800.00	350.00-450.00	9.00-12.00
☐ Rossini, G.	250.00-300.00	325.00-425.00	7.00-10.00
☐ Rubinstein, Anton	150.00-200.00	225.00-280.00	4.00-6.00
☐ Saint-Saens, Camille	120.00-150.00	125.00-170.00	4.00-6.00
☐ Schonberg, Arnold	170.00-230.00	70.00-90.00	5.00-7.00
☐ Schubert, Franz.	3750.00-5500.00		80.00-120.00
☐ Schumann, Robert	1200.00-1700.00		13.00-18.00
☐ Schumann, William.	27.00-35.00	25.00-33.00	3.00-4.00
☐ Scriabin, Alex.	320.00-420.00	325.00-425.00	7.00-10.00
☐ Shostakovich, Dmitri	400.00-500.00	230.00-280.00	7.00-10.00
☐ Sibelius, Jean	180.00-250.00	210.00-260.00	7.00-10.00
☐ Smetana, Bedrich.	575.00-700.00	600.00-800.00	8.00-12.00
☐ Stockhausen, K.	26.00-33.00	25.00-30.00	3.00-4.00

	ALs	Signed Photo	Plain Signature
☐ **Strauss, Richard.**	200.00-250.00	150.00-200.00	7.00-10.00
☐ **Stravinsky, Igor.**	150.00-200.00	120.00-170.00	4.00-6.00
☐ **Tchaikovsky, Peter.**	900.00-1200.00	675.00-900.00	15.00-20.00
☐ **Thomas, Ambroise.**	150.00-175.00	175.00-225.00	5.00-7.00
☐ **Thomson, Virgil.**	35.00-50.00	25.00-35.00	3.00-4.00
☐ **Wagner, Richard**	550.00-750.00	675.00-950.00	25.00-30.00

INSTRUMENTAL RECORDINGS

The following recordings are all in 78rpm and issued mostly in the years between 1900 and 1925.

By and large the public of this era (1900-1925), while a fair segment of it understood and appreciated classical music, bought instrumental recordings for the composition — not for the artist, as is usually the situation with serious fans of classical music today. In fact, the name of the pianist, cellist, orchestra conductor, etc., was frequently not even noticed. Fortunately, the record companies made the necessary identifications on record labels, otherwise the collecting of these records would now be very confusing.

While the sound quality of full orchestral recordings made before about 1912 is somewhat short of pleasing, selections of concert or chamber work by instrumentalists are more satisfactory. The piano's sound was well captured on early recordings, the violin's perhaps even better, the cello's tolerably well. They failed to meld in orchestral recordings because of the archaic practice of trying to capture all the sound in a studio or hall through a single microphone or horn — a practice which, even if attempted with today's sophisticated equipment, would yield very mediocre results.

	Price Range	
☐ **ELMAN, MISCHA (violinist). VICTOR RED SEAL.** *"Moment Musical/Perpetual Mobile"*	5.00	7.00
☐ *"Fantasie" (Faust)*	5.00	7.00
☐ *"Swing Song"*	5.00	7.00
☐ *"Gavotte"*	5.00	7.00
☐ *"Serenade"*	5.00	7.00
☐ *"Minuet in G #2"*	5.00	7.00
☐ *"Les Farfadets"*	5.00	7.00
☐ *"Minuet in F"*	5.00	7.00
☐ *"Gavotte in G" (Idomeneo)*	5.00	7.00
☐ *"Traumerei"*	5.00	7.00
☐ *"Capricietto"*	5.00	7.00
☐ *"Waltz in E Flat"*	5.00	7.00
☐ *"Rondo Capriccioso"*	9.00	12.00
☐ *"Souvenir de Moscow"*	9.00	12.00
☐ *"Nocturne in E Flat Opus 9, #2"*	9.00	12.00
☐ *"Melodie Opus 42, # 3"*	9.00	12.00

	Price Range	
☐ *"Humoresque"*	9.00	12.00
☐ *"Caprice Basque"*	9.00	12.00
☐ *"Sicilienne and Rigaudon"*	9.00	12.00
☐ *"Cavatina Op. 85 #3"*	9.00	12.00
☐ *"Ave Maria"*	9.00	12.00
☐ *"Chanson Louis XIII"*	9.00	12.00
☐ *"Meditation" (Thais)*	9.00	12.00
☐ *"Vogel als Prophet Op. 82 #7"*	5.00	7.00
☐ *"Hungarian Dance #7"*	5.00	7.00
☐ *"In a Gondola"*	5.00	7.00
☐ *"Country Dance"*	5.00	7.00
☐ *"Minuet in D"*	5.00	7.00
☐ *"Rondino on a Theme by Beethoven"*	5.00	7.00
☐ *"Pastorale"*	5.00	7.00
☐ *"Orientale"*	5.00	7.00
☐ *"Capriccio"*	5.00	7.00
☐ *"Valse Caprice Op. 16"*	5.00	7.00
☐ *"Souvenir"*	5.00	7.00
☐ *"Tango"*	5.00	7.00
☐ *"Canto Amoroso"*	12.00	17.00
☐ *"Dans les Bois"*	12.00	17.00
☐ **HEIFETZ, JASCHA (violinist). VICTOR RED SEAL.** *"Valse Bluette"*	5.00	7.00
☐ *"Ruins of Athens"*	5.00	7.00
☐ *"Capricieuse Op. 17"*	5.00	7.00
☐ *"Meditation Op. 32"*	5.00	7.00
☐ *"Guitarre Op. 45 #2"*	5.00	7.00
☐ *"Caprice #20"*	5.00	7.00
☐ *"Minuet"*	5.00	7.00
☐ *"Sicilienne and Rigaudon"*	5.00	7.00
☐ *"Serenade Op. 4"*	5.00	7.00
☐ *"Caprice #13"*	5.00	7.00
☐ *"Zapateado Op. 23 #6"*	5.00	7.00
☐ *"Spanish Dance"*	5.00	7.00
☐ *"Hungarian Dance #1 in G Minor"*	5.00	7.00
☐ *"Slavonic Dance #1 in G Minor"*	5.00	7.00
☐ *"Hebrew Lullaby"*	5.00	7.00
☐ *"Minuet in D"*	5.00	7.00
☐ *"Widmung"*	5.00	7.00
☐ *"Scherzo Tarantelle Op. 16"*	9.00	12.00
☐ *"Ave Marie"*	9.00	12.00
☐ *"Hebrew Melody"*	9.00	12.00
☐ *"Spanish Dance Op. 21 #1"*	9.00	12.00
☐ *"Ronde des Lutins"*	9.00	12.00
☐ *"Moto Perpetuo"*	17.00	23.00
☐ *"On Wings of Song"*	9.00	12.00
☐ *"Concert Op. 22"*	9.00	12.00
☐ *"Nocturne in E Flat Op. 9 #2"*	9.00	12.00
☐ *"Introduction and Tarantelle Op. 43"*	9.00	12.00
☐ *"Serenade Op. 48 - Valse"*	9.00	12.00
☐ *"Symphonie Espagnole - Andante"*	9.00	12.00
☐ *"Violin Concerto - Canzonetta"*	9.00	12.00
☐ *"Zigeunerweisen #1"*	9.00	12.00

	Price Range	
☐ *"Zigeunerweisen #2"*	9.00	12.00
☐ *"Serenade Melancolique Op. 26"*	9.00	12.00
☐ *"Concerto in E Minor - Finale"*	9.00	12.00
☐ *"Rondo in G"*	9.00	12.00
☐ *"Concerto in A Minor Op. 28 - Andante"*	9.00	12.00
☐ *"Nocturne Op. 27 #2"*	9.00	12.00
☐ *"Slavonic Dance #2 in E Minor"*	9.00	12.00
☐ *"Slavonic Dance #3 in G"*	9.00	12.00
☐ **KREISLER, FRITZ (violinist). VICTOR RED SEAL.** *"Old Refrain"*	5.00	7.00
☐ *"Song Without Words #25"*	5.00	7.00
☐ *"Spanish Dance"*	5.00	7.00
☐ *"Songs My Mother Taught Me"*	5.00	7.00
☐ *"Berceuse Romantique"*	5.00	7.00
☐ *"Rondino on a Theme by Beethoven"*	5.00	7.00
☐ *"Arlesienne Suite: Adagietto"*	5.00	7.00
☐ *"Minuet"*	5.00	7.00
☐ *"Bohemian Fantasie"*	9.00	12.00
☐ *"Humoresque"*	9.00	12.00
☐ *"Meditation" (Thais)*	9.00	12.00
☐ *"Liebesfreud"*	9.00	12.00
☐ *"Caprice Viennois"*	9.00	12.00
☐ *"Moment Musical"*	9.00	12.00
☐ *"Tambourin Chinois"*	9.00	12.00
☐ *"Scherzo"*	9.00	12.00
☐ *"Chanson"*	9.00	12.00
☐ *"Praeludium"*	9.00	12.00
☐ *"Liebeslied"*	9.00	12.00
☐ *"Indian Lament"*	9.00	12.00
☐ *"Slavonic Dance #2 in E Minor"*	9.00	12.00
☐ *"Wienerisch"*	9.00	12.00
☐ *"Concerto for Two Violins Part I"*	20.00	25.00
☐ *"Concerto for Two Violins Part II"*	20.00	25.00
☐ *"Concerto for Two Violins Part III"*	20.00	25.00
☐ *"Poor Butterfly"*	5.00	7.00
☐ *"Underneath the Stars"*	5.00	7.00
☐ *"Rosamunde Ballet"*	5.00	7.00
☐ *"Paraphrase on Minuet"*	5.00	7.00
☐ *"Dream of Youth"*	5.00	7.00
☐ *"Polichinelle Serenade"*	5.00	7.00
☐ *"Beautiful Ohio"*	5.00	7.00
☐ *"Nobody Knows the Trouble I See"*	5.00	7.00
☐ *"Gypsy Serenade"*	5.00	7.00
☐ *"Forsaken"*	5.00	7.00
☐ *"Who Can Tell"*	5.00	7.00
☐ *"Love Nest"*	5.00	7.00
☐ *"On Miami Shore"*	5.00	7.00
☐ *"Melody in A"*	5.00	7.00
☐ *"Souvenir"*	5.00	7.00
☐ *"To Spring Op. 43 #6"*	5.00	7.00
☐ *"La Gitana"*	5.00	7.00
☐ *"Paradise"*	5.00	7.00
☐ *"Waltz Op. 39 #15"*	5.00	7.00

	Price Range	
☐ *"Aucassin and Nicolette"*	5.00	7.00
☐ *"Pale Moon"*	5.00	7.00
☐ *"Toy Soldier's March"*	5.00	7.00
☐ *"Midnight Bells"*	5.00	7.00
☐ *"Mazurka Op. 33 #2"*	5.00	7.00
☐ *"Melodie Op. 16 #2"*	5.00	7.00
☐ *"Cherry Ripe"*	5.00	7.00
☐ *"Entr'acte"*	5.00	7.00
☐ *"Love Sends a Little Gift of Roses"*	5.00	7.00
☐ *"The World is Waiting For the Sunrise"*	5.00	7.00
☐ *"Old French Gavotte"*	5.00	7.00
☐ *"From the Land of the Sky Blue Water"*	5.00	7.00
☐ *"Farewell to Cucullain"*	5.00	7.00
☐ *"Serenade"*	5.00	7.00
☐ *"Miniature"*	5.00	7.00
☐ *"Syncopation"*	5.00	7.00
☐ **PADEREWSKI, JAN (pianist). VICTOR RED SEAL.** *"Minuet in G"*	20.00	25.00
☐ *"Valse Brilliante Op. 34 #1"*	20.00	25.00
☐ *"Hark Hark the Lark"*	20.00	25.00
☐ *"La Campanella"*	20.00	25.00
☐ *"Etude in F Minor"*	20.00	25.00
☐ *"Maiden's Wish Op. 74 #1"*	20.00	25.00
☐ *"Chant d'Amour"*	20.00	25.00
☐ *"Berceuse"*	20.00	25.00
☐ *"Aufschwung"*	20.00	25.00
☐ *"La Bandoline"*	20.00	25.00
☐ *"Carrillon de Cythere"*	20.00	25.00
☐ *"Warum"*	20.00	25.00
☐ *"Etude in G Flat Op. 25 #9"*	12.00	16.00
☐ *"Spinning Song"*	12.00	16.00
☐ *"Chant du Voyageur"*	12.00	16.00
☐ *"Nocturne in F Sharp Op. 15 #2"*	12.00	16.00
☐ *"Polonaise Militaire Op. 40 #1"*	12.00	16.00
☐ *"Minuet in G"*	12.00	16.00
☐ *"Cracovienne Fantastique"*	12.00	16.00
☐ *"Waltz in C Sharp Minor Op. 64 #2"*	12.00	16.00
☐ *"Nocturne in F Op. 15 #1"*	12.00	16.00
☐ *"Valse Brilliante Op. 34 #1"*	12.00	16.00
☐ *"Hark Hark the Lark"*	12.00	16.00
☐ *"La Bandoline"*	12.00	16.00
☐ *"Warum"*	12.00	16.00
☐ *"La Campanella"*	12.00	16.00
☐ *"Nocturne in B Flat"*	12.00	16.00
☐ *"Maiden's Wish Op. 74 #1"*	12.00	16.00
☐ *"Hungarian Rhapsody #10"*	12.00	16.00
☐ *"Valse in A Flat Op. 42"*	12.00	16.00
☐ *"Hungarian Rhapsody #2 Part I"*	12.00	16.00
☐ *"Hungarian Rhapsody #2 Part II"*	12.00	16.00
☐ **POWELL, MAUD (violinist). VICTOR RED SEAL.** *Sault d' amour"*	7.00	10.00
☐ *"Gavotte" (Mignon)*	7.00	10.00
☐ *"Barcarolle" (Tales of Hoffmann)*	7.00	10.00

	Price Range	
☐ *"Chanson a Bercer".*	7.00	10.00
☐ *"Silver Threads Among the Gold".*	7.00	10.00
☐ *"Tambourin".*	7.00	10.00
☐ *"Gondoliers".*	7.00	10.00
☐ *"Molly on the Shore".*	7.00	10.00
☐ *"Love's Delight".*	7.00	10.00
☐ *"Petite Valse".*	7.00	10.00
☐ *"Sonata in E, Second Movement".*	7.00	10.00
☐ *"Sonata in E, Fourth Movement".*	7.00	10.00
☐ *"Minuet in G".*	7.00	10.00
☐ *"Kol Nidre".*	7.00	10.00
☐ *"Guitarrero".*	7.00	10.00
☐ *"Little Firefly".*	7.00	10.00
☐ *"Poupee Valsante".*	7.00	10.00
☐ *"Valse Triste".*	7.00	10.00
☐ *"Largo" (Serse).*	7.00	10.00
☐ *"Concerto in G, Allegro Maestoso".*	7.00	10.00
☐ *"Concerto in G, Andante Tranquillo".*	7.00	10.00
☐ *"Concerto in G, Allegro Moderato".*	7.00	10.00
☐ *"Humoresque".*	7.00	10.00
☐ *"Fifth Nocturne".*	7.00	10.00
☐ *"Four American Folk Songs".*	7.00	10.00
☐ **RACHMANINOFF, SERGIE (pianist). VICTOR RED SEAL.** *"Lilacs".*	23.00	30.00
☐ *"Le Coucou".*	12.00	16.00
☐ *"Spinning Song".*	12.00	16.00
☐ *"Dr. Gradus ad Parnassum".*	12.00	16.00
☐ *"Prelude in G Sharp Minor Op. 23 #12".*	12.00	16.00
☐ *"Waltz in D Flat Op. 64 #1".*	12.00	16.00
☐ *"Golliwog's Cake-walk".*	12.00	16.00
☐ *"Waltz in G Flat Major".*	12.00	16.00
☐ *"Prelude in C Sharp Minor Op. 3 #2".*	12.00	16.00
☐ *"Etude in F Minor".*	12.00	16.00
☐ *"Waltz and Elfin Dance".*	12.00	16.00
☐ *"Serenade Op. 3 #5".*	12.00	16.00
☐ *"La Jongleuse".*	23.00	30.00
☐ *"Waltz in A Flat Op. 40 #8".*	23.00	30.00
☐ *"Waltz in B Minor Op. 69 #2".*	23.00	30.00
☐ *"Mazurka in C Sharp Minor Op. 63 #3".*	23.00	30.00
☐ *"If I Were a Bird".*	23.00	30.00
☐ *"Prelude in G Minor Op. 23 #5".*	12.00	16.00
☐ *"Troika en traineaux".*	12.00	16.00
☐ *"Prelude in G Major Op. 32 #5".*	12.00	16.00
☐ *"Liebeslied".*	12.00	16.00
☐ *"Polka de W.R.".*	12.00	16.00
☐ *"Polichinelle".*	12.00	16.00
☐ *"Nocturne in F Sharp Minor Op. 15 #2".*	23.00	30.00
☐ **ZIMBALIST, EFREM (violinist). VICTOR RED SEAL.** *"Humoresque."*	5.00	7.00
☐ *"Orientale".*	5.00	7.00
☐ *"Long Ago".*	5.00	7.00
☐ *"Larghetto".*	5.00	7.00
☐ *"Hebraisches Lied und Tanz".*	5.00	7.00
☐ *"Sonata Op. 42 #2, Andantino".*	5.00	7.00

	Price Range	
☐ "Polish Dance".	5.00	7.00
☐ "Serenata".	5.00	7.00
☐ "Chant d'Automne".	5.00	7.00
☐ "Massa's in de Cold, Cold Ground".	5.00	7.00
☐ "Old Black Joe".	5.00	7.00
☐ "Chant Negre".	5.00	7.00
☐ "Chant de la Veslomoy".	5.00	7.00
☐ "Russian Dance".	5.00	7.00
☐ "Spring Song".	5.00	7.00
☐ "Salut d'amour".	5.00	7.00
☐ "Song Without Words".	5.00	7.00
☐ "Madrigale".	9.00	12.00
☐ "Petite Serenade".	7.00	10.00
☐ "Improvisation".	7.00	10.00
☐ "Entr'acte".	7.00	10.00
☐ "Gypsy Love Song" (Fortune Teller).	7.00	10.00
☐ "Hungarian Dances #20 and 21".	7.00	10.00
☐ "Legende".	7.00	10.00
☐ "Alabama".	7.00	10.00
☐ "Broken Melody".	7.00	10.00
☐ "Millions d'Arlequin".	7.00	10.00
☐ "The Lark".	7.00	10.00

COUNTRY AND WESTERN

MEMORABILIA

For reasons not entirely explainable, fans of country and western music have traditionally been more avid collectors of star-related memorabilia than fans of most other kinds of music. From at least as early as the 1930's, devotees of country and western have sought out and devotedly preserved photographs, clothing, instruments, and virtually anything connected with their favorite artists. For a long while, however, this sort of collecting activity was confined to the so-called country and western belt — Tennessee, Kentucky, West Virginia and other states where this music originated. This is hardly surprising, as it was not until the mid-1950's that country and western recordings began to receive disc-jockey play nationwide. Until then, many of the biggest country and western stars were virtually unknown outside the south and southwest. Today, collecting interest in country and western memorabilia is not only national but international, with strongest buying activity for items pertaining to the early pioneers and big old-time stars, those who recorded in the 1920-39 period. Material relating to modern and current country and western performers is, of course, collected also but prices on the whole tend to be much lower.

Some early country and western memorabilia are very, very scarce. The star system that exists today was unknown in the country and western field 40, 50 and 60 years ago. Many of the early artists never posed for publicity photos, and the only shots that exist are candid ones or family-type photos. Some of these are known in just one specimen — which may be wrinkled and stained but still dear to the hearts of collectors.

Collectors of country and western memorabilia can purchase from dealers, but a much more exciting — and usually less expensive — way of obtaining this material is "at the source", from attics and garages of southern music fans, as well as southern secondhand shops. Troves of it certainly exist which have not yet reached the hands of collectors, but are waiting to be discovered. In the case of early country and western artists who are still alive, a letter to them (when the address can be learned) almost always brings a signed photo or other reply.

Beware of printed signatures on photos of semi-modern and modern stars, especially Gene Autry, Roy Rogers, Roy Acuff, Ernest Tubb, Eddy Arnold, Johnny Cash. Photos of these performers with stenciled or facsimile signatures were distributed in large numbers.

	Price Range	
☐ **ACUFF, ROY.** *c. 1948. Map of Nashville, Tenn., signed by him and several other country and western stars.*	100.00	125.00
☐ **ACUFF, ROY.** *Small colored photo on card, unsigned, early.*	11.00	16.00
☐ **ACUFF, ROY.** *c. 1955. 8x10 color photo, signed and inscribed, laminated.*	60.00	80.00
☐ **ACUFF, ROY.** *c. 1940. Fiddle used by him.*	1100.00	1500.00
☐ **ACUFF, ROY.** *Necktie reputedly worn by him at Grand Old Opry performance.*	110.00	135.00
☐ **ACUFF, ROY.** *Sheet music to "Wabash Cannonball", signed and inscribed, stained.*	95.00	120.00
☐ **ACUFF, ROY.** *c. 1938-72. Collection of c. 200 press cuttings on his career.*	110.00	140.00
☐ **ACUFF, ROY.** *Three large scrapbooks (14x17) with c. 2,500 items pertaining to him, 23 autographed photos, about 200 snapshots and candid photos, some unsigned publicity photos, c. 1,000 press cuttings, etc., mostly in well-preserved condition.*	3700.00	4500.00
☐ **ACUFF, ROY.** *c. 1958. Typed letter, signed.*	32.00	40.00
☐ **ALLEN, REX.** *8x10 photo, signed.*	11.00	16.00
☐ **ALLEN, REX.** *c. 1950's. Copy of "Rex Allen Comics", published by Dell.*	4.60	6.00
☐ **ALLEN, REX.** *Autographed copy "Rex Allen Comics".*	15.00	20.00
☐ **ALLEN, REX.** *Button with his name and picture.*	5.00	7.00
☐ **ARNOLD, EDDY.** *7x9 color photo mounted on stiff paper, signed twice, in original mailing envelope.*	35.00	45.00
☐ **ARNOLD, EDDY.** *8x10 photo, signed.*	15.00	20.00
☐ **ARNOLD, EDDY.** *16" 78rpm transcription of a radio show.*	120.00	150.00
☐ **ARNOLD, EDDY.** *Pair of tan leather boots reputedly worn by him.*	110.00	140.00
☐ **ATKINS, CHET.** *c. 1956. 6x7 photo with guitar, signed and dated.*	20.00	25.00
☐ **ATKINS, CHET.** *LP record album cover, signed, no record.*	33.00	42.00
☐ **ATKINS, CHET.** *Two small colored photos, unsigned.*	7.00	10.00
☐ **ATKINS, CHET.** *c. 1963. Typewritten letter, signed.*	9.00	12.00
☐ **ATKINS, CHET.** *Grand Old Opry poster with his name.*	16.00	22.00
☐ **ATKINS, CHET.** *8x10 photo with Little Jimmie Dickens, signed by both, inscribed.*	35.00	45.00

Eddy Arnold

	Price Range	
☐ **ATKINS, CHET.** *Postcard photo with facsimile signature.*	4.00	6.00
☐ **ATKINS, CHET.** *Two pieces of sheet music with notes in his hand.*	35.00	45.00
☐ **ATKINS, CHET.** *Collection of 67 news cuttings.*	55.00	70.00
☐ **AUTRY, GENE.** *c. 1948. "Autry's Aces". Fan club newsletter.*	30.00	40.00
☐ **AUTRY, GENE.** *Gene Autry Flying A Ranch decal, 5x8.*	20.00	25.00
☐ **AUTRY, GENE.** *c. 1940's. 5x7 photo, printed inscription "From your pal, Gene Autry".*	13.00	17.00
☐ **AUTRY, GENE.** *c. 1950. 8x10 photo, signed and inscribed.*	40.00	50.00
☐ **AUTRY, GENE.** *c. 1950. Button with his name and picture.*	15.00	20.00
☐ **AUTRY, GENE.** *Signature on rodeo souvenir booklet, Madison Square Garden, N.Y.*	35.00	50.00
☐ **AUTRY, GENE.** *Cowboy hat reputedly worn by him in film.*	100.00	115.00
☐ **AUTRY, GENE.** *Membership card in Gene Autry Fan Club.*	15.00	20.00
☐ **AUTRY, GENE.** *4x6 photo on horse, signed.*	17.00	22.00
☐ **BRITT, ELTON.** *c. 1946. 8x10 photo, signed and inscribed.*	16.00	21.00
☐ **BRITT, ELTON.** *c. 1932. ALs, two pp.*	23.00	33.00
☐ **BRITT, ELTON.** *78rpm record, signed on the label.*	50.00	65.00
☐ **BRITT, ELTON.** *Two small snapshot photos, one signed.*	15.00	20.00
☐ **BRITT, ELTON.** *Page with photo and biography cut from book, signed, framed.*	20.00	25.00
☐ **BRITT, ELTON.** *Photo with Cowboy Copas, signed by Britt.*	16.00	22.00
☐ **BRITT, ELTON.** *c. 1951. 78rpm record sleeve, signed, dated.*	13.00	18.00

	Price Range	
☐ **CARLISLE, CLIFF.** *8x10 studio photo, signed.*	15.00	20.00
☐ **CARLISLE, CLIFF.** *Photo in front of radio mike, signed.*	15.00	20.00
☐ **CARLISLE, CLIFF.** *Photo with Dellmore Bros., signed by Carlisle only.*	16.00	22.00
☐ **CARLISLE, CLIFF.** *Postcard photo, unsigned.*	4.00	5.00
☐ **CARLISLE, CLIFF.** *Signature on advertising poster.*	10.00	13.00
☐ **CARLISLE, CLIFF.** *Collection of 32 photos, none signed, mostly cut from magazines and mounted on cards.*	9.00	12.00
☐ **CARTER, WILF ("MONTANA SLIM").** *c. 1948. 8x10 photo, signed.*	20.00	25.00
☐ **CARTER, WILF.** *c. 1934. ALs, two pp., with envelope.*	15.00	20.00
☐ **CARTER, WILF.** *c. 1941 and 1947. Two postcards in his hand.*	11.00	16.00
☐ **CARTER, WILF.** *c. 1932. 4x5 photo, signed, creased.*	13.00	18.00
☐ **CARTER, WILF.** *c. 1975. Typewritten letter, signed.*	7.00	10.00
☐ **CARTER, WILF.** *Record company ad circular, signed.*	6.00	8.00
☐ **CARTER, WILF.** *8x10 photo signed "Montana Slim".*	15.00	20.00
☐ **COPAS, COWBOY.** *Sheet music, "Filipino Baby", signed.*	25.00	35.00
☐ **COPAS, COWBOY.** *c. 1957. ALs, one page.*	24.00	33.00
☐ **COPAS, COWBOY.** *c. 1955. 8x10 photo, signed and inscribed.*	33.00	40.00
☐ **COPAS, COWBOY.** *Brief memo in his hand, undated, early.*	15.00	20.00
☐ **DALHART, VERNON.** *c. 1925. 8x10 photo, signed.*	50.00	65.00
☐ **DALHART, VERNON.** *c. 1920's. Sheet music, "John T. Scopes Trial", signed, in a metal frame.*	125.00	160.00
☐ **DALHART, VERNON.** *5x7 photo wearing suit and tie, signed.*	30.00	40.00
☐ **DALHART, VERNON.** *Photo with Riley Puckett, signed by Dalhart only, browned.*	70.00	90.00
☐ **DAVIS, JIMMIE.** *8x10 close-up, signed.*	13.00	16.00
☐ **DAVIS, JIMMIE.** *Typewritten letter as Governor of Louisiana, 1½ pp., relating to a farm bill, signed.*	30.00	40.00
☐ **DAVIS, JIMMIE.** *Typewritten letter as Governor of Louisiana, about speculation on his seeking a second term, signed.*	45.00	60.00
☐ **DAVIS, JIMMIE.** *Signature on a calling card.*	5.00	7.00
☐ **DAVIS, JIMMIE.** *78rpm record, signed on the label.*	50.00	70.00
☐ **DAVIS, JIMMIE.** *Bumper sticker "Davis for Governor".* (*This is the value as a country and western collectible; collectors of political items would probably pay much less.)	15.00	*20.00
☐ **DAVIS, JIMMIE.** *Celluloid pin, "Davis for Gov.".*	9.00	12.00
☐ **DAVIS, JIMMIE.** *Photo behind desk in governor's mansion, signed.*	42.00	52.00
☐ **DAVIS, JIMMIE.** *Three Louisiana newspapers with headlines "Davis elected" or other headlines to that effect.*	9.00	12.00
☐ **DEXTER, AL.** *8x10 photo, signed.*	11.00	15.00
☐ **DEXTER, AL.** *78rpm record, signed on the label.*	30.00	37.00
☐ **DEXTER, AL.** *Sheet music, "Pistol Packin' Mama", signed.*	17.00	24.00
☐ **DEXTER, AL.** *c. 1941. ALs, with envelope.*	15.00	20.00
☐ **JONES, GRANDPA.** *8x10 signed photo.*	8.00	11.00
☐ **JONES, GRANDPA.** *c. 1972. Signed photo with "Hee Haw" cast.*	7.00	10.00
☐ **JONES, GRANDPA.** *c. 1933. 5x7 photo at early age, seated with banjo at radio mike, signed.*	20.00	25.00

	Price Range	
☐ **JONES, GRANDPA.** *TV Guide issue with feature on "Hee Haw", signed.*	7.00	10.00
☐ **JONES, GRANDPA.** *LP record album cover, signed, record missing.*	33.00	42.00
☐ **JONES, GRANDPA.** *c. 1940's. Banjo reputedly used by him.*	500.00	700.00
☐ **JONES, GRANDPA.** *Photo with Buck Owens, signed by Jones.*	7.00	10.00
☐ **JONES, GRANDPA.** *Photo of Dave Macon inscribed to Grandpa Jones.*	125.00	155.00
☐ **KINCAID, BRADLEY.** *c. 1940's. 8x10 close-up photo, signed.*	15.00	20.00
☐ **KINCAID, BRADLEY.** *Photo wearing cowboy outfit, signed.*	16.00	21.00
☐ **KINCAID, BRADLEY.** *c. 1930's. Record company brochure, signed.*	9.00	12.00
☐ **KINCAID, BRADLEY.** *c. 1930's. Photo on stage, signed.*	15.00	20.00
☐ **KINCAID, BRADLEY.** *Two snapshot photos, unsigned.*	6.00	8.00
☐ **KINCAID, BRADLEY.** *c. 1930. ALs, with envelope.*	22.00	27.00
☐ **KINCAID, BRADLEY.** *Poster advertising an appearance.*	16.00	22.00
☐ **KINCAID, BRADLEY.** *Postcard photo, facsimile signature.*	5.00	7.00
☐ **KINCAID, BRADLEY.** *Photo on street in Nashville, signed.*	13.00	17.00
☐ **LONG, JIMMIE.** *c. 1934. 8x10 photo, signed.*	24.00	33.00
☐ **LONG, JIMMIE.** *c. Early 1930's. 5x7 photo with Gene Autry, signed by both.*	90.00	110.00
☐ **LONG, JIMMIE.** *c. 1938. 78rpm record, signed.*	60.00	80.00
☐ **MACON, "UNCLE" DAVE.** *c. 1920. Banjo reputedly used by him, with several vintage photographs and other items, in a box.*	1350.00	1700.00
☐ **MACON, "UNCLE" DAVE.** *c. 1950. 30-minute reel-to-reel tape of an amateur interview with him, discussing his career.*	95.00	120.00
☐ **MACON, "UNCLE" DAVE.** *c. 1937. 4x5 photo, signed.*	32.00	40.00
☐ **MACON, "UNCLE" DAVE.** *c. 1949. ALs, four pages, reminiscences on his career, written in crayon.*	250.00	330.00
☐ **MAINER, J. E.** *8x10 photo with his group, signed by him and one other.*	90.00	115.00
☐ **MAINER, J. E.** *c. 1930. 4x5 photo, signed and inscribed.*	45.00	65.00
☐ **MAINER, J. E.** *Theater bill with his name.*	55.00	75.00
☐ **McMICHEN, CLAYTON.** *8x10 photo, signed, worn, creased.*	55.00	77.00
☐ **McMICHEN, CLAYTON.** *78rpm record, signed on the label.*	70.00	95.00
☐ **MONROE, BILL.** *c. 1942. ALs, two pages.*	10.00	13.00
☐ **MONROE, BILL.** *Postcard photo, facsimile signature.*	4.00	6.00
☐ **MONROE, BILL.** *c. 1953. Photo of him on stage, signed, dated.*	7.00	10.00
☐ **MONROE, BILL.** *Printed photo, "Blue Grass Boys", signed.*	10.00	14.00
☐ **MONROE, BILL.** *8x10 photo, signed and inscribed.*	9.00	12.00
☐ **MONROE, BILL.** *c. 1970's. Two snapshot photos, unsigned.*	4.00	6.00
☐ **MONROE, BILL.** *Necktie reputedly worn by him.*	22.00	30.00
☐ **MONROE, BILL.** *Scrapbook with 300-odd clippings, photos.*	120.00	150.00
☐ **MONROE, BILL.** *LP record album cover, signed, no record.*	35.00	45.00
☐ **MONROE, BILL.** *Photo with Ernest Tubb, signed by Monroe.*	11.00	15.00
☐ **MONROE, BILL.** *Signature on a card.*	4.00	5.00
☐ **MULLICAN, MOON.** *c. 1953. Photo of him at piano, signed.*	10.00	13.00

	Price Range	
☐ **MULLICAN, MOON.** *8x10 studio portrait, signed.*	11.00	16.00
☐ **MULLICAN, MOON.** *Printed discography of his recordings, signed.*	8.00	11.00
☐ **MULLICAN, MOON.** *Large poster with his name and picture.*	30.00	40.00
☐ **POOLE, CHARLIE.** *5x7 photo of him, signed, framed.*	27.00	37.00
☐ **POOLE, CHARLIE.** *c. 1928. Printed picture, "North Carolina Ramblers", signed.*	40.00	55.00
☐ **RITTER, TEX.** *c. 1958. Check endorsed by him.*	33.00	44.00
☐ **RITTER, TEX.** *Motion picture still, signed.*	17.00	22.00
☐ **RITTER, TEX.** *78rpm record, "High Noon", signed on label.*	70.00	95.00
☐ **RITTER, TEX.** *Printed postcard photo, facsimile signature.*	7.00	10.00
☐ **RITTER, TEX.** *Western style belt worn by him.*	70.00	95.00
☐ **RITTER, TEX.** *Sheet music, "Old Chisum Trail", signed.*	35.00	45.00
☐ **RITTER, TEX.** *c. 1946. Cover of a 78rpm record album set, signed, two records present (incomplete).*	125.00	150.00
☐ **RITTER, TEX.** *3 7 motion picture stills, unsigned.*	90.00	120.00
☐ **RITTER, TEX.** *Motion picture lobby card, 27x41.*	90.00	120.00
☐ **RITTER, TEX.** *8x10 photo, signed and inscribed.*	22.00	33.00
☐ **RITTER, TEX.** *c. 1968-74. Six snapshot photos.*	17.00	22.00
☐ **RITTER, TEX.** *Membership card "Tex Ritter Fan Club".*	13.00	16.00
☐ **RITTER, TEX.** *c. 1936. ALs, one page, torn.*	33.00	44.00
☐ **RITTER, TEX.** *Photo with Gary Cooper, signed by both.*	350.00	450.00
☐ **ROBERTSON, TEXAS JIM.** *c. 1940's. 5x7 photo, signed.*	10.00	14.00
☐ **ROBERTSON, TEXAS JIM.** *Full color photo, 3x4, signed on back.*	11.00	15.00
☐ **ROBERTSON, TEXAS JIM.** *78rpm record, signed on label.*	40.00	55.00
☐ **ROBERTSON, TEXAS JIM.** *8x10 photo, signed and inscribed.*	15.00	20.00
☐ **ROBERTSON, TEXAS JIM.** *Signature on a record company brochure.*	6.00	8.00
☐ **ROBERTSON, TEXAS JIM.** *Printed postcard photo, facsimile signature.*	4.00	6.00
☐ **ROBISON, CARSON.** *c. 1945. Small snapshot, inscribed "With best wishes, Carson Robison". Ink somewhat faded, mounted on stiff grey cardboard with traces of glue on the back.*	22.00	30.00
☐ **ROBISON, CARSON.** *Postcard dated 1938, three lines in his handwriting with signature "Carson", sent to a friend.*	20.00	25.00
☐ **ROBISON, CARSON.** *Scrap album containing c. 65 press cuttings and other material relating to him, mostly 1940's, a few unsigned and one small signed photograph, the album damaged, contents mostly in good condition.*	120.00	150.00
☐ **ROBISON, CARSON.** *c. Early 1940's. Photo with Roy Acuff, signed by both, probably taken at Nashville, framed.*	80.00	105.00
☐ **RODGERS, JIMMIE.** *c. 1932. 8x10 photo with banjo, signed.*	275.00	350.00
☐ **RODGERS, JIMMIE.** *4x5 postcard photo, facsimile signature.*	33.00	40.00
☐ **RODGERS, JIMMIE.** *Photo with Will Rogers, signed by both, shortly before J. R.'s death.*	575.00	770.00
☐ **RODGERS, JIMMIE.** *Sheet music, "Waiting for a Train", signed.*	450.00	570.00
☐ **RODGERS, JIMMIE.** *c. 1929. ALs, one page.*	500.00	675.00

	Price Range	
☐ **RODGERS, JIMMIE.** *Signature on a card*.* (*Beware of fakes. I have not seen any but they are rumored to exist.)	120.00	160.00
☐ **RODGERS, JIMMIE.** *c. 1933. Obituary notice from N.Y. Times.*	9.00	12.00
☐ **RODGERS, JIMMIE.** *Letter to him from record company executive.*	27.00	35.00
☐ **ROGERS, ROY.** *c. Probably 1950. White china plate with colored illustration of Roy and Trigger, lettered "Roy Rogers and Trigger - Many Happy Trails", nine inches in diameter.*	60.00	80.00
☐ **ROGERS, ROY.** *Child's clothes rack, wood, 4 feet tall, die-cut figure of Roy and Trigger, decorated with cattle brands.*	125.00	160.00
☐ **ROGERS, ROY.** *Child's cloth bathrobe, grey background with cowboy motifs and Roy's name, belt missing.*	85.00	110.00
☐ **ROGERS, ROY.** *Pair of child's gloves, black cloth and plastic, illustration of Roy and Trigger on each glove.*	22.00	33.00
☐ **ROGERS, ROY.** *c. 1955. "Roy Rogers and the Man From Dodge City", booklet advertising Dodge autos, 16 pp., 5x8.*	15.00	20.00
☐ **ROGERS, ROY.** *c. Probably 1950's. "Roy Rogers Fix-It Stagecoach". Plastic toy stagecoach with two horses, strongbox, rifle, driver, etc. In original box.*	125.00	160.00
☐ **ROGERS, ROY.** *c. 1955. "Roy Rogers Ranch Set". Marx playset with cowboys, fence, metal bunkhouse, animals, furniture, in a 9x21 box.*	125.00	165.00
☐ **ROGERS, ROY.** *"Roy Rogers Hauler and Van Trailer with Nellybelle Jeep". With plastic figures of Roy, Dale Evans, etc. The horse hauler is all metal in red, blue and yellow with illustration of Roy and Trigger on both sides. The tailgate drops and inside is a red plastic jeep and additional pieces, 15" long.*	80.00	110.00
☐ **ROGERS, ROY.** *c. Early 1950's. Nellybelle jeep with Pat Brady, Dale Evans, Bullet. Jeep is all metal, painted gray, 12x5, movable hood, windshield and steering wheel, plastic motor.*	80.00	110.00
☐ **ROGERS, ROY.** *"Roy Rogers Bank". White metal bank in the shape of a book, 6" tall.*	42.00	52.00
☐ **ROGERS, ROY.** *"Roy Rogers Darts". Two foot by two foot masonite board with full color target and picture of Roy.*	55.00	70.00
☐ **ROGERS, ROY.** *"Roy Rogers and Trigger 620 Snap Shot Camera". Black plastic and metal camera with flash attachment.*	50.00	70.00
☐ **ROGERS, ROY.** *"Roy Rogers and Trigger plastic binoculars". Brown plastic.*	27.00	37.00
☐ **ROGERS, ROY.** *c. 1952. "Roy Rogers, King of the Cowboys drinking mug", plastic.*	22.00	30.00
☐ **SNOW, HANK.** *c. 1960. 8x10 photo, signed and inscribed.*	10.00	13.00
☐ **SNOW, HANK.** *c. 1950's. Guitar used by him, with his name elaborately fashioned on it.*	1000.00	1500.00
☐ **SNOW, HANK.** *5x6½ photo, signed.*	8.00	11.00
☐ **SNOW, HANK.** *78rpm record, signed on the label.*	22.00	27.00
☐ **SNOW, HANK.** *LP record album cover, signed, record missing.*	33.00	45.00
☐ **SNOW, HANK.** *c. 1930's. Three snapshot photos, unsigned.*	7.00	10.00

Item	Price Range	
☐ **SNOW, HANK.** *Signature on a card.*	4.00	5.00
☐ **SNOW, HANK.** *c. 1931. ALs, about his future plans.*	25.00	30.00
☐ **SNOW, HANK.** *Photo with Ernest Tubb, signed by Snow.*	13.00	17.00
☐ **SNOW, HANK.** *c. 1974. Photo standing outside Country Music Hall of Fame, signed.*	11.00	16.00
☐ **SNOW, HANK.** *Sheet music, signed.*	27.00	35.00
☐ **SNOW, HANK.** *c. Early. Membership card, "Hank Snow Fan Club"*	7.00	10.00
☐ **STONEMAN, E. V.** *8x10 photo, signed, mounted.*	37.00	50.00
☐ **TANNER, GID.** *Photo playing fiddle, signed.*	55.00	70.00
☐ **TANNER, GID.** *Photo with Riley Puckett, signed by Tanner.*	50.00	65.00
☐ **TANNER, GID.** *c. 1930. Poster advertising "Gid Tanner and His Skillet Lickers", 22x30.*	100.00	120.00
☐ **TUBB, ERNEST.** *8x10 close-up photo, signed.*	8.00	11.00
☐ **TUBB, ERNEST.** *c. 1972. Catalogue issued by his record shop, Nashville, Tenn.*	2.00	3.00
☐ **TUBB, ERNEST.** *Photo of Mrs. Ernest Tubb and Mrs. Hank Snow, signed by Mrs. Ernest Tubb.*	6.00	8.00
☐ **TUBB, ERNEST.** *Sheet music, "Walking the Floor Over You", signed.*	22.00	27.00
☐ **TUBB, ERNEST.** *4x5 photo, signed.*	6.00	8.00
☐ **TUBB, ERNEST.** *78rpm record, signed on the label.*	35.00	45.00
☐ **TUBB, ERNEST.** *c. 1975. Photo in front of his record shop, Nashville, signed.*	8.00	11.00
☐ **TUBB, ERNEST.** *Signature on a 45rpm record sleeve.*	4.00	5.00
☐ **TUBB, ERNEST.** *Necktie with his name and likeness on it.*	13.00	16.00
☐ **TUBB, ERNEST.** *Wallet with his name and words "Music City U.S.A.".*	22.00	27.00
☐ **TYLER, T. TEXAS.** *8x10 portrait photo, signed.*	13.00	17.00
☐ **TYLER, T. TEXAS.** *Sheet music, "Deck of Cards" signed.*	25.00	33.00
☐ **WILLIAMS, HANK.** *c. 1945. ALs, with envelope.*	95.00	120.00
☐ **WILLIAMS, HANK.** *c. 1952. Cover of a 78rpm record album, signed, records missing, issued by MGM.*	160.00	220.00
☐ **WILLIAMS, HANK.** *8x10 portrait photo, signed, inscribed.*	85.00	110.00
☐ **WILLIAMS, HANK.** *c. 1950. Color photo, unsigned.*	15.00	20.00
☐ **WILLIAMS, HANK.** *Signature on a card.*	17.00	22.00
☐ **WILLS, BOB.** *8x10 photo with "The Texas Playboys", signed by Wills and one other member of group.*	55.00	70.00

78's

In this section are included all types of recordings that could be classified under the catch-all heading of country and western, including bluegrass, hillbilly, mountain music, cowboy, etc.

The market for 78rpm country records, or "country classics", has grown enormously in recent years. Tens of thousands of such recordings exist, many of them (perhaps most) by artists of whom little or nothing is known today. They span the period from 1924 — when Vernon Dalhart recorded the first country and western million-seller and alerted music producers to the salability of country records — to about 1954, when most record companies ceased producing records in 78rpm. In those 30 years, country and western music was a bigger money-maker than pop or jazz or any other form of commercial recordings. Every major record label had its country and western subsidiary company with a stable of artists, and throughout the country (not just in the South) there were innumerable small labels specializing in country and western. Many of the latter were of a "fly by night" nature, working out of barns or wagons, recording non-professional local talent without contracts and — usually — without pay. Most of the records they produced were naturally of mediocre quality, but quite a few are rare and, amidst the slush, one will discover occasional gems of talent that deserved to be discovered. All these records are "collectible", though it is not easy to find two collectors who agree on their merits or values. One collector's trash is another's treasure. But it is fairly safe to say that, at least as examples of American folk artistry, they do have some claim to attention.

The most valuable and sought-after country and western 78's are, mainly, early releases by artists who subsequently became stars, such as Gene Autry, Ernest Tubb, Jimmie Davis, Hank Snow, etc. There are important exceptions, however. In the case of Jimmie Rodgers — "The Singing Brakeman" — every single one of his recordings (more than 50 of them) is valuable, worth at minimum $50 in VF condition. This includes records released after he achieved mass popularity, some of which must have been pressed in quantities approaching 500,000. There is no easy explanation for this, except the very strong collector interest in Jimmie Rodgers records. They are certainly obtainable (most of them, at any rate), but the demand outpaces the supply. The fact that many of his recordings have been repressed into LP albums has not only failed to diminish interest in the originals, it has seemed to create an even greater market for them. Their values have more than doubled in the past four to five years.

The collector of country and western 78's should keep in mind that many artists recorded under different names early in their careers, or even later; the classic example is Wilf Carter/"Montana Slim", who made numerous recordings under both names. Gene Autry recorded under about half a dozen names. The country and western connoisseur will recognize the voice even if the name is unfamiliar.

Also: be sure you do not confuse the value of a **recording** with that of a **song.** Many tunes were re-recorded by the same artists several times, for different labels or the same label, and the values of each recording can **vary considerably.** Usually, a version of a song done by an artist for a small label, before he signed with a major recording company, is more valuable that the same song subsequently recorded by the big label. In some cases these are actually not remakes but merely repressings.

	Price Range	
☐ **ACUFF, ROY. Columbia.** *"Waiting for My Call to Glory/Tell Me Now or Tell Me Never"*.	5.00	7.00
☐ *"It's Too Late Now to Worry Anymore/Wait for the Light to Shine"*.	5.00	7.00
☐ *"Blues in My Mind/I Heard a Silver Trumpet"*.	6.00	9.00
☐ *"Write Me Sweetheart/I'll Forgive You but I Can't Forget"*. . . .	5.00	7.00

	Price Range	
☐ "The Prodigal Son/Not a Word From Home"	5.00	7.00
☐ "I'll Reap My Harvest in Heaven/Don't Make Me Go to Bed"	6.50	9.00
☐ "Night Train to Memphis/Low and Lonely"	5.00	7.00
☐ "Fireball Mail/Wreck on the Highway"	5.00	7.00
☐ "Be Honest With Me/Worried Mind"	5.00	7.00
☐ "Come Back Little Pal/The Precious Jewel"	5.00	7.00
☐ "Beneath That Lonely Mound of Clay/Blue Eyed Darling"	5.00	7.00
☐ "We Live in Two Different Worlds/Pins and Needles"	5.00	7.00
☐ "No One Will Ever Know/I Think I'll Go Home and Cry"	5.00	7.00
☐ "All the World is Lonely Now/That Glory Bound Train"	5.00	7.00
☐ "Great Speckled Bird/My Mountain Home Sweet Home"	5.50	8.00
☐ "Great Speckled Bird #2/Tell Mother I'll Be There"	4.50	7.00
☐ "Steel Guitar Chimes/Steel Guitar Blues"	8.00	12.00
☐ "Wabash Cannonball/Freight Train Blues"	7.00	10.00
☐ "Streamlined Cannonball/Mule Skinner Blues"	7.00	10.00
☐ "Let Me Be the First to Say I'm Sorry/Gone, Gone, Gone"	5.00	7.00
☐ "Jole Blon/Tennessee Central"	5.00	7.00
☐ "There's a Big Rock in the Road/Po' Folks"	5.00	7.00
☐ "It Won't Be Long/Just Inside the Pearly Gates"	5.00	7.00
☐ "Things That Might Have Been/No Letter in the Mail"	5.00	7.00
☐ "Brother Take Warning/The Great Judgment Morning"	5.00	7.00
☐ "You're My Darling/Branded Wherever I Go"	5.00	7.00
☐ "Are You Thinking of Me Darling?/I Called and Nobody Answered"	5.00	7.00
☐ "I Talk to Myself About You/Short Changed in Love"	5.00	7.00
☐ "New Greenback Dollar/Steamboat Whistle Blues"	5.00	7.00
☐ "Smoky Mountain Rag/Smoky Mountain Moon"	5.00	7.00
☐ "Blue Eyes Crying in the Rain/The Devil's Train"	8.00	12.00
☐ "They Can Only Fill One Grave/Do You Wonder Why?"	5.00	7.00
☐ "Easy Rockin' Chair/Golden Treasure"	5.00	7.00
☐ "The Songbirds are Singing in Heaven/The Waltz of the Wind"	6.00	9.00
☐ "I Saw the Light/Thank God"	5.00	7.00
☐ "Unloved and Unclaimed/I Had a Dream"	5.00	7.00
☐ "Blues in My Mind/I Heard a Silver Trumpet"	6.00	9.00
☐ "That Beautiful Picture/Do You Wonder Why"	5.00	7.00
☐ "Blue Ridge Sweetheart/Just to Ease My Worried Mind"	5.00	7.00
☐ "What Would You Do With Gabriel's Trumpet?/Farther Along"	5.00	7.00
☐ "Heartaches and Flowers/When They Take That Last Look at Me"	5.00	7.00
☐ "Lonesome Old River Blues/It's Just About Time"	9.00	12.00
☐ "You'll Reap These Tears/I'll Always Care"	5.00	7.00
☐ **Conqueror.** "Great Speckled Bird/My Mountain Home Sweet Home"	22.00	30.00
☐ "You're the Only Star/She No Longer Belongs to Me"	22.00	30.00
☐ "Gonna Have a Big Time Tonight/Yes Sir, That's My Baby"	22.00	30.00
☐ "Great Speckled Bird #2/Tell Mother I'll Be There"	24.00	33.00
☐ "Steel Guitar Chimes/Steel Guitar Blues"	22.00	30.00

	Price Range	
☐ *"Singing My Way to Glory/Lonesome Valley"*	28.00	39.00
☐ *"Wabash Cannonball/Freight Train Blues"*	22.00	30.00
☐ *"New Greenback Dollar/Steamboat Whistle Blues"*	22.00	30.00
☐ *"When Lulu's Gone/Doin' it the Old Fashioned Way"*	22.00	30.00
☐ *"An Old Three Room Shack/Bonnie Blue Eyes"*	22.00	30.00
☐ *"One Old Shirt/Tonky Tonk Mamas"*	22.00	30.00
☐ *"Old Fashioned Love/Mule Skinner Blues"*	25.00	35.00
☐ *"Answer to Sparkling Blue Eyes/Mother's Prayers Guide Me"*	22.00	30.00
☐ *"Ida Red/Just to Ease My Worried Mind"*	22.00	30.00
☐ *"Haven of Dreams/Old Age Pension Check"*	22.00	30.00
☐ **ALLEN BROTHERS. Vocalion.** *"Long Gone from Bowling Green/Red Pajama Sal"*	8.00	12.00
☐ *"Salty Dog Blues/Hey Hey Hey Hey"*	15.00	21.00
☐ *"Misbehavin' Mama/Midnight Mama"*	9.00	12.00
☐ *"Baby When You Come Back Home/Daddy Park Your Car"*	9.00	12.00
☐ *"The Prisoner's Dream/Mercy Mercy Blues"*	9.00	12.00
☐ *"Can I Get You Now/New Deal Blues"*	9.00	12.00
☐ *"Tipple Blues/Mary's Breakdown"*	9.00	12.00
☐ **ALLEN, ROSALIE. Bluebird.** *"Guitar Polka/I Want to Be a Cowboy's Sweetheart"*	15.00	21.00
☐ *"Me Go Where You Go/A Rose of the Alamo"*	12.00	18.00
☐ *"Hitler Lives/I Can't Tell that Lie to My Heart"*	9.00	12.00
☐ *"Never Trust a Man/Take it Back and Change it for a Boy"*	9.00	12.00
☐ **ARNOLD, EDDY. Bluebird.** *"Mommy, Please Stay Home With Me/Mother's Prayer"*	40.00	55.00
☐ *"Cattle Call/Each Year Seems a Million Years"*	35.00	45.00
☐ *"Did You See My Daddy Over There/I Walk Alone"*	35.00	45.00
☐ *"You Must Walk the Line/Many Years Ago"*	30.00	40.00
☐ *"I Talk to Myself About You/Live and Learn"*	25.00	35.00
☐ *"Can't Win, Can't Place, Can't Show/All Alone in This World Without You"*	25.00	35.00
☐ *"Mommy, Please Stay Home With Me/Many Tears Ago"*	25.00	35.00
☐ *"That's How Much I Love You/Chained to a Memory"*	25.00	35.00
☐ *"I'll Hold You in My Heart/Don't Bother to Cry"*	14.00	19.00
☐ *"Easy Rocking Chair/To My Sorrow"*	14.00	19.00
☐ **AUTRY, GENE. Champion.** *"Cowboy Yodel/Hobo Yodel"*	70.00	90.00
☐ *"Dust Pan Blues/Texas Blues"*	70.00	90.00
☐ *"In the Jailhouse Now #2/Anniversary Blue Yodel #7"*	70.00	90.00
☐ *"Blue Yodel #8/Mean Mama Blues"*	80.00	110.00
☐ *"Pistol Packin' Papa/Any Old Time"*	80.00	90.00
☐ *"Blue Days/Money Ain't No Use Anyhow"*	70.00	90.00
☐ *"T.B. Blues/I've Got the Jailhouse Blues"*	80.00	110.00
☐ **Clarion.** *"Hobo Yodel/That's Why I Left the Mountains"*	60.00	80.00
☐ *"No One to Call Me Darling/Frankie and Johnny"*	60.00	80.00
☐ *"I'll Be Thinking of You, Little Girl/Why Don't You Come Back to Me"*	60.00	80.00
☐ *"My Alabama Home/Cowboy Yodel"*	60.00	80.00
☐ *"Lullaby Yodel/Red River Valley" (with Carson Robison)*	55.00	75.00
☐ *"Pictures of My Mother/True Blue Bill"*	60.00	80.00
☐ *"A Gangster's Warning/That's How I Got My Start"*	60.00	80.00

	Price Range	
☐ **Columbia.** *"Don't Hang Around Me Anymore/Address Unknown"*	11.00	15.00
☐ *"I Want to be Sure/Don't Live a Lie"*	11.00	15.00
☐ *"Over and Over Again/Wave to Me, Lady"*	9.00	14.00
☐ *"Nobody's Darlin' But Mine/Don't Waste Your Tears on Me"*	9.00	14.00
☐ *"There's a Gold Mine in the Sky/Sail Along Silv'ry Moon"*	9.00	14.00
☐ *"End of My Round-Up Days/I Want a Pardon for Daddy"*	22.00	30.00
☐ *"Back in the Saddle Again/Little Old Band of Gold"*	9.00	12.00
☐ *"When I'm Gone You'll Soon Forget/Goodbye, Little Darlin', Goodbye"*	9.00	14.00
☐ *"You Waited Too Long/That Little Kid Sister of Mine"*	8.00	14.00
☐ *"You Are My Sunshine/It Makes No Difference Now"*	9.00	14.00
☐ *"Take Me Back into Your Heart/Tweedle-o-Twill"*	9.00	14.00
☐ *"Rainbow on the Rio Colorado/Private Buckaroo"*	9.00	14.00
☐ *"Yesterday's Roses/Call For Me and I'll Be There"*	9.00	14.00
☐ *"If You Only Believed in Me/Purple Sage in the Twilight"*	9.00	14.00
☐ *"I'll Be Back/At Mail Call Today"*	9.00	14.00
☐ *"Have I Told You Lately That I Love You/Someday You'll Want Me to Want You"*	9.00	14.00
☐ *"Tumbling Tumbleweeds/Back in the Saddle Again"*	9.00	14.00
☐ *"Home on the Range/Red River Valley"*	9.00	14.00
☐ *"Mexicali Rose/South of the Border"*	9.00	14.00
☐ *"Ridin' Down the Canyon/Twilight on the Trail"*	9.00	14.00
☐ *"Ages and Ages Ago/You Laughed and I Cried"*	9.00	14.00
☐ *"When the Snowbirds Cross the Rockies/The Angel Song"*	12.00	20.00
☐ *"Jingle Jangle Jingle/I'm A Cowpoke Pokin' Along"*	9.00	14.00
☐ *"Keep Rollin' Lazy Longhorns/Deep in the Heart of Texas"*	9.00	14.00
☐ *"I Hang My Head and Cry/You'll be Sorry"*	9.00	14.00
☐ **BATES, DR. HUMPHREY. "And his Possum Hunters". Brunswick.** *"Going Up-Town/How Many Biscuits Can You Eat"*	70.00	95.00
☐ *"Billy in the Low Ground/8th of January"*	70.00	95.00
☐ **BLUE SKY BOYS. Bluebird.** *"Sunny Side of Life/Where the Soul Never Dies"*	35.00	52.00
☐ *"Down on the Banks of the Ohio/Midnight on the Stormy Sea"*	35.00	52.00
☐ *"There'll Come a Time/I'm Troubled, I'm Troubled"*	35.00	52.00
☐ **BOYD, BILL.** *(NOTE: This was not the Bill Boyd who portrayed "Hopalong Cassidy".)* **Bluebird.** *"Train Song/Under the Double Eagle"*	9.00	13.00
☐ *"Boyd's Blues/David Blues"*	9.00	13.00
☐ *"The Sweetest Girl/Rio Grande Waltz"*	9.00	13.00
☐ *"Mama Don't Like No Music/Wind Swept Desert"*	9.00	13.00
☐ *"Floatin' Down/Beale Street Blues"*	15.00	20.00
☐ *"Hobo's Paradise/Ramshackle Shack"*	15.00	20.00
☐ *"Put Me in Your Pocket/Way Out There"*	9.00	13.00
☐ *"Ain't She Coming Out Tonight?/You Shall Be Free Monah"*	9.00	13.00
☐ *"Draggin' it Around/Right or Wrong"*	9.00	13.00
☐ *"Jennie Lee/You're Tired of Me"*	9.00	13.00
☐ **BRITT, ELTON. Bluebird.** –*"Goodbye, Little Darlin', Goodbye/I'll Never Smile Again"*	9.00	14.00
☐ *"She Taught Me to Yodel/Where Are You Now?"*	9.00	14.00
☐ *"There's a Star Spangled Banner Waving Somewhere/When the Roses Bloom Again"*	9.00	14.00

	Price Range	
☐ *"Buddy Boy/I Hung My Head and Cried"*	9.00	14.00
☐ *"I'm a Convict With Old Glory in My Heart/The Best of Travel"*	9.00	14.00
☐ *"Someday/Weep No More My Darlin' "*	9.00	14.00
☐ **RCA Victor.** *"Wave to Me, My Lady/Blueberry Lane"*	6.00	9.00
☐ *"Make Room in Your Heart For a Friend/Detour"*	6.00	9.00
☐ *"Thanks For the Heartaches/Blue Texas Moonlight"*	6.00	9.00
☐ *"Rogue River Valley/Too Tired to Care"*	6.00	9.00
☐ *"There's a Star Spangled Banner Waving Somewhere/I Hung My Head and Cried"*	8.00	11.00
☐ *"Blue Eyes Crying in the Rain/I'd Trade All of My Tomorrows"*	8.00	11.00
☐ *"Candlelight and Roses/I Wish You the Best of Everything"*	6.00	9.00
☐ **CARLISLE, CLIFF. Bluebird.** *"Look Out, I'm Shifting Gears/Get Her by the Tail"*	37.00	55.00
☐ *"A Wildcat Woman and a Tomcat Man/Rambling Yodler"*	37.00	55.00
☐ *"My Lovin' Kathleen/A Stretch of 28 Years"*	30.00	40.00
☐ *"In a Box Car Around the World/Cowboy Johnny's Last Ride"*	30.00	40.00
☐ *"You'll Miss Me When I'm Gone/When the Evening's Sun Goes Down"*	30.00	40.00
☐ *"Shufflin' Gal/Wigglin' Mama"*	30.00	40.00
☐ *"That Good Old Utah Trail/My Old Saddle Horse is Missing"*	22.00	30.00
☐ *"Still There's a Spark of Love/Cowgirl Jean"*	22.00	30.00
☐ *"That Nasty Swing/It Ain't No Fault of Mine"*	22.00	30.00
☐ *"My Rocking Mama/When I'm Dead and Gone"*	22.00	30.00
☐ *"A Little White Rose/Handsome Blues"*	22.00	30.00
☐ **CARSON, FIDDLIN' JOHN. Bluebird.** *"Georgia's $3 Tag/The New 'Comin' Round the Mountain' "*	75.00	100.00
☐ *"When the Saints Go Marching In/Bear Me Away on Your Snowy White Wings"*	75.00	100.00
☐ *"The Honest Farmer/Taxes on the Farmer Feeds Them All"*	75.00	100.00
☐ **CARTER, WILF ("MONTANA SLIM"). Bluebird.** *"I Long For Old Wyoming/My Little Swiss and Me"*	30.00	40.00
☐ *"Keep Smiling, Old Pal/Rescue From Moses River Goldmine"*	30.00	40.00
☐ *"The Fate of Old Strawberry Roan/Yodeling Hillbilly"*	30.00	40.00
☐ *"Broken-Down Cowboy/Old Barn Dance"*	30.00	40.00
☐ *"Dreamy Prairie Moon/Sweetheart of My Childhood Days"*	30.00	40.00
☐ *"The Fate of Sunset Trail/Midnight the Unconquered Outlaw"*	30.00	40.00
☐ *"Memories of My Grey-Haired Mother/Roll Along Moonlight Yodel"*	30.00	40.00
☐ *"Goodbye, Little Pal of My Dreams/The Hobo's Yodel"*	30.00	40.00
☐ *"Rose of My Heart/Under the Light of the Texas Moon"*	30.00	40.00
☐ *"Round-up Time in Heaven/Put My Little Shoes Away"*	30.00	40.00
☐ *"There's a Love-Knot in My Lariat/My Little Yoho Lady"*	30.00	40.00
☐ *"Where is My Boy Tonight?/Answer to Swiss Moonlight Lullaby"*	30.00	40.00
☐ *"When the Sun Says Goodnight to the Prairie/The Hindenburg Disaster"*	30.00	40.00
☐ *"How My Yodeling Days Began/Covered Wagon Headin' West"*	30.00	40.00
☐ *"Pete Knight's Last Ride/The Last Ride Down Lariat Trail"*	30.00	40.00
☐ *"Old Alberta Plains/Won't You Be the Same Old Pal"*	30.00	40.00

	Price Range	
☐ *"I Loved Her Till She Done Me Wrong/My Faithful Pinto Pal"*	30.00	40.00
☐ *"The Preacher and the Cowboy/Roll on Texas Dreamy Moon"*	30.00	40.00
☐ *"Dusty Trails/Everybody's Been Some Mother's Darlin' "*	30.00	40.00
☐ *"You'll Always Be Mine in My Dreams/I Wish I Had Never Seen Sunshine"*	30.00	40.00
☐ *"The Cowboy Wedding in May/I'm Still Waiting For You"*	30.00	40.00
☐ *"Round-Up Time in Sunny Old Alberta/When the Bright Prairie Moon is Rollin' "*	30.00	40.00
☐ *"By the Grave of Nobody's Darling/There'll Be No Blues Up Yonder"*	30.00	40.00
☐ *"Longing For my Mississippi Home/Don't Let Me Down, Old Pal"*	30.00	40.00
☐ *"The Cowboy's Heavenly Dream/Ridin' a Maverick"*	30.00	40.00
☐ *"That Tumbledown Shack By the Trail/My Old Montana Home"*	30.00	40.00
☐ *"What a Friend We Have in Mother/Down the Yodeling Trail at Twilight"*	30.00	40.00
☐ *"It Makes No Difference Now/We'll Meet Again in Peaceful Valley"*	30.00	40.00
☐ *"I'm Only a Dude in Cowboy Clothes/My Honeymoon Bridge Broke Down"*	30.00	40.00
☐ **DALHART, VERNON. Brunswick.** *"Jim Blake/The Death of Laura Parsons"*	25.00	35.00
☐ *"The Miner's Doom/Return of Mary Vickery"*	15.00	20.00
☐ *"The Dying Cowboy/A Home on the Range"*	15.00	20.00
☐ *"Barbara Allen/Wreck of the C & O #5"*	28.00	39.00
☐ *"The House at the End of the Lane/My Blue Ridge Mountain Home" (with Carson Robison)*	15.00	20.00
☐ *"Wreck of the Royal Palm/Wreck of the #9"*	25.00	35.00
☐ *"Down on the Farm/My Mother's Old Red Shawl"*	15.00	20.00
☐ *"The Gypsy's Warning/Molling Darling"*	15.00	20.00
☐ *"Billy Richardson's Last Ride/My Little Home in Tennessee"*	25.00	35.00
☐ *"A Cowboy's Herding Song/Cowboy's Evening Song"*	15.00	20.00
☐ *"The Jealous Lover of Lone Green/Nellie Dare and Charlie Brooks"*	15.00	20.00
☐ *"The Engineer's Dream/The Mississippi Floor"*	15.00	20.00
☐ *"Billy the Kid/The Three Drowned Sisters"*	17.00	25.00
☐ **Clarion.** *"When the Work's All Done Next Fall/The Cowboy's Lament" (with Mack Allen)*	25.00	35.00
☐ *"The Pony Express/Don't Marry a Widow"*	17.00	25.00
☐ **Columbia.** *"Prisoner's Song/Ain't Ya Coming Out Tonight"*	25.00	35.00
☐ *"Mother and Home/Chain Gang Song"*	27.00	37.00
☐ *"Oh Bury Me Not on the Lone Prairie/Get Away Old Man"*	15.00	20.00
☐ *"Lindbergh/Lucky Lindy"*	35.00	45.00
☐ *"Boy's Best Friend is His Mother/In the Baggage Coach Ahead"*	27.00	37.00
☐ *"Crepe on the Little Cabin Door/We Will Meet at the End of the Trail"*	26.00	36.00
☐ *"Dying Girl's Message/Fatal Wedding"*	33.00	42.00
☐ *"Putting on the Style/Goin' to Have a Big Time Tonight"*	15.00	20.00
☐ *"When the Moon Shines Down Upon the Mountain/Golden Slippers" (with Carson Robison, billed as Charlie Wells on this recording)*	27.00	37.00

	Price Range	
☐ *"John T Scopes Trial/Santa Barbara Earthquake"*	27.00	37.00
☐ *"Wreck of the Shenandoah/Stone Mountain Memorial"*	35.00	45.00
☐ **RCA Victor.** *"Prisoner's Song/Wreck of Old 97"*	35.00	45.00
☐ *"Death of Floyd Collins/Dream of a Miner's Child"*	35.00	45.00
☐ *"Letter Edged in Black/Lightning Express"*	35.00	45.00
☐ *"Little Rosewood Casket/Convict and Rose"*	35.00	46.00
☐ **DAVIS, JIMMIE. Bluebird.** *"Bear Cat Mama from Horners Corners/She's a Hum Dinger"*	65.00	95.00
☐ *"When It's Roundup Time in Heaven/I Wonder if She's Blue"*	50.00	70.00
☐ *"Beautiful Texas/The Tramp's Mother"*	50.00	70.00
☐ *"The Shotgun Wedding/Arabelle Blues"*	50.00	70.00
☐ *"I'll Be Happy Today/My Arkansas Sweetheart"*	35.00	50.00
☐ *"Midnight Blues/The Davis Limited"*	35.00	50.00
☐ *"Yo Yo Mama/Hold 'er, Newt"*	35.00	50.00
☐ **Decca.** *"Nobody's Darlin' But Mine/Have You Ever Been in Heaven"*	35.00	50.00
☐ *"Greatest Mistake of My Life/One, Two, Three, Four"*	35.00	50.00
☐ *"It's Been Years/Beautiful Mary"*	35.00	50.00
☐ *"Good Time Papa Blues/Shirt Tail Blues"*	45.00	70.00
☐ *"Jellyroll Blues/Graveyard Blues"*	45.00	70.00
☐ **DELMORE BROTHERS. Bluebird.** *"Gonna Lay Down My Old Guitar/Lonesome Yodel Blues"*	45.00	70.00
☐ *"The Frozen Girl/Bury Me Out on the Prairie"*	60.00	85.00
☐ *"I'm Leaving You/I'm Goin' Back to Alabama"*	50.00	75.00
☐ *"I Ain't Gonna Stay Here Long/I'm Mississippi Bound"*	45.00	70.00
☐ *"Smoky Mountain Bill and His Song/The Girls Don't Worry My Mind"*	45.00	70.00
☐ *"A New Salt Dog/Brown's Ferry Blues"*	45.00	70.00
☐ *"I've Got the Big River Blues/Blue Railroad Train"*	45.00	70.00
☐ *"I Ain't Got Nowhere to Travel/Ramblin' Minded Blues"*	45.00	70.00
☐ *"Lonesome Jailhouse Blues/By the Banks of the Rio Grande"*	45.00	70.00
☐ *"Blow Yo' Whistle, Freight Train/Lorena the Slave"*	35.00	50.00
☐ *"I Believe it For My Mother Told Me So/Hey! Hey! I'm Memphis Bound"*	35.00	50.00
☐ *"I'm Going Away/Brown's Ferry Blues (Part 2)"*	35.00	50.00
☐ *"Down South/Alabama Lullaby"*	35.00	50.00
☐ *"The Fugitive's Lament/Keep the Campfires Burning"*	35.00	50.00
☐ *"I Guess I've Got to Be Goin'/Kansas City Blues"*	35.00	50.00
☐ *"I Long to See My Mother/When it's Summer Time in a Southern Clime"*	35.00	50.00
☐ *"Lonesome Yodel Blues #2/Happy Hickey the Hobo"*	35.00	50.00
☐ *"I'm Worried Now/I'm Gonna Change My Way"*	35.00	50.00
☐ *"I Know I'll Be Happy in Heaven/Don't Let Me Be in the Way"*	35.00	50.00
☐ *"Nashville Blues/It's Takin' Me Down"*	35.00	50.00
☐ *"No Drunkard Can Enter There/Blind Child"*	35.00	50.00
☐ *"Southern Moon/I Don't Know Why I Love Her"*	35.00	50.00
☐ *"Don't You See That Train/The Lover's Warning"*	35.00	50.00
☐ *"Put Me on the Train to Carolina/Carry Me Back to Alabama"*	35.00	50.00
☐ *"False Hearted Girl/Memories of My Carolina Girl"*	35.00	50.00
☐ *"Take Away This Lonesome Day/No One"*	35.00	50.00
☐ *"Till the Roses Bloom Again/The Budded Rose"*	35.00	50.00
☐ **Columbia.** *"Alabama Lullaby/Got the Kansas City Blues"*	75.00	115.00

	Price Range	
☐ **DIXON BROTHERS. Bluebird.** *"Sales Tax on the Women/Intoxicated Rat"*	32.00	42.00
☐ *"Two Little Rosebuds/Weave Room Blues"*	32.00	42.00
☐ **FOLEY, RED. Decca.** *"Chiquita/Will You Wait for Me"*	9.00	13.00
☐ *"I'm Looking for a Sweetheart/Is It True?"*	9.00	13.00
☐ *"Pals of the Saddle/Someday Somewhere Sweetheart"*	9.00	13.00
☐ *"Smoke on the Water/There's a Blue Star Shining Bright"*	9.00	13.00
☐ **FOX, CURLY. King.** *"It's Your Time to be Blue/Soldier's Return"*	25.00	39.00
☐ *"Black Mountain Rag/Come Here Son"*	25.00	39.00
☐ **GUTHRIE, JACK. Capitol.** *"Oklahoma Hills/I'm Branding My Darling With My Heart"*	20.00	31.00
☐ *"When the Cactus is in Bloom/I Loved You Once"*	9.00	13.00
☐ *"Chained to a Memory/I'm Telling You"*	9.00	13.00
☐ *"Oakie Boogie/The Clouds Rained Trouble Down"*	9.00	13.00
☐ *"You Laughed and I Cried/It's Too Late to Change Your Mind"*	9.00	13.00
☐ **HAWKINS, HAWKSHAW. King.** *"After All/The Way I Love You"*	14.00	23.00
☐ *"I'll Never Cry Over You/I Ain't Goin' Honky Tonkin' Anymore"*	12.00	20.00
☐ *"There's a Little Bit of Everything in Texas/Soldier's Last Letter"*	9.00	12.00
☐ *"Blue-Eyed Elaine/Try Me One More Time"*	9.00	12.00
☐ *"You Nearly Lost Your Mind/Are You Waiting Just for Me?"*	9.00	12.00
☐ *"Walking the Floor Over You/I'll Get Along Somehow"*	9.00	12.00
☐ *"Mean Mama Blues/Mean Old Bedbug Blues"*	12.00	19.00
☐ *"That's When It's Coming Home to You/I'm Wondering How"*	5.00	8.00
☐ **JONES, GRANDPA. King.** *"It's Raining Here This Morning/I'll Be Around If You Need Me"*	13.00	21.00
☐ *"I'll Never Lose That Loneliness For You/That's a Grave in the Wave of the Ocean"*	13.00	21.00
☐ *"Steppin' Out Kind/You'll Be Lonesome Too"*	13.00	21.00
☐ *"Don't Sweet Talk Me/Maybe You'll Miss Me When I'm Gone"*	13.00	21.00
☐ **KINCAID, BRADLEY. Decca.** *"Ain't We Crazy/The Little Shirt That Mother Made For Me"*	7.00	11.00
☐ *"Old Wooden Rocker/My Mother's Beautiful Hands"*	7.00	11.00
☐ *"Red River Valley/Cowboy's Dream"*	7.00	11.00
☐ **MACON, "UNCLE" DAVE. Bluebird.** *"We Won the Heart of Sarah Jane/She's Got the Money Too"*	75.00	100.00
☐ *"When the Harvest Days are Over/One More River to Cross"*	75.00	100.00
☐ *"I'll Tickle Nancy/I'll Keep My Skillet Good and Greasy"*	80.00	130.00
☐ *"Over the Mountain/Just One Way to the Pearly Gates"*	75.00	100.00
☐ *"Honest Confession/From Jerusalem to Jericho"*	75.00	100.00
☐ *"Two in One Chewing Gum/Travelin' Down the Road"*	75.00	100.00
☐ *"Allin, Down and Out Blues/The Bum Hotel"*	75.00	100.00
☐ *"Johnny Grey/The Gayest Old Dude That's Out"*	75.00	100.00
☐ *"Give Me Back My Five Dollars/Railroadin' and Gamblin'"*	75.00	100.00
☐ *"Cumberland Mountain Deer Race/Country Ham and Red Gravy"*	75.00	100.00
☐ *"Things I Don't Like to See/Working for My Lord"*	75.00	100.00

	Price Range	
☐ **Brunswick.** *"Gal That Got Stuck on Everything She Said/Worthy of Estimation" (with Sam McGee).*	110.00	165.00
☐ *"Hold on to the Sleigh/Cross-Eyed Butcher".*	110.00	165.00
☐ *"Never Make Love No More/Diamond in the Rough".*	110.00	165.00
☐ *"'Comin' Round the Mountain/Gov. Al Smith" (with Sam McGee).*	110.00	165.00
☐ *"Tennessee Jubilee/Uncle Dave's Travels".*	110.00	165.00
☐ *"New Coon in Town/Uncle Dave's Travels, Part 1".*	110.00	165.00
☐ *"Over the Road I'm Bound to Go/From Earth to Heaven" (with Sam McGee).*	110.00	165.00
☐ *"Since Baby's Learned to Talk/Uncle Dave's Travels, Part 4".*	110.00	165.00
☐ *"Rock About, My Sara Jane/Death of John Henry" (billed as "Uncle" Dave Macon and the Fruit Jar Drinkers).*	110.00	165.00
☐ **MAINER, J. E. Bluebird.** *"Greenback Dollar/Broken-Hearted Blues".*	42.00	70.00
☐ *"Maple on the Hill/Take Me in the Lifeboat".*	42.00	70.00
☐ *"Ship Sailing Now/This World's Not My Home".*	42.00	70.00
☐ *"New Curly Headed Baby/Let Her Go, God Bless Her".*	42.00	70.00
☐ *"The Longest Train I Ever Saw/Ride On".*	36.00	70.00
☐ *"Lights in the Valley/City on the Hill".*	42.00	70.00
☐ *"Searching For a Pair of Blue Eyes/Write a Letter to Mother".*	42.00	70.00
☐ *"Fatal Wreck of the Bus/One to Love Me".*	35.00	51.00
☐ *"A Leaf From the Sea/Brown Eyes" (with Wade Mainer).*	35.00	51.00
☐ *"My Little Red Ford/My Wife Went Away and Left Me" (with John Love).*	35.00	51.00
☐ *"Satisfied/Don't Cause Mother's Hair to Turn Grey".*	35.00	51.00
☐ *"Maple on the Hill, Part 2/Where the Red, Red Roses Grow".*	35.00	51.00
☐ **O'DAY, MOLLY. Columbia.** *"The Tramp on the Street/Put My Rubber Doll Away".*	20.00	30.00
☐ *"The Drunken Driver/Six More Miles".*	20.00	30.00
☐ *"When God Comes to Gather His Jewels/The Tear Stained Letter".*	20.00	30.00
☐ **RENO, DON and RED SMILEY. King.** *"Hear Jerusalem Mourn/I'm Using My Bible for a Roadmap".*	5.00	8.00
☐ *"Lord's Last Supper/Highway to Heaven".*	5.00	8.00
☐ *"Choking the Strings/I'm the Talk of the Town".*	5.00	8.00
☐ *"He's Coming Back to Earth Again/My Mother's Bible".*	5.00	8.00
☐ *"Tennessee Breakdown/My Mother's Bible".*	5.00	8.00
☐ *"I Can Hear the Angels Singing/Mountain Church".*	5.00	8.00
☐ *"Tree of Life/Someone Will Love Me in Heaven".*	5.00	8.00
☐ **ROBERTSON, TEXAS JIM. RCA Victor.** *"Filipino Baby/Rainbow at Midnight".*	8.00	11.00
☐ *"Don't Look Now/It Takes a Long, Long Train".*	8.00	11.00
☐ *"Land, Sky and Water/Seven Women to One".*	8.00	11.00
☐ *"Miz O'Reilly's Daugher/Too Blue to Cry".*	8.00	11.00
☐ **RODGERS, JIMMIE. Bluebird.** *"Years Ago/Jimmie Rodger's Last Blue Yodel".*	100.00	140.00
☐ *"The Carter Family and Jimmie Rodgers in Texas/Where is My Sailor Boy" (second side by Monroe Bros.).*	100.00	140.00
☐ *"Why There's a Tear in My Eye/We Miss Him When the Evening Shadows Fall" (second side by Mrs. Jimmie Rodgers).*	150.00	200.00
☐ *"The One Rose/Yodeling My Way Back Home".*	100.00	140.00
☐ *"Take Me Back Again/Dreaming With Tears in My Eyes".*	100.00	140.00

	Price Range	
☐ *"I've Only Loved Three Women/The Wonderful City"*	100.00	140.00
☐ *"My Good Gal's Gone Blues/Blue Yodel #11"*	100.00	140.00
☐ *"I've Ranged, Roamed, I've Traveled/Why Did You Give Me Your Love"*	100.00	140.00
☐ **RCA Victor.** *"Sleep, Baby, Sleep/Soldier's Sweetheart"*	150.00	200.00
☐ *"Whippin' That Old T.B./No Hard Times"*	350.00	450.00
☐ *"In the Hills of Tennessee/Miss the Mississippi and You"*	300.00	400.00
☐ *"Hobo's Meditation/Down That Old Road to Home"*	120.00	200.00
☐ *"Waiting For a Train/Blue Yodel #4"*	120.00	175.00
☐ *"Rock All Our Babies to Sleep/Mother the Queen of My Heart"*	150.00	200.00
☐ *"My Blue Eyed Jane/Jimmie the Kid"*	100.00	140.00
☐ *"Hobo Bill's Last Ride/That's Why I'm Blue"*	100.00	140.00
☐ *"Train Whistle Blues/Jimmie's Texas Blues"*	100.00	140.00
☐ *"Blue Yodel #3/Never No More Blues"*	70.00	100.00
☐ *"Treasures Untold/Mother Was a Lady"*	70.00	100.00
☐ *"Ben Dew Berry's Final Run/In the Jailhouse Now #1"*	70.00	100.00
☐ *"Blue Yodel #1/Away Out on the Mountain"*	70.00	100.00
☐ *"Blue Yodel #2/Brakeman's Blues"*	70.00	100.00
☐ *"Blue Yodel #10/Mississippi Moon"*	150.00	200.00
☐ *"Home Call/She Was Happy Till She Met You"*	150.00	200.00
☐ *"99 Year Blues/My Time Ain't Long"*	185.00	230.00
☐ *"Roll Along Kentucky Moon/For the Sake of Days Gone By"*	150.00	200.00
☐ *"Gambling Polka Dot Blues/When the Cactus is in Bloom"*	150.00	200.00
☐ *"Let Me Be Your Sidetrack/Rodgers' Puzzle Record"*	150.00	200.00
☐ *"What's It/Why Should I Be Lonely"*	150.00	200.00
☐ *"Blue Yodel #9/Looking For a New Mama"*	150.00	200.00
☐ *"Moonlight and Skies/Jimmie Rodgers Visits the Carter Family"*	150.00	200.00
☐ *"Traveling Blues/I'm Lonesome Too"*	100.00	140.00
☐ *"T.B. Blues/MIssissippi River Blues"*	125.00	185.00
☐ *"Nobody Knows But Me/The Mystery of Number Five"*	100.00	140.00
☐ *"Blue Yodel #8/Jimmie's Mean Mama Blues"*	100.00	140.00
☐ *"Those Gambler's Blues/Pistol Packin' Papa"*	100.00	140.00
☐ *"High Powered Mama/In the Jailhouse Now #2"*	100.00	140.00
☐ *"A Drunkard's Child/Whisper Your Mother's Name"*	100.00	140.00
☐ *"Blue Yodel #6/Yodeling Cowbow"*	100.00	140.00
☐ *"My Rough and Rowdy Ways/Tuck Away My Lonesome Blues"*	100.00	150.00
☐ *"The Sailor's Plea/I'm Lonely and Blue"*	100.00	150.00
☐ *"My Little Lady/You and My Old Guitar"*	100.00	150.00
☐ *"My Carolina Sunshine Girl/Desert Blues"*	100.00	150.00
☐ *"Blue Yodel #5/I'm Sorry We Met"*	100.00	150.00
☐ *"Frankie and Johnnie/Everybody Does it in Hawaii"*	100.00	150.00
☐ *"Long Tall Mama Blues/Gambling Barroom Blues"*	250.00	350.00
☐ *"Southern Cannonball/Land of My Boyhood Dreams"*	250.00	350.00
☐ *"Old Love Letters/Somewhere Below the Dixon Line"*	300.00	425.00
☐ *"Blue Yodel #12/Cowhand's Last Ride"*	300.00	425.00
☐ *"Old Pal of My Heart/Mississippi Delta Blues"*	250.00	350.00
☐ *"Blue Yodel #12/Cowhand's Last Ride" (picture record with large portrait of Jimmie Rodgers on the record itself)* (This is the most valuable of all country and western 78rpm records.)	2000.00	3000.00

	Price Range	
☐ **ROGERS, ROY. Decca.** *"Nobody's Fault But My Own/You Waited Too Long"*	5.00	8.00
☐ *"O Come All Ye Faithful/Silent Night, Holy Night"*	5.00	8.00
☐ *"Chapel in the Valley/No Matter What Happens"*	5.00	8.00
☐ *"New Worried Mind/Melody of the Plains"*	5.00	8.00
☐ *"Yesterday/Time Changes Everything"*	4.00	6.00
☐ *"Life Won't Be the Same/Wondering Why"*	5.00	8.00
☐ *"Don't Be Blue, Little Pal/I'm Trusting in You"*	5.00	6.00
☐ *"Down By the Old Alamo/A Gay Ranchero"*	5.00	8.00
☐ **STANLEY BROTHERS. King.** *"Train 45/She's More to be Pitied"*	8.00	12.00
☐ *"Midnight Ramble/Love Me Darling Just Tonight"*	8.00	12.00
☐ *"How Can We Thank Him?/That Home Far Away"*	8.00	12.00
☐ *"Suwanee River Hoedown/The Memory of Your Smile"*	8.00	12.00
☐ *"Mother's Footsteps Guide Me On/White Dove"*	8.00	12.00
☐ *"I'm a Man of Constant Sorrow/How Mountain Girls Can Love"*	8.00	12.00
☐ **STONEMAN, ERNEST V. (& HIS DIXIE MOUNTAINEERS). RCA Victor.** *"Little Old Log/Sourwood Mountain"*	50.00	85.00
☐ *"I Love to Walk/Hallelujah Side"*	45.00	70.00
☐ *"Old Joe Clark/Ida Red"*	45.00	70.00
☐ *"Going Up Cripple Creek/Sugar in Gourd"*	50.00	85.00
☐ *"All Go Hungry/West Virginia"*	45.00	70.00
☐ **TANNER, GID (& HIS SKILLET LICKERS). Bluebird.** *"Tanner's Rag/Tanner's Hornpipe"*	40.00	55.00
☐ *"Cotton Patch/Whoa, Mule, Whoa"*	40.00	55.00
☐ *"Georgia Wagner/Mississippi Lawyer"*	40.00	55.00
☐ *"Skillet Licker Breakdown/Hawkin's Rag"*	40.00	55.00
☐ *"Ida Red/Git Along"*	40.00	55.00
☐ *"Down Yonder/Back Up and Push"*	40.00	55.00
☐ *"Soldier's Joy/Flop Eared Mule"*	40.00	55.00
☐ *"Keep Your Gal at Home/I Ain't No Better Now"*	40.00	55.00
☐ **Columbia.** *"Rocky Pallet/Hell's Broke Loose in Georgia"*	60.00	85.00
☐ *"Leather Breeches/New Arkansas Traveler"*	60.00	85.00
☐ *"Georgia Wagner/Sugar in the Gourd"*	60.00	85.00
☐ *"Soldier's Joy/Rock That Cradle Lucy"*	65.00	90.00
☐ *"Cripple Creek/Bonaparte's Retreat"*	65.00	90.00
☐ *"Flatwoods/Never Seen the Like"*	65.00	90.00
☐ *"Mississippi Sawyer/Goin' on Down Town"*	60.00	85.00
☐ *"Fox Chase/Arkansas Traveler" (with Riley Puckett)*	70.00	100.00
☐ *"Georgia Railroad/John Henry" (with Riley Puckett)*	70.00	100.00
☐ *"Just Gimme the Leavings/Old Time Tunes"*	60.00	85.00
☐ *"Darktown Strutter's Ball/Drink 'er Down"*	60.00	85.00
☐ **WILLIAMS, HANK. Sterling.** *"Calling You/Never Again"*	500.00	800.00
☐ *"Wealth Won't Save Your Soul/When God Comes and Gathers His Jewels"*	400.00	600.00
☐ *"My Love For You/I Don't Care"*	320.00	450.00
☐ *"Honky Tonkin'/Pan American"*	250.00	375.00
☐ **MGM.** *"Kaw-liga/Your Cheatin' Heart"*	14.00	20.00
☐ *"I'll Never Get Out of This World Alive/I Could Never Be Ashamed of You"*	14.00	20.00
☐ *"Jambalaya/Window Shopping"*	14.00	20.00
☐ *"Settin' the Woods on Fire/You Win Again"*	14.00	20.00

	Price Range	
☐ *"Half as Much/Let's Turn Back the Years"*.	14.00	20.00
☐ *"Honky Tonk Blues/I'm Sorry For You, My Friend"*.	14.00	20.00
☐ *"May You Never Be Alone/I Just Don't Like This Kind of Livin' "*.	17.00	23.00
☐ *"Lovesick Blues/Never Again"*.	14.00	20.00
☐ *"Wedding Bells/I've Just Told Mama Goodbye"*.	14.00	20.00
☐ *"Dear Brother/Lost on the River"*.	14.00	20.00
☐ *"My Son Calls Another Man Daddy/Long Ago Lonesome Blues"*.	14.00	20.00
☐ *"I Can't Help It/Howlin' at the Moon"*.	14.00	20.00
☐ *"Cold Cold Heart/Dear John"*.	14.00	20.00
☐ *"Moanin' the Blues/Nobody's Lonesome For Me"*.	14.00	20.00
☐ *"My Bucket's Got a Hole in It/I'm So Lonesome I Could Cry"*.	14.00	20.00
☐ *"I Saw the Light/Six More Miles"*.	14.00	20.00
☐ *"I'm a Long Gone Daddy/The Blues Come Around"*.	14.00	20.00
☐ *"Mansion on the Hill/I Can't Get You Off My Mind"*.	14.00	20.00
☐ *"Pan American/I Don't Care"*.	14.00	20.00
☐ **WILLS, BOB (& HIS TEXAS PLAYBOYS). Bluebird.** *"Nancy Jane/Sunbonnet Sue"*.	375.00	550.00
☐ **Columbia.** *"I Knew the Moment I Lost You/Oh! You Pretty Woman"*.	17.00	24.00
☐ *"Trouble in Mind/New San Antonio Rose"*.	12.00	19.00
☐ *"It's All Your Fault/Dusty Skies"*.	15.00	21.00
☐ *"New Texas Playboy Rag/Texarkana Baby"*.	15.00	21.00
☐ *"Empty Chairs at the Christmas Table/White Cross on Okinawa"*.	15.00	21.00
☐ *"Roly Poly/New Spanish Two-Step"*.	15.00	21.00
☐ *"New Worried Mind/Take Me Back to Tulsa"*.	12.00	19.00
☐ **Okeh.** *"Lil Liza Jane/Bob Wills' Stomp"*.	15.00	19.00
☐ *"I Don't Love a Nobody/Lone Star Rag"*.	15.00	21.00
☐ *"San Antonio Rose/Convict and the Rose"*.	15.00	21.00
☐ *"You're From Texas/We Might as Well Forget It"*.	15.00	21.00
☐ **Vocalion.** *"Alexander's Ragtime Band/Gambling Polka Dot Blues"*.	185.00	300.00
☐ *"Little Girl, Go Ask Your Mama/Whoa Babe"*.	100.00	140.00
☐ *"Oozlin' Daddy Blues/New St. Louis Blues"*.	100.00	140.00

CYLINDER RECORDINGS

The earliest phonograph recordings were of the cylinder type: a hollow tube with the sound grooves cut on the outside. In principle it worked just like a modern disc record but looked very different. When placed on a rotating arm, the cylinder turned and the phonograph needle engaged the sound grooves. Wax cylinders began to be manufactured in the late 1870's. They continued to be made up to the early 1900's, but sales sharply declined in the 1890's. By then, disc records were available and just about everybody preferred them over cylinders. The first disc records were introduced in 1887 — originally in zinc, then around 1898 in the standard wax type that remained in production up to the early 1950's. Cylinder records are, of course, highly collectible and have many fans among devotees of music history. They are not really difficult to find. Even though they were in production for only a little more than 30 years — and in peak production about 20 years — literally millions of specimens were turned out, to serve the owners of pioneer "talking machines." Finding them in *good condition* is another matter. For every 50 or 60 you'll run across, only about one can really be classified as "mint". And even an absolutely mint cylinder recording, just the way it came from the factory back in the 1880's or 1890's, sounds extremely lame compared to recording of a later era. If poor sound quality bothers you, you aren't going to be pleased with cylinder recordings. Most of those who collect cylinders are totally undisturbed by this: they approach them as historical objects, relics of the dawning days of recorded sound, and as such they really have no equals. Another thing to keep in mind (if you need to give yourself a pep talk) is that many things are captured on cylinder recordings which would not be preserved in any other way, such as the voices of early Presidents and eyewitness accounts of Queen Victoria's funeral procession.

At first, the makers of cylinder recordings did not pay any great attention to what they offered. During the early days of the cylinders, just about anything was slapped on them. When you bought a phonograph in 1880 or 1885, a few cylinder recordings came with it. These showed that the phonograph worked, and of course it was a big novelty to hear sound coming out of a machine — any kind of sound — in those days. If you wanted more, the phonograph dealer had them. Or you could send away to Mr. Edison in New Jersey, who regularly published long lists of his available cylinders. The phonograph companies made the cylinders and had a complete monopoly on the market. But it's very apparent that they were more concerned about selling phonographs than selling cylinders. That's where the money was, at that time, as phonographs by the multi thousands went into the homes of persons who had never before owned one. And at $15 or $20 for a machine, compared to 50¢ for a cylinder, you can hardly criticize that line of reasoning. Some folks were so thrilled at the novelty of it all that they just kept replaying the complimentary cylinders, and bought others only when the groove wore clear off the complimentaries. The phonograph, you have to remember, was the thing. People would say to their neighbors, "Come over and hear my phonograph", not "Come over and hear my new records". Hardly anybody really cared about the records — at first. It was the era of *"Be the first on your block to own . . ."*, and if you owned one of Edison's magical contraptions, that put you among the elite.

Many of the pioneer cylinders featured talking rather than music. The reasons were obvious. A talking record was much cheaper and simpler to cut than hiring a band, and the bad sound quality was less noticeable on such records. Another thing is that volume was hard to get out of the old machines. The more you cranked up the volume (if there was a volume control at all, which there often wasn't), the more scratchiness and paint-peeling screeches you heard. This is why the early ads show members of a family gathered AROUND the phonograph, leaning their ears as close as possible. The best way to listen was to keep the volume soft and move in close. Since voices did not need to project as much as music, they were better suited for that kind of equipment. What were the voices saying? Mostly they were reciting patriotic speeches or poems, or reading something out of *Hamlet.* This was great to kick off the phonograph on its path to commercial stardom, but of course the public got tired of that kind of thing. Gradually the cylinder makers had to provide more alluring material. Little by little, music, vocals, minstrels, funny stories, and all sorts of things worked their way on cylinders. The big push at variety came in the late 1880's and early 1890's when Thomas Edison tried his best (for a while) to make his cylinder records competitive with the disc records of Emile Berliner. When you come across a really groovy (pun, pun) cylinder recording, the odds are very good that it dates somewhere between 1887 and about 1892. Needless to say, the best ones are invariably found in the worst condition, since a dance-hall cylinder got played far more often than someone reciting, "By the shores of the gitchy goomy, by the shining big sea waters . . ." When these are in reasonable shape, they're certainly worth buying at the right price (see listings for rough guidelines).

In the next five or six years between the time that cylinder manufacturers woke up and put as much emphasis on the cylinder as on the phonograph, and the cylinder's death at the hands of disc records, some really worthy material got pressed. Most of the "progressive" cylinder recordings fell into one of the following categories (and remember that the world of entertainment was, in the Victorian era, quite a different scene than it later became — our ancestors were totally captivated by many types of performances that would bore us to tears):

MARCHES. Just by pure coincidence this was the era of John Philip Sousa, the "March King". Sousa composed — and played — stirring patriotic marches with lots of loud brassy punch. Great-grandpa thought Sousa's marches were spine-tingling. They were the rage of the age. Every amateur band from Pittsburgh to Podunk played them, and no parade was complete without several — at least. Tre patri age. Every amateur band from Pittsburgh to Podunk played them, and no parade was complete without several — at least. The patriotic spirit engendered by Sousa's marches was said to have been responsible for many enlistments for the Spanish-American War. You might not be quite so moved by them, hearing them on 90-year-old cylinder recordings. Their effect depended a lot on the ear-crunching volume of their sound, and that just doesn't come across on cylinders. Anyway, plenty of them were pressed, and they're interesting as curiosities even if nothing else. Compared to cylinder recordings on the whole, their values are not prohibitive.

BANJO SOLOS. Don't laugh — our ancestors were very fond of banjo solos. The "modern" era of vaudeville was just coming in, and every vaudeville troupe had a banjo soloist. In the intervening years, from then to now, the banjo has slipped a little in prestige as a solo instrument. The 1880's and 1890's were definitely its salad days. Why? Chiefly because there were several dozen musicians who could play a banjo, for every one who had a trace of talent on the piano or violin. Nearly all of them got started out in minstrel shows, which employed gangs of banjo-players. They were mostly self-taught and, if you listened closely, that fact was painfully evident. But it was not an overly-critical age. A good rollicking banjo solo, thumped out by somebody with heart, found plenty of sympathetic ears. They were a natural for early records, because they (unlike band music) presented no problems in microphone placement. You just stood the mike in front of the banjo-twanger and let him rip.

INSTRUMENTALS. Mostly these were called "Orchestra Records" in their day, because the word "orchestra" implied class and culture. Classical selections were not presented, however. The fare among instrumentals was largely a mixed bag taken from the music halls and minstrel show stages, heavy on the strings and light on the brass. Some of it comprised the "Top 40" of the day (though of course there were no popularity charts at the time), blended in with traditional tunes that might be as old as George Washington. These records were cut by the hundreds, possibly by the thousands, and surface wherever cylinders are found. If you want to make a collection, you can get most of them pretty reasonably — under $25. For an instrumental-on-cylinder to go as high as $35 or $40, it has to either be in fantastic condition or rank as something genuinely unusual. Premiums are usually attached to minstrel-type numbers with racist titles, having "coon", "nigger", or "darkie" in the title. Most such tunes were not pressed as instrumental recordings, however, but as Minstrels (see below). The difference was that in an orchestral recording there was more back-up. A number cut as a "Minstrel Tune" would usually be played with banjos only. One of the more valuable and worth-looking-for instrumental cylinders is Columbia 515063, "Night Alarm", which features the clanging bell of a fire engine. This was first-rate creativity for the time.

MINSTREL TUNES. On the whole these are the most valuable, monetarily, of cylinder records. They capture a form of entertainment which totally vanished from the American scene not long thereafter — replaced by vaudeville, movies, radio, etc. Therefore, minstrel records are considered more historical than the bulk of cylinder records. The magnitude of the minstrel industry is hard to conceive today. From 1850 to the 1890's, it was THE thing in U.S. entertainment. There were more minstrel groups active than grains of sand on the beach — touring around, going in every which direction, some making fortunes and others living like a pack of derelicts. A typical minstrel show consisted of banjo music, vocals, foot-stomping, and comedy. The performers were mostly white but painted their faces black, in the belief that this type of entertainment originated among slaves on the southern plantations. Actually, minstrel music as presented on stages bore little resemblance to any native "folk" music, but nobody really cared one way or the other. Some minstrel troupes WERE all-black, but these were very much in the minority. They were always advertised as "genuine" minstrels. It is highly questionable whether any of the all-black troupes were recorded on cylinder records. If such records exist and could be identified, they would be worth large premium prices. However, the practice in retailing cylinders was to indicate the selection's title and omit the performer's name or names. So it's not too likely that we're ever going to know. As things stand today, the most valuable minstrel cylinders are those of tunes which were recorded infrequently, especially those with racist titles.

MALE QUARTETTES. Male quartettes featured on cylinder records (tons of them) bear no resemblance to the Beatles. This was the age of so-called "barbershop singing". How that phrase got started is open to question, but every male quartette in the later 1800's was invariably referred to as a "barbershop quartette" (maybe people sang to pass the time, waiting for their turn for a shave). Most barbershop quartettes were amateur. They entertained at local civic functions and other events, just for the joy of belting loose in song. When you hear the ones captured on cylinder recordings you will not hesitate in concluding that they, too, were amateurs. That may or may not have been the case. Usually, barbershop quartettes sang without music, and this is how you'll hear them on most cylinder recordings. Their repertoire included everything from Stephen Foster to lullabies. They also sang — and are best remembered for — the popular tunes of their era, which of course seem as antique as parchment scrolls today. But if you like "In the Good Old Summertime" and "In the Shade of the Old Apple Tree", you may end up mainlining Male Quartette cylinders. One thing you have to say for them: they're authentic. Most of these records are not too expensive.

BARITONE SOLOS, TENOR SOLOS. Whenever a male vocalist sang solo, the cylinder record companies never put "John Smith" on the label. They identified such records as "Baritone Solo" or "Tenor Solor", relegating the poor artist to a lifetime of anonymity. Why? Largely because there were very few recognized names in the world of vocal music at that time. Just about the only "stars" who existed were on the operatic stage, and cylinder companies had no intention of paying them the kind of money they'd demand for warbling "Wait Till the Sun Shines Nellie". Why print a name on a label, when not a single buyer would know the name anyway? Or care? The philosophy was that everybody was interested in the tune, not in the performer, and this was probably 99% correct — though it did not remain so for very long (disc records ushered in the era of star recordings, when the name meant much MORE than the tune). Male solos on cylinder recordings are usually performed to the accompanyment of a piano, which can be heard faintly pinging away in the background. The talent is fair — but while you're blaming the artist, don't forget to blame the archaic recording and acoustical gear of the time, too. The tunes are nearly all in the "pop" category or what passed for it, pretty much the same as on Male Quartettes. In fact some of the singers may be the same, too. If multiple-track mixing were possible at that time (it wasn't), you'd almost believe that four Male Solo cuts were blended to make Male Quartette records.

SOPRANO SOLOS. Some fabulous operatic sopranos were active in the era of cylinder recordings. Unfortunately, they were not the ones who cut Soprano Solo records. Just who these artists were, is difficult to say. One thing you have to realize: the word "soprano" now denotes a classical artist, but in the 1800's any female who sang, and whose voice was more or less in the soprano range, was billed as a soprano — even if she sang exclusively dance-hall or minstrel tunes. That's just what cylinder Soprano Solos are, popular and not-so-popular songs, rather than anything with even a hint of classicism. They included dance-hall numbers that were considered highly risque in their time, with naughty titles like "I Just Can't Make My Eyes Behave" and "Everyone is in Slumberland But You and Me." The bad thing about Soprano Solo cylinders is too much treble and too little bass, resulting in many words going into such a high octave range that your cocker spaniel will catch them better than you do. Don't play these if you have a nervous dog in the house.

VAUDEVILLE NUMBERS. These comprise a large percentage of cylinder recordings, especially of those pressed in the period from 1887 until the cylinder record demise some years thereafter. Vaudeville was making its splash, pushing out the old traditional minstrel shows, and of course the cylinder manufacturers wanted to bring this new novelty into America's parlors. The term "vaudeville" was already in use when a man named B. F. Keith — a vaudeville manager — inaugurated continuous performances which ran all through the day. Thereafter it soared like no entertainment medium before had ever done. Vaudeville theatres grew up all across the land, most of which later turned into movie houses. Scores of great stars got their start — or spent the bulk of their careers — on the vaudeville stage. It was a tough proving ground, since five or six shows a day was enough to kill the show business ambition of just about anybody. But if you're looking for star recordings among cylinder records, save your time. Recordings labeled "Vaudeville Numbers" feature tunes made popular in that medium, but performed by house artists whose names did not become household words. In fact their names are not even on the records. Nevertheless this is a nostalgic group of cylinders, in which the long-ago echoes of Old Broadway can be heard. You might like them.

COMIC MONOLOGUES. This is probably the single most intriguing of all the groups of cylinder recordings — NOT because the monologues are funny or the performances are good (which is rare), but because of their uniqueness. They show what America was laughing at, 90 and 100 years ago, and in that sense are social documents of the highest order. The cylinder record was ideal for comic (or any other type of) monologues. They could be edited down or rewritten to fit recording time requirements much better than a song. Also, they simply sounded better when you played them, as they still do today: the lack of tonal balancing did not hurt the spoken word as much as music, or even as much as the singing voice. Cylinder manufacturers liked to advertise that their comic monologues were taken straight off the vaudeville stage. Some of them no doubt were, but with vaudeville reusing the same routines over and over endlessly, there weren't nearly enough comic monologues to go around. So they made up their own, and some very weird things found their way on the cylinders, with titles like "Krausmeyer and His Dog" and "Reuben Haskins' Ride on a Cyclone Auto". A large portion of comic monologues were of an ethnic or racial nature, which was par for the course at that time in show biz: foreigners who spoke with accents were heavily lampooned by comics. In fact, Americans who spoke with accents came in for their share of ribbing, too. There are many comic monologue records in which the joke is turned on New England Yankees. Comic monologue selections tend to be snapped up very fast wherever cylinders appear. Even those who don't really collect them have a curiosity interest in them, much more so than in most types of cylinder recordings.

Having said all of the above, we need to point out one more thing: that to play cylinder recordings, you need a cylinder phonograph. This is a fair-sized investment but for anybody who has intentions of being a serious collector it will be more than repaid in listening pleasure. Just make sure, before putting down any cash, that the machine is in proper operating condition. See the section on mechanical instruments for further information.

COLUMBIA WAX CYLINDER RECORDINGS

Recordings on the Columbia label (yes, the firm is still in business today) were slightly more expensive, originally, than those of Oxford. Musically and technically they were of about equal quality, but Columbia had the bigger reputation and — especially in the classical field — the bigger artists.

		Price Range	
BAND — MARCHES			
☐ **51544**	*Admiral's Favorite March.*	16.00	22.00
☐ **51514**	*America.*	16.00	22.00
☐ **532311**	*Anona.*	20.00	26.00
☐ **532362**	*Any Rags.*	16.00	22.00
☐ **531867**	*Arkansas Husking Bee.*	16.00	22.00
☐ **532389**	*Bedella.*	20.00	25.00
BANJO SOLOS			
☐ **53861**	*Bunch of Rags.*	34.00	51.00
☐ **531412**	*Coon Band Contest.*	45.00	60.00
☐ **53816**	*Darky's Dream.*	45.00	60.00
☐ **53825**	*El Capitan March.*	23.00	38.00
☐ **53856**	*Eli Green's Cakewalk.*	29.00	49.00
☐ **53860**	*Old Folks at Home.*	29.00	49.00
☐ **53830**	*Rag Time Medley ("All Coons Look Alike to Me").*	37.00	58.00
☐ **53859**	*Whistling Rufus.*	25.00	41.00
INSTRUMENTALS (originally called Orchestra Records)			
☐ **515132**	*Angel's Serenade.*	15.00	20.00
☐ **515162**	*Blue Danube Waltz.*	15.00	20.00
☐ **515206**	*Bugler's Dream.*	16.00	23.00
☐ **531688**	*Creole Belle.*	20.00	30.00
☐ **515010**	*Dancing in the Kitchen.*	20.00	30.00
☐ **515145**	*Darky's Dream.*	20.00	30.00
☐ **515159**	*Darky's Tickle.*	21.00	35.00
☐ **532191**	*Dixieland March.*	18.00	30.00
☐ **515064**	*Down on the Suwanee River.*	27.00	42.00
☐ **515114**	*Flora Waltz.*	15.00	21.00
☐ **515202**	*Georgia Camp Meeting.*	15.00	21.00
☐ **515007**	*Happy Days in Dixie.*	20.00	32.00
☐ **515142**	*Husking Bee.*	20.00	32.00
☐ **532283**	*Laughing Water.*	15.00	20.00
☐ **515121**	*Let Her Rip.*	15.00	20.00
☐ **515063**	*Night Alarm (with fire-engine sound effects).*	34.00	52.00
☐ **515044**	*Rose From the South Waltz.*	15.00	20.00
☐ **515059**	*Virginia Skedaddle.*	20.00	31.00
☐ **515203**	*Whistling Rufus.*	15.00	21.00
MINSTREL TUNES			
☐ **31609**	*Coon, Coon, Coon.*	50.00	71.00
☐ **13000**	*Dese Bones Shall Rise Again.*	65.00	95.00
☐ **32986**	*Dixie Dear.*	35.00	55.00
☐ **32952**	*Goodbye, Mr. Greenback.*	35.00	55.00
☐ **13001**	*High Old Time.*	65.00	100.00
☐ **31691**	*I'd Leave My Happy Home For You.*	45.00	75.00
☐ **13004**	*Laughing Song.*	72.00	105.00
☐ **33031**	*Moses Andrew Jackson.*	72.00	105.00
☐ **13002**	*Old Log Cabin.*	35.00	51.00
☐ **33104**	*San Antonio.*	35.00	51.00

			Price Range	
QUARTETTES — MALE				
☐	**33048**	*Ain't You Coming Back to New Hampshire, Molly?*	**16.00**	**22.00**
☐	**33049**	*Alice, Where Art Thou Going?*	**16.00**	**22.00**
☐	**33201**	*Black Jim.*	**30.00**	**44.00**
☐	**32931**	*Call to Arms.*	**30.00**	**44.00**
☐	**33033**	*Christmas Morning at Flanagan's.*	**25.00**	**39.00**
☐	**32836**	*Darling Nellie Gray.*	**16.00**	**22.00**
☐	**32907**	*Down in Chinkapin Lan.*	**27.00**	**45.00**
☐	**9037**	*Farmyard Medley.*	**23.00**	**38.00**
☐	**32690**	*Goodbye Sis.*	**23.00**	**38.00**
☐	**32237**	*Hoosier Hollow Quilting Party.*	**23.00**	**38.00**
☐	**32764**	*In the Shade of the Old Apple Tree.*	**16.00**	**24.00**
☐	**32722**	*In the Sweet Bye and Bye.*	**16.00**	**24.00**
☐	**9045**	*My Old New Hampshire Home.*	**16.00**	**24.00**
☐	**9042**	*Nationality Medley.*	**20.00**	**35.00**
☐	**32704**	*Nelle Was a Lady.*	**25.00**	**41.00**
☐	**9030**	*The Old Folks at Home.*	**25.00**	**41.00**
☐	**9029**	*Way Down Yonder in the Cornfield.*	**27.00**	**45.00**
☐	**33070**	*When Daddy Sings the Little Ones to Sleep.*	**16.00**	**24.00**
☐	**32989**	*While the Old Mill Wheel is Turning.*	**14.00**	**23.00**

OXFORD LABEL WAX CYLINDER RECORDINGS

The following cylinders are all Oxford label and date from circa 1905.

BAND MUSIC				
☐	**31529**	*American Students' Waltz.*	**19.00**	**15.00**
☐	**32413**	*By The Sycamore Tree Medley.*	**9.00**	**14.00**
☐	**32982**	Dixie Queen March.	**10.00**	**15.00**
☐	**514**	*El Capitan March.*	**16.00**	**22.00**
☐	**501**	*High School Cadets' March.*	**15.00**	**21.00**
☐	**32735**	*Hobo Band.*	**15.00**	**21.00**
☐	**500**	*Liberty Bell March.*	**16.00**	**22.00**
☐	**32816**	*Me and My Banjo.*	**20.00**	**32.00**
☐	**1537**	*O Promise Me.*	**25.00**	**40.00**
☐	**32749**	*Roosevelt's Inaugural Parade.*	**25.00**	**40.00**
☐	**32815**	*Whistler and His Dog.*	**23.00**	**32.00**
BARITONE SOLOS				
☐	**32615**	*Abraham (minstrel song).*	**50.00**	**75.00**
☐	**32820**	*And the World Goes On.*	**30.00**	**51.00**
☐	**32589**	*Come Take a Trip in My Airship.*	**50.00**	**75.00**
☐	**32811**	*Girl Who Cares For Me.*	**30.00**	**50.00**
☐	**32854**	*Home Sweet Home.*	**23.00**	**38.00**
☐	**33058**	*I Love the Last One Best of All.*	**30.00**	**50.00**
☐	**32805**	*In Dear Old Georgia.*	**37.00**	**51.00**
☐	**33123**	*My Irish Rosie.*	**37.00**	**51.00**
☐	**32960**	*The Poor Old Man.*	**30.00**	**50.00**
☐	**32882**	*Wait Till the Sun Shines Nelly.*	**25.00**	**38.00**
☐	**33057**	*We'll Be Sweethearts to the End.*	**30.00**	**51.00**
☐	**32889**	*When the Mocking Birds are Singing.*	**30.00**	**51.00**
☐	**32939**	*You Look Awfully Good to Father.*	**35.00**	**58.00**
☐	**32605**	*You Must Think I'm Santa Claus.*	**30.00**	**51.00**
☐	**32976**	*You're Just the Girl I'm Looking For.*	**35.00**	**58.00**

	Price Range	
COMIC MONOLOGUES, ETC.		
☐ **11102** *Backyard Conversation Between Two Jealous Irish Washwerwomen.*	50.00	81.00
☐ **330243** *An Evening at Mrs. Clancy's Boarding House.*	40.00	60.00
☐ **32949** *Flanagan's Night Off.*	40.00	60.00
☐ **32623** *Hand of Fate.*	35.00	55.00
☐ **32655** *Krausmeyer and His Dog.*	50.00	75.00
☐ **32603** *Night Before Christmas.*	27.00	40.00
☐ **33001** *Punch and Judy.*	27.00	40.00
☐ **32249** *Reuben Haskins' Ride on a Cyclone Auto.*	40.00	60.00
☐ **32569** *Rheumatism Cure in Jayville Center.*	50.00	75.00
SOPRANO SOLOS		
☐ **33082** *Everyone is in Slumberland But You and Me.*	16.00	22.00
☐ **33063** *Fancy Little Nancy.*	20.00	31.00
☐ **33083** *If the Man in the Moon Were a Coon.*	28.00	42.00
☐ **33097** *I Just Can't Make My Eyes Believe.*	20.00	30.00
☐ **33004** *It's All Right in the Summer Time.*	28.00	42.00
☐ **32911** *So Long, Mary.*	22.00	35.00
☐ **32746** *You Ain't the Man I Thought You Was.*	20.00	32.00
☐ **32972** *Waiting at the Church.*	20.00	32.00
TENOR SOLOS		
☐ **32533** *A Bit o' Blarney.*	20.00	32.00
☐ **33179** *Always Leave Them Laughing When You Say Good-bye.*	16.00	22.00
☐ **32945** *Anxious.*	21.00	36.00
☐ **33140** *Ask Me Not.*	16.00	25.00
☐ **32641** *Bunker Hill.*	16.00	25.00
☐ **32476** *By the Old Oak Tree.*	15.00	25.00
☐ **32946** *Can't You See I'm Lonely.*	16.00	25.00
☐ **33127** *Captain Baby Bunting.*	20.00	32.00
☐ **33023** *Cheer Up, Mary.*	16.00	23.00
☐ **32887** *Will You Love Me in December?*	11.00	15.00
☐ **33178** *Dreaming.*	20.00	31.00
☐ **32732** *Farewell, Soldier Boy (Spanish-American War).*	20.00	32.00
☐ **32844** *Girl of the U.S.A.*	22.00	38.00
☐ **32812** *Goodbye, Sweet Old Manhattan Isle.*	30.00	45.00
☐ **32875** *Goodnight, Little Girl.*	21.00	33.00
☐ **32997** *Good Old U.S.A.*	16.00	22.00
☐ **32806** *I'll Be Waiting in the Gloaming.*	30.00	45.00
☐ **32582** *I'm Longing For You, Sweetheart.*	16.00	22.00
☐ **32664** *In the Shade of the Old Apple Tree.*	10.00	14.00
☐ **32943** *Is There Any Room in Heaven?*	30.00	45.00
☐ **32658** *It Makes Me Think of Home.*	20.00	33.00
☐ **32726** *Just Across the Bridge of Gold.*	16.00	23.00
☐ **32860** *Just a Little Rocking Chair and You.*	20.00	31.00
☐ **32798** *Keep a Little Cozy Corner in Your Heart.*	23.00	37.00
☐ **32942** *Keep on the Sunny Side.*	20.00	32.00
☐ **33080** *Lemon in the Garden of Love.*	27.00	40.00
☐ **32908** *Let Me Write What I Never Dared to Tell.*	22.00	37.00
☐ **32566** *Little Boy Called Taps.*	27.00	40.00
☐ **33168** *Little Suit of Blue.*	25.00	37.00
☐ **32718** *Longing For You.*	25.00	37.00
☐ **32619** *Mamma's Boy.*	15.00	23.00

			Price Range	
☐	32909	*Mayor of Tokio, I Like You.*	30.00	45.00
☐	32465	*My Cosy Corner Girl.*	25.00	36.00
☐	32778	*My Irish Molly O.*	25.00	36.00
☐	33015	*Not Because Your Hair is Curly.*	20.00	33.00
☐	32919	*Nothing Like That in Our Family.*	22.00	37.00
☐	32773	*On a Summer Night.*	22.00	37.00
☐	32877	*Only 45 Minutes From Broadway.*	30.00	45.00
☐	32774	*Picnic For Two.*	25.00	37.00
☐	32859	*Robinson Crusoe's Isle.*	25.00	37.00
☐	32427	*Runaway Motor Car.*	27.00	42.00
☐	33128	*School Days.*	13.00	30.00
☐	32852	*Somebody's Sweetheart.*	22.00	38.00
☐	33062	*Street of New York.*	22.00	38.00
☐	32513	*Sweetest Girl in Dixie.*	20.00	33.00
☐	32828	*Sweethearts in Every Town.*	25.00	36.00
☐	33196	*Take Me Back to New York Town.*	25.00	36.00
☐	32560	*Teasing.*	20.00	35.00
☐	33205	*Two Blue Eyes.*	20.00	35.00
☐	32941	*We Parted as the Sun Went Down.*	20.00	35.00
☐	32881	*What Has the Night Time to Do With the Girl?*	22.00	36.00
☐	33060	*When the Flowers Bloom in the Springtime.*	16.00	23.00
☐	32458	*When the Sunset Turns the Ocean's Blue to Gold.*	20.00	33.00
☐	32470	*When the Trees are White With Blossoms I'll Return.*	16.00	22.00
☐	32814	*Where the Morning Glories Twine.*	16.00	22.00
☐	32619	*Why Don't They Play With Me?*	22.00	37.00
☐	32887	*Will You Love Me in December?*	11.00	15.00
☐	32970	*With the Robins I'll Return.*	23.00	32.00
☐	32625	*Yankee Doodle Boy.*	16.00	22.00
☐	32853	*You Don't Seem Like the Girl I Used to Know.*	22.00	35.00
☐	33157	*You'll Have to Get Off and Walk.*	20.00	33.00

VAUDEVILLE NUMBERS

☐	32795	*Anthony and Cleopatra (satire on Shakespeare).*	35.00	52.00
☐	33182	*At the Village Post Office.*	40.00	59.00
☐	33000	*Barnyard Serenade.*	30.00	43.00
☐	11024	*Blazing Ray.*	30.00	43.00
☐	33206	*Bronco Bob.*	40.00	53.00
☐	32981	*Coming Home From Coney Island.*	40.00	53.00
☐	32980	*Darktown Courtship.*	50.00	70.00
☐	32628	*Down the Pike at the St. Louis Exposition.*	40.00	52.00
☐	32730	*Ev'ry Little Bit Helps.*	30.00	42.00
☐	33170	*Flanagan at the Barber's.*	37.00	55.00
☐	33198	*Flanagan at the Doctor's.*	37.00	55.00
☐	33183	*Flanagan at the Vocal Teacher's.*	37.00	55.00
☐	33129	*Flanagan on a Broadway Car.*	37.00	55.00
☐	33144	*Flanagan on a Farm.*	35.00	55.00
☐	32868	*Fritz and Louisa.*	32.00	50.00
☐	32738	*Heinie.*	37.00	55.00
☐	33169	*Herman and Minnie.*	32.00	50.00
☐	33064	*Jealous.*	37.00	55.00
☐	32947	*Maggie Clancy's New Piano.*	32.00	50.00
☐	33143	*Meet Me Down at the Corner.*	32.00	50.00
☐	32998	*Monkey on a String.*	22.00	35.00
☐	32766	*Mr. and Mrs. 'Awkins.*	27.00	39.00
☐	32780	*Mr. and Mrs. Murphy.*	27.00	39.00

		Price Range	
☐ 33014	*Mrs. Hiram Offen Discharges Bridget Sullivan.*	35.00	50.00
☐ 32948	*Mrs. Hiram Offen Engaging Bridget Sullivan.*	35.00	50.00
☐ 33002	*Mrs. Reilly's Troubles With the Dumb Waiter.*	35.00	50.00
☐ 32700	*Musical Congress of Nations.*	27.00	40.00
☐ 32901	*Original Cohens.*	60.00	90.00

VOCAL DUETS (MALE)

☐ 33150	*And a Little Bit More.*	16.00	22.00
☐ 33050	*Arrah Wanna.*	16.00	22.00
☐ 33105	*Bake Dat Chicken Pie.*	20.00	31.00
☐ 32894	*Central, Give Me Back My Dime.*	20.00	31.00
☐ 32621	*Coax Me.*	22.00	37.00
☐ 32777	*Come Along, Little Girl.*	20.00	31.00
☐ 33009	*Come, Take a Skate With Me.*	20.00	31.00
☐ 32485	*Dixie.*	20.00	31.00

FOLK

MEMORABILIA

Only in the past 10-15 years has folk music memorabilia been actively collected. Undoubtedly this material is, as a whole, still undervalued and is likely to increase in price in the future.

☐ **BAEZ, JOAN.** *Photo cut from "Life" Magazine, signed and inscribed.*	7.00	10.00
☐ **BAEZ, JOAN.** *10x12 color photo, signed on the back. Glue marks on back.*	8.00	11.00
☐ **BAEZ, JOAN.** *8x10 studio portrait with guitar, signed, dated 1964.*	6.00	9.00
☐ **BAEZ, JOAN.** *8x10 photo blown up from candid shot, shows her seated on grass in park, signed, inscribed. c. 1967.*	15.00	20.00
☐ **BAEZ, JOAN.** *45rpm recording, "The Night They Drove Old Dixie Down", signed on the label.*	15.00	20.00
☐ **BAEZ, JOAN.** *Six snapshot photos, mostly 3½x4, two of them signed. Mounted on a stiff cardboard sheet.*	17.00	22.00
☐ **BRAND, OSCAR.** *Book, "The Ballad Mongers", signed and inscribed on front endleaf.*	7.00	10.00
☐ **BRAND, OSCAR.** *Typewritten letter, signed, radio station letterhead, 1968.*	3.00	4.00
☐ **BRAND, OSCAR.** *Postcard in his hand, three lines. 1958.*	2.00	3.00
☐ **BRAND, OSCAR.** *Signature on a card.*	1.00	2.00
☐ **BRAND, OSCAR.** *8x10 studio portrait, signed and inscribed, dated 1962.*	4.00	5.00
☐ **BRAND, OSCAR.** *3½x4 snapshot with fan, signed on the back.*	2.00	3.00
☐ **BRAND, OSCAR.** *T-shirt with his name and likeness.*	7.00	10.00
☐ **BRAND, OSCAR.** *Concert program, signed.*	2.00	3.00
☐ **BRAND, OSCAR.** *Magazine article, signed.*	2.00	3.00
☐ **BRAND, OSCAR.** *Two checks endorsed by him, 1971 and 1977.*	7.00	10.00

Joan Baez

	Price Range	
☐ **BRAND, OSCAR.** *Scrapbook with 41 photos of him, some with other folk music celebrities, a few signed.*	70.00	90.00
☐ **CLANCY BROTHERS.** *8x10 group photo, signed by all, 1961.*	13.00	20.00
☐ **COLLINS, JUDY.** *8x10 studio photo, signed and inscribed, dated 1968.*	4.00	6.00
☐ **COLLINS, JUDY.** *Photo cut from LP album cover, signed.*	7.00	10.00
☐ **COLLINS, JUDY.** *ALs, two pages, with envelope. 1961.*	4.00	6.00
☐ **COLLINS, JUDY.** *Signature on a card.*	2.00	3.00
☐ **COLLINS, JUDY.** *Signature on a record company press release.*	3.00	5.00
☐ **COLLINS, JUDY.** *5x7 color photo, signed on the back.*	4.00	6.00
☐ **COLLINS, JUDY.** *Book, "Poems of the Scottish Highlands", signed by her inside front cover.*	6.00	9.00
☐ **COLLINS, JUDY.** *News cutting (record review), signed. Laminated.*	2.00	3.00
☐ **COLLINS, JUDY.** *LP phono record, signed on the label.*	20.00	30.00
☐ **COLLINS, JUDY.** *Concert program, signed.*	3.00	5.00
☐ **COLLINS, JUDY.** *Record company contract, signed twice.*	20.00	25.00
☐ **HOUSTON, CISCO.** *EP album sleeve, signed, record missing.*	22.00	33.00
☐ **HOUSTON, CISCO.** *ALs, two pages, 1951.*	17.00	25.00
☐ **HOUSTON, CISCO.** *Concert program, signed.*	8.00	11.00
☐ **HOUSTON, CISCO.** *Book, "Songs of the American West", signed on front flyleaf.*	15.00	20.00

	Price Range	
☐ **HOUSTON, CISCO.** *8x10 studio portrait, signed, c. 1955.*	18.00	27.00
☐ **HOUSTON, CISCO.** *78rpm phono record, signed on the label.*	60.00	80.00
☐ **HOUSTON, CISCO.** *Signature on a card.*	3.00	5.00
☐ **HOUSTON, CISCO.** *Check endorsed by him, 1947.*	35.00	50.00
☐ **HOUSTON, CISCO.** *Concert appearance contract, signed.*	30.00	40.00
☐ **IVES, BURL.** *8x10 portrait photo, signed, dated 1950.*	4.00	6.00
☐ **IVES, BURL.** *Sailor's cap reputedly worn by him in concert.*	15.00	20.00
☐ **IVES, BURL.** *Motion picture still, "Cat on a Hot Tin Roof", signed.*	7.00	10.00
☐ **IVES, BURL.** *Theatrical poster, signed, framed, 18x28.*	40.00	55.00
☐ **IVES, BURL.** *Check endorsed by him, 1961.*	15.00	22.00
☐ **IVES, BURL.** *ALs, three pages, New York, 1941.*	20.00	28.00
☐ **IVES, BURL.** *Postcard sent by him in 1949, six lines, stained.*	4.00	5.00
☐ **IVES, BURL.** *Photo with John Daly, signed by Ives only.*	5.00	6.00
☐ **IVES, BURL.** *Article from "TV-Radio Life", signed.*	6.00	7.00
☐ **IVES, BURL.** *78rpm phono record, signed on the label.*	18.00	24.00
☐ **IVES, BURL.** *Record company contract, signed.*	20.00	26.00
☐ **IVES, BURL.** *T-shirt with his name and likeness.*	8.00	11.00
☐ **NILES, JOHN JACOB.** *ALs, two pages, 1935.*	22.00	33.00
☐ **NILES, JOHN JACOB.** *ALs, 1½ pages, to Carl Sandburg.*	80.00	110.00
☐ **NILES, JOHN JACOB.** *Copy of book, Carl Sandburg's "American Songbag", inscribed by Sandburg to Niles, with notes by Niles.*	130.00	175.00
☐ **NILES, JOHN JACOB.** *78rpm record, signed on the label.*	40.00	55.00
☐ **NILES, JOHN JACOB.** *5x6½ photo, signed and inscribed, c. 1930.*	18.00	24.00
☐ **NILES, JOHN JACOB.** *Signature on a card.*	5.00	7.00
☐ **OCHS, PHIL.** *8x10 studio portrait, signed and inscribed, dated 1966.*	25.00	33.00
☐ **OCHS, PHIL.** *Concert program, signed.*	20.00	28.00
☐ **OCHS, PHIL.** *LP record album cover, signed, record missing.*	80.00	105.00
☐ **OCHS, PHIL.** *Signature on a card.*	8.00	11.00
☐ **OCHS, PHIL.** *ALs, one page, 1960.*	37.00	53.00
☐ **ODETTA.** *8x10 studio photo, signed and inscribed.*	5.00	7.00
☐ **ODETTA.** *Sheet music, "The Golden Vanity", signed.*	4.00	5.00
☐ **ODETTA.** *Copy of magazine "Thirteen", signed.*	4.00	5.00
☐ **ODETTA.** *Snapshot photo on stage, signed on the back.*	4.00	5.00
☐ **ODETTA.** *ALs, two pages, 1969.*	5.00	6.00
☐ **ODETTA.** *ALs, 1½ pages, with autographed photo enclosed, 1973.*	7.00	10.00
☐ **ODETTA.** *Guitar reputedly used by her in TV appearance.*	550.00	800.00
☐ **ODETTA.** *Book, "Songs of the Southern Highlands", signed on front flyleaf.*	8.00	11.00
☐ **ODETTA.** *Scrapbook on her career, containing six 8x10 photos, three of them signed, 56 news cuttings and other items.*	70.00	90.00
☐ **PAXTON, TOM.** *8x10 studio photo, signed and inscribed.*	5.00	7.00
☐ **PAXTON, TOM.** *Concert contract, signed.*	11.00	16.00
☐ **PAXTON, TOM.** *ALs, ½ page, 1968.*	5.00	6.00

	Price Range	
☐ **PAXTON, TOM.** *LP record album cover, signed, record missing.*	13.00	19.00
☐ **PAXTON, TOM.** *Signature on a card.*	2.00	3.00
☐ **PAXTON, TOM.** *Photo with Phil Ochs, signed by both.*	70.00	90.00
☐ **PAXTON, TOM.** *T-shirt with his name and likeness.*	7.00	10.00
☐ **PAXTON, TOM.** *Postcard sent by him in 1961.*	4.00	5.00
☐ **PAXTON, TOM.** *Two 5x6 snapshot photos, signed on the backs.*	7.00	10.00
☐ **PAXTON, TOM.** *Check endorsed by him, 1970.*	11.00	15.00
☐ **PAXTON, TOM.** *LP phono record, signed on the label.*	20.00	25.00
☐ **SEEGER, PETE.** *8x10 studio portrait, signed, dated 1958.*	6.00	8.00
☐ **SEEGER, PETE.** *Three small snapshot photos, two signed, 1970-75.*	8.00	11.00
☐ **SEEGER, PETE.** *ALs, two pages, 1961.*	6.00	8.00
☐ **SEEGER, PETE.** *Concert poster (Carnegie Hall, New York), framed under glass, not signed.*	13.00	19.00
☐ **SEEGER, PETE.** *Signature on a card.*	1.50	2.00
☐ **SEEGER, PETE.** *Copy of "Rolling Stone" magazine, signed.*	5.00	7.00
☐ **SEEGER, PETE.** *6x7½ photo standing on shipboard, signed.*	5.00	7.00
☐ **SEEGER, PETE.** *Concert program, signed.*	4.00	5.00
☐ **SEEGER, PETE.** *Check endorsed by him, 1974.*	11.00	16.00
☐ **SEEGER, PETE.** *647 news cuttings relating to his career, housed in a set of four 14x17 leatherette albums.*	55.00	75.00
☐ **SEEGER, PETE.** *LP record album cover, signed, record missing.*	15.00	20.00
☐ **WHITE, JOSH.** *ALs, two pages, 1937.*	40.00	55.00
☐ **WHITE, JOSH.** *8x10 photo, signed and inscribed.*	16.00	22.00
☐ **WHITE, JOSH.** *Cover of 78rpm album set, signed.*	16.00	22.00

78's

The traditional definition of folk music is music (or ballads, or whatever) not originally created to be recorded or performed professionally. Mountain ballads of Kentucky are a perfect and indisputable example of folk music; so are sea shanties and the earlier Polish polkas. But today the term folk music, as commonly interpreted, also encompasses a great deal else. Almost any recording made by a recognized folk music artist is labeled folk music, and there is not doubt but that buyers are just as interested — if not more so — in the artist as in his music. Therefore it is difficult to set guidelines for the collector.

Whether the recordings made by current folk artists will be highly regarded by future generations is questionable. In any case, the fact that modern LP albums are pressed in very large quantities, and, being made of vinyl, preserve far better than recordings of the pre-1950 era, it is not likely they will become "collectors' items" to quite the same degree as the old 78's.

Folk music was recorded from the turn-of-the-century onward; it is found even on wax cylinders pre-dating disc records. Nearly all early recordings, however, up to World War I, had the songs performed by popular or operatic artists, which rendered them far from authentic-sounding. John McCormack doing an Irish folk ballad made sense, even though the original singers of these songs probably did not have opera-trained voices; but very often such songs, of whatever origin or nationality, were done in far too dignified and artistic a manner for folk music. It was only later, around 1920, that record companies began to press folk music performed by artists who gave it a suitable rendering.

There is much difference of opinion as to what may or may not be included in a collection of "authentic" folk music. Nor can any strict guidelines be laid. Many of the records listed in our section on Country and Western 78rpms could easily be termed "folk", especially those of such artists as Dave Macon, Gid Tanner, J. E. Mainer and Ernest Stoneman. They were mountain or bluegrass ballads, performed by natives of the land. "Overlapping" is common in folk music: a tune can fall into several categories. I am sure that there are people who collect the Beatles as folk music, too, even though this seems as improper as classifying Johnny Cash records with those of Vernon Dalhart.

	Price Range	
☐ **BATES, DR. HUMPHREY and HIS POSSUM HUNTERS. Brunswick 239.** *"Eighth of January"*.	**36.00**	**57.00**
☐ **Brunswick 275.** *"Run, Nigger, Run"*.	**45.00**	**65.00**
☐ **BAUMAN, MORDY. Musicraft M-75** *(album; 4 10-inch records). "Songs of American Sailormen"*.	**50.00**	**75.00**
☐ **BEIRNE and DONOVAN. Decca 12244.** *"Green Mossy Banks of the Lee/What Will You Do, Love?"*.	**8.00**	**12.00**
☐ **DYER-BENNETT, RICHARD. Packard D-6.** *"Come All Ye/ Leprechaun"*.	**15.00**	**21.00**
☐ **Asch 461** *(album; 3 12-inch records). "Ballads"*.	**85.00**	**130.00**
☐ **Vox 633** *(album; 4 10-inch records). "Singing Minstrel Songs of Germany". (Performed in English)*.	**75.00**	**115.00**
☐ **Keynote K-108** *(album; 3 10-inch records). "Ballads and Folk-songs"**.	**150.00**	**200.00**
*NOTE: Apparently there was a switch in record-company policy sometime during the marketing of this album, as some copies contain different records than others.)		
☐ **GUTHRIE, WOODY. Disc 610** *(album). "Dust Bowl Ballads"*...	**250.00**	**350.00**
☐ **Stinson-Asch 347** *(album). "Woody Guthrie, Vol. 1"*.	**175.00**	**250.00**
☐ **Stinson-Asch 360** *(album). "American Documentary"*.	**175.00**	**250.00**
☐ **Stinson-Asch 347, Part II.** *"Songs by Woody Guthrie" (with Cisco Houston and Blind Sonny Terry)*.	**175.00**	**250.00**
☐ **HADDOCK, G. MARSTON. Musicraft 55** *(album; 4 10-inch records). "English Folk Songs and Ballads"*.	**75.00**	**115.00**
☐ **HARLAN MINERS FIDDLERS. Montgomery Ward 3025.** *"Skip to My Lou/The Roving Gambler"*.	**12.00**	**19.00**
☐ **SANDBURG, CARL. Musicraft M-11** *(album; four 10-inch records). "American Songbag"*.	**110.00**	**150.00**
☐ **Decca A-356** *(album; four 10-inch records). "Cowboy Songs and Negro Spirituals"*.	**95.00**	**130.00**
☐ **SCOTT, TOM. Signature S-5** *(album; four 10-inch records). "Sing of America"*.	**110.00**	**145.00**

	Price Range	
☐ **SEEGER, PETE. Commodore CR-11.** *"Sea Chanteys and Whaling Ballads" (with Woody Guthrie, Peter Hawes and Millard Lampell).*	80.00	115.00
☐ **Disc 604** *(album). "School Days" (with Cisco Houston, Charity Bailey and "Leadbelly").*	60.00	95.00
☐ **Charter C-500.** *"Cumberland Mt. Bear Chase/Keep My Skillet Good and Greasy".*	10.00	15.00
☐ **Charter album** *(three 10-inch records). "Bawdy Ballads and Real Sad Songs" (with Betty Sanders)*	70.00	110.00

LP's

AXTON, Hoyt		
☐ **A and M SP-4376** *(stereo) Less Than A Song.*	12.00	20.00
☐ **SP-4422** *(stereo) Life Machine.*	12.00	20.00
☐ **SP-4510** *(stereo) Southbound.*	12.00	20.00
☐ **SP-4571** *(stereo) Fearless.*	12.00	20.00
☐ **SP-4669** *(stereo) Road Songs.*	12.00	20.00
☐ **Horizon WP-1601** *(stereo) The Balladeer.*	14.00	24.00
BROONZY, Big Bill & Pete Seeger		
☐ **Folkways FVS-9008** *(stereo) Bill Bill Broonzy & Pete Seeger.*	19.00	28.00
COLLINS, Judy		
☐ **Elektra EKS-7222** *(stereo) Golden Apples Of The Sun.*	14.00	24.00
☐ **EKS7-243** *(stereo) Judy Collins #3.*	14.00	24.00
☐ **EKS7-300** *(stereo) Judy Collins' Fifth Album.*	14.00	24.00
☐ **EKS7-320** *(stereo) In My Life.*	14.00	24.00
☐ **EKS7-4012** *(stereo) Wildflowers.*	12.00	20.00
☐ **EKS7-4033** *(stereo) Who Knows Where The Time Goes?*	12.00	20.00
☐ **EKS7-4055** *(stereo) Recollections.*	12.00	20.00
FOGELBERG, Dan		
☐ **Columbia KC-31751** *(stereo) Home Free.*	10.00	16.00
☐ **Epic PE-33499** *(stereo) Captured Angel.*	10.00	16.00
GUTHRIE, Arlo		
☐ **Reprise MS-2183** *(stereo) Arlo Guthrie.*	8.00	18.00
☐ **RS-6267** *(stereo) Alice's Restaurant.*	8.00	18.00
☐ **RS-6299** *(stereo) Arlo.*	8.00	18.00
☐ **RS-6346** *(stereo) Running Down The Road.*	8.00	18.00
HENSKE, Judy		
☐ **Mercury SR-61010** *(stereo) Little Bit of Sunshine.*	19.00	28.00
HESTER, Carolyn		
☐ **Columbia CL-8596** *(mono) Carolyn Hester.*	23.00	34.00
HURT, Mississippi John		
☐ **Piedmont PLP-13157** *(mono) Folksongs And Blues, Volume I. Though billed as Volume I, no further volumes were issued.*	20.00	30.00
IVES, Burl		
☐ **Decca DL7-8886** *(stereo) Cheers.*	10.00	20.00
☐ **MCA 318** *(stereo) Paying My Dues Again.*	8.00	15.00
☐ **2-4089** *(stereo) The Best Of Burl Ives.*	8.00	15.00

	Price Range	
☐ **Columbia CL-1459** *(mono) Return Of The Wayfaring Stranger.*	15.00	20.00
☐ **United Artists UAS-6060** *(stereo) Ballads.*	9.00	15.00
LIGHTFOOT, Gordon		
☐ **Reprise 2206** *(stereo) Cold On The Shoulder.*	9.00	15.00
☐ **United Artists UAS-6649** *(stereo) Did She Mention My Name.*	9.00	15.00
LOMAX, Alan		
☐ **United Artists 4027** *(stereo) Blues In The Mississippi Night.*	7.00	16.00
MITCHELL, Chad (Trio)		
☐ **Colpix SCP-411** *(stereo) The Chad Mitchell Trio Arrives.*	20.00	28.00
☐ **Kapp KS-3262** *(stereo) A Mighty Day On Campus.*	14.00	23.00
☐ **KS-3313** *(stereo) Blowin' In The Wind.*	14.00	23.00
☐ **KS-3324** *(stereo) Best Of The Chad Mitchell Trio.*	14.00	23.00
☐ **Mercury SR-60838** *(stereo) Singin' Our Mind.*	14.00	23.00
☐ **SR-60891** *(stereo) Reflecting.*	14.00	23.00
☐ **SR-61067** *(stereo) Violets Of Dan.*	14.00	23.00
MITCHELL, Joni		
☐ **Reprise RS-6293** *(stereo) Joni Mitchell.*	10.00	18.00
☐ **RS-6376** *(stereo) Ladies Ot The Canyon.*	10.00	18.00
☐ **Asylum 202** *(stereo) Miles Of Aisles.*	10.00	18.00
NEW CHRISTY MINSTRELS		
☐ **Columbia CS-8672** *(stereo) Presenting The New Christy Minstrels.*	8.00	12.00
☐ **CS-8817** *(stereo) Tall Tales.*	6.00	10.00
☐ **CS-8896** *(stereo) Merry Christmas.*	6.00	10.00
☐ **CS-9103** *(stereo) Cowboys & Indians.*	6.00	10.00
The New Christy Minstrels took their name from an old-time blackface band called The Christy Minstrels.		
OCHS, Phil		
☐ **Elektra EKS-7269** *(stereo) All The News That's Fit To Sing.*	12.00	16.00
☐ **EKS-7287** *(stereo) I Ain't Marching Anymore.*	12.00	16.00
☐ **EKS-7310** *(stereo) Phil Ochs In Concert.*	12.00	16.00
☐ **A & M SP-4133** *(stereo) Pleasures Of The Harbor.*	10.00	15.00
☐ **SP-4148** *(stereo) Tape From California.*	10.00	15.00
☐ **SP-4181** *(stereo) Rehearsals For Retirement.*	10.00	15.00
ODETTA		
☐ **Vanguard VSD-2046** *(stereo) My Eyes Have Seen.*	18.00	25.00
☐ **VSD-2057** *(stereo) Ballad For Americans.*	18.00	25.00
☐ **VSD-2072** *(stereo) Odetta At Carnegie Hall.*	18.00	25.00
☐ **Riverside RLP-9417** *(stereo) Odetta & The Blues.*	18.00	25.00
PAXTON, Tom		
☐ **Anchor 2012** *(stereo) The Paxton Brothers.*	10.00	18.00
☐ **Reprise 2096** *(stereo) Peace Will Come.*	9.00	17.00
☐ **2144** *(stereo) New Songs From Old Friends.*	9.00	17.00
☐ **Elektra 74043** *(stereo) Things I Notice Now.*	9.00	17.00
☐ **74066** *(stereo) Tom Paxton 6.*	9.00	17.00
PETER, PAUL & MARY		
☐ **Warner Brothers WS-1449** *(stereo) Peter, Paul & Mary.*	15.00	23.00
☐ **WS-1473** *(stereo) Moving.*	15.00	23.00
☐ **WS-1507** *(stereo) In The Wind.*	15.00	23.00

☐ **WS-1555** *(stereo) In Concert.*	**15.00**	**23.00**
☐ **WS-1589** *(stereo) A Song Will Rise.*	**12.00**	**17.00**
☐ **WS-1648** *(stereo) The Peter, Paul & Mary Album.*	**12.00**	**17.00**
SEEGER, Pete		
☐ **Aravel AB-1006** *(mono) Live Hootenanny.*	**20.00**	**30.00**
☐ **Folkways FH-5210** *(mono) Champlain Valley SongBAG.*	**10.00**	**15.00**
☐ **31040** *(stereo) Banks Of Marble.*	**10.00**	**15.00**
☐ **Tradition 2107** *(stereo) Pete Seeger Sings Folk Music OF THE WORLD.*	**10.00**	**15.00**
☐ **Columbia CS-8448** *(stereo) Pete Seeger Story Songs.*	**12.00**	**18.00**
☐ **CS-8901** *(mono) We Shall Overcome.*	**12.00**	**18.00**
SHANKAR, Ravi		
☐ **Columbia WL-119** *(mono) The Sounds Of India.*	**25.00**	**35.00**

HUMOROUS 77-81s

This section consists of 77-81rpm recordings released prior to 1920. The word "humorous" may be misleading, as this suggests to most modern readers monologues of comedians, etc. However, in the terminology of the early recording industry (1900-1925), "humorous records" were primarily songs and song-poems that did not fall into the classification of opera, standard or celebrity recordings. They were, in a sense, the "pop records" of their day, including show tunes, vaudeville routines, popular ditties and novelty items. Some would still be considered humorous in the true sense of the word — Ethel Levey's "Where Did Robinson Crusoe Go With Friday on Saturday Night?" — but many a ballad or near-ballad went into the humorous section of record catalogues, too, including all of Harry Lauder's recordings.

It should be remembered that the pre-1920 era was without disc jockeys or "Top 40" lists, so there is no tangible evidence, in most instances, of the popularity attained by these recordings in their time. There is no question, though, about some becoming "hits". In nearly all instances, the artists were public figures before making recordings, having attained reputations in music halls or vaudeville. Very rarely were recording contracts granted to unknowns, no matter how talented or promising, in the theory that sales were made on the artist's reputation. Persons, for example, who saw Harry Lauder in the music halls and enjoyed his songs might buy his records. The public was not likely to gamble its $1 (or whatever the price happened to be) on a performer it had not seen and heard. In the absence of radio, it would be very unlikely that anyone would have heard any of these songs except in a public performance.

Though early record companies prided themselves on their more serious releases — it seems almost criminal that, in the case of Lauder, RCA Victor did not place his recordings on its "celebrity" label — humorous records sold just as well and were produced in nearly equal numbers. A full listing of all such records pressed before 1920 would run to hundreds of pages.

Because humorous recordings did not require the full orchestration of classical, they did not place such challenges on early techniques and equipment. Therefore, the performances were captured somewhat more successfully and can be heard today, even on **very** old records, truer to the originals than one could expect of grand opera. You get the feeling of being in the vaudeville house or music hall much more readily with a humorous record than you do of being at LaScala when listening to a 78rpm of Caruso.

It would be normal to assume that the values of these discs should depend upon artist popularity — that the records made by more celebrated artists, those whose names are still remembered today, ought to outsell those of vaguely-recalled performers. Such is not always the situation. The more popular the artist, the better his (or her) records would sell, and the greater quantities would be manufactured. Thus they tend to be less scarce and, often, not worth so much money as one might expect. On the other hand, the records of lesser-known artists might be pressed in fewer numbers, have a limited sale, and be much harder to get today. Anyone who collects rock records of the 1950's knows that the million-sellers are seldom valued above $3 or $4, while obscure recordings by long-forgotten groups or artists can be valuable.

COLUMBIA—AMERICAN *(10-inch records, dating from c. 1920-22)*

The following are all 10-inch recordings on the Columbia label, dating from c. 1920-1922.

	Price Range	
☐ **CASEY, MICHAEL.** *"Casey at the Dentist's/Casey as a Doctor".*	7.00	10.00
☐ *"Casey at Home/Marriage Difficulties (second side by Golden & Marlow).*	6.00	9.00
☐ **DUPREZ, FRED.** *"Happy Tho' Married/Cohen on the Telephone" (second side by Joe Hayman).*	9.00	12.00
☐ **GOLDEN and HUGHES.** *"Whistling Pete/Turkey in the Straw" (second side by Billy Golden).*	6.00	9.00
☐ **PORTER, STEVE.** *"Flanagan on a Farm/Down on the Farm" (second side by Columbia Male Quartette).*	6.00	9.00
☐ **ROSE, JULIAN.** *"Levinsky at the Wedding I/Levinsky at the Wedding II".*	12.00	20.00
☐ *Levinsky at the Wedding III/Levinsky at the Wedding IV".*	12.00	20.00
☐ **STEWART, CAL.** *"Wedding of Uncle Josh and Aunt Nancy/Uncle Josh at Delmonico's".*	10.00	15.00
☐ *"War Talk at Pumpkin Center/Moving Pictures at Pumpkin Center".*	12.00	19.00
☐ *"Uncle Josh and the Insurance Company/Uncle Josh on an Automobile".*	10.00	15.00
☐ *"Uncle Josh at the Dentist's/Uncle Josh and Aunt Nancy Put Up Kitchen Stove"(first side Stewart and Browne, second side Stewart and Jones).*	12.00	20.00
☐ *Uncle Josh at the Opera/Uncle Josh and Aunt Nancy Visit New York".*	12.00	20.00
☐ *"Uncle Josh at Roller Rink/Uncle Josh Has His Photo Taken".*	10.00	15.00
☐ *"Uncle Josh in a Cafeteria/Uncle Josh and the Sailor".*	10.00	15.00

	Price Range	
☐ *"Uncle Josh Invites City Folks/Two Rubies in Eating House" (second side by Stanley and Harlan).*	12.00	20.00
☐ *Christmas at Punkin' Center/Evening at Punkin' Center" (both with Jones Quartette).*	12.00	20.00
☐ **WILLIAMS, BERT.** *"Ten Little Bottles/Unlucky Blues".*	20.00	30.00
☐ *"Eve Cost Adam Just One Bone/You'll Never Need a Doctor".*	15.00	21.00
☐ *"The Moon Shines on Moonshine/Somebody".*	18.00	29.00
☐ *"Save a Little Dram for Me/Lonesome Alimony Blues.*	15.00	21.00
☐ *"Never Me/Purpostus".*	15.00	21.00
☐ *"I Wish It Was Sunday Night/All the Silver from Silvery Moon".*	15.00	21.00
☐ *"I'm Sorry I Ain't Got It Blues/Checkers".*	18.00	29.00
☐ **WILLIAMS, BILLY.** *"Where Does Daddy Go?/When Father Papered the Parlor".*	18.00	29.00
☐ **WILLS, NAT.** *"No News, or What Killed the Dog/Head Waiter, Colored Social Club".*	24.00	37.00

JAZZ

MEMORABILIA

The collecting of jazz memorabilia had its beginnings in the night clubs and bistros of New Orleans, New York and elsewhere, where, from as early as the 1920's, the wall were often lined with inscribed photographs of the stars who performed there. Around 1950, "jazz collecting" began to take on interest as a hobby with private collectors. Many of the old-time jazz greats were still alive at that time, and ambitious collectors succeeded in obtaining from them a variety of personal momentos. Though no special cash value was then attached to much of this material, the growth of jazz-memorabilia collecting has rendered it quite valuable.

☐ **ADDERLEY, JULIAN.** *Article from "Downbeat" magazine, signed and inscribed.*	11.00	15.00
☐ **ADDERLEY, JULIAN.** *Mimeographed flyer advertising a concert appearance.*	6.00	8.00
☐ **ADDERLEY, JULIAN.** *Polaroid color snapshot, backstage at a theater, mounted on a card, signed on the card.*	17.50	22.00
☐ **ADDERLEY, JULIAN.** *Collection of obituaries from various newspapers, including NY Times, Washington Post, LA Times, etc..*	12.00	16.00
☐ **ALLEN, "RED".** *8x10 photo, signed, thumbtack holes.*	9.00	12.00
☐ **ALLEN, "RED".** *Two small photos, one signed.*	5.00	7.00
☐ **AMMONS, ALBERT.** *Piano score, with notations in his hand.*	32.00	40.00
☐ **AMMONS, ALBERT.** *Poster advertising an appearance in a New Orleans cafe, folded, worn at the folds.*	47.00	59.00
☐ **ARMSTRONG, LOUIS.** *Cover of "Life" magazine picturing him, signed in red crayon, matted in green plush and framed.*	175.00	250.00
☐ **ARMSTRONG, LOUIS.** *c. 1932. Trumpet reputedly used by him early in career, in a worn leather box.*	2375.00	3200.00
☐ **ARMSTRONG, LOUIS.** *c. 1975. Plastic figurine in his likeness.*	25.00	33.00

	Price Range	
☐ **ARMSTRONG, LOUIS.** *c. 1970. Pen and wash drawing of him playing trumpet, 11x14, matted to 14x17, framed.*	65.00	85.00
☐ **ARMSTRONG, LOUIS.** *Photograph of him at age c. 18, somewhat worn.*	40.00	55.00
☐ **ARMSTRONG, LOUIS.** *c. 1962. 8x10 photo with Carol Channing, signed by both.*	80.00	100.00
☐ **ARMSTRONG, LOUIS.** *c. 1955. 8x10 portrait photo, signed.*	60.00	80.00
☐ **ARMSTRONG, LOUIS.** *c. 1942. 8x10 sepia photo, signed.*	100.00	130.00
☐ **ARMSTRONG, LOUIS.** *c. 1955. LP album cover, "Louis Armstrong Plays W. C. Handy", signed, record lacking.*	85.00	110.00
☐ **ARMSTRONG, LOUIS.** *Pair of cuff links reputedly worn by him.*	60.00	80.00
☐ **ARMSTRONG, LOUIS.** *Oil portrait on canvas, 33x48, probably copied from a photograph and dating from c. 1975.*	120.00	160.00
☐ **ARMSTRONG, LOUIS.** *Signature on a theater program.*	30.00	40.00
☐ **BAILEY, MILDRED.** *c. 1940's. 5x8 photo, signed, ink faded.*	39.00	50.00
☐ **BAILEY, MILDRED.** *Postcard sent by her, brief message.*	35.00	45.00
☐ **BASIE, "COUNT".** *8x10 photo seated at piano, signed.*	15.00	20.00
☐ **BASIE, "COUNT".** *Pair of white gloves reputedly worn by him, sold with two small unsigned photos and a letter from a previous owner.*	60.00	80.00
☐ **BASIE, "COUNT".** *5x7 photo, signed, framed with a 78rpm recording.*	70.00	90.00
☐ **BASIE, "COUNT".** *Signature on a calling card.*	8.00	11.00
☐ **BEIDERBECKE, BIX.** *8x10 photo standing outside club, signed in white ink, also signed by two others, corners clipped.*	50.00	70.00
☐ **BEIDERBECKE, BIX.** *c. 1930. Typed letter, signed, with original envelope (stained).*	60.00	80.00
☐ **BEIDERBECKE, BIX.** *One page of music notations, unsigned.*	100.00	130.00
☐ **BEIDERBECKE, BIX.** *c. 1927 and 1929. Two postcards addressed to him.*	30.00	38.00
☐ **BERIGAN, BUNNY.** *c. 1935. Photo with orchestra, signed by him and several other musicians.*	50.00	65.00
☐ **BERIGAN, BUNNY.** *c. 1928. 3x4 snapshot photo.*	6.00	8.00
☐ **BERIGAN, BUNNY.** *Signature on cafe cocktail list.*	7.50	10.00
☐ **BLAKEY, ART.** *8x10 photo playing drums, signed.*	6.00	8.00
☐ **BLAKEY, ART.** *Pair of drumsticks used by him.*	15.00	20.00
☐ **BLANTON, JIMMY.** *6x7 photo, signed and inscribed across almost the entire photo.*	30.00	40.00
☐ **BOLDEN, CHARLES.** *Signature on a memo sheet.*	6.00	8.00
☐ **BOLDEN, CHARLES.** *Contract bearing his signature.*	23.00	29.00
☐ **BOLDEN, CHARLES.** *c. 1890's. Poster advertising his band.*	100.00	130.00
☐ **BOLDEN, CHARLES.** *8x10 sepia photo, damaged, unsigned.*	6.00	8.00
☐ **BROONZY, BILL.** *7x9 color photo, boldly signed.*	20.00	27.00
☐ **BROONZY, BILL.** *Collection of articles and news cuttings, mostly from "Billboard" and "DownBeat" magazines.*	16.00	21.00
☐ **BROONZY, BILL.** *Signature on an insurance company circular.*	7.00	10.00
☐ **BRUBECK, DAVE.** *c. 1958. Charcoal drawing of him at piano, 12x12, matted and framed.*	75.00	100.00

	Price Range	
☐ **BRUBECK, DAVE.** *Typed letter, signed, to a theatrical agent.*	8.00	11.00
☐ **BRUBECK, DAVE.** *Two LP record album covers, signed, records missing.*	40.00	55.00
☐ **BRUBECK, DAVE.** *8x10 photo, signed in brown ink.*	7.00	10.00
☐ **CARNEY, HARRY.** *Three small candid photos, one signed on the back.*	5.50	7.50
☐ **CARTER, BENNY.** *8x10 photo, signed, small corner crease.*	5.00	7.00
☐ **CARTER, BENNY.** *Signature on an otherwise blank card.*	2.50	3.50
☐ **CATLETT, SIDNEY.** *4x5 photo, inscribed, signed with initials.*	15.00	20.00
☐ **CHRISTIAN, CHARLIE.** *c. 1940. Envelope addressed by him, letter missing.*	15.00	20.00
☐ **CHRISTIAN, CHARLIE.** *5x4 photo, signed, margins cut.*	25.00	33.00
☐ **CHRISTIAN, CHARLIE.** *Small photo with guitar, signed.*	30.00	40.00
☐ **CLAYTON, BUCK.** *8x10 photo with two other musicians, signed by all three.*	9.00	12.00
☐ **CLAYTON, BUCK.** *Trumpet carrying case once owned by him.*	23.00	30.00
☐ **CLAYTON, BUCK.** *Two magazine articles about him, one signed.*	8.00	11.00
☐ **CLAYTON, BUCK.** *½-page note in his hand, signed.*	7.00	10.00
☐ **COHN, AL.** *Two 8x10 photos, one signed.*	9.00	12.00
☐ **COHN, AL.** *c. 1967. Typed letter, signed, with envelope.*	8.00	11.00
☐ **COHN, AL.** *Postcard in his handwriting.*	6.00	8.00
☐ **COLTRANE, JOHN.** *8x10 photo, signed in red ink, matted and inscribed on the mat, signed again, framed.*	30.00	40.00
☐ **COLTRANE, JOHN.** *Signature on a theatrical agent's card.*	5.00	7.00
☐ **COLTRANE, JOHN.** *Signature on an advertising circular.*	5.00	7.00
☐ **CONDON, EDDIE.** *11x14 color photo, signed in the margin.*	35.00	45.00
☐ **CONDON, EDDIE.** *Scrapbook with c. 220 items pertaining to him, mostly news cuttings, two signed photos, etc.*	75.00	95.00
☐ **CONDON, EDDIE.** *Xerox copy of a photo of him, signed on the Xerox.*	7.00	10.00
☐ **DAVIS, MILES.** *LP album cover inscribed and signed on the back, record missing.*	40.00	55.00
☐ **DAVIS, MILES.** *Small photo cut from magazine, signed, mounted on heavy card.*	12.00	17.00
☐ **DAVIS, MILES.** *Three 8x10 portrait photos, unsigned.*	7.00	10.00
☐ **DeFRANCO, BUDDY.** *8x10 photo, signed and inscribed on the back, tape marks at corners.*	6.00	8.00
☐ **DESMOND, PAUL.** *16 photos, mostly snapshots, one 8x10 signed studio photo, in a cloth folding case.*	50.00	65.00
☐ **DESMOND, PAUL.** *c. 1971. Three-page handwritten letter.*	52.00	70.00
☐ **DODDS, WARREN.** *Circular advertising a cafe appearance.*	7.00	10.00
☐ **DODDS, WARREN.** *5x6 photo, signed.*	8.00	11.00
☐ **DODDS, WARREN.** *Notebook used by him, various memos.*	40.00	50.00
☐ **DORSEY, JIMMY.** *c. 1943. Poster, 27x41, advertising a concert appearance, New York.*	110.00	140.00
☐ **DORSEY, JIMMY.** *Collection of 14 motion picture stills, unsigned.*	30.00	37.00
☐ **DORSEY, JIMMY.** *8x10 studio photo, signed and inscribed.*	30.00	40.00

	Price Range	
☐ **DORSEY, JIMMY.** *c. 1949. 8x10 photo, signed and inscribed to Toots Shore.*	50.00	65.00
☐ **DORSEY, JIMMY.** *Record company circular, signed.*	30.00	37.00
☐ **DORSEY, JIMMY.** *c. 1947. 8x10 photo with Tommy Dorsey, signed by both.*	90.00	115.00
☐ **DORSEY, JIMMY.** *c. 1952. One-page typewritten letter, signed.*	20.00	25.00
☐ **DORSEY, JIMMY.** *c. 1944-46. Six snapshot photos.*	16.00	21.00
☐ **DORSEY, TOMMY.** *8x10 studio photo, with trombone, signed.*	28.00	36.00
☐ **DORSEY, TOMMY.** *Five motion picture stills, one creased.*	11.00	15.00
☐ **DORSEY, TOMMY.** *Two scrapbooks relating to his career, containing c. 43 photos, mostly cut from magazines, 500 news cuttings, several letters and miscellaneous items.*	300.00	400.00
☐ **DORSEY, TOMMY.** *8x10 photo with Bing Crosby, signed by both.*	75.00	100.00
☐ **ELDRIDGE, ROY.** *5x4 photo, signed.*	6.00	8.00
☐ **ELDRIDGE, ROY.** *Signature on restaurant menu (faded).*	5.00	7.00
☐ **ELLINGTON, DUKE.** *Oil on canvas, 23x29, seated at piano, signed "Clark Tillman", date unknown, possibly copied from a photograph, unframed.*	100.00	140.00
☐ **ELLINGTON, DUKE.** *Two piano scores with notes in his hand.*	110.00	150.00
☐ **ELLINGTON, DUKE.** *c. 1927. Early photo of him at piano.*	25.00	35.00
☐ **ELLINGTON, DUKE.** *Seven pages from scrap album with various photos, including of him as a youth, two of them signed.*	175.00	250.00
☐ **ELLINGTON, DUKE.** *Magazine cover portrait of him, colored, signed, framed.*	75.00	100.00
☐ **ELLINGTON, DUKE.** *Caricature in ink, 7x9, artist unknown.*	50.00	70.00
☐ **ELLINGTON, DUKE.** *Piano stool reputedly used by him.*	85.00	110.00
☐ **ELLINGTON, DUKE.** *Program of a concert appearance.*	7.00	10.00
☐ **ELLINGTON, DUKE.** *Photo with Count Basie, signed by both.*	100.00	150.00
☐ **ELLINGTON, DUKE.** *Signature on cover of sheet music.*	25.00	35.00
☐ **ELLINGTON, DUKE.** *Envelope of obituary notices from various newspapers, some foreign.*	40.00	55.00
☐ **EVANS, BILL.** *8x10 photo, signed.*	7.00	10.00
☐ **EVANS, BILL.** *c. 1940's. 4x5 photo as a youth, unsigned.*	5.00	7.00
☐ **FITZGERALD, ELLA.** *LP album cover, signed in violet magic marker, record lacking, with two news cuttings.*	50.00	65.00
☐ **FITZGERALD, ELLA.** *Sheet music to "A Tisket, A Tasket", signed with large crayon signature.*	40.00	55.00
☐ **FITZGERALD, ELLA.** *8x10 studio portrait, signed.*	12.00	16.00
☐ **FITZGERALD, ELLA.** *Scrapbook with c. 75 news cuttings, etc.*	60.00	80.00
☐ **FITZGERALD, ELLA.** *45rpm phono record, signed on label.*	15.00	20.00
☐ **FITZGERALD, ELLA.** *Magazine article, signed, two pages.*	9.00	12.00
☐ **FITZGERALD, ELLA.** *Three unsigned 8x10 photos, one dated from the 1940's, mounted on cards.*	8.00	11.00
☐ **FITZGERALD, ELLA.** *Photo with Count Basie, signed by Fitzgerald only.*	15.00	20.00
☐ **FITZGERALD, ELLA.** *Photo with Duke Ellington, signed by both.*	45.00	60.00
☐ **FITZGERALD, ELLA.** *Interview in "DownBeat" magazine, signed.*	7.00	10.00

	Price Range	
☐ **FITZGERALD, ELLA.** *Two small snapshot photos, one signed.*	9.00	12.00
☐ **GARNER, ERROLL.** *c. 1960. 8x10 photo at piano, signed.*	10.00	15.00
☐ **GARNER, ERROLL.** *Two items of sheet music, signed.*	35.00	45.00
☐ **GARNER, ERROLL.** *Record album cover, signed, no record.*	30.00	40.00
☐ **GARNER, ERROLL.** *Cuff links reputedly worn by him.*	32.00	41.00
☐ **GARNER, ERROLL.** *Photo with Art Tatum, signed by Garner.*	22.00	33.00
☐ **GARNER, ERROLL.** *Collection of news cuttings and magazine articles, one signed photo, in a cloth folder.*	75.00	100.00
☐ **GARNER, ERROLL.** *Signature on a business card.*	3.00	4.00
☐ **GARNER, ERROLL.** *c. 1974. Color photo, 5x6½, signed.*	17.00	23.00
☐ **GETZ, STAN.** *Photo playing sax, signed, inscribed.*	5.00	6.00
☐ **GETZ, STAN.** *8x10 studio photo, signed, matted.*	6.00	8.00
☐ **GETZ, STAN.** *Magazine photo, signed, mounted on card.*	4.00	5.00
☐ **GETZ, STAN.** *c. 1965. Letter to him from record company official.*	3.00	4.00
☐ **GETZ, STAN.** *Two snapshots, one signed, New Orleans.*	4.00	5.00
☐ **GETZ, STAN.** *Magazine photo with Zutty Singleton, signed by Getz only.*	5.00	6.00
☐ **GETZ, STAN.** *Book, "Pictorial History of Jazz", signed by him and Gene Krupa.*	25.00	32.00
☐ **GETZ, STAN.** *Two items of sheet music, with notes in his hand, not signed.*	15.00	20.00
☐ **GIBBS, TERRY.** *8x10 studio photo, signed.*	4.00	5.00
☐ **GIBBS, TERRY.** *c. 1970. Poster advertising an appearance.*	12.00	15.00
☐ **GIBBS, TERRY.** *c. 1950. ALs, one page, with envelope.*	4.00	5.00
☐ **GIBBS, TERRY.** *Novelty $1 bill with his picture in center.*	2.00	3.00
☐ **GIBBS, TERRY.** *6x7 photo at vibes, signed and inscribed.*	4.00	5.00
☐ **GILLESPIE, DIZZY.** *Trumpet reputedly used by him early in career, in carrying case.*	500.00	650.00
☐ **GILLESPIE, DIZZY.** *LP record album cover, signed, record missing.*	35.00	45.00
☐ **GILLESPIE, DIZZY.** *Two 8x10 photos, signed, one inscribed.*	23.00	29.00
☐ **GILLESPIE, DIZZY.** *Signature on a postcard.*	3.75	5.00
☐ **GILLESPIE, DIZZY.** *c. 1958. Magazine article, signed.*	4.50	6.00
☐ **GILLESPIE, DIZZY.** *Photo with Billy Taylor, unsigned.*	2.50	3.50
☐ **GILLESPIE, DIZZY.** *Associated Press photo, unsigned.*	2.50	3.50
☐ **GILLESPIE, DIZZY.** *Sheet music with notes in his hand.*	45.00	60.00
☐ **GILLESPIE, DIZZY.** *Photo with John Lewis, signed by both.*	25.00	32.00
☐ **GILLESPIE, DIZZY.** *c. 1947-52. Five small snapshots.*	7.00	10.00
☐ **GILLESPIE, DIZZY.** *T-shirt with his likeness.*	9.00	12.00
☐ **GILLESPIE, DIZZY.** *Close-up cover photo playing horn, signed, matted, framed, signed again on the mat.*	35.00	45.00
☐ **GOODMAN, BENNY.** *c. 1942. 8x10 studio portrait wearing white jacket, holding clarinet, signed.*	20.00	25.00
☐ **GOODMAN, BENNY.** *Three motion picture stills, signed.*	45.00	58.00
☐ **GOODMAN, BENNY.** *c. 1938. Photo with Glenn Miller, unsigned.*	6.00	9.00
☐ **GOODMAN, BENNY.** *78rpm record, signed on the label.*	35.00	45.00
☐ **GOODMAN, BENNY.** *Concert program, signed.*	7.00	10.00
☐ **GOODMAN, BENNY.** *Signature on cafe menu.*	5.00	7.00

	Price Range	
☐ **GOODMAN, BENNY.** *c. 1946. 8x10 photo with band, signed.*	23.00	30.00
☐ **GOODMAN, BENNY.** *8x10 photo with Paul Whiteman, signed by Goodman only.*	25.00	32.00
☐ **GOODMAN, BENNY.** *c. 1958. Magazine article, signed.*	7.00	10.00
☐ **GOODMAN, BENNY.** *c. 1974. Typewritten letter, signed.*	9.00	12.00
☐ **GOODMAN, BENNY.** *c. 1951. Memo in his hand.*	7.00	10.00
☐ **GOODMAN, BENNY.** *Photo with Jimmy Dorsey, signed by both.*	60.00	80.00
☐ **HACKETT, BOBBY.** *5x7 photo playing trumpet, signed.*	8.00	11.00
☐ **HACKETT, BOBBY.** *c. 1961. ALs, one page, with envelope.*	11.00	15.00
☐ **HACKETT, BOBBY.** *Signature on a card.*	2.50	3.75
☐ **HACKETT, BOBBY.** *Magazine photo, signed and inscribed.*	5.00	7.00
☐ **HACKETT, BOBBY.** *Two 8x10 unsigned photos.*	4.00	6.00
☐ **HACKETT, BOBBY.** *Musical score with notes in his hand.*	23.00	30.00
☐ **HACKETT, BOBBY.** *c. 1966. Tiny snapshot photo, signed on back.*	3.00	4.00
☐ **HACKETT, BOBBY.** *c. 1972. Typewritten letter, signed.*	4.00	6.00
☐ **HAMPTON, LIONEL.** *Set of drumsticks used by him, autographed by him, in a velvet case.*	110.00	135.00
☐ **HAMPTON, LIONEL.** *Biography of him from jazz book, signed.*	7.00	10.00
☐ **HAMPTON, LIONEL.** *LP record album cover, signed, no record.*	32.00	40.00
☐ **HAMPTON, LIONEL.** *c. 1948. 8x10 studio portrait, signed.*	20.00	25.00
☐ **HAMPTON, LIONEL.** *Photo with John Kirby, signed by Hampton only.*	20.00	25.00
☐ **HAMPTON, LIONEL.** *c. 1942. ALs, with envelope.*	20.00	25.00
☐ **HAMPTON, LIONEL.** *Photo with Perry Como, signed by Hampton only.*	15.00	20.00
☐ **HAMPTON, LIONEL.** *Signature on a record company circular.*	2.50	3.50
☐ **HAMPTON, LIONEL.** *Scrapbook of c. 320 news cuttings, etc.*	100.00	130.00
☐ **HAMPTON, LIONEL.** *c. 1950's. Two short notes in his hand.*	7.00	10.00
☐ **HAMPTON, LIONEL.** *c. 1930's. Three early snapshot photos.*	8.00	11.00
☐ **HARRIS, BILL.** *8x10 studio photo, signed.*	4.00	5.00
☐ **HARRIS, BILL.** *Article from "Variety", signed.*	3.00	4.00
☐ **HARRIS, BILL.** *Musical score with notes in his hand.*	12.00	17.00
☐ **HARRIS, BILL.** *Photo with trombone, signed, framed.*	12.00	17.00
☐ **HAWKINS, COLEMAN.** *Sheet music, "Body and Soul", with notes in his hand.*	170.00	240.00
☐ **HAWKINS, COLEMAN.** *8x10 photo with orchestra, signed.*	30.00	40.00
☐ **HAWKINS, COLEMAN.** *78rpm record album signed on the front cover, records missing.*	90.00	120.00
☐ **HAWKINS, COLEMAN.** *Signature on back of a letter.*	10.00	15.00
☐ **HAWKINS, COLEMAN.** *Letter to him from an agent.*	5.00	7.00
☐ **HAWKINS, COLEMAN.** *c. 1964. Check endorsed by him.*	42.00	60.00
☐ **HAWKINS, COLEMAN.** *Photo playing sax, signed.*	32.00	43.00
☐ **HAWKINS, COLEMAN.** *c. 1950's. Two 8x10 unsigned photos.*	7.00	10.00
☐ **HAWKINS, COLEMAN.** *c. 1950. Photo with Charlie Parker, signed by both, framed.*	120.00	150.00
☐ **HENDERSON, FLETCHER.** *8x10 photo, signed, creased.*	7.00	10.00

	Price Range	
☐ **HENDERSON, FLETCHER.** *Photo from magazine, signed.*	6.00	8.00
☐ **HENDERSON, FLETCHER.** *One page of music score, signed.*	15.00	20.00
☐ **HENDERSON, FLETCHER.** *78rpm record, signed on the label.*	25.00	32.00
☐ **HENDERSON, FLETCHER.** *Record company advertising poster, signed.*	32.00	41.00
☐ **HENDERSON, FLETCHER.** *Photo in Times Square, NY, signed.*	6.00	8.00
☐ **HENDERSON, FLETCHER.** *c. 1930's. Two snapshots, one signed.*	7.00	10.00
☐ **HERMAN, WOODY.** *Photo with clarinet, signed, inscribed.*	8.00	11.00
☐ **HERMAN, WOODY.** *c. 1940's. Photo with Benny Goodman, each holding clarinet, signed by Herman only.*	17.00	23.00
☐ **HERMAN, WOODY.** *Caricature in ink, 8x10, unsigned.*	22.00	30.00
☐ **HERMAN, WOODY.** *4x5 photo as a youth, signed, stained.*	11.00	15.00
☐ **HERMAN, WOODY.** *Signature on cover of sheet music.*	13.00	20.00
☐ **HERMAN, WOODY.** *Signature on a concert program.*	6.00	9.00
☐ **HERMAN, WOODY.** *c. 1956. 8x10 studio portrait, signed.*	7.00	10.00
☐ **HERMAN, WOODY.** *Three letters to him from record company executives.*	9.00	12.00
☐ **HERMAN, WOODY.** *Magazine article, signed.*	4.00	6.00
☐ **HIGGINBOTHAM, JAY C.** *8x10 portrait photo, signed.*	12.00	17.00
☐ **HILL, BERTHA.** *5x6 portrait photo, signed.*	35.00	45.00
☐ **HINES, EARL.** *Photo at piano, signed, matted and framed.*	11.00	15.00
☐ **HINES, EARL.** *c. 1950's. Musical score, signed.*	25.00	35.00
☐ **HINES, EARL.** *Photo with George Shearing, signed by Hines.*	12.00	17.00
☐ **HINES, EARL.** *c. 1930's. Two 5x6 photos, unsigned.*	5.00	7.00
☐ **HINES, EARL.** *8x10 portrait photo at piano, large signature.*	12.00	17.00
☐ **HINES, EARL.** *11x14 photo, signed in the margin.*	16.00	22.00
☐ **HINES, EARL.** *Signature on a card.*	3.00	4.00
☐ **HINES, EARL.** *Scrapbook with reviews, photos, etc.*	65.00	85.00
☐ **HODGES, JOHNNY.** *Signature on a card, also signed by Max Roach.*	3.00	4.00
☐ **HODGES, JOHNNY.** *8x10 studio photo, signed.*	4.00	5.00
☐ **HODGES, JOHNNY.** *Notes on back of record company catalogue.*	4.00	5.00
☐ **HODGES, JOHNNY.** *Photo outside Philadelphia night club, signed.*	3.00	4.00
☐ **KRUPA, GENE.** *LP record album cover, signed, no record.*	40.00	55.00
☐ **KRUPA, GENE.** *c. 1958. Brochure issued by his drum school.*	4.00	6.00
☐ **KRUPA, GENE.** *c. 1936. 8x10 photo at drums, early, signed.*	20.00	27.00
☐ **KRUPA, GENE.** *c. 1962. Typewritten letter, signed.*	5.00	7.00
☐ **KRUPA, GENE.** *c. 1941. ALs, half page, with envelope.*	14.00	20.00
☐ **KRUPA, GENE.** *Signature on a business card.*	3.00	4.00
☐ **KRUPA, GENE.** *8x10 color portrait photo, signed on back.*	13.00	18.00
☐ **KRUPA, GENE.** *c. 1937. 4x5 snapshot photo, signed.*	8.00	11.00
☐ **KRUPA, GENE.** *c. 1956. Magazine article, signed.*	4.00	5.00
☐ **KRUPA, GENE.** *Photo with Miles Davis, signed by both.*	25.00	32.00
☐ **LADNIER, TOMMY.** *Photo cut from newspaper, signed.*	12.00	17.00
☐ **LADNIER, TOMMY.** *8x10 photo, signed, inscribed.*	22.00	30.00

	Price Range	
☐ **LADNIER, TOMMY.** *c. 1930. Poster advertising an appearance.*	40.00	55.00
☐ **LADNIER, TOMMY.** *Signature on a music company catalogue.*	7.00	10.00
☐ **LADNIER, TOMMY.** *c. 1920's. Snapshot photo, signed.*	20.00	25.00
☐ **LANG, EDDIE.** *Photo with guitar, signed, faded.*	40.00	55.00
☐ **LANG, EDDIE.** *c. 1925. Two small snapshots, one signed.*	28.00	36.00
☐ **LANG, EDDIE.** *c. 1928. ALs, Atlanta.*	45.00	60.00
☐ **LEDBETTER, HUDDIE ("LEADBELLY").** *c. 1940's. 5x7 photo, signed, laminated and mounted on a card.*	60.00	80.00
☐ **LEWIS, JOHN.** *Four lines of music composition in his hand.*	30.00	40.00
☐ **LEWIS, JOHN.** *8x10 studio portrait, signed.*	6.00	9.00
☐ **LEWIS, JOHN.** *Signature on a card.*	2.50	3.50
☐ **LEWIS, JOHN.** *c. 1971. Typewritten letter, signed.*	4.50	6.00
☐ **LEWIS, JOHN.** *c. 1960's. Photo with combo, signed.*	6.00	9.00
☐ **LEWIS, JOHN.** *Article in "Variety", signed.*	3.50	5.00
☐ **LUNCEFORD, JIMMIE.** *c. 1942. 8x10 studio portrait, signed, dated.*	22.00	30.00
☐ **LUNCEFORD, JIMMIE.** *c. 1930's. Two snapshots, signed.*	20.00	27.00
☐ **MANNE, SHELLY.** *8x10 photo at drums, signed.*	4.50	6.00
☐ **MANNE, SHELLY.** *c. 1978. Postcard in his hand, 4 lines.*	3.50	5.00
☐ **MANNE, SHELLY.** *c. 1954. ALs, half page.*	5.50	7.00
☐ **MANNE, SHELLY.** *c. 1967. Photo with Gene Krupa, signed by both.*	16.00	22.00
☐ **MANNE, SHELLY.** *Photo with Billy Taylor, signed by Manne.*	6.00	8.00
☐ **MANNE, SHELLY.** *½-hour amateur tape of "jam session" with him at drums.*	17.00	23.00
☐ **MANNE, SHELLY.** *Signature on a card.*	2.00	3.00
☐ **MANNE, SHELLY.** *Photo in front of New York night club, signed.*	3.50	5.00
☐ **MANNE, SHELLY.** *Article from "DownBeat" magazine, signed.*	3.50	5.00
☐ **McPARTLAND, JIMMY.** *Sheet music autographed.*	18.00	25.00
☐ **McPARTLAND, JIMMY.** *Two 6x8 photos, signed.*	12.00	17.00
☐ **McPARTLAND, JIMMY.** *8x10 studio photo with horn, signed.*	9.00	12.00
☐ **McPARTLAND, JIMMY.** *Colored photo cut from magazine or book, signed, inscribed, matted and framed.*	22.00	30.00
☐ **McPARTLAND, JIMMY.** *Signature on restaurant check.*	2.50	3.50
☐ **McPARTLAND, JIMMY.** *Typewritten letter to him from booking agent.*	2.50	3.50
☐ **McPARTLAND, JIMMY.** *c. 1947. ALs, two pp.*	11.00	15.00
☐ **McPARTLAND, JIMMY.** *Photo with L. Armstrong, signed by both.*	60.00	75.00
☐ **McPARTLAND, JIMMY.** *Straw hat reputedly worn by him.*	10.00	20.00
☐ **McPARTLAND, JIMMY.** *Two small snapshot photos, unsigned.*	2.00	3.00
☐ **MILLER, GLENN.** *78rpm phono record, signed on the label.*	90.00	110.00
☐ **MILLER, GLENN.** *8x10 studio portrait, signed, inscribed.*	60.00	80.00
☐ **MILLER, GLENN.** *c. 1938. Check endorsed by him.*	75.00	95.00

	Price Range	
☐ **MILLER, GLENN.** *Collection of 36 motion picture stills, unsigned, housed in a cloth folder.*	75.00	100.00
☐ **MILLER, GLENN.** *c. 1943. Typewritten letter to a fan, signed.*	75.00	100.00
☐ **MILLER, GLENN.** *8x10 photo with trombone, signed, inscribed, framed along with a 78rpm recording, overall size 26x19.*	230.00	300.00
☐ **MILLER, GLENN.** *Brief memo in his hand, two lines.*	25.00	32.00
☐ **MILLER, GLENN.** *Signature on a dance program.*	12.00	12.00
☐ **MILLER, GLENN.** *c. 1940. Signature with brief note on a restaurant menu.*	26.00	35.00
☐ **MILLER, GLENN.** *c. 1942. 8x10 photo with Benny Goodman, signed by both.*	150.00	200.00
☐ **MILLER, GLENN.** *78rpm record sleeve, signed.*	20.00	25.00
☐ **MILLER, GLENN.** *Sheet music, "In the Mood", signed.*	120.00	140.00
☐ **MILLER, GLENN.** *Sheet music, "Pennsylvania 6-5000", signed.*	120.00	150.00
☐ **MILLER, GLENN.** *Printed postcard photo, facsimile signature.*	20.00	25.00
☐ **MILLER, GLENN.** *c. 1937. Large poster advertising his band (size not stated), color illustration.*	230.00	300.00
☐ **MILLER, GLENN.** *c. 1932. Envelope addressed by him, postmarked 1932.*	35.00	45.00
☐ **MINGUS, CHARLIE.** *8x10 studio portrait, signed.*	6.00	9.00
☐ **MINGUS, CHARLIE.** *Two pages of notes in his hand.*	9.00	12.00
☐ **MINGUS, CHARLIE.** *LP album cover, signed, no record.*	20.00	25.00
☐ **MINGUS, CHARLIE.** *Cover of "DownBeat" magazine, signed.*	3.50	5.00
☐ **MINGUS, CHARLIE.** *Signature on a card.*	2.50	3.50
☐ **MINGUS, CHARLIE.** *Photo with band, signed by him and several others, framed.*	9.00	12.00
☐ **MINGUS, CHARLIE.** *Three snapshot photos, one signed.*	8.00	11.00
☐ **MINGUS, CHARLIE.** *Two 8x10 photos, unsigned.*	3.50	5.00
☐ **MONK, THEOLONIUS.** *Sheet music, signed.*	22.00	29.00
☐ **MONK, THEOLONIUS.** *c. 1961. Two typewritten letters to publisher, with envelopes.*	20.00	25.00
☐ **MONK, THEOLONIUS.** *One page of musical composition in his hand, creased.*	23.00	30.00
☐ **MONK, THEOLONIUS.** *8x10 photo with Charlie Parker, signed by Monk only.*	20.00	25.00
☐ **MONK, THEOLONIUS.** *Magazine interview, signed.*	3.50	4.50
☐ **MONK, THEOLONIUS.** *8x10 studio portrait, signed.*	6.00	8.00
☐ **MONTGOMERY, WES.** *Large color photo with guitar, signed.*	9.00	12.00
☐ **MONTGOMERY, WES.** *Signature on passport application.*	7.00	10.00
☐ **MONTGOMERY, WES.** *8x10 studio portrait, signed.*	4.00	6.00
☐ **MONTGOMERY, WES.** *3x4½ snapshot photo, signed.*	2.00	3.00
☐ **MONTGOMERY, WES.** *Guitar instructional book, signed on the flyleaf.*	7.00	10.00
☐ **MONTGOMERY, WES.** *c. 1959. Photo with boxer Ezzard Charles, signed by Montgomery only.*	6.00	8.50
☐ **MONTGOMERY, WES.** *Signature on a bus schedule folder.*	2.00	3.00

	Price Range	
☐ **MONTGOMERY, WES.** *Collection of 326 news cuttings, articles, pictures relating to his career, in an album.*	85.00	110.00
☐ **MORTON, JELLY ROLL.** *8x10 photo at piano in club, signed, framed. Photo somewhat faded.*	140.00	180.00
☐ **MORTON, JELLY ROLL.** *78rpm record, signed on the label.*	110.00	140.00
☐ **MORTON, JELLY ROLL.** *8x10 photo with W. C. Handy, unsigned, notation on back (perhaps by a third party).*	30.00	37.00
☐ **MORTON, JELLY ROLL.** *Piano score with notes in his hand, soiled, front cover torn, in a cello bag.*	220.00	265.00
☐ **MORTON, JELLY ROLL.** *c. 1920. Early photo at piano, unsigned.*	20.00	25.00
☐ **MORTON, JELLY ROLL.** *c. 1930. New Orleans cafe bill advertising him.*	100.00	120.00
☐ **MORTON, JELLY ROLL.** *Signature on a card.*	20.00	25.00
☐ **MOTEN, BENNIE.** *8x10 sepia photo, signed.*	25.00	32.00
☐ **MOTEN, BENNIE.** *c. 1916. ALs, three pages.*	75.00	100.00
☐ **MOTEN, BENNIE.** *Canceled check, signed by him.*	45.00	60.00
☐ **MULLIGAN, GERRY.** *8x10 studio portrait, signed.*	4.50	6.00
☐ **MULLIGAN, GERRY.** *11x14 montage of small photos clipped from magazines and books, signed, inscribed, framed.*	17.00	25.00
☐ **MULLIGAN, GERRY.** *Cover of "DownBeat" magazine, signed.*	2.50	3.50
☐ **MULLIGAN, GERRY.** *LP album cover, signed, record missing.*	17.00	25.00
☐ **MULLIGAN, GERRY.** *8x10 photo with sax, signed and inscribed.*	4.50	6.00
☐ **MULLIGAN, GERRY.** *c. 1954. Two brief memos in his hand.*	5.50	7.50
☐ **MULLIGAN, GERRY.** *LP record, signed on the label.*	22.00	30.00
☐ **MULLIGAN, GERRY.** *Saxophone reputedly owned by him.*	900.00	1200.00
☐ **MURPHY, TURK.** *c. 1926. Photo as a youth, unsigned.*	1.75	2.50
☐ **MURPHY, TURK.** *c. 1975. Typewritten letter, signed, ½-page.*	2.50	3.50
☐ **MURPHY, TURK.** *c. 1961. 8x10 studio portrait, signed.*	3.50	5.00
☐ **MURPHY, TURK.** *Photo with several other musicians, signed.*	2.50	3.50
☐ **MURPHY, TURK.** *Magazine interview, signed.*	2.50	3.50
☐ **NAVARRO, FATS.** *c. 1947. 4x5 photo, signed.*	11.00	16.00
☐ **NAVARRO, FATS.** *Three 8x10 photos, one signed.*	25.00	34.00
☐ **NAVARRO, FATS.** *Letter to a recording company, typewritten, signed.*	15.00	20.00
☐ **NICHOLS, RED.** *c. 1942. Theater poster advertising "Red Nichols & his Five Pennies". 27x41.*	70.00	90.00
☐ **NICHOLS, RED.** *78rpm record, signed on the label.*	23.00	29.00
☐ **NICHOLS, RED.** *8x10 photo with Sammy Kaye, signed by both.*	15.00	20.00
☐ **NICHOLS, RED.** *8x10 photo with Jack Benny, signed by Nichols only.*	7.00	10.00
☐ **NICHOLS, RED.** *8x10 studio photo, signed.*	4.50	6.00
☐ **NICHOLS, RED.** *Printed postcard photo, facsimile signature.*	1.75	2.50
☐ **NICHOLS, RED.** *c. 1953. Check endorsed by him.*	23.00	29.00
☐ **NICHOLS, RED.** *Scrapbook containing 6 signed photos, 35 unsigned studio photos and snapshots, 217 news cuttings and various miscellaneous.*	230.00	300.00

	Price Range	
☐ **NICHOLS, RED.** *c. 1964. Typewritten letter, signed.*	6.00	9.00
☐ **NICHOLS, RED.** *c. 1948. Music instrument catalog, signed.*	3.50	5.00
☐ **NOONE, JIMMIE.** *8x10 studio portrait, signed.*	22.00	30.00
☐ **NOONE, JIMMIE.** *Two small snapshot photos.*	3.50	5.00
☐ **NORVO, RED.** *Photo with Lionel Hampton, signed by both.*	20.00	27.00
☐ **NORVO, RED.** *Printed poster, "King of the Vibes".*	4.50	6.00
☐ **NORVO, RED.** *c. 1972. 8x10 photo, signed.*	3.50	5.00
☐ **NORVO, RED.** *Signature on a restaurant menu.*	1.75	2.75
☐ **NORVO, RED.** *Three pages of notations in his hand.*	7.00	10.00
☐ **OLIVER, KING.** *8x10 sepia photo with band, King Oliver stands holding cornet, faded, signed.*	200.00	250.00
☐ **OLIVER, KING.** *Music hall bill advertising his band.*	115.00	140.00
☐ **ORY, KID.** *8x10 portrait photo, signed in purple ink.*	5.00	7.50
☐ **ORY, KID.** *c. 1971. 4x5 Polaroid photo, mounted on signed card.*	6.00	8.50
☐ **ORY, KID.** *c. 1932. ALs, two pages, with envelope.*	12.00	17.00
☐ **ORY, KID.** *Sheet music, "Muskrat Ramble", signed.*	65.00	80.00
☐ **ORY, KID.** *Three bars from "Muskrat Ramble" in his hand, signed, framed along with a photo (unsigned).*	75.00	95.00
☐ **ORY, KID.** *c. 1943. 8x10 photo with trombone, signed.*	6.00	9.00
☐ **ORY, KID.** *Two small photos dating from c. 1930, unsigned.*	2.50	3.50
☐ **PARKER, CHARLIE.** *8x10 portrait photo, signed.*	60.00	80.00
☐ **PARKER, CHARLIE.** *Sheet of musical composition.*	135.00	180.00
☐ **PARKER, CHARLIE.** *Two photos cut from "DownBeat" magazine, signed.*	60.00	80.00
☐ **PETERSON, OSCAR.** *c. 1977. Check endorsed by him.*	11.00	15.00
☐ **PETERSON, OSCAR.** *Signature on a card.*	1.75	2.75
☐ **PETERSON, OSCAR.** *8x10 studio portrait, signed.*	4.50	6.00
☐ **PETERSON, OSCAR.** *Photo with Joe Turner, signed by both.*	8.00	11.00
☐ **PETERSON, OSCAR.** *Three small snapshot photos, unsigned.*	3.50	5.00
☐ **PETERSON, OSCAR.** *8x10 photo at piano, matted, signed on the mat.*	7.00	10.00
☐ **PETERSON, OSCAR.** *Signature on a store receipt.*	2.00	3.00
☐ **PETERSON, OSCAR.** *Envelope with about 250 news cuttings relating to him, reviews, etc.*	7.00	10.00
☐ **PETTIFORD, OSCAR.** *8x10 studio photo, signed.*	20.00	25.00
☐ **PETTIFORD, OSCAR.** *c. 1958. Typewritten letter, signed.*	11.00	15.00
☐ **PETTIFORD, OSCAR.** *Bowstring reputedly used by him.*	45.00	60.00
☐ **PETTIFORD, OSCAR.** *Biography of him from book, signed.*	15.00	20.00
☐ **PETTIFORD, OSCAR.** *Signature on a union card.*	27.00	34.00
☐ **PETTIFORD, OSCAR.** *His Social Security card, signed.*	35.00	45.00
☐ **PETTIFORD, OSCAR.** *6x8 photo in group outside hotel, signed.*	15.00	20.00
☐ **PETTIFORD, OSCAR.** *LP record album cover, signed, no record.*	65.00	85.00
☐ **POWELL, BUD.** *8x10 publicity photo, signed and inscribed.*	9.00	12.00
☐ **POWELL, BUD.** *9x12 color photo at piano, signed.*	15.00	20.00
☐ **POWELL, BUD.** *c. 1947. ALs, ½-page.*	20.00	25.00
☐ **POWELL, BUD.** *c. 1945. Two postcards in his hand, signed.*	11.00	15.00

	Price Range	
☐ **POWELL, BUD.** *Signature on a card.*	4.50	6.00
☐ **POWELL, BUD.** *c. 1930's. Two 4x5 snapshot photos, unsigned.*	4.50	6.00
☐ **RAINEY, GERTRUDE.** *c. 1908. Photo standing on lawn, cut down to 6x8½ (margins trimmed away and photo cut into), signed.*	115.00	150.00
☐ **REDMAN, DON.** *Two pages of musical composition in his hand.*	32.00	40.00
☐ **REDMAN, DON.** *Photo with Jimmy Dorsey, signed by Redman.*	15.00	20.00
☐ **REDMAN, DON.** *c. 1938. 8x10 studio portrait, signed.*	10.00	14.00
☐ **REDMAN, DON.** *c. 1939. Check endorsed by him.*	22.00	30.00
☐ **REDMAN, DON.** *c. 1941. ALs, one and ½-page.*	20.00	25.00
☐ **REDMAN, DON.** *Scrapbook with 16 photos (3 signed), news cuttings, articles, other memorabilia, album damaged.*	100.00	140.00
☐ **RICH, BUDDY.** *8x10 photo with drums, signed and inscribed.*	7.00	10.00
☐ **RICH, BUDDY.** *Photo with Gene Krupa, signed by both.*	22.00	28.00
☐ **RICH, BUDDY.** *Signature on a card.*	2.50	3.50
☐ **RICH, BUDDY.** *Set of drumsticks autographed by him.*	75.00	100.00
☐ **RICH, BUDDY.** *c. 1956. 6x7 photo in night club, signed.*	4.50	6.00
☐ **RICH, BUDDY.** *8x10 studio portrait, signed.*	6.00	8.00
☐ **RICH, BUDDY.** *8x10 studio portrait, signed and inscribed, matted and framed.*	20.00	25.00
☐ **RICH, BUDDY.** *Advertising poster, signed.*	4.50	6.00
☐ **RICH, BUDDY.** *Three small snapshots, one signed.*	6.00	8.00
☐ **ROACH, MAX.** *8x10 photo with Gene Krupa, signed by Roach.*	9.00	12.00
☐ **ROACH, MAX.** *Theater pass, signed.*	3.00	4.00
☐ **ROACH, MAX.** *c. 1962. ALs, with envelope.*	4.00	6.00
☐ **ROACH, MAX.** *Signature on a card.*	1.50	2.50
☐ **ROACH, MAX.** *8x10 studio portrait, signed.*	3.00	4.00
☐ **ROACH, MAX.** *Two snapshots, signed on the backs.*	4.00	6.00
☐ **ROACH, MAX.** *LP album cover, signed, record missing.*	13.00	18.00
☐ **ROGERS, SHORTY.** *Two pages of music composition in his hand.*	25.00	32.00
☐ **ROGERS, SHORTY.** *c. 1960. 8x10 studio portrait, signed.*	4.00	5.00
☐ **ROGERS, SHORTY.** *Signature on a card.*	2.00	3.00
☐ **ROGERS, SHORTY.** *c. 1968. Postcard in his hand, 17 words.*	4.00	5.50
☐ **ROGERS, SHORTY.** *$1 bill, signed by him.*	4.00	5.50
☐ **ROGERS, SHORTY.** *LP record, signed on the label.*	30.00	40.00
☐ **ROGERS, SHORTY.** *c. 1959. ALs, one page.*	7.00	10.00
☐ **ROLLINS, SONNY.** *c. 1975. 8x10 photo with sax, signed.*	3.00	4.00
☐ **ROLLINS, SONNY.** *Magazine article, signed.*	2.00	3.00
☐ **ROLLINS, SONNY.** *Snapshot with a fan, signed and inscribed.*	2.50	3.50
☐ **ROLLINS, SONNY.** *Printed sheet music, signed.*	5.00	8.00
☐ **ROLLINS, SONNY.** *Two typewritten letters, signed.*	4.00	6.00
☐ **RUGOLO, PETE.** *Musical score, signed, in a folder.*	17.00	22.00
☐ **RUGOLO, PETE.** *Photo with Johnny Hodges, signed by Rugolo.*	11.00	15.00
☐ **RUGOLO, PETE.** *Photo with Red Norvo, signed by both.*	25.00	30.00

	Price Range	
☐ **RUGOLO, PETE.** *Notebook used by him, c. 62 pp. with musical jottings, addresses, etc.*	30.00	37.00
☐ **RUGOLO, PETE.** *LP album cover, signed, record missing.*	22.00	27.00
☐ **RUGOLO, PETE.** *c. 1968. ½-hour tape interview.*	7.00	10.00
☐ **RUGOLO, PETE.** *8x10 studio portrait in color, unsigned.*	2.00	3.00
☐ **RUGOLO, PETE.** *Article from "Encyclopedia of Jazz", signed.*	3.50	5.00
☐ **RUGOLO, PETE.** *Signature on a card.*	2.00	3.00
☐ **RUGOLO, PETE.** *Collection of c. 200 news cuttings and magazine articles.*	13.00	17.00
☐ **RUSSELL, PEE WEE.** *c. 1938. Photo with clarinet, signed and dated, framed.*	23.00	30.00
☐ **RUSSELL, PEE WEE.** *8x10 studio photo, signed.*	13.00	17.00
☐ **RUSSELL, PEE WEE.** *c. 1930's. Three early snapshots, signed.*	17.00	23.00
☐ **RUSSELL, PEE WEE.** *78rpm recording, signed on the label.*	30.00	40.00
☐ **RUSSELL, PEE WEE.** *Photo with Dave Tough, signed by Russell.*	15.00	20.00
☐ **RUSSELL, PEE WEE.** *Photo with Red Nichols, signed by both.*	30.00	40.00
☐ **RUSSELL, PEE WEE.** *Magazine article, signed.*	8.00	11.00
☐ **SHAW, ARTIE.** *c. 1950. Photo with band, signed by him and several others, dated.*	17.00	23.00
☐ **SHAW, ARTIE.** *c. 1948. Poster, signed.*	30.00	38.00
☐ **SHAW, ARTIE.** *Magazine cover, signed.*	6.00	9.00
☐ **SHAW, ARTIE.** *c. 1952. Snapshot with fan, signed on back.*	7.00	10.00
☐ **SHAW, ARTIE.** *Musical score, signed.*	23.00	30.00
☐ **SHAW, ARTIE.** *Collection of 132 news cuttings and photos.*	45.00	60.00
☐ **SHAW, ARTIE.** *Scrapbook with 12 signed photos, news cuttings, miscellaneous items.*	115.00	150.00
☐ **SHAW, ARTIE.** *c. 1955. 8x10 studio photo, signed.*	6.00	9.00
☐ **SHAW, ARTIE.** *Three early magazine articles, one signed.*	9.00	12.00
☐ **SHAW, ARTIE.** *c. 1938-67. 27 snapshot photos, 12 signed, mounted on large cards, laminated.*	95.00	120.00
☐ **SHAW, ARTIE.** *78rpm recording "Begin the Beguine", signed on the label.*	75.00	100.00
☐ **SHAW, ARTIE.** *Sheet music, "Begin the Beguine", signed.*	45.00	65.00
☐ **SILVER, HORACE.** *8x10 studio portrait, color, signed.*	6.00	9.00
☐ **SILVER, HORACE.** *c. 1970. Check endorsed by him.*	11.00	16.00
☐ **SILVER, HORACE.** *c. 1965. ALs, two pages, with envelope.*	6.00	9.00
☐ **SILVER, HORACE.** *Poster picture (from a photo), 16x23, signed.*	13.00	17.00
☐ **SILVER, HORACE.** *T-shirt with his likeness and name.*	8.00	11.00
☐ **SILVER, HORACE.** *Signature on a card.*	1.50	2.50
☐ **SIMS, ZOOT.** *c. 1954. 8x10 photo with several unidentified persons, signed, inscribed, dated.*	4.50	6.00
☐ **SIMS, ZOOT.** *Signature on a cafe menu.*	2.00	3.00
☐ **SIMS, ZOOT.** *Two small snapshot photos, unsigned.*	2.50	3.50
☐ **SIMS, ZOOT.** *Three 8x10 photos, one signed.*	7.00	10.00
☐ **SIMS, ZOOT.** *c. 1963. Check endorsed by him.*	20.00	25.00
☐ **SIMS, ZOOT.** *Album cover, signed, record missing.*	40.00	50.00

	Price Range	
☐ **SIMS, ZOOT.** *Galley proofs of a magazine article, signed.*	4.50	6.00
☐ **SIMS, ZOOT.** *Printed poster, signed, creased, stained.*	9.00	12.00
☐ **SIMS, ZOOT.** *Record company catalogue, signed on front cover.*	11.00	16.00
☐ **SINGLETON, ZUTTY.** *Pair of drumsticks used by him, framed along with a signed 8x10 photo in a gold-colored frame.*	150.00	185.00
☐ **SINGLETON, ZUTTY.** *c. 1961. 8x10 studio photo, signed.*	6.00	8.50
☐ **SINGLETON, ZUTTY.** *Signature on a card.*	2.50	3.75
☐ **SINGLETON, ZUTTY.** *c. 1936. ALs, ½-page, stained.*	4.50	6.00
☐ **SINGLETON, ZUTTY.** *Three small snapshot photos, signed.*	13.00	17.00
☐ **SINGLETON, ZUTTY.** *Magazine photo, signed and inscribed.*	3.50	5.00
☐ **SINGLETON, ZUTTY.** *c. 1949. Check endorsed by him.*	22.00	30.00
☐ **SINGLETON, ZUTTY.** *Photo with Don Redman, signed by both.*	20.00	25.00
☐ **SINGLETON, ZUTTY.** *Photo with Nat Hentoff, signed by both.*	15.00	20.00
☐ **SINGLETON, ZUTTY.** *c. 1944. Postcard in his hand, four lines.*	4.50	6.00
☐ **SINGLETON, ZUTTY.** *78rpm record, signed on the label.*	30.00	42.00
☐ **SINGLETON, ZUTTY.** *Collection of c. 450 news cuttings, etc.*	85.00	110.00
☐ **SINGLETON, ZUTTY.** *Two 8x10 sepia photos, unsigned, early.*	6.00	8.50
☐ **SMITH, BESSIE.** *8x10 photo, signed and inscribed.*	200.00	275.00
☐ **SMITH, BESSIE.** *c. 1934. Poster advertising her appearance at a cafe, framed.*	185.00	240.00
☐ **SMITH, CLARENCE.** *c. 1926. ALs, four lines.*	75.00	100.00
☐ **SMITH, JOE.** *8x10 photo, signed and inscribed, creased.*	22.00	30.00
☐ **SMITH, JOE.** *c. 1922. 4x5 photo, unsigned.*	7.00	10.00
☐ **SMITH, WILLIE.** *8x10 studio photo, signed and inscribed.*	5.00	8.00
☐ **SMITH, WILLIE.** *Signature on a union card.*	35.00	45.00
☐ **SMITH, WILLIE.** *c. 1950's. Four snapshot photos, one signed.*	20.00	25.00
☐ **SMITH, WILLIE.** *78rpm recording, signed on the label.*	55.00	75.00
☐ **SMITH, WILLIE.** *c. 1962. Check endorsed by him.*	40.00	55.00
☐ **SMITH, WILLIE.** *c. 1941. 8x10 photo at piano, signed.*	12.00	17.00
☐ **SPANIER, MUGGSY.** *8x10 publicity photo, signed, trimmed.*	5.00	7.50
☐ **SPANIER, MUGGSY.** *LP record album cover, signed, no record.*	55.00	75.00
☐ **SPANIER, MUGGSY.** *Signature on a card.*	2.00	3.00
☐ **STITT, SONNY.** *8x10 studio photo, signed and inscribed.*	3.50	5.00
☐ **STITT, SONNY.** *Three small snapshots, one signed.*	4.00	6.00
☐ **STITT, SONNY.** *LP album cover, signed, record missing.*	17.00	23.00
☐ **STITT, SONNY.** *Two lines of musical notation, unsigned.*	6.00	9.00
☐ **TATUM, ART.** *c. 1948. 8x10 photo, signed and inscribed.*	30.00	40.00
☐ **TATUM, ART.** *c. 1930's. Poster advertising a cafe appearance.*	110.00	150.00
☐ **TATUM, ART.** *78rpm recording, signed on the label.*	75.00	100.00
☐ **TATUM, ART.** *5x6 photo at piano, signed in the margin.*	35.00	45.00
☐ **TATUM, ART.** *Printed score with notes in his hand.*	60.00	80.00
☐ **TATUM, ART.** *c. 1950. Check endorsed by him.*	35.00	45.00
☐ **TATUM, ART.** *c. 1925. Snapshot photo, signed.*	45.00	60.00
☐ **TATUM, ART.** *Scrapbook of 56 photos, 6 signed, other items.*	500.00	650.00

	Price Range	
☐ **TAYLOR, BILLY.** *8x10 photo at piano, signed.*	3.50	5.00
☐ **TAYLOR, BILLY.** *Signature on a card.*	2.00	3.00
☐ **TEAGARDEN, JACK.** *78rpm recording, signed on the label.*	75.00	95.00
☐ **TEAGARDEN, JACK.** *Signature on a card.*	3.50	5.00
☐ **TEAGARDEN, JACK.** *c. 1932. 8x10 studio photo, signed.*	30.00	40.00
☐ **WALLER, FATS.** *c. 1939. 8x10 photo, signed and inscribed.*	95.00	120.00
☐ **WALLER, FATS.** *Three snap photos, various sizes, unsigned.*	15.00	20.00
☐ **WALLER, FATS.** *78rpm recording, signed on the label.*	110.00	140.00
☐ **WEATHERFORD, TEDDY.** *c. 1936. ALs, one page.*	15.00	20.00
☐ **WEBB, CHICK.** *8x10 studio photo, signed.*	17.00	23.00
☐ **WHITEMAN, PAUL.** *c. 1922. Check endorsed by him.*	60.00	80.00
☐ **WHITEMAN, PAUL.** *c. 1930. Photo holding baton, signed.*	22.00	30.00
☐ **WHITEMAN, PAUL.** *Snapshot photo at age 21, unsigned.*	7.00	10.00
☐ **WILLIAMS, COOTIE.** *8x10 studio photo, signed.*	3.50	5.00
☐ **WINDING, KAI.** *"DownBeat" magazine article, signed.*	4.50	6.50
☐ **WINDING, KAI.** *LP album cover, signed, record missing.*	22.00	30.00
☐ **YANCEY, JIMMY.** *8x10 photo, signed, framed.*	33.00	45.00
☐ **YANCEY, JIMMY.** *Signature on a card.*	2.50	3.50
☐ **YOUNG, LESTER.** *8x10 photo, signed.*	20.00	25.00

78's

ALABAMA WASHBOARD STOMPERS		
☐ **Vocalion 1546** *I Want a Little Girl.*	24.00	39.00
☐ **1587** *Who Stole the Lock?*	24.00	39.00
☐ **1626** *I Surrender, Dear.*	24.00	39.00
☐ **1635** *I Need Lovin'.*	21.00	33.00
ALEXANDER, Texas		
☐ **Okeh 8511** *Corn-Bread Blues.*	17.00	28.00
☐ **8526** *Farm Hand Blues.*	17.00	28.00
☐ **8542** *Sabine River Blues.*	17.00	28.00
☐ **8563** *Bell Cow Blues.*	17.00	28.00
☐ **8578** *Death Bed Blues.*	15.00	23.00
☐ **8591** *Deep Blues Sea Blues.*	15.00	23.00
☐ **8603** *West Texas Blues.*	15.00	23.00
☐ **8624** *Sittin' On a Log.*	15.00	23.00
☐ **8640** *Blue Devil Blues.*	16.00	24.00
☐ **8658** *'Frisco Train Blues.*	40.00	70.00
☐ **8688** *St. Louis Fair Blues.*	18.00	27.00
☐ **8705** *Gold Tooth Blues.*	15.00	25.00
☐ **8731** *Awful Moaning Blues.*	15.00	25.00
☐ **8751** *Peaceful Blues.*	15.00	25.00
☐ **8764** *Broken Yo Yo.*	15.00	25.00
☐ **8771** *Texas Special.*	15.00	25.00
☐ **8785** *Thirty Day Blues.*	15.00	25.00
☐ **8813** *She's So Far.*	28.00	47.00
☐ **8823** *Last Stage Blues.*	30.00	55.00
☐ **8835** *Days Is Lonesome.*	28.00	47.00
☐ **8890** *Seen Better Days.*	28.00	47.00

		Price Range	
☐ **Vocalion 02743**	*Blues In My Mind.*	13.00	20.00
☐ **02764**	*Prairie Dog Hole Blues.*	13.00	20.00
☐ **02772**	*Worried Blues.*	13.00	20.00
☐ **02856**	*Justice Blues.*	13.00	20.00
☐ **02876**	*Lonesome Valley Blues.*	13.00	20.00
☐ **02912**	*Deceitful Blues.*	13.00	20.00
ANDERSON, Jelly Roll			
☐ **Gennett 6135**	*Free Women Blues.*	55.00	90.00
☐ **6181**	*Good Time Blues.*	45.00	80.00
☐ **Herwin 92014**	*Salt Tear Blues.*	75.00	120.00
☐ **92020**	*Free Women Blues.*	85.00	135.00
ANTRIM, Roosevelt			
☐ **Bluebird 7149**	*Complaint to Make.*	13.00	20.00
☐ **7475**	*Station Boy Blues.*	13.00	20.00
ARMSTRONG, Louis			
☐ **Columbia 2574-D**	*Star Dust.*	10.00	17.00
☐ **2606-D**	*All of Me.*	11.00	18.00
☐ **2631-D**	*The New Tiger Rag.*	10.00	17.00
☐ **2688-D**	*Rockin' Chair.*	10.00	17.00
☐ **2709-D**	*Body and Soul.*	11.00	18.00
☐ **2727-D**	*After You've Gone.*	11.00	18.00
☐ **Okeh 8299**	*Oriental Strut.*	45.00	80.00
☐ **8300**	*Heebie Jeebies.*	50.00	90.00
☐ **8318**	*Georgia Grind.*	50.00	90.00
☐ **8320**	*Cornet Chop Suey.*	52.00	95.00
☐ **8343**	*I'm Gonna Gitcha.*	45.00	80.00
☐ **8379**	*Sweet Little Papa.*	50.00	90.00
☐ **8396**	*The King of the Zulus.*	52.00	95.00
☐ **8423**	*Big Butter and Egg Man.*	50.00	90.00
☐ **8436**	*Jazz Lips.*	50.00	90.00
☐ **8447**	*Irish Black Bottom.*	45.00	80.00
☐ **8474**	*Wild Man Blues.*	50.00	90.00
☐ **8482**	*Willie the Weeper.*	40.00	75.00
☐ **8496**	*Keyhole Blues.*	45.00	80.00
☐ **8503**	*Potatoe Head Blues.*	45.00	80.00
☐ **8535**	*Savoy Blues.*	50.00	90.00
☐ **8551**	*Got No Blues.*	45.00	80.00
☐ **8566**	*Struttin' with Some Barbeque.*	45.00	80.00
☐ **8597**	*West End Blues.*	32.00	57.00
☐ **8609**	*Suger Foot Strut.*	35.00	60.00
☐ **8631**	*Knee Drops.*	30.00	53.00
☐ **8641**	*Squeeze Me.*	30.00	53.00
☐ **8657**	*Save It, Pretty Mama.*	27.00	50.00
☐ **8669**	*No-One Else But You.*	27.00	50.00
☐ **8690**	*Basin Street Blues.*	27.00	50.00
☐ **8703**	*Knockin' a Jug.*	26.00	47.00
☐ **8714**	*Ain't Misbehavin'.*	23.00	39.00
☐ **8717**	*That Rhythm Man.*	23.00	39.00
☐ **8729**	*Some of These Days.*	23.00	39.00
☐ **8756**	*Rockin' Chair.*	23.00	39.00
☐ **8774**	*Bessie Couldn't Help It.*	23.00	39.00
☐ **41078**	*Fireworks.*	21.00	37.00
☐ **41157**	*Knee Drops.*	12.00	18.00

		Price Range	
☐	**41180** *Save It, Pretty Mama.*	12.00	18.00
☐	**41241** *Basin Street Blues.*	17.00	24.00
☐	**41276** *Black and Blue.*	17.00	24.00
☐	**41281** *Sweet Savannah Sue.*	22.00	36.00
☐	**41298** *Some of These Days.*	22.00	36.00
☐	**41350** *After You've Gone.*	22.00	36.00
☐	**41415** *My Sweet.*	22.00	36.00
☐	**41423** *Exactly Like You.*	20.00	33.00
☐	**41442** *I'm a Ding Dong Daddy.*	20.00	33.00
☐	**41448** *Confessin'.*	20.00	33.00
☐	**41454** *Weather Bird.*	26.00	47.00
☐	**41468** *Body and Soul.*	17.00	30.00
☐	**41478** *You're Drivin' Me Crazy.*	16.00	27.00
☐	**41486** *Shine.*	16.00	27.00
☐	**41497** *Walkin' My Baby Back Home.*	17.00	30.00
☐	**41501** *Them There Eyes.*	16.00	27.00
☐	**41504** *When It's Sleepy Time Down South.*	15.00	26.00
☐	**41530** *Star Dust.*	15.00	26.00
☐	**41534** *Chinatown, My Chinatown.*	14.00	25.00
☐	**41538** *The Lonesome Road.*	14.00	25.00
☐	**41550** *Kickin' the Gong Around.*	14.00	25.00
☐	**41552** *All of Me.*	13.00	24.00
☐	**41557** *The New Tiger Rag.*	13.00	24.00
☐	**41560** *Keepin' Out of Mischief Now.*	13.00	24.00
AUSTIN, Lovie			
☐	**Paramount 12255** *Steppin' On the Blues.*	50.00	76.00
☐	**12278** *Charleston Mad.*	45.00	70.00
☐	**12283** *Heebie Jeebies.*	44.00	67.00
☐	**12300** *Rampart Street Blues.*	35.00	56.00
☐	**12313** *Too Sweet For Words.*	33.00	53.00
☐	**12361** *Frog Tongue Stomp.*	125.00	180.00
☐	**12380** *Chicago Mess Around.*	130.00	185.00
☐	**12391** *In the Alley Blues.*	130.00	185.00
BAILEY, De Ford			
☐	**Bluebird 5147** *Ice Water Blues.*	10.00	15.00
☐	**Brunswick 146** *Pan-American Blues.*	22.00	35.00
☐	**147** *Muscle Shoals Blues.*	22.00	35.00
☐	**148** *Alcoholic Blues.*	22.00	35.00
☐	**434** *Up Country Blues.*	17.00	25.00
☐	**Victor 23336** *John Henry.*	45.00	70.00
☐	**23831** *John Henry.*	40.00	62.00
☐	**38014** *Ice Water Blues.*	17.00	25.00
BAKER, Katherine			
☐	**Gennett 6125** *I Helped You, Sick Man*	65.00	100.00
☐	**6157** *Chicago Fire Blues.*	65.00	110.00
☐	**6228** *Money Women Blues.*	65.00	100.00
☐	**6321** *Mistreated Blues.*	65.00	100.00
☐	**Herwin 92017** *My Man Left Me Blues.*	75.00	120.00
☐	**92037** *Daddy Sunshine Blues.*	70.00	115.00
☐	**92038** *Wild Women Blues.*	70.00	115.00
☐	**92039** *Mistreated Blues.*	70.00	115.00

		Price Range	
BARBECUE BOB			
☐ **Columbia 14222-D**	*Mississippi Heavy Water Blues.*	12.00	19.00
☐ **15246-D**	*Honey You Don't Know My Mind.*	12.00	19.00
☐ **14257-D**	*Brown-Skin Gal.*	12.00	19.00
☐ **14268-D**	*It Won't Be Long Now.*	12.00	19.00
☐ **14280-D**	*Crooked Woman Blues.*	12.00	19.00
☐ **14299-D**	*Thinkin' Funny Blues.*	12.00	19.00
☐ **14331-D**	*Waycross Georgia Blues.*	15.00	25.00
☐ **14350-D**	*My Mistake Blues.*	15.00	25.00
☐ **14372-D**	*Blind Pig Blues.*	15.00	25.00
☐ **14383-D**	*Cold Wave Blues.*	15.00	25.00
☐ **14412-D**	*Dollar Down Blues.*	15.00	25.00
☐ **14436-D**	*It's a Funny Little Thing.*	15.00	25.00
☐ **14461-D**	*Bad Time Blues.*	15.00	25.00
☐ **14507-D**	*Me and My Whiskey.*	24.00	38.00
☐ **14523-D**	*Yo Yo Blues No. 2.*	24.00	38.00
☐ **14546-D**	*Telling It To You.*	24.00	38.00
☐ **14558-D**	*The Spider and the Fly.*	24.00	38.00
☐ **14573-D**	*California Blues.*	24.00	38.00
☐ **14581-D**	*Jambooger Blues.*	24.00	38.00
☐ **14591-D**	*Atlanta Moon.*	24.00	38.00
BLAKE, Eubie			
☐ **Crown 3086**	*When Your Lover Has Gone.*	23.00	35.00
☐ **3090**	*I'm No Account Any More.*	20.00	32.00
☐ **3105**	*It Looks Like Love.*	20.00	32.00
☐ **3130**	*Nobody's Sweetheart.*	23.00	35.00
☐ **3193**	*River Stay 'Way From My Door.*	20.00	32.00
☐ **3197**	*Sweet Georgia Brown.*	25.00	40.00
☐ **Victor 22735**	*My Blue Days Blew Over.*	25.00	40.00
☐ **22737**	*Thumpin And Bumpin'.*	27.00	42.00
BLIND BLAKE			
☐ **Paramount 12413**	*Skeedle Loo Doo Blues.*	37.00	56.00
☐ **12431**	*Too Tight.*	35.00	53.00
☐ **12442**	*Tampa Bound.*	34.00	52.00
☐ **12464**	*Buck-Town Blues.*	34.00	52.00
☐ **12479**	*One Time Blues.*	33.00	50.00
☐ **12565**	*Southern Rag.*	32.00	50.00
☐ **12583**	*Hard Road Blues.*	33.00	50.00
☐ **12597**	*Wabash Rag.*	32.00	49.00
☐ **12606**	*Brownskin Mama Blues.*	34.00	52.00
☐ **12643**	*Tootie Blues.*	39.00	60.00
☐ **12657**	*Detroit Bound Blues.*	38.00	57.00
☐ **12673**	*Hot Potatoes.*	50.00	75.00
☐ **12695**	*Low Down Loving Gal.*	38.00	57.00
☐ **12710**	*Back Door Slam Blues.*	37.00	55.00
☐ **12723**	*No Dough Blues.*	37.00	55.00
☐ **12737**	*Search Warrant Blues.*	36.00	53.00
☐ **12754**	*Notoriety Woman Blues.*	36.00	53.00
☐ **12767**	*Ramblin' Mama Blues.*	37.00	55.00
☐ **12810**	*Poker Woman Blues.*	37.00	55.00
☐ **12824**	*Georgia Bound.*	36.00	53.00
☐ **12863**	*Fightin' the Jug.*	65.00	100.00
☐ **12888**	*Police Dog Blues.*	47.00	72.00
☐ **12904**	*Ice Man Blues.*	45.00	69.00

	Price Range	
BLIND WILLIE		
☐ **Regal 3260** *How About You*	20.00	30.00
☐ **Vocalion 02568** *Weary Hearted Blues*	16.00	26.00
☐ **02577** *Death Cell Blues*	15.00	25.00
☐ **02595** *Warm It Up To Me*	15.00	25.00
☐ **02623** *Lord Have Mercy If You Please*	14.00	23.00
☐ **02668** *My Baby's Gone*	14.00	23.00
BLYTHE'S BLUE BOYS		
☐ **Champion 15344** *There'll Come a Day*	125.00	190.00
☐ **15528** *My Baby*	115.00	165.00
☐ **15551** *Pleasure Mad*	110.00	160.00
☐ **15570** *Tell Me, Cutie*	110.00	160.00
☐ **15676** *Oriental Man*	110.00	160.00
☐ **40023** *Oriental Man*	15.00	25.00
☐ **40062** *Tack It Down*	14.00	23.00
☐ **40115** *Tell Me, Cutie*	14.00	23.00
BOGAN, Lucille		
☐ **Brunswick 7083** *Coffee Grindin' Blues*	29.00	43.00
☐ **7145** *My Georgia Blues*	24.00	37.00
☐ **7186** *Black Angel Blues*	20.00	31.00
☐ **7193** *Crawlin' Lizard Blues*	23.00	36.00
☐ **Paramount 12459** *Sweet Patunia*	34.00	60.00
☐ **12504** *Kind Stella Blues*	32.00	55.00
☐ **12514** *Doggone Wicked Blues*	31.00	53.00
☐ **12560** *War Time Man Blues*	31.00	53.00
BOOKER, John Lee		
☐ **Chance 1108** *Miss Lorraine*	10.00	18.00
☐ **1110** *Graveyard Blues*	10.00	18.00
☐ **1122** *609 Boogie*	10.00	18.00
☐ **De Luxe 6032** *Stuttering Blues*	6.00	11.00
☐ **6046** *Real Real Gone*	6.00	11.00
☐ **Rockin' 525** *Pouring Down Rain*	7.00	12.00
BROWN, Bessie		
☐ **Banner 1833** *What's the Matter Now?*	11.00	18.00
☐ **Brunswick 4346** *The Blues Singer from Alabam*	20.00	35.00
☐ **4409** *He Just Don't Appeal to Me*	20.00	35.00
☐ **Regal 8143** *What's the Matter Now?*	11.00	18.00
☐ **Vocalion 1182** *Arkansas Blues*	13.00	22.00
☐ **15688** *The Man I Love*	10.00	17.00
BROWN, Henry		
☐ **Paramount 12825** *Twenty-First Street Stomp*	75.00	115.00
☐ **12934** *Blues Stomp*	70.00	110.00
☐ **12988** *Eastern Chimes Blues*	65.00	105.00
BRYANT, Gladys		
☐ **Harmograph 818** *Beale Street Mama*	35.00	52.00
☐ **2539** *Triflin' Blues*	20.00	32.00
☐ **2540** *Laughin' Cryin' Blues*	20.00	32.00
☐ **Paramount 12026** *Laughin' Cryin' Blues*	20.00	32.00
☐ **12031** *Beale Street Mama*	30.00	45.00

	Price Range	
BUMBLE BEE SLIM		
☐ **Decca 7021** *Cruel Hearted Woman Blues.*	13.00	23.00
☐ **7045** *The Longest Day You Live.*	12.00	21.00
☐ **7053** *Bleeding Heart Blues.*	12.00	21.00
☐ **7054** *Let's Pitch a Boogie Woogie.*	12.00	21.00
☐ **7071** *My Black Gal Blues.*	17.00	25.00
☐ **7079** *Mean Bloody Murder Blues.*	12.00	21.00
☐ **7089** *Good Evening Blues.*	12.00	21.00
☐ **7101** *Sail On Sail On Blues.*	12.00	21.00
☐ **7121** *I'll Take You Back.*	12.00	21.00
☐ **7126** *Smoky Mountain Blues.*	12.00	21.00
☐ **7138** *Happy Life Blues.*	12.00	21.00
☐ **7145** *Some Old Rainy Day.*	12.00	20.00
☐ **7162** *Deep Bass Blues.*	12.00	20.00
☐ **7170** *No Good Woman.*	13.00	21.00
☐ **Fidelity 3004** *Ida Red.*	11.00	18.00
☐ **Paramount 13102** *Yo Yo String Blues.*	65.00	105.00
☐ **13109** *Chain Gang Bound.*	70.00	115.00
☐ **13132** *Honey Bee Blues.*	65.00	105.00
☐ **Vocalion 1691** *Piney Woods Working Man.*	34.00	57.00
☐ **1719** *Greasy Greens.*	34.00	62.00
☐ **02728** *Baby So Long.*	12.00	19.00
☐ **02742** *East St. Louis Blues.*	10.00	16.00
☐ **02773** *Wrecked Life Blues.*	12.00	19.00
☐ **02809** *Helping Hand Blues.*	10.00	16.00
☐ **02829** *Rough Road Blues.*	9.00	15.00
☐ **02865** *Cold-Blooded Murder.*	12.00	19.00
☐ **02885** *Burned Down Mill.*	10.00	16.00
☐ **02903** *Running Bad Luck Blues.*	10.00	16.00
☐ **02930** *Blues Before Daylight.*	9.00	15.00
☐ **02970** *Way Down in Georgia.*	9.00	15.00
☐ **03005** *Lemon Squeezing Blues.*	10.00	16.00
☐ **03037** *I Keep on Drinking.*	12.00	19.00
☐ **03054** *When the Sun Goes Down.*	10.00	16.00
☐ **03090** *Big 80 Blues.*	9.00	15.00
☐ **03165** *Cold Blooded Murder No. 2.*	12.00	19.00
☐ **03197** *When Somebody Loses.*	9.00	15.00
☐ **03209** *Can't You Trust Me No More?*	10.00	16.00
☐ **03221** *Dumb Tricks Blues.*	10.00	16.00
☐ **03242** *Back in Jail Again.*	10.00	16.00
☐ **03267** *Wet Clothes Blues.*	12.00	19.00
☐ **03298** *Any Time at Night.*	10.00	16.00
☐ **03328** *Hard Rocks in My Bed.*	12.00	19.00
☐ **03384** *Meet Me at the Landing.*	9.00	15.00
☐ **03446** *Fast Life Blues.*	10.00	16.00
☐ **03473** *12 O'Clock Midnight.*	9.00	15.00
☐ **03506** *She Never.*	10.00	16.00
☐ **03550** *Big Six.*	9.00	15.00
☐ **03582** *Woman for Every Man.*	10.00	16.00
☐ **03611** *Good Bye.*	9.00	15.00
☐ **03637** *Rough Treatment.*	12.00	19.00
☐ **03698** *Just Yesterday.*	10.00	16.00

	Price Range	
☐ **03767** *This Old Life I'm Living.*	9.00	15.00
☐ **03870** *When Your Deal Goes Down.*	9.00	15.00
☐ **03929** *Rock Hearted Woman.*	9.00	15.00
☐ **04661** *Where Was You Last Night?*	9.00	15.00
BUNCH, Frank		
☐ **Gennett 6278** *Fuzzy Wuzzy.*	80.00	130.00
☐ **6293** *Fourth Avenue Stomp.*	70.00	110.00
☐ **Herwin 92044** *Congo Stomp.*	100.00	160.00
BURSTON, Clara		
☐ **Champion 16125** *Try That Man O'Mine.*	45.00	75.00
☐ **16216** *Pay with Money.*	42.00	70.00
☐ **16756** *Good and Hot.*	42.00	70.00
☐ **Paramount 12881** *Georgia Man Blues.*	35.00	60.00
☐ **13003** *C. P. Blues.*	33.00	56.00
☐ **13045** *Ginger Snappin'.*	35.00	60.00
CAMPBELL, Gene		
☐ **Brunswick 7139** *Bended Knee Blues.*	36.00	60.00
☐ **7154** *Western Plain Blues.*	33.00	52.00
☐ **7161** *Freight Train Yodeling Blues.*	32.00	50.00
☐ **7170** *Wandering Blues.*	32.00	50.00
☐ **7177** *Wash and Iron Woman Blues.*	31.00	50.00
☐ **7197** *Wedding Day Blues.*	31.00	50.00
☐ **7206** *Face to Face Blues.*	30.00	50.00
☐ **7214** *Doggone Mean Blues.*	31.00	50.00
☐ **7225** *Crooked Woman Blues.*	32.00	53.00
☐ **7226** *Turned Out Blues.*	30.00	50.00
☐ **7227** *Married Life Blues.*	30.00	50.00
CARR, Leroy		
☐ **Bluebird 5915** *Big Four Blues.*	11.00	18.00
☐ **5946** *Just a Rag.*	11.00	18.00
☐ **5963** *Going Back Home.*	11.00	18.00
☐ **Vocalion 1191** *My Own Lonesome Blues.*	15.00	25.00
☐ **1200** *Tennessee Blues.*	18.00	33.00
☐ **1214** *Low Down Dirty Blues.*	19.00	35.00
☐ **1232** *Truthful Blues.*	18.00	33.00
☐ **1241** *Prison Bound Blues.*	26.00	41.00
☐ **1259** *How About Me?*	25.00	40.00
☐ **1261** *Tired of Your Low Down Ways.*	25.00	40.00
☐ **1290** *Straight Alky Blues.*	26.00	41.00
☐ **1400** *Naptown Blues.*	25.00	40.00
☐ **1405** *Wrong Man Blues.*	25.00	40.00
☐ **1423** *Gettin' All Wet.*	26.00	41.00
☐ **1432** *Prison Cell Blues.*	25.00	38.00
☐ **1435** *Love Hides All Faults.*	25.00	38.00
☐ **1454** *The Dirty Dozen.*	25.00	38.00
☐ **1473** *Rainy Day Blues.*	23.00	36.00
☐ **1483** *That's Tellin' 'em.*	23.00	36.00
☐ **1499** *Blue with the Blues.*	22.00	35.00
☐ **1519** *I Know That I'll Be Blue.*	22.00	35.00
☐ **1527** *Memphis Town.*	22.00	35.00
☐ **1541** *Sloppy Drunk Blues.*	25.00	37.00
☐ **1549** *Four Day Rider.*	25.00	37.00

		Price Range	
☐	**1574** *Jail Cell Blues.*	24.00	36.00
☐	**1585** *Big House Blues.*	24.00	36.00
☐	**1593** *Papa's on the House Top.*	23.00	35.00
☐	**1605** *Low Down Dog Blues.*	23.00	35.00
☐	**1624** *Let's Disagree.*	23.00	35.00
☐	**1636** *Papa's Got Your Water On.*	24.00	36.00
☐	**1651** *What More Can I Do?*	23.00	35.00
☐	**1693** *The Depression Blues.*	25.00	37.00
☐	**1703** *Midnight Hour Blues.*	22.00	34.00
☐	**1709** *I Keep the Blues.*	22.00	34.00
☐	**1716** *Quittin' Papa.*	22.00	34.00
☐	**02875** *Longing For My Sister*	14.00	22.00
☐	**02893** *Cruel Woman Blues.*	14.00	22.00
☐	**02922** *Stormy Weather Blues.*	14.00	24.00
☐	**02950** *My Woman's Gone Wrong.*	14.00	24.00
☐	**02969** *Bo Bo Stomp.*	14.00	24.00
☐	**02986** *George Street Blues.*	14.00	24.00
☐	**03034** *Tight Time Blues.*	14.00	24.00
☐	**03067** *Black Wagon Blues.*	12.00	21.00
☐	**03107** *Muddy Water.*	13.00	22.00
☐	**03157** *My Good for Nothin' Gal.*	12.00	21.00
☐	**03233** *Blue Night Blues.*	13.00	22.00
☐	**03296** *Good Woman Blues.*	13.00	22.00
☐	**03349** *Big Four Blues.*	13.00	22.00
CARTER, Bo (& Walter Jacobs)			
☐	**Bluebird 5489** *Bo Carter Special.*	14.00	23.00
☐	**5536** *Howlin' Tom Cat Blues.*	14.00	22.00
☐	**5594** *Pin in Your Cushion.*	14.00	22.00
☐	**5629** *Beans.*	12.00	21.00
☐	**5704** *Nobody's Business.*	12.00	21.00
☐	**5825** *Backache Blues.*	14.00	22.00
☐	**5861** *Old Shoe Blues.*	12.00	20.00
☐	**5912** *Mashing That Thing.*	14.00	22.00
☐	**5997** *Skin Ball Blues.*	14.00	22.00
☐	**6024** *Blue Runner Blues.*	12.00	21.00
☐	**6058** *Please Warm My Weiner.*	17.00	28.00
☐	**6295** *Cigarette Blues.*	17.00	28.00
☐	**6315** *Ride My Mule.*	12.00	21.00
☐	**6363** *Rolling Blues.*	12.00	21.00
☐	**6407** *It's Too Wet.*	14.00	22.00
☐	**6444** *Fat Mouth Blues.*	14.00	22.00
☐	**6529** *T Baby Blues.*	14.00	23.00
☐	**6589** *I Get the Blues.*	12.00	20.00
☐	**6659** *Doubled Up in a Knot.*	12.00	20.00
☐	**6735** *Worried G Blues.*	12.00	20.00
☐	**7073** *Got to Work Somewhere.*	12.00	19.00
☐	**7213** *The Ins and Outs of My Girl.*	14.00	23.00
☐	**7927** *Shake 'em on Down.*	12.00	19.00
☐	**7952** *Lucille, Lucille.*	12.00	19.00
☐	**7968** *Shoo That Chicken.*	12.00	19.00
☐	**8045** *Let's Get Drunk Again.*	12.00	19.00
☐	**8093** *Old Devil.*	10.00	17.00
☐	**8122** *Whiskey Blues.*	11.00	19.00
☐	**8147** *Santa Claus.*	10.00	17.00

		Price Range	
☐	**8159** *Trouble in Blues.*	10.00	17.00
☐	**8397** *The County Farm Blues.*	10.00	17.00
☐	**8423** *Lock the Lock.*	11.00	19.00
☐	**8459** *Baby Ruth.*	14.00	23.00
☐	**8495** *Policy Blues.*	10.00	17.00
☐	**8514** *My Little Mind.*	10.00	16.00
☐	**8555** *Honey.*	10.00	16.00
☐	**Okeh 8852** *I'm an Old Bumble Bee.*	30.00	50.00
☐	**8858** *Times is Tight Like That.*	28.00	48.00
☐	**8870** *Mean Feeling Blues.*	27.00	45.00
☐	**8887** *Pin in Your Cushion.*	27.00	45.00
☐	**8888** *Loveless Love.*	26.00	44.00
☐	**8889** *Howling Tom Cat Blues.*	25.00	43.00
☐	**8897** *Ants in My Pants.*	25.00	43.00
☐	**8923** *What Kind of Scent is This?*	27.00	46.00
☐	**8930** *Last Go Round.*	25.00	42.00
☐	**8935** *I Want You to Know.*	25.00	42.00
☐	**8952** *Baby, How Can It Be?*	25.00	42.00

CELESTIN'S TUXEDO JAZZ ORCHESTRA

☐	**Columbia 636-D** *Station Calls.*	17.00	28.00
☐	**14200-D** *I'm Satisfied You Love Me.*	16.00	26.00
☐	**14220-D** *Papa's Got the Jim-Jams.*	16.00	26.00
☐	**14259-D** *As You Like It.*	15.00	25.00
☐	**14396-D** *The Sweetheart of T.K.O.*	14.00	25.00

COLLINS, Sam

☐	**Gennett 6167** *The Jail House Blues.*	50.00	70.00
☐	**6181** *Devil in the Lion's Den.*	43.00	68.00
☐	**6260** *Dark Cloudy Blues.*	42.00	66.00
☐	**6291** *Lead Me All the Way.*	41.00	65.00
☐	**6307** *Midnight Special Blues.*	42.00	66.00
☐	**6379** *Hesitation Blues.*	42.00	66.00

COX, Ida

☐	**Paramount 12022** *Come Right In.*	12.00	20.00
☐	**12044** *Weary Way Blues.*	24.00	37.00
☐	**12045** *Bama Bound Blues.*	15.00	25.00
☐	**12053** *Blue Monday Blues.*	15.00	25.00
☐	**12056** *Chicago Bound Blues.*	15.00	25.00
☐	**12063** *I've Got the Blues for Rampart Street.*	27.00	44.00
☐	**12064** *Moanin' Groanin' Blues.*	26.00	43.00
☐	**12085** *Worried Mama Blues.*	26.00	43.00
☐	**12086** *Confidential Blues.*	25.00	41.00
☐	**12087** *Mail Man Blues.*	25.00	41.00
☐	**12094** *Down the Road Bound Blues.*	16.00	24.00
☐	**12097** *Mean Paper Turn Your Key.*	26.00	43.00
☐	**12202** *Chicago Monkey Man Blues.*	15.00	23.00
☐	**12220** *Kentucky Man Blues.*	14.00	22.00
☐	**12228** *Cherry Picking Blues.*	13.00	20.00
☐	**12251** *Mississippi River Blues.*	27.00	44.00
☐	**12258** *Misery Blues.*	26.00	42.00
☐	**12263** *Georgia Hound Blues.*	25.00	41.00
☐	**12275** *Mister Man.*	16.00	24.00
☐	**12282** *Someday Blues.*	15.00	23.00
☐	**12291** *Black Crepe Blues.*	14.00	22.00

			Price Range	
☐	12298	*Southern Woman's Blues.*	14.00	22.00
☐	12298	*Lonesome Blues.*	14.00	22.00
☐	12318	*Coffin Blues.*	75.00	120.00
☐	12325	*One Time Woman Blues.*	27.00	44.00
☐	12344	*Trouble Trouble Blues.*	26.00	43.00
☐	12353	*Night and Day Blues.*	26.00	43.00
☐	12381	*Don't Blame Me.*	26.00	43.00
☐	12502	*Mercy Blues.*	20.00	33.00
☐	12513	*Pleading Blues.*	18.00	30.00
☐	12540	*Mojo Hand Blues.*	20.00	33.00
☐	12556	*Seven Day Blues.*	18.00	30.00
☐	12582	*Midnight Hour Blues.*	17.00	28.00
☐	12664	*Bone Orchard Blues.*	25.00	38.00
☐	12667	*Broadcasting Blues.*	26.00	40.00
☐	12690	*Fogyism.*	25.00	37.00
☐	12704	*You Stole My Man.*	25.00	37.00
☐	12727	*Separated Blues.*	23.00	36.00
☐	12965	*Jailhouse Blues.*	55.00	90.00
DAVIS, Walter				
☐	**Bluebird 5031**	*M. & O. BLUES.*	10.00	16.00
☐	5038	*Blue Sea Blues.*	9.00	15.00
☐	5077	*Howling Wind Blues.*	9.00	15.00
☐	5094	*Hijack Blues.*	9.00	15.00
☐	5129	*Worried Man Blues.*	8.00	14.00
☐	5143	*Red Cross Blues.*	8.00	14.00
☐	5192	*Moonlight Blues.*	8.00	14.00
☐	5228	*Evil Woman.*	9.00	15.00
☐	5305	*Red Cross Blues—No. 2.*	9.00	15.00
☐	5324	*You Don't Smell Right.*	11.00	17.00
☐	5361	*What's the Use of Worryin'?*	10.00	16.00
☐	5879	*Sloppy Drunk Again.*	12.00	20.00
☐	5931	*Sweet Sixteen.*	7.00	13.00
☐	5965	*Minute Man Blues.*	7.00	13.00
☐	5982	*Sad and Lonesome Blues.*	6.00	11.00
☐	6040	*Dentist Blues.*	9.00	16.00
☐	6059	*I Can Tell By the Way You Smell.*	12.00	20.00
☐	6074	*Pearly May.*	7.00	13.00
☐	6125	*Santa Claus.*	6.00	12.00
☐	6167	*Moonlight Is My Spread.*	6.00	12.00
☐	6201	*Katy Blues.*	6.00	12.00
☐	6228	*Blues at Midnight.*	6.00	12.00
☐	6354	*Carpenter Man.*	7.00	13.00
☐	6410	*Fallin' Rain.*	6.00	11.00
☐	6468	*Jacksonville.*	7.00	13.00
☐	6996	*Good Gal.*	7.00	13.00
☐	7021	*Fifth Avenue Blues.*	10.00	18.00
☐	7064	*Angel Child.*	7.00	12.00
☐	7292	*Guiding Rod.*	7.00	12.00
☐	7329	*Holiday Blues.*	7.00	12.00
☐	7375	*Black Jack Engine Blues.*	7.00	12.00
☐	7512	*Walking the Avenue.*	7.00	12.00
☐	7551	*Easy Goin' Mama.*	7.00	12.00
☐	7589	*Million-Dollar Baby.*	7.00	12.00
☐	7643	*Candy Man.*	7.00	12.00

	Price Range	
☐ **7663** *Friendless Blues.*	7.00	12.00
☐ **7745** *Call Me Anytime.*	7.00	12.00
☐ **7792** *Love Will Kill You.*	8.00	15.00
☐ **7978** *Cuttin' Off My Days.*	7.00	12.00
☐ **8002** *Early This Mornin'.*	7.00	12.00
☐ **8026** *Smoky Mountain.*	8.00	15.00
☐ **8058** *Mercy Blues.*	8.00	15.00
☐ **8107** *Troubled and Weary.*	8.00	15.00
☐ **8261** *Big Four Blues.*	8.00	15.00
☐ **8282** *Green and Lucky.*	7.00	12.00
☐ **8312** *Bachelor Blues.*	7.00	13.00
☐ **8343** *Froggy Bottom.*	7.00	13.00
☐ **8367** *Doctor Blues.*	6.00	11.00
☐ **8393** *Sundown Blues.*	7.00	13.00
☐ **8434** *Jungle Blues.*	7.00	13.00
☐ **8470** *Western Land.*	6.00	11.00
☐ **8510** *Come Back Baby.*	6.00	11.00
DEE, Mercy		
☐ **Bayou 003** *Please Understand.*	14.00	25.00
☐ **013** *Happy Bachelor.*	13.00	23.00
☐ **Colony 102** *Straight and Narrow.*	12.00	21.00
☐ **111** *Birdbrain Baby.*	11.00	18.00
☐ **Imperial 5104** *Empty Life.*	12.00	20.00
☐ **5110** *Big Foot Country.*	12.00	20.00
☐ **5118** *Bought Love.*	11.00	18.00
☐ **5127** *Pay Off.*	11.00	18.00
☐ **Spire 11-001** *Lonesome Cabin Blues.*	14.00	25.00
☐ **11-002** *Travelin' Alone Blues.*	13.00	22.00
DIXIE JAZZ BAND		
☐ **Challenge 958** *Icky Blues.*	16.00	25.00
☐ **999** *Makin' Friends.*	11.00	19.00
☐ **Jewel 5547** *Icky Blues.*	13.00	22.00
☐ **5569** *Makin' Friends.*	11.00	18.00
☐ **5575** *Sweet Liza.*	11.00	18.00
☐ **5648** *Twelfth Street Rag.*	11.00	18.00
☐ **5685** *It's So Good.*	16.00	25.00
☐ **5729** *The Way He Loves is Just Too Bad.*	15.00	27.00
☐ **5730** *Broadway Rhythm.*	19.00	30.00
☐ **Oriole 565** *Wait Till See You My Baby Do the Charleston.*	13.00	21.00
☐ **717** *Old Folks' Shuffle.*	13.00	21.00
☐ **880** *I'm in Love Again.*	10.00	17.00
☐ **883** *Rosy Cheeks.*	9.00	16.00
☐ **952** *Memphis Blues.*	9.00	16.00
☐ **984** *Tiger Rag.*	11.00	18.00
☐ **1100** *Sorry.*	9.00	16.00
☐ **1515** *Icky Blues.*	11.00	18.00
☐ **1540** *Sweet Liza.*	9.00	16.00
☐ **1624** *Twelfth Street Rad.*	11.00	18.00
☐ **1668** *It's So Good.*	12.00	20.00
☐ **1726** *The Way He Loves is Just Too Bad.*	13.00	21.00
☐ **1728** *Broadway Rhythm.*	14.00	23.00
☐ **1730** *Doin' the Voom Voom.*	15.00	25.00
☐ **Regal 8874** *Flaming Youth.*	22.00	35.00

		Price Range	
ELLINGTON, Duke			
☐ **Brunswick 3480**	*Birmingham Breakdown.*	13.00	21.00
☐ **3987**	*Tishomingo Blues.*	12.00	20.00
☐ **4110**	*Louisiana.*	12.00	20.00
☐ **4122**	*The Mooche.*	13.00	21.00
☐ **4705**	*Jolly Wog.*	12.00	20.00
☐ **6093**	*Creole Rhapsody.*	13.00	21.00
☐ **Buddy 8010**	*If You Can't Hold the Man You Love.*	70.00	110.00
☐ **8063**	*Animal Crackers.*	70.00	110.00
☐ **Columbia 953-D**	*Hop Head.*	18.00	32.00
☐ **1076-D**	*Down in Our Alley Blues.*	16.00	26.00
☐ **Gennett 3291**	*Wanna Go Back Again Blues.*	45.00	70.00
☐ **3342**	*Animal Crackers.*	50.00	75.00
☐ **Okeh 8521**	*Black and Tan Fantasy.*	20.00	30.00
☐ **8602**	*Diga Diga Doo.*	20.00	32.00
☐ **8636**	*Black Beauty.*	18.00	28.00
☐ **8662**	*Misty Mornin'.*	18.00	28.00
☐ **40955**	*Black and Tan Fantasy.*	18.00	28.00
☐ **41013**	*Jubilee Stomp.*	18.00	28.00
☐ **Pathe-Actuelle 7504**	*Georgia Grind.*	70.00	100.00
☐ **Perfect 104**	*Georgia Grind.*	50.00	70.00
☐ **14514**	*Trombone Blues.*	40.00	65.00
☐ **Victor 21137**	*Creole Love Call.*	13.00	21.00
☐ **21284**	*Washington Wobble.*	12.00	20.00
☐ **21490**	*The Blues I Love to Sing.*	13.00	21.00
☐ **21580**	*Black Beauty.*	12.00	20.00
☐ **21703**	*Got Everything But You.*	12.00	20.00
☐ **22528**	*Three Little Words.*	8.00	12.00
☐ **22586**	*What Good Am I Without You?*	12.00	20.00
☐ **22587**	*Mood Indigo.*	9.00	14.00
☐ **22603**	*Blue Again.*	9.00	14.00
☐ **22614**	*Keep a Song in Your Soul.*	13.00	22.00
☐ **22743**	*Limehouse Blues.*	10.00	16.00
☐ **22791**	*It's Glory.*	13.00	22.00
☐ **22800**	*The Mystery Song.*	11.00	17.00
☐ **22938**	*Bugle Call Rag.*	12.00	20.00
☐ **23017**	*You're Lucky to Me.*	25.00	34.00
☐ **23022**	*Jungle Nights in Harlem.*	30.00	47.00
☐ **23036**	*Sam and Delilah.*	16.00	27.00
☐ **23041**	*Shout 'em, Aunt Tillie.*	23.00	31.00
☐ **24431**	*Rude Interlude.*	13.00	21.00
☐ **24501**	*Daybreak Express.*	8.00	12.00
☐ **24622**	*Ebony Rhapsody.*	10.00	17.00
☐ **24651**	*My Old Flame.*	9.00	16.00
☐ **24755**	*Delta Seranade.*	9.00	16.00
☐ **38007**	*Bandanna Babies.*	11.00	17.00
☐ **38008**	*Diga Diga Doo.*	11.00	17.00
☐ **38034**	*The Mooche.*	35.00	50.00
☐ **38035**	*Flaming Youth.*	20.00	34.00
☐ **38036**	*Saturday Night Function.*	20.00	34.00
☐ **38053**	*Stevedore Stomp.*	19.00	32.00
☐ **38058**	*Saratoga Swing.*	19.00	32.00
☐ **38065**	*Hot Feet.*	20.00	35.00
☐ **38079**	*Cotton Club Stomp.*	20.00	35.00

		Price Range	
ELKINS, W. C.			
☐ **QRS 7045**	*Climbing Up the Mountain.*	23.00	37.00
☐ **7046**	*Oh, Mother, Don't You Weep.*	21.00	35.00
☐ **7047**	*Roll, Roll, Chariot.*	20.00	36.00
☐ **7063**	*Eloi.*	20.00	36.00
☐ **7068**	*A Wheel in a Wheel.*	20.00	36.00
ESTES, John			
☐ **Bluebird 8871**	*Little Laura Blues.*	12.00	20.00
☐ **8950**	*Working Man Blues.*	11.00	19.00
☐ **Champion 50001**	*Stop That Thing.*	17.00	29.00
☐ **50048**	*Drop Down Mama.*	16.00	28.00
☐ **50068**	*Someday Baby Blues.*	15.00	26.00
☐ **Decca 7279**	*Someday Baby Blues.*	11.00	18.00
☐ **7289**	*Married Woman Blues.*	10.00	17.00
☐ **7325**	*Down South Blues.*	11.00	18.00
☐ **7342**	*Vernita Blues.*	11.00	18.00
☐ **7354**	*Hobo Jungle Blues.*	10.00	17.00
☐ **7365**	*Need More Blues.*	9.00	16.00
☐ **7414**	*Government Money.*	9.00	16.00
☐ **7442**	*Floating Bridge.*	10.00	17.00
☐ **7473**	*Brownsville Blues.*	9.00	16.00
☐ **7491**	*Liquor Store Blues.*	8.00	14.00
☐ **7516**	*Easin' Back to Tennessee.*	8.00	14.00
☐ **7571**	*Everybody Oughta Make a Change.*	9.00	16.00
☐ **7766**	*Drop Down.*	8.00	14.00
☐ **7814**	*Jailhouse Blues.*	8.00	14.00
☐ **Victor 23318**	*Expressman Blues.*	8.00	14.00
☐ **23397**	*Stack O'Dollars.*	70.00	115.00
☐ **38549**	*Diving Duck Blues.*	65.00	105.00
☐ **38582**	*Black Mattie Blues.*	70.00	115.00
☐ **38595**	*T-Bone Steak Blues.*	60.00	100.00
☐ **38628**	*Poor John Blues.*	60.00	100.00
EZELL, Will			
☐ **Paramount 12688**	*Mixed Up Rag.*	55.00	85.00
☐ **12729**	*Crawlin' Spider Blues.*	52.00	80.00
☐ **12753**	*Barrel House Woman.*	50.00	78.00
☐ **12773**	*Bucket of Blood.*	55.00	80.00
☐ **12914**	*Freakish Mistreater Blues.*	55.00	80.00
FOSTER, Jim			
☐ **Champion 15301**	*Riverside Blues.*	45.00	70.00
☐ **15320**	*The Jail House Blues.*	42.00	67.00
☐ **15397**	*Dark Cloudy Blues.*	40.00	63.00
☐ **15453**	*It Won't Be Long.*	38.00	62.00
☐ **15472**	*Hesitation Blues.*	38.00	62.00
GEORGIA MELODIANS			
☐ **Edison 51336**	*Wop Blues.*	15.00	24.00
☐ **51338**	*Wait'll You See My Gal.*	10.00	17.00
☐ **51346**	*Savannah.*	11.00	18.00
☐ **51347**	*Tea Pot Dome Blues.*	10.00	17.00
☐ **51359**	*How You Gonna Keep Kool?*	9.00	16.00
☐ **51378**	*Why Did You Do It?*	9.00	16.00
☐ **51412**	*San.*	9.00	16.00

	Price Range	
☐ **51419** *Everybody Loves My Baby.*	9.00	16.00
☐ **51420** *Do Wacka Doo.*	8.00	14.00
☐ **51425** *I'm Satisfied Beside That Sweetie O'Mine.*	9.00	16.00
☐ **51437** *I'm Bound for Tennessee.*	9.00	16.00
☐ **51588** *Give Us the Charleston.*	12.00	20.00
☐ **51598** *She's Drivin' Me Wild.*	12.00	20.00
☐ **51678** *Charleston Ball.*	12.00	20.00
☐ **51730** *Rhythm of the Day.*	12.00	20.00
GEORGIA TOM		
☐ **Champion 16237** *Been Mistreated Blues.*	55.00	80.00
☐ **16360** *Don't Leave Me Blues.*	45.00	72.00
☐ **Decca 7362** *Levee Bound Blues.*	6.00	9.00
☐ **Gennett 6919** *My Texas Blues.*	42.00	75.00
☐ **6933** *Suicide Blues.*	40.00	70.00
☐ **7008** *Pig Meat Blues.*	42.00	75.00
☐ **7041** *Rollin' Mill Stomp.*	43.00	75.00
☐ **7130** *Six Shooter Blues.*	41.00	70.00
☐ **Supertone 9506** *My Texas Blues.*	41.00	70.00
☐ **9507** *Pig Meat Blues.*	44.00	75.00
☐ **9508** *Eagle Ridin' Papa.*	41.00	70.00
☐ **9512** *Rollin' Mill Stomp.*	41.00	70.00
☐ **Vocalion 1216** *Grievin' Me Blues.*	20.00	31.00
☐ **1246** *Lonesome Man Blues.*	18.00	30.00
☐ **1282** *If You Want Me to Love You.*	18.00	30.00
☐ **1685** *Don't Leave Me Here.*	13.00	22.00
GIBSON, Clifford		
☐ **Paramount 12866** *Tired of Being Mistreated.*	55.00	80.00
☐ **12923** *Stop Your Rambling.*	50.00	76.00
☐ **QRS 7079** *Tired of Being Mistreated.*	100.00	150.00
☐ **7082** *No No Blues.*	110.00	170.00
☐ **7083** *Stop Your Rambling.*	90.00	140.00
☐ **7087** *Whiskey Moan Blues.*	100.00	150.00
☐ **7090** *Morgan Street Blues.*	100.00	150.00
☐ **Victor 23255** *Old Time Rider.*	45.00	75.00
☐ **38562** *Ice and Snow Blues.*	41.00	70.00
☐ **38572** *Don't Put That Thing On Me.*	40.00	65.00
☐ **38577** *Levee Camp Moan.*	34.00	62.00
☐ **38290** *Bad Luck Dice.*	40.00	65.00
☐ **38612** *Society Blues.*	40.00	65.00
GLINN, Lillian		
☐ **Columbia 14275-D** *Doggin' Me Blues.*	10.00	17.00
☐ **14300-D** *Come Home Daddy.*	9.00	16.00
☐ **14315-D** *Shake It Down.*	9.00	16.00
☐ **14360-D** *Lost Letter Blues.*	9.00	16.00
☐ **14421-D** *Atlanta Blues.*	15.00	27.00
☐ **14433-D** *Black Man Blues.*	14.00	25.00
☐ **14493-D** *Don't Leave Me Daddy.*	14.00	25.00
☐ **14559-D** *I Love That Thing.*	13.00	23.00
☐ **14617-D** *Cannon Ball Blues.*	14.00	25.00
GORDON, Roscoe		
☐ **Duke 109** *Too Many Women.*	6.00	9.00
☐ **Flip 227** *Weeping Blues.*	12.00	20.00

	Price Range	
☐ **RPM 322** *Roscoe's Boogie*	6.00	9.00
☐ **336** *Dime a Dozen*	6.00	9.00
☐ **350** *No More Doggin'*	6.00	9.00
☐ **365** *Two Kinds of Women*	6.00	9.00
☐ **Sun 227** *Weeping Blues*	15.00	22.00
GRIFFIN, Tommy		
☐ **Bluebird 6696** *I'm Gonna Try That Meat*	10.00	17.00
☐ **6734** *Young Heifer Blues*	9.00	15.00
☐ **6756** *Dream Book Blues*	9.00	15.00
☐ **6793** *On My Way Blues*	9.00	15.00
☐ **6834** *Dying Sinner Blues—Part 2*	10.00	17.00
☐ **Vocalion 1479** *Bell Tolling Blues*	23.00	37.00
☐ **1507** *Mistreatment Blues*	21.00	34.00
GROSS, Helen		
☐ **Ajaz 17042** *I Wanna Jazz Some More*	36.00	52.00
☐ **17046** *Rockin' Chair Blues*	34.00	50.00
☐ **17049** *What'll I Do?*	33.00	50.00
☐ **17051** *My Man Ain't Yo' Man*	32.00	49.00
☐ **17060** *Ticket Agent, Ease Your Window Down*	31.00	47.00
☐ **17062** *Chicago Monkey Man Blues*	32.00	48.00
☐ **17071** *Neglected Blues*	33.00	49.00
☐ **17077** *If You Can't Ride Slow and Easy*	32.00	48.00
☐ **17082** *Conjure Man Blues*	33.00	49.00
☐ **17086** *Bitter Feelin' Blues*	31.00	47.00
☐ **17090** *Last Journey Blues*	30.00	46.00
☐ **17133** *Workin' Woman's Blues*	33.00	49.00
HANDY, W. C.		
☐ **Banner 1036** *St. Louis Blues*	17.00	27.00
☐ **1053** *She's a Mean Job*	16.00	25.00
☐ **Black Swan 2053** *Yellow Dog Blues*	25.00	40.00
☐ **2054** *Muscle Shoals Blues*	27.00	42.00
☐ **Lyratone 4211** *Beale Street Blues*	21.00	34.00
☐ **4212** *Yellow Dog Blues*	20.00	32.00
☐ **Paramount 20098** *St. Louis Blues*	15.00	22.00
☐ **20012** *She's a Mean Job*	14.00	21.00
HARLEM FOOTWARMERS		
☐ **Columbia 14670-D** *Sweet Chariot*	29.00	45.00
☐ **Okeh 8720** *Jungle Jamboree*	28.00	43.00
☐ **8746** *Syncopated Shuffle*	24.00	40.00
☐ **8760** *Lazy Duke*	28.00	43.00
☐ **8836** *Big House Blues*	29.00	45.00
☐ **8869** *Old Man Blues*	27.00	42.00

HARRIS, William	Price Range	
☐ **Gennett 6306** *I'm Leavin' Town.*	36.00	55.00
☐ **6661** *Bull Frog Blues.*	35.00	53.00
☐ **6677** *Kitchen Range Blues.*	34.00	50.00
☐ **6693** *Leavin' Here Blues.*	36.00	52.00
☐ **6707** *Kansas City Blues.*	36.00	52.00
☐ **6737** *I'm a Roamin' Gambler.*	33.00	51.00
☐ **6752** *Electric Chair Blues.*	35.00	52.00
☐ **6904** *Nothin' Right Blues.*	32.00	50.00
HAYES, Clifford		
☐ **Victor 20955** *Blue Guitar Stomp.*	12.00	20.00
☐ **21489** *Bare-Foot Stomp.*	26.00	41.00
☐ **21583** *Blue Harmony.*	13.00	21.00
☐ **23346** *Tenor Guitar Fiend.*	37.00	52.00
☐ **23407** *Automobile Blues.*	55.00	90.00
☐ **38011** *Clef Club Stomp.*	26.00	41.00
☐ **38022** *Ool Chord's Stomp.*	25.00	39.00
☐ **38514** *Frog Hop.*	33.00	53.00
☐ **38557** *Hey! Am I Blue.*	40.00	60.00
HENDERSON, Fletcher		
☐ **Ajax 17016** *Bull Blues.*	24.00	37.00
☐ **17017** *Chattanooga.*	23.00	35.00
☐ **17022** *Mistreatin' Daddy.*	22.00	34.00
☐ **17023** *House Rent Ball.*	23.00	35.00
☐ **17029** *Just Blues.*	22.00	34.00
☐ **17030** *I'm Crazy Over You.*	23.00	35.00
☐ **17109** *Everybody Loves My Baby.*	50.00	70.00
☐ **17113** *Alabama Bound.*	27.00	45.00
☐ **17114** *I'll See You in My Dreams.*	27.00	44.00
☐ **17123** *Why Couldn't It Be Poor Little Me?*	25.00	41.00
☐ **Apex 8300** *Everybody Loves My Baby.*	43.00	63.00
☐ **8309** *Alabamy Bound.*	12.00	22.00
☐ **8311** *I'll See You in My Dreams.*	12.00	22.00
☐ **8316** *Why Couldn't It Be Poor Little Me?*	12.00	22.00
☐ **8419** *Sleepy Time Gal.*	12.00	22.00
☐ **Black Swan 2022** *My Oriental Rose.*	13.00	21.00
☐ **2026** *The Unknown Blues.*	22.00	34.00
☐ **2076** *Love Days.*	14.00	25.00
☐ **2079** *Blue.*	14.00	25.00
☐ **10072** *Love Days.*	14.00	25.00
☐ **10075** *Blue.*	13.00	21.00
☐ **10083** *Dumbell.*	12.00	19.00
☐ **Bluebird 5682** *Hocus Pocus.*	9.00	16.00
☐ **Brunswick 2592** *War Horse Mama.*	6.00	9.00
☐ **3460** *Stockholm Stomp.*	11.00	19.00
☐ **3521** *Sensation.*	11.00	19.00
☐ **4119** *Hop Off.*	11.00	19.00
☐ **Cameo 9033** *Old Black Joe's Blues.*	12.00	20.00
☐ **9174** *Freeze and Melt.*	11.00	17.00
☐ **9175** *Raisin' the Roof.*	10.00	16.00
☐ **Columbia 1543-D** *King Porter Stomp.*	8.00	13.00
☐ **1913-D** *Blazin'.*	7.00	12.00
☐ **126-D** *Somebody Stole My Gal.*	9.00	16.00
☐ **164-D** *Muscle Shoals Blues.*	8.00	15.00

	Record	Title	Price Range	
☐	202-D	*That's Georgia*	8.00	15.00
☐	209-D	*He's the Hottest Man in Town*	7.00	13.00
☐	228-D	*Manda*	13.00	21.00
☐	249-D	*The Meanest Kind of Blues*	12.00	20.00
☐	292-D	*Play Me Slow*	11.00	18.00
☐	383-D	*Money Blues*	14.00	23.00
☐	395-D	*Sugar Foot Stomp*	13.00	23.00
☐	509-D	*Carolina Stomp*	13.00	23.00
☐	532-D	*Pensacola*	14.00	25.00
☐	654-D	*The Stampede*	13.00	23.00
☐	817-D	*The Chant*	14.00	25.00
☐	854-D	*Sweet Thing*	12.00	21.00
☐	970-D	*Rocky Mountain Blues*	14.00	25.00
☐	1059-D	*Whiteman Stomp*	15.00	26.00
☐	1543-D	*King Porter Stomp*	11.00	18.00
☐	1913-D	*Blazin'*	13.00	22.00
☐	2329-D	*Somebody Loves Me*	13.00	22.00
☐	2353-D	*Keep a Song In Your Soul*	14.00	23.00
☐	2414-D	*Sweet and Hot*	13.00	22.00
☐	2513-D	*Clarinet Marmalade*	13.00	22.00
☐	2559-D	*Sugar*	14.00	23.00
☐	2565-D	*Singin' the Blues*	14.00	23.00
☐	2586-D	*My Gal Sal*	13.00	22.00
☐	2615-D	*Business in F*	14.00	23.00
☐	2732-D	*Honeysuckle Rose*	14.00	23.00
☐	2825-D	*Nagasaki*	15.00	25.00
☐	A-3995	*Dicty Blues*	9.00	16.00
☐	14392-D	*Easy Money*	21.00	32.00
☐	2329-D	*Somebody Loves Me*	14.00	23.00
☐	2352-D	*Keep a Song In Your Soul*	13.00	22.00
☐	2414-D	*Sweet and Hot*	14.00	25.00
☐	2513-D	*Clarinet Marmalade*	13.00	22.00
☐	2559-D	*Sugar*	14.00	25.00
☐	2586-D	*My Gal Sal*	14.00	25.00
☐	2615-D	*Business in F*	13.00	21.00
☐	2732-D	*Honeysuckle Rose*	14.00	25.00
☐	2825-D	*Nagasaki*	17.00	30.00
☐	14392-D	*Easy Money*	14.00	23.00
☐	**Crown 3093**	*After You've Gone*	18.00	28.00
☐	3107	*Tiger Rag*	17.00	27.00
☐	**Edison 51276**	*Shake Your Feet*	10.00	12.00
☐	51277	*Linger Awhile*	10.00	12.00
☐	**Emerson 10714**	*Steppin' Out*	12.00	20.00
☐	10744	*Ghost of the Blues*	13.00	22.00
☐	**Gennett 3285**	*When Spring Comes Peeping Through*	19.00	29.00
☐	3286	*Honeybunch*	17.00	28.00
☐	**Lincoln 3062**	*Old Black Joe's Blues*	12.00	17.00
☐	3201	*Freeze and Melt*	15.00	23.00
☐	3202	*Raisin' the Roof*	14.00	22.00
☐	**Paramount 12143**	*Chime Blues*	20.00	30.00
☐	12486	*Off to Buffalo*	28.00	40.00
☐	20367	*Prince of Wails*	37.00	60.00

		Price Range	
☐ **Romeo 837**	*Old Black Joe's Blues.*	12.00	21.00
☐ **976**	*Freeze and Melt.*	13.00	22.00
☐ **977**	*Raisin' the Roof.*	12.00	21.00
☐ **Victor 22775**	*Malinda's Wedding Day.*	9.00	16.00
☐ **22786**	*Oh, It Looks Like Rain.*	9.00	16.00
☐ **22955**	*Strangers.*	9.00	16.00
☐ **24008**	*Poor Old Joe.*	9.00	16.00
☐ **24699**	*Harlem Madness.*	9.00	16.00
☐ **Vocalion 14636**	*Gulf Coast Blues.*	10.00	16.00
☐ **14654**	*Dicty Blues.*	11.00	18.00
☐ **14691**	*Just Hot.*	10.00	16.00
☐ **14726**	*Charleston Crazy.*	10.00	16.00
☐ **14740**	*Potomac River Blues.*	9.00	13.00
☐ **14759**	*Lots O'Mama.*	10.00	16.00
☐ **14788**	*Chicago Blues.*	11.00	17.00
☐ **14828**	*Strutter's Drag.*	11.00	17.00
☐ **14838**	*Do That Thing.*	11.00	17.00
☐ **14880**	*A New Kind of Man.*	11.00	17.00
☐ **14892**	*Forsaken Blues.*	9.00	15.00
☐ **14926**	*Copenhagen.*	16.00	27.00
☐ **14935**	*Shanghai Shuffle.*	16.00	27.00
☐ **15030**	*Memphis Bound.*	36.00	60.00
HICKS, Edna			
☐ **Ajax 17006**	*Just Thinkin'.*	18.00	30.00
☐ **Paramount 12023**	*Hard Luck Blues.*	17.00	26.00
☐ **12089**	*Cemetery Blues.*	18.00	29.00
☐ **12090**	*Where Can That Somebody Be?*	16.00	25.00
☐ **12204**	*Down on the Levee Blues.*	17.00	26.00
☐ **Vocalion 14650**	*You've Got Everything.*	14.00	23.00
HOKUM BOYS			
☐ **Broadway 5060**	*It's All Worn Out.*	33.00	50.00
☐ **5078**	*Cut That Out.*	33.00	50.00
☐ **Champion 16081**	*Pig Meat Strut.*	70.00	110.00
☐ **16237**	*Hip Shakin' Strut.*	60.00	95.00
☐ **16360**	*Hokum Stomp.*	60.00	95.00
☐ **Okeh 8747**	*Gin Mill Blues.*	27.00	45.00
☐ **8788**	*That's My Business.*	26.00	43.00
☐ **Paramount 12714**	*Selling That Stuff.*	25.00	42.00
☐ **12746**	*Pat-A-Foot Blues.*	24.00	41.00
☐ **12777**	*Better Cut That Out.*	30.00	47.00
☐ **12778**	*Selling That Stuff.*	28.00	46.00
☐ **12811**	*Hokum Blues.*	30.00	47.00
☐ **12821**	*Ain't Goin' That Way.*	26.00	43.00
☐ **12858**	*Went To His Head.*	26.00	43.00
☐ **12882**	*I Was Afraid of That.*	27.00	45.00
☐ **12897**	*Let Me Have It.*	26.00	43.00
☐ **12919**	*Gambler's Blues—No. 2.*	26.00	43.00
☐ **12935**	*The Folks Down Stairs.*	27.00	45.00
HOWELL, Peg Leg			
☐ **Columbia 14194-D**	*Coal Man Blues.*	18.00	30.00
☐ **14210-D**	*New Jelly Roll Blues.*	17.00	27.00
☐ **14238-D**	*Sadie Lee Blues.*	16.00	26.00
☐ **14270-D**	*Hobo Blues.*	17.00	27.00

		Price Range	
☐	**14298-D** *Peg Leg Stomp.*	16.00	26.00
☐	**14320-D** *Rock and Gravel Blues.*	15.00	25.00
☐	**14356-D** *Fairy Blues.*	16.00	27.00
☐	**14426-D** *Monkey Man Blues.*	16.00	27.00
☐	**14438-D** *Rolling Mill Blues.*	15.00	25.00
☐	**14456-D** *Turtle Dove Blues.*	15.00	25.00
☐	**14473-D** *Skin Game Blues.*	18.00	30.00

HUNTER, Alberta

☐	**Black Swan 2008** *Bring Back the Joys.*	32.00	50.00
☐	**2019** *Someday Sweetheart.*	27.00	46.00
☐	**Columbia 14450-D** *My Particular Man.*	14.00	24.00
☐	**Okeh 8268** *Your Jelly Roll Is Good.*	17.00	28.00
☐	**8278** *Everybody Does It Now.*	12.00	20.00
☐	**8294** *I'm Hard to Satisfy.*	12.00	20.00
☐	**8315** *Empty Cellar Blues.*	12.00	20.00
☐	**8365** *You For Me, Me For You.*	9.00	14.00
☐	**8383** *Everybody Mess Around.*	14.00	21.00
☐	**8393** *Wasn't It Nice?*	12.00	20.00
☐	**8409** *Don't Forget to Mess Around.*	11.00	18.00
☐	**Paramount 12001** *Daddy Blues.*	12.00	20.00
☐	**12005** *Down Hearted Blues.*	13.00	21.00
☐	**12006** *Jazzin' Baby Blues.*	13.00	21.00
☐	**12008** *You Can't Have It All.*	12.00	20.00
☐	**12010** *After All These Years.*	12.00	20.00
☐	**12012** *Someday Sweetheart.*	11.00	18.00
☐	**12014** *Bring Back the Joys.*	12.00	20.00
☐	**12016** *'Tain't Nobody's Bizness.*	11.00	18.00
☐	**12017** *Chirping the Blues.*	12.00	20.00
☐	**12018** *Bring It With You When You Come.*	17.00	28.00
☐	**12019** *Loveless Love.*	16.00	26.00
☐	**12021** *Bleeding Hearted Blues.*	17.00	30.00
☐	**12036** *Michigan Water Blues.*	18.00	32.00
☐	**12043** *Mistreated Blues.*	17.00	30.00
☐	**12049** *Stingaree Blues.*	17.00	30.00
☐	**12065** *Experience Blues.*	22.00	36.00
☐	**12093** *Old-Fashioned Love.*	13.00	22.00
☐	**Victor 20497** *I'll Forgive You 'Cause I Love You.*	12.00	21.00
☐	**20651** *My Old Daddy's Got a Brand New*	11.00	20.00
☐	**20771** *Sugar.*	14.00	25.00
☐	**21539** *I'm Going to See My Ma.*	23.00	35.00

JACKSON, Charlie

☐	**Okeh 8954** *Skoodle-Um-Skoo.*	15.00	23.00
☐	**8957** *If I Got What You Want.*	16.00	25.00
☐	**Paramount 12219** *Papa's Lawdy Lawdy Blues.*	12.00	20.00
☐	**12236** *Salty Dog Blues.*	13.00	21.00
☐	**12259** *The Cat's Got the Measles.*	12.00	20.00
☐	**12264** *Coffee Pot Blues.*	12.00	20.00
☐	**12281** *Shake That Thing.*	12.00	20.00
☐	**12289** *Drop That Sack.*	12.00	20.00
☐	**12305** *Mama, Don't You Think I Know?*	12.00	20.00
☐	**12320** *Maxwell Street Blues.*	12.00	20.00
☐	**12335** *Texas Blues.*	10.00	16.00
☐	**12348** *Jackson's Blues.*	10.00	17.00

		Price Range	
☐	**12358** *Butter and Egg Man Blues.*	9.00	16.00
☐	**12366** *The Judge Cliff Davis Blues.*	11.00	18.00
☐	**12375** *Up the Way Bound.*	11.00	18.00
☐	**12383** *Bad Luck Woman Blues.*	10.00	17.00
☐	**12422** *Fat Mouth Blues.*	11.00	18.00
☐	**12461** *Coal Man Blues.*	13.00	22.00
☐	**12501** *Skoodle Um Skoo.*	13.00	22.00
☐	**12574** *Bright Eyes.*	14.00	23.00
☐	**12602** *Long Gone Lost John.*	13.00	21.00
☐	**12660** *Ash Tray Blues.*	14.00	23.00
☐	**12700** *Lexington Kentucky Blues.*	16.00	27.00
☐	**12721** *Corn Liquor Blues.*	17.00	28.00
☐	**12736** *Don't Break Down On Me.*	17.00	28.00
☐	**12765** *We Can't Buy It No More.*	20.00	30.00
☐	**12797** *Tailor Made Lover.*	17.00	29.00
☐	**12853** *Forgotten Blues.*	17.00	29.00
☐	**12905** *I'll Be Gone Babe.*	16.00	25.00
☐	**12911** *Papa Charlie and Blind Blake Talk About It.*	36.00	55.00
☐	**12956** *Self Experience.*	24.00	38.00

JACKSON, Jim

☐	**Victor 21268** *Bootlegging Blues.*	18.00	30.00
☐	**21387** *Old Dog Blue.*	17.00	27.00
☐	**21671** *I'm Gonna Move to Louisiana.*	18.00	30.00
☐	**38505** *What a Time.*	16.00	25.00
☐	**38517** *Traveling Man.*	17.00	27.00
☐	**38525** *Going 'Round the Mountain.*	17.00	27.00
☐	**Vocalion 1145** *Mobile Central Blues.*	18.00	29.00
☐	**1146** *He's in the Jailhouse Now.*	17.00	26.00
☐	**1164** *I'm a Bad Bad Man.*	17.00	26.00
☐	**1284** *Hey Mama, It's Nice Like That.*	18.00	29.00
☐	**1295** *Foot Achin' Blues.*	17.00	26.00
☐	**1413** *Ain't You Sorry Mama?*	16.00	25.00
☐	**1428** *Jim Jackson's Jamboree.*	16.00	24.00
☐	**1477** *Hesitation Blues.*	15.00	23.00

JAMES, Skip

☐	**Paramount 13065** *Cherry Ball Blues.*	120.00	185.00
☐	**13066** *22-20 Blues.*	130.00	210.00
☐	**13072** *Illinois Blues.*	120.00	185.00
☐	**13085** *How Long 'Buck'.*	110.00	175.00
☐	**13088** *Devil Got My Woman.*	120.00	185.00
☐	**13098** *Special Rider Blues.*	110.00	175.00
☐	**13106** *Hard Luck Child.*	110.00	175.00
☐	**13108** *Be Ready When He Comes.*	105.00	170.00
☐	**13111** *Drunken Spree.*	120.00	185.00

JEFFERSON, Blind Lemon

☐	**Paramount 12347** *Booster Blues.*	27.00	42.00
☐	**12354** *Got the Blues.*	26.00	40.00
☐	**12367** *Black Horse Blues.*	27.00	41.00
☐	**12373** *Jack O'Diamond Blues.*	26.00	40.00
☐	**12394** *Beggin' Back.*	25.00	38.00
☐	**12407** *Stockin' Feet Blues.*	25.00	38.00
☐	**12425** *Wartime Blues.*	25.00	38.00
☐	**12443** *Bad Luck Blues.*	24.00	37.00

		Price Range	
☐	**12454** *Rabbit Foot Blues.*	**24.00**	**37.00**
☐	**12493** *Weary Dog Blues.*	**34.00**	**50.00**
☐	**12510** *Right of Way Blues.*	**33.00**	**48.00**
☐	**12541** *Rambler Blues.*	**30.00**	**47.00**
☐	**12551** *Chinch Bug Blues.*	**31.00**	**48.00**
☐	**12578** *Gone Dead on You Blues.*	**32.00**	**50.00**
☐	**12585** *He Arose from the Dead.*	**34.00**	**52.00**
☐	**12593** *Lonesome House Blues.*	**34.00**	**52.00**
☐	**12608** *'Lectric Chair Blues.*	**35.00**	**54.00**
☐	**12622** *Prison Cell Blues.*	**35.00**	**54.00**
☐	**12631** *Mean Jumper Blues.*	**33.00**	**52.00**
☐	**12639** *Lemon's Cannon Ball Moan.*	**32.00**	**50.00**
☐	**12650** *Piney Woods Mama Blues.*	**31.00**	**49.00**
☐	**12666** *Blind Lemon's Penitentiary Blues.*	**45.00**	**70.00**
☐	**12679** *Lock Step Blues.*	**31.00**	**52.00**
☐	**12685** *How Long How Long.*	**31.00**	**52.00**
☐	**12712** *Maltese Cat Blues.*	**31.00**	**52.00**
☐	**12728** *Competition Bed Blues.*	**32.00**	**55.00**
☐	**12739** *Eagle Eyed Mama.*	**31.00**	**48.00**
☐	**12756** *Tin Cup Blues.*	**32.00**	**55.00**
☐	**12771** *Oil Well Blues.*	**31.00**	**48.00**
☐	**12801** *Peach Orchard Mama.*	**31.00**	**48.00**
☐	**12852** *Long Distance Moan.*	**30.00**	**47.00**
☐	**12872** *Bed Springs Blues.*	**32.00**	**55.00**
☐	**12880** *Pneumonia Blues.*	**31.00**	**48.00**
☐	**12921** *Cat Man Blues.*	**31.00**	**48.00**
☐	**12933** *The Cheaters Spell.*	**31.00**	**48.00**
☐	**12946** *Empty House Blues.*	**30.00**	**47.00**
JEFFRIES, SPEED			
☐	**Superior 2648** *Georgia Grind.*	**85.00**	**135.00**
☐	**2670** *Kentucky Blues.*	**80.00**	**125.00**
☐	**2728** *Stomp Your Stuff.*	**80.00**	**125.00**
☐	**2755** *Tiger Moan.*	**80.00**	**125.00**
☐	**2797** *Richmond Stomp.*	**75.00**	**120.00**
JACKSON, Big Bill			
☐	**Champion 16081** *Saturday Night Rub.*	**50.00**	**75.00**
☐	**16172** *That Won't Do.*	**48.00**	**72.00**
☐	**16327** *The Baker's Blues.*	**47.00**	**70.00**
☐	**16396** *Worried in Mind Blues.*	**46.00**	**70.00**
☐	**16426** *Mr. Conductor Man.*	**47.00**	**70.00**
☐	**50060** *Big Bill Blues.*	**13.00**	**22.00**
☐	**50069** *Too Too Train Blues.*	**13.00**	**22.00**
JOHNSON, Lonnie			
☐	**Columbia 14667-D** *Home Wreckers Blues.*	**27.00**	**40.00**
☐	**14674-D** *Unselfish Love.*	**26.00**	**37.00**
☐	**Okeh 8253** *Mr. Johnson's Blues.*	**16.00**	**26.00**
☐	**8282** *Love Story Blues.*	**14.00**	**23.00**
☐	**8291** *Bed of Sand.*	**13.00**	**23.00**
☐	**8340** *A Good Happy Home.*	**13.00**	**23.00**
☐	**8358** *Good Old Wagon.*	**15.00**	**23.00**
☐	**8376** *Baby Please Tell Me.*	**15.00**	**23.00**
☐	**8391** *Oh! Doctor, The Blues.*	**13.00**	**23.00**
☐	**8417** *Johnson Trio Stomp.*	**15.00**	**23.00**

		Price Range	
☐ 8435	*Ball and Chain Blues.*	13.00	23.00
☐ 8451	*You Drove a Good Man Away.*	12.00	21.00
☐ 8466	*South Bound Water.*	14.00	23.00
☐ 8484	*Treat 'em Right.*	14.00	23.00
☐ 8505	*Fickle Mamma Blues.*	14.00	23.00
☐ 8512	*St. Louis Cyclone Blues.*	14.00	23.00
☐ 8524	*Tin Can Alley Blues.*	14.00	23.00
☐ 8537	*Kansas City Blues.*	13.00	23.00
☐ 8557	*Life Saver Blues.*	13.00	23.00
☐ 8558	*Playing With the Strings.*	13.00	23.00
☐ 8574	*Crowing Rooster Blues.*	12.00	21.00
☐ 8575	*Blues in G.*	13.00	23.00
☐ 8586	*Bed Bug Blues No. 2.*	13.00	22.00
☐ 8601	*Wrong Woman Blues.*	14.00	23.00
☐ 8618	*Broken Levee Blues.*	13.00	22.00
☐ 8635	*Careless Love.*	13.00	22.00
☐ 8664	*It Feels So Good—Part 1/2.*	9.00	14.00
☐ 8691	*Death is on Your Track.*	13.00	22.00
☐ 8695	*Bull Frog Moan.*	12.00	20.00
☐ 8697	*It Feels So Good—Part 3/4.*	9.00	14.00
☐ 8709	*Mr. Johnson's Blues—No. 2.*	13.00	22.00
☐ 8754	*Sundown Blues.*	13.00	22.00
☐ 8762	*Wipe It Off.*	20.00	34.00
☐ 8768	*She's Making Whoopee in Hell Tonight.*	22.00	35.00
☐ 8775	*The Dirty Dozen.*	20.00	32.00
☐ 8786	*Headed for Southland.*	18.00	31.00
☐ 8796	*Don't Drive Me From Your Door.*	16.00	27.00
☐ 8802	*The Bull Frog and the Toad.*	17.00	30.00
☐ 8812	*Keep it to Yourself.*	15.00	26.00
☐ 8822	*Deep Sea Blues.*	15.00	26.00
☐ 8831	*No More Troubles Now.*	17.00	27.00
☐ 8846	*Let All Married Women Alone.*	17.00	27.00
☐ 8875	*Just a Roaming Man.*	18.00	28.00
☐ 8886	*I Just Can't Stand These Blues.*	18.00	28.00
☐ 8898	*Beautiful But Dumb.*	18.00	28.00
☐ 8909	*I Have To Do My Time.*	16.00	27.00
☐ 8916	*The Best Jockey in Town.*	16.00	27.00
☐ 8926	*Sleepy Water Blues.*	18.00	28.00
☐ 8937	*Sam, You're Just a Rat.*	16.00	27.00
☐ 8946	*Racketeers Blues.*	17.00	28.00
☐ 40695	*Nile of Genago.*	9.00	13.00
☐ Paradise 110	*Tomorrow Night.*	15.00	26.00
☐ 123	*Lonesome Day Blues.*	15.00	26.00

JOHNSON, Margaret

☐ Okeh 8107	*E Flat Blues.*	10.00	15.00
☐ 8162	*Absent Minded Blues.*	10.00	15.00
☐ 8185	*Changeable Daddy of Mine.*	27.00	41.00
☐ 8193	*Who'll Chop Your Suey When I'm Gone.*	15.00	24.00
☐ 8220	*Nobody's Blues But Mine.*	11.00	18.00
☐ 8230	*I'm a Good-Hearted Mama.*	17.00	26.00
☐ 8405	*Mama, Papa Don't Wanna Come Back Home.*	9.00	16.00
☐ 8506	*Stinging Bee Blues.*	14.00	23.00

		Price Range	
☐ **Victor 20178**	*My Man's Done Me Dirty.*	9.00	16.00
☐ **20333**	*Graysom Street Blues.*	18.00	30.00
☐ **20982**	*Dead Drunk Blues.*	17.00	27.00
JOHNSON, Stump			
☐ **Bluebird 5159**	*Don't Give My Lard Away.*	13.00	22.00
☐ **5247**	*Money Johnson.*	12.00	20.00
☐ **Paramount 12862**	*Kind Babe Blues.*	45.00	70.00
☐ **12906**	*Soaking Wet Blues.*	43.00	67.00
☐ **12938**	*You Buzzard You.*	41.00	65.00
☐ **Victor 23327**	*Barrel of Whiskey Blues.*	43.00	67.00
BLIND WILLIE JOHNSON			
☐ **Columbia 14303-D**	*Nobody's Fault But Mine.*	15.00	22.00
☐ **14343-D**	*Mother's Children Have a Hard Time.*	13.00	21.00
☐ **14391-D**	*Jesus is Coming Soon.*	15.00	22.00
☐ **14490-D**	*Let Your Light Shine On.*	14.00	21.00
☐ **14520-D**	*God Moves on the Water.*	14.00	21.00
☐ **14530-D**	*John the Revelator.*	42.00	65.00
☐ **14537-D**	*The Rain Don't Fall on Me.*	15.00	21.00
☐ **14545-D**	*When the War Was On.*	15.00	23.00
☐ **14556-D**	*Can't Nobody Hide From God.*	15.00	23.00
☐ **14582-D**	*The Soul of a Man.*	14.00	21.00
☐ **14597-D**	*Go With Me to That Land.*	14.00	21.00
☐ **14624-D**	*Take Your Stand.*	14.00	21.00
JONES, Alberta			
☐ **Buddy 8024**	*Sud Bustin' Blues.*	29.00	42.00
☐ **8025**	*Home Alone Blues.*	27.00	40.00
☐ **8033**	*It Must Be Hard.*	58.00	90.00
☐ **8034**	*Take Your Fingers Off It.*	62.00	100.00
☐ **Gennett 3306**	*Take Your Fingers Off It.*	12.00	20.00
☐ **3402**	*Lucky Number Blues.*	33.00	50.00
☐ **6424**	*Dying Blues.*	29.00	43.00
☐ **6439**	*Shake a Little Bit.*	27.00	40.00
☐ **6535**	*My Slow and Easy Man.*	25.00	38.00
☐ **6642**	*Wild Geese Blues.*	37.00	59.00
☐ **7252**	*On Revival Day.*	27.00	39.00
☐ **7274**	*I Lost My Man.*	28.00	41.00
☐ **Silvertone 4052**	*Home Alone Blues.*	12.00	20.00
☐ **5025**	*Lucky Number Blues.*	27.00	41.00
☐ **Supertone 9284**	*Dying Blues.*	23.00	34.00
JUNGLE BAND			
☐ **Brunswick 3956**	*Tiger Rag.*	9.00	15.00
☐ **4238**	*Tiger Rad.*	12.00	20.00
☐ **4309**	*Paducah.*	11.00	19.00
☐ **4345**	*Doin' the Voom Voom.*	11.00	19.00
☐ **4450**	*Dog Bottom.*	13.00	21.00
☐ **4492**	*Jungle Jamboree.*	11.00	19.00
☐ **4760**	*Sweet Mama.*	12.00	20.00
☐ **4776**	*Maori.*	11.00	19.00
☐ **4783**	*Double Check Stomp.*	11.00	19.00
☐ **4889**	*Wall Street Wall.*	9.00	16.00
☐ **4936**	*St. Louis Blues.*	12.00	20.00
☐ **4952**	*Runnin' Wild.*	12.00	20.00

		Price Range	
☐	6038 *Rockin' in Rhythm.*	10.00	17.00
☐	6732 *Rockin' Chair.*	8.00	13.00
KANSAS JOE			
☐	**Bluebird 6260** *Something Gonna Happen to You.*	10.00	16.00
☐	**Columbia 14439-D** *When the Levee Breaks.*	18.00	29.00
☐	14542-D *I Want That.*	17.00	26.00
☐	**Vocalion 1500** *What Fault You Find of Me?*	16.00	25.00
☐	1523 *Can I Do It For You?*	17.00	26.00
☐	1535 *Cherry Ball Blues.*	16.00	25.00
☐	1550 *North Memphis Blues.*	15.00	24.00
☐	1570 *Botherin' That Thing.*	15.00	24.00
☐	1612 *Pile Drivin' Blues.*	16.00	25.00
☐	1631 *I Called Up This Morning.*	16.00	25.00
☐	1643 *Preachers Blues.*	15.00	24.00
☐	1660 *Pickin' the Blues.*	22.00	38.00
☐	1668 *My Wash Woman's Gone.*	15.00	24.00
☐	1686 *Joliet Bound.*	14.00	23.00
☐	1688 *You Stole My Cake.*	15.00	25.00
☐	1705 *Dresser Drawer Blues.*	21.00	36.00
KELLY, Willie			
☐	**Victor 23259** *Kelly's Special.*	50.00	85.00
☐	23263 *Side Door Blues.*	48.00	80.00
☐	23270 *Big Time Woman.*	47.00	75.00
☐	23299 *Nasty But It's Clean.*	47.00	75.00
☐	23320 *Hard Luck Man Blues.*	45.00	70.00
☐	23416 *Sad and Lonely Day.*	45.00	70.00
☐	38619 *32-20 Blues.*	40.00	60.00
KIRK, Andy			
☐	**Brunswick 4694** *Blue Clarinet Stomp.*	18.00	30.00
☐	4803 *I Lost My Gal From Memphis.*	17.00	28.00
☐	4863 *Once or Twice.*	18.00	30.00
☐	4878 *Snag It.*	19.00	32.00
☐	4893 *Froggy Bottom.*	18.00	30.00
☐	4981 *Honey, Just For You.*	17.00	28.00
LENOIR, J. B.			
☐	**Chess 1449** *My Baby Told Me.*	11.00	18.00
☐	1463 *Deep in Debt Blues.*	10.00	16.00
☐	**J.O.B. 112** *Let's Roll.*	13.00	21.00
☐	1008 *The Mountain.*	7.00	12.00
☐	1012 *The Mojo.*	6.00	10.00
☐	1016 *I'll Die Trying.*	7.00	12.00
☐	**Parrot 802** *Eisenhower Blues/I'm in Korea.*	9.00	15.00
☐	802 *Tax Paying Blues/I'm in Korea.*	9.00	15.00
☐	809 *Mama Talk to Your Daughter.*	6.00	9.00
☐	814 *What Have I Done.*	7.00	10.00
LOUISIANA RHYTHM KINGS:			
☐	**Vocalion 15657** *Nobody's Sweetheart.*	18.00	27.00
☐	15710 *I Can't Give You Anything But Love.*	23.00	33.00
☐	15716 *Dusky Stevedore.*	20.00	30.00
☐	15729 *Skinner's Sock.*	18.00	27.00
☐	15779 *Futuristic Rythm.*	22.00	32.00
☐	15784 *That's a Plenty.*	23.00	34.00

	Price Range	
☐ **15810** *I'm Walking Through Clover.*	33.00	49.00
☐ **15815** *Last Cent.*	35.00	52.00
☐ **15828** *Ballin' the Jack.*	35.00	52.00
☐ **15841** *Little by Little.*	31.00	47.00
LOVIN' SAM		
☐ **Bluebird 7514, 7629, 7916.**	7.00	12.00
☐ **Brunswick 7073** *She's Givin' It Away.*	17.00	28.00
☐ **7075** *What You Gonna Do?.*	16.00	27.00
☐ **7090** *Get Your Mind On It.*	16.00	27.00
☐ **7098** *You Rascal You.*	17.00	29.00
☐ **7117** *Huggin' and Kissin' Gwine On.*	17.00	29.00
☐ **7131** *Get It In Front.*	18.00	30.00
☐ **7167** *You Rascal! You—No. 2.*	16.00	27.00
☐ **7198** *Three Sixes.*	16.00	27.00
☐ **7218** *That New Kinda Stuff.*	15.00	24.00
☐ **Vocalion 03686** *Spo-Dee-O-Dee.*	9.00	15.00
MACK, Alura		
☐ **Gennett 6767** *Old Fashioned Blues.*	35.00	55.00
☐ **6813** *West End Blues.*	32.00	50.00
☐ **6876** *Loose Like That.*	32.00	50.00
☐ **6890** *Beef Blood Blues.*	33.00	52.00
☐ **6964** *The Long Lost Blues.*	32.00	50.00
☐ **7295** *Everybody's Man is Mine.*	31.00	49.00
McCLENNAN, Tommy		
☐ **Bluebird 8347** *You Can Mistreat Me Here.*	8.00	12.00
☐ **8373** *Bottle It Up and Go.*	9.00	15.00
☐ **8408** *Cotton Patch Blues.*	8.00	12.00
☐ **8444** *Brown Skin Girl.*	7.00	11.00
☐ **8545** *My Baby's Doggin' Me.*	9.00	15.00
☐ **8605** *My Little Girl.*	8.00	12.00
☐ **8669** *My Baby's Gone.*	8.00	12.00
McCRACKLIN, Jimmy		
☐ **Aladdin 3089** *Bad Luck and Trouble.*	6.00	10.00
☐ **Courtney 123** *You Had Your Chance.*	9.00	15.00
☐ **Down Town 2023** *Bad Condition Blues.*	10.00	16.00
☐ **2027** *Low Down Mood.*	11.00	17.00
☐ **Excelsior 182** *You Deceived Me.*	12.00	20.00
☐ **Globe 102** *Miss Mattie Left Me.*	6.00	9.00
☐ **104** *Highway 101.*	7.00	10.00
☐ **109** *Street Loafin' Woman.*	7.00	10.00
☐ **J & M Fullbright 123** *Special For You.*	9.00	15.00
☐ **124** *Rock and Rye.*	9.00	15.00
☐ **RPM 317** *Your Heart Ain't Right.*	7.00	10.00
☐ **Trilon 197** *Rock and Rye.*	8.00	12.00
☐ **231** *Big Foot Mama.*	8.00	12.00
MEMPHIS MINNIE & KANSAS JOE		
☐ **Bluebird 6187** *When the Sun Goes Down.*	10.00	16.00
☐ **6199** *Doctor, Doctor Blues.*	9.00	15.00
☐ **6202** *Hustlin' Woman Blues.*	9.00	15.00
☐ **Checker 771** *Me and My Chauffeur.*	7.00	11.00

	Price Range	
☐ **Decca 7019** *Chickasaw Train Blues.*	10.00	17.00
☐ **7023** *Hole in the Wall.*	9.00	14.00
☐ **7037** *Keep It To Yourself.*	9.00	14.00
☐ **7038** *You Got To Move.*	8.00	13.00
☐ **7048** *You Can't Give It Away.*	10.00	17.00
☐ **7084** *Sylvester and His Mule Blues.*	9.00	15.00
☐ **7102** *Down in New Orleans.*	9.00	15.00
☐ **7125** *Jockey Man Blues.*	8.00	14.00
☐ **7146** *Squat It.*	8.00	14.00
☐ **J.O.B. 1101** *Kissing in the Dark.*	9.00	15.00
☐ **Okeh 8948** *My Butcher Man.*	13.00	21.00
☐ **Regal 3259** *Kidman Blues.*	11.00	17.00
☐ **Vocalion 1476** *Bumble Bee.*	11.00	17.00
☐ **1512** *I'm Gonna Bake My Biscuits.*	12.00	20.00
☐ **1556** *Bumble Bee—No. 2.*	12.00	20.00
☐ **1588** *Frankie Jean.*	11.00	17.00
☐ **1601** *Garage Fire Blues.*	26.00	45.00
☐ **1603** *Good Girl Blues.*	14.00	21.00
☐ **1618** *New Dirty Dozen.*	13.00	20.00
☐ **1631** *Plymouth Rock Blues.*	13.00	20.00
☐ **1638** *Dirt Dauber Blues.*	12.00	20.00
☐ **1653** *Tricks Ain't Walkin' No More.*	11.00	19.00
☐ **1673** *Don't Bother It.*	11.00	19.00
☐ **1682** *Minnie Minnie Bumble Bee.*	13.00	20.00
☐ **1688** *Socket Blues.*	11.00	19.00
☐ **1698** *Outdoor Blues.*	11.00	19.00
☐ **1711** *Fishin' Blues.*	9.00	15.00
☐ **1718** *Jailhouse Trouble Blues.*	17.00	28.00
☐ **02711** *Stinging Snake Blues.*	14.00	21.00
MILES, Josie		
☐ **Ajax 17057** *Lovin' Henry Blues.*	32.00	53.00
☐ **17066** *Believe Me, Hot Mama.*	31.00	50.00
☐ **17070** *South Bound Blues.*	30.00	49.00
☐ **17076** *Sweet Man Joe.*	31.00	50.00
☐ **17080** *A to Z Blues.*	32.00	53.00
☐ **17083** *Picnic Time.*	19.00	29.00
☐ **17087** *Cross Word Papa.*	17.00	26.00
☐ **17092** *It Ain't Gonna Rain No Mo.*	13.00	21.00
☐ **17127** *At the Cake Walk Steppers Ball.*	31.00	48.00
☐ **17134** *Give Me Just a Little Bit of Love.*	30.00	47.00
☐ **Banner 1498** *Bitter Feelin' Blues.*	10.00	16.00
☐ **1499** *Let's Agree to Disagree.*	13.00	19.00
☐ **1516** *Ghost Walkin' Blues.*	14.00	21.00
☐ **1534** *Low Down Daddy Blues.*	10.00	16.00
☐ **Black Swan 14133** *When I Dream of Old Tennessee Blues.*	19.00	31.00
☐ **14136** *Four O'Clock Blues.*	18.00	23.00
☐ **14139** *Low Down 'Bama Blues.*	16.00	28.00
☐ **Domino 3468** *Bitter Feelin' Blues.*	10.00	16.00
☐ **3469** *Let's Agree to Disagree.*	13.00	19.00
☐ **3485** *Ghost Walkin' Blues.*	13.00	21.00
☐ **3504** *Low Down Daddy Blues.*	10.00	16.00
☐ **Edison 51476** *Sweet Man Joe.*	50.00	80.00
☐ **51477** *Temper'mental Papa.*	55.00	85.00

		Price Range	
☐	**Gennett 5359** *War Horse Mama.*	13.00	21.00
☐	**Paramount 12157** *If You Want to Keep Your Daddy Home.*	20.00	30.00
☐	**12158** *When I Dream of Old Tennessee Blues.*	13.00	22.00
☐	**12159** *Four O'Clock Blues.*	13.00	22.00
☐	**12160** *Low Down 'Bama Blues.*	14.00	22.00
☐	**Regal 9796** *Let's Agree to Disagree.*	11.00	17.00
☐	**9797** *Bitter Feelin' Blues.*	10.00	15.00
☐	**9831** *Low Down Daddy Blues.*	9.00	14.00
	LUCKY MILLINDER		
☐	**Brunswick 6156** *Moanin'.*	20.00	35.00
☐	**6199** *Snake Hips.*	11.00	20.00
☐	**6229** *Savage Rhythm.*	12.00	20.00
☐	**Columbia 2963-D** *Let's Have a Jubilee.*	11.00	20.00
☐	**2994-D** *Keep the Rhythm Going.*	10.00	17.00
☐	**3020-D** *Back Beats.*	9.00	15.00
☐	**3038-D** *African Lullaby.*	12.00	20.00
☐	**3071-D** *Harlen Heat.*	12.00	20.00
☐	**3078-D** *Truckin'.*	10.00	17.00
☐	**3087-D** *Congo Caravan.*	9.00	15.00
☐	**3111-D** *Yes! Yes!*	10.00	17.00
☐	**3134-D** *Everything is Still Okay.*	9.00	16.00
☐	**3147-D** *Merry-Go-Round.*	9.00	16.00
☐	**3148-D** *In a Sentimental Mood.*	9.00	16.00
☐	**3156-D** *Balloonacy.*	8.00	14.00
☐	**3157-D** *Showboat Shuffle.*	9.00	16.00
☐	**3158-D** *Algiers Stomp.*	9.00	16.00
☐	**3162-D** *Big John's Special.*	8.00	14.00
☐	**Variety 503** *Jungle Madness.*	7.00	13.00
☐	**546** *Rhythm Jam.*	7.00	13.00
☐	**604** *The Lucky Swing.*	8.00	15.00
☐	**624** *Camp Meeting Jamboree.*	7.00	14.00
☐	**634** *Jammin' For the Jack-Pot.*	7.00	14.00
☐	**Victor 22763** *Heebie Jeebies.*	8.00	15.00
☐	**22800** *Moanin'.*	8.00	15.00
☐	**24442** *Harlem After Midnight.*	15.00	27.00
☐	**24482** *Break It Down.*	12.00	23.00
☐	**Vocalion 3808** *Blue Rhythm Fantasy.*	7.00	13.00
	MILLER, Al		
☐	**Black Patti 8047** *Someday Sweetheart.*	60.00	100.00
☐	**8049** *Saturday Night Hymn.*	55.00	95.00
☐	**Champion 50067** *Truckin' Old Fool.*	13.00	22.00
☐	**50072** *Ain't That a Mess?*	14.00	23.00
☐	**Gennett 6875** *Mister Mary Blues.*	38.00	55.00
	OLIVER, Joe ("King Oliver")		
☐	**Autograph 617** *King Porter.*	500.00	900.00
☐	**Brunswick 3398** *Showboat Shuffle.*	15.00	23.00
☐	**3741** *Farewell Blues.*	15.00	27.00
☐	**4028** *Four or Five Times.*	23.00	40.00
☐	**4469** *I'm Watching the Clock.*	24.00	43.00
☐	**6053** *Papa De Da Da.*	24.00	43.00
☐	**6065** *I'm Crazy 'Bout My Baby.*	23.00	40.00

		Price Range	
☐	**Claxtonola 40292** *Riverside Blues.*	110.00	170.00
☐	**Columbia 13003-D** *Chattanooga Stomp.*	37.00	51.00
☐	**14003-D** *Camp Meeting Clues.*	34.00	46.00
☐	**Gennett 5132** *Weather Bird Rag.*	165.00	280.00
☐	**5133** *Cana Street Blues.*	175.00	300.00
☐	**5134** *Mandy Lee Blues.*	165.00	280.00
☐	**5135** *Froggie Moore.*	160.00	265.00
☐	**5184** *Snake Rag.*	165.00	280.00
☐	**5274** *Krooked Blues.*	220.00	350.00
☐	**5275** *Zulus Blues.*	900.00	1300.00
☐	**Okeh 4906** *Sobbin' Blues.*	90.00	135.00
☐	**4918** *Dipper Mouth Blues.*	95.00	145.00
☐	**4933** *Snake Rag.*	95.00	145.00
☐	**4975** *Jazzin' Babies' Blues.*	110.00	165.00
☐	**8148** *Room Rent Blues.*	90.00	135.00
☐	**8235** *Mabel's Dream.*	85.00	125.00
☐	**40000** *Buddy's Habits.*	85.00	125.00
☐	**40034** *Riverside Blues.*	95.00	135.00
☐	**Paramount 20292** *Mabel's Dream.*	80.00	125.00
☐	**Puritan 11292** *Mabel's Dream.*	85.00	130.00
☐	**Victor 22298** *When You're Smiling.*	10.00	15.00
☐	**22681** *Olga.*	20.00	30.00
☐	**23001** *Struggle Buggy.*	32.00	47.00
☐	**23009** *Shake It and Break It.*	33.00	50.00
☐	**23011** *You Were Only Passing Time With Me.*	33.00	50.00
☐	**23029** *I Can't Stop Loving You.*	32.00	49.00
☐	**23388** *New Orleans Shout.*	65.00	100.00
☐	**38034** *West End Blues.*	22.00	35.00
☐	**38039** *Call of the Freaks.*	36.00	50.00
☐	**38090** *Too Late.*	35.00	47.00
☐	**38101** *Sweet Like This.*	34.00	47.00
☐	**38109** *Frankie and Johnny.*	34.00	47.00
☐	**38134** *Boogie Woogie.*	34.00	47.00
☐	**38137** *Edna.*	33.00	45.00
☐	**38521** *Freakish Light Blues.*	32.00	44.00
☐	**Vocalion 1007** *Too Bad.*	42.00	63.00
☐	**1014** *Jackass Blues.*	43.00	65.00
☐	**1033** *Sugar Foot Stomp.*	43.00	65.00
☐	**1049** *Tack Annie.*	65.00	95.00
☐	**1059** *Dead Man Blues.*	26.00	39.00
☐	**1112** *Willie the Weeper.*	67.00	100.00
☐	**1114** *Showboat Shuffle.*	65.00	90.00
☐	**1152** *Farewell Blues.*	45.00	70.00
☐	**1189** *West End Blues.*	65.00	95.00
☐	**1190** *Sweet Emmaline.*	61.00	90.00
☐	**1225** *Speakeasy Blues.*	61.00	90.00
☐	**15394** *Deep Henderson.*	31.00	50.00
☐	**15493** *Dead Mans Blues.*	32.00	55.00
☐	**15503** *Snag It.*	32.00	55.00

ORIGINAL WOLVERINES

☐	**Brunswick 3707** *Shim-Me-Sha-Wabble.*	13.00	21.00
☐	**Vocalion 15635** *Royal Garden Blues.*	18.00	30.00
☐	**15708** *Limehouse Blues.*	20.00	32.00

			Price Range	
☐	15732	*There's a Rainbow Round My Shoulder.*	12.00	18.00
☐	15751	*Sweethearts on Parade.*	12.00	18.00
☐	15768	*I'll Never Ask for More.*	12.00	20.00
☐	15784	*He, She and Me.*	24.00	35.00
☐	15795	*Some Sweet Day.*	12.00	20.00
PATTON, Charley				
☐	**Paramount 12792**	*Banty Rooster Blues.*	75.00	120.00
☐	12854	*It Won't Be Long.*	72.00	115.00
☐	12869	*A Spoonful Blues.*	70.00	110.00
☐	12877	*Pea Vine Blues.*	68.00	105.00
☐	12883	*Lord I'm Discouraged.*	65.00	100.00
☐	12909	*High Water Everywhere.*	75.00	120.00
☐	12924	*Rattlesnake Blues.*	65.00	95.00
☐	12943	*Magnolia Blues.*	80.00	130.00
☐	12972	*Green River Blues.*	85.00	135.00
☐	12986	*I Shall Not Be Moved.*	85.00	135.00
☐	12998	*Hammer Blues.*	95.00	140.00
☐	13014	*Moon Going Down.*	85.00	135.00
☐	13031	*Some Happy Day.*	90.00	140.00
☐	13040	*Devil Sent the Train*	100.00	150.00
☐	13070	*Dry Well Blues.*	90.00	140.00
☐	13110	*Frankie and Albert.*	95.00	150.00
☐	13133	*Joe Kirby.*	100.00	165.00
☐	**Vocalion 02651**	*Poor Me.*	22.00	37.00
☐	02680	*High Sheriff Blues.*	21.00	35.00
☐	02782	*Love My Stuff.*	21.00	35.00
☐	02931	*Revenue Man Blues.*	20.00	34.00
PARHAM, Tiny				
☐	**Victor 21553**	*Cuckoo Blues.*	33.00	48.00
☐	21659	*Snake Eyes.*	30.00	45.00
☐	22778	*Sud Buster's Dream.*	31.00	46.00
☐	22842	*Rock Bottom.*	26.00	41.00
☐	23027	*Blue Moon Blues.*	34.00	49.00
☐	23386	*Nervous Tension.*	75.00	110.00
☐	23410	*Steel String Blues.*	80.00	120.00
☐	23426	*Golden Lily.*	75.00	110.00
☐	38009	*Jogo Rhythm.*	27.00	41.00
☐	38041	*Subway Sobs.*	26.00	39.00
☐	38047	*Blue Melody Blues.*	25.00	38.00
☐	38060	*Stompin' on Down.*	32.00	49.00
☐	38076	*Echo Blues.*	33.00	51.00
RAINEY, Ma				
☐	**Paramount 12080**	*Last Minute Blues.*	22.00	38.00
☐	12081	*Bad Luck Blues.*	21.00	36.00
☐	12082	*Walking Blues.*	22.00	38.00
☐	12083	*Southern Blues.*	23.00	40.00
☐	12098	*Dream Blues.*	15.00	25.00
☐	12200	*Ma Rainey's Mystery Record.*	26.00	42.00
☐	12215	*Lucky Rock Blues.*	25.00	42.00
☐	12222	*Farewell Daddy Blues.*	18.00	30.00
☐	12227	*South Bound Blues.*	33.00	47.00
☐	12238	*Jelly Bean Blues.*	95.00	135.00
☐	12242	*Toad Frog Blues.*	30.00	47.00

		Price Range	
☐	**12252** *See See Rider Blues.*	100.00	145.00
☐	**12257** *Cell Bound Blues.*	32.00	50.00
☐	**12284** *Explaining the Blues.*	31.00	48.00
☐	**12290** *Louisiana Hoo Doo Blues.*	30.00	46.00
☐	**12295** *Stormy Sea Blues.*	31.00	48.00
☐	**12303** *Night Time Blues.*	30.00	46.00
☐	**12311** *Rough and Tumble Blues.*	30.00	45.00
☐	**12332** *Slave to the Blues.*	30.00	45.00
☐	**12338** *Chain Gang Blues.*	28.00	42.00
☐	**12357** *Stack O'Lee Blues.*	28.00	42.00
☐	**12364** *Broken Hearted Blues.*	27.00	41.00
☐	**12374** *Titanic Man Blues.*	27.00	41.00
☐	**12384** *Sissy Blues.*	28.00	43.00
☐	**12395** *Down in the Basement.*	28.00	43.00
☐	**12419** *Grievin' Hearted Blues.*	24.00	37.00
☐	**12438** *Don't Fish In My Sea.*	23.00	36.00
☐	**12508** *Misery Blues.*	70.00	110.00
☐	**12526** *Gone Daddy Blues.*	60.00	95.00
☐	**12548** *Big Boy Blues.*	60.00	95.00
☐	**12566** *Oh Papa Blues.*	70.00	110.00
☐	**12590** *Georgia Cake Walk.*	50.00	95.00
☐	**12603** *Moonshine Blues.*	52.00	100.00
☐	**12612** *Ice Bag Papa.*	52.00	100.00
☐	**12668** *Prove It On Me Blues.*	53.00	105.00
☐	**12687** *Victim of the Blues.*	51.00	100.00
☐	**12706** *Traveling Blues.*	51.00	100.00
☐	**12718** *Big Feeling Blues.*	30.00	50.00
☐	**12735** *Tough Luck Blues.*	28.00	48.00
☐	**12760** *Sleep Talking Blues.*	28.00	48.00
☐	**12804** *Log Camp Blues.*	50.00	90.00
☐	**12902** *Runaway Blues.*	33.00	55.00
☐	**12926** *Sweet Rough Man.*	32.00	53.00
REDMAN, Don			
☐	**Brunswick 6211** *Chant of the Weed.*	14.00	24.00
☐	**6233** *I Heard.*	13.00	21.00
☐	**6273** *How'm I Doin'?*	10.00	19.00
☐	**6344** *It's a Great World After All.*	10.00	19.00
☐	**6354** *Tea for Two.*	9.00	16.00
☐	**6368** *Hot and Anxious.*	9.00	16.00
☐	**6401** *Ain't I The Lucky One?*	9.00	15.00
☐	**6412** *Two-Time Man.*	9.00	15.00
☐	**6429** *Nagasaki.*	9.00	15.00
☐	**6517** *Doin' the New Low-Down.*	9.00	15.00
☐	**6523** *How Ya Feelin'?*	9.00	15.00
☐	**6560** *Sophisticated Lady.*	7.00	12.00
☐	**6585** *I Won't Tell.*	8.00	14.00
☐	**6622** *Lazy Bones.*	9.00	16.00
☐	**6684** *I Found a New Way to Go.*	9.00	15.00
☐	**6745** *Got the Jitters.*	9.00	15.00
☐	**6935** *Lonely Cabin*	9.00	15.00
ROBINSON, Elzadie			
☐	**Paramount 12417** *Barrel House Man.*	50.00	95.00
☐	**12420** *Houston Bound.*	48.00	90.00
☐	**12469** *Baltimore Blues.*	47.00	87.00

		Price Range	
☐	**12509** *Whiskey Blues.*	45.00	85.00
☐	**12544** *Tick Tock Blues.*	42.00	80.00
☐	**12573** *St. Louis Cyclone Blues.*	38.00	62.00
☐	**12627** *Love Crazy Blues.*	36.00	59.00
☐	**12635** *Elzadie's Policy Blues.*	42.00	80.00
☐	**12676** *Mad Blues.*	39.00	70.00
☐	**12689** *Wicked Daddy.*	39.00	70.00
☐	**12701** *Arkansas Mill Blues.*	40.00	75.00
☐	**12745** *Unsatisfied Blues.*	39.00	70.00
☐	**12768** *Cheatin' Daddy.*	39.00	70.00
☐	**12900** *Driving Me South.*	38.00	65.00
RUSSELL, Luis			
☐	**Okeh 8424** *Plantation Joys.*	22.00	36.00
☐	**8454** *Sweet Mumtaz.*	21.00	34.00
☐	**8656** *The Call of the Freaks.*	21.00	34.00
☐	**8734** *Jersey Lightnin'.*	20.00	33.00
☐	**8760** *Savoy Shout.*	20.00	33.00
☐	**8780** *Saratoga Shout.*	19.00	32.00
☐	**8811** *Louisiana Swing.*	21.00	35.00
☐	**8830** *Muggin' Lightly.*	21.00	35.00
☐	**8849** *High Tension.*	19.00	32.00
☐	**Victor 22789** *Goin' to Town.*	22.00	36.00
☐	**22793** *You Rascal, You.*	21.00	35.00
☐	**22815** *Freakish Blues.*	21.00	35.00
SCOTT, Sonny			
☐	**Vocalion 02533** *No Good Biddie.*	20.00	34.00
☐	**02586** *Black Horse Blues.*	18.00	30.00
☐	**02614** *Fire Wood Man.*	17.00	29.00
☐	**25012** *Noal Mountain Blues.*	17.00	29.00
☐	**25013** *Working Man's Moan.*	18.00	30.00
☐	**25017** *Red Rooster Blues.*	17.00	29.00
SCRUGGS, Irene			
☐	**Champion 16102** *Borrowed Love.*	26.00	41.00
☐	**16148** *My Back to the Wall.*	25.00	40.00
☐	**16756** *The Voice of the Blues.*	25.00	39.00
☐	**Gennett 7296** *You've Got What I Want.*	25.00	39.00
☐	**Paramount 13023** *Good Meat Grinder.*	37.00	58.00
☐	**13046** *Back to the Wall.*	36.00	56.00
☐	**Vocalion 1017** *Home Town Blues.*	62.00	90.00
SMITH, Bessie			
☐	**Columbia 14042-D** *Weeping Willow Blues.*	14.00	23.00
☐	**14056-D** *Sobbin' Hearted Blues.*	17.00	30.00
☐	**14064-D** *Cold in Hand Blues.*	16.00	27.00
☐	**14075-D** *Soft Pedal Blues.*	11.00	20.00
☐	**14079-D** *You've Been a Good Old Wagon.*	19.00	29.00
☐	**14083-D** *Careless Love.*	19.00	29.00
☐	**14090-D** *Nashville Woman's Blues.*	19.00	29.00
☐	**14095-D** *J. C. Holmes Blues.*	11.00	19.00
☐	**14115-D** *Red Mountain Blues.*	12.00	21.00
☐	**14179-D** *Young Woman's Blues.*	11.00	19.00
☐	**14197-D** *After You've Gone.*	12.00	21.00
☐	**14209-D** *Them's Graveyard Words.*	11.00	19.00

		Price Range	
☐ **14219-D**	*Alexander's Ragtime Band*	10.00	18.00
☐ **14232-D**	*Trombone Cholly*	10.00	18.00
☐ **14260-D**	*Sweet Mistreater*	11.00	19.00
☐ **14273-D**	*Dyin' By the Hour*	12.00	23.00
☐ **14435-D**	*I've Got What It Takes*	11.00	19.00
☐ **14451-D**	*Take It Right Back*	11.00	19.00
☐ **14464-D**	*He's Got Me Goin'*	12.00	23.00
☐ **14476-D**	*Wasted Life Blues*	13.00	24.00
☐ **14487-D**	*You Don't Understand*	13.00	24.00
☐ **14527-D**	*Blue Spirit Blues*	13.00	24.00
☐ **14538-D**	*Moan, You Moaners*	13.00	24.00
☐ **14554-D**	*Hustlin' Dan*	15.00	27.00
☐ **14569-D**	*Hot Springs Blues*	15.00	27.00
☐ **14611-D**	*In the House Blues*	20.00	36.00
☐ **14634-D**	*Safety Mama*	18.00	34.00
☐ **14663-D**	*Shipwreck Blues*	18.00	34.00
SMITH, Clara			
☐ **Black Patti 8034**	*Sand Raisin' Blues*	70.00	110.00
☐ **Columbia 14062-D**	*Broken Busted Blues*	15.00	25.00
☐ **14073-D**	*Courthouse Blues*	15.00	24.00
☐ **14077-D**	*My John Blues*	15.00	24.00
☐ **14419-D**	*Got My Mind On That Thing*	15.00	24.00
☐ **14462-D**	*Papa I Don't Need You Now*	15.00	24.00
☐ **14536-D**	*Where Is My Man?*	12.00	20.00
☐ **14553-D**	*Don't Fool Around on Me*	9.00	15.00
☐ **14568-D**	*You're Getting Old on Your Job*	10.00	16.00
☐ **14580-D**	*Woman to Woman*	9.00	15.00
☐ **14592-D**	*Good Times*	9.00	15.00
☐ **14619-D**	*Ol' Sam Tages*	9.00	15.00
☐ **14633-D**	*You Dirty Dog*	12.00	20.00
☐ **14653-D**	*So Long Jim*	12.00	20.00
SMITH, Ivy			
☐ **Gennett 6829**	*Shadow Blues*	37.00	60.00
☐ **6861**	*Gin House Blues*	34.00	51.00
☐ **6875**	*Mistreated Mama Blues*	37.00	60.00
☐ **7024**	*Wringin' and Twistin' Papa*	36.00	57.00
☐ **7040**	*Doin' That Thing*	36.00	57.00
☐ **7101**	*Cheating Only Blues*	37.00	60.00
☐ **7231**	*That's the Kind of Girl I'm Looking For*	35.00	52.00
☐ **7251**	*Milkman Blues*	35.00	52.00
☐ **Paramount 12436**	*Rising Sun Blues*	42.00	70.00
☐ **12472**	*Barrel House Mojo*	45.00	75.00
☐ **12496**	*Ninety-Nine Years Blues*	42.00	69.00
SMITH, Susie			
☐ **Ajax 17064**	*House Rent Blues*	23.00	40.00
☐ **17073**	*Salt Water Blues*	22.00	39.00
☐ **17079**	*The Bye Bye Blues*	21.00	36.00
☐ **17081**	*Meat Man Pete*	23.00	40.00
☐ **17089**	*Sore Bunion Blues*	23.00	40.00
☐ **17093**	*Scandal Blues*	22.00	39.00
☐ **17095**	*How Can I Miss You*	21.00	36.00
☐ **17127**	*Texas Special Blues*	21.00	36.00
☐ **17132**	*Undertaker's Blues*	21.00	36.00
☐ **17134**	*Crepe Hanger Blues*	21.00	36.00

SMITH, Trixie	Price Range	
☐ **Black Swan 2039** *Trixie's Blues*	19.00	28.00
☐ **2044** *Long Lost Weary Blues*	20.00	30.00
☐ **14114** *Pensacola Blues*	19.00	28.00
☐ **14127** *My Man Rocks Me*	18.00	27.00
☐ **14132** *I'm Through With You*	19.00	28.00
☐ **14138** *I'm Gonna Get You*	16.00	27.00
☐ **14142** *Log Cabin Blues*	16.00	27.00
☐ **14149** *Triflin' Blues*	17.00	27.00
☐ **Paramount 12161** *Trixie's Blues*	14.00	23.00
☐ **12162** *Long Lost Weary Blues*	14.00	23.00
☐ **12163** *Pensacola Blues*	14.00	23.00
☐ **12164** *My Man Rocks Me*	14.00	23.00
☐ **12165** *I'm Through With You*	14.00	23.00
☐ **12167** *Log Cabin Blues*	12.00	20.00
☐ **12168** *Triflin' Blues*	12.00	20.00
☐ **12208** *Sorrowful Blues*	23.00	36.00
☐ **12211** *Freight Train Blues*	22.00	34.00
☐ **12232** *Praying Blues*	23.00	36.00
☐ **12262** *Railroad Blues*	65.00	110.00
☐ **12330** *Love Me Life You Used To Do*	32.00	50.00
☐ **12336** *Black Bottom Hop*	32.00	50.00
TENNESSEE MUSIC MEN		
☐ **Clarion 5389-C** *Georgia On My Mind*	15.00	25.00
☐ **5446-C** *Loveless Love*	12.00	20.00
☐ **5461-C** *Bugle Call Rag*	13.00	22.00
☐ **5467-C** *Choo Choo*	15.00	25.00
☐ **5469-C** *Baby Won't You Please Come Home*	13.00	22.00
☐ **5474-C** *Shim-Me-Sha-Wabble*	12.00	20.00
☐ **Harmony 1378-H** *You Rascal You*	15.00	25.00
☐ **1406-H** *Loveless Love*	13.00	22.00
☐ **1415-H** *Bugle Call Rag*	11.00	19.00
☐ **1420-H** *Choo Choo*	12.00	20.00
☐ **1422-H** *Baby, Won't You Please Come Home*	12.00	20.00
☐ **1427-H** *Shim-Me-Sha-Wabble*	13.00	22.00
☐ **Velvet Tone 2453-V** *Georgia On My Mind*	12.00	20.00
☐ **2456-V** *You Rascal You*	13.00	22.00
☐ **2506-V** *Loveless Love*	12.00	20.00
☐ **2521-V** *Bugle Call Rag*	11.00	19.00
☐ **2527-V** *Choo Choo*	11.00	19.00
☐ **2529-V** *Baby, Won't You Please Come Home*	12.00	20.00
☐ **2534-V** *Shim-Me-Sha-Wabble*	12.00	20.00
THOMAS, Henry		
☐ **Bluebird 5343** *My Sweet Candy*	11.00	18.00
☐ **5411** *Sick with the Blues*	12.00	20.00
☐ **Vocalion 1094** *John Henry*	21.00	36.00
☐ **1137** *Red River Blues*	23.00	37.00
☐ **1138** *The Little Red Caboose*	23.00	37.00
☐ **1139** *Woodhouse Blues*	21.00	36.00
☐ **1141** *Run, Mollie, Run*	23.00	37.00
☐ **1197** *Texas Easy Street Blues*	24.00	41.00
☐ **1230** *Bull Doze Blues*	23.00	39.00
☐ **1249** *Texas Worried Blues*	24.00	41.00
☐ **1443** *Don't Leave Me Here*	23.00	39.00
☐ **1468** *Lovin' Babe*	24.00	41.00

	Price Range	
THOMAS, Ramblin'		
☐ **Paramount 12616** *Sawmill Moan.*	55.00	80.00
☐ **12637** *Lock and Key Blues.*	52.00	75.00
☐ **12670** *No Baby Blues.*	60.00	85.00
☐ **12708** *Jig Head Blues.*	55.00	80.00
☐ **12722** *Ramblin' Man.*	53.00	75.00
☐ **12752** *Good Time Blues.*	53.00	75.00
THREE JOLLY MINERS		
☐ **Vocalion 1003** *Pig Alley Stomp.*	13.00	21.00
☐ **1004** *Chicago Back Step.*	12.00	20.00
☐ **15009** *Freakish Blues.*	12.00	20.00
☐ **15051** *Black Cat Blues.*	13.00	21.00
☐ **15087** *Lake George Blues.*	11.00	18.00
☐ **15141** *Texas Shuffle.*	12.00	19.00
☐ **15164** *House Party Stomp.*	13.00	21.00
☐ **15269** *Pig Alley Stomp.*	11.00	18.00
TUCKER, Bessie		
☐ **Victor 21692** *Black Name Moan.*	16.00	27.00
☐ **21708** *The Dummy.*	16.00	27.00
☐ **23385** *Bogey Man Blues.*	27.00	41.00
☐ **23392** *T. B. Moan.*	26.00	40.00
☐ **38018** *Fryin' Pan Skillet Blues.*	17.00	29.00
☐ **38538** *Old Black Mary.*	17.00	29.00
☐ **38542** *Katy Blues.*	17.00	29.00
VENUTI, Joe		
☐ **Columbia 2535-D** *There's No Other Girl.*	11.00	18.00
☐ **2589-D** *The Wolf Wobble.*	11.00	18.00
☐ **2765-D** *Raggin' the Scale.*	11.00	18.00
☐ **2782-D** *Vibraphonia.*	11.00	18.00
☐ **2783-D** *Isn't It Heavenly?*	11.00	18.00
☐ **2834-D** *Doin' the Uptown Lowdown.*	12.00	20.00
☐ **3103-D** *Eeny Meeny Miney Mo.*	11.00	18.00
☐ **3104-D** *Stop, Look and Listen.*	10.00	16.00
☐ **3105-D** *Red Velvet.*	10.00	16.00
☐ **Melotone 12277** *Farewell Blues.*	29.00	44.00
☐ **12294** *Beale Street Blues.*	25.00	39.00
☐ **Okeh 40762** *Wild Cat.*	10.00	16.00
☐ **40825** *Doin' Things.*	9.00	15.00
☐ **40853** *Kickin' the Cat.*	11.00	19.00
☐ **40897** *A Mug of Ale.*	10.00	18.00
☐ **40947** *Penn Beach Blues.*	11.00	18.00
☐ **41025** *The Wild Dog.*	12.00	20.00
☐ **41051** *'Tain't So, Honey, 'Tain't So.*	11.00	18.00
☐ **41076** *The Man From the South.*	11.00	18.00
☐ **41087** *Pickin' Cotton.*	10.00	17.00
☐ **41133** *I Must Have That Man.*	10.00	17.00
☐ **41144** *The Blue Room.*	11.00	18.00
☐ **41251** *My Honey's Lovin' Arms.*	11.00	18.00
☐ **41263** *I'm In Seventh Heaven.*	9.00	15.00
☐ **41320** *Chant of the Jungle.*	11.00	18.00
☐ **41361** *Apple Blossoms.*	10.00	17.00
☐ **41432** *Raggin' the Scale.*	12.00	20.00
☐ **41451** *Out of Breath.*	12.00	20.00
☐ **41469** *I've Found a New Baby.*	12.00	20.00

		Price Range	
☐ 41506	*Pardon Me, Pretty Baby.*	12.00	20.00
☐ 41586	*Fiddlesticks.*	12.00	20.00
☐ **Victor 21561**	*Doin' Things.*	16.00	27.00
☐ 23015	*My Man from Caroline.*	17.00	28.00
☐ 23018	*Wasting My Love On You.*	16.00	27.00
☐ 23039	*Gettin' Hot.*	21.00	37.00
☐ **Vocalion 15858**	*Farewell Blues.*	27.00	45.00
☐ 15864	*Beale Street Blues.*	31.00	50.00
WALLER, Fats			
☐ **Columbia 14593-D**	*I'm Crazy 'Bout My Baby.*	35.00	55.00
☐ **Okeh 4757**	*Birmingham Blues.*	29.00	46.00
☐ **Victor 20357**	*St. Louis Blues.*	12.00	20.00
☐ 20470	*Soothin' Syrup Stomp.*	19.00	32.00
☐ 20492	*Rusty Pail.*	18.00	30.00
☐ 20655	*Stompin' the Bug.*	19.00	32.00
☐ 20890	*Beale Street Blues.*	21.00	35.00
☐ 21127	*I Ain't Got Nobody.*	19.00	32.00
☐ 21202	*He's Gone Away.*	18.00	30.00
☐ 21525	*Hog Maw Stomp.*	18.00	30.00
☐ 22092	*Ain't Misbehavin'.*	12.00	20.00
☐ 22108	*Sweet Savannah Sue.*	14.00	25.00
☐ 22371	*St. Louis Blues.*	9.00	15.00
☐ 23260	*That's All.*	33.00	51.00
☐ 23331	*Sugar.*	21.00	34.00
☐ **Victor 38050**	*Harlem Fuss.*	34.00	51.00
☐ 38086	*Lookin' Good But Feelin' Bad.*	31.00	46.00
☐ 38110	*When I'm Alone.*	32.00	47.00
☐ 38119	*Ridin' But Walkin'.*	32.00	47.00
☐ 38508	*Numb Fumblin'.*	18.00	30.00
☐ 38554	*Valentine Stomp.*	27.00	41.00
☐ 38568	*Turn on the Heat.*	18.00	30.00
☐ 38613	*Smashing Thirds.*	23.00	35.00
WASHBOARD RHYTHM BOYS			
☐ **Bluebird 6157**	*Arlena.*	11.00	19.00
☐ 6186	*Street Walkin' Blues.*	12.00	20.00
☐ 6278	*Hot Nuts.*	11.00	19.00
☐ **Victor 22719**	*A Porter's Love Song to a Chambermaid.*	19.00	30.00
☐ 22814	*Shoot 'em.*	18.00	27.00
☐ 22958	*Pepper Steak.*	35.00	51.00
☐ 23301	*Georgia on My Mind.*	29.00	46.00
☐ 23323	*If You Don't Love Me.*	28.00	45.00
☐ 23337	*All This World is Made of Glass.*	29.00	46.00
☐ 23348	*My Silent Love.*	25.00	43.00
☐ 23357	*Depression Stomp.*	28.00	46.00
☐ 23364	*Say It Isn't So.*	25.00	43.00
☐ 23368	*The Boy in the Boat.*	26.00	46.00
☐ 23373	*How Deep is the Ocean?*	27.00	43.00
☐ 23375	*A Nickel for a Pickle.*	23.00	41.00
☐ 23380	*Sloppy Drunk Blues.*	24.00	40.00
☐ 23403	*Nobody's Sweetheart.*	24.00	40.00
☐ 23405	*Sophisticated Lady.*	24.00	40.00
☐ 23408	*Bug-A-Boo.*	24.00	40.00
☐ 23415	*Hard Corn.*	27.00	43.00

	Price Range	
☐ **Vocalion 1725** *The Scat Song.*	19.00	32.00
☐ **1729** *Syncopate Your Sins Away.*	18.00	31.00
☐ **1730** *Oh! You Sweet Thing.*	18.00	31.00
☐ **1731** *Angeline.*	17.00	30.00
☐ **1732** *Blue Drag.*	18.00	31.00
☐ **1733** *Old Yazoo.*	17.00	30.00
☐ **1734** *Spider Crawl.*	16.00	28.00
WATERS, Ethel		
☐ **Black Swan 2010** *Down Home Blues.*	22.00	37.00
☐ **2021** *There'll Be Some Changes Made.*	21.00	36.00
☐ **2035** *Royal Garden Blues.*	21.00	35.00
☐ **2037** *Bugle Blues.*	20.00	33.00
☐ **2038** *Dyin' with the Blues.*	21.00	36.00
☐ **2074** *Struggle.*	20.00	33.00
☐ **2077** *Tiger Rag.*	21.00	36.00
☐ **10077** *Struggle.*	20.00	31.00
☐ **14117** *Jazzin' Babies Blues.*	20.00	31.00
☐ **14120** *Georgia Blues.*	22.00	36.00
☐ **14128** *At the New Jump Steady Ball.*	22.00	35.00
☐ **14145** *Brown Baby.*	24.00	39.00
☐ **14146** *Memphis Man.*	20.00	31.00
☐ **14148** *Long-Lost Mama.*	20.00	31.00
☐ **14151** *Lost Out Blues.*	19.00	29.00
☐ **14155** *All the Time.*	19.00	29.00
☐ **Cardinal 2036** *The New York Guide.*	24.00	37.00
☐ **Columbia 2222-D** *My Kind of Man.*	10.00	17.00
☐ **2346-D** *I Got Rhythm.*	12.00	20.00
☐ **2409-D** *When Your Lover Has Gone.*	14.00	23.00
☐ **2481-D** *Without That Gal.*	13.00	21.00
☐ **2511-D** *River, Stay 'Way From My Door.*	14.00	23.00
☐ **2826-D** *Harlem On My Mind.*	15.00	26.00
☐ **2853-D** *A Hundred Years from Today.*	13.00	21.00
☐ **14353-D** *My Handy Man.*	9.00	16.00
☐ **14380-D** *Do What You Did Last Night.*	9.00	16.00
☐ **14411-D** *Lonesome Swallow.*	11.00	17.00
☐ **14458-D** *Long Lean Lanky Mama.*	9.00	15.00
☐ **14565-D** *Georgia Blues.*	9.00	15.00
☐ **Paramount 12169** *Down Home Blues.*	13.00	21.00
☐ **12170** *There'll Be Some Changes Made.*	14.00	23.00
☐ **12171** *Royal Garden Blues.*	13.00	21.00
☐ **12173** *Bugle Blues.*	15.00	24.00
☐ **12174** *Dying with the Blues.*	15.00	24.00
☐ **12175** *Jazzin' Babies Blues.*	15.00	24.00
☐ **12176** *At the New Jump Steady Ball.*	15.00	24.00
☐ **12178** *Brown Baby.*	13.00	21.00
☐ **12179** *Memphis Man.*	14.00	23.00
☐ **12180** *Long-Lost Mama.*	13.00	21.00
☐ **12181** *Lost Our Blues.*	13.00	21.00
☐ **12182** *Ethel Sings 'em.*	14.00	25.00
☐ **12189** *All the Time.*	13.00	21.00
☐ **12214** *Tell 'em 'Bout Me.*	12.00	20.00
☐ **12230** *Black Splatch Blues.*	27.00	41.00
☐ **12313** *Craving Blues.*	29.00	43.00

	Price Range	
WASHINGTON, Lizzie		
☐ **Black Patti 8054** *Mexico Blues.*	100.00	150.00
☐ **Champion 15282** *Skeleton Key Blues.*	90.00	135.00
☐ **15303** *East Coast Blues.*	37.00	56.00
☐ **15319** *Sport Model Mamma Blues.*	40.00	62.00
☐ **Gennett 6126** *Working Man Blues.*	37.00	56.00
☐ **6134** *Skeleton Key Blues.*	35.00	52.00
☐ **6321** *Brick Flat Blues.*	36.00	54.00
☐ **Herwin 92013** *East Coast Blues.*	41.00	67.00
☐ **92021** *My Low Down Brown.*	43.00	69.00
☐ **92039** *Lord Have Mercy Blues.*	41.00	67.00
☐ **92040** *Mexico Blues.*	44.00	70.00
☐ **92041** *Brick Flat Blues.*	41.00	67.00
☐ **Vocalion 1459** *Whiskey Head Blues.*	20.00	33.00
WHEATSTRAW, Peetie		
☐ **Bluebird 5451** *Devil's Son-in-Law.*	12.00	20.00
☐ **5626** *Ice and Snow Blues.*	12.00	20.00
☐ **Conqueror 8858, 8858, 8925, 9027, 9028.**	10.00	16.00
☐ **Decca 7007** *Doin' the Best I Can.*	11.00	18.00
☐ **7018** *Throw Me in the Alley.*	12.00	20.00
☐ **7061** *Good Home Blues.*	12.00	20.00
☐ **7082** *Numbers Blues.*	12.00	20.00
☐ **Vocalion 1552** *Tennessee Peaches Blues.*	29.00	49.00
☐ **1569** *School Days.*	26.00	43.00
☐ **1597** *Strange Man Blues.*	27.00	46.00
☐ **1620** *Mama's Advice.*	26.00	43.00
☐ **1649** *Ain't It a Pity and a Shame.*	27.00	46.00
☐ **1672** *C and A Blues.*	25.00	40.00
☐ **1722** *Police Station Blues.*	25.00	40.00
☐ **1727** *Can't See Blues.*	25.00	40.00
☐ **02783** *Back Door Blues.*	15.00	25.00
☐ **02810** *C and A Train Blues.*	15.00	25.00
☐ **02843** *Keyhole Blues.*	15.00	25.00
☐ **03066** *King of Spades.*	11.00	16.00
☐ **03119** *Sorrow Hearted Blues.*	10.00	15.00
☐ **03155** *Johnnie Blues.*	10.00	15.00
WHOOPEE MAKERS		
☐ **Banner 6548** *Saturday Night Function.*	15.00	24.00
☐ **Cameo 9036** *Hottentot.*	13.00	21.00
☐ **9037** *Misty Mornin'.*	14.00	24.00
☐ **9306** *Saturday Night Function.*	12.00	20.00
☐ **Conqueror 7428** *Flaming Youth.*	12.00	20.00
☐ **Lincoln 3065** *Hottentot.*	12.00	20.00
☐ **3066** *Misty Morning.*	11.00	18.00
☐ **3330** *Saturday Night Function.*	11.00	18.00
☐ **Pathe-Acuelle 36781** *Jubilee Stomp.*	15.00	26.00
☐ **36787** *Take It Easy.*	14.00	23.00
☐ **36899** *The Mooche.*	14.00	21.00
☐ **36915** *Hot and Bothered.*	15.00	21.00
☐ **36923** *Misty Mornin'.*	14.00	23.00
☐ **36945** *Bugle Call Rag.*	13.00	21.00
☐ **37013** *Tiger Rag.*	11.00	17.00
☐ **37042** *Dirty Dog.*	10.00	16.00
☐ **37059** *Doin' the Voom Voom.*	16.00	26.00

		Price Range	
☐	**Perfect 14962** *East St. Louis Toodle-oo.*	17.00	29.00
☐	**14968** *Take It Easy.*	17.00	26.00
☐	**15080** *Move Over.*	17.00	29.00
☐	**15096** *Hot and Bothered.*	18.00	32.00
☐	**15104** *Misty Mornin'.*	18.00	32.00
☐	**15194** *Tiger Rag.*	11.00	18.00
☐	**15217** *Twelfth Street Rag.*	10.00	17.00
☐	**15223** *The Sorority Stomp.*	10.00	17.00
☐	**15376** *Happy Feet.*	9.00	15.00
☐	**15418** *Them There Eyes.*	11.00	18.00
☐	**Romeo 840** *Misty Mornin'.*	11.00	18.00

WILLIAMS, Clarence

☐	**Oriole 2141** *Papa De-Da-Da.*	11.00	18.00
☐	**2164** *Hot Lovin'.*	10.00	17.00
☐	**Paramount 12435** *Shut Your Mouth.*	47.00	65.00
☐	**12517** *Bottomland.*	32.00	53.00
☐	**12839** *Midnight Stomp.*	90.00	140.00
☐	**12870** *Pane in the Glass.*	110.00	155.00
☐	**12884** *Speakeasy.*	95.00	145.00
☐	**12885** *Squeeze Me.*	90.00	140.00
☐	**Perfect 15403** *Hot Lovin'.*	11.00	20.00
☐	**QRS 7004** *Speakeasy.*	110.00	175.00
☐	**7005** *Squeeze Me.*	100.00	160.00
☐	**7039** *Midnight Stomp.*	110.00	175.00
☐	**7034** *Bozo.*	110.00	175.00
☐	**7044** *Sister Kate.*	105.00	160.00
☐	**Romeo 1529** *Hot Lovin'.*	12.00	20.00
☐	**Victor 38063** *Lazy Mama.*	21.00	33.00
☐	**38524** *Too Low.*	23.00	36.00
☐	**38630** *I'm Not Worryin'.*	31.00	50.00
☐	**Vocalion 2541** *Breeze.*	7.00	11.00
☐	**2563** *The Right Key But the Wrong Keyhole.*	12.00	20.00
☐	**2584** *Chocolate Avenue.*	11.00	19.00
☐	**2602** *Harlem Rhythm Dance.*	10.00	17.00
☐	**2616** *Swaller-Tail Coat.*	11.00	18.00
☐	**2629** *Jimmy Had a Nickel.*	9.00	16.00
☐	**2630** *How Can I Get It?*	11.00	18.00
☐	**2654** *New Orleans Hop Scop Blues.*	11.00	18.00
☐	**2674** *As Long As I Live.*	10.00	18.00
☐	**2676** *St. Louis Blues.*	11.00	19.00
☐	**2689** *I Can't Dance, I Got Ants In My Pants.*	11.00	19.00
☐	**2718** *Pretty Baby, Is It Yes or No?*	10.00	17.00
☐	**2736** *After Tonight.*	9.00	15.00
☐	**2759** *Let's Have a Showdown.*	10.00	17.00
☐	**2778** *Bimbo.*	9.00	15.00
☐	**2788** *Trouble.*	10.00	17.00
☐	**2838** *Big Fat Mama.*	10.00	17.00
☐	**2854** *Chizzlin' Sam.*	9.00	15.00
☐	**2871** *Organ Grinder Blues.*	10.00	17.00
☐	**2889** *Tell the Truth.*	11.00	18.00
☐	**2899** *I Saw Stars.*	10.00	17.00
☐	**2909** *Jungle Crawl.*	9.00	15.00
☐	**2938** *Black Gal.*	10.00	17.00
☐	**2958** *I Can See You All Over the Place.*	10.00	17.00

WILLIAMSON, Sonny Boy — Price Range

	Title	Low	High
☐	**Bluebird 7012** *Skinny Woman*	12.00	18.00
☐	**7059** *Sugar Mama Blues*	12.00	18.00
☐	**7098** *Blue Bird Blues*	12.00	18.00
☐	**7302** *Early in the Morning*	12.00	18.00
☐	**7352** *Suzanne Blues*	12.00	18.00
☐	**7404** *Frigidaire Blues*	12.00	18.00
☐	**7428** *Collector Man Blues*	12.00	18.00
☐	**7500** *Sunny Land*	10.00	16.00
☐	**7536** *You Can Lead Me*	12.00	18.00
☐	**7576** *Miss Louisa Blues*	10.00	16.00
☐	**7665** *Decoration Blues*	10.00	16.00
☐	**7707** *Honey Bee Blues*	9.00	15.00
☐	**7756** *You Give an Account*	10.00	16.00
☐	**7805** *Deep Down in the Ground*	10.00	16.00
☐	**7847** *Shannon Street Blues*	9.00	15.00
☐	**Bluebird 8034, 8094**	9.00	15.00
☐	**8237** *Good for Nothing Blues*	10.00	16.00
☐	**8265** *Bad Luck Blues*	10.00	16.00
☐	**8307** *Doggin' My Love Around*	12.00	18.00
☐	**8333** *T. B. Blues*	12.00	18.00
☐	**8357** *Good Gal Blues*	10.00	16.00
☐	**8383** *New Jail House Blues*	12.00	18.00
☐	**8403** *Joe Louis and John Henry Blues*	12.00	18.00
☐	**8439** *Miss Ida Lee*	10.00	16.00
☐	**8474** *Honey Bee Blues*	12.00	18.00
☐	**Trumpet 139** *Do It If You Wanna*	9.00	15.00
☐	**140** *Stop Crying*	9.00	15.00
☐	**144** *West Memphis Blues*	3.00	13.00
☐	**145** *Pontiac Blues*	8.00	13.00

OPERA

MEMORABILIA

	Item	Low	High
☐	**ADLER, KURT.** *8x10 photograph, signed and inscribed.*	15.00	22.00
☐	**ADLER, KURT.** *c. Mid-1950's. Printed score of "The Magic Flute", signed and inscribed.*	10.00	15.00
☐	**ALBANESE, LICIA.** *5x7 photo in "Butterfly" costume, signed in light blue ink, mounted on stiff paper, laminated, signature somewhat faded.*	17.00	22.00
☐	**ALBANESE, LICIA.** *c. 1947. Typewritten letter, signed, half page.*	15.00	20.00
☐	**ALBANESE, LICIA.** *Four photos of her, ranging in size from 4x3 to 8x10, two in costume, one signed, one damaged.*	33.00	45.00
☐	**ALCOCK, MERLE.** *c. 1920's. Photo in costume from "Amico Fritz", 8x10, signed in the margin.*	30.00	40.00
☐	**ALDA, FRANCES.** *c. 1920. Sepia photo, 12x14½, with lengthy inscription and large bold signature.*	52.00	75.00
☐	**ALDA, FRANCES.** *Metropolitan Opera program, signed (also signed by several others).*	26.00	40.00
☐	**ALDA, FRANCES.** *Two candid snapshots, one creased.*	8.00	11.00
☐	**ALTGLASS, MAX.** *7x9 photo in costume from "Boris", signed in green ink, framed under glass.*	43.00	55.00

	Price Range	
☐ **ALVARY, LORENZO.** *8x10 studio photo, signed.*	10.00	13.00
☐ **ALVARY, LORENZO.** *Six photos, various sizes, in costume, four of them signed, in a cloth folding case.*	77.00	100.00
☐ **ALVARY, LORENZO.** *Hotel menu signed, stained.*	8.00	13.00
☐ **AMARA, LUCINE.** *Article from "Opera News" magazine, signed and with handwritten comments.*	12.00	17.00
☐ **AMARA, LUCINE.** *Pair of 8x10 photos, signed, one in costume, one framed against green velvet in a simple wood frame.*	53.00	70.00
☐ **AMARA, LUCINE.** *Pair of long black gloves worn by her in an operatic role.*	30.00	40.00
☐ **AMARA, LUCINE.** *Plain signature on an otherwise blank sheet.*	5.00	6.00
☐ **ANTHONY, CHARLES.** *8x10 photo, signed.*	9.00	12.00
☐ **BACCALONI, SALVATORE.** *8x10 photo signed, framed.*	25.00	35.00
☐ **BACCALONI, SALVATORE.** *c. 1940's. Poster advertising a concert appearance.*	12.00	17.00
☐ **BACCALONI, SALVATORE.** *14x17 photo in costume, signed and inscribed, mounted on bristol board.*	65.00	85.00
☐ **BADA, ANGELO.** *4x3 photo, signed, wrinkled.*	10.00	14.00
☐ **BADA, ANGELO.** *c. 1932. Postcard with handwritten message and signature.*	12.00	17.00
☐ **BAMPTON, ROSE.** *c. 1938. Typed letter signed, NY*	32.00	42.00
☐ **BAUM, KURT.** *8x10 photo in costume, signed twice.*	20.00	25.00
☐ **BERGONZI, CARLO.** *Newspaper review of an opera, signed in pencil.*	10.00	15.00
☐ **BERGONZI, CARLO.** *Small printed card, signed.*	7.00	10.00
☐ **BJOERLING, JUSSI.** *8x10 photo in "Boheme" costume, signed.*	25.00	33.00
☐ **BJOERLING, JUSSI.** *Scrapbook on his career, with c. 200 news cuttings, several 8x10 and other photos, a few signed items.*	110.00	150.00
☐ **BORI, LUCREZIA.** *8x10 sepia photo, signed and inscribed.*	35.00	44.00
☐ **BORI, LUCREZIA.** *c. 1917. Handwritten letter, signed, with the original envelope. Sold with two small unsigned photos.*	90.00	115.00
☐ **BRANZELL, KARIN.** *Seven photos, 3x4 to 8x10, two duplicates, one signed. Enclosed in a leatherette envelope.*	35.00	44.00
☐ **BROWNLEE, JOHN.** *c. 1940. 8x10 photo in "Rigoletto" costume, signed.*	21.00	30.00
☐ **BROWNLEE, JOHN.** *5x7½ color photo from magazine, signed and inscribed. Mounted on stiff paper.*	17.00	23.00
☐ **BROWNLEE, JOHN.** *Check endorsed by him.*	10.00	14.00
☐ **BROWNLEE, JOHN.** *Artist's caricature of him in role, 5x7, pen and wash, matted.*	45.00	60.00
☐ **CABALLE, MONTSERRAT.** *8x10 photo in costume, signed.*	10.00	14.00
☐ **CABALLE, MONTSERRAT.** *Seven different 8x10 photos, three of them signed, along with several news cuttings.*	50.00	63.00
☐ **CABALLE, MONTSERRAT.** *LP album cover, signed and inscribed (lacking record).*	44.00	55.00
☐ **CARUSO, ENRICO.** *c. 1911. Handwritten letter, signed.*	175.00	220.00
☐ **CARUSO, ENRICO.** *c. 1915. Two-page letter, typed, signed.*	150.00	190.00

	Price Range	
☐ **CARUSO, ENRICO.** *Handwritten letter with caricature of old man and dog, signed, framed in a metal frame.*	250.00	320.00
☐ **CARUSO, ENRICO.** *Caricature of bearded man holding umbrella, on 6x7½ sheet of greenish paper, a few handwritten notes, signed.*	185.00	240.00
☐ **CARUSO, ENRICO.** *c. 1915. Restaurant menu with small caricature, signed, stained and worn.*	170.00	210.00
☐ **CARUSO, ENRICO.** *c. 1908. Restaurant menu, signed.*	115.00	150.00
☐ **CARUSO, ENRICO.** *Signature on calling card.*	65.00	85.00
☐ **CARUSO, ENRICO.** *c. 1902. Check endorsed by him.*	100.00	130.00
☐ **CARUSO, ENRICO.** *Handwritten note on stationery of the Ansonia Hotel, New York.*	175.00	225.00
☐ **CARUSO, ENRICO.** *8x10 photo in "I Pagliacci" costume, signed and inscribed, matted and framed.*	220.00	300.00
☐ **CARUSO, ENRICO.** *5x7 photo in "Rigoletto" costume, signed, ink faded, lightly watermarked.*	150.00	200.00
☐ **CARUSO, ENRICO.** *8x10 photo in "Girl of the Golden West" costume, matted, unsigned.*	65.00	85.00
☐ **CARUSO, ENRICO.** *8x10 photo in "Barber" costume, signed in dark brown ink, framed.*	200.00	245.00
☐ **CARUSO, ENRICO.** *Half-page handwritten note, framed along with a signed 5x7 portrait and a 78rpm recording in a 17x22 wood frame.*	385.00	450.00
☐ **CARUSO, ENRICO.** *c. 1906. 8x10 portrait photo in street dress, signed and inscribed.*	170.00	220.00
☐ **CARUSO, ENRICO.** *Two 3x4 photos, one on shipboard.*	45.00	60.00
☐ **CARUSO, ENRICO.** *Opera review from the New York Times, signed. Enclosed in a cloth folding case, along with an unsigned photo.*	110.00	130.00
☐ **CARUSO, ENRICO.** *Scrapbook with 27 photos, 17 of them signed, and c. 300 other items, news cuttings, tickets, etc.*	1800.00	2300.00
☐ **CARUSO, ENRICO.** *Poster advertising his appearance in a Metropolitan Opera production.*	250.00	330.00
☐ **CASSEL, WALTER.** *8x10 photo, signed.*	15.00	22.00
☐ **CHALIAPIN, FYODOR.** *8x10 sepia photo, signed as "Boris".*	230.00	330.00
☐ **CHALIAPIN, FYODOR.** *Handwritten letter, signed, in Russian.*	475.00	650.00
☐ **CHALIAPIN, FYODOR.** *Five 8x10 movie stills, unsigned.*	33.00	45.00
☐ **CHALIAPIN, FYODOR.** *c. 1925. 5x7 portrait photo, signed.*	210.00	275.00
☐ **CHALIAPIN, FYODOR.** *22x31 poster as "Boris", apparently a recent enlargement by a collector from a small early Metropolitan Opera photo.*	45.00	66.00
☐ **CHALIAPIN, FYODOR.** *Signature on an otherwise blank sheet.*	60.00	80.00
☐ **CHOOKASIAN, LILI.** *8x10 portrait photo (unsigned).*	3.00	4.00
☐ **CLAUSSEN, JULIA.** *c. 1920's. Series of five letters to her, mostly on musical matters.*	45.00	65.00
☐ **CLEVA, FAUSTO.** *8x10 photo with baton, boldly signed.*	45.00	67.00
☐ **CONNER, NADINE.** *6x7½ color photo, trimmed into margins, inscribed and signed.*	22.00	30.00
☐ **CONTINI, LUDOVICO.** *5x7 photo in "Faust" costume, signed.*	62.00	80.00

		Price Range	
☐	**CORELLI, FRANCO.** *Two 8x10 photos, signed.*	25.00	35.00
☐	**CORELLI, FRANCO.** *Concert program, signed.*	11.00	15.00
☐	**CRESPIN, REGINE.** *8x10 color photo, signed and inscribed, mounted on stiff paper, laminated and framed.*	28.00	37.00
☐	**CRESPIN, REGINE.** *LP album cover signed, record missing.*	12.00	16.00
☐	**CRESPIN, REGINE.** *Copy of "Metropolitan Opera Annual", signed.*	10.00	14.00
☐	**DAVIDSON, LAWRENCE.** *4x5 photo, inscribed and signed.*	6.00	9.00
☐	**DELLA CASA, LISA.** *Collection of 7 photos, c. 35 press cuttings and various miscellaneous items, three signatures, in a manila envelope.*	55.00	75.00
☐	**DeLOS ANGELES, VICTORIA.** *8x10 photo in "Faust" costume, with lengthy inscription and signature, thumbtack holes at corners.*	45.00	60.00
☐	**DeLOS ANGELES, VICTORIA.** *Signature on page torn from a magazine.*	9.00	13.00
☐	**DELUCA, GIUSEPPE.** *Small sepia photo in "Barber" costume, signed in pencil.*	25.00	35.00
☐	**DELUCA, GIUSEPPE.** *Opera contract signed by him, stained.*	75.00	100.00
☐	**DESTINN, EMMY.** *8x10 photo, signed in violet ink, framed.*	100.00	125.00
☐	**DESTINN, EMMY.** *Three unsigned early photos, one in costume.*	23.00	31.00
☐	**DESTINN, EMMY.** *c. 1909. Handwritten letter, ¾ths page.*	80.00	105.00
☐	**DIAZ, JUSTINO.** *Copy of "Opera News" magazine, with photo of him on front cover, signed on the cover.*	25.00	35.00
☐	**DIAZ, JUSTINO.** *8x10 photo, signed.*	10.00	14.00
☐	**DIAZ, JUSTINO.** *Small color photo of him and Beverly Sills in rehearsal, signed and inscribed by him.*	12.00	16.00
☐	**DIAZ, JUSTINO.** *Sword used by him in Metropolitan Opera.*	50.00	70.00
☐	**DIAZ, JUSTINO.** *Helmet worn by him in Metropolitan Opera production, gold colored.*	55.00	75.00
☐	**DUNN, MIGNON.** *8x10 photo, signed and inscribed.*	12.00	16.00
☐	**DUNN, MIGNON.** *Two 5x7 photos, one cut from a magazine. Not signed, mounted on a card.*	7.00	10.00
☐	**ELIAS, ROSALIND.** *8x10 photo in costume, signed.*	10.00	14.00
☐	**ELIAS, ROSALIND.** *Magazine article, signed, worn.*	9.00	13.00
☐	**ELIAS, ROSALIND.** *Small color photo from "Walkure", signed.*	11.00	15.00
☐	**FARRAR, GERALDINE.** *8x10 photo in "Butterfly" costume, inscribed and signed, framed.*	100.00	125.00
☐	**FARRAR, GERALDINE.** *c. 1921-1942. Six letters written by her, all but one in holograph.*	200.00	250.00
☐	**FARRAR, GERALDINE.** *8x10 photo as "Juliet", signed, somewhat damaged.*	85.00	115.00
☐	**FARRAR, GERALDINE.** *c. 1933. Postcard, handwritten.*	40.00	55.00
☐	**FARRELL, EILEEN.** *8x10 photo, signed.*	9.00	12.00
☐	**FLAGSTAD, KIRSTEN.** *Six 8x10 photos, signed, four in costume, two with inscriptions, all collected into one frame along with a short handwritten note.*	325.00	400.00
☐	**FLAGSTAD, KIRSTEN.** *c. 1930's. 8x10 photo in costume, signed.*	40.00	55.00

	Price Range	
☐ **FLAGSTAD, KIRSTEN.** *Inscribed Metropolitan Opera program.*	39.00	50.00
☐ **FLAGSTAD, KIRSTEN.** *78rpm record album cover, signed, records missing.*	60.00	80.00
☐ **FLAGSTAD, KIRSTEN.** *U.S. $1 bill, signed.*	50.00	66.00
☐ **GALLI-CURCI, AMELITA.** *5x4 photo in "Traviata" costume, signed in the margin.*	40.00	55.00
☐ **GALLI-CURCI, AMELITA.** *8x10 photo, matted to 11x13½. Not signed.*	26.00	36.00
☐ **GALLI-CURCI, AMELITA.** *Scrapbook with c. 85 new cuttings relating to her career, also a few items on other artists.*	90.00	115.00
☐ **GEDDA, NICOLAI.** *Opera poster, signed in crayon.*	23.00	28.00
☐ **GEDDA, NICOLAI.** *Photo in costume, signed, size not given.*	10.00	13.00
☐ **GOBBI, TITO.** *c. 1959. 8x10 photo, signed and dated.*	30.00	38.00
☐ **GOBBI, TITO.** *26 photographs, some cut from publications, two of them signed.*	80.00	100.00
☐ **GOBBI, TITO.** *Western Union telegram addressed to him.*	10.00	14.00
☐ **GRAMM. DONALD.** *c. 1975. 8x10 portrait photo, signed.*	12.00	17.00
☐ **GRAMM, DONALD.** *8x10 photo in costume, signed in margin, matted.*	20.00	25.00
☐ **HUNT, LOIS.** *6x7½ photo, signed, with brief note in her handwriting, signed.*	15.00	20.00
☐ **JERITZA, MARIA.** *Photo in "Tote Stadt" costume, signed on the back. Traces of glue staining.*	55.00	70.00
☐ **JERITZA, MARIA.** *c. 1923. Two-page letter in her hand, signed, with original envelope.*	90.00	115.00
☐ **KEITH, GEORGE.** *Libretto to "Tosca", signed in pencil.*	7.00	10.00
☐ **KIRSTEN, DOROTHY.** *Framed montage consisting of two small signed photos of her, a 78rpm record and three press cuttings.*	120.00	150.00
☐ **KIRSTEN, DOROTHY.** *Envelope addressed by her (contents missing).*	12.00	17.00
☐ **KIRSTEN, DOROTHY.** *8x10 studio photo, hand-colored, signed.*	55.00	75.00
☐ **KIRSTEN, DOROTHY.** *Huge poster photo, 27x41, unsigned, mounted on thin wooden board, some defects.*	60.00	80.00
☐ **LOVE, SHIRLEY.** *8x10 photo in costume, signed.*	10.00	14.00
☐ **MARTINELLI, GUISEPPI.** *10x12 sepia portrait photo, signed.*	70.00	90.00
☐ **McCORMACK, JOHN.** *Sheet music "When Irish Eyes Are Smiling", signed and inscribed.*	90.00	110.00
☐ **McCORMACK, JOHN.** *c. 1928. Typed letter, signed.*	33.00	45.00
☐ **McCORMACK, JOHN.** *c. 1915. 8x10 photo in "Traviata" costume, signed.*	55.00	70.00
☐ **McCORMACK, JOHN.** *Card signed, "Best Wishes, John McCormack".*	23.00	35.00
☐ **McCORMACK, JOHN.** *Small snapshot photo. Corner creased.*	12.00	16.00
☐ **McCRACKEN, JAMES.** *8x10 photo in costume, signed.*	10.00	14.00
☐ **McCRACKEN, JAMES.** *Color photo from cover of "Opera News" magazine, signed in Magic Marker.*	12.00	16.00

	Price Range	
☐ **McCRACKEN, JAMES.** *Three LP album covers signed, with records.*	70.00	90.00
☐ **MELBA, NELLIE.** *c. 1901. One-page holograph letter on her stationery, framed against pink velvet along with a photograph.*	90.00	115.00
☐ **MELBA, NELLIE.** *7x9 photo signed, brief inscription.*	120.00	150.00
☐ **MELCHIOR, LAURITZ.** *8x10 photo in Wagnerian costume, with lengthy inscription and signature.*	80.00	100.00
☐ **MELCHIOR, LAURITZ.** *c. 1925-1945. Collection of 17 posters advertising his appearances in operas and concerts.*	225.00	300.00
☐ **MELCHIOR, LAURITZ.** *Photo of him and Jimmy Durante, signed by both.*	65.00	85.00
☐ **MELCHIOR, LAURITZ.** *Snapshot photo of him in Central Park, New York, signed on the back.*	40.00	53.00
☐ **MELCHIOR, LAURITZ.** *Five unsigned photos, various sizes.*	45.00	60.00
☐ **MELCHIOR, LAURITZ.** *Letter to him from James J. Rorimer, president of the Metropolitan Museum, New York, regarding artworks given to the museum by Melchior.*	40.00	55.00
☐ **MELTON, JAMES.** *8x10 photo in costume, signed.*	22.00	34.00
☐ **MELTON, JAMES.** *Typed letter, signed.*	30.00	38.00
☐ **MELTON, JAMES.** *Collection of c. 150 press cuttings relating to his career, contained in a vinyl-covered album.*	60.00	80.00
☐ **MERRILL, ROBERT.** *Photo of him with Danny Kaye, signed by both.*	35.00	45.00
☐ **MERRILL, ROBERT.** *Copy of his autobiography, inscribed on the flyleaf.*	20.00	25.00
☐ **MERRILL, ROBERT.** *c. 1952. 8x10 portrait photo, signed.*	19.00	24.00
☐ **MERRILL, ROBERT.** *Record company contract, signed by him.*	43.00	57.00
☐ **MERRILL, ROBERT.** *6x8 color photo in costume, signed.*	25.00	32.00
☐ **MERRILL, ROBERT and JAN PEERCE.** *8x10 photo of both in costume, signed by both.*	80.00	110.00
☐ **MILANOV, ZINKA.** *Magazine article signed in blue pencil.*	20.00	26.00
☐ **MILANOV, ZINKA.** *Pair of earrings worn by her.*	60.00	80.00
☐ **MILANOV, ZINKA.** *8x10 photo in costume, signed.*	22.00	33.00
☐ **MILANOV, ZINKA.** *LP record album cover, signed (no record).*	45.00	63.00
☐ **MILNES, SHERRILL.** *Small photo cut from magazine, mounted on card, signed on the card, inscribed on back of card.*	20.00	26.00
☐ **MILNES, SHERRILL.** *Three 8x10 photos, one in costume, all signed.*	38.00	48.00
☐ **MILNES, SHERRILL.** *c. 1969. Photo of him with Leontyne Price, signed by him.*	20.00	25.00
☐ **MOFFO, ANNA.** *Article on her from "Life" magazine, signed.*	30.00	37.00
☐ **MOFFO, ANNA.** *Card signed "Best Wishes, Anna Moffo".*	9.00	13.00
☐ **MOFFO, ANNA.** *Christmas card sent by her, signed.*	21.00	27.00
☐ **MOFFO, ANNA.** *8x10 photo in costume, signed.*	25.00	33.00
☐ **MOFFO, ANNA.** *LP album cover, signed, record missing.*	33.00	45.00
☐ **MOFFO, ANNA.** *17x22 color photo of her on stage, unsigned.*	45.00	60.00
☐ **MOORE, GRACE.** *Photo with Bob Hope, signed by both.*	27.00	37.00
☐ **MOORE, GRACE.** *Six motion picture stills, unsigned.*	13.00	17.00

	Price Range	
☐ **MOORE, GRACE.** *c. 1935. 8x10 photo, signed and inscribed.*	20.00	28.00
☐ **MOORE, GRACE.** *Photo as Mimi in "Boheme", signed.*	35.00	45.00
☐ **MOORE, GRACE.** *Signature on a news cutting.*	8.00	11.00
☐ **MOORE, GRACE.** *Fan used by her in opera production.*	30.00	40.00
☐ **MOORE, GRACE.** *Five small snapshot photos, one signed.*	25.00	33.00
☐ **MORELL, BARRY.** *8x10 photo in costume, signed.*	8.00	11.00
☐ **MORELL, BARRY.** *LP record album cover, signed, record missing.*	12.00	16.00
☐ **MORELL, BARRY.** *Signature on opera libretto.*	6.00	8.00
☐ **MORELL, BARRY.** *Photo with James Levine, signed by both.*	25.00	33.00
☐ **MUNSEL, PATRICE.** *Pair of long silver gloves worn by her in opera production, with letter of authentication.*	42.00	55.00
☐ **MUNSEL, PATRICE.** *8x10 photo, signed and inscribed.*	12.00	16.00
☐ **MUNSEL, PATRICE.** *c. 1940's. Two 8x10 studio portraits, one of them signed.*	15.00	22.00
☐ **MUNSEL, PATRICE.** *Signature on an opera company contract.*	31.00	40.00
☐ **MUNSEL, PATRICE.** *Article from "TV Guide", signed.*	8.00	11.00
☐ **MUNSEL, PATRICE.** *Photo with Helen Traubel, signed by Munsel only, framed, glass cracked.*	20.00	26.00
☐ **MUNSEL, PATRICE.** *Two small snapshot photos, signed.*	12.00	16.00
☐ **MUNSEL, PATRICE.** *Libretto to "Boheme", signed.*	21.00	28.00
☐ **MUNSEL, PATRICE.** *Photo in "Mignon" costume, signed.*	27.00	35.00
☐ **MUNSEL, PATRICE.** *6x8 color photo, laminated, signed.*	21.00	28.00
☐ **NAGY, ROBERT.** *8x10 photo, signed.*	7.00	10.00
☐ **NILSSON, BIRGIT.** *Photo in "Tristan" costume, signed.*	20.00	28.00
☐ **NILSSON, BIRGIT.** *LP album cover signed, records missing.*	27.00	35.00
☐ **NILSSON, BIRGIT.** *Cover of "Opera News" magazine, signed.*	15.00	22.00
☐ **NILSSON, BIRGIT.** *Helmet reputedly worn by her on stage.*	80.00	105.00
☐ **NILSSON, BIRGIT.** *Scrapbook containing c. 800 items pertaining to her, press cuttings, photos, several signed, etc. Bound in ½ green leather, 19½x24½ inches. In a buckram slipcase.*	800.00	1000.00
☐ **NILSSON, BIRGIT.** *Signature on an opera circular.*	6.00	8.00
☐ **ORDASSY, CARLOTTA.** *8x10 studio photo, signed and inscribed.*	9.00	12.00
☐ **ORDASSY, CARLOTTA.** *Libretto, "Walkure", signed.*	12.00	16.00
☐ **PATTI, ADELINA.** *c. 1893. ALs, with envelope.*	55.00	70.00
☐ **PATTI, ADELINA.** *c. 1897. ALs, 2½ pp. regarding her role in an opera.*	110.00	140.00
☐ **PATTI, ADELINA.** *7x9½ photo in costume, framed, soiled, not signed.*	20.00	26.00
☐ **PATTI, ADELINA.** *Oil on canvas portrait, 25x38, seated in chair with flowers, framed.*	1000.00	1250.00
☐ **PATTI, ADELINA.** *8x10 photo, signed and inscribed, framed.*	160.00	200.00
☐ **PATTI, ADELINA.** *Typed letter, signed, ½ page.*	25.00	32.00
☐ **PATTI, ADELINA.** *Two small unsigned photos.*	12.00	16.00
☐ **PATTI, ADELINA.** *Signature cut from a letter, glue stained.*	8.00	11.00

	Price Range	
☐ **PEERCE, JAN.** *8x10 photo with Richard Tucker, signed by Peerce only, both in costume.*	75.00	110.00
☐ **PEERCE, JAN.** *c. 1950. 8x10 studio portrait, signed.*	20.00	26.00
☐ **PEERCE, JAN.** *Photo in costume, signed and inscribed.*	23.00	30.00
☐ **PEERCE, JAN.** *c. 1971. Typed letter, signed.*	23.00	30.00
☐ **PEERCE, JAN.** *c. 1970. Brief handwritten note, undated.*	20.00	26.00
☐ **PEERCE, JAN.** *Photo with Robert Merrill, signed by Peerce only, matted and framed.*	70.00	90.00
☐ **PEERCE, JAN.** *Signature on opera program.*	12.00	16.00
☐ **PEERCE, JAN.** *8x10 photo in costume, signed.*	20.00	27.00
☐ **PEERCE, JAN.** *Magazine article on opera, signed by him and several others.*	33.00	42.00
☐ **PEERCE, JAN.** *c. 1950's. Five snapshots, unsigned.*	15.00	20.00
☐ **PETERS, ROBERTA.** *c. 1965. LP record album cover, signed, record missing.*	65.00	80.00
☐ **PETERS, ROBERTA.** *8x10 photo standing next to piano, long gown, signed and inscribed.*	35.00	45.00
☐ **PETERS, ROBERTA.** *Concert program, signed.*	9.00	12.00
☐ **PETERS, ROBERTA.** *c. 1968. Christmas card, signed.*	20.00	26.00
☐ **PETERS, ROBERTA.** *Photo in "Don Giovanni" costume, signed.*	15.00	20.00
☐ **PETERS, ROBERTA.** *c. 1972. Colored magazine photo, signed.*	12.00	16.00
☐ **PETERS, ROBERTA.** *c. 1965. ALs, half page.*	15.00	20.00
☐ **PINZA, EZIO.** *8x10 photo in "Carmen" costume, signed.*	40.00	53.00
☐ **PINZA, EZIO.** *c. 1923. ALs, two pp. with envelope.*	60.00	80.00
☐ **PINZA, EZIO.** *c. 1932. ALs, mentions Lawrence Tibbett.*	66.00	85.00
☐ **PINZA, EZIO.** *4x5 portrait, signed, framed along with a 78rpm phono record.*	75.00	95.00
☐ **PINZA, EZIO.** *c. 1948. 8x10 portrait photo, inscribed.*	33.00	50.00
☐ **PINZA, EZIO.** *Photo with cast of "Fanny", signed.*	32.00	45.00
☐ **PINZA, EZIO.** *Printed score, "Fanny", signed.*	32.00	45.00
☐ **PINZA, EZIO.** *Sheet music, "Some Enchanted Evening", signed.*	39.00	50.00
☐ **PINZA, EZIO.** *8x10 photo with Lauritz Melchior, signed by both.*	95.00	120.00
☐ **PINZA, EZIO.** *Signature on a news cutting.*	10.00	14.00
☐ **PINZA, EZIO.** *c. 1928-1940. Six Metropolitan Opera posters advertising his appearances in various operas, unsigned.*	180.00	235.00
☐ **PONS, LILY.** *c. 1930's. 8x10 photo with drum from "Daughter of the Regiment", signed and inscribed.*	45.00	60.00
☐ **PONS, LILY.** *c. 1937. 8x10 studio photo, signed.*	35.00	47.00
☐ **PONS, LILY.** *Printed score, "Traviata", signed.*	32.00	37.00
☐ **PONS, LILY.** *c. 1935, ALs, one page, about an opera role.*	50.00	65.00
☐ **PONS, LILY.** *c. 1946. ALs, one page, declining an invitation.*	35.00	45.00
☐ **PONS, LILY.** *Signature on an opera libretto.*	27.00	35.00
☐ **PONS, LILY.** *8x10 photo with Robert Merrill, signed by Pons only.*	30.00	40.00
☐ **PONS, LILY.** *8x10 signed photo, framed with a 78rpm phonograph record and two news cuttings.*	60.00	80.00
☐ **PONS, LILY.** *Scrapbook with c. 200 items pertaining to her career, mostly magazine and news cuttings, a few snapshot photos, etc.*	200.00	250.00

	Price Range	
☐ **PONS, LILY.** *c. 1975. Late photo of her, signed.*	38.00	47.00
☐ **PONSELLE, ROSA.** *11x14 sepia photo in costume, signed in blue ink with lengthy inscription, matted and framed (frame damaged).*	190.00	240.00
☐ **PONSELLE, ROSA.** *6x8 photo in "Forza" costume, signed.*	60.00	80.00
☐ **PONSELLE, ROSA.** *c. 1917, ALs, ½ page, with envelope.*	70.00	100.00
☐ **PONSELLE, ROSA.** *c. 1976. Typewritten letter, signed, lengthy, 5 pp., discussing her life in opera, etc.*	235.00	300.00
☐ **PONSELLE, ROSA.** *Signature on an opera libretto.*	35.00	43.00
☐ **PONSELLE, ROSA.** *c. 1937. 8x10 studio portrait, signed.*	44.00	59.00
☐ **PONSELLE, ROSA.** *Four small photos, unsigned, mounted.*	12.00	16.00
☐ **PONSELLE, ROSA.** *78rpm record signed on the label.*	30.00	38.00
☐ **PONSELLE, ROSA.** *c. 1920's. Hand-colored photo in costume.*	12.00	16.00
☐ **PRICE, LEONTYNE.** *Photo from "Opera News" cover, signed.*	12.00	16.00
☐ **PRICE, LEONTYNE.** *8x10 portrait photo, signed and inscribed.*	15.00	20.00
☐ **PRICE, LEONTYNE.** *T-shirt with her likeness.*	8.00	11.00
☐ **PRICE, LEONTYNE.** *c. 1972. Typewritten letter, signed.*	23.00	28.00
☐ **PRICE, LEONTYNE.** *8x10 color photo in costume, signed.*	33.00	40.00
☐ **PRICE, LEONTYNE.** *Two LP record album covers, signed, one with records present.*	125.00	165.00
☐ **PRICE, LEONTYNE.** *Photo with Justino Diaz, signed by Price only.*	20.00	28.00
☐ **PRICE, LEONTYNE.** *Six 8x10 photos in costume, unsigned.*	10.00	14.00
☐ **PRICE, LEONTYNE.** *Gold-colored bracelet worn by her in opera production, sold at benefit auction.*	60.00	80.00
☐ **PRICE, LEONTYNE.** *27x41 poster portrait.*	75.00	95.00
☐ **PRICE, LEONTYNE.** *Signature on a card.*	7.00	10.00
☐ **RASKIN, JUDITH.** *8x10 studio portrait, signed.*	7.00	10.00
☐ **RESNIK, REGINA.** *c. 1948. Opera libretto, signed.*	12.00	16.00
☐ **RESNIK, REGINA.** *8x10 photo in costume, signed.*	12.00	16.00
☐ **RESNIK, REGINA.** *Magazine article with colored photos, signed.*	15.00	20.00
☐ **RESNIK, REGINA.** *c. 1952. Signature on an opera company brochure.*	7.00	10.00
☐ **RESNIK, REGINA.** *Two 8x10 photos in costume, one signed.*	20.00	28.00
☐ **RESNIK, REGINA.** *Photo with Mario Lanza, signed by both.*	45.00	60.00
☐ **RESNIK, REGINA.** *c. 1945-1965. Collection of 325 news cuttings.*	105.00	130.00
☐ **RESNIK, REGINA.** *Two snapshots taken by fans, signed on the backs.*	8.00	11.00
☐ **SAYAO, BIDU.** *c. 1930's. 8x10 photo in costume, matted, signed on the mount. Sold with several news cuttings.*	70.00	90.00
☐ **SAYAO, BIDU.** *c. 1940. 78rpm phono record, signed on the label.*	25.00	33.00
☐ **SAYAO, BIDU.** *Opera libretto, signed and inscribed (in Spanish).*	32.00	40.00
☐ **SAYAO, BIDU.** *c. 1929. ALs, one page (in Spanish).*	41.00	50.00
☐ **SAYAO, BIDU.** *c. 1932. Handwritten note (in Spanish).*	33.00	42.00
☐ **SAYAO, BIDU.** *Book, "Folk Songs of South America", signed.*	31.00	39.00

	Price Range	
☐ **SCHWARZKOPF, ELIZABETH.** *Color cover of "Opera News" magazine, signed and inscribed, framed.*	20.00	25.00
☐ **SCHWARZKOPF, ELIZABETH.** *c. 1955. 8x10 photo in costume, signed.*	26.00	33.00
☐ **SCHWARZKOPF, ELIZABETH.** *Three unsigned 8x10 studio portraits.*	10.00	15.00
☐ **SCHWARZKOPF, ELIZABETH.** *c. 1960's. Signed concert program.*	9.00	13.00
☐ **SCHWARZKOPF, ELIZABETH.** *Watercolor sketch of her, 14x20, bristol board, matted and framed.*	310.00	375.00
☐ **SCHWARZKOPF, ELIZABETH.** *LP record album cover, signed, record missing.*	33.00	41.00
☐ **SCHWARZKOPF, ELIZABETH.** *Three snapshots, signed on backs.*	21.00	28.00
☐ **SCHWARZKOPF, ELIZABETH.** *c. 1959. ALs, 2½ pp., N.Y. hotel stationery.*	30.00	40.00
☐ **SCHWARZKOPF, ELIZABETH.** *c. 1962. ALs, one page.*	21.00	27.00
☐ **SCHWARZKOPF, ELIZABETH.** *Signature on a greeting card.*	21.00	27.00
☐ **SCHWARZKOPF, ELIZABETH.** *Photo cut from album cover, signed.*	12.00	17.00
☐ **SIEPI, CESARE.** *8x10 photo in costume, signed.*	8.00	11.00
☐ **SIEPI, CESARE.** *6x8 photo with Richard Tucker, signed by Siepi only.*	11.00	15.00
☐ **SIEPI, CESARE.** *c. 1978. Typewritten letter, signed.*	7.00	10.00
☐ **SIEPI, CESARE.** *8x10 portrait photo, signed and inscribed.*	10.00	14.00
☐ **SIEPI, CESARE.** *c. 1969. Check endorsed by him.*	21.00	28.00
☐ **SIEPI, CESARE.** *Opera libretto, signed.*	12.00	16.00
☐ **SIEPI, CESARE.** *Three small unsigned photos (candid).*	9.00	12.00
☐ **SIEPI, CESARE.** *Signature on a card.*	4.00	6.00
☐ **SILLS, BEVERLY.** *Als from Pittsburgh hotel, mentioning bad weather.*	21.00	30.00
☐ **SILLS, BEVERLY.** *8x10 photo in "Daughter of the Regiment" costume, signed.*	25.00	35.00
☐ **SILLS, BEVERLY.** *Huge portrait of her mounted on heart-shaped heavy cardboard, c. three feet, in color, inscribed.*	100.00	125.00
☐ **SILLS, BEVERLY.** *Copy of her autobiography, "Bubbles", signed.*	31.00	40.00
☐ **SILLS, BEVERLY.** *8x10 portrait photo, signed.*	20.00	27.00
☐ **SILLS, BEVERLY.** *c. 1975. Large poster of the New York City Opera, picturing her in roles from the "Three Queens", signed by her in magic marker*.* (*The unfairly low price of this item — which under normal conditions would be worth at least $50 — results from the fact that she signed hundreds of these posters so they could be sold at the New York City Opera's gift shop.)	13.00	20.00
☐ **SILLS, BEVERLY.** *T-shirt with her likeness in color.*	12.00	15.00
☐ **SUTHERLAND, JOAN.** *8x10 photo in "Traviata" costume, signed.*	14.00	20.00
☐ **SUTHERLAND, JOAN.** *Two unsigned 8x10 photos in costume.*	7.00	10.00

	Price Range	
☐ **SUTHERLAND, JOAN.** *LP record album set, signed on box, records present.*	125.00	150.00
☐ **SUTHERLAND, JOAN.** *Review of a concert from the "London Times", signed.*	8.00	11.00
☐ **SUTHERLAND, JOAN.** *c. 1948. ALs, one page.*	35.00	45.00
☐ **SUTHERLAND, JOAN.** *Colored magazine cover, signed.*	25.00	31.00
☐ **SUTHERLAND, JOAN.** *c. 1971. Opera libretto, signed.*	20.00	26.00
☐ **SUTHERLAND, JOAN.** *8x10 photo with Richard Bonynge, signed by both.*	55.00	71.00
☐ **SUTHERLAND, JOAN.** *Christmas card, signed by her and Richard Bonynge.*	45.00	60.00
☐ **SUTHERLAND, JOAN.** *c. 1968. 8x10 studio portrait, signed.*	15.00	21.00
☐ **SUTHERLAND, JOAN.** *22x30 color blow-up of a photo of her in costume, signed with large signature, framed.*	90.00	115.00
☐ **SUTHERLAND, JOAN.** *Six scrapbooks with c. 1,500 items on her career, including 56 signed photos, mostly cut from magazines, etc.*	1500.00	1900.00
☐ **SUTHERLAND, JOAN.** *Signature on a restaurant menu.*	7.00	10.00
☐ **SUTHERLAND, JOAN.** *Snapshot photo at age about 18, unsigned, mounted.*	5.00	7.00
☐ **SUTHERLAND, JOAN.** *c. 1975. Typewritten letter, signed, Brooklyn.*	20.00	27.00
☐ **SUTHERLAND, JOAN.** *Five photos mounted on heavy paper, signed on the paper, inscribed, dated 1976.*	90.00	115.00
☐ **SWARTHOUT, GLADYS.** *8x10 portrait photo, signed.*	15.00	21.00
☐ **SWARTHOUT, GLADYS.** *8x10 photo in costume, signed.*	20.00	25.00
☐ **SWARTHOUT, GLADYS.** *c. 1932. ALs, 1½ pp., with envelope.*	36.00	45.00
☐ **SWARTHOUT, GLADYS.** *78rpm record, signed on the label.*	25.00	33.00
☐ **SWARTHOUT, GLADYS.** *Signature on opera libretto.*	10.00	15.00
☐ **THOMAS, JOHN CHARLES.** *Copy of book, "Songs of Stephen Foster", signed on flyleaf.*	25.00	35.00
☐ **THOMAS, JOHN CHARLES.** *5x6 photo in dressing room, signed.*	17.00	23.00
☐ **THOMAS, JOHN CHARLES.** *c. 1945. 8x10 studio portrait, signed and inscribed.*	20.00	28.00
☐ **THOMAS, JOHN CHARLES.** *8x10 photo, signed, framed along with a 78rpm record.*	55.00	75.00
☐ **THOMAS, JOHN CHARLES.** *Typewritten letter, signed, undated.*	15.00	22.00
☐ **THOMAS, JOHN CHARLES.** *Early photo at age c. 15, signed.*	31.00	43.00
☐ **THOMAS, JOHN CHARLES.** *Two small snapshots, unsigned.*	6.00	9.00
☐ **THOMAS, JOHN CHARLES.** *c. 1948. 78rpm record album set, signed on the front cover, records present.*	70.00	90.00
☐ **THOMAS, JOHN CHARLES.** *Signature on a card.*	5.00	7.00
☐ **TIBBETT, LAWRENCE.** *8x10 photo from "Emperor Jones", matted, signed on the mat, framed.*	120.00	150.00
☐ **TIBBETT, LAWRENCE.** *Printed score, "Emperor Jones", signed.*	70.00	90.00
☐ **TIBBETT, LAWRENCE.** *8x10 photo in costume, signed.*	44.00	60.00
☐ **TIBBETT, LAWRENCE.** *c. 1926. ALs, 1½ pp.*	77.00	100.00

	Price Range	
☐ **TIBBETT, LAWRENCE.** *8x10 photo with Amelita Galli-Curci, signed by both, framed.*	120.00	150.00
☐ **TIBBETT, LAWRENCE.** *Metropolitan opera poster for "Emperor Jones", signed.*	250.00	350.00
☐ **TRAUBEL, HELEN.** *c. 1952. 8x10 photo with Jimmy Durante, signed by both, matted and framed.*	60.00	80.00
☐ **TRAUBEL, HELEN.** *c. 1940's. 8x10 photo in "Tristan" costume, signed.*	50.00	65.00
☐ **TRAUBEL, HELEN.** *5x7 photo with Lauritz Melchior in scene from opera, signed by Traubel only.*	42.00	55.00
☐ **TRAUBEL, HELEN.** *Signature on opera libretto.*	12.00	17.00
☐ **TRAUBEL, HELEN.** *4x5 snapshot photo on street, unsigned.*	6.00	7.00
☐ **TRAUBEL, HELEN.** *c. 1961. Typewritten letter, signed.*	12.00	17.00
☐ **TRAUBEL, HELEN.** *8x10 studio portrait, signed, thumbtack holes in corners.*	15.00	20.00
☐ **TUCKER, RICHARD.** *c. 1948, 8x10 studio portrait, signed.*	12.00	17.00
☐ **TUCKER, RICHARD.** *Two photos in costume, one signed.*	20.00	30.00
☐ **TUCKER, RICHARD.** *c. 1974. Typewritten letter, signed.*	12.00	17.00
☐ **TUCKER, RICHARD.** *Colored photo from magazine, signed.*	15.00	20.00
☐ **TUCKER, RICHARD.** *Signature on opera program.*	7.00	10.00
☐ **TUCKER, RICHARD.** *LP album cover signed, no record.*	42.00	55.00
☐ **TUCKER, RICHARD.** *c. 1962. Magazine cover photo, signed.*	20.00	27.00
☐ **WARREN, LEONARD.** *8x10 photo in costume, signed.*	36.00	46.00
☐ **WARREN, LEONARD.** *5x7 portrait photo, signed.*	20.00	25.00

POSTERS

A thorough listing of opera posters from the 19th-century to today would be exhaustive, insofar as virtually every opera company in the world — even small companies that perform out of auditoriums rather than actual opera theaters — uses posters of one kind or another to promote its productions. All of these are collectible to varying degrees. Of course, the most desirable and usually most expensive posters are (a) the oldest, (b) those of acclaimed opera companies, (c) posters with names of celebrated artists, (d) highly pictorial posters, especially those with graphic work by noted artists. The price range of opera posters goes from about $5 to at least $500 — not counting special copies that carry signatures of artists or are in some other way specially desirable (some of which will be found listed in the above section with star memorabilia).

Certainly, posters dating from before 1900 are very highly collectible and seem to be the overall favorite of collectors. Standards of condition are rather high, as it is possible in most cases to find specimens of these posters in nearly mint condition.

☐ **Foreign Opera Houses.** *Posters 1850-99.*	50.00	220.00
☐ **Foreign Opera Houses.** *Posters pre-1900, with names of artists who later became celebrated in U.S.*	100.00	285.00
☐ **Foreign Opera Houses.** *Pre-1800 (generally rather small and printed on thinner paper than later posters; these were designed to be pasted on walls).*	250.00	500.00
☐ **Foreign Opera Posters.** *Pre-1700. Very rare.*	500.00	2000.00

	Price Range	
☐ **Metropolitan Opera House.** *Unillustrated posters dating before 1900*	75.00	100.00
☐ **Metropolitan Opera House.** *Unillustrated posters, 1900-10.*	50.00	75.00
☐ **Metropolitan Opera House.** *Unillustrated posters, 1911-20.*	45.00	60.00
☐ **Metropolitan Opera House.** *Posters 1900-10 with illustration of a member or members of the cast*	90.00	150.00
☐ **Metropolitan Opera House.** *Most illustrated posters, 1911-20.*	75.00	125.00
☐ **Metropolitan Opera House.** *Most illustrated posters, 1920's.*	65.00	125.00
☐ **Metropolitan Opera House.** *Most illustrated posters, 1965-75.*	15.00	25.00
☐ **New York City Opera.** *Most posters prior to 1970.*	15.00	30.00
☐ **U.S. Opera Houses outside New York.** *Most posters before 1900*	70.00	110.00

(The values of posters are increased by framing. The proportion of increase depends upon the type of framing and, of course, the value of the frame itself. Generally, a poster in a frame of average design is worth $20 to $40 more than unframed, but this is only a rough guideline.)

SCRAPBOOKS

Since about 1890, the keeping of scrapbooks has been a favorite pastime among opera fans. Scrapbooks are found pertaining to individual artists as well as to opera in general, and range in scope from collections of news cuttings to autographed photographs and, sometimes, letters by the artists to the scrapbook keeper. It is not a simple matter to place value guidelines on these collections, as each differs from the other. As a general rule, the older scrapbooks are of greater interest and value than the newer, as they are likely to contain out-of-print photographs and other memorabilia which is no longer easily obtainable. News cuttings, however, even those of an early vintage, have very little cash value; nor do snippings from magazines, unless autographed, as the magazines from which they were obtained can usually be supplied by "back-date" dealers at a nominal cost.

The values of scrapbooks can **roughly** be figured as follows:

In scrapbooks in which the majority of material dates before 1920, figure $4 to $8 for original photographs (not cut from magazines or books) of major artists, 50¢-$1 for significant news cuttings, and add to this the values of any autographed items which might be included, referring to the list of artists' memorabilia as a guide.

Subtract 10-20 percent from the values of items which are pasted down, and make any necessary allowance for material in poor condition. The physical condition of the album itself is generally not important.

RECORDINGS

CARUSO, ENRICO

Listed below are exclusively 78 (or, as was occasionally the case, 79) rpm recordings, the great majority of them issued while Caruso was alive (he died in 1921). Some posthumous releases are included, **but none dating later than the 1920's.**

Of course, Caruso was prevailed upon to make a great number of recordings. His name on a record, after he achieved fame at the Metropolitan and other opera houses, guaranteed a good sale. Many persons bought Caruso records who never bought other classical music. He was, in fact, the only operatic performer of the time (1903-21) who could be called popular with the average record-buying public. Though most of his records were of operatic arias or selections, he also recorded a number of non-operatic light-classical songs and even an occasional folk song (such as "O Solo Mio").

The sound quality on his earlier recordings is understandably quite pitiable. They date to as early as 1903, when recording techniques and equipment still remained in a primitive state. However, his later records are surprisingly good technically, and if one can lay hands on near-mint specimens, the great Caruso voice can be heard fairly close to the way in which it must have sounded in life.

These recordings, ancient though some may be, are by no means impossible to find, and the building of a complete collection of original "Carusos" is certainly attainable with time, patience and some care. If you choose to collect Caruso 78rpms, do not "settle for" worn-out copies of the earlier discs, in the belief that their vast age would make it unlikely to find better ones. Well-preserved specimens of all the Caruso recordings are available and can be found; they cost somewhat more than worn copies but are well worth the investment.

I do not advise that you play these records too often. Most (or nearly all) are available on LP repressings, if you wish to **listen** to them — though listening to records is often the last thing a collector has in mind. If you have Caruso 78's which are not to be found in LP repressing, and want to listen to them, my advice is to play them once, record them, and use the recording instead. In any event, you are apt to be far more pleased with the tonal quality of LP repressings than with the original records. A record made in 1905 or 1910 was not designed for play on modern equipment. Tone arms of present-day phonographs are too light; they do not dig deeply enough into the grooves to bring out the full sound. And if you use an old phono with a heavy tone arm, the record will be that much more rapidly worn out. The record companies can play these "oldies" better than you or I can, and achieve very satisfactory results on their repressings.

The prices given are for specimens in VG and VF condition, but of course one must realize that these standards, for records 60-70 years old, are not quite the same as for more recent recordings. **Surface noise** is inevitable even in well-preserved specimens, but is more noticeable on worn copies.

	Price Range	
☐ **VICTOR RED SEAL (IMPORTED)** *1903. "Celeste Aida" (Aida).*	45.00	70.00
☐ *"Cielo e mar" (Gioconda).*	45.00	70.00
☐ *"E lucevan le stelle" (Tosca).*	45.00	70.00
☐ *"La Mia Canzone".*	45.00	70.00
☐ *"Siciliana (Cavalleria Rusticana).*	45.00	70.00
☐ *"Non t'amo piu".*	72.00	110.00
☐ *"Vesti la giubba" (Pagliacci).*	42.00	62.00
☐ **VICTOR RED SEAL** *1904-1905. "Questa o quella" (Rigoletto).*	17.00	25.00
☐ *"La donna e mobile" (Rigoletto).*	17.00	25.00
☐ *"Una furtiva lagrima", Part One (Elisir d'Amore).*	20.00	30.00

	Price Range	
☐ *"E lucevan le stelle" (Tosca).*	17.00	25.00
☐ *"Recondita armonia" (Tosca).*	22.00	35.00
☐ *"Siciliana" (Cavalleria Rusticana).*	17.00	25.00
☐ *"Il sogno (Manon).*	22.00	35.00
☐ *"Vesti la giubba (Pagliacci)*.*	18.00	27.00
(*The first phonograph recording to sell one million copies.)		
☐ *"Brindisi" (Cavalleria Rusticana).*	17.00	25.00
☐ *"Una furtiva lagrima", Part Two (Elisir d'Amore).*	37.00	55.00
☐ *"Celeste Aida" (Aida).*	23.00	32.00
☐ *"Com'e gentil" (Don Pasquale).*	26.00	35.00
☐ *"Canzone del fior" (Carmen).*	37.00	54.00
☐ *"Cielo e mar" (Gioconda).*	31.00	43.00
☐ *"Bianca al par" (Hugenots).*	37.00	55.00
☐ **VICTOR RED SEAL** *1906-1908. "Di quella pira" (Trovatore).*	19.00	27.00
☐ *"La donna e mobile" (Rigoletto).*	12.00	19.00
☐ *"Questa o quella" (Rigoletto).*	12.00	19.00
☐ *"M'appari" (Martha).*	12.00	19.00
☐ *"Che gelida manina" (Boheme).*	23.00	34.00
☐ *"Salut demeure" (Faust).*	23.00	34.00
☐ *"Spirto gentil" (La Favorita).*	23.00	34.00
☐ *"Triste Ritorno".*	23.00	34.00
☐ *"Ideale".*	20.00	30.00
☐ *"O Paradiso" (Africana).*	20.00	30.00
☐ *"Improviso" (Andrea Chenier).*	20.00	32.00
☐ *"Vesti la giubba" (Pagliacci).*	17.00	25.00
☐ *"In terra sola" (Don Sebastiano).*	21.00	33.00
☐ *"Adorables tourments".*	21.00	33.00
☐ *"Lolita".*	17.00	25.00
☐ *"Ah se ben mio" (Trovatore).*	21.00	32.00
☐ *"Celeste Aida" (Aida).*	12.00	17.00
☐ *"Solenne" (Forza del Destino) — with Scotti.*	14.00	22.00
☐ *"Ah Mimi" (Boheme) — with Scotti.*	14.00	22.00
☐ *"Del Tempio" Pearl Fishers.*	22.00	32.00
☐ *"O quanti occhi" (Butterfly) — with Geraldine Farrar*.*	22.00	33.00
(*This was the first duet recording made by Caruso and Geraldine Farrar and is considered a prize collectors' item. They later teamed up again for selections from *Faust* and other recordings.)		
☐ *"Ai nostri monti" (Trovatore).*	20.00	30.00
☐ *"O Soave fanciulla" (Boheme) — with Nellie Melba.*	32.00	45.00
☐ *"Quartet" (Rigoletto), record #96000.*	21.00	31.00
☐ *"Quartet" (Rigoletto), record #96001.*	20.00	30.00
☐ *"Addio dolce" (Boheme).*	22.00	31.00
☐ *"Sextet" (Lucia).*	20.00	30.00
☐ **VICTOR RED SEAL** *1909-1911. "Magiche note" (Queen of Sheba).*	31.00	43.00
☐ *"Pour un baiser".*	21.00	31.00
☐ *"Recondita armonia" (Tosca).*	12.00	18.00
☐ *"E lucevan le stelle" (Tosca).*	17.00	18.00
☐ *"Studenti, udite" (Germania).*	31.00	46.00
☐ *"Non chiuder" (Germania).*	30.00	44.00
☐ *"For You Alone".*	10.00	15.00
☐ *"Ora e per sempre addio" (Otello).*	30.00	44.00
☐ *"Siciliana" (Cavalleria Rusticana).*	10.00	15.00

		Price Range	
☐	*"Mamma Mia".*	12.00	19.00
☐	*"O tu che in seno" (Forza del Destino).*	12.00	19.00
☐	*"Air de la fleur" (Carmen).*	25.00	36.00
☐	*"Canzone del fior" (Carmen).*	21.00	32.00
☐	*"Bianca al par" (Hugenots).*	25.00	36.00
☐	*"Cielo e mar" (Gioconda).*	20.00	29.00
☐	*"No, Pagliaccio non son" (Pagliacci).*	15.00	23.00
☐	*"Addio".*	10.00	15.00
☐	*"La fatal pietra" (Aida).*	21.00	34.00
☐	*"O terra addio" (Aida).*	21.00	34.00
☐	*"Miserere" (Trovatore).*	10.00	15.00
☐	*"Eternelle" (Faust).*	20.00	30.00
☐	*"Laisse-moi" (Faust).*	20.00	30.00
☐	*"Mon coeur" (Faust).*	23.00	34.00
☐	*"Voici la rue" (Faust).*	23.00	34.00
☐	*"Solo, profugo" (Martha).*	23.00	34.00
☐	*"O Merveille" (Faust).*	12.00	18.00
☐	*"Amore o grillo" (Butterfly).*	23.00	34.00
☐	*"Ve lo dissi" (Butterfly).*	23.00	34.00
☐	*"Mal reggendo" (Trovatore).*	19.00	29.00
☐	*"Gia i sacerdoti" (Aida).*	23.00	34.00
☐	*"Aida a me togliesti" (Aida).*	23.00	34.00
☐	*"Alerte" (Faust).*	19.00	29.00
☐	*"Seigneur Dieu" (Faust).*	23.00	32.00
☐	*"Eh quoi" (Faust).*	27.00	40.00
☐	*"Que voulez-vouz" (Faust).*	23.00	34.00
☐	**VICTOR RED SEAL** *1912-1915. "Barcarola" (Masked Ball).*	10.00	15.00
☐	*"Canta pe'me".*	14.00	21.00
☐	*"Love is Mine".*	10.00	15.00
☐	*"Because".*	15.00	23.00
☐	*"Pimpinella".*	15.00	23.00
☐	*"Donna non vidi mai" (Manon Lescaut).*	20.00	30.00
☐	*"Your Eyes Have Told".*	14.00	21.00
☐	*"Lasciati amar".*	20.00	29.00
☐	*"Guardann'a luna".*	21.00	32.00
☐	*"Serenade Espagnole".*	21.00	32.00
☐	*"Amor Mio".*	20.00	29.00
☐	*"Parted".*	15.00	23.00
☐	*"Trusting Eyes".*	15.00	23.00
☐	*"Hantise d'amour".*	25.00	40.00
☐	*"La Mia Canzone".*	14.00	21.00
☐	*"Cielo Turchino".*	20.00	29.00
☐	*"Brindisi" (Traviata).*	20.00	29.00
☐	*"Celeste Aida" (Aida).*	10.00	15.00
☐	*"Testa adorata" (Boheme).*	20.00	30.00
☐	*"Eternamente".*	20.00	30.00
☐	*"Core 'ngrato".*	20.00	30.00
☐	*"Io non ho" (Boheme).*	20.00	30.00
☐	*"Una furtiva lagrima" (Elisir d'Amore).*	10.00	15.00
☐	*"Quando Nascesti Tu" (Lo Schiavo).*	24.00	38.00
☐	*"Ma se m'e forza" (Masked Ball).*	24.00	35.00
☐	*"Tarantella Sincera".*	16.00	24.00
☐	*"Ah fuyez" (Manon).*	25.00	37.00
☐	*"Danza".*	16.00	24.00

	Price Range	
☐ *"Dreams of Long Ago"*	12.00	19.00
☐ *"Lost Chord"*	12.00	19.00
☐ *"Hosanna"*	16.00	27.00
☐ *"Agnus dei"*	16.00	27.00
☐ *"Parmi veder le lagrime" (Rigoletto)*	15.00	27.00
☐ *"Fenesta che lucive"*	15.00	27.00
☐ *"Addio alla madre" (Cavalleria Rusticana)*	22.00	30.00
☐ *"Les Rameaux"*	16.00	27.00
☐ *"Cuius Animam" (Stabat Mater)*	16.00	27.00
☐ *"Manella Mia"*	22.00	30.00
☐ *"Tiempo antico"*	22.00	30.00
☐ *"Ingemisco" (Requiem)*	22.00	30.00
☐ *"Angelo casto" (The Duke of Alba)*	27.00	42.00
☐ *"Pecche"*	21.00	30.00
☐ *"Invano, Alvaro" (Forza del Destino)*	25.00	39.00
☐ *"Le minaccie" (Forza del Destino)*	25.00	39.00
☐ *"Crucifix"*	21.00	29.00
☐ *"On l'appelle" (Manon)*	26.00	39.00
☐ *"Ai nostri monti" (Trovatore)*	16.00	25.00
☐ *"Dio che nell'alma" (Don Carlos)*	24.00	37.00
☐ *"Elegie"*	12.00	17.00
☐ *"Si per ceil (Othello)*	21.00	30.00
☐ *"E scherzo" (Masked Ball)*	28.00	40.00
☐ *"La rivedro" (Masked Ball)*	28.00	40.00
☐ *"Sento un forza" (Guarany)*	31.00	48.00
☐ *"Si vous l'avez compris"*	15.00	27.00
☐ *"Deux Serenades"*	15.00	27.00
☐ *"Siam giunti" (Martha)*	22.00	29.00
☐ *"Che vuol dir" (Martha)*	22.00	29.00
☐ *"Presto, Presto" (Martha)*	22.00	29.00
☐ *"Quartetto Notturno" (Martha)*	16.00	25.00
☐ *"Qual volutta" (Lombardi)*	25.00	36.00
☐ *"Sextet" (Lucia)*	25.00	36.00
☐ **VICTOR RED SEAL** *1916-20, and some later. "Luna d'estate"*	18.00	26.00
☐ *"O Solo Mio"*	12.00	19.00
☐ *"Come un bel di" (Andrea Chernier)*	21.00	30.00
☐ *"De mon amie" (Pearl Fishers)*	21.00	30.00
☐ *"Pourquoi"*	18.00	26.00
☐ *"L'Alba separa"*	18.00	26.00
☐ *"Over There"*	21.00	30.00
☐ *"Inno de Garibaldi"*	21.00	30.00
☐ *"A Vucchella"*	18.00	26.00
☐ *"Vieni sul mar"*	12.00	19.00
☐ *"Addio a Napoli"*	12.00	19.00
☐ *"A Dream"*	8.00	11.00
☐ *"Messe Solenelle"*	21.00	29.00
☐ *"Nina"*	18.00	26.00
☐ *"M'appari" (Martha)*	12.00	19.00
☐ *"Inspirez-moi" (Queen of Sheba)*	25.00	38.00
☐ *"O Souverain" (El Cid)*	25.00	38.00
☐ *"Mia sposa"*	25.00	38.00
☐ *"La Procession"*	23.00	32.00
☐ *"Ah la paterna mano" (Macbeth)*	27.00	40.00
☐ *"Sancta Maria"*	23.00	32.00

	Price Range	
☐ *"Santa Lucia"*	17.00	25.00
☐ *"Noel"*	17.00	25.00
☐ *"Chanson de Juin"*	23.00	32.00
☐ *"Je crois entendre" (Pearl Fishers)*	12.00	19.00
☐ *"Vois, ma misere" (Samson)*	23.00	32.00
☐ *"Echo lontain" (Eugene Onegin)*	27.00	39.00
☐ *"Musica Proibita"*	23.00	32.00
☐ *"Uocchie Celeste"*	23.00	32.00
☐ *"Ah mon sort" (Nero)*	27.00	39.00
☐ *"Pieta Signore"*	23.00	32.00
☐ *"Regiment de Sambre et Meuse"*	21.00	30.00
☐ *"Campana de San Giusto"*	17.00	25.00
☐ *"Compane a Sera"*	17.00	25.00
☐ *"Love Me or Not"*	21.00	33.00
☐ *"Largo" (Serse)*	16.00	25.00
☐ *"A Granada"*	16.00	25.00
☐ *"Rachel quand du Seigneur" (La Juive)*	12.00	18.00
☐ *"Mia piccirella" (Salvator Rosa)*	21.00	30.00
☐ *"A la luz de la Luna"*	17.00	25.00
☐ *"Il segreto fu dunque" (Forza del Destino)*	23.00	34.00
☐ *"Je viens celebrer" (Samson)*	23.00	34.00
☐ *"Venti scudi" (Elisir d'Amore)*	23.00	34.00
☐ *"Quartet" (Rigoletto)*	12.00	19.00
☐ *"Sextet" (Lucia)*	12.00	19.00
HOMER, LOUISE		
☐ **VICTOR RED SEAL** *1903-1905. "Le parlate d'amor" (Faust)*	23.00	32.00
☐ *"Annie Laurie"*	21.00	29.00
☐ *"May Day"*	30.00	42.00
☐ *"Sing Me a Song"*	23.00	32.00
☐ *"Stella del mariner" (La Giaconda)*	37.00	51.00
☐ *"Old Folks at Home"*	23.00	32.00
☐ *"Habanera" (Carmen)*	37.00	51.00
☐ *"Filles de Cadiz"*	37.00	51.00
☐ *"Scene de la prison" (La Phophete)*	57.00	82.00
☐ *"Nobil Signori" (Huguenots)*	41.00	58.00
☐ *"He Shall Feed His Flock (Messiah)*	35.00	46.00
☐ *"Mon coeur" (Samson)*	38.00	50.00
☐ *"Away with Crying" (Orfeo)*	48.00	61.00
☐ *"O don fatale" (Don Carlos)*	46.00	60.00
☐ *"Turn Ye to Me"*	38.00	50.00
☐ *"O Rest in the Lord" (Elijah)*	31.00	43.00
☐ *"Ah mon fils" (La Prophete)*	38.00	55.00
☐ **VICTOR RED SEAL** *1906-1911. "Stride la vamps" (Trovatore)*	23.00	33.00
☐ *"Voce di donna" (La Gioconda)*	25.00	38.00
☐ *"Esser mesto" (Martha)*	40.00	59.00
☐ *"Quanto a te lieta" (Faust)*	31.00	45.00
☐ *"Le parlate d'amor" (Faust)*	29.00	40.00
☐ *"Acerbe volunta" (Adriana Lecouvreur)*	39.00	51.00
☐ *"At Parting"*	17.00	25.00
☐ *"Banjo Song"*	8.00	14.00
☐ *"Vengeance at Last" (Samson)*	29.00	40.00
☐ *"Lost Chord"*	12.00	19.00
☐ *"Old Black Joe"*	12.00	19.00

	Price Range	
☐ *"Fac ut portem" (Stabat Mater).*	16.00	23.00
☐ *"Quando a te lieta" (Faust).*	25.00	40.00
☐ *"Amour, viens aider" (Samson).*	16.00	23.00
☐ *"Die Lorelei".*	16.00	23.00
☐ *"Die Allmacht".*	35.00	51.00
☐ *"Che faro senza Euridice" (Orfeo).*	16.00	22.00
☐ *"Fatal Divinita" (Alceste).*	35.00	51.00
☐ *"There is a Green Tree'.*	12.00	19.00
☐ *"Mesta ognor" (Martha).*	44.00	65.00
☐ *"Dome epais" (Lakme).*	44.00	65.00
☐ *"Du Aermste" (Lohengrin).*	44.00	65.00
☐ **VICTOR RED SEAL** *1912-1918. "I Cannot Sing the Old Songs".*	8.00	14.00
☐ *"Boats Sail/Sing to Me".*	12.00	17.00
☐ *"Annie Laurie".*	8.00	14.00
☐ *"Oh Promise Me" (Robin Hood).*	8.00	14.00
☐ *"Last Night".*	8.00	14.00
☐ *"Janet's Choice".*	12.00	19.00
☐ *"Don't Cease".*	12.00	19.00
☐ *"Where is My Boy Tonight?".*	8.00	14.00
☐ *"Nur wer die Sehnsucht kennst".*	8.00	14.00
☐ *"Star Spangled Banner".*	12.00	19.00
☐ *"Come Unto Me".*	25.00	40.00
☐ *"Dearest" (Requiem).*	25.00	40.00
☐ *"Babylon".*	25.00	40.00
☐ *"He Was Despised" (Messiah).*	16.00	23.00
☐ *"My Heart Ever Faithful".*	16.00	23.00
☐ *"Largo" (Serse).*	16.00	23.00
☐ *"Love's Old Sweet Song".*	12.00	17.00
☐ **VICTOR RED SEAL** *1919-1925. "I Love to Tell the Story".*	8.00	14.00
☐ *"Hard Times".*	8.00	14.00
☐ *"Oh, Boys, Carry Me 'Long".*	8.00	14.00
☐ *"When the Roses Bloom".*	8.00	14.00
☐ *"Just for Today".*	8.00	14.00
☐ *"My Ain Folk".*	8.00	14.00
☐ *"My Ain Countrie".*	8.00	14.00
☐ *"Christ the Lord".*	8.00	14.00
☐ *"Lane to Ballybree".*	8.00	14.00
☐ *"Ring Out Wild Bells".*	17.00	25.00
☐ *"Sheep and Lambs".*	17.00	25.00
☐ *"Auld Scotch Sangs".*	17.00	25.00
☐ *"Barnyard Song".*	17.00	25.00
☐ *"Little Orphant Annie".*	27.00	40.00

McCORMACK, JOHN

John McCormack was the all-around singer supreme, at home with folk songs, popular tunes and operatic arias. Although best remembered today as the classic balladeer of Irish traditional melodies, he also enjoyed a long career on the opera stage, notably at the Metropolitan, and made a number of operatic recordings. Most of his records are, however, in the nature of ballads or comic ditties, sung to the accompaniment of a piano only. They have been repressed to death, but collectors, being collectors, will always persist in searching out the originals.

The discs listed here date from the period 1910-1925 and are, of course, one-sided. On the whole, the sound quality of McCormack's recordings was not too bad, though one can only wonder how he might have sounded with modern recording techniques. He was under exclusive contract with the Eldridge Johnson Victor Co., and all his records were released on the Victor "red seal" label, that label being assigned to classical music and what were then called "celebrity recordings".

	Price Range	
☐ **VICTOR RED SEAL** *1910-1912. "The Minstrel Boy".*	**8.00**	**14.00**
☐ *"I Hear You Calling Me".*	**8.00**	**14.00**
☐ *"When Shadows Gather".*	**14.00**	**20.00**
☐ *"Annie Laurie".*	**8.00**	**14.00**
☐ *"Dear Little Shamrock".*	**8.00**	**14.00**
☐ *"My Lagen Love".*	**16.00**	**23.00**
☐ *"I'm Falling in Love" (Naughty Marietta).*	**12.00**	**19.00**
☐ *"Believe Me if All Those Endearing Young Charms".*	**8.00**	**14.00**
☐ *"Mother Machree".*	**8.00**	**14.00**
☐ *"Take, Oh Take Those Lips Away".*	**8.00**	**14.00**
☐ *"A Child's Song".*	**15.00**	**22.00**
☐ *"A Farewell".*	**15.00**	**22.00**
☐ *"I Know of Two Bright Eyes".*	**15.00**	**22.00**
☐ *"Eileen Aroon".*	**15.00**	**22.00**
☐ *"The Rosary".*	**8.00**	**14.00**
☐ *"The Wearing of the Green".*	**8.00**	**14.00**
☐ *"The Harp That Once Thro' Tara's Halls".*	**8.00**	**14.00**
☐ *"Silver Threads Among the Gold".*	**8.00**	**14.00**
☐ *"Killarney".*	**12.00**	**19.00**
☐ *"Come Back to Erin".*	**12.00**	**19.00**
☐ *"Snowy Breasted Pearl".*	**12.00**	**19.00**
☐ *"Molly Bawn".*	**12.00**	**19.00**
☐ *"Has Sorrow Thy Young Days Shaded".*	**12.00**	**19.00**
☐ *"Drink To Me Only With Thine Eyes".*	**12.00**	**19.00**
☐ *"Ah, Moon of My Delight".*	**14.00**	**20.00**
☐ *"Kathleen Mavoureen".*	**12.00**	**19.00**
☐ *"Irish Emigrant".*	**12.00**	**19.00**
☐ *"She is Far From the Land".*	**12.00**	**19.00**
☐ *"An Evening Song".*	**12.00**	**19.00**
☐ *"Paul's Address" (Natoma).*	**27.00**	**39.00**
☐ *"Like Stars Above".*	**21.00**	**30.00**
☐ *"Marie, My Girl".*	**21.00**	**30.00**
☐ *"Asthore".*	**14.00**	**20.00**
☐ *"Vieni al contento" (Lakme).*	**21.00**	**30.00**
☐ *"Li Mariani".*	**29.00**	**45.00**
☐ *"Del Tempio" (Pearl Fishers).*	**29.00**	**45.00**
☐ *"Fra poco a me" (Lucia).*	**29.00**	**45.00**
☐ *"Canzone del fior" (Carmen).*	**29.00**	**45.00**
☐ *"Una furtiva lagrima" (Elisir d'Amore).*	**29.00**	**45.00**
☐ *"Che gelida manina" (Boheme).*	**29.00**	**45.00**
☐ *"Salve dimora" (Faust).*	**29.00**	**45.00**
☐ *"Per viver vicino (Daughter of the Regiment).*	**29.00**	**45.00**
☐ *"Tu che a Dio" (Lucia).*	**29.00**	**45.00**
☐ *"Ah Mimi" (Boheme).*	**35.00**	**50.00**

	Price Range	
☐ **VICTOR RED SEAL** *1913-1915. "At Dawning".*	8.00	12.00
☐ *"Dai campi" (Mefistofele).*	17.00	25.00
☐ *"Giunto sul passo" (Mefistofele).*	17.00	25.00
☐ *"Mi par d'udire (Pearl Fishers).*	17.00	25.00
☐ *"There is a Flower" (Maritana).*	14.00	20.00
☐ *"Sweet Genevieve".*	8.00	12.00
☐ *"My Dreams".*	8.00	12.00
☐ *"Where the River Shannon Flows".*	8.00	12.00
☐ *"Il sogno" (Manon).*	21.00	33.00
☐ *"Molly Brannigan".*	12.00	19.00
☐ *"Within the Garden of My Heart".*	8.00	14.00
☐ *"Dear Love, Remember Me".*	8.00	14.00
☐ *"Foggy Dew".*	8.00	14.00
☐ *"Say Au Revoir".*	8.00	14.00
☐ *"Low Back'd Car".*	8.00	14.00
☐ *"Down in the Forest.*	14.00	25.00
☐ *"Mother o' Mine".*	8.00	14.00
☐ *"Sospiri Miei".*	21.00	30.00
☐ *"I Hear a Thrush at Eve".*	8.00	14.00
☐ *"Eileen Allanna".*	12.00	17.00
☐ *"Good Bye, Sweetheart".*	8.00	14.00
☐ *"A Little Love".*	8.00	14.00
☐ *"Questa o quella" (Rigoletto).*	15.00	25.00
☐ *"Nearer, My God, to Thee".*	8.00	14.00
☐ *"Le Portrait".*	26.00	40.00
☐ *"I'll Sing Thee Songs of Araby".*	8.00	14.00
☐ *"Somewhere a Voice is Calling".*	8.00	14.00
☐ *"Mavis".*	8.00	14.00
☐ *"Come Where My Love Lies".*	8.00	14.00
☐ *"Who Knows".*	8.00	14.00
☐ *"Little Grey Home".*	8.00	14.00
☐ *"My Wild Irish Rose".*	8.00	14.00
☐ *"Bonnie Wee Thing".*	8.00	14.00
☐ *"Beautiful Isle of Somewhere".*	15.00	23.00
☐ *"Golden Love".*	8.00	14.00
☐ *"Because".*	15.00	23.00
☐ *"Mavoureen".*	8.00	14.00
☐ *"Mary of Argyle".*	8.00	14.00
☐ *"Ben Bolt".*	8.00	14.00
☐ *"A Dream".*	8.00	14.00
☐ *"Funiculi Funicula".*	15.00	22.00
☐ *"Lily of Killarney".*	13.00	19.00
☐ *"It's a Long, Long Way to Tipperray".*	8.00	14.00
☐ *"Until".*	8.00	14.00
☐ *"Evening Song".*	8.00	14.00
☐ *"When the Dew is Falling".*	8.00	14.00
☐ *"Morning".*	15.00	22.00
☐ *"Vacant Chair".*	8.00	14.00
☐ *"De' miei bollenti spiriti" (Traviata).*	35.00	50.00
☐ *"Nirvana".*	21.00	30.00
☐ *"Parle-moi de ma mere" (Carmen).*	25.00	37.00
☐ *"Good Bye".*	11.00	19.00
☐ *"O terra addio" (Aida).*	20.00	30.00
☐ *"When My Ships Come Sailing Home".*	13.00	19.00

	Price Range	
☐ *"The Trumpeter"*	13.00	19.00
☐ *"Come Into the Garden"*	13.00	19.00
☐ *"Turn Ye to Me"*	22.00	35.00
☐ *"Adeste Fideles"*	13.00	19.00
☐ *"Serenade"*	13.00	19.00
☐ *"Ave Marie" (record #87192)*	13.00	19.00
☐ *"Serenata"*	13.00	19.00
☐ *"Carme"*	16.00	25.00
☐ *"Flirtation"*	11.00	17.00
☐ *"Calm as the Night"*	11.00	17.00
☐ *"O soave fanciulla" (Boheme)*	15.00	23.00
☐ *"Parigi o cara" (Traviata)*	20.00	30.00
☐ *"Angel's Serenade"*	15.00	23.00
☐ *"Ave Maria" (record #88481)*	15.00	23.00
☐ *"Le Nil"*	15.00	23.00
☐ *"Berceuse" (Jocelyn)*	15.00	23.00
☐ *"Ave Maria" (record #88484)*	15.00	23.00
☐ *"Quartet" (Rigoletto)*	20.00	30.00
☐ **VICTOR RED SEAL** *1916-1919. "Sing, Sing Birds on the Wing"*	8.00	14.00
☐ *"A Little Bit of Heaven"*	7.00	13.00
☐ *"Forgotten"*	7.00	13.00
☐ *"Venetian Song"*	7.00	13.00
☐ *"Old Refrain"*	7.00	13.00
☐ *"Parted"*	7.00	13.00
☐ *"Then You'll Remember Me" (Bohemian Girl)*	11.00	19.00
☐ *"Dreams"*	8.00	14.00
☐ *"Your Eyes"*	8.00	14.00
☐ *"Little Boy Blue"*	8.00	14.00
☐ *"Cradle Song 1915"*	8.00	14.00
☐ *"Sunshine of Your Smile"*	8.00	14.00
☐ *"Love, Here is My Heart"*	8.00	14.00
☐ *"Tommy Lad"*	8.00	14.00
☐ *"When Irish Eyes are Smiling"*	8.00	14.00
☐ *"Star Spangled Banner"*	12.00	19.00
☐ *"Ireland My Sireland" (Eileen)*	12.00	19.00
☐ *"Eileen Alanna Asthore" (Eileen)*	12.00	19.00
☐ *"There's a Long, Long Trail"*	8.00	14.00
☐ *"Keep the Home Fires Burning"*	8.00	14.00
☐ *"Any Place is Heaven"*	8.00	14.00
☐ *"Crucifix"*	8.00	14.00
☐ *"Lord is My Light"*	8.00	14.00
☐ *"Rainbow of Love"*	8.00	14.00
☐ *"Trumpet Call"*	12.00	19.00
☐ *"Send Me Away With a Smile"*	12.00	19.00
☐ *"God Be With Our Boys"*	12.00	19.00
☐ *"Little Mother of Mine"*	8.00	14.00
☐ *"Dear Old Pal of Mine"*	8.00	14.00
☐ *"Love's Garden of Roses"*	8.00	14.00
☐ *"When You Come Back"*	12.00	19.00
☐ *"My Irish Song of Songs"*	8.00	14.00
☐ *"Calling Me Home to You"*	8.00	14.00
☐ *"When You Look in the Heart of a Rose"*	8.00	14.00
☐ *"First Rose of Summer"*	8.00	14.00

	Price Range	
☐ "Roses of Picardy".	8.00	14.00
☐ "Prize Song" (Meistersinger).	12.00	20.00
☐ "Il mio tesoro" (Don Giovanni).	14.00	21.00
☐ "Kerry Dance".	10.00	15.00
☐ "Non e ver".	18.00	27.00
☐ "Champs paternels" (Joseph).	21.00	32.00
☐ "Barcarolle" (Tales of Hoffman).	10.00	15.00
☐ **VICTOR RED SEAL** *1920-1925. "The Tumble-Down Shack".*	6.50	11.00
☐ "Only You".	6.50	11.00
☐ "Your Eyes".	6.50	11.00
☐ "Barefoot Trail".	6.50	11.00
☐ "Thank God for a Garden".	6.50	11.00
☐ "Honour & Love" (Monsieur Beaucaire).	10.00	15.00
☐ "When You & I Were Young".	6.50	11.00
☐ "'Tis an Irish Girl".	6.50	11.00
☐ "Next Market Day".	10.00	15.00
☐ "Beneath the Moon of Lombardy".	6.50	11.00
☐ "Somewhere".	6.50	11.00
☐ "Learn to Smile".	6.50	12.00
☐ "Little Town in Ould County Down".	6.50	11.00
☐ "Rose of My Heart".	6.50	11.00
☐ "The Road That Brought You".	6.50	11.00
☐ "Sweet Peggy O'Neil".	6.50	11.00
☐ "Wonderful World of Romance".	6.50	11.00
☐ "O Sleep" (Semele).	6.50	11.00
☐ "Three O'Clock in the Morning".	12.00	19.00
☐ "Mother in Ireland".	6.50	11.00
☐ "Jesus, My Lord".	6.50	11.00
☐ "Kingdom Within Your Eyes".	6.50	11.00
☐ "Remember the Rose".	6.50	11.00
☐ "Sometime You'll Remember".	6.50	11.00
☐ "Love Sends a Little Gift of Roses".	6.50	11.00
☐ "Wonderful One".	6.50	11.00
☐ "Somewhere in the World".	6.50	11.00
☐ "Where the Rainbow Ends".	6.50	11.00
☐ "Bard of Armagh".	11.00	17.00
☐ "Would God I Were the Tender Apple Blossom".	6.50	11.00
☐ "Take a Look Molly".	6.50	11.00
☐ "Marcheta".	11.00	17.00
☐ "Indiana Moon".	11.00	17.00
☐ "Lost Chord".	6.50	11.00
☐ "When Night Descends".	11.00	17.00
☐ "Since You Went Away".	11.00	17.00
☐ "O Cease Thy Singing".	11.00	17.00
☐ "The Last Hour".	6.50	11.00

MELBA, NELLIE

Nellie Melba's recordings are collectors' items in the truest sense of the term. Having reached the peak of her stardom not long after the introduction of 78rpm records, her voice was among the most frequently recorded of early 20th-century opera artists. A star she was in every respect, the only female opera singer before 1910 whose public notoriety could be said to equal Caruso's. Modern opinion of her talents do not perhaps equal those of her contemporaries, nevertheless her recordings are still very much in demand.

	Price Range	
☐ **IMPORTED VICTOR MAUVE LABEL** *1904-1905. "Les Anges Pleurent".*	30.00	44.00
☐ *"Chant Venetien".*	30.00	44.00
☐ *"Come Back to Erin".*	22.00	30.00
☐ *"Auld Lang Syne".*	22.00	30.00
☐ *"Old Folks at Home".*	22.00	30.00
☐ *"Good Night".*	22.00	35.00
☐ *"Away on the Hill".*	22.00	35.00
☐ *"Goodbye".*	27.00	37.00
☐ *"Mad scene" (Lucia).*	38.00	53.00
☐ *"Ah fors e lui" (Traviata).*	38.00	53.00
☐ *"Sempre libera" (Traviata).*	38.00	53.00
☐ *"Sweet Bird" (Penseroso).*	38.00	53.00
☐ *"Three Green Bonnets".*	38.00	53.00
☐ *"Caro nome" (Rigoletto).*	38.00	53.00
☐ *"Se Saran Rose".*	38.00	53.00
☐ *"A vos jeux" (Hamlet).*	38.00	53.00
☐ *"Pale et blonde" (Hamlet).*	38.00	53.00
☐ *"Martinata" (Tosti).*	38.00	53.00
☐ *"Nymphes et Sylvainus".*	38.00	53.00
☐ *"Si Mes Vers".*	38.00	53.00
☐ *"Porgi amor" (Marriage of Figaro).*	38.00	53.00
☐ *"Home Sweet Home".*	27.00	40.00
☐ *"Lo, Hear the Gentle Lark".*	27.00	40.00
☐ *"Sur le Lac".*	36.00	51.00

NIELSEN, ALICE

The rich soprano voice of Alice Nielsen, who long enticed opera audiences with her renditions of roles from **Tosca, Butterfly, Marriage of Figaro** and others, was well represented on recordings, of which the following is only a mere selection. On the whole her recordings are somewhat more valuable than those of most other opera singers.

☐ **COLUMBIA** *1911-1915. "Deh Vieni" (Marraige of Figaro).*	30.00	43.00
☐ *"Le roi de Thule" (Faust).*	30.00	43.00
☐ *"Annie Laurie".*	15.00	22.00
☐ *"Kathleen Mavoureen.*	15.00	22.00
☐ *"From the Land of the Sky Blue Water".*	30.00	45.00
☐ *"Chonita's Prayer" (Sacrifice).*	30.00	45.00
☐ *"Home Sweet Home".*	20.00	30.00
☐ *"Il Bacio".*	20.00	30.00
☐ *"Ancora un passo" (Butterfly).*	30.00	45.00
☐ *"Piccolo Iddio" (Butterfly).*	30.00	45.00
☐ *"Un beldi" (Butterfly).*	30.00	45.00
☐ *"Addio" (Boheme).*	20.00	30.00
☐ *"L'altra notte" (Mefistofele).*	30.00	45.00
☐ *"Viss d'art" (Tosca).*	30.00	45.00
☐ *"Je dis que rien" (Carmen).*	30.00	45.00
☐ *"Ieri son salito" (Butterfly).*	30.00	45.00
☐ *"Fardi si fa" (Faust).*	36.00	51.00
☐ *"Sweet Genevieve".*	16.00	25.00
☐ *"In the Gloaming".*	16.00	25.00
☐ *"Oh I'm Not Myself.*	16.00	25.00
☐ *"Believe Me if All Those Endearing Young Charms".*	16.00	25.00

	Price Range	
☐ *"Love's Old Sweet Song"*	16.00	25.00
☐ *"Bendemeer's Stream"*	16.00	25.00
☐ *"Day is Done"*	16.00	25.00
☐ *"Spirit Flower"*	16.00	25.00
☐ *"Low Back'd Car"*	16.00	25.00
☐ *"Killarney"*	16.00	25.00
☐ *"Barney O'Hea"*	16.00	25.00
☐ *"By the Water of Minnetonka"*	12.00	19.00
☐ *"From the Land of Sky-Blue Water"*	12.00	19.00

ROSA, PONSELLE

The voice of Rosa Ponselle, a long-time favorite at the Metropolitan and other opera houses, is still regarded by those who heard it "in the flesh" as one of the finest in operatic history. On these recordings she tackled a wide range of selections, usually with memorable results.

☐ **COLUMBIA RECORDS** *1919-1923. "O Patria mia" (Aida).*	17.00	25.00
☐ *"La vergine" (Forza del Destino).*	17.00	25.00
☐ *"D'amor sull'ali" (Trovatore).*	17.00	25.00
☐ *"Good Bye"*	17.00	25.00
☐ *"Vissi d'arte" (Tosca).*	17.00	25.00
☐ *"Un beldi" (Butterfly).*	17.00	25.00
☐ *"Keep the Home Fires Burning"*	17.00	25.00
☐ *"Bolero" (Vespri Siciliani).*	21.00	32.00
☐ *"Casta diva" (Norma).*	17.00	25.00
☐ *"O terra addio" (Aida).*	17.00	25.00
☐ *"Suicidio" (Gioconda).*	17.00	25.00
☐ *"Pace, pace" (Forza del Destino).*	17.00	25.00
☐ *"Kiss Me Again" (Mme. Modiste).*	17.00	25.00
☐ *"Maria Mari"*	17.00	25.00
☐ *"Song of India" (Sadko).*	17.00	25.00
☐ *"Mira d'acerbe" (Trovatore).*	19.00	25.00
☐ *"Rachem"*	17.00	25.00
☐ *"Old Folks at Home"*	12.00	17.00
☐ *"Home Sweet Home"*	12.00	17.00
☐ *"Scenes That Are Brightest" (Maritana).*	17.00	24.00
☐ *"O Solo Mio"*	18.00	25.00

RUFFO, TITTA

Unfortunately the early recordings of this noted baritone were made at a time when equipment and techniques did not permit the full range of his voice to be captured at its best. Still, his records are of historical interest and popular with collectors.

☐ **IMPORTED VICTOR RED SEAL** *1907-1909. "Veglia of donna" (Rigoletto).*	20.00	32.00
☐ *"Si vendetta" (Rigoletto).*	20.00	32.00
☐ *"Brindis" (Hamlet).*	20.00	32.00
☐ *"Per me giunto" (Don Carlos).*	20.00	32.00
☐ *"Largo al factotum" (Barber of Seville).*	15.00	23.00
☐ *"Prologo" (Pagliacci).*	15.00	23.00
☐ *"Pari siamo" (Rigoletto).*	22.00	34.00

	Price Range	
☐ *"Monologo - Essere onon essere" (Hamlet).*	22.00	34.00
☐ *"Dio possente" (Faust).*	22.00	34.00
☐ *"Come il romito Fior" (Hamlet).*	22.00	34.00
☐ *"Canzon del toreador" (Carmen).*	22.00	34.00
☐ *"Cortigiani (Rigoletto).*	22.00	34.00
☐ *"Nega se puoi la luce" (Hamlet).*	25.00	38.00
☐ *"Dungue io son" (Barger of Seville).*	22.00	34.00
☐ *"Piangi Fanciulla" (Rigoletto).*	22.00	34.00
☐ *"Dite alla giovine" (Traviata).*	22.00	34.00
☐ *"Le minaccie" (Forza del Destino).*	25.00	42.00
☐ *"La ci darem" (Don Giovanni).*	21.00	30.00
☐ *"Lassu in cielo" (Rigoletto).*	25.00	42.00

SCOTTI, ANTONIO

The 78rpm discography of Antonio Scotti includes a number of rare and costly recordings. He was one of the comparatively few artists to switch labels, beginning with Columbia and going over to the then-more-prestigious Victor.

☐ **COLUMBIA RECORDS** *1903. "Canzone del Toreador" (Carmen).*	215.00	325.00
☐ *"Prologo" (Pagliacci).*	215.00	325.00
☐ *"Serenata" (Don Giovanni).*	215.00	325.00
☐ *"Canzone del Toreador" (Carmen) (reissue).*	140.00	215.00
☐ **VICTOR RED SEAL** *1903 – 1905. "Dio possente" (Faust).*	65.00	110.00
☐ *"Prologo" (Pagliacci).*	28.00	45.00
☐ *"Dio possente" (Faust).*	28.00	45.00
☐ *"Suo padre" (Aida).*	28.00	45.00
☐ *"Bella siccome unangelo" (Don Pasquale).*	28.00	45.00
☐ *"Brindis" (Othello).*	28.00	45.00
☐ *"Mandolinata".*	23.00	34.00
☐ *"O casto fior" (Rio de Lahore).*	27.00	43.00
☐ *"Alla vita" (Masked Ball).*	27.00	43.00
☐ *"Deh non pariare" (Rigoletto).*	55.00	80.00
☐ *"Fin ch'han dal vino" (Don Giovanni).*	55.00	80.00
☐ *"Eri tu" (Masked Ball).*	55.00	80.00
☐ *"Credo" (Othello).*	55.00	80.00
☐ *"Per megi unto" (Don Carlos).*	55.00	80.00
☐ *"Come pande vezzoso" (Elisir d'Amore).*	55.00	80.00
☐ *"Triste Aprile".*	40.00	57.00

STRACCIARA, RICCARDO

A baritone popular in his day, who is now much better known to record collectors than to the public.

☐ **COLUMBIA RECORDS** *1907-1912. "Prologo" (Pagliacci).*	17.00	25.00
☐ *"Largo al Factotum" (Barber of Seville).*	17.00	25.00
☐ *"Dio Possente" (Faust).*	17.00	25.00
☐ *"Di Provenza" (Traviata).*	17.00	25.00
☐ *"Il balen" (Trovatore).*	17.00	25.00
☐ *"Eri tu" (Masked Ball).*	17.00	25.00
☐ *"Elegie".*	17.00	25.00

	Price Range	
☐ *"There's a Long, Long Trail"*	17.00	25.00
☐ *"The Sunshine of Your Smile"*	13.00	19.00
☐ *"Solenne" (Forza del Destino)*	17.00	25.00
☐ *" 'Cause of You"*	17.00	25.00
☐ *"La Paloma"*	13.00	19.00
☐ *"Mira d'acerbe" (Trovatore)*	21.00	30.00
☐ *"Canzone del Toreador" (Carmen)*	17.00	25.00
☐ *"Ideale"*	17.00	25.00
☐ *"Pari siamo" (Rigoletto)*	17.00	25.00
☐ *"Elegie"*	13.00	19.00
☐ *"O Solo Mio"*	13.00	19.00
☐ *"Untill"*	13.00	19.00
☐ *"Santa Lucia"*	13.00	19.00
☐ *"Canta pe'me"*	13.00	19.00
☐ *"When the Evening Bells are Ringing"*	13.00	19.00

WILSON, MARGARET WOODROW

Margaret Woodrow Wilson, daughter of the President, aspired to be an opera singer and, in the opinion of some, thanks only to the celebrity of her father she succeeded in obtaining a recording contract with Columbia Records. Her records were mostly in the folk song category.

☐ **COLUMBIA RECORDS** *1914-1918. "Low Back'd Car"*	8.00	13.00
☐ *"Will Ye No Come Back"*	8.00	13.00
☐ *"My Laddie"*	7.00	11.00
☐ *"My Lovely Celia"*	7.00	11.00
☐ *"Leezie Lindsay"*	7.00	11.00
☐ *"Star Spangled Banner"*	7.00	11.00
☐ *"My Old Kentucky Home"*	7.00	11.00

ORCHESTRA LEADERS AND MUSICIANS MEMORABILIA

☐ **ALPERT, HERB.** *8x10 photo with combo, signed, dated 1966.*	7.00	10.00
☐ **ALPERT, HERB.** *Restaurant menu, signed, with small sketch of man playing horn.*	8.00	11.00
☐ **ALPERT, HERB.** *LP record album cover, signed, record missing.*	20.00	30.00
☐ **ALPERT, HERB.** *Record company contract, signed, three pages.*	15.00	20.00
☐ **ALPERT, HERB.** *Postcard in his hand, three lines, 1961.*	5.00	7.00
☐ **ALPERT, HERB.** *Two typed letters, signed, 1972 and 1973.*	7.00	10.00
☐ **ALPERT, HERB.** *Poster, advertising "Tijuana Brass". Matted, framed, 27x41, c. 1968.*	27.00	35.00
☐ **ALPERT, HERB.** *Three Polaroid snapshots taken by fans, not signed.*	3.00	4.00
☐ **ARNAZ, DESI.** *8x10 studio photo, inscribed and signed, 1945.*	15.00	20.00
☐ **ARNAZ, DESI.** *8x10 portrait with Lucille Ball, signed by both, matted and framed, c. 1953.*	45.00	60.00
☐ **ARNAZ, DESI.** *Magazine cover, signed, corner torn.*	6.00	8.00
☐ **ARNAZ, DESI.** *Article from "TV Guide", signed, c. 1951.*	8.00	11.00
☐ **ARNAZ, DESI.** *Motion picture company publicity photo on card, facsimile signature, 5x6½, c. 1949.*	3.00	4.00

	Price Range	
☐ **ARNAZ, DESI.** *Mexican-style hat reputedly worn by him in revue, c. 1946.*	60.00	80.00
☐ **ARNAZ, DESI.** *Signature on a card.*	3.00	4.00
☐ **ARNAZ, DESI.** *Postcard from him to film producer, 1950.*	7.00	10.00
☐ **ARNAZ, DESI.** *Typewritten letter, signed, Desilou letterhead, 1955.*	7.00	10.00
☐ **ARNAZ, DESI.** *Desilou Productions contract, signed by him and several others, 1956.*	11.00	15.00
☐ **ARRAU, CLAUDIO.** *Concert program, signed, 1955.*	13.00	18.00
☐ **ARRAU, CLAUDIO.** *8x10 studio portrait, signed, 1968.*	15.00	20.00
☐ **ARRAU, CLAUDIO.** *Scrapbook containing mementos of his career, with 34 photos, mostly candid, 7 signed, three postcards written by him, two letters, one contract, 61 news cuttings and other items.*	235.00	330.00
☐ **ARRAU, CLAUDIO.** *5x7 photo, signed and inscribed.*	12.00	16.00
☐ **ARRAU, CLAUDIO.** *Copy of "Opera News", signed on interior page.*	7.00	10.00
☐ **ARRAU, CLAUDIO.** *Signature on a 3x5 sheet of paper.*	4.00	5.00
☐ **ARRAU, CLAUDIO.** *Signature on label of a 12" LP record.*	45.00	60.00
☐ **ARRAU, CLAUDIO.** *Candid snapshot outside Alice Tully Hall, N.Y., signed on the back.*	10.00	15.00
☐ **ARRAU, CLAUDIO.** *ALs, three pages, with envelope, 1946.*	30.00	40.00
☐ **BERNSTEIN, LEONARD.** *ALs, one page, NY, 1951.*	25.00	35.00
☐ **BERNSTEIN, LEONARD.** *6x8 color photo, signed and inscribed.*	16.00	23.00
☐ **BERNSTEIN, LEONARD.** *Musical score, "The Mass", signed.*	13.00	18.00
☐ **BERNSTEIN, LEONARD.** *Four sheets of original manuscript composition for "The Mass", in plastic folder.*	115.00	150.00
☐ **BERNSTEIN, LEONARD.** *Concert program, signed.*	13.00	20.00
☐ **BERNSTEIN, LEONARD.** *Membership card, "ASCAP", signed.*	35.00	45.00
☐ **BERNSTEIN, LEONARD.** *Performance contract, signed three times, 1961.*	70.00	100.00
☐ **BERNSTEIN, LEONARD.** *LP record album cover, signed, record missing.*	55.00	75.00
☐ **BERNSTEIN, LEONARD.** *Signature on a card.*	5.00	7.00
☐ **BLOCH, RAY.** *8x10 photo, signed, 1955.*	4.00	6.00
☐ **BLOCH, RAY.** *ALs, two pages, 1967.*	5.00	7.00
☐ **BLOCH, RAY.** *Photo with Milton DeLugg, signed by both, 1967.*	10.00	14.00
☐ **BLOCH, RAY.** *Photo with Rosemary Clooney, signed by Bloch only.*	6.00	8.00
☐ **BLOCH, RAY.** *Magazine article, signed, c. 1957.*	3.00	4.00
☐ **BLOCH, RAY.** *TV contract, signed, seven pages.*	12.00	16.00
☐ **BLOCH, RAY.** *Photo with orchestra, signed by him and 7 members of orchestra, c. 1954.*	9.00	13.00
☐ **CASALS, PABLO.** *Instructional booklet on cello playing, signed and inscribed, dated 1928.*	60.00	80.00
☐ **CASALS, PABLO.** *8x10 photo with cello, signed, c. 1968.*	50.00	65.00

	Price Range	
☐ **CASALS, PABLO.** *Handwritten postcard from Mrs. Jacqueline K. Onassis to Pablo Casals, four lines, large signature, 1966.*	220.00	300.00
☐ **CASALS, PABLO.** *5x7 photo at age about 50, signed on back, pinholes in corners, traces of glue on back.*	60.00	80.00
☐ **CASALS, PABLO.** *ALs, four pages, in Spanish, concerns musical engagements, 1919.*	150.00	200.00
☐ **CASALS, PABLO.** *ALs, one page, 1927.*	80.00	105.00
☐ **CASALS, PABLO.** *ALs, half page, declining a speaking invitation, 1951.*	65.00	80.00
☐ **CASALS, PABLO.** *ALs, two pages, concerning cello lessons for a student, 1958.*	120.00	160.00
☐ **CASALS, PABLO.** *Envelope addressed by him, 1957.*	45.00	60.00
☐ **CASALS, PABLO.** *Concert program, signed.*	75.00	100.00
☐ **CASALS, PABLO.** *Poster advertising an appearance at Carnegie Hall, New York, unsigned.*	26.00	34.00
☐ **CAVALLARO, CARMEN.** *8x10 photo with band, signed.*	7.00	10.00
☐ **CAVALLARO, CARMEN.** *Handbill advertising his appearance at a Chicago cafe, signed.*	5.00	7.00
☐ **CAVALLARO, CARMEN.** *ALs, two pages, 1960.*	7.00	10.00
☐ **CAVALLARO, CARMEN.** *Two-page article from newspaper, signed and inscribed, laminated.*	8.00	11.00
☐ **CAVALLARO, CARMEN.** *Book, "The Big Bands", inscribed on front endleaf.*	7.00	10.00
☐ **CAVALLARO, CARMEN.** *Two 4x5½ snapshot photos, one signed on the back, the other unsigned.*	4.00	5.00
☐ **CAVALLARO, CARMEN.** *Signature on a card.*	2.00	2.75
☐ **CAVALLARO, CARMEN.** *Postcard written by him to newspaper columnist, 1952.*	4.00	5.00
☐ **CAVALLARO, CARMEN.** *Photo with Sammy Kaye, signed by Cavallaro only.*	4.00	5.00
☐ **CLIBURN, VAN.** *8x10 photo, signed, at piano, 1958.*	20.00	25.00
☐ **CLIBURN, VAN.** *Photo of him in Red Square, Moscow, signed.*	14.00	18.00
☐ **CLIBURN, VAN.** *Printed musical score, signed, inscribed.*	25.00	32.00
☐ **CLIBURN, VAN.** *Collection of 327 news cuttings relating to his career, mostly from Philadelphia Inquirer and Life magazine. Mounted in three loose-leaf albums.*	70.00	90.00
☐ **CLIBURN, VAN.** *ALs, half page, with envelope, 1959.*	25.00	31.00
☐ **CLIBURN, VAN.** *Contract for a concert appearance, signed twice.*	40.00	50.00
☐ **CLIBURN, VAN.** *Signature on a concert program.*	13.00	18.00
☐ **CLIBURN, VAN.** *LP record album cover, signed, record missing.*	45.00	60.00
☐ **CLIBURN, VAN.** *Two 4x5 fan snapshots, unsigned, c. 1958.*	4.00	5.00
☐ **CLIBURN, VAN.** *Signature on a small concert poster.*	25.00	35.00
☐ **CONNIFF, RAY.** *8x10 studio portrait, signed.*	4.00	5.50
☐ **CONNIFF, RAY.** *12" LP recording, signed on label.*	25.00	35.00
☐ **CONNIFF, RAY.** *8x10 color photo with Perry Como, signed by Conniff only.*	7.00	10.00

	Price Range	
☐ **CONNIFF, RAY.** *Scrapbook containing c. 200 items on him, including 16 photos, most of them autographed, news cuttings, etc., Also some material on other music personalities. Album worn, cover detached.*	150.00	200.00
☐ **CONNIFF, RAY.** *22x30 blow-up poster of him, full color, homemade, not signed, c. 1970.*	4.00	5.00
☐ **CONNIFF, RAY.** *45rpm record sleeve, signed (no record).*	2.00	2.50
☐ **CONNIFF, RAY.** *Signature on a card.*	1.00	2.00
☐ **CONNIFF, RAY.** *Magazine article, signed.*	3.00	4.00
☐ **CUGAT, XAVIER.** *8x10 studio photo, signed on back.*	7.00	10.00
☐ **CUGAT, XAVIER.** *ALs, 1½ pages, in Spanish, regarding Spanish Civil War, with envelope, 1938.*	45.00	65.00
☐ **CUGAT, XAVIER.** *ALs, one page, about an engagement in Los Angeles, 1948.*	9.00	12.00
☐ **CUGAT, XAVIER.** *Pencil sketch of him, 9x12", matted and framed, signed "S.W.L., 1967".*	15.00	21.00
☐ **CUGAT, XAVIER.** *5x7 photo of living room in his Manhattan apartment, lengthy inscription on reverse, not signed.*	8.00	11.00
☐ **CUGAT, XAVIER.** *8x10 photo with Abby Lane, signed by both.*	25.00	32.00
☐ **CUGAT, XAVIER.** *Magazine cover boldly signed in pink ink.*	7.00	10.00
☐ **CUGAT, XAVIER.** *Three photo of him in early 1920's, unsigned, in a wallet-like folder, worn.*	7.00	10.00
☐ **CUGAT, XAVIER.** *Signature on a card.*	2.00	3.00
☐ **DUCHIN, PETER.** *LP record album cover, signed, record missing.*	13.00	20.00
☐ **DUCHIN, PETER.** *8x10 studio photo, signed and inscribed.*	4.00	5.00
☐ **DUCHIN, PETER.** *Motion picture company contract, signed in three places, in a cloth folder.*	20.00	25.00
☐ **DUCHIN, PETER.** *ALs, one page, 1971.*	6.00	8.00
☐ **DUCHIN, PETER.** *Photo with Peggy Lee, signed by Duchin only.*	7.00	10.00
☐ **DUCHIN, PETER.** *Check endorsed by him, 1975.*	13.00	20.00
☐ **DUCHIN, PETER.** *Magazine article, signed.*	3.00	4.00
☐ **DUCHIN, PETER.** *Three Polaroid snapshots made by fans, mounted on heavy paper, one signed.*	5.00	7.00
☐ **DUCHIN, PETER.** *45rpm phonograph record, signed on the label.*	7.00	10.00
☐ **DUCHIN, PETER.** *Collection of 227 news cuttings and photos, no autographs, covering the period 1962-1977, in a manila portfolio.*	55.00	70.00
☐ **ELGART, LES.** *8x10 studio photo, signed, dated 1944.*	4.00	6.00
☐ **ELGART, LES.** *8x10 portrait, Associated Press stamp on back, signed in margin.*	4.00	6.00
☐ **ELGART, LES.** *Postcard in his hand, seven lines, New Orleans, 1961.*	4.00	6.00
☐ **ELGART, LES.** *8x10 color photo with Larry Elgart, signed by both, dated 1969.*	13.00	20.00
☐ **ELGART, LES.** *Two-page printed musical score, signed.*	5.00	7.00
☐ **ELGART, LES.** *ALs, two pages, with envelope, 1949.*	7.00	10.00
☐ **ELGART, LES.** *Record company contract, signed, three pages.*	13.00	20.00

	Price Range	
☐ **ELGART, LES.** *Signature on a restaurant menu.*	3.00	4.00
☐ **ELGART, LES.** *Signature on a card.*	2.00	2.75
☐ **ELGART, LES.** *Page of notes kept by him, addresses, etc.*	3.00	4.00
☐ **FIEDLER, ARTHUR.** *LP record album cover, signed, record missing.*	45.00	60.00
☐ **FIEDLER, ARTHUR.** *Copy of "Thirteen" magazine, signed on the cover.*	8.00	11.00
☐ **FIEDLER, ARTHUR.** *8x10 studio portrait, signed, c. 1940.*	13.00	20.00
☐ **FIEDLER, ARTHUR.** *8x10 photo with baton, signed, c. 1947.*	15.00	21.00
☐ **FIEDLER, ARTHUR.** *Magazine article, signed.*	10.00	15.00
☐ **FIEDLER, ARTHUR.** *ALs, three pages, with envelope, 1933.*	35.00	45.00
☐ **FIEDLER, ARTHUR.** *ALs, one page, to Columbia Records, 1945.*	20.00	25.00
☐ **FIEDLER, ARTHUR.** *328 news cuttings relating to his career, mounted in three leatherette albums, 1936-1978.*	100.00	130.00
☐ **FIEDLER, ARTHUR.** *Check endorsed by him, 1951.*	33.00	44.00
☐ **FIEDLER, ARTHUR.** *5x7 color glossy photo on podium, signed.*	21.00	28.00
☐ **FIEDLER, ARTHUR.** *Printed musical score, signed.*	25.00	35.00
☐ **GRECO, BUDDY.** *8x10 photo, signed and inscribed, dated 1955.*	7.00	10.00
☐ **GRECO, BUDDY.** *Three 5½x7 photos, two signed, various dates.*	10.00	15.00
☐ **GRECO, BUDDY.** *Colletion of 18 pieces of sheet music, signed by him.*	85.00	110.00
☐ **GRECO, BUDDY.** *Signature on cafe menu, dated 1960.*	4.00	6.00
☐ **GRECO, BUDDY.** *Check endorsed by him, 1966.*	13.00	20.00
☐ **GRECO, BUDDY.** *Postcard sent by him, large signature.*	5.00	7.00
☐ **GRECO, BUDDY.** *Photo with Guy Lombardo, signed by Greco only.*	7.00	10.00
☐ **GRECO, BUDDY.** *Typewritten letter, signed, 1969.*	4.00	6.00
☐ **GRECO, BUDDY.** *Two small pocket photos, signed and inscribed for fans.*	5.00	7.00
☐ **HEIFETZ, JASCHA.** *ALs, two pages (written at age 17), 1918.*	60.00	80.00
☐ **HEIFETZ, JASCHA.** *ALs, one page, regarding an engagement, 1931.*	35.00	47.00
☐ **HEIFETZ, JASCHA.** *ALs, ½ page, regarding state of the arts in America as a result of the war and financial depression, 1941.*	43.00	60.00
☐ **HEIFETZ, JASCHA.** *ALs, ½ page, declining an invitation, 1962.*	25.00	35.00
☐ **HEIFETZ, JASCHA.** *Check endorsed by him, 1950.*	50.00	65.00
☐ **HEIFETZ, JASCHA.** *Photo of him as a youth, not signed, dated 1916.*	11.00	15.00
☐ **HEIFETZ, JASCHA.** *8x10 studio portrait at an early age, signed and inscribed, photo touched with hand-coloring, matted and framed, c. 1930.*	45.00	60.00
☐ **HEIFETZ, JASCHA.** *Magazine photo, signed, c. 1960.*	9.00	12.00
☐ **HEIFETZ, JASCHA.** *Studio portrait, signed, inscribed, dated 1968.*	25.00	32.00

	Price Range	
☐ **HEIFETZ, JASCHA.** *Signature on a concert program.*	15.00	21.00
☐ **HEIFETZ, JASCHA.** *Signature on a card.*	5.00	7.00
☐ **HEIFETZ, JASCHA.** *Booklet on violin instruction, signed.*	25.00	32.00
☐ **HEIFETZ, JASCHA.** *Copy of "Hi-Fi-Stereo Review", signed.*	8.00	11.00
☐ **HENDERSON, SKITCH.** *8x10 studio photo, signed, dated 1958.*	4.00	6.00
☐ **HENDERSON, SKITCH.** *Photo with Sammy Kaye, signed by Henderson only.*	5.00	7.00
☐ **HENDERSON, SKITCH.** *Photo with Steve Allen, signed by both.*	8.00	11.00
☐ **HENDERSON, SKITCH.** *Check endorsed by him, 1966.*	12.00	17.00
☐ **HENDERSON, SKITCH.** *Taped radio interview, 30 minutes, c. 1964.*	7.00	10.00
☐ **HENDERSON, SKITCH.** *T-shirt with his likeness and name.*	8.00	11.00
☐ **HENDERSON, SKITCH.** *Signature on a restaurant napkin.*	3.00	4.00
☐ **HENDERSON, SKITCH.** *Record company contract, signed (three signatures).*	13.00	20.00
☐ **HENDERSON, SKITCH.** *Copy of "Billboard" magazine, signed on front page.*	4.00	6.00
☐ **HENDERSON, SKITCH.** *Two 5x7 photos, signed.*	6.00	8.00
☐ **HENDERSON, SKITCH.** *Copy of "TV Guide", signed on interior page. Also signed by several other musicians.*	12.00	16.00
☐ **HENDERSON, SKITCH.** *Signature on a card.*	2.00	2.50
☐ **HIRT, AL.** *Poster advertising his appearance at a New Orleans club, signed, c. 1972.*	20.00	30.00
☐ **HIRT, AL.** *8x10 studio photo with trumpet, signed, dated 1975.*	6.00	8.00
☐ **HIRT, AL.** *Celluloid button with his likeness and name, 2" diameter, c. 1970.*	4.00	6.00
☐ **HIRT, AL.** *ALs, two pages, with envelope, 1953.*	8.00	11.00
☐ **HIRT, AL.** *8x10 publicity photo, in street parade, signed on back, with lengthy inscription.*	10.00	15.00
☐ **HIRT, AL.** *T-shirt with his name and likeness.*	8.00	11.00
☐ **HIRT, AL.** *8x10 studio photo, close-up, signed, dated 1966.*	5.00	7.00
☐ **HIRT, AL.** *4x5½ snapshot photo with Benny Goodman, signed by Hirt only.*	5.00	7.00
☐ **HIRT, AL.** *Magazine article, signed.*	3.00	4.00
☐ **HIRT, AL.** *Signature on a card.*	2.25	3.00
☐ **HIRT, AL.** *12" LP record, signed on the label.*	26.00	36.00
☐ **HOROWITZ, VLADIMIR.** *ALs, four pages, one page stained, in a cloth folder with morocco spine, 1923.*	95.00	115.00
☐ **HOROWITZ, VLADIMIR.** *ALs, 1½ pages, 1941.*	60.00	80.00
☐ **HOROWITZ, VLADIMIR.** *ALs, two pages, on music theory, 1947.*	85.00	110.00
☐ **HOROWITZ, VLADIMIR.** *Concert program, signed, 1971.*	15.00	21.00
☐ **HOROWITZ, VLADIMIR.** *5x7 color photo mounted on stiff card, signed on the card.*	20.00	30.00
☐ **HOROWITZ, VLADIMIR.** *8x10 studio photo, sepia, signed and inscribed, c. 1935.*	55.00	70.00
☐ **HOROWITZ, VLADIMIR.** *8x10 photo, signed, dated 1969.*	26.00	38.00
☐ **HOROWITZ, VLADIMIR.** *Signature on a receipt.*	15.00	22.00

	Price Range	
☐ **HOROWITZ, VLADIMIR.** *Signature on LP record album box, records missing.*	50.00	70.00
☐ **HOROWITZ, VLADIMIR.** *Concert contract, signed three times.*	85.00	110.00
☐ **HOROWITZ, VLADIMIR.** *Signature on a card.*	5.00	7.00
☐ **HOROWITZ, VLADIMIR.** *Musical score (printed), signed.*	50.00	65.00
☐ **HOROWITZ, VLADIMIR.** *Poster advertising an appearance at Carnegie Hall, NY., not signed.*	7.00	10.00
☐ **ITURBI, JOSE.** *8x10 studio portrait, signed on front and back.*	20.00	30.00
☐ **ITURBI, JOSE.** *Cartoon sketch of him in charcoal by "Franz S.", bristol board, unframed, 11x14, c. 1960.*	35.00	45.00
☐ **ITURBI, JOSE.** *ALs, in Spanish, with envelope, 1917.*	31.00	40.00
☐ **ITURBI, JOSE.** *ALs, two pages, 1933.*	34.00	45.00
☐ **ITURBI, JOSE.** *Concert poster, signed in Magic Marker, matted and framed.*	65.00	90.00
☐ **ITURBI, JOSE.** *LP record album cover, signed, record missing.*	35.00	45.00
☐ **ITURBI, JOSE.** *Cancelled check, endorsed by him.*	30.00	42.00
☐ **ITURBI, JOSE.** *Five postcards in his hand, three sent from London, total of 25 lines of writing, mounted on album sheets.*	60.00	80.00
☐ **ITURBI, JOSE.** *Photo with James Levine, signed by Iturbi only.*	14.00	20.00
☐ **ITURBI, JOSE.** *Christmas card sent by him in 1973, inscribed.*	26.00	33.00
☐ **ITURBI, JOSE.** *Signature on a card.*	3.00	4.00
☐ **KAYE, SAMMY.** *Newspaper article, signed and inscribed, 1948.*	6.00	8.00
☐ **KAYE, SAMMY.** *Baton autographed by him.*	13.00	19.00
☐ **KAYE, SAMMY.** *TV Guide article, signed, framed along with an unsigned portrait.*	14.00	20.00
☐ **KAYE, SAMMY.** *8x10 studio photo, signed, dated 1950.*	4.00	5.00
☐ **KAYE, SAMMY.** *78rpm phonograph record, signed on the label.*	18.00	27.00
☐ **KAYE, SAMMY.** *Photo with Hoagy Carmichael, signed by both.*	13.00	17.00
☐ **KAYE, SAMMY.** *Collection of 22 candid snapshots, mostly on street, not signed, mostly from the 1940's.*	7.00	10.00
☐ **KAYE, SAMMY.** *Check endorsed by him, 1969.*	14.00	20.00
☐ **KAYE, SAMMY.** *LP record album cover, signed, record missing.*	18.00	27.00
☐ **KAYE, SAMMY.** *Pair of kidskin gloves reputedly owned by him.*	13.00	17.00
☐ **KLEMPERER, WERNER.** *8x10 studio portrait, signed.*	14.00	20.00
☐ **KLEMPERER, WERNER.** *ALs, in German, two pages, 1944.*	33.00	45.00
☐ **KLEMPERER, WERNER.** *Signature on a card.*	5.00	7.00
☐ **KLEMPERER, WERNER.** *Record company contract, signed.*	40.00	50.00
☐ **KLEMPERER, WERNER.** *Two 8x10 blow-ups of candid photos, one signed.*	22.00	30.00
☐ **KLEMPERER, WERNER.** *LP record album cover, signed, record missing.*	40.00	55.00
☐ **KLEMPERER, WERNER.** *Concert poster, signed in margin.*	30.00	40.00

	Price Range	
☐ **KLEMPERER, WERNER.** *Check endorsed by him, 1977.*	21.00	27.00
☐ **KLEMPERER, WERNER.** *Signature on a restaurant menu.*	6.00	8.00
☐ **KOSTELANETZ, ANDRE.** *ALs, two pages, with envelope, 1926.*	10.00	15.00
☐ **KOSTELANETZ, ANDRE.** *ALs, ½ page, about appearing on a TV show, 1971.*	6.00	8.00
☐ **KOSTELANETZ, ANDRE.** *8x10 studio portrait, signed, c. 1955.*	8.00	11.00
☐ **KOSTELANETZ, ANDRE.** *8x10 color portrait photo, inscribed on back, dated 1958.*	13.00	20.00
☐ **KOSTELANETZ, ANDRE.** *Letter to him from NBC program department.*	3.00	4.00
☐ **KOSTELANETZ, ANDRE.** *LP record, signed on the label.*	24.00	35.00
☐ **KOSTELANETZ, ANDRE.** *Two postcards sent by him in 1966.*	10.00	15.00
☐ **KOSTELANETZ, ANDRE.** *Record company contract, signed in two places.*	26.00	33.00
☐ **KOSTELANETZ, ANDRE.** *Two 5x7 color photos cut from periodicals, signed and inscribed, mounted on stiff cards.*	13.00	20.00
☐ **KOSTELANETZ, ANDRE.** *Signature on a card.*	3.00	4.00
☐ **KYSER, KAY.** *Photo with Bing Crosby, signed by both, dated 1942.*	75.00	100.00
☐ **KYSER, KAY.** *Printed postcard photo, facsimile signature.*	7.00	10.00
☐ **LEINSDORF, ERICH.** *ALs, two pages, in German, 1930.*	30.00	40.00
☐ **LEINSDORF, ERICH.** *Concert poster, signed, 22x28.*	60.00	80.00
☐ **LEINSDORF, ERICH.** *8x10 studio portrait, signed on back.*	15.00	21.00
☐ **LEINSDORF, ERICH.** *Photo with Martina Arroyo, signed by Leinsdorf only.*	20.00	26.00
☐ **LEINSDORF, ERICH.** *Check endorsed by him, 1977.*	35.00	45.00
☐ **LEINSDORF, ERICH.** *Copy of "Opera News", signed on front cover.*	11.00	15.00
☐ **LEINSDORF, ERICH.** *Photo debarking from plane, signed.*	9.00	14.00
☐ **LEINSDORF, ERICH.** *Printed musical score, signed.*	26.00	32.00
☐ **LEINSDORF, ERICH.** *Book, "Complete Opera Book", signed on front endleaf.*	13.00	18.00
☐ **LEINSDORF, ERICH.** *LP record album cover, signed, record missing.*	35.00	45.00
☐ **LEINSDORF, ERICH.** *Two postcards sent by him from Paris.*	20.00	27.00
☐ **LEINSDORF, ERICH.** *Three 5x6½ snapshot photos, signed.*	20.00	27.00
☐ **LEINSDORF, ERICH.** *Signature on an opera libretto.*	8.00	11.00
☐ **LEINSDORF, ERICH.** *Signature on a card.*	3.00	4.00
☐ **LIBERACE.** *Copy of "TV Guide", signed on cover.*	20.00	27.00
☐ **LIBERACE.** *8x10 photo in costume at piano, signed, 1952.*	15.00	20.00
☐ **LIBERACE.** *8x10 photo in front of swimming pool, signed, undated.*	11.00	16.00
☐ **LIBERACE.** *8x10 studio portrait, signed, c. 1953.*	11.00	16.00
☐ **LIBERACE.** *Postcard photo (printed), facsimile signature.*	4.00	5.00
☐ **LIBERACE.** *Magazine article, signed (fan magazine), signed, c. 1951.*	10.00	15.00
☐ **LIBERACE.** *Scrapbook containing 33 photos, 11 of them signed, four ALs's, several typed letters and other items related to him.*	350.00	425.00

	Price Range	
☐ **LIBERACE.** *Jacket said to have been worn by him, pink silk with sequins.*	205.00	240.00
☐ **LIBERACE.** *Check endorsed by him, 1954.*	40.00	50.00
☐ **LIBERACE.** *Printed musical score (Chopin), signed.*	30.00	39.00
☐ **LIBERACE.** *Signature on a card.*	3.00	4.00
☐ **LIBERACE.** *TV contract, signed (three signatures).*	70.00	90.00
☐ **LIBERACE.** *78rpm record, signed on the label.*	35.00	45.00
☐ **LOMBARDO, GUY.** *Check endorsed by him, 1940.*	41.00	55.00
☐ **LOMBARDO, GUY.** *8x10 photo with Ted Weems, signed by both.*	40.00	55.00
☐ **LOPEZ, TRINI.** *8x10 studio portrait, signed, dated 1969.*	5.00	7.00
☐ **LOPEZ, TRINI.** *45rpm record, signed on the label.*	9.00	13.00
☐ **LOPEZ, TRINI.** *Record company contract, signed.*	33.00	41.00
☐ **LOPEZ, TRINI.** *Copy of "Billboard" magazine, signed.*	7.00	10.00
☐ **LOPEZ, TRINI.** *Collection of 41 news cuttings relating to his career, reviews of his records, etc., 1968-1975.*	12.00	16.00
☐ **LOPEZ, TRINI.** *8x10 color photo with band, signed by him and several band members.*	13.00	18.00
☐ **LOPEZ, TRINI.** *ALs, one page, on hotel stationery, 1970.*	6.00	8.00
☐ **LOPEZ, TRINI.** *Poster in full colors, 17x24", signed.*	10.00	13.00
☐ **LOPEZ, TRINI.** *Two small snapshot photos, one signed on the back.*	4.00	6.00
☐ **LOPEZ, TRINI.** *Check endorsed by him, 1977.*	13.00	18.00
☐ **LOPEZ, TRINI.** *Photo with Mac Davidson, signed by Lopez only.*	5.00	7.00
☐ **MAAZEL, LORIN.** *ALs, two pages, in French, 1950.*	10.00	13.00
☐ **MAAZEL, LORIN.** *ALs, 1½ pages, with envelope, 1956.*	8.00	11.00
☐ **MAAZEL, LORIN.** *8x10 studio portrait, signed and inscribed.*	10.00	13.00
☐ **MAAZEL, LORIN.** *Concert program, signed, 1971.*	7.00	10.00
☐ **MAAZEL, LORIN.** *Two postcards sent by him, lengthy messages, 1976 and 1977.*	7.00	10.00
☐ **MAAZEL, LORIN.** *11x14 color portrait photo with baton, signed and inscribed, matted and framed along with an LP phonograph record.*	50.00	65.00
☐ **MAAZEL, LORIN.** *LP record album cover, signed, record missing.*	25.00	33.00
☐ **MAAZEL, LORIN.** *Check endorsed by him, stained, 1971.*	10.00	13.00
☐ **MAAZEL, LORIN.** *Typewritten letter, signed, large signature.*	5.00	7.00
☐ **MAAZEL, LORIN.** *Copy of "Hi-Fi-Stereo Review", signed.*	5.00	7.00
☐ **MAAZEL, LORIN.** *Signature on a card.*	2.00	3.00
☐ **MAAZEL, LORIN.** *Collection of 31 unsigned snapshot photos, mostly dating from 1957-1975.*	20.00	28.00
☐ **MANTOVANI, ANNUZIO.** *Check endorsed by him, 1955.*	15.00	20.00
☐ **MANTOVANI, ANNUZIO.** *8x10 portrait photo, signed and inscribed.*	8.00	11.00
☐ **MANTOVANI, ANNUZIO.** *ALs, two pages, 1955.*	14.00	20.00
☐ **MANTOVANI, ANNUZIO.** *Postcard sent by him in 1961.*	6.00	8.00
☐ **MANTOVANI, ANNUZIO.** *Sheet music, signed.*	14.00	20.00
☐ **MANTOVANI, ANNUZIO.** *Two 4x5 snapshots, one signed on the back.*	8.00	11.00

	Price Range	
☐ **MANTOVANI, ANNUZIO.** *LP record album cover, signed, record missing*	18.00	26.00
☐ **MANTOVANI, ANNUZIO.** *Concert poster, signed, 1961.*	12.00	16.00
☐ **MANTOVANI, ANNUZIO.** *45rpm phonograph record, signed on the label*	15.00	20.00
☐ **MANTOVANI, ANNUZIO.** *Magazine article, signed twice, preserved in a cloth folder along with an unsigned snapshot photo*	10.00	13.00
☐ **MENUHIN, YEHUDI.** *8x10 portrait photo in concert, signed on the back.*	40.00	52.00
☐ **MENUHIN, YEHUDI.** *8x10 color photo, close-up, signed and inscribed, dated 1974.*	52.00	70.00
☐ **MENUHIN, YEHUDI.** *Musical score (printed), signed.*	30.00	38.00
☐ **MENUHIN, YEHUDI.** *ALs, New York, two pages, 1938*	35.00	45.00
☐ **MENUHIN, YEHUDI.** *Concert program, signed, 1970*	13.00	20.00
☐ **MENUHIN, YEHUDI.** *Two postcards sent by him from London, total of 11 lines of writing*	20.00	28.00
☐ **MENUHIN, YEHUDI.** *Envelope addressed by him, postmarked 1950*	7.00	10.00
☐ **MENUHIN, YEHUDI.** *4x5 photo, signed and inscribed.*	15.00	21.00
☐ **MENUHIN, YEHUDI.** *LP record album cover, signed, record missing*	40.00	50.00
☐ **MENUHIN, YEHUDI.** *Three snapshot photos, various sizes, one signed and dated 1968, others unsigned, mounted on a 14x16 card.*	20.00	26.00
☐ **MENUHIN, YEHUDI.** *Cancelled check, endorsed by him, 1975.*	35.00	45.00
☐ **MENUHIN, YEHUDI.** *Typewritten letter, signed, ½ page, 1976*	11.00	15.00
☐ **SCHIPPERS, THOMAS.** *8x10 photo, signed, dated 1978*	9.00	12.00
☐ **SCHIPPERS, THOMAS.** *Opera libretto, signed.*	7.00	10.00
☐ **SCHIPPERS, THOMAS.** *Check endorsed by him, 1971.*	22.00	26.00
☐ **SCHIPPERS, THOMAS.** *Baton used by him in leading orchestra, signed.*	50.00	65.00
☐ **SCHIPPERS, THOMAS.** *Photo cut from "Opera News", signed, framed.*	13.00	18.00
☐ **SCHIPPERS, THOMAS.** *Concert program, signed*	6.00	9.00
☐ **SCHIPPERS, THOMAS.** *Two 4x5 snapshot photos outside Metropolitan Opera House, signed on the backs*	9.00	12.00
☐ **SERKIN, RUDOLF.** *ALs, three pages, in German, 1929.*	30.00	38.00
☐ **SERKIN, RUDOLF.** *8x10 portrait photo, signed and inscribed, 1976*	15.00	20.00
☐ **SERKIN, RUDOLF.** *8x10 color photo, matted and framed, signed in pencil on the mat*	20.00	25.00
☐ **SERKIN, RUDOLF.** *Postcard sent by him in 1973, three lines.*	8.00	11.00
☐ **SERKIN, RUDOLF.** *Concert program, signed*	9.00	12.00
☐ **SERKIN, RUDOLF.** *Pen-and-ink caricature, 8x10, matted and framed, artist unknown*	20.00	28.00

	Price Range	
☐ **SERKIN, RUDOLF.** *Set of three scrapbooks containing 15 photos, nine of them signed, plus numerous memorabilia relating to his career.*	200.00	245.00
☐ **SERKIN, RUDOLF.** *Snapshot photo, signed on the back.*	6.00	9.00
☐ **SOLTI, GEORGE.** *8x10 portrait photo, signed and inscribed.*	10.00	14.00
☐ **SOLTI, GEORGE.** *News cutting, signed (review of an LP recording).*	6.00	9.00
☐ **SOLTI, GEORGE.** *ALs, one page, New York, 1961.*	11.00	15.00
☐ **SOLTI, GEORGE.** *ALs, 3½ pages, Los Angeles, with envelope, 1974.*	16.00	22.00
☐ **SOLTI, GEORGE.** *Check endorsed by him, 1971.*	20.00	29.00
☐ **SOLTI, GEORGE.** *Concert program, signed.*	8.00	11.00
☐ **SOLTI, GEORGE.** *LP record album cover, signed, record missing.*	30.00	38.00
☐ **SOLTI, GEORGE.** *5x7 color photo, signed on the back.*	11.00	15.00
☐ **SOLTI, GEORGE.** *Six postcards sent by him, 1971-1976.*	35.00	45.00
☐ **SOLTI, GEORGE.** *Collection of 147 news cuttings relating to his career, enclosed in a vinyl folder.*	40.00	50.00
☐ **STERN, ISAAC.** *ALs, two pages, New York, 1967.*	30.00	37.00
☐ **STERN, ISAAC.** *Photo with Beverly Sills, signed by Stern only.*	27.00	35.00
☐ **STERN, ISAAC.** *Carnegie Hall recital poster, signed in crayon, matted and framed.*	85.00	110.00
☐ **STERN, ISAAC.** *New York Philharmonic program, signed.*	15.00	20.00
☐ **STERN, ISAAC.** *Two 4x5½ snapshot photos with fans, one signed.*	15.00	20.00
☐ **STERN, ISAAC.** *Typewritten letter, signed, one page, 1977.*	16.00	22.00
☐ **STERN, ISAAC.** *8x10 portrait photo, signed and inscribed, with violin.*	20.00	25.00
☐ **STERN, ISAAC.** *Check endorsed by him, 1966.*	45.00	65.00
☐ **STERN, ISAAC.** *LP record, signed on the label.*	70.00	95.00
☐ **STERN, ISAAC.** *Concert program, signed twice, mounted and framed along with an unsigned snapshot photo.*	35.00	45.00
☐ **STOKOWSKI, LEOPOLD.** *Poster for "Fantasia", signed by Walt Disney and Stokowski, matted and framed.*	675.00	800.00
☐ **STOKOWSKI, LEOPOLD.** *ALs, two pages, London, 1906.*	45.00	60.00
☐ **STOKOWSKI, LEOPOLD.** *Concert program, signed.*	17.00	25.00
☐ **STOKOWSKI, LEOPOLD.** *Check endorsed by him, 1931.*	55.00	75.00
☐ **STOKOWSKI, LEOPOLD.** *LP record album cover, signed, record missing, matted and framed.*	75.00	100.00
☐ **STOKOWSKI, LEOPOLD.** *8x10 portrait photo, sepia, signed, dated 1929.*	30.00	37.00
☐ **STOKOWSKI, LEOPOLD.** *8x10 studio photo, signed and inscribed, c. 1955.*	23.00	32.00
☐ **STOKOWSKI, LEOPOLD.** *Photo with Fritz Chrysler, signed by both.*	65.00	80.00
☐ **STOKOWSKI, LEOPOLD.** *Signature on a card.*	6.00	9.00
☐ **ZIMBALIST, EFREM, SR.** *8x10 portrait photo, signed.*	15.00	20.00

POPULAR MUSIC

ARTISTS' MEMORABILIA

Though "pop" (short for "popular", as opposed to classical) music has been around since the 1800's, and available on commercial recordings since the 1890's, the collecting of pop memorabilia did not become a major hobby until the 1950's. Elvis Presley's impact on his fans is thought by some to have started it all; others feel that the Beatles made collectors out of pop music fans. In any event, the collecting of pop memorabilia was not taken seriously until pretty recently. Most collectors were the very young, who obtained autographs in person at concerts, etc., and who adoringly preserved shirts, neckties, or other personal items that once belonged to their favorites, while adults scoffed at the possibility of this material ever having more than emotional value. Gradually, as a market developed (in the 1960's), dealers began to print up catalogues and auction lists of this memorabilia, with prices that were at first very modest. Today, pop music memorabilia is big business all across the country. It is sold by specialist dealers as well as by dealers in comic books, movie memorabilia, and nostalgia, and some of it fetches healthy sums indeed. Many souvenirs obtained free at stage doors by admiring fans are now worth $10, $20 or even more, depending on the star and the item's nature.

Nostalgia buffs, many of them born too late to remember stars of the 1940's or earlier, are buying the early material, or, as it might be called, pre-Presley items. Because of space limitations, the following listings exclude material relating to stars whose careers were completed before 1940. This should not be taken to mean that such memorabilia is not of value; it surely is, and in many instances of greater value than more modern items. We hope to include it in a future edition.

	Price Range	
☐ **ALDA, ROBERT.** *c. 1952. 8x10 studio photo, signed.*	5.00	7.00
☐ **ALDA, ROBERT.** *Printed copy, "Guys and Dolls", signed.*	8.00	11.00
☐ **ALDA, ROBERT.** *c. 1958. Typed letter, signed, one page*	7.00	10.00
☐ **ALDA, ROBERT.** *Collection of 26 motion picture stills, none of them signed.*	55.00	70.00
☐ **ALDA, ROBERT.** *8x10 color photo in "Guys and Dolls" costume, signed.*	12.00	16.00
☐ **ALPERT, HERB.** *c. 1969. Fan magazine article, signed.*	11.00	15.00
☐ **ALPERT, HERB.** *8x10 studio portrait, signed.*	11.00	15.00
☐ **ALPERT, HERB.** *Photo with band, signed twice.*	12.00	17.00
☐ **ALPERT, HERB.** *Two LP album covers, signed, records missing.*	50.00	65.00
☐ **AMES, ED.** *c. 1956. 8x10 photo of group "The Ames Bros.", signed by all.*	35.00	45.00
☐ **AMES, ED.** *Snapshot photo taken by fan, signed on back.*	5.00	7.00
☐ **AMES, ED.** *Magazine photo, signed, pasted on card.*	4.00	6.00
☐ **AMES, ED.** *45rpm phono record signed on label (indistinct).*	10.00	14.00
☐ **AMES, ED.** *8x10 color photo, signed and inscribed.*	12.00	16.00

	Price Range	
☐ **ANDERSON, LYNN.** *Sheet music, "Rose Garden", signed, framed along with a colored magazine photo (unsigned).*	36.00	45.00
☐ **ANDERSON, LYNN.** *8x10 studio portrait, signed.*	8.00	11.00
☐ **ANDERSON, LYNN.** *Two small outdoor snapshots, Polaroid.*	5.00	7.00
☐ **ANDREWS, JULIE.** *Lobby card, "Sound of Music", signed.*	27.00	35.00
☐ **ANDREWS, JULIE.** *Sheet music, "A Spoonful of Sugar", signed.*	20.00	27.00
(NOTE: "Spoonful of Sugar", in the motion picture "Mary Poppins", was mouthed by Julie Andrews but sung on the soundtrack by Marni Nixon.)		
☐ **ANDREWS, JULIE.** *Press review, "Sound of Music", signed.*	8.00	11.00
☐ **ANDREWS, JULIE.** *Fan magazine photo, signed and inscribed.*	9.00	12.00
☐ **ANDREWS, JULIE.** *Collection of 76 motion picture stills, unsigned.*	180.00	210.00
☐ **ANDREWS, JULIE.** *Gown worn by her at Academy Awards presentation, with letter of authentication.*	325.00	420.00
☐ **ANDREWS, JULIE.** *5x7 photo signed, with balloon.*	8.00	11.00
☐ **ANDREWS, JULIE.** *Strip of 32mm film (41 frames), scene from "Mary Poppins". Framed along with a signed photo.*	120.00	165.00
☐ **ANDREWS, PATTY.** *c. 1947. Typed letter, signed.*	10.00	14.00
☐ **ANDREWS, PATTY.** *Signature on a card.*	4.00	5.00
☐ **ANDREWS, PATTY.** *8x10 photo, signed and inscribed.*	10.00	14.00
☐ **ANDREWS, PATTY.** *8x10 photo with Bing Crosby, signed by Andrews only.*	20.00	28.00
☐ **ANN-MARGRET (OLSON).** *Color photo from "Playboy" magazine, signed.*	25.00	33.00
☐ **ANN-MARGRET.** *Motion picture still with Elvis Presley, signed by Ann-Margret only.*	50.00	65.00
☐ **ANN-MARGRET.** *8x10 photo (pin-up), signed.*	26.00	36.00
☐ **ANN-MARGRET.** *Six stills from the motion picture "Tommy", three of them signed, in a folder.*	38.00	49.00
☐ **ANN-MARGRET.** *Photo with Anthony Hopkins, signed by her only.*	15.00	23.00
☐ **ANN-MARGRET.** *Small photo of her, topless, from a movie scene, cut from a magazine or book, matted, signed on the mat.*	36.00	45.00
☐ **BELAFONTE, HARRY.** *8x10 motion picture still with Sidney Poitier, signed by both.*	80.00	100.00
☐ **BELAFONTE, HARRY.** *Sheet music, "Banana Boat Song", signed.*	20.00	26.00
☐ **BELAFONTE, HARRY.** *LP record album cover signed, no record.*	33.00	43.00
☐ **BELAFONTE, HARRY.** *Colored photo from "Life" magazine, signed.*	20.00	25.00
☐ **BELAFONTE, HARRY.** *Two 8x10 studio portraits, one signed.*	20.00	25.00
☐ **BELAFONTE, HARRY.** *Signature on a concert program, NY.*	8.00	11.00
☐ **BELAFONTE, HARRY.** *Five miscellaneous items signed by him.*	22.00	33.00
☐ **BELAFONTE, HARRY.** *c. 1955. 8x10 photo in calypso outfit, signed.*	26.00	35.00

	Price Range	
☐ **BENNETT, TONY.** *Sheet music, "I Left My Heart in San Francisco", signed, inscribed. Framed along with a portrait and a 45rpm record.*	110.00	140.00
☐ **BENNETT, TONY.** *Sheet music (as above), signed.*	30.00	38.00
☐ **BENNETT, TONY.** *8x10 studio portrait, signed and inscribed.*	10.00	14.00
☐ **BENNETT, TONY.** *Snapshot on stage, signed in crayon.*	8.00	11.00
☐ **BENNETT, TONY.** *c. 1971. Canceled check endorsed by him.*	20.00	25.00
☐ **BENNETT, TONY.** *Lock of hair reputedly his, framed with an unsigned photo.*	32.00	40.00
(We list items of this nature only out of curiosity interest; collectors should be wary of them, as they frequently are not authentic.)		
☐ **BENNETT, TONY.** *Early LP record album cover signed, record missing.*	36.00	45.00
☐ **BENNETT, TONY.** *Signature on concert program.*	12.00	16.00
☐ **BENNETT, TONY.** *c. 1966. Typed letter to a fan, signed.*	12.00	16.00
☐ **BERGEN, POLLY.** *c. 1956. 8x10 photo signed.*	8.00	11.00
☐ **BERGEN, POLLY.** *Ad for skin cream, signed.*	10.00	14.00
☐ **BERGEN, POLLY.** *Signature on the back of an envelope.*	4.00	5.00
☐ **BERGEN, POLLY.** *c. 1968. Typed letter, signed.*	6.00	9.00
☐ **BERGEN, POLLY.** *8x10 color portrait photo, unsigned.*	5.00	7.00
☐ **BREWER, TERESA.** *c. 1957. 8x10 photo in stage costume (probably from a TV show), signed.*	8.00	12.00
☐ **BREWER, TERESA.** *45rpm phono record, "Ricochet Romance", signed on the label, framed.*	20.00	26.00
☐ **BREWER, TERESA.** *5x7 photo as a girl of c. 15.*	5.00	7.00
☐ **BREWER, TERESA.** *8x10 studio portrait, signed and inscribed.*	9.00	12.00
☐ **BREWER, TERESA.** *Signature on leaf from autograph book.*	3.00	4.00
☐ **CANTRELL, LANA.** *5x6 photo from magazine, full color, signed in red magic marker.*	5.00	7.00
☐ **CANTRELL, LANA.** *c. 1977. 8x10 studio photo, signed.*	6.00	8.00
☐ **CANTRELL, LANA.** *LP record album cover signed, no record.*	14.00	18.00
☐ **CANTRELL, LANA.** *c. 1975. Signature on a fan club card.*	5.00	7.00
☐ **CARPENTER, KAREN.** *Sheet music to four of her song hits, signed, in a large plastic frame.*	75.00	90.00
☐ **CARPENTER, KAREN.** *c. 1976. Small photo taken by fan, mounted on a card, signed on the card.*	9.00	12.00
☐ **CARPENTER, KAREN.** *c. 1975. 8x10 studio photo with Richard Carpenter, signed by both.*	20.00	30.00
☐ **CARPENTER, KAREN.** *Signature on a concert brochure.*	8.00	11.00
☐ **CARR, VICKI.** *c. 1963. Typed letter, signed.*	6.00	9.00
☐ **CARR, VICKI.** *Brief memo on pink stationery, undated.*	5.00	7.00
☐ **CARR, VICKI.** *T-shirt with her photo.*	8.00	11.00
☐ **CARR, VICKI.** *Christmas card signed by her.*	8.00	11.00
☐ **CARR, VICKI.** *Magazine ad signed.*	4.00	5.00
☐ **CARR, VICKI.** *Photo clipped from magazine, signed, mounted.*	5.00	7.00
☐ **CARROLL, DIAHANN.** *Two motion picture stills, signed.*	12.00	16.00
☐ **CARROLL, DIAHANN.** *8x10 photo with Alan Alda, signed by Carroll only.*	9.00	13.00

	Price Range	
☐ **CARROLL, DIAHANN.** *8x10 photo inscribed to David Frost...*	30.00	40.00
☐ **CARROLL, DIAHANN.** *Studio portrait, inscribed and signed...*	9.00	13.00
☐ **CARROLL, DIAHANN.** *LP record album cover signed, no record.*	15.00	20.00
☐ **CARROLL, DIAHANN.** *c. 1971. Typed letter, signed.*	8.00	11.00
☐ **CHANNING, CAROL.** *Printed score, "Hello Dolly", signed and inscribed. Framed along with an unsigned photo.*	90.00	115.00
☐ **CHANNING, CAROL.** *Review of show "Gentlemen Prefer Blondes", clipped from N.Y. Times, signed, framed.*	41.00	55.00
☐ **CHANNING, CAROL.** *8x10 photo in "Dolly" costume, signed...*	36.00	46.00
☐ **CHANNING, CAROL.** *8x10 color photo with Barbra Streisand, both dressed as "Dolly", signed by both.*	100.00	120.00
☐ **CHANNING, CAROL.** *8x10 color photo with Louis Armstrong, signed by Channing only.*	90.00	115.00
☐ **CHANNING, CAROL.** *Hat worn by her in "Hello Dolly", sold at benefit auction.*	125.00	140.00
☐ **CHANNING, CAROL.** *Book "The Matchmaker", signed on flyleaf, signed again on interior page. Soft covered.*	60.00	80.00
☐ **CHANNING, CAROL.** *Signature on a theater program.*	9.00	12.00
☐ **CLARK, PETULA.** *Sheet music, "Downtown", signed.*	15.00	20.00
☐ **CLARK, PETULA.** *Article from British fan magazine, signed.*	8.00	11.00
☐ **CLARK, PETULA.** *8x10 photo performing on stage.*	3.00	4.00
☐ **CLARK, PETULA.** *Postcard photo with facsimile signature...*	4.00	5.00
☐ **CLARK, PETULA.** *Poster advertising a concert, 24x37.*	70.00	90.00
☐ **CLARK, PETULA.** *Signature on a shop circular.*	5.00	7.00
☐ **CLOONEY, ROSEMARY.** *c. 1957. 8x10 studio portrait, signed.*	10.00	13.00
☐ **CLOONEY, ROSEMARY.** *Color photo from fan magazine, cover signed.*	7.00	10.00
☐ **CLOONEY, ROSEMARY.** *Sheet music, "This Old House", signed.*	20.00	26.00
☐ **CLOONEY, ROSEMARY.** *Snapshot with Perry Como, signed by Clooney only.*	13.00	17.00
☐ **CLOONEY, ROSEMARY.** *c. 1964. LP record album cover signed on the back with lengthy message, record present.*	70.00	90.00
☐ **COLLINS, DOROTHY.** *"TV Guide" article on "Your Hit Parade", signed, also signed by S. Lanson, G. MacKenzie, two others.*	40.00	55.00
☐ **COLLINS, DOROTHY.** *c. 1952. 8x10 studio portrait, signed...*	12.00	16.00
☐ **COLLINS, DOROTHY.** *c. 1959. Handwritten note, signed.*	10.00	13.00
☐ **COLLINS, DOROTHY.** *5x6 photo, signed, margins cut.*	5.00	7.00
☐ **COLLINS, DOROTHY.** *Two signed snapshots, one dated 1954.*	6.00	8.00
☐ **COLLINS, DOROTHY.** *Color photo from magazine or book, signed.*	8.00	11.00
☐ **COMO, PERRY.** *c. 1930. Handwritten letter, 1½ pp.*	56.00	70.00
☐ **COMO, PERRY.** *c. 1925. Exercise book used by him in grade school.*	80.00	100.00
☐ **COMO, PERRY.** *8x10 photo with Dinah Shore, signed by both.*	34.00	44.00
☐ **COMO, PERRY.** *c. 1953. 8x10 photo on stage, possibly TV....*	5.00	7.00

Perry Como

	Price Range	
☐ **COMO, PERRY.** *Three signed and inscribed 8x10 photos.*	33.00	42.00
☐ **COMO, PERRY.** *c. 1960. Christmas card, signed.*	25.00	33.00
☐ **COMO, PERRY.** *c. 1964. LP album cover, signed, no record.* . .	36.00	44.00
☐ **COMO, PERRY.** *Typed letter, signed, regarding his TV show.* . .	22.00	30.00
☐ **COMO, PERRY.** *Signature on a record sleeve.*	6.00	8.00
☐ **COMO, PERRY.** *Book "Pictorial History of Television", signed by him.*	25.00	34.00
☐ **CONNIFF, RAY.** *c. 1967. Photo with orchestra, signed.*	8.00	11.00
☐ **CONNIFF, RAY.** *c. 1971. Typed letter, signed.*	6.00	9.00
☐ **CONNIFF, RAY.** *Photo with Mike Douglas, signed by Conniff.*	11.00	16.00
☐ **CONNIFF, RAY.** *Signature on an advertising circular.*	3.00	4.00
☐ **CONNIFF, RAY.** *LP record album cover signed, record inside also signed (on the label).*	35.00	45.00
☐ **CROSBY, BING.** *c. 1932. 8x10 photo, signed and inscribed.* . .	70.00	90.00
☐ **CROSBY, BING.** *Collection of 236 motion picture stills, six of them signed, housed in looseleaf albums.*	600.00	750.00
☐ **CROSBY, BING.** *Pipe smoked by him, sold at auction in War Bonds drive.*	85.00	100.00
☐ **CROSBY, BING.** *78rpm record album cover, signed and inscribed, all four records missing, somewhat worn*.* . . . . (*The value would not be so high, if it were not possible to replace the records.)	110.00	140.00
☐ **CROSBY, BING.** *8x10 photo with Barry FitzGerald, signed by both.*	130.00	175.00
☐ **CROSBY, BING.** *c. 1948. 6x8 photo cut from magazine, signed and inscribed.*	25.00	33.00

	Price Range	
☐ **CROSBY, BING.** *5x6 color photo with Danny Kaye, signed by both.*	45.00	60.00
☐ **CROSBY, BING.** *Motion picture poster "Country Girl", signed at the top, stained.*	350.00	450.00
☐ **CROSBY, BING.** *Golf ball signed by him.*	90.00	130.00
☐ **CROSBY, BING.** *Baseball autographed by him and Mel Allen.*	120.00	160.00
☐ **CROSBY, BING.** *c. 1970. Typed letter, signed.*	20.00	25.00
☐ **CROSBY, BING.** *Signature on a hotel desk receipt.*	8.00	11.00
☐ **CROSBY, BING.** *8x10 photo with Harry James, unsigned.*	5.00	7.00
☐ **DAMONE, VIC.** *c. 1955. 8x10 studio portrait, signed.*	10.00	13.00
☐ **DAMONE, VIC.** *c. 1958. Cabaret handbill advertising him, with small photo.*	4.00	5.00
☐ **DAMONE, VIC.** *Color cover of a fan magazine, signed.*	10.00	13.00
☐ **DAMONE, VIC.** *"Top 60" chart from "Cashbox" magazine, signed and inscribed, framed.*	25.00	33.00
☐ **DAMONE, VIC.** *4x5 snapshot photo on street, signed on back.*	5.00	7.00
☐ **DAMONE, VIC.** *Two 8x10 studio photos, unsigned, early.*	6.00	8.00
☐ **DAMONE, VIC.** *c. 1961. Typed letter, signed.*	5.00	7.00
☐ **DAMONE, VIC.** *Large cardboard figure of him, almost life-size, apparently from a theater display.*	55.00	70.00
☐ **DAVIS, SAMMY, JR.** *c. 1960. 8x10 photo with Frank Sinatra and Dean Martin, signed by all.*	120.00	150.00
☐ **DAVIS, SAMMY, JR.** *LP record album cover signed, no record.*	45.00	65.00
☐ **DAVIS, SAMMY, JR.** *Signature on a milk carton (indistinct).*	10.00	13.00
☐ **DAVIS, SAMMY, JR.** *Early 1950's. Bill advertising Will Maston Trio.*	6.00	8.00
☐ **DAVIS, SAMMY, JR.** *c. 1953. ALs, nearly one full page.*	30.00	38.00
☐ **DAVIS, SAMMY, JR.** *Photo with Peter Lawford, signed by Davis only.*	31.00	40.00
☐ **DAVIS, SAMMY, JR.** *8x10 studio portrait, signed and inscribed.*	12.00	16.00
☐ **DAVIS, SAMMY, JR.** *Three snapshots on stage, unsigned.*	9.00	12.00
☐ **DAVIS, SAMMY, JR.** *c. 1968. Check endorsed by him.*	30.00	40.00
☐ **DAVIS, SAMMY, JR.** *c. 1957-1974. Collection of 64 magazine articles on him, unbound, in a folder.*	110.00	140.00
☐ **DAY, DORIS.** *Large photo from "Life" magazine, signed.*	12.00	16.00
☐ **DAY, DORIS.** *Sheet music, "Secret Love", signed and inscribed.*	42.00	60.00
☐ **DAY, DORIS.** *c. 1948. 8x10 publicity photo.*	4.00	6.00
☐ **DAY, DORIS.** *Collection of 91 motion picture stills from about 15 films, none signed.*	220.00	275.00
☐ **DAY, DORIS.** *"Doris Day Coloring Book", mint.*	15.00	20.00
☐ **DAY, DORIS.** *Sheet music, "Ten Cents a Dance", signed.*	25.00	35.00
☐ **DAY, DORIS.** *Matted, signed photo of Ruth Etting, signed on the mat by Doris Day (who portrayed her in motion picture).*	130.00	155.00
☐ **DAY, DORIS.** *11x14 color photo, signed.*	24.00	34.00
☐ **DAY, DORIS.** *EP record album cover, signed, no record.*	36.00	46.00
☐ **DAY, DORIS.** *8x10 photo with James Cagney, signed by both.*	70.00	90.00
☐ **DeHAVEN, GLORIA.** *8x10 motion picture still, signed.*	10.00	14.00
☐ **DESMOND, JOHNNY.** *c. 1957. Concert program, signed.*	5.00	7.00

	Price Range	
☐ **DESMOND, JOHNNY.** *Membership card "Johnny Desmond Fan Club".*	8.00	11.00
☐ **DESMOND, JOHNNY.** *8x10 portrait photo, signed.*	9.00	13.00
☐ **DESMOND, JOHNNY.** *Two fan magazine covers from the 1950's with his portrait in color, unsigned.*	4.00	5.00
☐ **DESMOND, JOHNNY.** *c. 1963. Typed letter, signed, with envelope.*	6.00	8.00
☐ **DESMOND, JOHNNY.** *c. 1956. Signature on cafe check.*	6.00	8.00
☐ **DESMOND, JOHNNY.** *Photo with Vic Damone, signed by both.*	25.00	35.00
☐ **DESMOND, JOHNNY.** *45rpm record, "That Old Gang of Mine", signed on the label.*	15.00	20.00
☐ **DOWNEY, MORTON.** *c. 1941. Check endorsed by him.*	19.00	26.00
☐ **DOWNEY, MORTON.** *Postcard photo with facsimile signature.*	6.00	8.00
☐ **EDDY, NELSON.** *c. 1938. 8x10 studio portrait, signed and inscribed.*	21.00	27.00
☐ **EDDY, NELSON.** *8x10 motion picture still with Jeanette MacDonald, signed by both.*	85.00	110.00
☐ **EDDY, NELSON.** *Collection of 57 motion picture stills.*	130.00	160.00
☐ **EDDY, NELSON.** *Series of 8 scrapbooks 11x14 inches, containing items on his life and career, 23 signed photos, c. 250 unsigned photos (including motion picture stills), magazine articles, news cuttings.*	1500.00	2000.00
☐ **EDDY, NELSON.** *Sheet music, "Shortnin' Bread", signed.*	130.00	160.00
☐ **EDDY, NELSON.** *c. 1945. Pen and wash caricature by Al Capp.*	300.00	350.00
☐ **EDDY, NELSON.** *Bulletin of the "Nelson Eddy Fan Club".*	25.00	33.00
☐ **EDDY, NELSON.** *c. 1939. Postcard photo with facsimile signature.*	12.00	16.00
☐ **FISHER, EDDIE.** *c. 1953. 8x10 studio portrait, signed.*	21.00	26.00
☐ **FISHER, EDDIE.** *Magazine cover photo with Elizabeth Taylor.*	4.00	6.00
☐ **FISHER, EDDIE.** *c. 1953. "Enjoy Coke Time with Eddie Fisher", 11x14 ad, signed.*	26.00	32.00
☐ **FISHER, EDDIE.** *Signature on a "TV Guide" cover.*	6.00	9.00
☐ **FISHER, EDDIE.** *45rpm record, "O My Papa", signed on the label. Framed along with a small unsigned portrait.*	80.00	100.00
☐ **FISHER, EDDIE.** *c. 1968. 5x7 photo, signed.*	8.00	11.00
☐ **FISHER, EDDIE.** *c. 1978. 6x8 photo with Carrie Fisher, signed by both.*	12.00	16.00
☐ **FISHER, EDDIE.** *8x10 photo with Debbie Reynolds.*	5.00	7.00
☐ **FROMAN, JANE.** *c. 1952. 8x10 studio portrait, signed.*	7.00	10.00
☐ **GARLAND, JUDY.** *c. 1969. N.Y. Times newspaper with story on her death.*	9.00	13.00
☐ **GARLAND, JUDY.** *c. 1946. 8x10 photo, signed and inscribed.*	180.00	240.00
☐ **GARLAND, JUDY.** *Sheet music, "Over the Rainbow", signed, framed along with a signed, inscribed early photo.*	500.00	650.00
☐ **GARLAND, JUDY.** *Concert program, Palace Theater, NY, unsigned.*	22.00	28.00

	Price Range	
☐ **GARLAND, JUDY.** *Three stills from "The Wizard of Oz", all signed by her, two also signed by Jack Haley, one by Jack Haley and Bert Lahr. In a brown leatherette folder.*	550.00	700.00
☐ **GARLAND, JUDY.** *c. 1962. Typed letter, signed.*	100.00	120.00
☐ **GARLAND, JUDY.** *c. 1937. ALs, two pp., Hollywood.*	400.00	500.00
☐ **GARLAND, JUDY.** *LP record album cover, signed, no record.*	310.00	390.00
☐ **GARLAND, JUDY.** *Newspaper clipping, signed.*	85.00	110.00
☐ **GORME, EYDIE.** *8x10 photo with Steve Lawrence, signed by both.*	21.00	26.00
☐ **GORME, EYDIE.** *Record company ad, signed by her.*	8.00	11.00
☐ **GORME, EYDIE.** *5x7 photo on stage, signed on the back.*	9.00	12.00
☐ **GORME, EYDIE.** *Signature on a card.*	4.00	5.00
☐ **GORME, EYDIE.** *Scrapbook with c. 250 news cuttings, photos, a few signed, other items pertaining to her and Steve Lawrence.*	95.00	115.00
☐ **GORME, EYDIE.** *c. 1966. Typed letter, signed.*	6.00	8.00
☐ **HAYMES, DICK.** *c. 1947. 8x10 studio photo, signed.*	10.00	13.00
☐ **HAYMES, DICK.** *Magazine article, signed, soiled.*	6.00	8.00
☐ **HAYMES, DICK.** *c. 1951. Three-line memo on small sheet.*	6.00	8.00
☐ **HAYMES, DICK.** *8x10 photo on stage, signed, inscribed.*	12.00	16.00
☐ **HAYMES, DICK.** *4x5 fan snapshot, signed on the back.*	5.00	7.00
☐ **HUMPERDINCK, ENGELBERT.** *LP record album cover signed and inscribed to a fan, record present.*	50.00	70.00
☐ **HUMPERDINCK, ENGELBERT.** *8x10 studio portrait, signed.*	25.00	33.00
☐ **HUMPERDINCK, ENGELBERT.** *Collection of color photos from fan magazine covers, mounted on stiff paper sheets, unsigned.*	15.00	20.00
☐ **HUMPERDINCK, ENGELBERT.** *T-shirt with his likeness.*	10.00	13.00
☐ **HUMPERDINCK, ENGELBERT.** *Bumper sticker.*	8.00	11.00
☐ **HUMPERDINCK, ENGELBERT.** *Four 8x10 color photos, one signed.*	90.00	115.00
☐ **HUMPERDINCK, ENGELBERT.** *Membership card in his fan club.*	5.00	7.00
☐ **HUMPERDINCK, ENGELBERT.** *c. 1970. "Win a Date with Englebert", rules for promotional contest, one page.*	4.00	5.00
☐ **HUMPERDINCK, ENGELBERT.** *Signature on a card.*	6.00	8.00
☐ **HUNTER, TAB.** *c. 1958. 8x10 photo, signed.*	5.00	7.00
☐ **JOLSON, AL.** *c. 1920's. 8x10 sepia photo, signed and inscribed.*	110.00	135.00
☐ **JOLSON, AL.** *Sheet music, "Mammy", signed, framed.*	150.00	210.00
☐ **JOLSON, AL.** *c. 1908. ALs, 1½ pp., with envelope.*	100.00	125.00
☐ **JOLSON, AL.** *Cardboard cut-out portrait of Jolson in blackface, possibly from a motion picture poster, signed.*	240.00	310.00
☐ **JOLSON, AL.** *c. 1944, Typewritten letter, two pages, concerning the war and his observations on its effect on show biz, signed.*	225.00	300.00
☐ **JOLSON, AL.** *c. 1940. 8x10 photo with Eddie Cantor, signed by Jolson only, framed.*	110.00	125.00
☐ **JOLSON, AL.** *c. 1936. Signature on the back of a press pass.*	16.00	21.00
☐ **JOLSON, AL.** *c. 1912. Vaudeville bill advertising him as one of the attractions.*	60.00	80.00

	Price	Range
☐ **JOLSON, AL.** *8x10 photo with George Jessel, unsigned.*	12.00	17.00
☐ **JOLSON, AL.** *8x10 motion picture still, boldly signed.*	100.00	115.00
☐ **JOLSON, AL.** *c. 1925. Handwritten memo, three lines.*	50.00	70.00
☐ **JOLSON, AL.** *17 unsigned publicity photos, various sizes.*	120.00	150.00
☐ **KAZAN, LAINIE.** *c. 1971. 8x10 photo, signed.*	9.00	13.00
☐ **KAZAN, LAINIE.** *LP record album cover, signed, no record.*	21.00	26.00
☐ **KAZAN, LAINIE.** *Signature on a food company brochure.*	4.00	6.00
☐ **KITT, EARTHA.** *c. 1956. 8x10 photo, signed.*	12.00	17.00
☐ **KITT, EARTHA.** *c. 1965. Christmas card, signed.*	16.00	22.00
☐ **KITT, EARTHA.** *Three items of sheet music signed by her.*	80.00	110.00
☐ **KITT, EARTHA.** *8x10 photo with Lena Horne, signed by both.*	44.00	60.00
☐ **KYSER, KAY.** *Postcard photo with facsimile signature.*	8.00	11.00
☐ **KYSER, KAY.** *c. 1944. 8x10 photo with band, signed.*	12.00	16.00
☐ **KYSER, KAY.** *Diploma in "Kollege of Musical Knowlege", facsimile signature.*	10.00	13.00
☐ **KYSER, KAY.** *c. 1941. Snapshot photo signed on back.*	6.00	8.00
☐ **KYSER, KAY.** *Photo with "Ish Kabibble", signed by both.*	17.00	25.00
☐ **KYSER, KAY.** *Photo with Bob Crosby, signed by both.*	15.00	20.00
☐ **LAINE, FRANKIE.** *Sheet music, "Mule Train", signed.*	55.00	70.00
☐ **LAINE, FRANKIE.** *c. 1954. Magazine article, signed.*	5.00	7.00
☐ **LAINE, FRANKIE.** *c. 1960. Typewritten letter, signed.*	8.00	11.00
☐ **LAINE, FRANKIE.** *LP album cover, signed, record inside also signed (on the label).*	60.00	80.00
☐ **LAINE, FRANKIE.** *c. 1952. Sheet music, "High Noon", signed.*	50.00	70.00
☐ **LAINE, FRANKIE.** *Photo with Tex Ritter, signed by both, framed along with sheet music of "High Noon" and 78rpm records of the song done by both.*	120.00	160.00
☐ **LAINE, FRANKIE.** *Signature on a cash voucher.*	4.00	5.00
☐ **LAINE, FRANKIE.** *c. 1958. 8x10 photo, signed.*	10.00	13.00
☐ **LANSON, SNOOKY.** *8x10 photo with Dorothy Collins, signed by Lanson only.*	6.00	8.00
☐ **LaROSA, JULIUS.** *c. 1956. 6x8 color photo from magazine, signed.*	6.00	8.00
☐ **LaROSA, JULIUS.** *c. early 1950's. Advertisement for Arthur Godfrey radio program with his picture and others.*	3.00	4.00
☐ **LaROSA, JULIUS.** *c. 1951. Handwritten letter, with envelope.*	8.00	11.00
☐ **LaROSA, JULIUS.** *c. 1953. 8x10 studio portrait.*	3.00	4.00
☐ **LaROSA, JULIUS.** *Collection of c. 85 news clippings on LaRosa/Godfrey affair.*	22.00	28.00
☐ **LaROSA, JULIUS.** *Two candid photos, one signed on back.*	9.00	12.00
☐ **LaROSA, JULIUS.** *Signature on cover of LP album, no record.*	21.00	28.00
☐ **LEE, PEGGY.** *8x10 studio portrait, signed and inscribed, framed along with a 45rpm recording.*	50.00	65.00
☐ **LEE, PEGGY.** *Sheet music, "Fever", signed.*	33.00	41.00
☐ **LEE, PEGGY.** *Typewritten letter to a music agent, signed.*	12.00	16.00
☐ **LEE, PEGGY.** *8x10 publicity photo, close-up, signed.*	15.00	20.00
☐ **LEE, PEGGY.** *Two 8x10 photos, one holding a gold record.*	12.00	16.00
☐ **LEE, PEGGY.** *Snapshot photo with Duke Ellington, signed by Lee only.*	17.00	25.00

	Price Range	
☐ **LEE, PEGGY.** *c. 1955. Photo in long gown, photo service stamp on back.*	4.00	5.00
☐ **LEE, PEGGY.** *Sheet music, "Is That All There Is?", signed.*	30.00	38.00
☐ **LEE, PEGGY.** *LP record album cover, signed, record missing.*	33.00	45.00
☐ **LEE, PEGGY.** *Poster advertising an album, signed.*	60.00	75.00
☐ **LONDON, JULIE.** *c. 1955. LP record album cover, signed.*	75.00	90.00
☐ **LONDON, JULIE.** *8x10 studio portrait wearing low-cut gown, signed, mounted on heavy paper.*	20.00	26.00
☐ **LONDON, JULIE.** *6x8 photo with Jack Webb, unsigned.*	6.00	8.00
☐ **LONDON, JULIE.** *c. 1961. Card inscribed and signed.*	9.00	12.00
☐ **MacRAE, GORDON.** *8x10 studio portrait, signed.*	5.00	7.00
☐ **MacRAE, GORDON.** *c. 1958. Three small fan snapshots.*	6.00	8.00
☐ **MacRAE, GORDON.** *c. 1963. 8x10 photo with Sheila MacRae, signed by both.*	25.00	33.00
☐ **MacRAE, GORDON.** *Photo with Vic Damone, signed by MacRae only.*	12.00	16.00
☐ **MacRAE, GORDON.** *Typewritten letter to a fan, signed.*	6.00	8.00
☐ **MacRAE, GORDON.** *Magazine article, signed.*	5.00	7.00
☐ **MacRAE, GORDON.** *c. 1960. Photo with Dean Martin, unsigned.*	4.00	5.00
☐ **MARTIN, DEAN.** *c. 1951. 8x10 photo with Jerry Lewis, signed by both, CBS stamp on back.*	70.00	90.00
☐ **MARTIN, DEAN.** *Photo-spread from "Life" magazine, signed.*	30.00	40.00
☐ **MARTIN, DEAN.** *8x10 portrait photo holding gold record, signed.*	13.00	18.00
☐ **MARTIN, DEAN.** *c. 1970. Signature on restaurant menu.*	5.00	7.00
☐ **MARTIN, DEAN.** *LP record album cover, signed and inscribed on the back, record missing.*	38.00	48.00
☐ **MARTIN, DEAN.** *45rpm record, "That's Amore", signed on the label.*	30.00	40.00
☐ **MARTIN, DEAN.** *c. 1954. Postcard photo with Jerry Lewis, facsimile signatures.*	6.00	8.00
☐ **MARTIN, DEAN.** *8x10 photo with Sammy Davis, Jr. and Frank Sinatra, signed by Martin only.*	30.00	40.00
☐ **MARTIN, DEAN.** *43 motion picture stills, two in color.*	115.00	145.00
☐ **MARTIN, DEAN.** *c. 1975. Typewritten letter, signed.*	9.00	13.00
☐ **MARTIN, DEAN.** *Sheet music, "That's Amore", signed.*	45.00	57.00
☐ **MERMAN, ETHEL.** *8x10 photo with Mary Martin, signed by both, matted and framed.*	110.00	145.00
☐ **MERMAN, ETHEL.** *Printed score, "Annie Get Your Gun", signed.*	50.00	65.00
☐ **MERMAN, ETHEL.** *c. 1944. 8x10 studio portrait, signed.*	42.00	50.00
☐ **MERMAN, ETHEL.** *c. 1948. 8x10 studio portrait, signed.*	36.00	45.00
☐ **MERMAN, ETHEL.** *8x10 photo in "Annie" costume, signed.*	50.00	70.00
☐ **MERMAN, ETHEL.** *c. 1970. 6x8 color photo, inscribed.*	26.00	33.00
☐ **MERMAN, ETHEL.** *Two pages from a notebook in her hand.*	31.00	40.00
☐ **MERMAN, ETHEL.** *Three small snapshots taken by fans.*	6.00	8.00
☐ **MERMAN, ETHEL.** *Poster advertising "Annie Get Your Gun", 27x41, color, soiled.*	160.00	210.00
☐ **MILLER, MITCH.** *Printed record company circular, signed.*	5.00	7.00

	Price Range	
☐ **MILLER, MITCH.** *Typewritten letter on Columbia Record Co. stationery, signed.*	9.00	12.00
☐ **MILLER, MITCH.** *Sheet music, "Yellow Rose of Texas", signed.*	31.00	36.00
☐ **MILLER, MITCH.** *c. 1958. 8x10 studio photo, signed.*	8.00	11.00
☐ **MILLER, MITCH.** *c. 1966. 7x8½ magazine photo with Skitch Henderson, signed by both.*	21.00	26.00
☐ **MILLER, MITCH.** *8x10 photo with Al Hirt, signed by Miller only.*	12.00	16.00
☐ **MILLER, MITCH.** *c. 1958 & 1960. Two checks endorsed by him.*	36.00	43.00
☐ **MILLER, MITCH.** *LP record album cover, signed, record missing.*	31.00	40.00
☐ **MILLER, MITCH.** *Signature on a notebook page.*	4.00	5.00
☐ **MITCHELL, GUY.** *c. 1957. 45rpm record, "Singing the Blues", autographed on the label, framed with an unsigned photo.*	31.00	40.00
☐ **MITCHELL, GUY.** *"Billboard" magazine Top 100 chart, showing "Singing the Blues" #1, signed.*	24.00	32.00
☐ **MITCHELL, GUY.** *8x10 photo on stage, signed, inscribed.*	10.00	13.00
☐ **MITCHELL, GUY.** *Sheet music to three songs recorded by him, signed.*	55.00	70.00
☐ **MITCHELL, GUY.** *4x5 snapshot photo in car, signed.*	7.00	9.00
☐ **MITCHELL, GUY.** *5x7 photo with Perry Como, signed by Mitchell only.*	9.00	12.00
☐ **MONROE, VAUGHN.** *Sheet music, "Ghost Riders in the Sky", signed, framed along with a photo and a 78rpm recording.*	80.00	100.00
☐ **MONROE, VAUGHN.** *8x10 studio portrait, signed.*	12.00	16.00
☐ **MONROE, VAUGHN.** *c. 1941. Typewritten letter, signed.*	14.00	19.00
☐ **MONROE, VAUGHN.** *c. 1949. Signature on a card.*	7.00	10.00
☐ **MONROE, VAUGHN.** *8x10 photo at party, signed.*	12.00	16.00
☐ **MONROE, VAUGHN.** *Scrapbook with 34 photos, 17 of them signed, c. 135 news cuttings and magazine articles relating to him.*	300.00	350.00
☐ **MONROE, VAUGHN.** *c. 1958. Christmas card, signed.*	12.00	16.00
☐ **MONROE, VAUGHN.** *Two small photos taken with fans, signed.*	15.00	20.00
☐ **MONROE, VAUGHN.** *8x10 photo, unsigned, Associated Press stamp on back.*	5.00	7.00
☐ **NEWLEY, ANTHONY.** *Printed score, "Stop the World", signed.*	14.00	18.00
☐ **NEWLEY, ANTHONY.** *LP record album cover, signed, no record.*	30.00	37.00
☐ **NEWLEY, ANTHONY.** *LP album cover, "Stop the World", original Broadway cast, signed on front, inscribed on back, no record.*	45.00	60.00
☐ **NEWLEY, ANTHONY.** *8x10 photo in costume, signed.*	12.00	16.00
☐ **NEWLEY, ANTHONY.** *4x5 photo, signed, mounted.*	8.00	11.00
☐ **NEWLEY, ANTHONY.** *Signature on a small slip of paper.*	3.00	4.00
☐ **O'CONNELL, HELEN.** *c. 1944. 8x10 photo in group, signed.*	9.00	12.00
☐ **O'CONNELL, HELEN.** *Color photo from magazine or book, signed.*	8.00	11.00
☐ **O'CONNELL, HELEN.** *c. 1953. Typewritten letter, signed.*	8.00	11.00

	Price Range	
☐ **O'CONNELL, HELEN.** *Record company reply to a fan of O'Connell's, detailing plans for releases of forthcoming records, etc.*	4.00	5.00
☐ **O'CONNELL, HELEN.** *c. 1936. Early photo of her, signed.*	9.00	12.00
☐ **O'CONNELL, HELEN.** *8x10 photo with Bob Hope, signed by O'Connell only.*	10.00	14.00
☐ **O'CONNELL, HELEN.** *Scrapbook with c. 350 news cuttings, etc.*	80.00	110.00
☐ **PAGE, PATTI.** *Sheet music, "How Much is That Doggie in the Window?", signed, framed.*	45.00	60.00
☐ **PAGE, PATTI.** *c. 1964. 8x10 studio photo, signed.*	8.00	11.00
☐ **PAGE, PATTI.** *Photo with two gold disc records, signed.*	10.00	13.00
☐ **PAGE, PATTI.** *Two news clippings, signed.*	5.00	7.00
☐ **PAGE, PATTI.** *Cover of a fan magazine with colored photo, signed.*	8.00	11.00
☐ **PAGE, PATTI.** *Signature on a 45rpm record sleeve.*	3.00	4.00
☐ **PAGE, PATTI.** *c. 1950's. Three 8x10 studio photos, unsigned.*	8.00	11.00
☐ **PAGE, PATTI.** *Photo with Perry Como, signed by both.*	25.00	33.00
☐ **RAY, JOHNNY.** *c. 1952. Sheet music, "Little White Cloud That Cried", signed.*	31.00	42.00
☐ **RAY, JOHNNY.** *8x10 photo with Liberace, signed by both.*	50.00	65.00
☐ **RAY, JOHNNY.** *Two small magazine photos mounted on card, signed on the card.*	10.00	13.00
☐ **RAY, JOHNNY.** *c. 1951. Typewritten letter, signed.*	12.00	16.00
☐ **REYNOLDS, DEBBIE.** *45rpm phono record, "Tammy", signed on the label, framed with a signed 8x10 photo.*	70.00	90.00
☐ **REYNOLDS, DEBBIE.** *Collection of 147 unsigned motion picture stills, 23 of them in color.*	370.00	450.00
☐ **REYNOLDS, DEBBIE.** *c. 1948. 8x10 photo, signed.*	10.00	13.00
☐ **REYNOLDS, DEBBIE.** *c. 1942. Photo as a youth, signed.*	15.00	20.00
☐ **REYNOLDS, DEBBIE.** *Five lobby cards of motion pictures.*	175.00	210.00
☐ **REYNOLDS, DEBBIE.** *c. 1959. 8x10 photo with Doris Day, signed by Reynolds only.*	12.00	16.00
☐ **REYNOLDS, DEBBIE.** *Typewritten letter to Warner Bros. studios, signed, with envelope.*	15.00	20.00
☐ **REYNOLDS, DEBBIE.** *Sheet music, "Abba Dabba Honeymoon", signed and inscribed.*	40.00	50.00
☐ **REYNOLDS, DEBBIE.** *c. 1961. Magazine article, signed.*	7.00	11.00
☐ **REYNOLDS, DEBBIE.** *8x10 color photo portrait, signed.*	15.00	21.00
☐ **SHORE, DINAH.** *c. 1973. 8x10 photo on golf course, signed.*	8.00	11.00
☐ **SHORE, DINAH.** *Signature on a department store receipt.*	4.00	5.00
☐ **SHORE, DINAH.** *c. 1951. Photo on stage (TV show), signed.*	8.00	11.00
☐ **SHORE, DINAH.** *c. 1949. ALs, one page, with envelope.*	9.00	12.00
☐ **SHORE, DINAH.** *List of recordings made by her, signed.*	5.00	7.00
☐ **SHORE, DINAH.** *Photo with Perry Como, signed by Shore only.*	12.00	16.00

	Price Range	
☐ **SHORE, DINAH.** *Photo with Montgomery Clift, signed by both.*	33.00	44.00
☐ **SHORE, DINAH.** *Christmas card, signed, undated.*	12.00	16.00
☐ **SHORE, DINAH.** *Photo in record studio, signed, mounted.*	12.00	16.00
☐ **SHORE, DINAH.** *Large portrait photo, 16x23, signed.*	26.00	31.00
☐ **SHORE, DINAH.** *Three items of sheet music, signed.*	44.00	52.00
☐ **SHORE, DINAH.** *Photo with Dean Martin, signed by Shore only.*	12.00	16.00
☐ **SINATRA, FRANK.** *c. 1941. Paramount theater poster advertising an appearance by him, unsigned.*	150.00	200.00
☐ **SINATRA, FRANK.** *c. 1957. 8x10 portrait photo, signed.*	30.00	40.00
☐ **SINATRA, FRANK.** *LP record album cover signed, no record.*	90.00	120.00
☐ **SINATRA, FRANK.** *c. 1960. Memo in his hand.*	15.00	20.00
☐ **SINATRA, FRANK.** *8x10 photo on stage, Madison Square Garden, NY, autographed, matted, framed.*	70.00	100.00
☐ **SINATRA, FRANK.** *c. 1962. Pen and ink caricature of him, 10x12, matted and framed.*	100.00	125.00
☐ **SINATRA, FRANK.** *Photo with Frank Jr., signed by both.*	70.00	100.00
☐ **SINATRA, FRANK.** *Photo with Dean Martin, signed by Sinatra only.*	35.00	45.00
☐ **SINATRA, FRANK.** *43 motion picture stills, black and white, one of them signed, several signed by other performers.*	120.00	150.00
☐ **SINATRA, FRANK.** *c. 1958. Photo holding a gold record, signed.*	30.00	40.00
☐ **SINATRA, FRANK.** *Sheet music, "My Way", signed, also signed by Paul Anka.*	150.00	200.00
☐ **SINATRA, FRANK.** *c. 1972. Photo with Paul Anka, signed by both.*	100.00	150.00
☐ **SINATRA, FRANK.** *45rpm record, "All the Way", signed on the label.*	75.00	100.00
☐ **SINATRA, FRANK.** *T-shirt with his likeness.*	10.00	13.00
☐ **SINATRA, FRANK.** *c. 1944. Membership card in fan club.*	15.00	20.00
☐ **SINATRA, FRANK.** *Photo at age 17, signed "Frank".*	60.00	80.00
☐ **SINATRA, FRANK.** *c. 1975. Photo with Nancy Sinatra, signed by both.*	70.00	100.00
☐ **SINATRA, FRANK.** *c. 1940's. Photo with Tommy Dorsey, signed by Sinatra only.*	65.00	90.00
☐ **SINATRA, FRANK.** *Motion picture still, "Man With the Golden Arm", signed, also signed by Kim Novak and Robert Strauss.*	100.00	160.00
☐ **SMITH, KATE.** *c. 1950. Sheet music, "When the Moon Comes Over the Mountain", signed and inscribed.*	44.00	60.00
☐ **SMITH, KATE.** *c. 1951. Photo from TV show, signed.*	9.00	12.00
☐ **SMITH, KATE.** *c. 1939. 8x10 portrait photo, signed.*	14.00	19.00
☐ **SMITH, KATE.** *8x10 photo on stage, signed.*	12.00	16.00
☐ **SMITH, KATE.** *c. 1955. Signature on theater program.*	4.00	5.00

	Price Range	
☐ **SMITH, KATE.** *c. 1974. Photo at hockey game, Canada, signed.*	8.00	11.00
☐ **SMITH, KATE.** *Two colored photos from magazine, signed.*	11.00	15.00
☐ **SMITH, KATE.** *c. 1957. Christmas card signed.*	12.00	16.00
☐ **SMITH, KATE.** *78rpm recording signed on the label.*	26.00	33.00
☐ **SMITH, KATE.** *Snapshot photo with fan, signed.*	5.00	6.00
☐ **STAFFORD, JO.** *c. 1952. 8x10 studio portrait, signed.*	9.00	12.00
☐ **STAFFORD, JO.** *c. 1953. Colored photo from magazine, signed.*	8.00	11.00
☐ **STAFFORD, JO.** *8x10 photo with Frankie Laine, signed by both.*	16.00	22.00
☐ **STAFFORD, JO.** *Signature on a card.*	3.00	4.00
☐ **STAFFORD, JO.** *c. 1969. Typewritten letter, signed.*	6.00	8.00
☐ **STAFFORD, JO.** *c. 1961. Brief memo in her hand.*	5.00	7.00
☐ **STARR, KAY.** *Sheet music, "Side by Side", signed.*	16.00	22.00
☐ **STARR, KAY.** *c. 1953. 8x10 studio portrait, signed.*	8.00	11.00
☐ **STARR, KAY.** *78rpm recording signed on the label.*	20.00	27.00
☐ **STARR, KAY.** *c. 1958. Postcard with five lines in her hand.*	5.00	7.00
☐ **STARR, KAY.** *8x10 photo on stage (possibly TV), signed.*	9.00	13.00
☐ **STARR, KAY.** *Snapshot photo at age about 16, signed.*	9.00	13.00
☐ **STARR, KAY.** *Record company contract signed.*	20.00	27.00
☐ **STARR, KAY.** *c. 1954. Magazine article, signed.*	5.00	7.00
☐ **STARR, KAY.** *Record company advertisement, signed.*	4.00	5.00
☐ **STARR, KAY.** *c. mostly 1952-56. Scrapbook with c. 90 news cuttings, several signed photos, etc.*	50.00	65.00
☐ **STREISAND, BARBRA.** *8x10 photo with Garry Moore, signed by Streisand only, age 19.*	30.00	40.00
☐ **STREISAND, BARBRA.** *Printed score, "Funny Girl", signed.*	40.00	55.00
☐ **STREISAND, BARBRA.** *Gown worn by her in film, sold at benefit auction.*	400.00	550.00
☐ **STREISAND, BARBRA.** *c. 1962. 8x10 studio portrait, signed.*	25.00	33.00
☐ **STREISAND, BARBRA.** *c. 1975. 8x10 studio portrait, signed.*	20.00	27.00
☐ **STREISAND, BARBRA.** *c. 1972. Typewritten letter, signed.*	20.00	27.00
☐ **STREISAND, BARBRA.** *c. 1968. ALs, one-page, with envelope.*	40.00	60.00
☐ **STREISAND, BARBRA.** *Collection of 166 motion picture stills, all black and white, none signed, in a cloth box.*	370.00	445.00
☐ **STREISAND, BARBRA.** *8x10 photo with Elliot Gould, signed by Streisand only.*	50.00	70.00
☐ **STREISAND, BARBRA.** *8x10 photo with Woody Allen, signed by both, framed.*	100.00	150.00
☐ **STREISAND, BARBRA.** *LP record album cover, signed, record missing.*	175.00	250.00
☐ **STREISAND, BARBRA.** *Two pages of notes in her hand.*	100.00	135.00

	Price Range	
☐ **STREISAND, BARBRA.** *Sheet music, "Memories", signed.*	75.00	100.00
☐ **STREISAND, BARBRA.** *T-shirt with her likeness.*	10.00	13.00
☐ **STREISAND, BARBRA.** *Pen sketch of her, 8x10, framed.*	23.00	30.00
☐ **STREISAND, BARBRA.** *Portrait of her done in stained glass, 22x25, framed.*	130.00	180.00
☐ **STREISAND, BARBRA.** *Photo of her with Oscar award, signed.*	80.00	110.00
☐ **TORME, MEL.** *c. 1954. 8x10 studio portrait, signed.*	8.00	11.00
☐ **TORME, MEL.** *c. 1949. ALs, half page.*	6.00	8.00
☐ **TORME, MEL.** *c. 1953. Hand puppet, "Velvet Frog" (after his nickname "Velvet Frog"), plush.*	12.00	16.00
☐ **TORME, MEL.** *8x10 photo on stage, signed.*	7.00	10.00
☐ **TORME, MEL.** *5x7 photo on street, signed, creased.*	4.00	5.00
☐ **TORME, MEL.** *Magazine photo in turtleneck sweater, signed.*	5.00	7.00
☐ **VALE, JERRY.** *c. 1960. 8x10 studio portrait, signed.*	8.00	11.00
☐ **VALE, JERRY.** *c. 1964. Restaurant ad, signed.*	6.00	8.00
☐ **VALE, JERRY.** *Three unsigned photos, various sizes.*	5.00	7.00
☐ **VALE, JERRY.** *c. 1972. Handwritten note.*	5.00	7.00
☐ **VALE, JERRY.** *LP album cover, signed, record present.*	14.00	20.00
☐ **VALE, JERRY.** *Signature on restaurant napkin.*	3.00	4.00
☐ **VALLEE, RUDY.** *c. 1930. 8x10 photo, signed and inscribed.*	25.00	33.00
☐ **VALLEE, RUDY.** *Score, "How to Succeed", signed.*	22.00	29.00
☐ **VALLEE, RUDY.** *c. 1934. Yale football pennant, signed.*	70.00	95.00
☐ **VALLEE, RUDY.** *Photo at age about 14, signed.*	50.00	65.00
☐ **VALLEE, RUDY.** *Photo with Robert Morse, signed by both.*	41.00	55.00
☐ **VALLEE, RUDY.** *78rpm recording, signed on the label.*	25.00	33.00
☐ **VALLEE, RUDY.** *c. 1959. 8x10 photo with microphone, signed.*	20.00	27.00
☐ **WILLIAMS, ANDY.** *4x5 snapshot, signed, mounted.*	5.00	7.00
☐ **WILLIAMS, ANDY.** *c. 1970. LP record album cover, signed.*	25.00	33.00
☐ **WILLIAMS, ANDY.** *8x10 color photo on golf course, signed.*	12.00	16.00
☐ **WILLIAMS, ANDY.** *c. 1969. Photo with gold records and other awards, signed.*	10.00	14.00

ROCK AND ROLL

Rock music's beginnings can be traced back to roots in country, bluegrass, and jazz; its closest ancestor was Negro rhythm and blues. A number of the earlier rock stars came out of rhythm and blues. To name the first pure rock record or rock performer would be impossible. Some would say Bill Haley & the Comets. This group had the first million-selling pure rock record, "Rock Around the Clock," in 1955. Without doubt, Bill Haley and his band were more of an influence on early rock performers than any other pioneers in the field. The success of "Rock Around the Clock" also encouraged record companies previously skeptical of rock's sales appeal to bring out rock records. By the end of 1955, rock was the biggest selling type of popular music.

The so-called "golden age" of rock was the 1950's, or more specifically the years from 1955 to 1959. All rock records of that era are collectible, though many carry just minimal value depending on the artist, label, recording, and scarcity. Many post-1960 records are also sought by rockaphiles. There is no line of demarcation on age. Undoubtedly, today's rock records will be collectors' items in time, perhaps a very short time.

As far as collectibility goes, in terms of artist, the most desirable rock recordings are early (pre-popularity) releases by artists who later became stars. It is very rare in the rock field — or in any form of pop music, for that matter — for an unknown artist's first recording to become a big hit. Usually, unknowns who score Top Ten hits have made previous recordings; the big hit is believed by the public to be their first record because few persons are aware earlier records were released. Everyone, including many disc jockeys, thought the Everly Brothers' "Bye Bye Love," a 1956 million-seller, was their first recording. It **was** their first on the Cadence label, but had been preceded by a Columbia disc (a flop). That Columbia recording, "Keep A-Loving Me/The Sun Keeps Shining," is now a prime collectors' item, worth $20-$30 depending on condition. "Bye Bye Love" brings $3 at most.

Generally speaking, records that made the hit charts are of minimal value, because of the vast quantities manufactured. Of a flop record, only ten or twenty thousand copies might have been pressed; in some cases less. As many as four million copies can exist of a super hit. Any recording that reached the Top Ten is likely to have been pressed in at least 500,000 copies. In fact, there have been many million sellers — "gold records" — that never made Number One.

With very few exceptions (such as early releases by Fats Domino), all collectible rock records are in 45rpm. Extended play and 33⅓rpm albums of rock artists are also collected. For more complete information on the field of rock music collecting, see "The Official Guide to Collectible Rock Records" by Randal C. Hill, published by House of Collectibles.

ROCK MUSIC COLLECTING. The logical and most popular approach is to concentrate on the recordings of a single artist, or several artists. Some collectors try to assemble a complete "Billboard" or "Cashbox" hit list — the fifty or sixty recordings that appeared on the list in a given week, but this will invariably include non-rock titles. Others make a specialty of recordings by artists who never became famous. These records, usually very popular among '50's cultists (more so today than originally), tend to be quite scarce and costly. Some had very limited pressings. They were issued by small companies with low budgets, which could not afford to take gambles. No complete list of all rock recordings has ever been compiled, so it is possible that some obscure releases of the 1950's or later exist that are not even known to collectors. Advanced collectors are also interested in demo records, many of which were never publicly released or, if released, were not identical to the demo.

The best source for rock records are the dealers who make a specialty of buying and selling them. Occasional "finds" may be made in junkshops, Salvation Army shops, etc., but in general the condition of records found in this fashion is undesirable. Specialist dealers stock only specimens in fine or better condition, and can supply hard-to-get titles that would probably not be obtainable anywhere else. Another possibility is to trade with fellow collectors, using this guide or dealer price lists to establish values.

AUTOGRAPHS

	8x10 Signed Photo	Plain Signature	Other
☐ **ACE, JOHNNY.**	3.00	2.00	
☐ **ADAMS, LINK.**	3.00	2.00	
☐ **ADDEO, NICKY.**	5.00	2.00	
☐ **ALAIMO, STEVE.**	3.00	1.50	
☐ **ALEXANDER, ARTHUR.**	3.00	1.50	
☐ **ALLEN, DAVIE.**	4.00	2.00	
☐ *Typed Letter with Signature.*			3.00
☐ **ALLEN, LEE.**	2.75	1.50	
☐ **ALPERT, HERB.**	4.00	2.00	
☐ **ANDREWS, LEE.**	4.00	2.00	
☐ **ANKA, PAUL.**	3.00	1.50	
☐ *Typed Letter.*			2.00
☐ *Signed cover of record album.*			10.00
☐ **ANNETTE.**	5.00	2.00	
☐ **AVALON, FRANKIE.**	3.00	2.00	
☐ **BAKER, KENNY.**	5.00	2.00	
☐ **BAKER, LAVERN.**	5.00	2.50	
☐ **BALIN, MARTY.**	6.00	3.00	
☐ **BALLARD, HANK.**	3.00	1.50	
☐ **BARRI, STEVE.**	3.00	1.50	
☐ **BARRY, JEFF.**	9.00	3.00	
Most Memorabilia is rather scarce.			
☐ **BEAUMONT, JIMMY.**	3.00	1.50	
☐ **BELLUS, TONY.**	5.00	2.00	
☐ **BENNETT, BOYD.**	4.00	2.00	
☐ **BERRY, CHUCK.**	4.00	2.00	
☐ *Signed album cover.*			15.00
☐ **BERRY, JAN.**	4.00	2.00	
☐ **BEST, PETER.**	25.00	5.00	
☐ **BIG BOPPER (J. P. Richardson).**	100.00	20.00	
☐ **BLACK, JACK.**	3.00	1.50	
☐ **BLAND, BILLY.**	3.00	1.50	
☐ **BLANE, MARCIE.**	3.00	1.50	
☐ **BONDS, GARY.**	5.00	1.50	
☐ **BONO, SONNY.**	4.00	1.50	
☐ **BOONE, PAT.**	4.00	1.50	
☐ *Signed album cover.*			15.00
☐ **BOWEN, JIMMY.**	10.00	3.00	
☐ **BOWIE, DAVID.**	25.00	8.00	
☐ **BOYCE, TOMMY.**	3.50	1.50	
☐ **BRADLEY, JAN.**	3.00	1.50	
☐ **BROOKS, DONNIE.**	3.00	1.50	
☐ **BROWN, RUTH.**	5.00	2.00	
☐ **BURNETTE, DORSEY.**	4.00	1.50	
☐ **BURNETTE, JOHNNY.**	20.00	5.00	
Most Memorabilia is scarce.			
☐ **BUTLER, JERRY.**	3.00	1.50	
☐ **BYRNES, ED.**	6.00	2.00	
☐ **CAMPBELL, GLEN.**	5.00	1.50	

	8x10 Signed Photo	Plain Signature	Other
☐ **CAMPBELL, JO-ANN.**	3.00	1.50	
☐ **CANNON, FREDDY.**	3.00	1.50	
☐ **CAPEHART, JERRY.**	6.00	3.00	
☐ **CARR, VICKI.**	4.00	1.50	
☐ **CASEY, AL.**	6.00	3.00	
☐ **CASTRO, VINCE.**	6.00	3.00	
☐ **CHANNEL, BRUCE.**	4.00	1.50	
☐ **CHECKER, CHUBBY.**	7.00	3.00	
☐ **CHRISTIE, LOU.**	6.00	3.00	
☐ **CLANTON, JIMMY.**	4.00	1.50	
☐ **CLARK, SANFORD.**	3.00	1.50	
☐ **CLIFFORD, BUZZ.**	4.00	1.50	
☐ **COCHRAN, EDDIE.**	6.00	3.00	
☐ **COCKER, JOE.**	6.00	3.00	
☐ **CONNORS, CAROL.**	6.00	3.00	
☐ **COOKE, SAM.**	25.00	5.00	
☐ *Signed album cover.*			75.00
☐ **COPELAND, KEN.**	3.00	1.50	
☐ **CORTEZ, DAVE.**	4.00	1.50	
☐ **CRAWFORD, JOHNNY.**	4.00	1.50	
☐ **CYMBAL, JOHNNY.**	4.00	1.50	
☐ **DALE, DICK.**	5.00	2.00	
☐ **DARIN, BOBBY.**	40.00	7.00	
☐ *Signed album cover.*			150.00
☐ **DARREN, JAMES.**	4.00	1.50	
☐ **DAVIES, DAVE.**	3.00	1.50	
☐ **DEANE, JANET.**	6.00	3.00	
☐ **DEE, JOHNNY.**	7.00	3.00	
☐ **DEE, TOMMY.**	5.00	2.00	
☐ **DENSON, LEE.**	6.00	2.00	
☐ **DeSHANNON, JACKIE.**	6.00	2.00	
☐ **DeVORZON, BARRY.**	4.00	1.50	
☐ **DIDDLEY, BO.**	13.00	4.00	
☐ **DINNING, MARK.**	3.00	1.50	
☐ **DION.**	6.00	2.00	
☐ **DOBKINS, CARL.**	4.00	1.50	
☐ **DOLENZ, MICKEY.**	7.00	2.00	
☐ **DOMINO, FATS.**	12.00	3.00	
☐ **DONNER, RAL.**	20.00	5.00	
☐ **DORMAN, HAROLD.**	2.00	1.00	
☐ **DYLAN, BOB.**	30.00	5.00	
Very strong collector interest in all memorabilia.			
☐ **EDDY, DUANE.**	5.00	2.00	
☐ **ENGLISH, SCOTT.**	5.00	2.00	
☐ **FABIAN.**	3.50	1.50	
☐ *Signed album cover.*			12.00
☐ **FAITH, ADAM.**	3.00	1.00	

	8x10 Signed Photo	Plain Signature	Other
☐ **FORD, FRANKIE.**	3.00	1.00	
☐ **FOWLEY, KIM.**	5.00	2.00	
☐ **FRAMPTON, PETER.**	25.00	5.00	
☐ **FRANCIS, CONNIE.**	4.00	1.00	
☐ **FREEMAN, BOBBY.**	5.00	1.50	
☐ **FRENCH, DON.**	4.00	1.00	
☐ **FULLER, JERRY.**	5.00	1.50	
☐ **FURY, BILLY.**	4.00	1.00	
☐ **GALLANT, BILLY.**	4.00	1.00	
☐ **GARFUNKEL, ART.**	9.00	1.50	
☐ **GATES, DAVID.**	5.00	1.50	
☐ **GAYE, MARVIN.**	25.00	5.00	
☐ **GIBBS, GEORGIA.**	5.00	1.50	
☐ *Signed contract with record company.*			22.00
☐ **GORE, LESLEY.**	2.00	1.00	
☐ **GRACIE, CHARLIE.**	4.00	1.50	
☐ **GRAMMER, BILLY.**	4.00	1.50	
☐ **GRANAHAN, JERRY.**	4.00	1.50	
☐ **HALEY, BILL.**	35.00	4.00	
☐ **HALL, LARRY.**	5.00	1.50	
☐ **HAMILTON, GEORGE.**	5.00	1.50	
☐ **HARRISON, WILBERT.**	8.00	2.00	
☐ **HART, BOBBY.**	3.00	1.00	
☐ **HAWKINS, DALE.**	5.00	1.50	
☐ **HAWKINS, RONNIE.**	5.00	1.50	
☐ **HAWKS, MICKEY.**	6.00	1.50	
☐ **HEAD, ROY.**	3.00	1.00	
☐ **HELMS, BOBBY.**	2.50	1.00	
☐ **HENDRIX, JIMI.**	40.00	8.00	
☐ **HICKEY, ERSEL.**	5.00	1.50	
☐ **HILL, JOEL.**	6.00	1.50	
☐ **HOLLY, BUDDY.**	120.00	20.00	
☐ **HUNTER, IVORY JOE.**	10.00	2.00	
☐ **HYLAND, BRIAN.**	6.00	1.50	
☐ **JARVIS, CAROL.**	3.00	1.00	
☐ **JOHNSON, MARV.**	4.00	1.00	
☐ **JONES, DAVY.**	7.50	2.00	
☐ **JONES, JIMMY.**	3.00	1.00	
☐ **JUSTIS, BILL.**	7.50	2.00	
☐ **KENNER, CHRIS.**	3.00	1.00	
☐ **KNIGHT, SONNY.**	7.50	2.00	
☐ **KNOX, BUDDY.**	15.00	3.00	
☐ *Signed album cover.*			50.00
☐ **LAUREN, ROD.**	4.00	1.50	
☐ **LEE, CURTIS.**	5.00	1.50	
☐ *4x5 photo signed from magazine.*			4.00

	8x10 Signed Photo	Plain Signature	Other
☐ **LEWIS, BOBBY.**	4.50	1.50	
☐ **LINDEN, KATHY.**	4.00	1.50	
☐ **LITTLE ANTHONY.**	8.00	3.00	
☐ **LITTLE EVA.**	6.00	2.00	
☐ **LITTLE RICHARD.**	10.00	3.00	
☐ **LUKE, ROBIN.**	5.00	2.00	
☐ **LYMON, FRANKIE.**	80.00	11.00	
☐ **MACK, LONNIE.**	4.00	2.00	
☐ **MANN, CARL.**	6.00	2.00	
☐ **MARENO, LEE.**	11.00	3.00	
☐ **MARSH, RITCHIE.**	8.00	3.00	
☐ **MARTIN, GEORGE.**	4.00	2.00	
☐ **MARTIN, JANIS.**	6.00	2.50	
☐ **MAYER, NATHANIEL.**	4.00	1.50	
☐ **McDANIELS, GENE.**	4.00	1.50	
☐ **McKUEN, ROD.**	11.00	4.00	
☐ **McPHATTER, CLYDE.**	10.00	3.00	
☐ **MILES, GARRY.**	4.00	1.50	
☐ **MILLS, HAYLEY.**	4.00	1.50	
☐ **MINEO, SAL.**	25.00	5.00	
☐ *Signed movie stills.*			30.00
☐ **MONTEZ, CHRIS.**	5.00	1.50	
☐ **NEAL, JERRY.**	6.00	2.00	
☐ **NELSON, RICKY.**	4.00	1.50	
☐ **NELSON, SANDY.**	6.00	2.00	
☐ **NESMITH, MIKE.**	8.00	3.00	
☐ **NEWMAN, TED.**	3.00	1.50	
☐ **NORVUS, NERVOUS.**	11.00	4.00	
☐ **ORBISON, ROY.**	4.00	1.50	
☐ **ORLANDO, TONY.**	6.00	1.50	
☐ *8x10 photo with "Dawn", signed by all.*			12.00
☐ **PARSONS, BILL.**	5.00	1.50	
☐ **PAXTON, GARY.**	4.00	1.50	
☐ **PETERSON, PAUL.**	4.50	1.50	
☐ **PHILLIPS, PHIL.**	6.00	2.00	
☐ **PITNEY, GENE.**	4.00	1.50	
☐ **POWERS, JOEY.**	3.00	1.50	
☐ **PRESTON, JOHNNY.**	6.00	2.00	
☐ **PRICE, LLOYD.**	9.00	3.00	
☐ **PROBY, P. J.**	4.00	1.50	
☐ **RANDAZZO, TEDDY.**	6.00	2.00	
☐ **RELF, KEITH.**	6.00	2.00	
☐ **RENAY, DIANE.**	4.00	1.50	
☐ **RESTIVO, JOHNNY.**	4.00	1.50	
☐ **REYNOLDS, JODY.**	3.00	1.50	
☐ **RICHARD, CLIFF.**	5.00	1.50	
☐ **RIVERS, JOHNNY.**	3.00	1.50	

	8x10 Signed Photo	Plain Signature	Other
☐ **ROBINSON, FLOYD**	3.50	1.50	
☐ **ROE, TOMMY**	3.00	1.50	
☐ **ROGERS, TIMMIE**	4.00	1.50	
☐ **RONSTADT, LINDA**	7.00	2.00	
☐ **RUSSELL, LEON**	6.00	2.00	
☐ **RYDELL, BOBBY**	6.00	1.50	
☐ **SANDS, TOMMY**	4.50	1.50	
☐ **SCOTT, JACK**	4.00	1.50	
☐ **SCOTT, LINDA**	3.50	1.50	
☐ **SEDAKA, NEIL**	3.00	1.50	
☐ **SELF, RONNIE**	6.00	2.00	
☐ **SHANNON, DEL**	3.50	1.50	
☐ **SHARP, DEE DEE**	3.00	1.50	
☐ **SHARPE, RAY**	3.00	1.50	
☐ **SHERMAN, BOBBY**	7.00	2.00	
☐ *"Bobby Sherman coloring book", 1971*			6.00
☐ **SHONDELL, TROY**	5.00	1.50	
☐ **SIMON, PAUL**	10.00	2.00	
☐ *Photo with Art Garfunkel, signed by both*			35.00
☐ **SMITH, HUEY**	8.00	3.00	
☐ **SMITH, RAY**	4.00	1.50	
☐ **SOUL, JIMMY**	5.00	1.50	
☐ **STAFFORD, TERRY**	3.00	1.50	
☐ **STANLEY, PAT**	6.00	2.00	
☐ **STEVENS, CONNIE**	5.00	1.50	
☐ **STITES, GARY**	3.00	1.50	
☐ **STORM, GALE**	3.00	1.50	
☐ **STRONG, BARRETT**	4.00	1.50	
☐ **SUMMERS, GENE**	7.00	2.00	
☐ **TAYLOR, AUSTIN**	4.00	1.50	
☐ **THOMAS, GENE**	3.50	1.50	
☐ **THOMPSON, SUE**	3.00	1.50	
☐ **TOROK, MITCHELL**	8.00	3.00	
☐ **TURNER, JOE**	11.00	4.00	
☐ **TWITTY, CONWAY**	4.00	1.50	
☐ **USHER, GARY**	8.00	3.00	
☐ **VALENS, RITCHIE**	75.00	10.00	
☐ **VEE, BOBBY**	5.00	1.50	
☐ **VINCENT, GENE**	50.00	8.00	
☐ *Signed album cover*			150.00
☐ **VINTON, BOBBY**	6.00	2.00	
☐ **WALLACE, JERRY**	4.00	1.50	
☐ **WARD, DALE**	4.00	1.50	
☐ **WAYNE, THOMAS**	5.00	1.50	
☐ **WILLIAMS, LARRY**	5.00	1.50	
☐ **WILLIS, CHUCK**	8.00	2.50	
☐ **WILSON, JACKIE**	8.00	2.50	

	8x10 Signed Photo	Plain Signature	Other
☐ **WRAY, LINK.**	6.00	1.50	
☐ **YOUNG, KATHY.**	4.00	1.50	

45's and LP's

PAUL ANKA — 45's	Price Range	
☐ **RPM 472** *I Confess/Blau-Wile Deveest Fontaine (with the Jacks).*	19.00	35.00
☐ **ABC-Paramount 9831** *Diana/Don't Gamble With Love.*	2.50	5.00
☐ **9855** *I Love You Baby/Tell Me That You Love Me.*	2.25	4.00
☐ **9880** *You Are My Destiny/When I Stop Loving You.*	2.25	4.00
☐ **9907** *Crazy Love/Let the Bells Keep Ringing.*	2.25	4.00
☐ **9937** *Midnight/Verboten.*	2.25	4.00
☐ **9956** *Just Young/So It's Goodbye.*	2.25	4.00
☐ **9987** *My Heart Sings/That's Love.*	2.25	4.00
☐ **10011** *I Miss You So/Late Last Night.*	2.25	4.00
☐ **10022** *Lonely Boy/Your Way.*	2.25	4.00
☐ **10040** *Put Your Head on My Shoulder/ Don't Ever Leave Me.*	2.25	4.00
☐ **10064** *It's Time to Cry/Something Has Changed Me.*	2.25	4.00
☐ **10082** *Puppy Love/Adam and Eve.*	2.25	4.00
☐ **10106** *My Home Town/Something Happened.*	2.25	4.00
☐ **10132** *Hello Young Lovers/ I Love You in the Same Old Way.*	2.25	4.00
☐ **10147** *Summer's Gone/I'd Have to Share.*	2.25	4.00
☐ **10163** *I Saw Mommy Kissing Santa Claus/ Rudolph the Red-Nosed Reindeer.*	3.00	5.00
☐ **10168** *The Story of My Love/Don't Say You're Sorry.*	2.00	3.50
☐ **10169** *Ii's Christmas Everywhere/ Rudolph the Red-Nosed Reindeer*	3.00	5.00
☐ **10194** *Tonight My Love Tonight/ I'm Just Your Fool Anyway.*	2.00	3.50
☐ **10220** *Dance on Little Girl/I Talk to You.*	2.00	3.50
☐ **10239** *Cinderella/Kissin' on the Phone.*	2.00	3.50
☐ **10279** *Loveland/The Bells at My Wedding.*	2.00	3.50
☐ **10282** *The Fool's Hall of Fame/ Far From the Lights of Town.*	2.00	3.50
☐ **10311** *I'd Never Find Another You/Uh Huh.*	2.00	3.50
☐ **10338** *I'm Coming Home/Cry.*	2.00	3.50
☐ **RCA 7977** *Love Me Warm and Tender/I'd Like to Know.*	1.75	3.00
☐ **8030** *A Steel Guitar and a Glass of Wine/ I Never Knew Your Name.*	1.75	3.00
☐ **8068** *Every Night/There You Go.*	1.75	3.00
☐ **8097** *Eso Beso/Give Me Back My Heart.*	1.75	3.00
☐ **8115** *Love/Crying in the Wind.*	1.75	3.00
☐ **8170** *Remember Diana/At Night.*	1.75	3.00
☐ **8195** *Hello Jim/You've Got the Nerve to Call This Love.*	1.75	3.00
☐ **8237** *Wondrous are the Ways of Love/ Hurry Up and Tell Me.*	1.75	3.00

		Price Range	
☐	**8272** *Did You Have a Happy Birthday?/ For No Good Reason at All.*	1.75	3.00
☐	**8311** *From Rocking Horse to Rocking Chair/Cheer Up.*	1.75	3.00
☐	**8349** *Baby's Coming Home/No, No.*	1.75	3.00
☐	**8396** *It's Easy to Say/In My Imagination.*	1.75	3.00

PAUL ANKA — ALBUMS

☐	**ABC-Paramount 240 (M)** *Paul Anka.*	29.00	38.00
☐	**240 (S)** *Paul Anka.*	35.00	45.00
☐	**296 (M)** *My Heart Sings.*	15.00	25.00
☐	**296 (S)** *My Heart Sings.*	30.00	40.00
☐	**323 (M)** *Paul Anka Sings His Big 15.*	20.00	30.00
☐	**323 (S)** *Paul Anka Sings His Big 15.*	35.00	45.00
☐	**347 (M)** *Swings for Young Lovers.*	15.00	22.00
☐	**347 (S)** *Swings for Young Lovers.*	25.00	35.00
☐	**353 (M)** *Anka at the Copa.*	15.00	25.00
☐	**353 (S)** *Anka at the Copa.*	20.00	30.00
☐	**360 (M)** *It's Christmas Everywhere.*	20.00	28.00
☐	**360 (S)** *It's Christmas Everywhere.*	23.00	27.00
☐	**371 (M)** *Strictly Instrumental.*	14.00	20.00
☐	**371 (S)** *Strictly Instrumental.*	20.00	30.00
☐	**390 (M)** *Paul Anka Sings His Big 15, Vol. II.*	17.00	27.00
☐	**390 (S)** *Paul Anka Sings His Big 15, Vol. II.*	25.00	35.00
☐	**409 (M)** *Paul Anka Sings His Big 15, Vol. III.*	17.00	28.00
☐	**409 (S)** *Paul Anka Sings His Big 15, Vol. III.*	23.00	33.00
☐	**420 (M)** *Diana.*	14.00	20.00
☐	**420 (S)** *Diana.*	15.00	25.00
☐	**RCA 2502 (M)** *Young, Alive and in Love.*	14.00	24.00
☐	**2502 (S)** *Young, Alive and in Love.*	17.00	27.00
☐	**2575 (M)** *Let's Sit This One Out.*	14.00	24.00
☐	**2575 (S)** *Let's Sit This One Out.*	17.00	27.00
☐	**2614 (M)** *Our Man Around the World.*	12.00	18.00
☐	**2614 (S)** *Our Man Around the World.*	14.00	24.00
☐	**2691 (M)** *21 Golden Hits (redone).*	10.00	20.00
☐	**2691 (S)** *21 Golden Hits (redone).*	12.00	16.00
☐	**2744 (M)** *Songs I Wish I'd Written.*	12.00	16.00
☐	**2744 (S)** *Songs I Wish I'd Written.*	14.00	24.00
☐	**2966 (M)** *Excitement on Park Avenue.*	12.00	18.00
☐	**2966 (S)** *Excitement on Park Avenue.*	10.00	18.00
☐	**3580 (M)** *Strictly Nashville.*	8.00	15.00

BEACH BOYS — 45's

☐	**X 301** *Surfin'/Luau.*	75.00	120.00
☐	**Candix 301** *Surfin'/Luau (without "Era Sales" on label).*	35.00	60.00
☐	**301** *Surfin'/Luau (with "Era Sales" on label).*	28.00	45.00
☐	**331** *Surfin'/Luau.*	28.00	45.00
☐	**Capitol 4777** *Surfin' Safari/409.*	3.00	5.00
☐	**4880** *Ten Little Indians/County Fair.*	3.50	6.00
☐	**4932** *Surfin' U.S.A./Shut Down.*	2.50	4.00
☐	**5009** *Surfer Girl/Little Deuce Coupe.*	2.50	4.00
☐	**5069** *Be True to Your School/In My Room.*	2.50	4.00
☐	**5096** *Little Saint Nick/The Lord's Prayer.*	5.00	8.00
☐	**5118** *Fun, Fun, Fun/Why Do Fools Fall in Love.*	2.00	3.50
☐	**5174** *I Get Around/Don't Worry Baby.*	2.00	3.50
☐	**5245** *When I Grow Up/She Knows Me Too Well.*	2.00	3.50

		Price Range	
☐	**5306** *Dance, Dance, Dance/The Warmth of the Sun*	1.75	3.50
☐	**5312** *The Man With All the Toys/Blue Christmas*	4.00	7.00
☐	**5372** *Do You Wanna Dance?/Please Let Me Wonder*	2.00	3.50
☐	**5395** *Help Me Rhonda/Kiss Me Baby*	2.00	3.50
☐	**5464** *California Girls/Let Him Run Wild*	2.00	3.50
☐	**5540** *The Little Girl I Once Knew/There's No Other*	2.00	3.50
☐	**5561** *Barbara Ann/Girl Don't Tell Me*	2.00	3.50
☐	**5602** *Sloop John B/You're So Good To Me*	2.00	3.50
☐	**5676** *Good Vibrations/Let's Go Away For Awhile*	2.00	3.50
☐	**5706** *Wouldn't It Be Nice/God Only Knows*	2.00	3.50
☐	**2028** *Wild Honey/Wind Chimes*	2.00	3.50
☐	**2068** *Darlin'/Here Today*	2.00	3.50
☐	**2160** *Friends/Little Bird*	2.50	4.00
☐	**2239** *Do It Again/Wake the World*	2.50	4.00
☐	**2360** *Bluebirds Over the Mountain/ Never Learn Not To Love*	3.00	5.00
☐	**2432** *I Can Hear Music/All I Want To Do*	2.50	4.00
☐	**2530** *Break Away/Celebrate the News*	5.00	9.00
☐	**2765** *Cotton Fields/The Nearest Faraway Place*	8.00	14.00
☐	**2937** *Salt Lake City/Amusement Parks U.S.A. (promotional)*	90.00	175.00
☐	**Capitol Custom** *Boogie Woodie/Spirit of America*	55.00	100.00
☐	**Brother 1001** *Heores and Villains/You're Welcome*	2.00	3.50
☐	**1002** *Gettin' Hungry/Devoted to You*	3.00	5.00
☐	**Reprise 0894** *Add Some Music to Your Day/ Susie Cincinatti*	2.50	4.00
☐	**0929** *This Whole World/Slip on Through*	3.00	5.00
☐	**0957** *Tears in the Morning/It's About Time*	3.00	5.00
☐	**0998** *Cool, Cool Water/Forever*	3.00	5.00
☐	**1015** *Long Promised Road/Deirdre*	3.00	5.00
☐	**1047** *Long Promised Road/Till I Die*	2.50	4.00
☐	**1058** *Surf's Up/Don't Go Near the Water*	3.00	5.00
☐	**1091** *Cuddle Up/You Need a Mess of Helf To Stand Alone*	7.00	12.00
☐	**1101** *Marcella/Hold On, Dear Brother*	3.50	6.00
☐	**1138** *Sail on Sailor/Only With You*	3.50	6.00
☐	**1156** *California Saga/Funky Pretty*	3.50	6.00
☐	**1321** *Child of Winter/Susie Cincinnati*	7.00	12.00
☐	**1325** *Sail on Sailor/Only With You*	2.50	4.00
☐	**Ode 66016** *Wouldn't It Be Nice/ The Times They Are A-Changin'*	6.00	10.00

BEACH BOYS — ALBUMS

☐	**Capitol 1808 (M)** *Surfin' Safari*	14.00	24.00
☐	**1890 (M)** *Surfin' U.S.A.*	12.00	22.00
☐	**1981 (M)** *Surfer Girl*	12.00	22.00
☐	**1998 (M)** *Little Deuce Coupe*	12.00	22.00
☐	**2027 (M)** *Shut Down, Vol. II*	12.00	22.00
☐	**2110 (M)** *All Summer Long*	12.00	22.00
☐	**2164 (M)** *The Beach Boys' Christmas Album*	14.00	24.00
☐	**2198 (M)** *The Beach Boys' Concer*	10.00	20.00
	STEREO VERSIONS OF THE ABOVE HAVE THE SAME VALUE		
☐	**2269 (M)** *The Beach Boys Today!*	12.00	22.00
☐	**2269 (S)** *The Beach Boys Today!*	10.00	20.00

		Price Range	
☐	**2354 (M)** *Summer Days (And Summer Nights).*	12.00	22.00
☐	**2354 (S)** *Summer Days (And Summer Nights).*	10.00	20.00
☐	**2398 (M)** *The Beach Boys' Party.*	10.00	20.00
☐	**2398 (S)** *The Beach Boys' Party.*	9.00	19.00
☐	**2458 (M)** *Pet Sounds.*	12.00	22.00
☐	**2458 (S)** *Pet Sounds.*	10.00	20.00
☐	**2545 (S)** *Best of the Beach Boys, Vol. I.*	9.00	19.00
☐	**2706 (S)** *Best of the Beach Boys, Vol. II.*	9.00	19.00
☐	**2859 (S)** *Wild Honey.*	12.00	22.00
☐	**2891 (S)** *Smiley Smile (black Capitol label).*	90.00	165.00
☐	**2893 (S)** *Stack-O-Tracks (with book).*	35.00	60.00
☐	**2893 (S)** *Stack-O-Tracks (without book).*	30.00	50.00
☐	**2895 (S)** *Friends.*	10.00	20.00
☐	**2945 (S)** *Best of the Beach Boys, Vol. III.*	10.00	20.00
☐	**Brother 9001 (S)** *Smiley Smile (reissue of rare Capitol album).*	12.00	22.00

CHUCK BERRY — 45's

☐	**Chess 1604** *Maybellene/Wee Wee Hours.*	4.00	7.00
☐	**1610** *Thirty Days/Together.*	5.00	9.00
☐	**1615** *No Money Down/The Downbound Train.*	5.00	9.00
☐	**1626** *Roll Over Beethoven/Drifting Heart.*	4.00	7.00
☐	**1635** *Too Much Monkey Business/ Brown Eyed Handsome Man*	5.00	9.00
☐	**1645** *You Can't Catch Me/Havana Moon.*	4.00	7.00
☐	**1653** *School Day/Deep Feeling.*	3.00	5.00
☐	**1664** *Oh Baby Doll/Lajunda.*	3.00	5.00
	ABOVE ISSUES FEATURED THE SILVER-AND-BLUE CHESS-TOP LABELS		
☐	**1671** *Rock and Roll Music/Blue Feeling.*	3.00	5.00
☐	**1683** *Sweet Little Sixteen/Reelin' and Rockin'.*	3.00	5.00
☐	**1691** *Johnny B. Goode/Around and Around.*	3.00	5.00
☐	**1697** *Beautiful Delilah/Vacation Time.*	2.50	4.00
☐	**1700** *Carol/Hey Pedro.*	2.50	4.00
☐	**1709** *Sweet Little Rock and Roll/Joe Joe Gun.*	2.50	4.00
☐	**1714** *Merry Christmas Baby/Run Rudolph Run.*	2.50	4.00
☐	**1716** *Anthony Boy/That's My Desire.*	2.50	4.00
☐	**1722** *Little Queenie/Almost Grown.*	2.00	3.50
☐	**1729** *Back in the U.S.A./Memphis, Tennessee.*	2.00	3.50
☐	**1736** *Childhood Sweetheart/Broken Arrow.*	2.00	3.50
☐	**1747** *Too Pooped to Pop/Let It Rock.*	2.00	3.50
☐	**1754** *Bye Bye Johnny/Worried Life Blues.*	2.00	3.50
☐	**1763** *Mad Lad/I Got to Finy My Baby.*	2.00	3.50
☐	**1767** *Jaguar and the Thunderbird/ Our Little Rendezvous.*	1.75	3.00
☐	**1779** *Little Star/I'm Talking About You.*	1.75	3.00
☐	**1799** *Go Go Go/Come On.*	1.75	3.00
☐	**1853** *I'm Talking About You/Diploma For Two.*	1.75	3.00
☐	**1866** *Sweet Little Sixteen/Memphis (reissue).*	1.75	3.00
☐	**1883** *Nadine/Orangutang.*	1.75	3.00
☐	**1898** *No Particular Place to Go/You Two.*	1.75	3.00
☐	**1906** *You Never Can Tell/Brenda Lee.*	1.75	3.00
☐	**1912** *Little Marie/Go Bobby Soxer.*	1.75	3.00
☐	**1916** *Promised Land/Things I Used To Do.*	1.75	3.00
☐	**1926** *Dear Dad/Lonely School Days.*	1.75	3.00

		Price Range	
☐	1943 *It Wasn't Me/Welcome Back Pretty Baby*	1.75	3.00
☐	1963 *Lonely School Days/Ramona, Say Yes*	1.75	3.00
☐	2090 *Tulane/Have Mercy Judge*	1.75	3.00
☐	2131 *My Ding-A-Ling/Johnny B. Goode*	1.75	3.00
☐	2136 *Reelin' and Rockin'/Let's Boogie*	1.75	3.00
☐	2140 *Bio/Roll 'em Pete*	1.75	3.00
☐	2169 *Shake, Rattle and Roll/ Baby What You Want Me to Do*	1.75	3.00

CHUCK BERRY — ALBUMS

☐	**Chess 1426 (M)** *After School Session*	25.00	35.00
☐	1432 (M) *One Dozen Berrys*	17.00	27.00
☐	1435 (M) *Chuck Berry is on Top*	14.00	24.00
☐	1448 (M) *Rockin' at the Hops*	14.00	24.00
☐	1456 (M) *More Juke Box Hits*	14.00	24.00
☐	1465 (M) *More Chuck Berry*	14.00	24.00
☐	1485 (M) *Chuck Berry's Greatest Hits*	14.00	24.00
☐	1488 (M) *St. Louis to Liverpool*	14.00	24.00
☐	1495 (M) *Chuck Berry in London*	14.00	24.00
☐	1498 (M) *Fresh Berry's*	12.00	22.00
☐	1514 (S) *Chuck Berry's Golden Decade*	8.00	18.00
☐	1550 (S) *Back Home*	8.00	18.00
☐	**Mercury 21103 (M)** *Golden Hits*	8.00	18.00
☐	61103 (S) *Golden Hits*	8.00	18.00
☐	21123 (M) *In Memphis*	8.00	18.00
☐	61123 (S) *In Memphis*	8.00	18.00
☐	21138 (M) *Live at Fillmore Auditorium*	8.00	18.00
☐	61138 (S) *Live at Fillmore Auditorium*	8.00	18.00
☐	61176 (S) *From St. Louis to Frisco*	8.00	18.00
☐	61223 (S) *Concerto in B. Goode*	8.00	18.00

FATS DOMINO — 45's

☐	**Imperial 5058** *The Fat Man/Detroit City Blues*	23.00	40.00
☐	5065 *Boogie Woogie Baby/Little Bee*	23.00	40.00
☐	5077 *She's My Baby/Hideaway Blues*	23.00	40.00
☐	5085 *Hey La Bas Boogie/Brand New Baby*	23.00	40.00
	THE FIRST FOUR RELEASES WERE ISSUED ONLY ON 78 RPM THE FOLLOWING REFLECT PRICES FOR 45 RPM DISCS		
☐	5099 *Korea Blues/Every Night About This Time*	30.00	50.00
☐	5114 *Tired of Crying/What's the Matter, Baby?*	20.00	35.00
☐	5123 *Don't You Lie to Me/Sometimes I Wonder*	20.00	35.00
☐	5138 *No, No Baby/Right From Wrong*	18.00	30.00
☐	5145 *Rockin' Chair/Careless Love*	18.00	30.00
☐	5167 *You Know I Miss You/I'll Be Gone*	15.00	25.00
☐	5180 *Goin' Home/Reeling and Rocking*	15.00	25.00
☐	5197 *Poor Poor Me/Trust In Me*	15.00	25.00
☐	5209 *How Long?/Dreaming*	12.00	20.00
☐	5220 *Nobody Loves Me/Cheatin'*	10.00	17.00
☐	5231 *Going to the River/Mardi Gras in New Orleans*	10.00	17.00
☐	5240 *Please Don't Leave Me/The Girl I Love*	8.00	14.00
☐	5251 *Rose Mary/You Said You Loved Me*	8.00	14.00
☐	5262 *Don't Leave Me This Way/Something's Wrong*	8.00	14.00
☐	5272 *Little School Girl/You Done Me Wrong*	8.00	14.00
☐	5283 *Baby, Please/Where Did You Stay?*	8.00	14.00
☐	5301 *You Can Pack Your Suitcase/I Lived My Life*	8.00	14.00

		Price Range	
☐	**5313** *Don't You Hear Me Calling You/Love Me.*	7.00	12.00
☐	**5323** *I Know/Thinking of You.*	6.00	10.00
☐	**5340** *Don't You Know/Helping Hand.*	5.00	8.50
☐	**5348** *Ain't It a Shame/La La.*	4.00	7.00
☐	**5357** *All By Myself/Troubles of My Own.*	4.00	7.00
☐	**5369** *Poor Me/I Can't Go On.*	3.50	6.00
☐	**5375** *Bo Weevil/Don't Blame It On Me.*	3.50	6.00
☐	**5386** *I'm in Love Again/My Blue Heaven.*	3.00	5.00
☐	**5396** *When My Dreamboat Comes Home/So-Long.*	3.00	5.00
☐	**5407** *Blueberry Hill/Honey Chile.*	3.00	5.00
☐	**5417** *Blue Monday/What's the Reason I'm Not Pleasing You.*	2.50	4.00
☐	**5428** *I'm Walkin'/I'm in the Mood for Love.*	2.50	4.00
☐	**5442** *Valley of Tears/It's You I Love.*	2.50	4.00
☐	**5454** *When I See You/What Will I Tell My Heart.*	2.50	4.00
☐	**5467** *Wait and See/I Still Love You.*	2.50	4.00
☐	**5477** *The Big Beat/I Want You to Know.*	2.00	3.50
☐	**5492** *Yes, My Darling/Don't You Know I Love You.*	2.00	3.50
☐	**5515** *Sick and Tired/No, No.*	2.00	3.50
☐	**5526** *Little Mary/Prisoner's Song.*	2.00	3.50
☐	**5537** *Young School Girl/It Must Be Love.*	2.00	3.50
☐	**5553** *Whole Lotta Loving/Coquette.*	2.00	3.50
☐	**5569** *When the Saints Go Marching In/Telling Lies.*	2.00	3.50
☐	**5585** *I'm Ready/Margie.*	2.00	3.50
☐	**5606** *I Want to Walk You Home/ I'm Gonna Be a Wheel Someday.*	2.00	3.50
☐	**5629** *Be My Guest/I've Been Around.*	2.00	3.50
☐	**5645** *Country Boy/If You Need Me.*	2.00	3.50
☐	**5660** *Tell Me That You Love Me/ Before I Grow Too Old.*	2.00	3.50
☐	**5675** *Walking to New Orleans/Don't Come Knocking.*	2.00	3.50
☐	**5687** *Three Nights a Week/ Put Your Arms Around Me Honey.*	2.00	3.50
☐	**5704** *My Girl Josephine/Natural Born Lover.*	2.00	3.50
☐	**5723** *What a Price/Ain't That Just Like a Woman.*	2.00	3.50
☐	**5734** *Shu Rah/Fell in Love on Monday.*	2.00	3.50
☐	**5753** *It Keeps Rainin'/I Just Cry.*	2.00	3.50
☐	**5764** *Let the Four Winds Blow/Good Hearted Man.*	2.00	3.50
☐	**5779** *What a Party/Rockin' Bicycle.*	2.00	3.50
☐	**5796** *Jambalaya (On the Bayou)/I Hear You Knocking.*	2.00	3.50

FATS DOMINO — ALBUMS

☐	**Imperial 9004 (M)** *Rock and Rollin' with Fats Domino.*	50.00	60.00
☐	**9009 (M)** *Rock and Rollin'.*	40.00	50.00
☐	**9028 (M)** *This is Fats Domino.*	40.00	50.00
☐	**9038 (M)** *Here Stands Fats Domino.*	40.00	50.00
☐	**9040 (M)** *This is Fats.*	30.00	40.00
☐	**9055 (M)** *The Fabulous Mr. D.*	30.00	40.00
☐	**9062 (M)** *Fats Domino Swings.*	25.00	35.00
☐	**9065 (M)** *Let's Play.*	25.00	35.00
☐	**9103 (M)** *Fats Domino Sings.*	20.00	30.00
☐	**9138 (M)** *A Lot of Dominos.*	20.00	30.00
☐	**9153 (M)** *Let the Four Winds Blow.*	20.00	30.00
☐	**9164 (M)** *What a Party.*	20.00	30.00

	Price Range	
BILL HALEY AND THE COMETS — 45's		
☐ **Essex 303** *Rock the Joint/Icy Heart.*	25.00	45.00
☐ **305** *Dance With the Dolly/Rocking Chair on the Moon.*	25.00	45.00
☐ **310** *Real Rock Drive/ Stop Beatin' 'Round the Mulberry Bush.*	20.00	35.00
☐ **321** *Crazy Man Crazy/Whatcha Gonna Do.*	15.00	30.00
☐ **327** *Fractured/Pat-A-Cake.*	15.00	30.00
☐ **332** *Live It Up/Farewell, So Long, Goodbye.*	10.00	20.00
☐ **340** *I'll Be True/Ten Little Indians.*	10.00	20.00
☐ **348** *Straight Jacket/Chattanooga Choo-Choo.*	10.00	20.00
☐ **374** *Sundown Boogie/Jukebox Cannonball.*	12.00	22.00
☐ **381** *Rocket 88/Green Tree Boogie.*	12.00	22.00
☐ **399** *Rock the Joing/Farewell, So Long, Goodbye.*	10.00	20.00
☐ **Trans World 718** *Real Rock Drive/Yes Indeed.*	10.00	20.00
☐ **Decca 29124** *Rock Around the Clock/Thirteen Women.*	8.00	16.00
☐ **29204** *Shake, Rattle and Roll/A.B.C. Boogie.*	8.00	16.00
☐ **29317** *Dim, Dim the Lights/Happy Baby.*	6.00	12.00
☐ **29418** *Mambo Rock/Birth of the Boogie.*	6.00	12.00
☐ **29552** *Razzle-Dazzle/Two Hound Dogs.*	6.00	12.00
☐ **29713** *Burn That Candle/Rock-A-Beatin' Boogie.*	6.00	12.00
☐ **29791** *See You Later Alligator/The Paper Boy.*	6.00	12.00
☐ **29870** *R-O-C-K/The Saints Rock 'n' Roll.*	5.00	10.00
☐ **29948** *Hot Dog Buddy Buddy/Rockin' Through the Rye.*	5.00	10.00
☐ **30028** *Rip It Up/Teenager's Mother.*	5.00	10.00
☐ **30085** *Rudy's Rock/Blue Comet Blues.*	5.00	10.00
☐ **30148** *Don't Knock the Rock/Cho Cho Ch'Boogie.*	5.00	10.00
☐ **30214** *Forty Cups of Coffee/Hook, Line and Sinker.*	4.50	8.50
☐ **30314** *Billy Goat/Rockin' Rollin' Rover.*	4.50	8.50
☐ **30394** *The Dipsy Doodle/Miss You.*	4.50	8.50
☐ **30461** *Rock the Joint/How Many.*	4.50	8.50
☐ **30530** *Mary, Mary Lou/It's a Sin.*	4.50	8.50
☐ **30592** *Skinny Minnie/Sway With Me.*	4.50	8.50
☐ **30681** *Lean Jean/Don't Nobody Move.*	4.50	8.50
☐ **30741** *Whoa Mabel/Chiquita Lina.*	4.50	8.50
☐ **30781** *Corrine, Corrina/ B. B. Plenty.*	4.50	8.50
☐ **30844** *I Got a Woman/Charmaine.*	4.50	8.50
☐ **30873** *A Fool Such As I/Where'd You Go Last Night?*	4.50	8.50
☐ **30926** *Caldonia/Shaky.*	4.50	8.50
☐ **30956** *Joey's Song/Ooh! Look-A-There Ain't She Pretty!*	4.50	8.50
BILL HALEY AND THE COMETS — ALBUMS		
☐ **Essex 202 (M)** *Rock with Bill Haley and His Comets.*	70.00	115.00
☐ **Trans World 202 (M)** *Rock with Bill Haley and His Comets.*	30.00	40.00
☐ **Decca 5560 (M)** *Shake Rattle and Roll (10" LP).*	65.00	110.00
☐ **8225 (M)** *Rock Around the Clock.*	25.00	35.00
☐ **8315 (M)** *He Digs Rock and Roll.*	20.00	30.00
☐ **8345 (M)** *Rock and Roll Stage Show.*	20.00	30.00
☐ **8569 (M)** *Rockin' the Oldies.*	20.00	30.00
☐ **8692 (M)** *Rockin' Around the World.*	20.00	30.00
☐ **8692 (S)** *Rockin' Around the World.*	25.00	35.00
☐ **8775 (M)** *Rockin' the Joint.*	25.00	35.00
☐ **8775 (S)** *Rockin' the Joint.*	25.00	40.00
☐ **8821 (M)** *Bill Haley's Chicks.*	15.00	25.00
☐ **8821 (S)** *Bill Haley's Chicks.*	20.00	30.00

	Price Range	
☐ **8964 (M)** *Strictly Instrumental.*	15.00	25.00
☐ **8964 (S)** *Strictly Instrumental.*	20.00	30.00
☐ **Warner Brothers 1378 (M)** *Bill Haley and His Comets.*	15.00	25.00
☐ **1378 (S)** *Bill Haley and His Comets.*	20.00	30.00
☐ **1391 (M)** *Haley's Juke Box.*	15.00	25.00
☐ **1391 (S)** *Haley's Juke Box.*	20.00	30.00

BUDDY HOLLY — 45's

☐ **Decca 29854** *Love Me/Blue Days, Black Nights.*	23.00	40.00
☐ **30166** *Modern Don Juan/You Are My One Desire.*	20.00	35.00
☐ **30534** *That'll Be the Day/Rock Around with Ollie Vee.*	28.00	45.00
☐ **30543** *Love Me/You Are My One Desire.*	18.00	30.00
☐ **30650** *Girl on My Mind/Ting-A-Ling.*	20.00	35.00
☐ **Coral 61852** *Words of Love/ Mailman, Bring Me No More Blues.*	50.00	90.00
☐ **61885** *Peggy Sue/Everyday.*	4.00	7.00
☐ **61947** *I'm Gonna Love You Too/Listen To Me.*	6.00	10.00
☐ **61985** *Rave On/Take Your Time.*	4.00	7.00
☐ **62006** *Early In the Morning/Now We're One.*	4.00	7.00
☐ **62051** *Heartbeat/Well . . . All Right.*	4.00	7.00
☐ **62074** *It Doesn't Matter Anymore/Raining in My Heart.*	4.00	7.00
☐ **62134** *Peggy Sue Got Married/Crying, Waiting, Hoping.*	15.00	25.00
☐ **62210** *True Love Ways/That Makes It Tough.*	15.00	25.00
☐ **62283** *You're So Square/ Valley of Tears (Canadian Release).*	15.00	25.00
☐ **62329** *Reminiscing/Wait Till the Sun Shines Nellie.*	8.00	14.00
☐ **62352** *True Love Ways/Bo Diddley.*	6.00	10.00
☐ **62369** *Brown Eyed Handsome Man/Wishing.*	6.00	10.00
☐ **62390** *I'm Gonna Love You Too/ Rock Around With Ollie Vee.*	6.00	10.00
☐ **62448** *Slippin' and Slidin'/What To Do.*	12.00	20.00
☐ **62554** *Rave On/Early in the Morning.*	8.00	14.00
☐ **62558** *Love is Strange/You're the One.*	7.00	12.00

BUDDY HOLLY — ALBUMS

☐ **Decca 8707 (M)** *That'll Be the Day (flat black label).*	125.00	225.00
☐ **8707 (M)** *That'll Be the Day (rainbow label).*	90.00	150.00
☐ **Coral 57210 (M)** *Buddy Holly.*	30.00	50.00
☐ **57279 (M)** *The Buddy Holly Story.*	20.00	30.00
☐ **57279 (S)** *The Buddy Holly Story.*	25.00	38.00
☐ **57326 (M)** *The Buddy Holly Story, Vol. II.*	20.00	30.00
☐ **57326 (S)** *The Buddy Holly Story, Vol. II.*	25.00	38.00
☐ **57405 (M)** *Buddy Holly and the Crickets.*	20.00	30.00
☐ **57405 (S)** *Buddy Holly and the Crickets.*	25.00	38.00
☐ **57426 (M)** *Reminiscing.*	20.00	30.00
☐ **57426 (S)** *Reminiscing.*	25.00	38.00
☐ **57450 (M)** *Showcase.*	15.00	25.00
☐ **57450 (S)** *Showcase.*	25.00	35.00
☐ **57463 (M)** *Holly in the Hills.*	17.00	27.00
☐ **57463 (S)** *Holly in the Hills.*	25.00	35.00
☐ **57492 (M)** *Greatest Hits.*	15.00	25.00
☐ **57492 (S)** *Greatest Hits.*	20.00	30.00

		Price Range	
BOBBY RYDELL			
☐	**Venise 201** *Fatty Fatty/Happy Happy*	10.00	17.00
☐	**Veko 731** *Fatty Fatty/Dream Age.*	6.00	12.00
☐	**Cameo 160** *Please Don't Be Mad/Makin' Time.*	12.00	20.00
☐	**164** *All I Want is You/For You, For You*	8.00	14.00
☐	**167** *Kissin' Time/You'll Never Tame Me.*	2.50	4.00
☐	**169** *We Got Love/I Dig Girls*	2.50	4.00
☐	**171** *Wild One/Itty Bitty Girl.*	2.50	4.00
☐	**175** *Swingin' School/Ding a Ling.*	2.50	4.00
☐	**179** *Volare/I'll Do It Again.*	2.00	3.50
☐	**182** *Sway/Groovy Tonight.*	2.00	3.50
☐	**186** *Good Time Baby/Cherie.*	2.00	3.50
☐	**190** *That Old Black Magic/Don't Be Afraid*	2.00	3.50
☐	**192** *The Fish/The Third House*	2.00	3.50
☐	**201** *I Wanna Thank You/The Door to Paradise.*	2.00	3.50
☐	**209** *I've Got Bonnie/Lose Her.*	2.00	3.50
☐	**217** *I'll Never Dance Again/Gee, It's Wonderful*	2.00	3.50
☐	**228** *The Cha-Cha-Cha/The Best Man Cried.*	2.00	3.50
☐	**242** *Butterfly Baby/Love is Blind*	1.75	3.00
☐	**252** *Wildwood Days/Will You Be My Baby.*	1.75	3.00
☐	**265** *Little Queenie/The Woodpecker Song*	1.75	3.00
☐	**272** *Let's Make Love Tonight/Childhood Sweetheart*	1.75	3.00
☐	**280** *Forget Him/Love, Love, Go Away*	1.75	3.00
☐	**309** *Make Me Forget/ Little Girl, I've Had a Busy Day*	1.75	3.00
☐	**320** *A World Without Love/Our Faded Love*	1.75	3.00
☐	**361** *Ciao Ciao Bambino/Voce De La Notte.*	2.00	3.50
☐	**1070** *Forget Him/A Message from Bobby.*	1.50	2.50
BOBBY RYDELL — ALBUMS			
☐	**Cameo 1006 (M)** *We Got Love*	20.00	30.00
☐	**1007 (M)** *Bobby Sings*	20.00	30.00
☐	**1009 (M)** *Biggest Hits.*	17.00	27.00
☐	**1010 (M)** *Bobby Rydell Salutes the Great Ones.*	17.00	27.00
☐	**1011 (M)** *Rydell at the Copa.*	14.00	24.00
☐	**1019 (M)** *All the Hits by Bobby Rydell.*	14.00	24.00
☐	**1028 (M)** *Biggest Hits, Vol. II.*	14.00	24.00
☐	**1040 (M)** *All the Hits by Bobby Rydell, Vol. II.*	14.00	24.00
☐	**1043 (M)** *Bye Bye Birdie*	14.00	24.00
☐	**1055 (M)** *Wild (Wood) Days*	12.00	22.00
☐	**1055 (S)** *Wild (Wood) Days*	12.00	22.00
☐	**1070 (M)** *Top Hits of '63*	12.00	22.00
☐	**1070 (S)** *Top Hits of '63.*	14.00	24.00
☐	**1080 (M)** *Forget Him.*	12.00	22.00
☐	**1080 (S)** *Forget Him*	14.00	24.00
☐	**2001 (M)** *16 Golden Hits*	12.00	22.00
☐	**2001 (S)** *16 Golden Hits*	14.00	24.00
☐	**4017 (M)** *An Era Reborn*	10.00	20.00
☐	**4017 (S)** *An Era Reborn*	12.00	22.00
☐	**Capitol 2281 (S)** *Somebody Loves You.*	9.00	19.00

	Price Range	
SIMON AND GARFUNKEL — 45's		
☐ **Columbia 43396** *Sounds of Silence/We've Got a Groovy Thing Goin'.*	1.75	3.00
☐ **43511** *Homeward Bound/Leaves That Are Green.*	1.75	3.00
☐ **43617** *I Am a Rock/Flowers Never Bend with the Rainfall.*	1.75	3.00
☐ **43728** *Dangling Conversation/Big Bright Green Pleasure Machine.*	1.75	3.00
☐ **43873** *A Hazy Shade of Winter/For Emily, Wherever I May Find Her.*	1.75	3.00
☐ **44046** *At the Zoo/59th Street Bridge Song (Feelin' Groovy).*	1.75	3.00
☐ **44232** *Fakin' It/ You Don't Know Where Your Interest Lies.*	1.75	3.00
☐ **44465** *Scarborough Fair/April Come She Will.*	1.75	3.00
☐ **44465** *Scarborough Fair/Canticle.*	1.75	3.00
☐ **44511** *Mrs. Robinson/Old Friends-Bookends.*	1.75	3.00
☐ **44785** *The Boxer/Baby Driver.*	1.75	3.00
☐ **45079** *Bridge Over Troubled Water/ Keep the Customer Satisfied.*	1.75	3.00
☐ **45133** *Cecelia/The Only Living Boy in New York City.*	1.75	3.00
☐ **45237** *El Condor Pasa/Why Don't You Write Me?*	1.75	3.00
☐ **45663** *For Emily, Wherever I May Find Her/America.*	1.75	3.00
☐ **10230** *My Little Town/Rag Doll-You're Kind.*	1.50	2.50
SIMON AND GARFUNKEL — ALBUMS		
☐ **Pickwick 3059 (S)** *Hit Sounds of Simon and Garfunkel (pre-Columbia material)*	30.00	40.00
☐ **Columbia 2249 (M)** *Wednesday Morning, 3 A.M.*	10.00	20.00
☐ **9049 (S)** *Wednesday Morning, 3 A.M.*	14.00	24.00
☐ **2469 (M)** *Sounds of Silence.*	10.00	20.00
☐ **9269 (S)** *Sounds of Silence*	12.00	22.00
☐ **2563 (M)** *Parsley, Sage, Rosemary & Thyme.*	10.00	20.00
☐ **9363 (S)** *Parsley, Sage, Rosemary & Thyme.*	12.00	22.00
☐ **9529 (S)** *Bookends*	9.00	19.00
☐ **9914 (S)** *Bridge Over Troubled Water.*	9.00	19.00
☐ **31350 (S)** *Greatest Hits.*	9.00	19.00
RITCHIE VALENS — 45's		
☐ **Del-Fi 4106** *Come On, Let's Go/Framed.*	4.00	7.00
☐ **4110** *Donna/La Bamba.*	3.00	5.00
☐ **4114** *That's My Little Suzie/In a Turkish Town.*	3.00	5.00
☐ **4117** *Little Girl/We Belong Together.*	3.50	6.00
☐ **4128** *Stay Beside Me/Big Baby Blues.*	3.50	6.00
☐ **4133** *Cry, Cry, Cry/Paddiwack Song.*	3.50	6.00
RITCHIE VALENS — ALBUMS		
☐ **Del-Fi 1201 (M)** *Ritchie Valens.*	35.00	45.00
☐ **1206 (M)** *Ritchie.*	40.00	50.00
☐ **1214 (M)** *In Concert at Pacoima Jr. High.*	70.00	80.00
☐ **1225 (M)** *His Greatest Hits.*	20.00	30.00
☐ **1247 (M)** *Greatest Hits, Vol. II.*	40.00	50.00
GENE VINCENT — 45's		
☐ **Capitol 3450** *Be-Bop-A-Lulu/Woman Love.*	4.00	7.00
☐ **3530** *Race with the Devil/Gonna Back Up Baby.*	5.00	8.00
☐ **3558** *Bluejean Bop/Who Slapped John*	4.50	7.50

		Price Range	
☐	**3617** *Crazy Legs/Important Words*	4.50	7.50
☐	**3678** *Five Days, Five Days/Bi-Bickey-Bi-Bo-Bo-Go.*	4.50	7.50
☐	**3763** *Lotta Lovin'/Wear My Ring.*	4.50	7.50
☐	**3839** *Dance to the Bop/I Got It.*	3.50	6.00
☐	**3874** *Walkin' Home from School/I Got a Baby.*	3.50	6.00
☐	**3959** *Baby Blue/True to You*	3.50	6.00
☐	**4010** *Rocky Road Blues/Yes, I Love You Baby.*	3.50	6.00
☐	**4051** *Little Lover/Git It*	3.50	3.00
☐	**4105** *Be Bop Boogie Baby/Say Mama*	3.50	6.00
☐	**4153** *Who's Pushin' Your Swing?/Over the Rainbow.*	3.50	6.00
☐	**4237** *Right Now/The Night is so Lonely.*	3.50	6.00
☐	**4313** *Wild Cat/Right Here on Earth*	3.50	6.00
☐	**4442** *Anna-Annabelle/Pistol Packin' Mama.*	3.50	6.00
☐	**4525** *If You Want My Lovin'/Mister Loneliness.*	3.50	6.00
☐	**4665** *Lucky Star/Baby Don't Believe Him*	3.50	6.00
☐	**Challenge 59337** *Bird Doggin'/Ain't That Too Much.*	2.25	4.00
☐	**59347** *I've Got My Eyes on You/Lonely Street.*	2.25	4.00
☐	**59365** *Born to be a Rolling Stone Hurting For You Baby.*	2.25	4.00
☐	**Playground 100** *Story of the Rockers/Pickin' Poppies.*	18.00	30.00
☐	**Forever 6001** *Story of the Rockers/Pickin' Poppies.*	3.00	5.00
☐	**Kama Sutra 514** *Sunshine/Geese*	2.00	3.50
☐	**518** *The Day the World Turned Blue/High on Life.*	2.00	3.50

GENE VINCENT—ALBUMS

☐	**Capitol 764 (M)** *Bluejean Bop*	50.00	90.00
☐	**811 (M)** *Gene Vincent and His Blue Caps*	50.00	65.00
☐	**970 (M)** *Gene Vincent Rocks and the Blue Caps Roll.*	50.00	65.00
☐	**1059 (M)** *A Gene Vincent Record Date*	50.00	65.00
☐	**1207 (M)** *Sounds Like Gene Vincent*	40.00	50.00
☐	**1342 (M)** *Crazy Times*	40.00	50.00
☐	**1342 (S)** *Crazy Times*	50.00	65.00
☐	**Dandelion 102 (S)** *I'm Back and I'm Proud*	12.00	20.00
☐	**Kama Sutra 2019 (S)** *Gene Vincent*	12.00	20.00
☐	**2027 (S)** *The Day the World Turned Blue*	12.00	20.00

THE BEATLES

Along with Elvis Presley, the Beatles rank as the most heavily collected of all recording personalities in history — both in terms of their records and memorabilia. Collecting interest is so intense that price records are continually eclipsed. While hobbyists may regret having to pay more and more, the price increases have served to fully vindicate their enthusiasm for Beatles material. Back in 1964 when the group first burst upon the American scene, autograph hunters were accused of wasting their time by seeking signatures of the Fab Four. Today these signatures, often scrawled on wrinkled bits of paper, are fetching higher sums than those of many Presidents and other historical celebrities. Furthermore the significance — social and financial — of Beatles memorabilia has been acknowledged by its appearance in the most prestigious auction sales, alongside furniture of

Louis XIV and gems of Tiffany. It has not only "arrived." It has far surpassed, in collecting interest and status, the wildest dreams of its most devoted collectors. Unbelievable though it may seem, Beatles items now rank on a level with souvenirs of Abraham Lincoln, when they appear for sale. And this may be only the beginning. Never in the history of collecting has any celebrity material soared so high in price within less than two decades.

The tragic death of John Lennon in December, 1980, has understandably resulted in higher prices for his autographs and other items, than those of the other Beatles. At the same time it has generated higher prices for all material bearing autographs of all four Beatles. Hobbyists (and investors) will now stretch further for these items, because of the Lennon autograph. But there is much more than just autographs for the Lennon collector. He left behind numerous drawings and other material, much of which has not yet reached the market. It may be another ten years, or longer, before we know the full extent of Lennon memorabilia that exists.

The extraordinary collecting activity on Beatles items has spilled over into those associated with them — a phenomenon which seldom occurs even in the case of great historical celebrities. Prices now being paid for autographs and other ephemera of Yoko Ono are virtually on a par with those of the Beatles themselves. There is likewise an active market for all memorabilia of Brian Epstein (the Beatles' first manager), Peter Best (the drummer who was replaced by Ringo Starr), and others. It seems almost as though whatever the Beatles touched turned to gold.

A comprehensive listing of collectible Beatles memorabilia would be long indeed. A selection is included here, but is — for reasons of space — far from complete. The interested buyer will discover an enormous variety offered by specialist dealers, and, as mentioned, in the auction galleries. Of course, a certain amount of discrimination needs to be exercised in collecting. Any autograph can be faked, and some fakes are quite skillful. As far as printed items, toys, dolls and the like are concerned, each piece must be judged on its merits for age and significance. The mere fact that something pictures the Beatles is no excuse for a price of $500 or $800. All of it may be worthy to collect, but it is certainly not equally rare or equally significant. Anyone can, today, stamp out a Beatles statuette and advertise it as a "collectors' item." Anyone can print the names of John, Paul, George and Ringo on a pencil or watchband. If an item is of recent origin and obviously not rare or exclusive, the fact that it relates to the Beatles is not, in itself, magic. Serious collectors want early material, so far as group items are concerned. Any souvenirs or toys picturing the Beatles, but manufactured after their break-up, is not considered as collectible as pre-1970 material.

In attempting to date items, which can be difficult at best, do not be misled by dates which may appear on the piece or by the physical appearance of the portraits. Manufacturers who want their items to be taken for collectors' pieces are careful to show the group as very youthful, to give the impression of mid-1960s origin. The best proof of an item's origin is to compare it against a listing in the pricelist of an established dealer. The dealers have done extensive research on most kinds of Beatles memorabilia — not as a social service but to protect THEMSELVES from getting taken by items of little or no value. The whole job is far from done yet, however. Newly discovered items turn up regularly.

Similar effort has been directed toward Beatles records and has borne even more fruit, simply because that task is not quite as challenging. Variations exists of covers, labels, etc., and fakes are inevitable from time to time; but the range of records is not nearly as extensive as that of memorabilia, and the pitfalls are fewer. An amateur could, by using the information in this book and supplementing this knowledge through dealers' catalogues, collect even the most expensive Beatles recordings without danger. With memorabilia he will need to use more care.

The following listings are broken down as follows:

1. Beatles singles, arranged alphabetically.
2. Beatles LP's, also arranged alphabetically.
3. Recordings made by individual Beatles members, after the group disbanded.
4. Memorabilia.

Prices are as accurate as possible at the time of going to press. The reader is reminded, though, that this is an extremely volatile market in which values can change within a matter of weeks.

Supplementary collecting and/or historical information has been supplied whenever possible.

Japanese releases. Many of the Beatles records were released in Japan, bearing labels with Japanese imprints. These are sought by collectors and have in recent years been entering the American market in increasing quantity. At this point the values on most Japanese pressings are fluctuating too sharply to establish fair market prices.

MEMORABILIA	Price Range	
☐ **Album, Help!,** *LP record album (Parlophone/EMI, 1965), autographed on the sleeve by each of the four Beatles.*	900.00	1085.00
☐ **"Bag One".** *"Bag One" was a set of 14 lithographs from drawings made by John Lennon in 1969, published in 1970 by the Cinnamon Press of New York. The drawings relate to Lennon's marriage and honeymoon. Each lithograph was limited to 300 numbered copies, and enclosed in a white leather portfolio. They measure 20" x 30". Of the 300 issued, it is believed that very few full sets are still in existence, as most owners broke them up for framing. The current market value for a full set is:*	35000.00	45000.00
The individual prints from this set have been selling in the range of 2,000.00/3,000.00.		
☐ **Belt Buckle,** *with "BEATLES" in swirled script-type lettering, and portrait illustrations.*	65.00	85.00
☐ **Bobbing Head Auto Mascots.** *Set of 4. Dating to the mid 1960's.*	700.00	900.00
When sold individually, the value is around 150.00/200.00, but the John Lennon specimen is worth a premium.		
☐ **Book,** *"A Cellarful of Noise" by Brian Epstein, published by Souvenir Press, 1964. This is the British first edition, with dust jacket. Issued when Epstein was still alive.*	125.00	175.00
For a copy autographed by him (and such do exist), the price would be at least double this amount.		
☐ **Book,** *"A Cellarful of Noise" by Brian Epstein, clothbound reprint of the now-scarce 1964 first edition.*	13.00	17.00

	Price Range	
☐ **Book,** *"A Day in the Life" by Tom Schultheiss, paperback, 334 pages.*	8.00	11.00
☐ **Book,** *"A Hard Day's Night" by John Burke, published by Dell, paperback.*	15.00	20.00
☐ **Book,** *"A Spaniard in the Works" by John Lennon, clothbound first edition.*	20.00	25.00
This price represents the average range but published offers differ considerably. When autographed by Lennon it is, of course, worth substantially more.		
☐ **Book,** *"A Spaniard in the Works" by John Lennon, paperback, 94 pages.*	4.00	6.00
☐ **Book,** *"A Tribute to John Lennon" by various authors, clothbound.*	7.00	10.00
☐ **Book,** *"A Twist of Lennon" by Cynthia Lennon, paperback, 190 pages.*	2.00	3.00
Cynthia was John's first wife.		
☐ **Book,** *"Abbey Road" by Brian Southall, clothbound, printed in Great Britain, 210 pages.*	12.00	16.00
☐ **Book,** *"All You Need is Ears" by George Martin, paperback, 285 pages.*	7.00	10.00
George Martin was a record producer who worked with the Beatles as well as with many other rock artists.		
☐ **Book,** *"Apple to the Core" by Peter McCabe and Robert D. Schonfeld, paperback, 209 pages.*	4.00	6.00
☐ **Book,** *"As I Write This Letter" by Marc Catone, clothbound, 254 pages.*	16.00	20.00
A collection of fan letters written to the Beatles.		
☐ **Book,** *"As Time Goes By" by Derek Taylor, clothbound, 231 pages, 1983 reprint.*	13.00	17.00
Derek Taylor was Brian Epstein's press agent.		
☐ **Book,** *"The Ballad of John and Yoko" by The Editors of Rolling Stone Magazine, paperback, 306 pages.*	10.00	13.00
☐ **Book,** *"The Beatles" by Geoffrey Stokes, clothbound, 245 pages.*	15.00	20.00
☐ **Book,** *"The Beatles" by Helen Spence, clothbound, 96 pages.*	7.00	10.00
☐ **Book,** *"Beatles Diary", published in Scotland, miniature 3"x4" size, 1965.*	50.00	70.00
☐ **Book,** *"The Beatles After the Beatles" by John Blake, paperback, 286 pages.*	7.00	10.00
The rather confusing title refers to the fact that this work deals with the Beatles after their break-up.		
☐ **Book,** *"The Beatles: An Illustrated Diary" by H. V. Fulpen, paperback, 176 pages.*	10.00	14.00
☐ **Book,** *"The Beatles: An Illustrated Record" by Roy Carr and Tony Tyler, paperback.*	8.00	11.00
☐ **Book,** *"The Beatles Again" by Harry Castleman and Walter Podrazik, clothbound, 302 pages.*	14.00	18.00
☐ **Book,** *"The Beatles Apart" by Bob Woffinden, paperback, unpaginated.*	8.00	11.00

Vee Jay 581, 45 r.p.m.

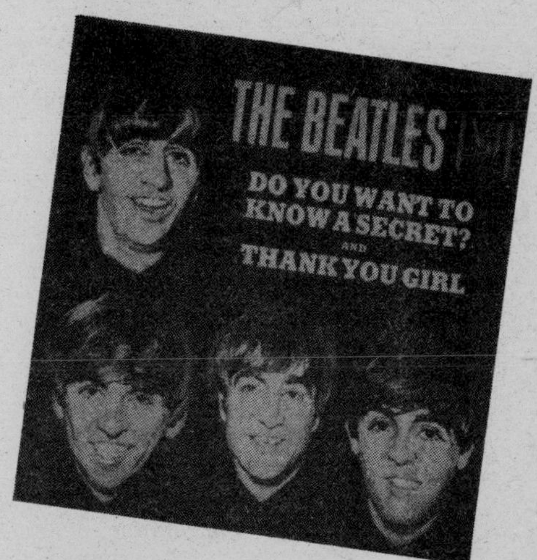

Vee Jay 587, 45 r.p.m.

	Price Range	
☐ **Book,** *"The Beatles at the Beeb" by Kevin Howlett, clothbound, unpaginated.*	11.00	14.00
"Beeb" is British slang for BBC, the British Broadcasting Company. This is the story of the various performances given by the Beatles for the BBC.		
☐ **Book,** *"The Beatles: The Biography" by Hunter Davis, clothbound, 380 pages.*	13.00	17.00
☐ **Book,** *"The Beatles Down Under" by Glenn Baker, paperback, 128 pages.*	13.00	17.00
Story of the group's Australian tour.		
☐ **Book,** *"The Beatles' England" by David Bacon and Norman Maslov, paperback, 138 pages.*	11.00	14.00
☐ **Book,** *"The Beatles for the Record", authorshipuncredited, 96 pages, measures 12" square.*	8.00	11.00
☐ **Book,** *"The Beatles Forever" by Nicholas Schaffner, clothbound, 218 pages.*	13.00	17.00
An identical edition in paperback is selling at $6-8.		
☐ **Book,** *"The Beatles in Their Own Words" by Miles (author who uses no last name), paperback.*	5.00	7.00
☐ **Book,** *"The Beatles on Record" by J. P. Russell, paperback, 682 pages.*	6.00	8.00
☐ **Book,** *"The Beatles' Record in Australia" by Bruce Hamlin, paperback, published in Australia.*	8.00	11.00
☐ **Book,** *"The Beatles Reader" by Charles P. Neises, clothbound.*	13.00	17.00
☐ **Book,** *"The Beatles Who's Who" by Bill Harry, paperback, 190 pages.*	8.00	11.00
Biographies of everyone who played a role in the Beatles' lives.		
☐ **Book,** *"The Book of Lennon" by Bill Harry, paperback, 223 pages.*	9.00	12.00
☐ **Book,** *"Come Together" by Jon Wiener, paperback, 379 pages.*	10.00	13.00
☐ **Book,** *"The Complete Beatles Quiz Book" by Edwin Goodgold and Dan Carlinsky, clothbound, 128 pages.*	3.00	3.50
☐ **Book,** *"Dakota Days" by John Green, clothbound, 260 pages.*	11.00	14.00
☐ **Book,** *"George Harrison Yesterday and Today" by Ross Michaels, paperback, 96 pages, published in Great Britain.*	6.00	8.00
☐ **Book,** *"Growing Up With the Beatles" by Rom Schaumburg, paperback, 160 pages.*	7.00	10.00
☐ **Book,** *"In His Own Write" by John Lennon, clothbound first edition.*	25.00	30.00
Multiply that by about ten if it's personally autographed.		
☐ **Book,** *"Lennon and Me" by Pete Shotton, paperback, 399 pages.*	3.50	4.50
☐ **Book,** *"Lennon and McCartney" by Malcolm Doney, clothbound, 126 pages.*	8.00	11.00
☐ **Book,** *"John Lennon: A Family Album" by Nishi F. Saimaru, paperback, 128 pages.*	32.00	40.00
☐ **Book,** *"John Lennon in His Own Words" by Miles (author who uses no last name), paperback.*	5.00	7.00

	Price Range	
☐ **Book,** *"John Lennon in His Own Write" by John Lennon, paperback, 79 pages.* *Lennon not only wrote and illustrated this book, but wrote reviews of it.*	4.50	6.00
☐ **Book,** *"John Lennon In My Life" by Pete Shotton and Nicholas Schaffner, paperback, 208 pages.* *Shotten was a childhood chum of Lennon in Liverpool.*	13.00	17.00
☐ **Book,** *"John Lennon: One Day At a Time" by Anthony Fawcett, paperback, 190 pages.*	8.00	11.00
☐ **Book,** *"Lennon: The Solo Years", author uncredited, paperback, 164 pages.*	12.00	15.00
☐ **Book,** *"John Lennon: The Summer of 1980" by Yoko Ono, paperback, 108 pages.*	8.00	11.00
☐ **Book,** *"The Literary Lennon" by James Sauceda, clothbound, 232 pages.* *Counting his books, letters and various miscellania, John Lennon did almost as much writing as a professional author.*	13.00	17.00
☐ **Book,** *"The Long and Winding Road" by John Tobler and Neville Stannard, paperback.*	7.00	10.00
☐ **Book,** *"The Longest Cocktail Party" by Richard DiLello, clothbound, 284 pages.* *An insight into the day to day operations of Apple Records while the Beatles were still together.*	16.00	20.00
☐ **Book,** *"The Love You Make" by Peter Brown and Steven Gaines, clothbound, 438 pages.*	13.00	17.00
☐ **Book,** *"Loving John" by May Pang, 335 pages.*	7.00	10.00
☐ **Book,** *"The Playbook Interviews With John Lennon and Yoko Ono" by David Sheff, paperback, 236 pages.*	3.00	4.00
☐ **Book,** *"Pocket Beatles for Guitar" by Milton Okun, paperback, 256 pages.*	4.00	6.00
☐ **Book,** *"Shout" by Philip Norman, paperback, 398 pages.*	7.00	10.00
☐ **Book,** *"Wings Tour USA", paperback.*	7.00	10.00
☐ **Book,** *"With the Beatles" by Dezo Hoffman, paperback, 130 pages.*	10.00	14.00
☐ **Book,** *"Working Class Heroes" by Neville Stannard, 240 pages.*	11.00	15.00
☐ **Book,** *"Yesterday: The Beatles From 1963 to 1965" by Robert Freeman, clothbound.*	10.00	13.00
☐ **Book,** *"You Can't Do That" by Charles Reinhart, clothbound, 410 pages.* *Deals with bootleg versions of the Beatles' records.*	14.00	19.00
☐ **Calendar,** *"Make a Date with the Beatles", mid 1960's. Mint condition.*	40.00	55.00
☐ **Cardboard Figures,** *set of 4 advertising promotion figures on very heavy cardboard, almost lifesize, issued for display in record shops in the mid 1960's. Full color. Self-standing.*	1200.00	1600.00
☐ **Coasters,** *set of six plastic coasters (different colors), each bearing the same illustration and wording, probably 1960's.*	30.00	40.00
☐ **Coloring Book.** *"Beatles Coloring Book" by the Saalfield Publishing Co., 1964. Softcovered.* *Value stated is for a copy in which no coloring has been attempted; otherwise, the price is lower.*	50.00	65.00

	Price Range	
☐ **Concert Tickets.** *Tickets to Beatles' concerts are scarce collectors' items.*	35.00	50.00
☐ **Drum Stick,** *autographed by Ringo Starr.*	800.00	1000.00
☐ **EPSTEIN, BRIAN.** *Candid snapshot photograph, signed. Undated.*	100.00	150.00
Brian Epstein managed the Beatles in their early years. He met a tragic death at an early age. All autograph material of his is scarce.		
☐ **Fan Club membership card.** *Measuring 4½" x 5½", picturing all four Beatles in characteristic pose, signed by each, 1963.*	900.00	1200.00
☐ **Gum Cards,** *set of 64 cards issued by Topps, 1964. Orange backs. Question and answer series, in color.*	50.00	65.00
Individual cards from this set normally sell for .65/.85.		
☐ **Gum Cards,** *set of 50 Yellow Submarine cards issued by Primrose Confectionary (Britain), 1968. Cards measure 1⁵⁄₁₆" by 2½". They were originally distributed in packets of candy cigarettes.*	95.00	125.00
Individual cards from this set normally sell for $1.25/1.75.		
☐ **Hairbrush,** *plastic hairbrush carrying cartoon likenesses of the Beatles, apparently marketed in the 1960's.*	60.00	80.00
☐ **HARRISON, GEORGE.** *Restaurant check signed (for wine), 1964.*	225.00	275.00
Even as early as 1964, the Beatles were signing their restaurant bills.		
☐ **HARRISON, GEORGE.** *Lock of hair (about 1") said to be that of George Harrison, enclosed in a plastic brooch-type mounting set with a chain. Accompanied by a written statement by the former owner, telling how it was obtained.*	100.00	135.00
Readers are cautioned that many items of this sort are not authentic, and that making a positive authentication is just about impossible. Hence their value — regardless of how much they may fetch at sales — is very questionable.		
☐ **Jigsaw Puzzle,** *"Illustrated Lyrics Puzzle in a Puzzle," bearing a copyright date of 1970, in the original box.*	40.00	55.00
☐ **LENNON, JOHN.** *Paperback book containing two writings by him,* **John Lennon in His Own Write** *and* **A Spaniard in the Works,** *published by Penguin Books. Signed by Lennon on the front flyleaf.*	475.00	600.00
Obviously it's the signature that makes the price. Plain copies of this book are still on the market.		
☐ **LENNON, JOHN.** *Restaurant check signed (for breakfast), 1964.*	325.00	400.00
☐ **LENNON, JOHN.** *"Two Virgins" LP record album (Apple Records, 1968), autographed on the sleeve. Accompanying the autograph is a small sketch.*	450.00	579.00
Though this record was released in 1968, the autograph and sketch date to 1979.		
☐ **LENNON, JOHN.** *Ink sketch on paper, a profile drawing of an unidentified male subject, signed on the back by Lennon and Ringo Starr, 5½" x 3". Undated.*	600.00	800.00

	Price Range	
☐ **LENNON, JOHN.** *"Whatever Gets You Through the Night", master disc used in the pressing of this 45 r.p.m. record. Signed by Lennon (first name only). Apple Records, 1974.* . .	450.00	550.00
☐ **LP Album,** *"Yesterday and Today", with the original "butcher" cover (see listings for description), signed by all four Beatles.*	1500.00	1900.00
☐ *as above, signed by John Lennon only.*	600.00	800.00
☐ *as above, signed by Ringo Starr only.*	250.00	350.00
☐ **Lunchbox,** *laminated tin, with colored portraits (drawings) of the Beatles, no contents.*	200.00	250.00
☐ **Magazine.** *"The Beatles Book", published in England, a complete run of 77 issues beginning August, 1963 and concluding December, 1969. This fan magazine terminated when the Beatles when their separate ways. It was a popular item but full sets are hard to find.*	350.00	450.00
☐ **McCARTNEY, PAUL.** *Small b/w snapshot showing him standing on a street, signed on the back in violet ink, with a pencil notation (in another hand) that the photo was snapped in Paris. Undated, probably c. 1970.*	290.00	360.00
☐ **McCARTNEY, PAUL.** *Pencil sketch by him of a young girl, signed, 8" x 5", 1965.*	525.00	650.00
Sketching has been merely a pasttime for Paul McCartney, but his skills with a pencil are clearly above average.		
☐ **McCARTNEY, PAUL.** *Small candid photograph of John Lennon, signed by Paul McCartney, 3½" x 5", 1968. Snapped at a press function.*	325.00	400.00
It wasn't too unusual for the Beatles to do zany things like autographing each other's pictures.		
☐ **McCARTNEY, PAUL.** *Picture postal card with 16 words in his handwriting plus partial signature ("Paul"), and some doodles. Apparently not sent through the mails. Creased at one corner.*	450.00	575.00
☐ **Pennant,** *a felt pennant (size not specified) with the name BEATLES printed in block letters and with likenesses of the group's members. Believed to date from 1964.*	50.00	65.00
☐ **Platinum Record,** *awarded to John Lennon for sales of his album "Rock 'n' Roll", 1975, signed by Lennon, enclosed in a simple frame. Overall size 20" x 16".*	9000.00	12000.00
☐ **Pocketbook or Carrybag,** *canvas, imprinted "BEATLES" with illustrations.*	45.00	60.00
☐ **Poster** *for the motion picture "A Hard Day's Night", approximately 22" x 30", colored illustration, stained in the margins from having been amateurishly mounted on a stiff backing.*	300.00	375.00
☐ **Poster.** *Italian poster for the motion picture "Yellow Submarine", 1969. Approximately 18½" x 26½".*	200.00	250.00
☐ **Poster.** *fan club souvenir poster dated 1968, measuring approximately 20" x 30", full color. With traces of old folds, mostly smoothed out.*	200.00	250.00
☐ **Press Kit** *for Paul McCartney and Wings, 1973.*	80.00	110.00

	Price Range	
☐ **Press Photographs.** *When these are unsigned (printed signatures do not count, of course), the value is quite low, because of large quantities distributed — in most instances no more than $5 unless very early.*		
☐ **Promotion Card** *issued by Parlophone Records for the Beatles in 1963, picturing all (looking* **very** *young) and signed by all. 5" x 7½".*	900.00	1150.00
☐ *above, without signatures.*	40.00	55.00
☐ **Record Shop Poster,** *4-color poster advertising "A Hard Day's Night", mint condition.*	180.00	230.00
☐ **Song Sheet,** *"Scrambled Egg", composed by John Lennon and Paul McCartney, signed and inscribed by John Lennon, dated 1978.*	800.00	1000.00
☐ **Strap** *for carrying schoolbooks, imprinted "BEATLES" with musical notes.*	17.00	23.00
☐ **Tablecloth,** *Beatles tablecloth printed with likenesses (each accompanied by the instrument he played).*	70.00	90.00
☐ **Wristwatch.** *Beatles Wristwatch, the dial consisting of a printed photograph of the Beatles in close-up. Above the portraits appears appear the words THE BEATLES, and the date "1964" beneath. With a corrugated leather band.*	275.00	350.00
The watch has no numerals, but simply stars where each numberal should appear. The price stated is for a specimen without the original box. In the original box it would have some slight premium. Collectors are cautioned that reproductions of an item such as this are very apt to turn up.		
☐ **Writing Tablet,** *a blank writing tablet (note size) with cover photo of the Beatles in color, dating to the mid or later 1960's.*	35.00	50.00
If any of the sheets were used or missing, the value would be somewhat less. For the cover alone, the value would be in the range of 18.00/25.00.		
☐ **Yellow Submarine.** *Animation cell, matted and framed, from the Beatles motion picture "Yellow Submarine".*	250.00	325.00
The range of price is rather wide as it depends to some extent on the scene. Cells showing all four Beatles normally fetch the highest sums — those with no members of the group go lowest. As of this date, comparatively few cells have reached the market.		
☐ **Yellow Submarine** *"flasher", a plastic disc measuring approximately 2½" in diameter, carrying on one side a colored picture printed on a plastic grid (network of impressed lines). When tilted, the picture appears to move. c. 1967.*	85.00	110.00

BEATLES 45's	**Price Range**	
☐ **Atco 6308.** *"Nobody's Child/Ain't She Sweet?", promo.*	27.00	62.00
☐ *as above, commercial, with picture sleeve.*	45.00	100.00
☐ *as above, commercial, without picture sleeve.*	3.50	7.50
When offered separately, the sleeve of Atco 6308 brings as much as $75 in mint condition. It is rare to be offered separately, however, as the accompanying record is easly obtainable — so most sellers will automatically take their empty sleeve and marry it up with a record.		
☐ **Polydor 52-317.** *"Ain't She Sweet?/If You Love Me, Baby", with picture sleeve.*	50.00	120.00
This is a German release dating to 1964. The label is red, the picture sleeve blue.		
☐ *as above, without picture sleeve.*	25.00	60.00
☐ **Polydor 52-317.** *"Ain't She Sweet?/Take Out Some Insurance", with picture sleeve.*	50.00	120.00
As you will note, the serial number of this disc is the same as that of the previous. Polydor used the 52-317 number for "Ain't She Sweet?", but issued two versions of the record, one backed with "If You Love Me, Baby" and the other with "Take Out Some Insurance". This practice is not uncommon in Germany. As with the previous, label is red but the picture sleeve is red rather than blue.		
☐ *as above, without picture sleeve.*	25.00	60.00
☐ **Apple 5964.** *"All You Need is Love/Baby, You're a Rich Man"*	2.00	4.00
☐ **Capitol 5964.** *"All You Need is Love/Baby, You're a Rich Man", promo.*	35.00	80.00
☐ *as above, commercial, orange label.*	2.00	4.50
☐ *as above, commercial, orange label, picture sleeve.*	7.00	11.00
☐ *as above, commercial, orange and yellow label.*	3.00	6.00
☐ *as above, commercial, orange an yellow label, picture sleeve.*	10.00	18.00
☐ *as above, commercial, red and orange "bullseye" label.*	6.00	12.00
☐ *as above, commercial, red and orange "bullseye" label, picture sleeve.*	12.00	20.00
☐ **Apple 5235.** *"And I Love Her/If I Fell".*	2.50	5.50
☐ **Capitol 5235.** *"And I Love Her/If I Fell", orange label.*	2.00	4.50
☐ *as above, orange and yellow label.*	3.00	6.00
☐ *as above, orange label, picture sleeve.*	12.00	25.00
☐ *as above, orange and yellow label.*	3.00	6.00
☐ *as above, orange and yellow label, picture sleeve.*	16.00	31.00
☐ *as above, red and orange "bullseye" label.*	7.00	13.00
☐ *as above, red and orange "bullseye" label, picture sleeve.*	23.00	45.00
No promotional copies have been discovered.		
☐ **Apple 2531.** *"The Ballad of John and Yoko/Old Brown Shoe".*	2.50	5.50
☐ *as above, picture sleeve.*	10.00	21.00
☐ *as above, bearing Apple and Capitol markings.*	7.00	17.00
☐ *as above, bearing apple and Capitol markings, picture sleeve.*	13.00	28.00
☐ *as above, Apple marking only, orange label.*	2.00	4.00
☐ *as above, Apple marking only, orange label, picture sleeve.*	9.00	18.00
☐ **Apple 5150.** *Can't Buy Me Love/You Can't Do That".*	3.00	5.50

	Price Range	
☐ **Capitol 5150.** *"Can't Buy Me Love/You Can't Do That", orange label.*	4.00	6.00
☐ *as above, orange label, picture sleeve.*	75.00	150.00
☐ *as above, orange and yellow label.*	7.00	13.00
☐ *as above, orange and yellow label, picture sleeve.*	85.00	185.00
☐ *as above, red and orange "bullseye" label.*	7.00	13.00
☐ *as above, red and orange "bullseye" label, picture sleeve...*	85.00	185.00
All existing picture sleeves for this disc bear the Capitol name. Apple did not issue a picture sleeve. However, it is possible to find an Apple pressing in a Capitol picture sleeve. The value would be around 75.00/150.00, almost wholly on the strength of the sleeve.		
☐ **Capitol Starline 6064.** *"Do You Want to Know a Secret?/ Thank You, Girl".*	7.00	17.00
☐ **VeeJay 587.** *"Do You Want to Know a Secret?/Thank You Girl", label name contained in brackets.*	6.00	13.00
☐ *as above, picture sleeve.*	25.00	55.00
☐ *as above, label name contained in oval.*	7.00	17.00
☐ *as above, label name contained in oval, picture sleeve.*	26.00	56.00
☐ *as above, promo (no picture sleeve).*	21.00	45.00
☐ **Oldies 149.** *"Do You Want to Know a Secret?/Thank You Girl".*	4.00	9.00
The picture sleeve was printed only for use on VeeJay pressings.		
☐ **Apple 5371.** *"8 Days a Week/I Don't Want to Spoil the Party".*	2.50	5.50
☐ **Capitol 5371.** *"8 Days a Week/I Don't Want to Spoil the Party", orange label.*	4.00	6.00
☐ *as above, orange label, picture sleeve.*	7.00	13.00
☐ *as above, orange and yellow label.*	3.00	5.50
☐ *as above, orange and yellow label, picture sleeve.*	8.00	17.00
☐ *as above, red and orange "bullseye" label.*	7.00	13.00
☐ *as above, red and orange "bullseye" label, picture sleeve...*	11.00	21.00
The picture sleeve was printed by Capitol only. So far there are no reports of discovery of promotional copies.		
☐ **VeeJay 522.** *"From Me to You/Thank You, Girl", promo.*	25.00	60.00
☐ *as above, commercial, label name contained in brackets...*	5.00	11.00
☐ *as above, commercial, label name contained in oval.*	8.00	19.00
No picture sleeves were printed for this disc.		
☐ **Apple 2490.** *"Get Back/Don't Let Me Down".*	3.00	6.50
☐ *as above, bearing Apple and Capitol markings.*	4.00	9.00
☐ **Capitol 2490.** *"Get Back/Don't Let Me Down".*	2.00	4.00
☐ **Capitol 4506.** *Girl/You're Gonna Lose That Girl", promo.*	35.00	80.00
☐ *as above, promo, picture sleeve.*	40.00	95.00
☐ **Apple 5222.** *"Hard Day's Night/I Should Have Known Better".*	2.50	5.50
☐ **Capitol 5222.** *"Hard Day's Night/I Should Have Known Better", orange label.*	2.00	4.50
☐ *as above, orange label, picture sleeve.*	11.00	21.00
☐ *as above, orange and yellow label.*	4.00	9.00
☐ *as above, orange and yellow label, picture sleeve.*	13.00	25.00
☐ *as above, red and orange "bullseye" label.*	6.00	13.00
☐ *as above, red and orange "bullseye" label, picture sleeve...*	16.00	33.00
The picture sleeve was printed by Capitol only.		

	Price Range	
☐ **Apple 2056.** *"Hello Goodbye/I Am The Walrus"*	2.50	5.50
No promotional copies have been found on Apple — nor picture sleeve bearing that label's name.		
☐ **Capitol 2056.** *"Hello Goodbye/I Am The Walrus", promo*	37.00	83.00
☐ *as above, commercial, orange label*	2.00	4.50
☐ *as above, commercial, orange label, picture sleeve*	13.00	25.00
☐ *as above, commercial, orange and yellow label*	3.00	6.00
☐ *as above, commercial, orange and yellow label, picture sleeve*	15.00	33.00
☐ *as above, commercial, red and orange "bullseye" label*	5.00	11.00
☐ *as above, commercial, red and orange "bullseye" label, picture sleeve*	19.00	40.00
☐ **Apple 5476.** *"Help/I'm Down"*	2.50	5.50
☐ **Capitol 5476.** *"Help/I'm Down", orange label*	2.00	4.50
☐ *as above, orange label, picture sleeve*	9.00	20.00
☐ *as above, orange and yellow label*	3.00	6.00
☐ *as above, orange and yellow label, picture sleeve*	10.00	23.00
☐ *as above, red and orange "bullseye" label*	6.00	13.00
☐ *as above, red and orange "bullseye" label, picture sleeve*	12.00	27.00
No promotion copies have been found.		
☐ **Capitol 4274.** *"Helter Skelter" (both sides), promo*	7.00	16.00
☐ **Capitol 4274.** *"Helter Skelter/Got to Get You Into My Life", promo*	7.00	16.00
☐ *as above, commercial*	2.00	4.50
Note that the serial numbers are the same on both promo pressings of "Helter Skelter", even though the reverse sides aren't.		
☐ **Apple 2276.** *"Hey Jude/Revolution"*	3.00	6.50
☐ *as above, bearing Apple and Capitol markings*	4.00	9.00
☐ **Capitol 2276.** *"Hey Jude/Revolution"*	2.00	4.50
☐ **Apple 5327.** *"I Feel Fine/She's A Woman"*	2.50	5.50
☐ **Capitol 5327.** *"I Feel Fine/She's A Woman", orange label*	2.00	4.50
☐ *as above, orange label, picture sleeve*	9.00	20.00
☐ *as above, orange and yellow label*	3.00	6.00
☐ *as above, orange and yellow label, picture sleeve*	10.00	23.00
☐ *as above, red and orange "bullseye" label*	6.00	13.00
☐ *as above, red and orange "bullseye" label, picture sleeve*	12.00	27.00
No promotional copies seem to have been pressed.		
☐ **Apple 5112.** *"I Want to Hold Your Hand/I Saw Her Standing There"*	2.50	5.50
☐ **Capitol 5112.** *"I Want to Hold Your Hand/I Saw Her Standing There", orange label*	4.00	7.50
☐ *as above, orange label, Capitol picture sleeve*	16.00	35.00
☐ *as above, orange label, WMCA picture sleeve*	400.00	900.00
The WMCA picture sleeve was printed by radio station WMCA in New York. It had the Capitol picture on the front with pictures of the WMCA "Good Guys" (the station's disc jockeys) on the back. It was used as part of a giveaway promotion, and the number of copies printed, compared to those of the regular Capitol sleeve, was apparently very small.		
☐ *as above, orange and yellow label*	6.00	13.00
☐ *as above, orange and yellow label, Capitol picture sleeve*	18.00	38.00

	Price Range	
☐ *as above, orange and yellow label, WMCA picture sleeve. . .*	450.00	975.00
☐ *as above, red and orange "bullseye" label. . . . .*	6.00	13.00
☐ *as above, red and orange "bullseye" label, Capitol picture sleeve. . . . .*	21.00	45.00
☐ *as above, red and orange "bullseye" label, WMCA picture sleeve. . . . .*	450.00	975.00
No promotional copies have been found.		
☐ **Apple 5235.** *"If I Fell/And I Love Her". . . . .*	2.50	5.50
☐ **Capitol 5235.** *"If I Fell/And I Love Her", orange label. . . . . .*	2.00	4.50
☐ *as above, orange label, picture sleeve. . . . .*	11.00	23.00
☐ *as above, orange and yellow label. . . . .*	3.00	6.00
☐ *as above, orange and yellow label, picture sleeve. . . . .*	13.00	26.00
☐ *as above, red and orange "bullseye" label. . . . .*	6.00	13.00
☐ *as above, red and orange "bullseye" label, picture sleeve. . .*	15.00	33.00
No promotional copies have been traced.		
☐ **Apple 5234.** *"I'll Cry Instead/I'm Happy Just to Dance With You". . . . .*	2.50	5.50
☐ **Capitol 5234.** *"I'll Cry Instead/I'm Happy Just to Dance With You", orange label. . . . .*	2.00	4.50
☐ *as above, orange label, picture sleeve. . . . .*	11.00	24.00
☐ *as above, orange and yellow label. . . . .*	3.00	6.00
☐ *as above, orange and yellow label, picture sleeve. . . . .*	13.00	28.00
☐ *as above, red and orange "bullseye" label. . . . .*	6.00	13.00
☐ *as above, red and orange "bullseye" label, picture sleeve. . .*	14.00	31.00
No promotional copies have been discovered.		
☐ **Swan 4152-1.** *"I'll Get You" (uniface). . . . .*	75.00	180.00
This one-sided disc was pressed as a promo in 1964. It was not turned into a commercial release.		
☐ **Capitol Starline 6066.** *"Kansas City/Boys", red and orange "bullseye" label. . . . .*	7.00	15.00
☐ *as above, green label. . . . .*	8.00	20.00
☐ **Apple 2138.** *"Lady Madonna/The Inner Light". . . . .*	2.50	5.50
☐ **Capitol 2138.** *"Lady Madonna/The Inner Light", promo. . . . .*	35.00	87.00
☐ *as above, commercial, orange label. . . . .*	2.00	4.50
☐ *as above, commercial, orange label, picture sleeve. . . . .*	10.00	23.00
☐ *as above, commercial, orange label, picture sleeve, accompanied by flyer on Beatles fan club. . . . .*	15.00	33.00
The Beatles fan club flyer was included only with discs in the picture sleeve. It frequently became separated, however, and copies (on any of the label variations) with both picture sleeve AND fan club flyer are worth more than with the picture sleeve alone.		
☐ *as above, commercial, orange and yellow label. . . . .*	3.00	6.00
☐ *as above, commercial, orange and yellow label, picture sleeve. . . . .*	11.00	23.00
☐ *as above, commercial, orange and yellow label, picture sleeve, accompanied by flyer on Beatles fan club. . . . .*	14.00	36.00
☐ *as above, commercial, red and orange "bullseye" label. . . .*	6.00	13.00
☐ *as above, commercial, red and orange "bullseye" label, picture sleeve. . . . .*	13.00	29.00
☐ *as above, commercial, red and orange "bullseye" label, picture sleeve, accompanied by flyer on Beatles fan club. . . . .*	17.00	39.00
☐ **Apple 2764.** *"Let It Be/You Know My Name". . . . .*	2.50	5.50

	Price Range	
☐ *as above, picture sleeve*	11.00	21.00
☐ *as above, bearing Apple and Capitol markings*	4.00	9.00
☐ *as above, bearing Apple and Capitol markings, picture sleeve*	13.00	28.00
☐ **Capitol 2764.** *"Let It Be/You Know My Name"*	2.00	4.00
☐ **Apple 2832.** *"Long and Winding Road/For You Blue"*	2.50	5.50
☐ *as above, picture sleeve*	9.00	19.00
☐ *as above, bearing Apple and Capitol markings*	6.00	13.00
☐ *as above, bearing Apple and Capitol markings, picture sleeve*	13.00	27.00
☐ **Capitol 2764.** *"Long and Winding Road/For You Blue"*	2.00	4.00
☐ **Capitol Starline 9008.** *"Love Me Do/P.S. I Love You"*	8.00	20.00
☐ **Oldies 151.** *"Love Me Do/P.S. I Love You"*	4.00	9.00
☐ **Tollie 9008.** *"Love Me Do/P.S. I Love You", promo*	30.00	70.00
☐ *as above, commercial*	3.50	7.50
☐ *as above, commercial, picture sleeve*	14.00	34.00
This might be more of a collector's item with the picture sleeve than meets the eye. It was the only picture sleeve ever printed by Tollie for a Beatles disc. This record was NOT pressed on the regular Capitol label, nor on Apple. (Apple Records was not in existence at the time of its release, in 1964.)		
☐ **Polydor 24 948.** *"Madison Kid/Let's Dance"*	240.00	610.00
One of the earliest examples of the Beatles on disc, this German release was billed as by Tony Sheridan and the Beat Brothers.		
☐ *as above, picture sleeve*	710.00	1750.00
☐ **Capitol Starline 6065.** *"Misery/Roll Over, Beethoven, green label.*	8.00	20.00
☐ *as above, red and orange "bullseye" label.*	7.00	14.00
☐ **Polydor 24 673.** *"My Bonnie/The Saints"*	420.00	950.00
☐ *as above, picture sleeve*	825.00	1950.00
The sleeve does not bill the Beat Brothers — it notes only that the recording is Tony Sheridan.		
☐ *as above, picture sleeve, with the numbers referred to as "twist" music on the sleeve*	865.00	2050.00
☐ **Polydor 52 273.** *"My Bonnie/The Saints", red label*	30.00	70.00
This disc was released two years after Polydor 24 673. It was on "red label Polydor", intended for circulation to Germany and Austria.		
☐ *as above, red label, picture sleeve.*	80.00	190.00
☐ **Polydor NH 66 833.** *"My Bonnie/The Saints"*	1400.00	3000.00
The most valuable Beatles 45. It dates to 1962 and gives the name of the group as Tony Sheridan and the Beatles (not Beat Brothers, as was the case on most Polydor releases). This disc was intended for circulation in England. Unfortunately — as it complicates the collector's life — a reissue appeared the following year, with the same serial number. They can be told apart only by the printing on the label, which is thinner and curvier on the original. Value of the reissue is less than 1/10th as much — 55.00/130.00		

	Price Range	
☐ **Decca 9-31382.** *"My Bonnie/The Saints", promo, pink label. The above, like all Decca pressings of "My Bonnie", is billed as by Tony Sheridan and the* **Beat Brothers.**	375.00	860.00
☐ *as above, commercial.*	1350.00	2850.00
☐ *as above, silver and black label (BNA release). This was the only appearance of the Beatles on Decca, which allowed a multi-billion dollar property slip away to Capitol.*	700.00	1500.00
☐ **MGM K-13213.** *"My Bonnie/The Saints", promo. Billed as by the Beatles with Tony Sheridan. This was released at about the time the group was making its first American tour.*	35.00	85.00
☐ *as above, commercial, with LP number on label.*	5.00	11.00
☐ *as above, commercial, without LP number on label.*	8.00	17.00
☐ **Apple 5587.** *"Nowhere Man/What Goes On".*	2.00	4.00
☐ **Capitol 5587.** *"Nowhere Man/What Goes On", orange label.*	2.00	4.50
☐ *as above, orange label, picture sleeve.*	7.00	16.00
☐ *as above, orange and yellow label.*	3.00	6.00
☐ *as above, orange and yellow label, picture sleeve.*	9.00	20.00
☐ *as above, red and orange "bullseye" label.*	5.00	12.00
☐ *as above, red and orange "bullseye" label, picture sleeve... No promotional copies seems to have been released.*	11.00	24.00
☐ **Capitol 4347.** *"Ob-La-Di Ob-La-Da/Julia", promo.*	6.00	13.00
☐ *as above, commercial.*	2.50	5.50
☐ *as above, commercial, picture sleeve. This disc was not pressed on the Apple label.*	5.00	11.00
☐ **Apple 5651.** *"Paperback Writer/Rain".*	2.00	4.00
☐ **Capitol 5651.** *"Paperback Writer/Rain", orange label.*	2.00	4.50
☐ *as above, orange label, picture sleeve.*	9.00	20.00
☐ *as above, orange and yellow label.*	3.00	6.00
☐ *as above, orange and yellow label, picture sleeve.*	11.00	23.00
☐ *as above, red and orange "bullseye" label.*	6.00	13.00
☐ *as above, red and orange "bullseye" label, picture sleeve... No promotional copies have been found.*	13.00	28.00
☐ **Apple 5810.** *"Penny Lane/Strawberry Fields Forever".*	2.00	4.00
☐ **Capitol 5810.** *"Penny Lane/Strawberry Fields Forever", orange label.*	2.00	4.50
☐ *as above, orange label, picture sleeve.*	20.00	40.00
☐ *as above, orange and yellow label.*	3.00	6.00
☐ *as above, orange and yellow label, picture sleeve.*	15.00	33.00
☐ *as above, red and orange "bullseye" label.*	5.00	11.00
☐ *as above, red and orange "bullseye" label, picture sleeve...*	22.00	46.00
☐ **Capitol Starline 6063.** *"Please Please Me/From Me To You".*	8.00	20.00
☐ **Oldies 150.** *"Please Please Me/From Me To You".*	4.00	9.00
☐ **VeeJay 498.** *"Please Please Me/Ask Me Why", promo.*	127.00	270.00
☐ *as above, commercial, label name contained within brackets.*	110.00	235.00
☐ *as above, commercial, label name contained within oval.*	130.00	275.00

	Price Range	
☐ as above, commercial, group's name shown as BEATTLES (two t's), thin lettering.	700.00	1475.00
There are two versions of the misspelled label rarity. The one listed above is the most desirable. They can be told apart only by the lettering style, which thin in the more valuable variety and thick in the less valuable. But the latter is by no means an items to be lightly regarded, as it sells for 130.00/275.00.		
☐ **VeeJay 581.** *"Please Please Me/From Me To You", promo.* .	35.00	75.00
☐ *as above, commercial, label name contained within brackets.*	6.00	12.50
☐ *as above, commercial, label name contained within brackets, picture sleeve.*	50.00	110.00
☐ *as above, commercial, label name contained within oval.* . .	13.00	27.00
☐ *as above, commercial, label name contained within oval, picture sleeve.*	55.00	120.00
VeeJay 581 was not simply a repressing of that label's #498. A new flip side was added, and this is the way it appeared when pressed by Capitol Starline. It was never issued by the regular Capitol label nor by Apple.		
☐ **Polydor 52 025.** *"Ruby Baby/What'd I Say?".*	280.00	580.00
Billed as by Tony Sheridan and the Beat Brothers. Issued on "red label Polydor" for circulation in Germany and Austria.		
☐ *as above, picture sleeve.*	600.00	1300.00
On this Polydor sleeve, the Beat Brothers were credited along with Tony Sheridan — not always the case with Polydor. This was the first Beatles 45 r.p.m. record, dating a full four years prior to their first American visit.		
☐ **Capitol 4612.** *"Sergeant Pepper's Lonely Hearts Club Band/ A Day in the Life".*	2.00	4.00
☐ *as above, picture sleeve.*	4.00	9.00
☐ **Swan 4152.** *"She Love You/I'll Get You", early pressing.*	75.00	125.00
Early pressing specimens are identified by the absence of the worlds DON'T DROP OUT on the label.		
☐ *as above, later pressing.*	30.00	65.00
Later pressings are identified by the presence of the words DON'T DROP OUT on the label.		
☐ *as above, final pressing.*	3.25	5.50
Final pressing specimens are identified by the black and silver coloring used on the label.		
☐ *as above, promo.*	90.00	175.00
This disc was also released (by Swan) with special labels showing the title of "She Loves You" in the German language. There are two variations, one in which the German and English are shown on the same line (13.00/30.00) and another in which the English equivalent is placed on a second line (6.00/12.00).		
☐ **Apple 5255.** *"Slow Down/Matchbox".*	2.00	4.50
☐ **Capitol 5255.** *"Slow Down/Matchbox", orange label.*	2.00	4.50
☐ *as above, orange label, picture sleeve.*	25.00	60.00
☐ *as above, orange and yellow label.*	3.00	6.00
☐ *as above, orange and yellow label, picture sleeve.*	28.00	69.00

	Price Range	
☐ *as above, red and orange "bullseye" label.*	6.00	13.00
☐ *as above, red and orange "bullseye" label, picture sleeve...*	32.00	75.00
Promotional copies have not been discovered. The value of an Apple disc in a Capitol picture sleeve would be in the neighborhood of 25.00/60.00.		
☐ **Apple 2645.** *"Something/Come Together"*	2.50	5.50
☐ *as above, bearing Apple and Capitol markings.*	5.00	11.00
There were no picture sleeves or promotional records issued for this disc, so far as can be determined.		
☐ **Atco 6302.** *"Sweet Georgia Brown/Take Out Some Insurance", promo.*	35.00	70.00
☐ *as above, commercial.*	8.50	20.00
☐ **Polydor 52 324.** *"Sweet Georgia Brown/Skinny Minny".*	35.00	72.00
This was a Polydor (German) "red label" release, for circulation in Germany and Austria. It dates from 1964.		
☐ *as above, picture sleeve.*	90.00	195.00
☐ **Apple 5407.** *"Ticket to Ride/Yes It Is".*	2.50	5.50
☐ **Capitol 5407.** *"Ticket to Ride/Yes It Is", orange label.*	4.00	6.00
☐ *as above, orange label, picture sleeve.*	11.00	23.00
☐ *as above, orange and yellow label.*	6.00	11.00
☐ *as above, orange and yellow label, picture sleeve.*	15.00	33.00
☐ *as above, red and orange "bullseye" label.*	8.00	18.00
☐ *as above, red and orange "bullseye" label, picture sleeve...*	20.00	41.00
No promotional copies have been discovered.		
☐ **Capitol Starline 6061.** *"Twist and Shout/There's a Place".*	8.00	20.00
☐ **Oldies 152.** *"Twist and Shout/There's a Place".*	4.00	9.00
☐ **Tollie 9001.** *"Twist and Shout/There a Place".*	4.50	9.50
☐ **Apple 5555.** *"We Can Work It Out/Day Tripper".*	2.50	5.50
☐ **Capitol 5555.** *"We Can Work It Out/Day Tripper", orange label.*	2.00	4.50
☐ *as above, orange label, picture sleeve.*	11.00	23.00
☐ *as above, orange and yellow label.*	3.00	6.00
☐ *as above, orange and yellow label, picture sleeve.*	13.00	28.00
☐ *as above, red and orange "bullseye" label.*	6.00	13.00
☐ *as above, red and orange "bullseye" label, picture sleeve...*	18.00	38.00
No promotional copies have been discovered.		
☐ **Polydor 0462.** *"What'd I Say?/Ya Ya".*	420.00	950.00
☐ **MGM K-13227.** *"Why/Cry For a Shadow", promo.*	35.00	80.00
Billed as by the Beatles with Tony Sheridan. This disc dates to 1964, when the group's meteoric rise to stardom prompted companies holding old Beatles tracks to dust them off and give them a fresh try.		
☐ *as above, commercial.*	11.00	18.00
☐ **Apple 5715.** *"Yellow Submarine/Eleanor Rigby".*	2.50	5.50
☐ **Capitol 5715.** *"Yellow Submarine/Eleanor Rigby", orange label.*	2.00	4.50
☐ *as above, orange label, picture sleeve.*	10.00	21.00
☐ *as above, orange and yellow label.*	3.00	6.00
☐ *as above, orange and yellow label, picture sleeve.*	12.00	25.00
☐ *as above, red and orange "bullseye" label.*	6.00	13.00
☐ *as above, red and orange "bullseye" label, picture sleeve...*	15.00	33.00
No promotional copies have been found.		

	Price Range	
☐ **Apple 5498.** *"Yesterday/Act Naturally".*	2.50	5.50
☐ **Capitol 5498.** *"Yesterday/Act Naturally", orange label.*	2.00	4.50
☐ *as above, orange label, picture sleeve.*	9.00	19.00
☐ *as above, orange and yellow label.*	3.00	6.00
☐ *as above, orange and yellow label, picture sleeve.*	12.00	27.00
☐ *as above, red and orange "bullseye" label.*	6.00	13.00
☐ *as above, red and orange "bullseye" label, picture sleeve... No promotional copies have turned up.*	16.00	35.00
☐ **Polydor 24 849.** *"You Are My Sunshine/Swanee". This was a German "red label Polydor" release. It billed the group as Tony Sheridan and the Beat Brothers.*	230.00	590.00
☐ *as above, picture sleeve.*	700.00	1700.00

BEATLES LP's

☐ **Apple SO-383.** *(stereo) "Abbey Road".*	8.00	20.00
☐ **R.P.N.** *(unnumbered) "The Beatles American Tour" (with Ed Ruby), #2. A collection of interviews, packaged with a booklet (which must still be present, to command the values stated).*	36.00	76.00
☐ **R.P.N.** *(unnumbered) "The Beatles American Tour" (with Ed Ruby), #3. Fakes have turned up. The ones reported to date lack printing on the sleeve's spine.*	25.00	63.00
☐ **Apple SWBO-101.** *(stereo) "The Beatles". Double-record album with embossed printing on the front cover. Can still be found at retail in some shops but fast disappearing.*	13.00	30.00
☐ **VeeJay LP-1085.** *(mono) "The Beatles and Frank Ifield on Stage".*	150.00	315.00
☐ *as above, stereo.*	285.00	550.00
☐ **Apple SBC-100.** *(stereo) "The Beatles Christmas Album".*	33.00	75.00
☐ **Apple SKBO-3403.** *(stereo) "The Beatles, 1962-1966". Still on retail sale at many record shops.*	6.00	13.00
☐ **Apple SKBO-3404.** *(stereo) "The Beatles, 1967-1970". Still on retail sale at many record shops.*	6.00	13.00
☐ **Capitol SXA-2080.** *(stereo) "The Beatles Second Album". A compact 33 r.p.m. extended play, to be used in jukeboxes. Copies that have been "on the route" (played in jukeboxes) aren't touched by collectors with a long pole.*	65.00	148.00
☐ **Capitol ST-2080.** *(stereo) "The Beatles Second Album", green label.*	10.00	24.00
☐ *as above, black label. This was the regular commercial version of SXA-2080 (see above).*	8.00	18.00
☐ **Apple ST-2080.** *(stereo) "The Beatles Second Album". Still readily available in the record shops.*	4.00	9.00
☐ *as above, bearing Capitol and Apple markings on the label. You can still find this one in the shops, too, but it may take a bit more looking.*	6.00	13.00
☐ **Apple ST-2358.** *(stereo) "Beatles VI".*	7.00	16.00
as above, bearing Capitol and Apple markings on the label.	5.00	11.00

	Price Range	
☐ **Capitol ST-2358.** *(stereo) "Beatles VI".*	4.00	8.50
as above, with sleeve reading "SEE LABEL FOR CORRECT PLAYING ORDER".	9.00	20.00
☐ **Apple ST-2228.** *(stereo) "Beatles '65".*	5.00	11.00
The label has both the Apple and Capitol names.		
☐ **VeeJay PRO-202.** *(mono) "Hear the Beatles Tell All".*	25.00	63400
An early interview album, played to death by radio stations as a substitute for a live Beatles interview.		
☐ **Apple SMAS-2386.** *(stereo) "Help".*	4.00	9.00
The label has both the Apple and Capitol names. Readily available in record shops.		
☐ **Capitol SMAS-2386.** *(stereo) "Help", green label.*	6.00	13.00
☐ *as above, black label.*	7.00	16.00
The Capitol pressing also exists in mono but is not the big collector's item in mono that some people mistakenly believe. Actually its value, even in mint, is under $15.		
☐ **Apple SW-385.** *(stereo) "Hey Jude".*	4.00	9.00
☐ **Polydor 24-4504.** *(stereo) "In The Beginning".*	5.00	11.00
☐ **Apple AR-34001.** *(stereo) "Let It Be".*	4.00	9.00
All three above albums should be easy to find in the record shops.		
☐ **Capitol SMAS-11638.** *(stereo) "Live at Hollywood Bowl".*	5.00	11.00
☐ **Lingasong 2-7001.** *"Live at the Star Club" (Hamburg).*	7.00	15.00
Cuts on this LP were recorded when the group was performing in Germany, very early in their career (when under contract to Polydor).		
☐ **Capitol SKBL-11711.** *(stereo) "Love Songs".*	5.00	11.00
☐ **Apple SMAL-2835.** *(stereo) "Magical Mystery Tour".*	6.00	13.00
The label has both the Apple and Capitol names.		
☐ **Capitol SMAL-2835.** *(mono) "Magical Mystery Tour".*	9.00	20.00
☐ *as above, stereo, green label.*	8.00	20.00
☐ *as above, stereo, black label.*	6.00	13.00
☐ **Apple ST-2047.** *(stereo) "Meet the Beatles".*	4.00	9.00
The label has both the Apple and Capitol names.		
☐ **Capitol ST-2407.** *(stereo) "Meet the Beatles", green label.*	7.00	13.00
☐ *as above, black label.*	8.00	23.00
This album also exists as a compact 33, for jukebox use. It is considerably scarcer in that form and carries a value of 60.00/139.00. However, copies that were actually used in jukeboxes (which comprise the majority) are not considered to be in "collector condition" and sell for much less. The serial number is SXA-2047.	75.00	150.00
☐ **Apple ST-2576.** *(stereo) "Revolver".*	6.00	13.00
The label has both the Apple and Capitol names.		
☐ **Capitol ST-2576.** *(stereo) "Revolver", green label.*	7.00	16.00
☐ *as above, black label.*	7.00	16.00
☐ **Capitol SKBO-11537.** *(stereo) "Rock and Roll Music".*	4.00	9.00
This album was not pressed on Apple.		
☐ **Apple ST-2442.** *(stereo) "Rubber Soul".*	5.00	11.00
The label has both the Apple and Capitol names.		
☐ **Capitol ST-2442.** *(stereo) "Rubber Soul", green label.*	6.00	13.00
☐ *as above, black label.*	7.00	16.00

	Price Range	
☐ **Savage BM-69.** *(mono) "Savage Young Beatles".*	12.00	29.00
☐ **Apple SMAS-2652.** *(stereo) "Sergeant Pepper's Lonely Hearts Club Band.*	5.00	11.00
The label has both the Apple and Capitol names.		
☐ **Capitol SMAS-2652.** *(stereo) "Sergeant Pepper's Lonely Hearts Club Band, green label.*	6.00	13.00
☐ *as above, black label.*	7.00	15.00
Not to be confused with the soundtrack album of the film "Sergeant Pepper," released a number of years later (which feature the BeeGees, not the Beatles).		
☐ **Apple ST-2108.** *(stereo) "Something New"*	5.00	11.00
The label has both the Apple and Capitol names.		
☐ **Capitol ST-2108.** *(stereo) "Something New", green label.*	6.00	13.00
☐ *as above, black label.*	8.00	19.00
This album also exists as a compact 33, for jukebox use. It is considerably scarcer in that form and carries a value of 77.00/195.00. However, copies that were actually used in jukeboxes (which comprises the majority) are not considered to be in "collector condition" and sell for much less. The serial number is SXA-2108.	85.00	200.00
☐ **Apple SW-153.** *(stereo) "Yellow Submarine" (soundtract).*	4.00	9.00
Still readily available in the record shops.		
☐ **Apple ST-2553.** *(stereo) "Yesterday and Today".*	13.00	20.00
☐ **Capitol T-2553** *(mono) "Yesterday and Today", butcher cover.*	145.00	300.00
☐ *as above, revised cover.*	85.00	195.00

ELVIS PRESLEY

When Elvis Presley first burst upon the recording scene, in 1956, critics called his meteoric popularity a fad. Once again, following his death in 1977 and the sharply increased prices paid for his records and memorabilia, the cry of "fad" was heard. All of this buying activity will soon subside, some claimed. Today, almost a decade later, it has not only failed to subside but has measurably grown. Collecting interest — and values — are stronger at the present time, in just about everything and anything connected with Elvis, than at any time in the past. In fact the RATE of increase, in market value, has outstripped most other types of music collectibles. There are now estimated to be more than a million Elvis collectors, scattered around the world. Of these, many (often because of financial circumstances, not a lack of enthusiasm) buy only the repressings of his records rather than the scarce originals, and ignore memorabilia. But there is certainly a considerable number of hobbyists competing for the cream of Elvis collectibles, spending sums of money which are said to reach sixty million dollars annually. They fit no special mold or type. Old and young are involved in the Elvis hobby, from fans who followed him since the earliest days of his career to persons far too young to remember "Love Me Tender" or "Hound Dog". During his 20 years in the spotlight, Elvis picked up many new fans along the way, and the same appears to be true of Elvis collecting. More and more individuals are coming into the hobby, some of whom, quite possibly, were not even Elvis fans in his lifetime.

The advanced Elvis specialists have brought their hobby down to a science. They've researched every aspect of Elvis' life and career, his family and friends. They've traced his day-to-day movements and know where he was, and what he was doing, virtually every day of his life — which is not really difficult in light of the enormous press coverage he received. They know what exists in the way of memorabilia, how scarce it is, and — usually — where to find it, and how much to pay for it. They can sort out the good from the not-so-good, the rare from the common, without any trouble. They know when to say "no", and when to stretch a few extra dollars — or even a few extra hundred — for a really exceptional item. To the beginner, the world of Elvis collecting may seem a vast jungle of potential pitfalls and entanglements. To a degree it is. The problems arise, of course, because of profiteers, who always stand ready to take advantage of a "good thing". If the public is anxious to buy Elvis Presley memorabilia, these individuals are just as anxious to provide it, even if it means manufacturing fakes, facsimiles and cheap souvenirs. This has been going on for quite some time and has saturated the market with Elvis "memorabilia" of very questionable nature and value. Thus, the first piece of advice to a beginner is: develop a sense of discrimination. Don't fall into the trap of believing that everything is collectible just because it carries Elvis' name or likeness. Anyone can put Elvis' name and picture on a button, pennant, scarf, etc., and call it a "collectors' item". The Elvis memorabilia now being sold in retail shops and in the souvenir stands around Graceland is of current manufacture. Obviously, there is a market for these things, but the serious collector ought to stay away from them. It is very doubtful if they will increase in value or even gain recognized collector status. The collectible Elvis memorabilia falls basically into two groups: personal items such as signed photographs, and souvenir-type merchandise manufactured during his lifetime. As far as the souvenir-type items are concerned (bowls, clocks, spoons, etc.), the older the better, with the highest level of desirability attached to those from the very earliest days of his popularity. These objects were made for sale to fans, not to entice hobbyists or investors. Although nationally and sometimes internationally sold, they were STILL manufactured in smaller quantities than most of today's Elvis souvenirs — and most of them were of better quality, too.

When modern items have gotten into private hands and are then offered for resale, it may be difficult to judge their age. Fortunately it is very easy to recognize many modern Elvis souvenirs as "non collectibles", or, at the very best, collectibles of secondary interest and value. Any object giving the dates of his birth and death were obviously manufactured after his death; and anything picturing an older Elvis is just as obviously not from the early years of his career. Likewise it can be automatically presumed that objects bearing slogans such as "The King Lives On" were manufactured after his passing. But some pieces exist — which would have to be categorized as fakes — that are of current or very recent manufacture, yet bear a youthful likeness of Elvis. These can easily be mistaken for originals dating from the fifties or early sixties. Sometimes the manufacturer will add to the aura of "age" by using a black-and-white photo, or imprinting one of Elvis' early song titles on the object. Proceed with caution, and do not pay a premium price unless you feel assured of the item's authenticity. Buying from established dealers in Elvis collectibles will eliminate most of the uncertainty. This is one of the advantages of the hobby's vast expansion. It is now profitable for specialist dealers to trade exclusively in Elvis collectibles. These people serve a very valuable purpose. They may charge "top of the market" prices (such as are indicated in our listings), but they succeed in turning up many Elvis collectibles that the hobbyist, operating on his own, would never encounter. Also, and perhaps most vitally, they screen out the fakes and doubtful pieces and offer only worthy material to their customers. The specialist dealers see and handle so much Elvis memorabilia that they can spot the good ones without much trouble.

Obviously, this hobby is never going to be as standardized as — say — coin collecting. We don't know (and aren't likely to, ever) how many Elvis souvenirs were manufactured during his lifetime, or how many specimens of each was placed on the market. There are no "Mint figures", and no hope of getting such info through manufacturer's files. Mistakes are probable. Some items may be scarcer than they're assumed to be; others may be more common than dealers and collectors believe. But the market itself is the final analyst. If something appears for sale very seldom on the market, it is presumed to be scarce or rare and this presumption must be treated as valid until proven otherwise. On the other hand, if an object is offered repeatedly by dealers and shows up in just about every auction sale of Elvis collectibles, no amount of sales talk can make anyone believe it to be scarce. With just a little experience in the market, you will learn which items and which TYPES of items are the scarcest.

There is no space to get into detail about the various techniques used by sellers, in advertising currently-made items to give them glamor and appearance. If they can give the suggestion that a current item is 10 or 15 or 20 years old, it naturally has a much greater sales potential. They are then in the position of having to "explain it away", because if the item was truly old and scarce, how could they be offering dozens or hundreds of them? Usually this is taken care of by the phrase WAREHOUSE FIND. It is not restricted to Elvis collectibles but is used throughout the collectibles market, as any reader of the antiques and hobbyist newspapers knows. The seller advertises that a lucky find occurred, in which "forgotten stock" was discovered in a manufacturer's warehouse. This not only satisfies the buyer's doubt about authenticity, but gives a good excuse for the items being in mint condition. This is not to say that EVERY claim of "warehouse find" is a fraud, but many of them are. You have been forewarned!

MEMORABILIA	**Price Range**	
☐ **Book,** *The Army Years by Nick Corvino, 93 pages, clothbound, 5½" x 8½".* *Fictionalized Story of the years spent by Elvis in the army.*	**5.00**	**7.00**
☐ **Book,** *The Complete Elvis by Martin Torgoff, paperback, 256 pages.*	**9.00**	**12.00**
☐ **Book,** *Elvis by Dave Marsh, clothbound, 246 pages.*	**30.00**	**40.00**
☐ **Book,** *Elvis by Albert Goldman, clothbound.*	**13.00**	**17.00**

	Price Range	
☐ **Book,** *Elvis: The Final Years by Jerry Hopkins, clothbound, 258 pages*	11.00	15.00
☐ **Book,** *Elvis: The Illustrated Discography by Martin Hawkins and Colin Escott, paperback*	5.00	7.00
☐ **Book,** *Elvis: The Illustrated Record by Roy Carr and Mick Farren, 12" square format*	11.00	15.00
☐ **Book,** *Elvis in His Own Words by Mick Farren and Pearce Marchbank, paperback, 128 pages*	5.00	7.00
☐ **Book,** *Elvis: The Legend and the Music by John Tobler and Richard Wooten, clothbound, 192 pages*	10.00	13.00
☐ **Book,** *Elvis Presley: A Complete Reference by Wendy Sauers, clothbound, 194 pages*	16.00	20.00
☐ **Book,** *Elvis Presley Reference Guide and Discography by John Whisler, clothbound, 250 pages*	13.00	17.00
☐ **Book,** *Elvis Presley: A Study in Music by Robert Matthew-Walker, paperback, 154 pages*	5.00	7.00
☐ **Book,** *Elvis Presley News Diary by Bill Johnson, 230 pages, spiral binding, 9½" x 12", 1981*	8.00	10.00
☐ **Book,** *The Illustrated Elvis by W. A. Harbinson, 160 pages, softbound, 8" x 10½"*	2.00	3.00
☐ **Book,** *Jailhouse Rock by Lee Cotten and Howard A. DeWitt, clothbound, 368 pages*	16.00	20.00
☐ **Book,** *Private Elvis, author uncredited, 199 pages, softbound, 8½" x 11", 1978*	10.00	13.00
☐ **Book,** *Up and Down With Elvis Presley by Marge Crumbaker and Gabe Tucker, clothbound, 254 pages*	11.00	15.00
☐ **Book,** *When Elvis Died by Neal Gregory and Janice Gregory, clothbound, 290 pages*	12.00	16.00
☐ *Elvis Presley child's guitar, plastic*	28.00	38.00
☐ *Elvis Presley school bag*	35.00	50.00
☐ *8x10 photo with guitar, signed and inscribed, 1957*	350.00	450.00
☐ *Printed postcard photo, facsimile signature*	5.00	8.00
☐ *Lifesize cardboard figure of Elvis, c. 1961, used for theater promotion, full color*	375.00	475.00
☐ *8x10 color photo, signed*	400.00	600.00
☐ *Signature on label of 45rpm record - add $225-$300 to value of record as listed above.*		
☐ *Signature on label of 33⅓rpm long-play record - add $275-$375 to value of album as listed above.*		
☐ *Signature on cover of 33⅓rpm long-play album - add $300-$400 to value of album if record is present. If record is not present, cover alone is worth $300-$400.*		
☐ *Elvis Presley drinking mug, ceramic, picture on side*	23.00	32.00
☐ *Handkerchief, colored silk, illustrated*	20.00	27.00
☐ *Typewritten note by Col. Tom Parker (his manager), signed.*	9.00	12.00
☐ *8x10 photo, unsigned, black and white*	2.00	4.00
☐ *8x10 motion picture still, unsigned, black and white*	1.50	3.00
☐ *8x10 color photo, unsigned (**not** clipped from magazine or book)*	6.00	10.00
☐ *8x10 motion picture still, unsigned, color*	5.00	8.00
☐ *8x10 motion picture still, black and white, signed*	250.00	375.00

RCA Victor, LSP 2426.

RCA Victor, LSP 4776

	Price Range	
☐ *8x10 motion picture still, color, signed.*	300.00	450.00
☐ *Typewritten letter, signed, ½ page*	150.00	225.00
☐ *Typewritten letter, signed, 1 page*	180.00	250.00
☐ *Typewritten letter, signed, 2 pages*	275.00	375.00
☐ *Handwritten letter, signed, ½ page*	275.00	375.00
☐ *Handwritten letter, signed, 1 page*	450.00	600.00
☐ *Handwritten letter, signed, 2 pages*	600.00	800.00
☐ *Handwritten letter, signed, 3 pages*	750.00	1100.00
☐ *Note in his handwriting, one line.*	150.00	200.00
☐ *Signature on an otherwise blank sheet of paper or card.*	80.00	100.00
☐ *Typewritten letter* **to him** *from record company executive.*	40.00	50.00
☐ *Typewritten letter* **to him** *from motion picture executive.*	35.00	49.00
☐ *Typewritten letter* **to him** *from TV producer.*	31.00	42.00
☐ *Typewritten letter* **to him** *from music agent.*	29.00	39.00
☐ *Typewritten letter* **to him** *from U.S. Armed Forces.*	235.00	310.00
☐ *Typewritten letter* **to him** *from author seeking an interview.*	9.00	14.00
☐ *Typewritten letter* **to him** *from Ed Sullivan.*	140.00	200.00
☐ *Draft card issued to him by Selective Service.*	1750.00	3000.00
☐ *Magazine cover with full color photo.*	.50	1.00
☐ *News cuttings (most).*	.50	2.00

ELVIS PRESLEY — 45 SINGLES

☐ **Sun 209** *That's All Right/Blue Moon of Kentucky.*	195.00	350.00
☐ **210** *Good Rockin' Tonight/ I Don't Care If the Sun Don't Shine.*	175.00	275.00
☐ **215** *Milkcow Blues Boogie/You're a Heartbreaker.*	250.00	375.00
☐ **217** *Baby Let's Play House/ I'm Left, Your Right, She's Gone.*	140.00	240.00
☐ **223** *Mystery Train/I Forgot to Remember to Forget.*	130.00	240.00
☐ **RCA6357** *Mystery Train/I Forgot to Remember to Forget.*	15.00	24.00
☐ **6380** *That's All Right/Blue Moon of Kentucky.*	15.00	24.00
☐ **6381** *Good Rockin' Tonight/ I Don't Care If the Sun Don't Shine.*	15.00	24.00
☐ **6382** *Milkcow Blues Boogie/You're a Heartbreaker.*	15.00	24.00
☐ **6383** *Baby Let's Play House/ I'm Left, You're Right, She's Gone.*	15.00	24.00
☐ **6420** *Heartbreak Hotel/I Was the One.*	5.00	9.00
☐ **6540** *I Want You, I Need You, I Love You/ My Baby Left Me.*	5.00	9.00
☐ **6604** *Don't Be Cruel/Hound Dog.*	5.00	9.00
☐ **6636** *Blue Suede Shoes/Tutti Fruitti.*	15.00	24.00
☐ **6637** *I Got a Woman/I'm Countin' on You.*	15.00	24.00
☐ **6638** *I'm Gonna Sit Right Down and Cry Over You/ I'll Never Let You Go.*	15.00	24.00
☐ **6639** *Tryin' to Get to You/I Love You Because.*	15.00	24.00
☐ **6640** *Blue Moon/Just Because.*	15.00	24.00
☐ **6641** *Money Honey/One-Sided Love Affair.*	15.00	24.00
☐ **6642** *Shake, Rattle and Roll/Lawdy Miss Clawdy.*	15.00	24.00
☐ **6643** *Love Me Tender/Anyway You Want Me.*	4.50	8.00
☐ **6800** *Too Much Playing For Keeps.*	4.50	8.00
☐ **6870** *All Shook Up/That's When Your Heartaches Begin.*	4.50	8.00
☐ **7000** *Teddy Bear/Loving You.*	4.50	8.00

		Price Range	
☐	**7035** *Jailhouse Rock/Treat Me Nice*	4.50	8.00
☐	**7150** *Don't/I Beg of You*	4.50	8.00
☐	**7240** *Wear My Ring Around Your Neck/ Doncha Think It's Time*	4.50	8.00
☐	**7280** *Hard Headed Woman/Don't Ask Me Why*	4.50	8.00
☐	**7410** *One Night/I Got Stung*	4.50	8.00
☐	**7506** *A Fool Such As I/I Need Your Love Tonight*	3.75	6.00
☐	**7600** *A Big Hunk O' Love/My Wish Came True*	3.75	6.00
☐	**7740** *Stuck on You/Fame and Fortune*	3.25	5.50
☐	**7740** *Stuck on You/Fame and Fortune (stereo single)*	70.00	125.00
☐	**7777** *It's Now or Never/A Mess of Blues*	3.25	5.50
☐	**7777** *It's Now or Never/A Mess of Blues (stereo single)*	70.00	125.00
☐	**7810** *Are You Lonesome Tonight?/I Gotta Know*	3.25	5.50
☐	**7810** *Are You Lonesome Tonight?/I Gotta Know (stereo single)*	70.00	125.00
☐	**7850** *Surrender/Lonely Man*	3.25	5.50
☐	**7850** *Surrender/Lonely Man (stereo single)*	95.00	165.00
☐	**7880** *I Feel So Bad/Wild in the Country*	3.25	5.50
☐	**7880** *I Feel So Bad/Wild in the Country (stereo single)*	95.00	165.00
☐	**098** *His Latest Flame/Little Sister*	3.00	5.00
☐	**7968** *Can't Help Falling in Love/Rock-A-Hula-Baby*	3.00	5.00
☐	**7992** *Good Luck Charm/Anything That's a Part of You*	3.00	5.00
☐	**8041** *She's Not You/Just Tell Her Jim Said Hello*	3.00	5.00
☐	**8100** *Return to Sender/Where Do You Come From?*	3.00	5.00
☐	**8134** *One Broken Heart For Sale/ They Remind Me Too Much of You*	3.00	5.00
☐	**8188** *Devil in Disguise/ Please Don't Drag That Sting Around*	3.00	5.00
☐	**8234** *Kissin' Cousins/It Hurts Me*	3.00	5.00
☐	**8360** *What's I Say/Viva Las Vegas*	3.00	5.00
☐	**8400** *Such a Night/Never Ending*	3.00	5.00
☐	**8440** *Ask Me/Ain't That Loving You Baby*	3.00	5.00
☐	**8500** *Do the Clam/You'll Be Gone*	3.00	5.00
☐	**8585** *(Such An) Easy Question/It Feels So Right*	3.00	5.00
☐	**8740** *Tell Me Why/Blue Rider*	3.00	5.00
☐	**8780** *Frankie and Johnny/Please Don't Stop Loving Me*	3.00	5.00
☐	**8870** *Love Letters/Come What May*	3.00	5.00
☐	**8941** *If Every Day Was Like Christmas/ How Would You Like To Be*	4.50	8.00
☐	**9056** *Indescribably Blue/Fools Fall in Love*	3.00	5.00
☐	**9115** *Long Legged Girl/ That's Someone You Never Forget*	3.00	5.00
☐	**9287** *There's Always Me/Judy*	3.00	5.00
☐	**9341** *Big Boss Man/You Don't Know Me*	3.00	5.00
☐	**94258** *Guitar Man/High Heeled Sneakers*	3.00	5.00
☐	**9465** *U.S. Male/Stay Away Joe*	3.00	5.00
☐	**9547** *Let Yourself Go/Your Time Hasn't Come Yet Baby*	3.00	5.00
☐	**9600** *You'll Never Walk Alone/We Call on Him*	3.00	5.00
☐	**9610** *A Little Less Conversation/Almost in Love*	3.00	5.00
☐	**9670** *If I Can Dream/Edge of Reality*	2.75	4.50
☐	**9731** *Memories/Charro*	2.75	4.50
☐	**9741** *In the Ghetto/Any Day Now*	2.75	4.50
☐	**9747** *Clean Up Your Own Back Yard/ The Fair is Moving On*	2.75	4.50
☐	**9764** *Suspicious Minds/You'll Think of Me*	2.75	4.50

		Price Range	
☐ **9768**	*Don't Cry Daddy/Rubberneckin'.*	2.75	4.50
☐ **9791**	*Kentucky Rain/My Little Friend.*	2.75	4.50
☐ **9835**	*The Wonder of You/Mama Liked the Roses.*	2.75	4.50
☐ **9873**	*I've Lost You/The Next Step is Love.*	2.75	4.50
☐ **9916**	*You Don't Have to Say You Love Me/Patch It Up.*	2.75	4.50
☐ **9960**	*I Really Don't Want To Know/ There Goes My Everything.*	2.75	4.50
☐ **9980**	*Where Did They Go, Lord?/Rags to Riches.*	2.75	4.50
☐ **9985**	*Life/Only Believe.*	2.75	4.50
☐ **9998**	*I'm Leavin'/Heart of Rome.*	2.75	4.50
☐ **1017**	*It's Only Love/The Sound of Your Cry.*	2.75	4.50
☐ **0619**	*Until It's Time for You to Go/ We Can Make the Morning.*	2.75	4.50
☐ **0672**	*An American Trilogy/ The First Time I Ever Saw Your Face.*	2.75	4.50
☐ **0769**	*Burning Love/It's a Matter of Time.*	2.50	4.00
☐ **0815**	*Separate Ways/Always on My Mind.*	2.50	4.00
☐ **0910**	*Steamroller Blues/Fool.*	2.50	4.00
☐ **0088**	*Raised on Rock/For Ol' Time Sake.*	2.50	4.00
☐ **0196**	*I've Got a Thing About You Baby/ Take Good Care of Her.*	2.50	4.00
☐ **0280**	*If You Talk in Your Sleep/Help Me.*	2.50	4.00
☐ **10074**	*Promised Land/It's Midnight.*	2.50	4.00
☐ **10191**	*My Boy/Thinking About You.*	2.50	4.00
☐ **10278**	*T-R-O-U-B-L-E/Mr. Songman.*	2.50	4.00
☐ **10401**	*Bringing It Back/Pieces of My Life.*	2.50	4.00
☐ **10601**	*Hurt/For the Heart.*	2.50	4.00
☐ **18057**	*Moody Blue/She Thinks I Still Care.*	2.50	4.00

EXTENDED PLAY (EP)

☐ **RCA 1254**	*Elvis Presley (double-pocket).*	90.00	165.00
☐ **747**	*Elvis Presley.*	12.00	25.00
☐ **821**	*Heartbreak HoteL.*	14.00	27.00
☐ **830**	*Elvis Presley.*	14.00	27.00
☐ **940**	*The Real Elvis.*	14.00	27.00
☐ **965**	*Anyway You Want Me.*	14.00	27.00
☐ **4006**	*Love Me Tender.*	12.00	25.00
☐ **992**	*Elvis, Vol. I.*	12.00	25.00
☐ **993**	*Elvis, Vol. II.*	14.00	27.00
☐ **994**	*Strictly Elvis.*	14.00	27.00
☐ **1-1515**	*Loving You, Vol. I.*	14.00	27.00
☐ **2-1515**	*Loving You, Vol. II.*	14.00	27.00
☐ **4041**	*Just for You.*	14.00	27.00
☐ **4054**	*Peace in the Valley.*	12.00	25.00
☐ **4108**	*Elvis Sings Christmas Songs.*	14.00	27.00
☐ **4114**	*Jailhouse Rock.*	14.00	27.00
☐ **4319**	*King Creole, Vol. I.*	14.00	27.00
☐ **4321**	*King Creole, Vol. II.*	14.00	27.00
☐ **4325**	*Elvis Sails.*	27.00	48.00
☐ **4340**	*Christmas with Elvis.*	14.00	27.00
☐ **4368**	*Follow That Dream.*	8.25	14.00
☐ **4371**	*Kid Galahad.*	8.25	14.00
☐ **4382**	*Easy Come, Easy Go.*	9.50	18.00
☐ **4383**	*Tickle Me.*	9.50	18.00
☐ **5088**	*A Touch of Gold, Vol. I (maroon label).*	35.00	56.00
☐ **5088**	*A Touch of Gold, Vol. I (black label).*	12.00	25.00

		Price Range	
☐	5120 *The Real Elvis (reissue) (maroon label).*	35.00	54.00
☐	5120 *The Real Elvis (reissue) (black label).*	9.50	15.00
☐	5121 *Peace in the Valley (reissue) (maroon label).*	35.00	54.00
☐	5151 *Peace in the Valley (reissue) (black label).*	9.50	15.00
☐	5122 *King Creole, Vol. I (reissue) (maroon label).*	35.00	54.00
☐	5122 *King Creole, Vol. I (reissue) (black label).*	9.50	15.00
☐	5101 *A Touch of Gold, Vol. II (maroon label).*	35.00	54.00
☐	5101 *A Touch of Gold, Vol. II (black label).*	12.00	25.00
☐	5141 *A Touch of Gold, Vol. II (maroon label).*	35.00	54.00
☐	5141 *A Touch of Gold, Vol. III (black label).*	12.00	25.00
☐	5157 *Elvis Sails (reissue) (maroon label).*	40.00	70.00
☐	5157 *Elvis Sails (reissue) (maroon label).*	12.00	25.00
COMPACT 33's			
☐	RCA 37-7850 *Surrender/Lonely Man.*	48.00	115.00
☐	37-7880 *I Feel So Bad/Wild in the Country.*	75.00	175.00
☐	37-7908 *His Latest Flame/Little Sister.*	75.00	175.00
☐	37-7968 *Can't Help Falling in Love/Rock-A-Hula Baby.*	75.00	175.00
☐	37-7992 *Good Luck Charm/Anything That's Part of You.*	75.00	175.00
☐	37-8041 *She's Not You/Just Tell Her Jim Said Hello.*	90.00	250.00
☐	37-8100 *Return to Sender/Where Do You Come From?*	90.00	250.00
LP'S			
	THE ALBUMS BELOW WERE FIRST ISSUED ONLY IN MONO		
☐	RCA 1254 (M) *Elvis Presley.*	25.00	56.00
☐	1382 (M) *Elvis.*	25.00	56.00
☐	1515 (M) *Loving You.*	17.00	39.00
☐	1035 (M) *Elvis' Christmas Album (double-pocket).*	75.00	190.00
☐	1707 (M) *Elvis' Golden Records.*	17.00	39.00
☐	1884 (M) *King Creole.*	17.00	39.00
☐	1951 (M) *Elvis' Christmas Album (reissue) (photo on back).*	17.00	39.00
☐	1990 (M) *For LP Fans Only.*	24.00	56.00
☐	2011 (M) *A Date with Elvis (double pocket).*	34.00	84.00
☐	2011 (M) *A Date with Elvis (single pocket).*	17.00	39.00
☐	2075 *Elvis' Golden Records, Vol. II.*	17.00	39.00
	THE ALBUMS BELOW HAVE EQUIVALENT VALUE IN MONO AND STEREO		
☐	2231 (M) *Elvis is Back.*	17.00	39.00
☐	2256 (M) *G.I. Blues.*	17.00	39.00
☐	2328 (M) *His Hand in Mine.*	12.00	29.00
☐	2370 (M) *Something for Everybody.*	17.00	39.00
☐	2436 (M) *Blue Hawaii.*	17.00	39.00
☐	2523 (M) *Pot Luck.*	17.00	39.00
☐	2621 (M) *Girls! Girls! Girls!*	17.00	39.00
☐	2697 (M) *It Happened at the World's Fair.*	17.00	39.00
☐	2697 (M) *Fun in Acapulco.*	15.00	35.00
☐	2765 (M) *Elvis' Golden Records, Vol. III.*	15.00	35.00
☐	2894 (M) *Kissin' Cousins.*	15.00	35.00
☐	2999 (M) *Roustabout.*	15.00	35.00
☐	3338 (M) *Girl Happy.*	15.00	35.00
☐	3450 (M) *Elvis for Everyone.*	15.00	35.00
☐	3468 (M) *Harum Scarum (with photo enclosed).*	20.00	35.00
☐	3553 (M) *Frankie and Johnny.*	17.00	39.00
☐	3643 (M) *Paradise, Hawaiian Style.*	15.00	35.00
☐	3702 (M) *Spinout.*	17.00	39.00
☐	3758 (M) *How Great Thou Art.*	15.00	35.00